Starting Out with Visual Basic .NET

Tony Gaddis
Haywood Community College

Kip Irvine
Florida International Unviersity

Bruce Denton
Haywood Community College

Scott/Jones Inc.
P.O. Box 696
El Granada, California 94018
Voice: 650-726-2436
Facsimile: 650-726-4693
e-mail: scotjones2@aol.com
Web page: www.scottjonespub.com

Starting Out with Visual Basic .NET, Second Edition
Tony Gaddis
Haywood Community College
Kip Irvine
Florida International University
Bruce Denton
Haywood Community College

ISBN: 1-57676-094-4

The publisher wishes to acknowledge the memory and influence of James F. Leisy. Thanks, Jim. We miss you.

Text Design: Darrell Judd
Cover Design: Nicole Clayton, Design Graphx
Composition: Diane DeMarco, Option C
Proofreading: Kristin Furino, Holbrook Communications
Book Manufacturing: Corley Printing Company

Scott/Jones Publishing Company
Editorial Group: Richard Jones, Mike Needham, Denise Simon, Leata Holloway, Joe Burns, and Patricia Miyaki
Production Management: Audrey Anderson
Marketing and Sales: Victoria Judy, Page Mead, Hazel Dunlap, Hester Winn and Donna Cross
Business Operations: Michelle Robelet, Cathy Glenn, Natasha Hoffmeyer and Bill Overfelt

A Word About Trademarks

Additional Titles of Interest from Scott/Jones

Computing with Java™: Programs, Objects, Graphics,
    Second Edition and Second Alternate Edition
From Objects to Components with the Java™ Platform
Advanced Java™ Internet Applications, Second Edition
    by Art Gittleman

Developing Web Applications with Active Server Pages
    by Thom Luce

Starting Out with Visual Basic
Standard Version of Starting Out with C++, Third Edition
Brief Version of Starting Out with C++, Third Edition
    by Tony Gaddis

Starting Out with C++, Third Alternate Edition
    by Tony Gaddis, Judy Walters, and Godfrey Muganda

C by Discovery, Third Edition
    by L.S. and Dusty Foster

Assembly Language for the IBM PC Family, Third Edition
    by William Jones

QuickStart to JavaScript
QuickStart to DOS for Windows 9X
    by Forest Lin

Advanced Visual Basic.Net, Third Edition
    by Kip Irvine

HTML for Web Developers
Server-Side Programming for Web Developers
    by John Avila

The Complete A+ Guide to PC Repair
The Complete Computer Repair Textbook, Third Edition
    by Cheryl Schmidt

Windows 2000 Professional Step-by-Step
Windows XP Professional Step-by-Step
    by Leslie Hardin and Deborah Tice

The Windows 2000 Professional Textbook
The Visual Basic 6 Coursebook, Fourth Edition
Prelude to Programming: Concepts and Design
The Windows XP Textbook
    by Stewart Venit

The Windows 2000 Server Lab Manual
    by Gerard Morris

Contents in Brief

CONTENTS

CHAPTER 7   Multiple Forms, Standard Modules, and Menus   401

CHAPTER 8   Arrays, Timers, and More   477

PREFACE

Starting Out with Visual Basic .NET is intended for use in an introductory programming course. Although it is designed for students with no prior programming background, even experienced students will benefit from its depth of detail and the chapters covering databases and advanced topics.

The book is written in clear, easy-to-understand language and covers all the necessary topics of an introductory programming course. The text is rich in example programs that are concise, practical, and real world oriented. This approach was taken so the student not only learns how to use the various controls, constructs, and features of Visual Basic .NET, but why and when.

Organization of the Text

This text teaches Visual Basic .NET in a step-by-step fashion. Each chapter covers a major set of programming topics, introduces controls and GUI elements, and builds knowledge as the student progresses through the book. Although the chapters can be easily taught in their existing sequence, some flexibility is provided. The following diagram suggests possible sequences of instruction.

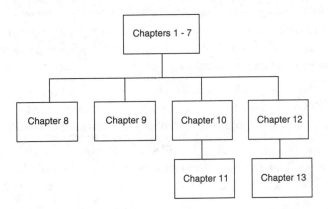

Chapters 1 through 7 cover the fundamentals of program design, flow control, modular programming, and the most important Visual Basic .NET controls. The instructor may then continue with Chapters 8, 9, 10, or 12. Chapter 11 should be covered after Chapter 10, and Chapter 13 should be covered after Chapter 12.

Brief Overview of Each Chapter

Chapter 1: Introduction to Programming and Visual Basic .NET. This chapter provides an introduction to programming, the programming process, and Visual Basic .NET. Object-oriented programming and the event-driven model are explained. The components of programs, such as key words, variables, operators, and punctuation are covered, and tools such as flow charts and pseudocode are presented. The student gets started using the Visual Basic .NET environment in a hands-on tutorial.

Chapter 2: Creating Applications with Visual Basic .NET. In this chapter the student starts by creating a simple application that displays a graphic image. In the tutorials that follow, the student adds controls, modifies properties, and enables the application to respond to events. An introduction to the Visual Basic .NET help system, with a tutorial on debugging, is given.

Chapter 3: Input, Variables, Constants, and Calculations. Variables, constants, and the Visual Basic .NET data types are introduced in this chapter. The student learns to gather input and create simple arithmetic statements. The intricacies of GUI design are introduced as the student learns about grouping controls with group boxes, assigning keyboard access keys, and setting the tab order. Debugging techniques for locating logic errors are covered.

Chapter 4: Making Decisions and Working with Strings. Here the student learns about relational operators and how to control the flow of a program with the `If...Then`, `If...Then...Else`, and `If...Then...ElseIf` statements. Logical operators are introduced, and the `Select Case` statement is covered. Important applications of these constructs are covered, such as testing numeric values, strings, and determining if a value lies within a range. Several string-handling functions and string methods are introduced. Class-level variables, message boxes, radio buttons, and check boxes are introduced.

Chapter 5: Lists, Loops, Validation, and More. This chapter begins by showing the student how to use input boxes as a quick and simple way to gather input. Next, list boxes and combo boxes are introduced. The chapter then covers the Visual Basic .NET repetition control structures: the `Do While`, `Do Until`, and `For...Next` loops. Counters, accumulators, running totals, and other application-related topics are discussed. Finally, the student learns about the CausesValidation property, the Validating event, the Validated event, and how these are used to perform input validation.

Chapter 6: Sub Procedures and Functions. The student learns how and why to modularize programs with general procedures and functions. Arguments, parameters, and return values are discussed. Debugging techniques for stepping into and over procedures are introduced.

Chapter 7: Multiple Forms, Standard Modules, and Menus. This chapter shows how to add multiple forms to a project and how to create a standard module to hold procedures and functions that are not associated with a specific form. Last, it covers creating a menu system, with commands and submenus that the user may select from.

Chapter 8: Arrays, Timers, and More. This chapter discusses both single dimension and multidimensional variable arrays. Many array programming techniques are presented, such as summing all the elements in an array, summing all the rows or columns in a two-dimensional array, searching an array for a specific value, and using parallel arrays. The disabled property, timer controls, and splash screens are covered, as well as programming techniques for generating random numbers.

Chapter 9: Files, Printing, and Structures. This chapter begins by discussing how to save data to sequential text files and then read the data back into an application. The OpenFileDialog, SaveFileDialog, FontDialog and ColorDialog controls are introduced. The PrintDocument control is discussed, with a special focus on printing reports. Last, the chapter shows the student how to create user-defined data types with structures.

Chapter 10: Working with Databases. This chapter discusses basic database terminology and introduces fundamental database concepts. ADO .NET is presented as a tool for accessing databases. The student learns how to connect to a database, create data adapters, datasets, and `CurrencyManager` objects. Many techniques for working with databases in code are presented.

Chapter 11: Advanced Database Programming and SQL. This chapter introduces the Structured Query Language (SQL) and gives a tutorial on different SQL statements. Techniques for using SQL to search for data using ADO .NET are discussed. The DataGrid control, which displays database data in rows and columns, similar to a spreadsheet, is introduced. The chapter concludes with a primer on good database design.

Chapter 12: Classes, Exceptions, Collections, and Scrollable Controls. This chapter introduces classes as a tool for creating abstract data types. The process of analyzing a problem and determining its classes is discussed, and techniques for creating objects, properties, and methods are introduced. Next, the chapter discusses exceptions and how to trap them during a program's execution. Collections are presented as structures for holding groups of objects. The Object Browser, which allows the student to see information about the classes, properties, methods, and events available to a project, is also covered. The chapter concludes by showing how to construct horizontal and vertical scroll bar and track bar controls.

Chapter 13: Inheritance, Custom Controls, and Using the Clipboard. This chapter introduces the student to inheritance, and shows how to create a class that is based on an existing class. Next, the chapter shows how to create custom, user-defined controls. The ability to equip applications with clipboard copy, cut, and paste operations is then covered.

Appendix A: User Interface Design Guidelines. Discusses how to design user interfaces that are simple, without distracting features, and that conform to Windows standards.

Appendix B: Visual Basic .NET Function and Method Reference. Provides a reference for all the intrinsic functions and methods that are covered in this text. The exceptions that may be caused by these functions and methods are also listed.

Appendix C: Binary and Random-Access Files. Describes programming techniques for creating and working with binary and random-access data files.

Appendix D: Converting Mathematical Expressions to Programming Statements. Shows the student how to convert a mathematical expression into a Visual Basic .NET programming statement.

Appendix E: Answers to Checkpoints. Students may test their own progress by comparing their answers to the Checkpoint exercises against this appendix. The answers to all Checkpoints are included.

Appendix F: Glossary. This appendix provides a glossary of all the key terms presented in the text.

Appendix G: (On the Student Disk CD): Answers to Odd-Numbered Review Questions. This appendix provides another tool that students can use to gauge their progress.

Features of the Text

Concept Statements	Each major section of the text starts with a concept statement. This statement concisely summarizes the meaning of the section.
Example Programs	The text has an abundant number of complete and partial example programs, each designed to highlight the topic currently being studied. In most cases, the programs are practical, real-world examples.
Tutorials	Each chapter has several hands-on tutorials that reinforce the chapter's topics.
Checkpoints	Checkpoints are questions placed at intervals throughout each chapter. They are designed to query the student's knowledge quickly after learning a new topic. The answers to the checkpoints are provided in Appendix E.
Notes	Notes are short explanations of interesting or often misunderstood points relevant to the topic at hand.
Tips	Tips appear regularly that advise the student on the best techniques for approaching different programming problems.
Warnings	Warnings caution the student about certain Visual Basic .NET features, programming techniques, or practices that can lead to malfunctioning programs or lost data.
If You Want to Know More	These sections go into greater detail about VB .NET features. Since they are easily identifiable, you can pick the ones you want to use in your class, and the ones you want to skip.
Case Studies	The Focus on Problem Solving sections provide case studies that simulate real-world applications. These case studies are designed to highlight the major topics of each chapter they appear in.
Review Questions	In the tradition of any Gaddis text, each chapter presents a thorough and diverse set of review questions. These include traditional fill-in-the-blank, true/false, multiple choice, and short answer questions. There are also unique tools for assessing a student's knowledge. For example, find the error questions ask the student to identify syntax or logic errors in brief code segments. Algorithm workbench questions ask the student to design code segments to satisfy a given problem. There are also questions labeled "What do you think?" that require the student to think critically and contemplate the topics presented in the chapter. The answers to the odd-numbered review questions appear in Appendix G, which is on the student disk CD-ROM.
Programming Challenges	Each chapter offers a pool of programming exercises designed to solidify the student's knowledge of the topics at hand. In most cases the assignments present real-world problems to be solved. When applicable, these exercises also include input validation rules.
Supplements	The following supplementary material is also available for this textbook:

- ◆ A student disk CD-ROM containing the source code and files required for the chapter tutorials. The CD also contains Appendix G: Answers to the Odd-Numbered Review Questions.

- Instructor's resources, containing answers to the even-numbered review questions, completed versions of the tutorial applications, and solutions to the programming challenges.

Web Resources

The Web site for *Starting Out with Visual Basic .NET* provides corrections and a password-protected instructor site. You may access it at http://www.gaddisbooks.com/vbnet

Acknowledgments

There have been many helping hands in the development and publication of this text. The authors would like to thank the following faculty reviewers for their helpful suggestions and expertise during the production of this manuscript:

Reviewers

Ronald Bass
Austin Community College

Zachory T. Beers
Microsoft Corporation

Bob Benavides
Collin County Community College District

Hal Broberg
Indiana Purdue University

William J. Dorin
Indiana University

David M. Himes
Oklahoma State University – Okmulgee

Corinne Hoisington
Central Virginia Community College

Greg Hodge
Northwestern Michigan College

Lee A. Hunt
Collin County Community College

Norman McNeal
Dakota County Technical College

Joan P. Mosey
Point Park College

Merrill B. Parker
Chattanooga State Technical Community College

Carol M. Peterson
South Plains Community College

Anita Philipp
Oklahoma City Community College

Robert L. Terrell
Walters State Community College

Margaret Warrick
Allan Hancock College

Catherine Wyman
DeVry Institute, Phoenix

The authors would like to thank their families for their tremendous support. We also thank everyone at Scott/Jones, especially our publisher Richard Jones, for his enthusiasm, guidance and expertise. In addition, Cathy Glenn and Michelle Windell were vital team members. We also owe a tremendous debt of gratitude to Audrey Anderson, Carol Noble, Diane DeMarco, Kristin Furino, and Darrell Judd. They made the production of this text a real pleasure.

About the Authors

Tony Gaddis teaches computer science courses at Haywood Community College in North Carolina. He has also taught programming for several corporations and government agencies, including NASA's Kennedy Space Center. He holds a B.S. in Management Information Systems and a master's degree in instructional technology. Tony is a highly acclaimed instructor who was selected as the North Carolina Community College "Teacher of the Year" in 1994; he received the Teaching Excellence award from the National Institute for Staff and Organizational Development in 1997. He is also the author of the *Starting Out with C++* series, published by Scott/Jones.

Kip Irvine holds a M.S. (computer science, 1995) and D.M.A. (music composition, 1982) from the University of Miami. He was a professor of Computer Information Systems at Miami-Dade Community College-Kendall from 1983-1999 and has been an instructor at Florida International University since 1999. His published textbooks include *COBOL for the IBM Personal Computer* (Prentice-Hall, 1987), *Assembly Language for Intel-Based Computers* (Prentice-Hall 1990, 1993, 1999, and 2002), *C++ and Object-Oriented Programming* (Prentice-Hall, 1997), and *Advanced Visual Basic .NET* (1998).

Bruce Denton is a systems analyst and has a B.S. in Journalism. He has been working with computers since 1983. His career includes consulting for Fortune 1000 companies, conducting corporate training in Visual Basic .NET, and teaching workforce development courses at Haywood Community College for professional programmers.

Introduction to Programming and Visual Basic .NET

► 1.1 Introduction

This book teaches programming using Microsoft Visual Basic .NET. Visual Basic .NET is a powerful software development system for creating applications that run in the Windows family of operating systems. With Visual Basic .NET, you may

- create applications with graphical windows, dialog boxes, menus, and so on
- create applications that work with databases
- create web applications and applications that use Internet technologies
- create applications that display graphics

Visual Basic is widely used in the academic world because students find its combination of visual design tools and BASIC programming language easy to learn. It is also a favorite tool among professional programmers. It allows developers to create powerful real-world applications in a relatively short period of time.

Before plunging right into learning Visual Basic, let us review the fundamentals of computer hardware and software, then build an understanding of how a Visual Basic .NET application is organized.

▶ 1.2 Computer Systems: Hardware and Software

Hardware

The term *hardware* refers to a computer's physical components. A computer, as we generally think of it, is not an individual device but a system of devices. Like the instruments in a symphony orchestra, each device plays its own part. A typical computer system consists of the following major components.

ALL COMPUTER SYSTEMS CONSIST OF SIMILAR HARDWARE DEVICES AND SOFTWARE COMPONENTS. THIS SECTION PROVIDES AN OVERVIEW OF COMPUTER HARDWARE AND SOFTWARE ORGANIZATION.

1. The central processing unit (CPU)
2. Main memory
3. Secondary storage devices
4. Input devices
5. Output devices

The organization of a computer system is depicted in Figure 1-1.

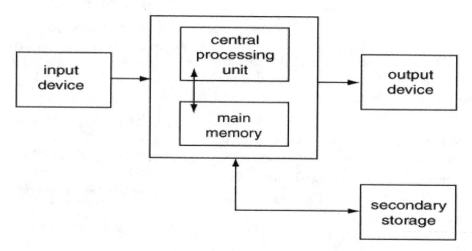

Figure 1-1   The organization of a computer system

The CPU

At the heart of a computer is its *central processing unit,* or CPU. The CPU's job is to fetch instructions, carry out the operations commanded by the instructions, and produce some outcome or resultant information. The CPU gets its instructions from a program. *A program* is a sequence of instructions stored in the computer's main memory. Computer programs are stored in memory as a series of binary numbers. A *binary number* is a sequence of 1s and 0s, such as

```
11011011
```

This number has no apparent meaning to you or me, but to the computer it might be an instruction to multiply two numbers or read another value from memory.

Main Memory

Commonly known as *random-access memory,* or *RAM,* the computer's main memory holds information. Specifically, main memory holds the sequences of instructions in the programs that are running and the data those programs are working with.

Memory is divided into sections known as bytes, each of which holds an equal amount of data. Each byte is assigned a unique number known as an *address.* The addresses are ordered from lowest to highest. A byte is identified by its address in much the same way a post office box is identified by an address. Figure 1-2 depicts a group of bytes with their addresses. In the illustration, sample data is stored in memory. The number 149 is stored in the byte with the address 16, and the number 72 is stored at address 23.

0	1	2	3	4	5	6	7	8	9
10	11	12	13	14	15	16 **149**	17	18	19
20	21	22	23 **72**	24	25	26	27	28	29

Figure 1-2   Bytes and their addresses

RAM is usually a volatile type of memory, used only for temporary storage. When the computer is turned off, the contents of RAM are erased.

Secondary Storage

Secondary storage is a nonvolatile type of memory, which means it can hold data for long periods of time, even when there is no power to the computer. Frequently used programs are stored in secondary memory, and loaded into main memory as needed. Important information, such as word processing documents, payroll data, and inventory figures, is saved to secondary storage as well.

The most common type of secondary storage device is the *disk drive.* A disk drive stores information by magnetically encoding it onto a circular disk. There are several different types of disks, each with advantages and disadvantages. The most common types are hard disks and floppy disks. Hard disks are capable of storing very large amounts of information and can access that information quickly. Hard disks are not portable, however. Floppy disks are portable but hold only a small amount of information. In addition, the access speed of a floppy disk drive is considerably slower than that of a hard disk.

Input Devices

Input is any information the computer collects from the outside world. The device that collects the information and sends it to the computer is called an *input device.* Common input devices are the keyboard and mouse. A disk drive can also be considered an input device because programs and information are retrieved from it and loaded into the computer's memory.

Output Devices

Output is information the computer sends to the outside world. It might be a sales report, a list of names, a graphic image, or a sound. The information is sent to an *output device,* which formats and presents it. Common output devices are video displays and printers. The disk drive can also be considered an output device because the CPU sends information to it in order to be saved.

Software

Software refers to the programs that run on a computer. There are two general categories of software: operating systems and application software. An *operating system* or *OS* is a set of programs that manages the computer's hardware devices and controls their processes. Windows 95, Windows 98, Windows NT, Windows ME, Windows 2000, and Windows XP are all operating systems.

Application software refers to programs that make the computer useful to the user. These programs, which are generally called applications, solve specific problems or perform general operations that satisfy the needs of the user. Word processing, spreadsheet, and database packages are all examples of application software. As you work through this book, you will develop application software using Visual Basic. Net.

✓ Checkpoint

1.1 List the five major hardware components of a computer system.

1.2 What is a memory address? What is its purpose?

1.3 Explain why computers have both main memory and secondary storage.

1.4 What are the two general categories of software?

► 1.3   Programs and Programming Languages

CONCEPT

A PROGRAM IS A SET OF INSTRUCTIONS A COMPUTER FOLLOWS IN ORDER TO PERFORM A TASK. A PROGRAMMING LANGUAGE IS A SPECIAL LANGUAGE USED TO WRITE COMPUTER PROGRAMS.

What Is a Program?

Computers are designed to follow instructions. A computer program is a set of instructions that enable the computer to solve a problem or perform a task. For example, suppose we want the computer to calculate someone's gross pay. Figure 1-3 shows a list of things the computer should do.

1. Display a message on the screen: "How many hours did you work?"
2. Allow the user to enter the number of hours worked.
3. Once the user enters a number, store it in memory.
4. Display a message on the screen: "How much do you get paid per hour?"
5. Allow the user to enter an hourly pay rate.
6. Once the user enters a number, store it in memory.
7. Once both the number of hours worked and the hourly pay rate are entered, multiply the two numbers and store the result in memory.
8. Display a message on the screen that shows the amount of money earned. The message must include the result of the calculation performed in step 7.

Figure 1-3

Collectively, the instructions in Figure 1-3 are called an *algorithm.* An algorithm is a set of well-defined steps for performing a task or solving a problem. Notice these steps are sequentially ordered. Step 1 should be performed before step 2, and so forth. It is important that these instructions be performed in their proper sequence.

In order for a computer to perform instructions such as the pay-calculating algorithm, the steps must be converted to a form the computer can process. As mentioned earlier, a program is stored in memory as a series of binary numbers. These numbers are known as *machine language instructions.* The CPU only processes instructions written in machine language.

The CPU interprets these binary or machine language numbers as commands. As you might imagine, the process of encoding an algorithm in machine language is tedious and difficult. *Programming languages,* which use words instead of numbers, were invented ease to this task. Programmers can write their applications in programming language statements, then use special software to convert the program into machine language.   ⌐ line of code

Many programming languages have been created. Table 1-1 lists a few of the well-known ones.

Table 1-1

Programming Languages

Language	Description
BASIC	Beginners All-purpose Symbolic Instruction Code, a general-purpose, procedural programming language. It was originally designed to be simple enough for beginners to learn.
FORTRAN	FORmula TRANslator is a procedural language designed for programming complex mathematical algorithms.
COBOL	Common Business-Oriented Language is a procedural language designed for business applications.
Pascal	A structured, general-purpose, procedural language designed primarily for teaching programming.
C	A structured, general-purpose, procedural language developed at Bell Laboratories.
C++	Based on the C language, C++ offers object-oriented features not found in C. C++ was also invented at Bell Laboratories.
Java	An object-oriented language invented at Sun Microsystems. In addition to programs that operate on a single computer, Java may be used to develop programs that run over the Internet, in a Web browser.

Visual Basic .NET is more than just a programming language. It is a programming environment, with tools for creating screen elements and programming language statements. Although Visual Basic, as a whole, is radically different from the original BASIC programming language, the programming statements used in each are similar.

Procedural and Object-Oriented Programming

There are primarily two methods of programming in use today: *procedural* and *object-oriented.* The earliest programming languages were procedural. This means that a program is made of one or more procedures. A *procedure* is a set of programming language statements that are executed by the The statements might gather input from the user, manipulate information stored in the computer's memory, perform calculations, or any other operation necessary to complete its task. The pay-calculating algorithm in Figure 1-3 can be thought of as a procedure. If the algorithm's eight steps are performed in order, one after the other, it will succeed in calculating and displaying the user's gross pay.

Procedural programming was the standard when users were interacting with text-based computer terminals. For example, Figure 1-4 illustrates the screen of an older MS-DOS computer running a program that performs the pay-calculating algorithm. The user has entered the numbers shown in bold.

```
How many hours did you work? 10
How much are you paid per hour? 15
You have earned $150.00
C>_
```

Figure 1-4   Wage Calculator Program

In text-based environments using procedural programs, the user responds to the program. Modern operating systems, such as the Windows family, use a graphical user interface, or *GUI* (pronounced "gooey"). Although GUIs have made programs friendlier and easier to interact with, they have not simplified the task of programming. GUIs make it necessary for the programmer to create a variety of on-screen elements such as windows, dialog boxes, buttons, and menus. Furthermore, the programmer must write statements that handle the user's interactions with these on-screen elements, in any order the user might choose to select them. No longer does the user respond to the program, now the program responds to the user.

This has helped influence the shift from procedural programming to object-oriented programming. Whereas procedural programming is centered on creating procedures, object-oriented programming is centered on creating *objects.* An object is a programming element that contains data and actions. The data contained in an object is known as its *attributes.* In Visual Basic, an object's attributes are called *properties.* The actions that an object performs are known as the object's *methods*. The object is, conceptually, a self-contained unit consisting of data (properties) and actions (methods).

Perhaps the best way to understand objects is to experience a program that uses them. The following steps guide you through the process of running a demonstration program located on the student disk. The program was created with Visual Basic .NET.

TUTORIAL 1-1:

Running an application that demonstrates objects

Step 1:   Insert the student disk into your CD-Rom drive.

Step 2:   Click the Start button. From the menu, click Run…

Step 3:   Assuming your CD-Rom drive is drive D, type the following in the Run dialog box:

D:\Chap1\Program1\bin\Program1.exe

Step 4:   Click the OK button. Once the program loads and executes, the window shown in Figure 1-5 should appear on the screen.

NOTE: *If your CD-Rom drive is a letter other than D, substitute that letter for D.*

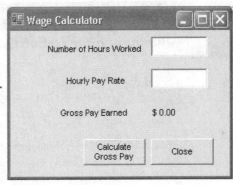

The window shown in Figure 1-5 can be thought of as an object. In Visual Basic .NET terminology, this window object is known as a *Form* object. The form also contains numerous other objects. As shown in Figure 1-6, it has four *Label* objects, two *TextBox* objects, and two *Button* objects. In Visual Basic, these objects are known as *controls.*

The appearance of a screen object, such as a form or other control, is determined by the object's properties. For example, each of the Label controls has a property known as Text. The value stored in the Text property becomes the text displayed by the label. For instance, the

Figure 1-5   Wage Calculator screen

Text property of the topmost label on the form is set to the value "Number of Hours Worked." Beneath it is another Label control, whose Text property is set to "Hourly Pay Rate." The Button controls also have a Text property. The Text property of the leftmost button is set to "Calculate Gross Pay," and the rightmost button has its Text property set to "Close." Even the window, or form, has a Text property, which determines the text displayed in the window's title bar. "Wage Calculator" is the value stored in this form's Text property. Part of the process of creating a Visual Basic .NET application is deciding what values to store in each object's properties.

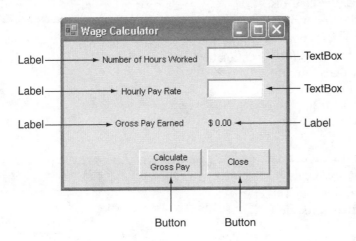

Figure 1-6   Control Names

Event-Driven Programming

Programs that operate in a GUI environment must be *event-driven.* An event is an action that takes place within a program, such as the clicking of a control. All Visual Basic .NET controls are capable of detecting various events. For example, a Button control can detect when it has been clicked, and a Text-Box control can detect when its contents have changed.

Names are assigned to all of the events that can be detected. For instance, when the user clicks a Button control, a `Click` event occurs. When the contents of a TextBox control changes, a `TextChanged` event occurs. If you wish for a control to respond to a specific event, you must write a special type of method known as an *event procedure.* An event procedure is a method that is executed when a specific event occurs. If an event occurs, and there is no event procedure to respond to that event, the event is ignored.

Part of the Visual Basic .NET programming process is designing and writing event procedures. The following steps demonstrate an event procedure using the wage calculator program you executed in Tutorial 1-1.

TUTORIAL 1-2:

Running an application that demonstrates event procedures

Step 1:   With the wage calculator program (\Chap1\Program1\bin\Program1.exe on the student disk) running, enter the value 10 in the first TextBox control. This is the number of hours worked.

Step 2:   Press the tab key. Notice that the cursor moves to the next TextBox control. Enter the value 15. This is the hourly pay rate. The window should look like that shown in Figure 1-7.

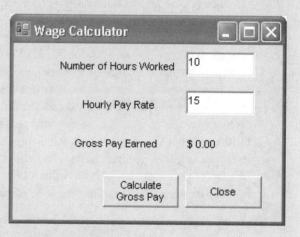

Figure 1-7   Text boxes filled in on Wage Calculator form

Step 3:   Click the Calculate Gross Pay button. Notice that in response to the mouse click, the application multiplies the values you entered in the TextBox controls, and displays the result in a Label control. This action is performed by an event procedure that responds to the button being clicked. The window should look like that shown in Figure 1-8.

Step 4:   Next, click the Close button. The application responds to this event by terminating. This is because an event procedure closes the application when the button is clicked.

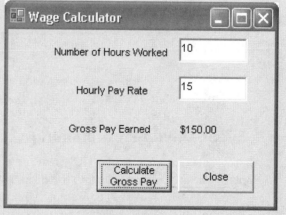

Figure 1-8   Gross pay calculated

This simple application demonstrates the essence of object-oriented, event-driven programming. In the next section, we examine the controls and event procedures more closely.

▶ 1.4 More About Controls and Programming

CONCEPT

AS A VISUAL BASIC .NET PROGRAMMER, YOU MUST DESIGN AND CREATE THE TWO MAJOR COMPONENTS OF AN APPLI-
CATION: <u>THE GUI ELEMENTS</u> (FORMS AND OTHER CONTROLS) AND TH<u>E PROGRAMMING STATEMENTS</u> THAT RESPOND
TO AND/OR PERFORM ACTIONS (EVENT PROCEDURES).

While creating a Visual Basic .NET application, you will primarily spend your time doing three things: creating the GUI elements that make up the application's user interface, setting the properties of the GUI elements, and writing programming language statements that respond to events and perform other operations. In this section, we take a closer look at both of these aspects of Visual Basic .NET programming.

Visual Basic .NET Controls

In the previous section, you saw examples of several GUI elements, or controls. Visual Basic .NET provides a wide assortment of controls for gathering input, displaying information, selecting values, showing graphics, and more. Table 1-2 lists some of the commonly used controls.

Table 1-2

Visual Basic .NET Controls

Control Type	Description
CheckBox	A box that is either checked or un-checked when clicked with the mouse
ComboBox	A control that is the combination of a ListBox and a TextBox
Button	A rectangular button-shaped object that performs an action when clicked with the mouse
Form	A window, onto which other controls may be placed
GroupBox	A rectangular border that functions as a container for other controls
HScrollBar	A horizontal scroll bar that, when moved with the mouse, increases or decreases a value
Label	A box that displays text that cannot be changed or entered by the user
ListBox	A box containing a list of items
RadioButton	A round button that is either selected or deselected when clicked with the mouse
PictureBox	A control that displays a graphic image
TextBox	A rectangular area in which the user can enter text, or the program can display text
VScrollBar	A vertical scroll bar that, when moved with the mouse, increases or decreases a value

If you have any experience using a Windows operating system, you are already familiar with most of the controls listed in Table 1-2. The student disk contains a simple demonstration program that will show you how a few of them work. Follow the steps in Tutorial 1-3 to run the program \Chap1\Program2\bin\Program2.exe, located on the student disk.

Tutorial 1-3:

Running an application that demonstrates various controls

Step 1:   Insert the student disk into your CD-Rom drive.

Step 2:   Click the Start button. From the menu, click Run…

Step 3:   Assuming your CD-Rom drive is drive D, type the following command in the Run dialog box. (As before, substitute your CD-Rom drive letter if it is something other than D.)

D:\Chap1\Program2\bin\Program2.exe

Step 4:   Click the Ok button. Once the program loads and executes, the window shown in Figure 1-9 should appear on the screen.

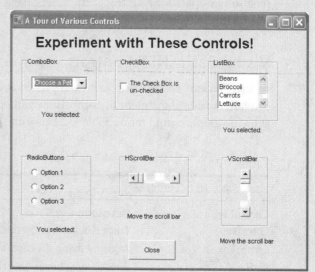

Step 5:   The program presents several Visual Basic .NET controls. Experiment with each one, noticing the following actions, which are performed by event procedures:

Figure 1-9   Control demonstration screen

- When you click on the small down arrow in the ComboBox control, you see a list of pets. When you select one the name of the pet appears below the combo box.

- When you click the CheckBox control, its text changes to indicate that the CheckBox is checked or unchecked.

- When you click an item in the ListBox control, the name of that item appears below the ListBox.

- When you select one of the RadioButton controls, the text below them changes to indicate which one you selected. You may only select one at a time.

- You move the horizontal scroll bar (HScrollBar) and the vertical scroll bar (VScrollBar) by:

- clicking either of the small arrows at each end of the bar

- clicking inside the bar on either side of the slider

- clicking on the slider and, while holding the mouse button down, moving the mouse to the right or left for the horizontal scroll bar, or, up or down for the vertical scroll bar.

◆ When you move either of the scroll bars, the text below it changes to a number. Moving the scroll bar in one direction increases the number, and moving it in the other direction decreases the number.

Step 6: Click the Close button to end the application.

The Name Property

You learned in Section 1.3 that the appearance of a control is determined by its properties. Some properties, however, establish non-visual characteristics. One such property is the control's name. When the programmer wishes to manipulate or access a control in a programming statement, he or she must refer to the control by its name.

When the programmer creates a control in Visual Basic, it automatically receives a *default name.* The first Label control created in an application receives the default name Label1. The second Label control created receives the default name Label2, and the default names continue in this fashion. The first TextBox created in an application is automatically named Text1. As you can imagine, the names for each subsequent TextBox are Text2, Text3, and so forth. Quite often, the programmer changes the control's default name to something more descriptive.

Table 1-3 lists all the controls, by name, that are in the wage calculator program (which you ran in Section 1.3), and Figure 1-10 shows where each is located.

Table 1-3

Wage Calculator controls

Control Name	Control Type	Description
Label1	Label	Displays the message "Number of Hours Worked."
Label2	Label	Displays the message "Hourly Pay Rate."
Label3	Label	Displays the message "Gross Pay Earned."
txtHoursWorked	Text Box	Allows the user to enter the number of hours worked.
txtPayRate	Text Box	Allows the user to enter the hourly pay rate.
lblGrossPay	Label	Displays the gross pay, after the btnCalcGrossPay button has been clicked.
btnCalcGrossPay	Button	When clicked, multiplies the number of hours worked by the hourly pay rate.
btnClose	Button	When clicked, terminates the application.

Control Naming Rules and Conventions

Notice that three of the controls in Figure 1-10, Label1, Label2, and Label3, still have their default names. The other five controls have programmer-defined names. This is because those five controls play an active role in the application's event procedures, which means their names will appear in the application's programming statements. Any control that activates programming statements or whose name appears in a programming statement should have a descriptive, *programmer-defined name.*

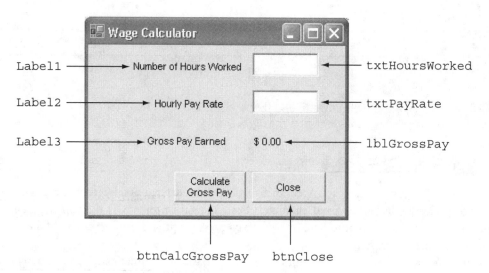

Figure 1-10 Wage Calculator Controls

NOTE: *Some programmers prefer to give all the controls in their application meaningful names, including the ones that do not activate programming statements or whose names do not appear in programming statements.*

Although programmers have a great deal of flexibility in naming controls, they should follow some standard guidelines. First, Visual Basic .NET requires that control names start with a letter. The remaining characters may only be letters, digits, or underscore characters. You cannot have spaces, special symbols, or punctuation characters in a control name. If a control name does not conform to this rule, it is not a legal name. In addition to this mandatory rule, there are three general guidelines to follow when naming controls:

1. The first three letters of the name should be a lowercase prefix that indicates the control's type. Notice that in the Wage Calculator program, the programmer-defined names use the following standard three-letter prefixes:

    lbl indicates a Label control.
    txt indicates a TextBox control.
    btn indicates a Button control.

    There are standard prefixes for other controls as well. These are discussed in Chapter 2.

2. The first letter after the prefix should be uppercase. In addition, if the name consists of multiple words, the first letter of each word should be capitalized. This makes the name more readable. For example, txtHoursWorked is easier to read than txthoursworked.

3. The part of the control name that appears after the three-letter prefix should describe the control's purpose in the application. This makes the control name very helpful to anyone reading the application's programming statements. For example, it is evident that the btnCalcGrossPay control is a button that calculates the gross pay.

Table 1-4 describes several fictitious controls and suggests appropriate programmer-defined names for them.

Table 1-4

Programmer-defined control name examples

Control Description	Suggested Name
A text box in which the user enters his or her age	`txtAge`
A button that, when clicked, calculates the total of an order	`btnCalcTotal`
A label that is used to display the distance from one city to another	`lblDistance`
A text box in which the user enters his or her last name	`txtLastName`
A button that, when clicked, adds a series of numbers	`btnAddNumbers`

These three guidelines are not mandatory rules, but they are standard conventions that other programmers follow. You should use these guidelines when naming the controls in your applications as well.

✓ **Checkpoint**

1.5   What is an algorithm?

1.6   Why were computer programming languages invented?

1.7   What are the two methods of programming in use today?

1.8   What does event-driven mean?

1.9   Describe the difference between a property and a method.

1.10   Why should the programmer change the name of a control from its default name?

1.11   If a control has the programmer-defined name `txtRadius`, what type of control is it?

1.12   What is the default name given to the first TextBox control created in an application?

1.13   Is `txtFirst+LastName` an acceptable control name? Why or why not?

Programming an Application

When a Visual Basic .NET programmer creates an object, such as a form or other control, he or she must also create many of the object's methods. You learned in Section 1.3 that an object's methods are the actions it can perform. In essence, a method is a script of detailed instructions that an object follows to perform an action. Event procedures are one example of an object's methods.

Methods are written in programming statements, which are generally referred to as *code*. The wage calculating program has two event procedures. One of them responds to the clicking of the `btnCalcGrossPay` control. The code for that event procedure is as follows.

```
Private Sub btnCalcGrossPay_Click(ByVal sender As System.Object, _
    ByVal e As System.EventArgs) Handles btnCalcGrossPay.Click
        Dim grossPay As Single
        ' The next line calculates the gross pay.
        grossPay = Val(txtHoursWorked.Text) * Val(txtPayRate.Text)
        lblGrossPay.Text = FormatCurrency(grossPay)
End Sub
```

The application's other event procedure responds to the clicking of the `btnClose` control. Its code is as follows.

```
Private Sub btnClose_Click(ByVal sender As System.Object, _
    ByVal e As System.EventArgs) Handles btnClose.Click
    ' End the application.
    End
End Sub
```

Don't worry if you do not understand any of this code. By the end of Chapter 2, you will not only understand code like this, you will also be able to write it. For now, let's try to understand the fundamental language elements of a Visual Basic .NET method. Table 1-5 lists the elements you should know about.

Table 1-5

Visual Basic .NET language elements

Language Element	Description
Key words	Words that have a special meaning in a programming language. Key words may only be used for their intended purpose. Some examples in Visual Basic .NET are Private, Sub, Dim, and End.
Programmer-defined names	Words or names defined by the programmer
Operators	Operators perform operations on one or more operands. An *operand* is usually a piece of data, such as a number. Some examples of operators are +, −, *, and /.
Remarks	Also known as *comments*, *remarks* are notes of explanation that document lines or sections in a method. Remarks are part of an application, but they are ignored when the application is running. They are intended for the programmer or others who might read the application's code.
Syntax	Rules that must be followed when constructing a method. *Syntax* dictates how key words, operators, and programmer-defined names may be used.

Let's look at some specific parts of the wage calculating program to see examples of each element listed in the Table 1-5. For your convenience, the wage calculating program's event procedures are listed as follows, this time with each line numbered.

```
1:   Private Sub btnCalcGrossPay_Click(ByVal sender As System.Object, _
2:       ByVal e As System.EventArgs) Handles btnCalcGrossPay.Click
3:       Dim grossPay As Single
4:       ' The next line calculates the gross pay.
5:       grossPay = Val(txtHoursWorked.Text) * Val(txtPayRate.Text)
6:       lblGrossPay.Text = FormatCurrency(grossPay)
7:   End Sub

8:   Private Sub btnClose_Click(ByVal sender As System.Object, _
9:       ByVal e As System.EventArgs) Handles btnClose.Click
10:      ' End the application.
11:      End
12:  End Sub
```

NOTE: *The line numbers are not part of the program. They are used in the following paragraphs to help point out specific parts of the program.*

Key Words

In line 1 are two key words: `Private` and `Sub`. These key words are repeated in line 8. The words `End` and `Sub`, which appear in lines 7 and 12, are key words, as is the word `Dim`, which appears in line 3. These words each have a special meaning in Visual Basic .NET and can only be used for their intended purpose. As you will see, the programmer is allowed to make up his or her own names for certain things in a program. Key words, however, are reserved and cannot be used for anything other than their designated purpose. Part of learning a programming language is learning what the key words are, what they mean, and how to use them.

Programmer-Defined Names

The word `grossPay` which appears in lines 3, 5, and 6, is a programmer-defined name. It is not part of the Visual Basic .NET language but is a name that is made up by the programmer. In this particular program, it is the name of a variable. As discussed in Chapter 3, variables are the names of memory locations that may hold data.

Operators

In line 5 the following statement appears.

```
grossPay = Val(txtHoursWorked.Text) * Val(txtPayRate.Text)
```

The = and * symbols are both operators. They perform operations on pieces of data, known as operands. The * operator multiplies two operands, and the = operator stores a value in a variable or a property. The word `Val` converts text to a number. You will learn more about it in Chapter 3.

Remarks

Line 4 reads

```
' The next line calculates the gross pay.
```

In addition, line 10 reads

```
' End the application.
```

Notice that each of these lines begins with an apostrophe. This symbol marks the beginning of a remark. A remark is meant for the human readers of an application's code, not the computer. When an application is running, the system ignores everything on a line that appears after an apostrophe symbol.

The remark in line 4 informs the reader what the next line does: It calculates the gross pay. The remark in line 10 indicates that the next line of code will end the application. It is important that you develop the habit of annotating your code with descriptive comments like this. It might take extra time now, but it will almost certainly save time in the future when you, or another programmer, attempt to modify or correct your application.

Syntax

Each of the statements in the event procedures is written according to the rules of the Visual Basic .NET language. These rules, which collectively are known as the language's syntax, define the correct way that key words, operators, and programmer-defined names may be used. If a programming statement violates the Visual Basic .NET syntax, the application will not run until it is corrected.

▶ 1.5   The Programming Process

Designing and Creating an Application

Now that you have been introduced to what a Visual Basic .NET application is, it's time to consider the process of creating one. Quite often, when inexperienced students are given programming assignments, they have trouble getting started because they don't know what to do first. If you find yourself facing this dilemma, the steps listed below may help. These are the steps recommended for developing a Visual Basic .NET application.

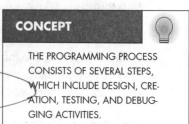

CONCEPT

THE PROGRAMMING PROCESS CONSISTS OF SEVERAL STEPS, WHICH INCLUDE DESIGN, CREATION, TESTING, AND DEBUGGING ACTIVITIES.

Steps for Developing a Visual Basic .NET Application

1. Clearly define what the application is to do.
2. Visualize the application running on the computer and design its user interface.
3. Make a list of the controls needed.
4. Define the values of each control's relevant properties.
5. Make a list of methods needed for each control.
6. Create a flowchart or pseudocode version of each method.
7. Check the flowchart or pseudocode for errors.
8. Start Visual Basic .NET and create the forms and other controls identified in step 3.
9. Write the code for the event procedures and other methods created in step 6.
10. Attempt to run the application. Correct any syntax errors found and repeat this step as many times as necessary.
11. Once all syntax errors are corrected, run the program with test data for input. Correct any run time errors. Repeat this step as many times as necessary.

These steps emphasize the importance of planning. Just as there are good ways and bad ways to paint a house, there are good ways and bad ways to write a program. A good program always begins with planning.

With the wage calculating program as our example, let's look at each of these steps in greater detail.

1. Clearly define what the program is to do.

This step requires that you identify the purpose of the program, the information that is to be input, the processing that is to take place, and the desired output. For example, these requirements for the wage calculating program are

Purpose: To calculate the user's gross pay.
Input: Number of hours worked, hourly pay rate.
Process: Multiply number of hours worked by hourly pay rate. The result is the user's gross pay.
Output: Display a message indicating the user's gross pay.

2. Visualize the application running on the computer and design its user interface.

Before you create an application on the computer, you should first create it in your mind. Step 2 is the visualization of the program. Try to imagine what the computer screen will look like while the application is running. Then, sketch the form or forms in the application. For instance, Figure 1-11 shows a sketch of the form presented by the wage calculator program.

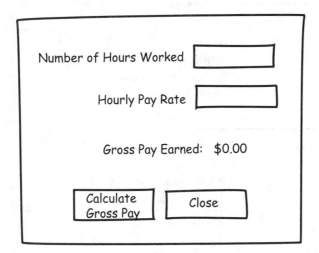

Figure 1-11   Sketch of the Wage Calculator form

3. Make a list of the controls needed.

The next step is to list all the controls needed. You should assign names to all the controls that will be accessed or manipulated in the application code and provide a brief description of each control. Table 1-6 lists the controls in the wage calculator application.

Table 1-6

Wage Calculator controls

Control Type	Control Name	Description
Form	(Default)	A small form that will serve as the window onto which the other controls will be placed
Label	(Default)	Displays the message "Number of Hours Worked."
Label	(Default)	Displays the message "Hourly Pay Rate."
Label	(Default)	Displays the message "Gross Pay Earned."
TextBox	txtHoursWorked	Allows the user to enter the number of hours worked.
TextBox	txtPayRate	Allows the user to enter the hourly pay rate.
Label	lblGrossPay	Displays the gross pay, after the btnCalcGrossPay button has been clicked.
Button	btnCalcGrossPay	When clicked, multiplies the number of hours worked by the hourly pay rate
Button	btnClose	When clicked, terminates the application

4. Define the values of each control's relevant properties.

Other than Name, Text is the only control property modified in the wage calculator application. Table 1-7 lists the value of each control's Text property.

Table 1-7

Wage Calculator control values

Control Type	Control Name	Text
Form	(Default)	"Wage Calculator"
Label	(Default)	"Number of Hours Worked"
Label	(Default)	"Hourly Pay Rate"
Label	(Default)	"Gross Pay Earned"
Label	lblGrossPay	"$0.00"
TextBox	txtHoursWorked	" "
TextBox	txtPayRate	" "
Button	btnCalcGrossPay	"Calculate Gross Pay"
Button	btnClose	"Close"

5. Make a list of methods needed for each control.

Next you should list the event procedures and other methods you will write. There are only two event procedures in the wage calculator application. Table 1-8 lists and describes them. Notice the Visual Basic .NET names for the event procedures. btnCalcGrossPay_Click is the name of the procedure invoked when the btnCalcGrossPay button is clicked, and btnClose_Click is the event procedure that executes when the btnClose button is clicked.

Table 1-8

Wage Calculator event procedures

Method	Description
btnCalcGrossPay_Click	Multiplies the number of hours worked by the hourly pay rate. These values are entered into the txtHoursWorked and txtPayRate TextBoxes. The result is stored in the lblGrossPay Text property.
btnClose_Click	Terminates the application.

6. Create a flowchart or pseudocode version of each method.

A flowchart is a diagram that graphically depicts the flow of a method. It uses boxes and other symbols to represent each step. Figure 1-12 shows a flowchart for the btnCalcGross Pay_Click event procedure.

Notice there are two types of boxes in the flowchart in Figure 1-12: ovals and rectangles. The flowchart begins with an oval labeled Start, and ends with another oval labeled End. The rectangles represent a computational process or other operation. Notice that the symbols are connected with arrows that indicate the direction of program flow.

Many programmers prefer to use pseudocode instead of flowcharts. *Pseudocode* is a cross between human language and a programming language. Although the computer can't understand pseudocode, programmers often find it helpful to plan an algorithm in a language that's almost a programming language but still very human-readable. Here is a pseudocode version of the btnCalcGrossPay_Click event procedure:

```
Store Number of Hours Worked times Hourly Pay Rate in grossPay.
Store the value in grossPay in lblGrossPay.Text.
```

7. Check the code for errors.

In this phase the programmer starts reading the flowcharts and/or pseudocode at the beginning and steps through each operation, pretending that he or she is the computer. A sheet of paper is often used in this process to jot down the current contents of variables and properties that change, and sketch what the screen looks like after each output operation. By stepping through each step, a programmer can locate and correct many errors.

8. Start Visual Basic .NET and create the forms and other controls identified in step 3.

This step is the first actual work done on the computer. Here, the programmer uses Visual Basic .NET to create the application's user interface and arrange the controls on each form.

9. Write code for the event procedures and other methods created in step 6.

This is the second step performed on the computer. The event procedures and other methods may be converted into code and entered into the computer using the Visual Basic .NET environment.

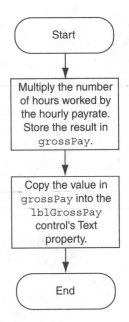

Figure 1-12
Flowchart for
`btnCalcGrossPay_`
`Click` event
procedure

10. Attempt to run the application. Correct any syntax errors found and repeat this step as many times as necessary.

If you have entered code with syntax errors or typing mistakes, this step will uncover them. A *syntax error* is the incorrect use of a programming language element, such as a key word, operator, or programmer-defined name. Correct your mistakes and repeat this step until the program runs.

11. Once all syntax errors are corrected, run the program with test data for input. Correct any run-time errors (errors found while running the program). Repeat this step as many times as necessary.

Run-time errors are mistakes that do not prevent an application from executing but cause it to produce incorrect results. For example, a mistake in a mathematical formula is a common type of run-time error. When run-time errors are found in a program, they must be corrected and the program retested. This step must be repeated until the program reliably produces satisfactory results.

✓ Checkpoint

1.14 What four items should be identified when defining what a program is to do?

1.15 Describe the importance of good planning in the process of creating a Visual Basic .NET application.

1.16 What does it mean to visualize a program running? What is the value of such an activity?

1.17 What is a flowchart?

1.18 What is pseudocode?

1.19 What is a run-time error?

1.20 What is the purpose of testing a program with sample data or input?

1.21 How much testing should you perform on a new program?

▶ 1.6   Visual Studio and the Visual Basic .NET Environment

In Chapter 2 you will build your first Visual Basic .NET application. First, you need to know how to start Visual Studio and understand its major components. Visual Studio is an *integrated development environment (IDE),* which is an application that provides all the tools necessary for creating, testing, and debugging software. Visual Studio is quite powerful, and can be used to create applications not only with Visual Basic, but other languages such as Visual C++ and C# (pronounced C-sharp). This section guides you through the Visual Studio startup process and gives you a hands-on tour of its tools for creating Visual Basic .NET applications.

CONCEPT

VISUAL STUDIO CONSISTS OF TOOLS THAT YOU USE TO BUILD VISUAL BASIC .NET APPLICATIONS. THE FIRST STEP IN VISUAL BASIC .NET IS LEARNING ABOUT THESE TOOLS.

TUTORIAL 1-4:

Starting Visual Studio

The following steps guide you through the Visual Studio startup process.

Step 1:   Click the Start button and open the Programs menu (or the All Programs menu if you are using Windows XP).

Step 2:   Click Microsoft Visual Studio.NET. Another menu appears. Click Microsoft Visual Studio.NET. You will momentarily see the Visual Studio logo screen. Visual Studio displays the Start Page similar to that shown in Figure 1-13.

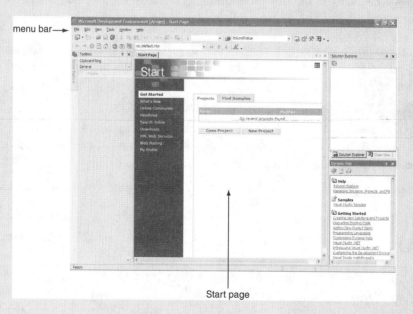

menu bar →

Start page

Figure 1-13   Visual Studio Start Page

NOTE: *Your screen may not appear exactly as that shown in Figure 1-13. For example, some of the windows shown in the figure may not be open on your screen. This chapter will show you how to control the appearance of Visual Studio .NET.*

TIP: If you do not see the Start page shown in Figure 1-13, click Help in the menu bar, then click Show Start Page.

Step 3:   Visual Studio allows you to select a profile that customizes it for a specific programming language. You should select a profile that customizes Visual Studio for Visual Basic. On the Start page click My Profile. This causes the Start page to display your current profile settings. Make sure that Visual Basic Developer is selected under Profile, as shown in Figure 1-14.

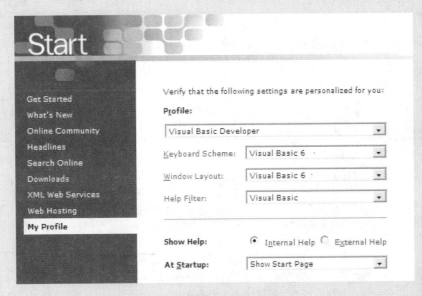

Figure 1-14   Start page with profile settings shown

Step 4:   Click Get Started on the Start page.

Step 5:   Each application you create with Visual Studio is a project. Now you will start a new project. Click the New Project button on the Start page.

   TIP: You may also click File on the menu bar, then click New, and then click Project.

   The New Project dialog box shown in Figure 1-15 appears.

Step 6:   The left pane, which is labeled Project Types, lists the different programming languages available in Visual Studio. The right pane, which is labeled Templates, shows the various types of applications that you may create in the selected language. Select Visual Basic Projects under Project Types and select Windows Application under Templates.

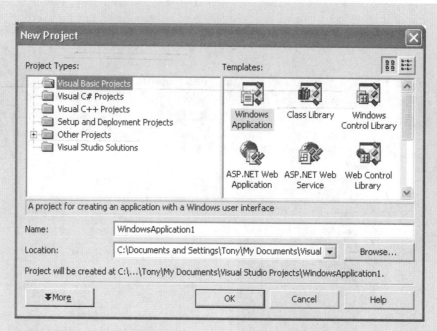

Figure 1-15   New Project dialog box

Step 7:   The Name text box is where you enter the name of your project. Visual Studio automatically fills this box with a default name. In Figure 1-15 the default name is WindowsApplication1. Change the project name to **Tutorial 1-1.**

NOTE: *A project consists of numerous files. When you begin a new project, Visual Studio stores the files in a folder with the same name as the project. As you create more and more projects, you will find that default names such as WindowsApplication1 do not help you remember what each project does. Therefore you should always change the name of a new project to something that describes the project's purpose.*

Step 8:   The Location text box shows where the project folder will be created on your system. If you wish to change the location, click the Browse button and select the desired drive and folder.

Step 9:   Click the OK button. You should now see the Visual Basic .NET environment similar to that shown in Figure 1-16.

NOTE: *Visual Basic .NET is customizable. Your screen might not appear exactly as shown in Figure 1-16. As you continue in this chapter, you will learn how to arrange the screen elements in different ways.*

Step 10:   Now you will set some of the Visual Basic .NET options so your screens and code will appear as the examples shown in this book. Click Tools on the menu bar. On the Tools menu, click Options... The Options dialog box appears. In the left pane click Text Editor, then click Basic. The dialog box should now appear as shown in Figure 1-16. With General selected in the left pane, make sure that your settings match those in Figure 1-17. Specifically, make sure that the auto list members, hide advanced members, parameter information, and enable single-click URL navigation options are checked. Also, make sure that the enable virtual space, word wrap, and line numbers options are unchecked.

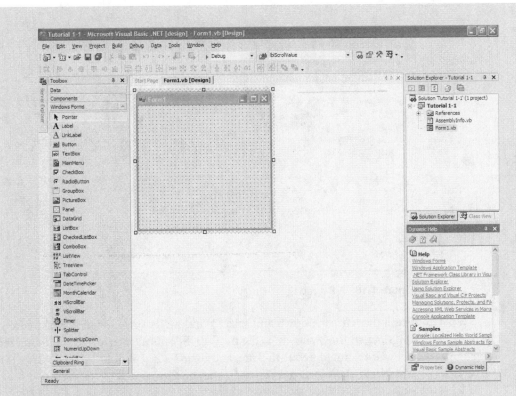

Figure 1-16   Visual Basic .NET environment with a new project open

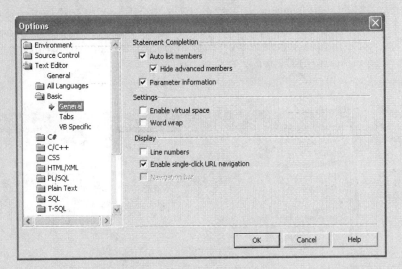

Figure 1-17   Options dialog box

Step 11:   In the left pane, click on VB Specific. Make sure the automatic insertion of end constructs, pretty listing (reformatting) of code, and enter outlining mode when files open options are selected, as shown in Figure 1-18.

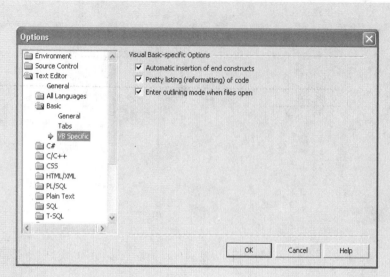

Figure 1-18   VB-specific settings

Step 12: Scroll the left pane down and select Windows Forms Designer. Make sure your settings match those shown in Figure 1-19. Specifically, GridSize should be set to 8, 8, ShowGrid should be set to True, and SnapToGrid should be set to True. These settings control the grid you will use to design forms.

TIP: To change the GridSize setting, click the area where the current setting is displayed, erase it, and enter **8**, **8** as the new setting. To change either the ShowGrid or SnapToGrid settings, click the area where the current setting is displayed, then click the down-arrow button ([▾]) that appears. Select True from the menu that drops down.

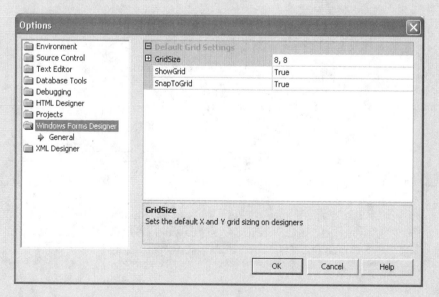

Figure 1-19   Windows Forms Designer settings

Step 13:   Click OK to close the dialog box.

> **NOTE:**   *The options you set in steps 10 through 13 will remain set until you or someone else changes them. If you are working in a shared computer lab and you find that your screens and/or the appearance of your code does not match the examples shown in this book, you will probably need to reset these options.*

The Visual Basic .NET Environment

The Visual Basic .NET environment consists of a number of windows and other components. Figure 1-20 shows the locations of the following components: the Design Window, the Solution Explorer window, the Dynamic Help window and Dynamic Help window tab, and the Properties window tab.

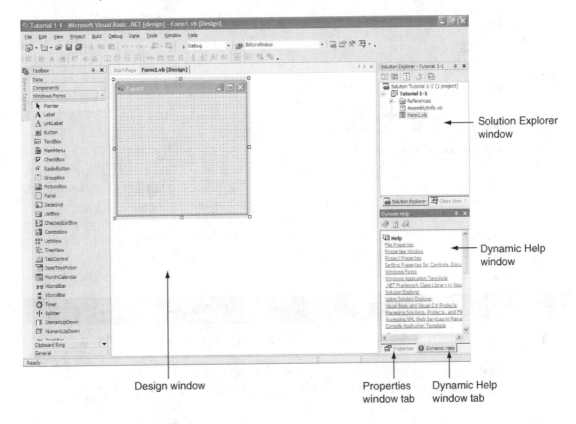

Figure 1-20   The Design window, Solution Explorer window, Dynamic Help window and Dynamic Help windows tab, and Properties windows tab

The Properties window and the Dynamic Help window share the same location on the screen. You click the Properties window tab to display the Properties window, and the Dynamic Help window tab to display the Dynamic Help window. Your system may show the Properties window displayed instead of the Dynamic Help window, as shown in Figure 1-21.

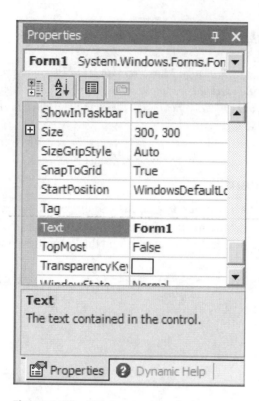

Figure 1-21   The Properties window

It is also possible that the Dynamic Help window is not displayed at all on your system. If this is the case, you will not see it or the Dynamic Help window tab.

You can move the windows around, so they may not appear in the exact location on your screen as shown in Figure 1-20. You can also close the windows so they do not appear at all. If you do not see one or more of them, follow the steps in Tutorial 1-5 to make them visible.

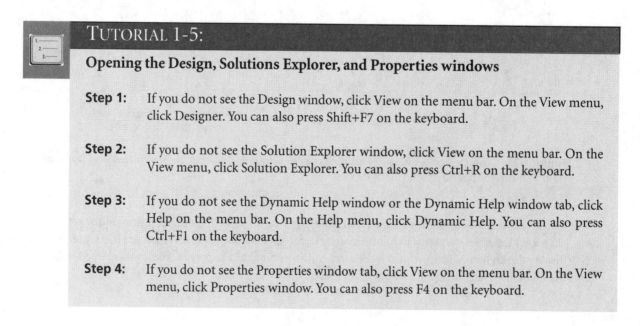

TUTORIAL 1-5:

Opening the Design, Solutions Explorer, and Properties windows

Step 1:   If you do not see the Design window, click View on the menu bar. On the View menu, click Designer. You can also press Shift+F7 on the keyboard.

Step 2:   If you do not see the Solution Explorer window, click View on the menu bar. On the View menu, click Solution Explorer. You can also press Ctrl+R on the keyboard.

Step 3:   If you do not see the Dynamic Help window or the Dynamic Help window tab, click Help on the menu bar. On the Help menu, click Dynamic Help. You can also press Ctrl+F1 on the keyboard.

Step 4:   If you do not see the Properties window tab, click View on the menu bar. On the View menu, click Properties window. You can also press F4 on the keyboard.

Step 5: Both the Properties window tab and the Dynamic Help window tab should be visible. Practice switching between the Properties window and the Dynamic Help window by clicking the tabs. When you are finished, leave the Properties window displayed.

Hidden Windows

Many of the windows in the Visual Basic .NET environment have a feature known as auto hide. When a window's *auto hide* feature is turned on, the window normally stays minimized as a tab along one of the edges of the screen. This gives you more room to view your application's forms and code. Figure 1-22 shows how the Solution Explorer and Properties windows appear when their auto hide feature is turned on. The figure shows the right edge of the screen.

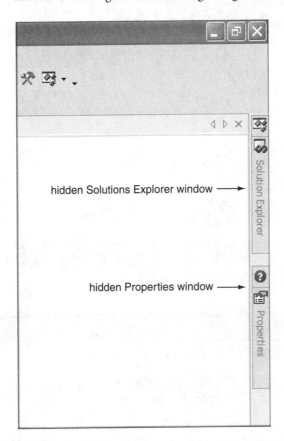

Figure 1-22 The Solution Explorer and Properties windows hidden

To display a hidden window, you simply position the mouse cursor over its tab. This pulls the window back into view. If you want the window to remain in view for a time, pull it into view and then click it. The window will remain displayed until you click outside of it. Tutorials 1-6 and 1-7 guide you through the steps of turning the auto hide feature on and off.

TUTORIAL 1-6:

Turning auto hide on

Step 1: Notice the pushpin icon (⬛) in the upper right corner of the Solution Explorer window. This icon controls the window's auto hide feature. Click the icon to turn auto hide on and move the mouse cursor away from the window. After a moment, the window slides out of view and is replaced by a tab on the right edge of the screen, as shown in Figure 1-23.

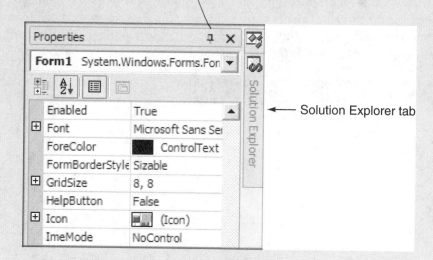

Figure 1-23   The Solution Explorer window hidden

> **TIP:** When a window's pushpin icon points down, as shown in Figure 1-23, that window's auto hide feature is turned off. When the pushpin icon points to the left, Auto hide is turned on.

Step 2: Turn the Properties window's auto hide feature on by clicking its pushpin icon. Move the mouse cursor away from the window. Now both the Solution Explorer and Properties windows are hidden and replaced with tabs.

Step 3: Position the mouse cursor over either of the tabs to display its window. When the window appears, click inside it to select it. The window will remain visible until you click outside it.

> **TIP:** You can also turn a window's auto hide feature on by selecting the window, then clicking Window on the menu bar, then clicking Auto Hide.

TUTORIAL 1-7:

Turning auto hide off

Step 1: Bring the Solutions Explorer window into view and click it. Click the pushpin button (⊟) to turn auto hide off. The window will now remain visible when it is not selected.

Step 2: Bring the Properties window into view and click it. Click the pushpin button (⊟) to turn auto hide off. The window will now remain visible when it is not selected.

> **TIP:** You can also turn a window's auto hide feature off by selecting the window, then clicking Window on the menu bar, then clicking Auto Hide.

Although you will learn more about the Design, Solution Explorer, Dynamic Help, and Properties windows as you progress through this book, a brief overview is given here.

Design Window

The *Design window contains your application's forms. This is where you design your application's user interface by creating forms and placing controls on them.*

> **NOTE:** *The tiny dots that appear on forms in the Design window are part of a grid that is only displayed while you are designing your application. The grid does not appear on the form while the application is running.*

Solution Explorer Window

A *solution* is a container for holding Visual Basic .NET projects. A project is a group of files that make up a Visual Basic .NET application. When you create a new project, a new solution is automatically created to contain it. The Solution Explorer window allows you to navigate quickly among the files in your Visual Basic .NET application.

The Dynamic Help Window

The *Dynamic Help window* displays a list of help topics that changes as you perform operations. The topics that are displayed are relevant to the operation you are currently performing.

The Properties Window

The *Properties window* shows most of the currently selected object's properties and those properties' values. For example, if a form is selected, the Properties window shows the form's properties and their values. The Properties window also allows you to change a property's value while you are designing an application.

> **NOTE:** *Some properties can only be set with code, while the application is running. The Properties window only shows the properties that may be set while you are designing the application.*

Docked and Floating Windows

Figure 1-20 shows the Project Explorer and Properties windows *docked*, which means they are attached to each other or to one of the edges of the Visual Basic .NET main window. When you click and drag one of these windows by its title bar, you move it out of the docked position, and the window becomes *floating*. Double-clicking the window's title bar produces the same effect. Figure 1-24 shows these windows floating.

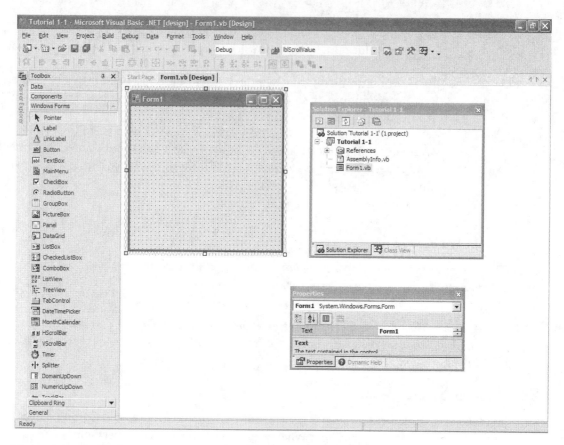

Figure 1-24   Solution Explorer and Properties windows floating

TIP: A window cannot float if its auto hide feature is turned on.

To dock one of these floating windows, double-click its title bar or drag it to one of the edges of the main window. You may use whichever style, docked or floating, you prefer. When these windows are floating, they behave as normal windows. You may move or resize them to suit your preference.

You now have the Visual Basic .NET environment set up properly to work with the projects in this book. Next, we will look at the other elements of the Visual Basic .NET environment. Figure 1-25 shows the Visual Basic .NET environment with additional components labeled.

The Title Bar

The title bar indicates the name of the project you are currently working on. The title bar in Figure 1-24 shows the name Tutorial 1-1. The [design] designator that appears on the title bar indicates that Visual Basic .NET is currently operating in design time. *Design time* is the mode in which you build an application. Chapter 2 covers run time, which is the mode in which you are running and testing an application, and break time, which is the mode in which an application is suspended for debugging purposes.

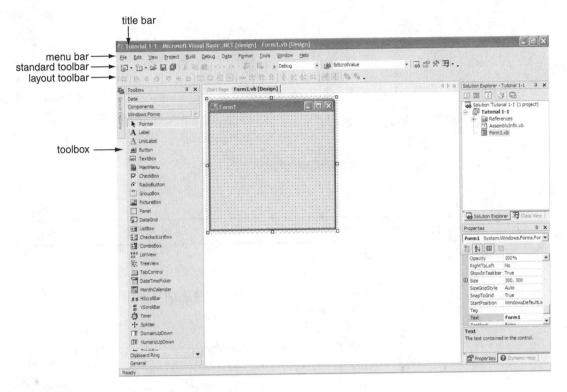

Figure 1-25   Visual Basic .NET environment

The Menu Bar

Below the title bar is the menu bar. This is where you access the Visual Basic .NET menus while you are building an application.

The Standard Toolbar

Below the menu bar is the standard toolbar. The standard toolbar contains numerous buttons that execute frequently used commands. All of the commands executed by the toolbar may also be executed from a menu, but the standard toolbar gives you quicker access to them. For example, in Tutorial 1-2 you were instructed to open the Solution Explorer and Properties windows if they were not already open. You opened these windows by clicking on the View menu, and then selecting the appropriate command. The standard toolbar contains a set of buttons that opens these windows in a single click.

Figure 1-26 points out the standard toolbar buttons, and Table 1-9 gives a brief description of each.

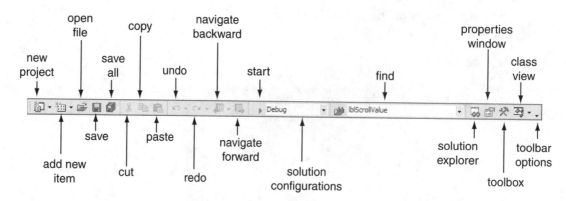

Figure 1-26   Visual Basic .NET standard toolbar

Table 1-9

Visual Basic .NET toolbar buttons

Toolbar Button	Description
New project	Starts a new project
Add new item	Adds a new item such as a form to the current project
Open file	Opens an existing file
Save	Saves the current file
Save all	Saves all of the files in the current project
Cut	Cuts the selected item to the clipboard
Copy	Copies the selected item to the clipboard
Paste	Pastes the contents of the clipboard
Undo	Undoes the most recent operation
Redo	Redoes the most recently undone operation
Navigate backward	Allows you to navigate backward through the items represented by the tabs at the top of the Design window
Navigate forward	Allows you to navigate forward through the items represented by the tabs at the top of the forms designer window
Start	Causes the current application to begin executing
Solution configurations	An advanced feature that allows you to set the solution's build configuration. The build configuration may be set to debug (while the application is under development), release (when the application is complete), or a custom configuration.
Find	Searches for text in your application code
Solution Explorer	Opens the Solution Explorer window
Properties Window	Opens the Properties window
Toolbox	Opens the toolbox
Class view	Provides a hierarchical, tree structured, object-oriented view of a project
Toolbar options	Allows you to add or remove buttons to the toolbar

NOTE: *As with most Windows applications, menu items and buttons cannot be used when they are grayed out.*

The Layout Toolbar

The buttons on the layout toolbar allow you to format the layout of controls on a form. There are buttons for aligning, sizing, spacing, centering, and ordering controls.

The Toolbox

Figure 1-27 shows the toolbox. It contains buttons, or tools, for the Visual Basic .NET controls. You use these tools to place controls on an application's form. The toolbox is divided into sections which are accessible by tabs. Figure 1-27 shows the toolbox with the Windows Forms tab open. This section contains tools for commonly used controls such as Buttons, Labels, and TextBoxes. Because all of the control tools cannot be displayed at once, the toolbox provides scroll arrows.

TIP: Don't confuse the toolbox with the toolbar. The toolbar usually appears under the menu bar, and provides quick access to frequently used commands. The toolbox allows you to place controls on a form.

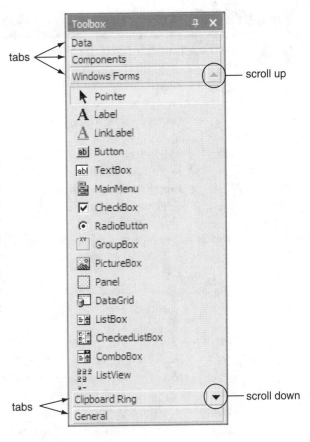

Figure 1-27 The Toolbox

Using Tooltips

A *tooltip* is a small box that is displayed when you hold the mouse cursor over a button on the toolbar or in the toolbox for a few seconds. The box gives a short description of what the button does. Figure 1-28 shows the tooltip that appears when the cursor is left sitting on the save all button. Use tooltips whenever you cannot remember a particular button's function.

Figure 1-28 Save All tooltip

TUTORIAL 1-8:

Getting familiar with the Visual Basic .NET environment

This activity should be continued from the previous tutorial. If Visual Basic .NET is not running on your computer, follow the steps in Tutorial 1-4. This exercise will give you practice working with elements of the Visual Basic .NET environment.

Step 1: Make sure auto hide is turned off for the Solution Explorer and Properties windows. (See Tutorials 1-6 and 1-7 if you cannot remember how.) If your Solution Explorer and Properties windows are in the docked position, double-click on each of their title bars to undock them. (If they are already floating, skip to step 2.)

Step 2: Practice moving the windows around on the screen by clicking and dragging their title bars.

Step 3: Double-click the title bars of each of the windows to move them back to their docked positions.

Step 4: The Solution Explorer, Properties window, Dynamic Help window, and toolbox each have a close button (❎) in their upper right corner. Close each of these four windows by clicking their close buttons.

Step 5: Do you remember which buttons on the toolbar restore the Solution Explorer, Properties window, and toolbox? If not, move your cursor over any button on the toolbar, and leave it there until the tooltip appears. Repeat this procedure on different buttons until you find the ones whose tooltips read "Solution Explorer", "Properties Window", and "Toolbox".

Step 6: Click the appropriate buttons on the toolbar to restore the Project Explorer, Properties, Dynamic Help, and Form Layout windows.

Step 7: Exit Visual Basic .NET by clicking File on the menu bar, then clicking Exit on the File menu. You may see a dialog box asking you if you wish to save changes to a number of items. Because we are just experimenting with the Visual Basic .NET environment, click No.

In this section, you have learned to start Visual Studio, interact with the Visual Basic .NET environment, and identify many of its on-screen tools and components. In Chapter 2, you will start building your first application.

✓ Checkpoint

1.22 Briefly describe the purpose of the Solution Explorer window.

1.23 Briefly describe the purpose of the Properties window.

1.24 Briefly describe the purpose of the Dynamic Help window.

1.25 Briefly describe the purposes of the standard toolbar and the layout toolbar.

1.26 What is design time? What is run time? What is break time?

1.27 What is the difference between the toolbar and the toolbox?

1.28 What is a tooltip?

SUMMARY

The major hardware components of a computer are the central processing unit (CPU), main memory, secondary storage devices, input devices, and output devices.

The CPU's job is to fetch instructions, carry out operations commanded by the instructions, and produce an outcome.

Computer programs are stored in machine language, as a series of binary numbers.

Main memory, or random-access memory (RAM) holds information. It is a volatile type of memory, used for temporary storage. Memory is divided into bytes, each of which is assigned a unique address.

Secondary storage holds information for long periods of time. The disk drive is an example of secondary storage.

Input is information the computer collects. Input devices are used to collect the information.

Output is information the computer sends to the outside world. Output devices are used to format and present the information.

Software refers to the programs that run on a computer. The two general categories of software are operating systems and application software.

An algorithm is a set of well-defined steps for performing a task or solving a problem.

Computer programming languages, which use words instead of numbers to program the computer, were invented to ease the task of programming.

The two primary methods of programming in use today are procedural and object-oriented.

An object is a programming element that contains data and actions. The data contained in an object is known as its attributes. In Visual Basic, an object's attributes are called properties. The actions that an object performs are known as the object's methods.

The advent of graphical user interfaces (GUIs) has influenced the shift from procedural programming to object-oriented.

There are several types of controls available in Visual Basic. Applications in this chapter contained forms, Labels, TextBoxes, Buttons, CheckBoxes, RadioButtons, ListBoxes, ComboBoxes, and scroll bars.

The appearance of a screen object, such as a form or other control, is determined by the object's properties.

An event-driven program is one that responds to events or actions that take place while the program is running.

All controls have a name. When the programmer wishes to manipulate or access a control in a programming statement, he or she must refer to the control by its name.

When the programmer creates a control in Visual Basic, it automatically receives a default name.

Any control whose name appears in a programming statement should have a descriptive, programmer-defined name.

Although programmers have a great deal of flexibility in naming controls, they should follow some standard guidelines.

The fundamental language elements of an event procedure or other method are key words, programmer-defined names, operators, remarks, and syntax.

This chapter outlines an 11-step process for designing and creating a Visual Basic .NET application.

The Visual Basic .NET environment, which is part of Visual Studio, consists of tools that are used to build Visual Basic .NET applications.

Visual Basic .NET can be used to create many different types of applications. The New Project dialog box is used to indicate what type of application is being created.

The Options dialog box is used to set various options in Visual Studio.

A solution is a container for holding projects. A project is a group of files that make up a software application.

The Design window contains your application's forms. This is where you design your application's user interface by creating forms and placing controls on them.

The Solution Explorer window allows you to navigate quickly among the files in your Visual Basic .NET application.

The Dynamic Help window displays a list of help topics that changes as you perform operations. The topics that are displayed are relevant to the operation you are currently performing.

The Properties window shows, and allows you to change, most of the currently selected object's properties and those properties' values.

The Solution Explorer and Properties windows may be docked or floating.

Design time is the mode in which an application is built.

Run time is the mode in which an application is run and tested.

The standard toolbar contains buttons that execute frequently used commands. The layout toolbar contains buttons for formatting the layout of controls on a form.

The toolbox contains buttons, or tools, that are used to place controls on a form.

A tooltip is a small box that is displayed when the cursor is held over a button on the toolbar or in the toolbox for a few seconds. The box gives a short description of what the button does.

KEY TERMS

Address	Desk-checking
Algorithm	Disk drive
Application software	Dynamic Help window
Attributes	Event procedure
Binary number	Event-driven
Button	Floating
Central processing unit (CPU)	Flowchart
CheckBox	Form
Code	Graphical user interface (GUI)
ComboBox	GroupBox
Control	Hardware
Default name	Horizontal scroll bar
Design time	Input device
Design window	Integrated development environment (IDE)

Key words

Label

ListBox

Machine language

Main memory

Methods

Name property

New Project dialog box

Object

Object-oriented programming

Operating system

Operator

Options dialog box

Output device

Picture box

Procedural programming

Procedure

Program

Programmer-assigned name

Programmer-defined names

Programming languages

Project

Properties

Properties window

Pseudocode

RadioButton

Random-access memory (RAM)

Remark

Run-time error

Secondary storage

Software

Solution

Syntax

Syntax error

Text property

TextBox

Toolbar, layout

Toolbar, standard

Toolbox

Tooltip

Vertical scroll bar

Review Questions

Fill-in-the-blank

1. The job of the _____ is to fetch instructions, carry out the operations commanded by the instructions, and produce some outcome or resultant information.

2. A(n) _____ is an example of a secondary storage device.

3. The two general categories of software are _____ and _____.

4. A program is a set of _____.

5. Since computers can't be programmed in natural human language, algorithms must be written in a(n) _____ language.

6. _____ is the only language computers really process.

7. Words that have special meaning in a programming language are called _____.

8. Words or names defined by the programmer are called _____.

9. _____ are characters or symbols that perform operations on one or more operands.

10. A(n) _____ is part of an application's code but is ignored by the computer. It is intended for documentation purposes only.

11. The rules that must be followed when constructing a program are called _____.

12. _____ is information a program gathers from the outside world.

13. _____ is information a program sends to the outside world.

14. A(n) _____ is a set of well-defined steps for performing a task or solving a problem.

15. A(n) _____ is a diagram that graphically illustrates the flow of a program.

16. _____ is a cross between human language and a programming language.

17. To set the Visual Basic .NET environment options, click the Options.... command, which is found on the _____ menu.

18. If you do not see the Solution Explorer, or Properties windows in the Visual Basic .NET environment, you may use the _____ menu to bring them up.

19. A(n) _____ is a container for holding a project.

20. A(n) _____ is a group of files that make up a software application.

21. The _____ window allows you to quickly navigate among the files in your project.

22. The _____ window shows most of the currently selected object's properties and those properties' values.

23. When windows are _____, it means they are attached to each other or to one of the edges of the Visual Basic .NET main window.

24. To dock a floating window, _____ its title bar or drag it to one of the edges of the main window.

25. Visual Basic's _____ indicates the name of the project you are working on and displays [design] while you are in design time.

26. All of the commands executed by the _____ may also be executed from a menu.

27. The _____ window contains your application's form. This is where you design your application's user interface by placing controls on the form that appears when your application executes.

28. You use the _____ to place controls on an application's form. It contains buttons for the commonly used Visual Basic .NET controls.

29. The _____ window displays help topics that are relevant to the operation you are currently performing in Visual Basic .NET.

30. A(n) _____ is a small box that is displayed when you hold the mouse cursor over a button on the toolbar or in the toolbox for a few seconds.

What Do You Think?

1. Are each of the following control names legal or illegal? If a name is illegal, indicate why.
   a. `txtUserName`
   b. `2001sales`
   c. `lblUser Age`
   d. `txtName/Address`
   e. `btnCalcSubtotal`

2. What type of control does each of the following prefixes usually indicate?
   a. `btn`

b. `lbl`

c. `txt`

3. For each of the following controls, make up a legal name that conforms to the standard control name convention described in this chapter.

   a. A `TextBox` in which the user enters his or her last name

   b. A button that, when clicked, calculates an annual interest rate

   c. A label used to display the total of an order

   d. A button that clears all the input fields on a form

4. The following six control names appear in a Visual Basic .NET application that is used in a retail store. Indicate what type of control each is and guess the control's purpose.

   a. `txtPriceEach`

   b. `txtQuantity`

   c. `txtTaxRate`

   d. `btnCalcSale`

   e. `lblSubTotal`

   f. `lblTotal`

Short Answer

1. Both main memory and secondary storage are types of memory. Describe the difference between the two.

2. What is the difference between operating system software and application software?

3. Briefly describe what procedural programming means.

4. Briefly describe what object-oriented programming means.

5. Briefly describe what event-driven programming means.

6. Why has the advent of graphical user interfaces (GUIs) influenced the shift from procedural programming to object-oriented/event-driven programming?

7. From what you have read in this chapter, describe the difference between a Label control and a TextBox control. When is it appropriate to use one or the other?

PROGRAMMING CHALLENGES

1. Carpet Size

You have been asked to create an application for a carpet sales and installation business. The application should allow the user to enter the length and width of a room, and calculate the room's area in square feet. The formula for this calculation is

area = length × width

In this exercise, you will gain practice using the first six steps of the programming process described in section 1.5:

1. Clearly define what the application is to do.

2. Visualize the application running on the computer and design its user interface.

3. Make a list of the controls needed.

4. Define the values of each control's properties.

5. Make a list of methods needed for each control.

6. Create a flowchart or pseudocode version of each method.

Step 1: Describe the following four characteristics of this application:
Purpose
Input
Process
Output

Step 2: Draw a sketch of the application's form and place all the controls that are needed.

Step 3: Make a list of the controls you included in your sketch. List the control type and the name of each control.

Step 4: List the value of the Text property for each control, as needed. (Remember, some controls do not have a Text property.)

Step 5: List each method needed. Give the name of each method and describe what each method does.

Step 6: For each method you listed in step 5, draw a flowchart or write pseudocode.

2. Available Credit

A retail store gives each of its customers a maximum amount of credit. A customer's available credit is determined by subtracting the amount of credit used by the customer from the customer's maximum amount of credit. As you did in Programming Challenge 1, perform the first six steps of the programming process to design an application that determines a customer's available credit.

3. Sales Tax

Perform the first six steps of the programming process to design an application that gets the amount of a retail sale and the sales tax rate from the user. The application should calculate the amount of the sales tax and the total of the sale.

4. Account Balance

Perform the first six steps of the programming process to design an application that gets from the user the starting balance of a savings account, the total dollar amount of the deposits made to the account, and the total dollar amount of withdrawals made from the account. The application should calculate the account balance.

2

Creating Applications with Visual Basic .NET

▶2.1 Introduction

In this chapter you develop your first application, which displays a map and written directions to the Highlander Hotel. This application uses a form with labels, a PictureBox control, and buttons. You also write your first event procedures in Visual Basic .NET code. You then learn to use the Label control's AutoSize, BorderStyle, and TextAlign properties. Clickable images are also covered. Dynamic help and context-sensitive help is then demonstrated. In addition, you are introduced to the debugging process in Visual Basic .NET.

▶2.2 Focus on Problem Solving: Building the Hotel Directions Application

CONCEPT

IN THIS SECTION YOU CREATE YOUR FIRST VISUAL BASIC .NET APPLICATION: A WINDOW THAT DISPLAYS A MAP AND ROAD DIRECTIONS TO A HOTEL. IN THE PROCESS YOU LEARN HOW TO PLACE CONTROLS ON A FORM AND MANIPULATE VARIOUS PROPERTIES.

The desk clerks at the historic Highlander Hotel frequently receive calls from guests requesting road directions. Some desk clerks are not familiar with the road numbers or exits, and inadvertently give unclear or incorrect directions. The hotel manager has asked you to create an application that displays a map to the hotel. The desk clerks can then refer to the application when giving directions to customers over the phone.

In Chapter 1, you learned an 11 step process for designing and creating a Visual Basic .NET application. Because the directions application simply displays a graphic image, and does not require an event procedure, we will use the first four steps of the process, and then jump to step 9. After step 9, we will run the application. (The steps between 4 and 9 deal with event procedures.) Here are the steps we will use:

- ◆ Clearly define what the application is to do.
- ◆ Visualize the application running on the computer, and design its user interface.
- ◆ Make a list of the controls needed.
- ◆ Define the values of each control's relevant properties.
- ◆ Start Visual Basic .NET and create the forms and other controls.

Now we will take a closer look at each of these steps.

Clearly define what the application is to do.

Purpose: Display a map to the Highlander hotel.
Input: None.
Process: Display a form.
Output: Display on the form a graphic image showing a map.

Visualize the application running on the computer and design its user interface.

Before you create an application on the computer, you should first create it in your mind. This step is the visualization of the program. Try to imagine what the computer screen will look like while the application is running. Then draw a sketch of the form or forms in the application. Figure 2-1 shows a sketch of the form presented by this application.

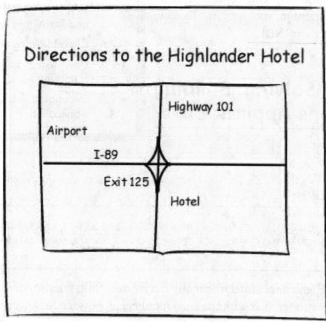

Figure 2-1   Sketch of hotel map form

Make a list of the controls needed.

In this step you list all the needed controls. You should assign names to all the controls that will be accessed or manipulated in the application code, and provide a brief description of each control. Our application only needs three controls, listed in Table 2-1. Because none of the controls are used in code, we will keep their default names.

Table 2-1

Hotel map application controls

Control Type	Control Name	Description
Form	(Default Name: `Form1`)	A small form that will serve as the window onto which the other controls will be placed
Label	(Default Name: `Label1`)	Displays the message "Directions to the Highlander Hotel"
PictureBox	(Default Name: `PictureBox1`)	Displays the graphic image showing the map to the hotel

Define the values of each control's relevant properties.

Each control's property settings are listed in Table 2-2.

Table 2-2

Hotel map application control properties

Form	
Name	`Form1`
Text	"Directions"
Label	
Name	`Label1`
Text	"Directions to the Highlander Hotel"
TextAlign	MiddleCenter
Font	Microsoft sans serif, bold, 18 point
PictureBox	
Name	`PictureBox1`
Picture	HotelMap.jpg
SizeMode	StretchImage

Notice that in addition to the Name and Text properties, we are setting the TextAlign and Font properties of the Label control. The TextAlign property determines how the text is aligned within the label. We will discuss this property in detail later.

In addition to its Name property, we are setting the PictureBox control's Image and SizeMode properties. The Image property lists the name of the file containing the graphic image. We will use HotelMap.jpg, which is located on the student disk in the Chap2 folder. The SizeMode property is set to StretchImage, which allows us to resize the image. If the image is too small, we can enlarge it (stretch it). If it is too large, we can shrink it.

Start Visual Basic .NET and create the forms and other controls

Now you are ready to construct the application's form. Tutorial 2-1 gets you started.

TUTORIAL 2-1:

Beginning the Directions application

In this tutorial you begin the Directions application. You will create the application's form and use the Properties window to set the form's Text property.

Step 1: Start Visual Studio .NET, just as you did in Chapter 1, and click the New Project button on the Start page. (If you do not see the Start page, click File on the menu bar, then click New, then click Project.) In the New Project dialog box, select Visual Basic Projects under Project Types, and Windows Application under Templates.

Each project has a name. A default name for the project, such as WindowsApplication1, will appear in the Name text box. Erase this name and type **Directions**. Next, look at the path name that is listed in the Location text box. This is where Visual Basic .NET will create a folder to hold the files related to this project. If you want to change this location, click the Browse button and select a suitable folder on your disk drive.

When you have set all of these items, click the OK button on the New Project dialog box.

NOTE: *If you are completing this tutorial in a computer lab, your instructor may give you a specific location for the project.*

Step 2: The Visual Basic .NET environment should be open with a blank form named Form1 displayed in the Design window, as shown in Figure 2-2. Click the form to select it.

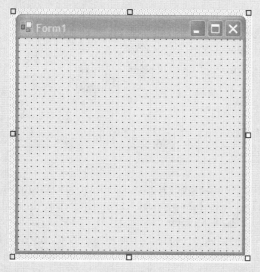

Figure 2-2 Form1 displayed in the Design window

Step 3: Look at the Properties window. It should appear as shown in Figure 2-3.

Because you have selected Form1, the Properties window displays the properties for the Form1 object. Notice that the drop-down list box at the top of the window shows the name of the selected object, Form1. Below that, the object's properties are displayed in two columns. The left column lists each property's name, and the right column shows each property's value. Below the list of properties is a brief description of the currently selected property.

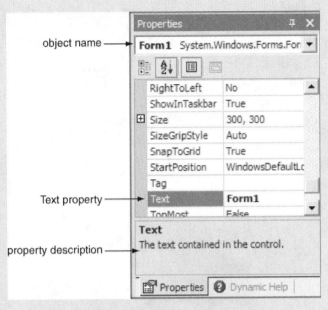

Figure 2-3   Properties window showing Form1

Notice that the Text property is highlighted, which means it is currently selected. Recall from Chapter 1 that a form's Text property determines the text that is displayed in the form's title bar. A form's Text property is initially set to the same value as the form's name, so this form's Text property is set to "Form1". Follow the instructions in steps 3 and 4 to change the Text property to "Directions".

Step 4: Double-click the word "Form1" that appears as the contents of the Text property.

Step 5: Delete the word "Form1" and type **Directions** in its place. Press the Enter key. Notice that the word "Directions" now appears in the form's title bar, as shown in Figure 2-4.

Step 6: Although you changed the form's Text property, you did not change its name. Scroll the Properties window up to the top of the list of properties, as shown in Figure 2-5. The Name property is still set to the default value, Form1.

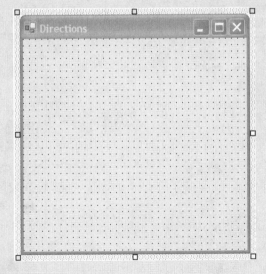

Figure 2-4   Directions in form title bar

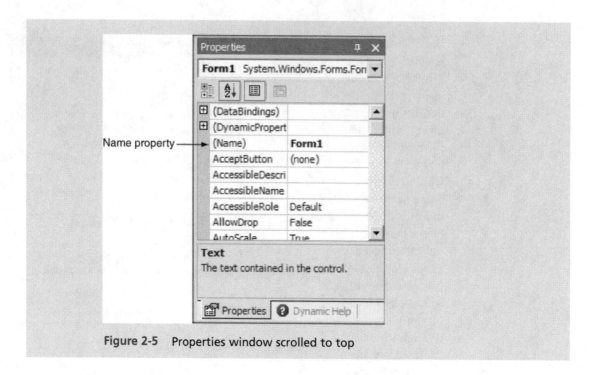

Name property

Figure 2-5 Properties window scrolled to top

The next step is to add a Label control to the form. Tutorial 2-2 guides you through the process.

TUTORIAL 2-2:

Adding a Label control

Step 1: Now you are ready to add the Label control to the form. As a reminder, Figure 2-6 shows where the Label control tool is located in the toolbox.

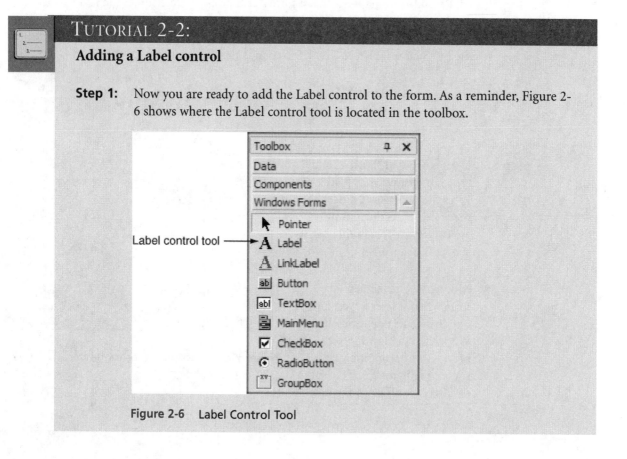

Label control tool

Figure 2-6 Label Control Tool

Double-click the Label control tool. A Label control appears on the form, as shown in Figure 2-7.

The label appears on the form as the word "Label1" surrounded by small squares. The squares are sizing handles. You use *sizing handles* to enlarge or shrink the control. Anytime you select an existing control, the sizing handles appear.

NOTE: *You might remember seeing sizing handles around the form when you selected it. Sizing handles always appear around the object that is currently selected in the Design window. In addition, the Properties window will display the currently selected object's properties.*

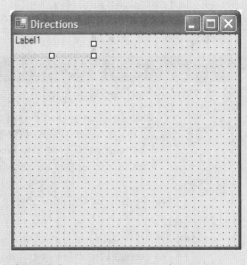

Figure 2-7   Label control on form

Step 2:   Look at the Properties window. Because the label you just placed on the form is currently selected, the Properties window now shows its properties, as shown in Figure 2-8.

Notice that the Text property is set, by default, to "Label1." Double-click on this value, delete it, and type **Directions to the Highlander Hotel** in its place. Press the Enter key. When you have typed the new text into the Text property, the form appears similar to Figure 2-9.

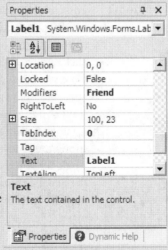

Figure 2-8   Properties window

Figure 2-9   Label with new text property value

Once you place a control on a form, you can move it by dragging it with the mouse. You can also resize a control using its sizing handles. In Tutorial 2-3 you move and resize the Label control.

TUTORIAL 2-3:

Moving and resizing the label

The Label control we created in Tutorial 2-2 was placed, by default, in the upper left corner of the form. We must move and resize the Label control so its position and size matches the sketch we drew during the application's planning phase. You move a control by selecting it and dragging it to its new location. You resize a control by dragging one of its sizing handles.

Step 1: If you do not see sizing handles around the label, click it to select it.

Step 2: Position the mouse cursor inside the selected Label control (not on a sizing handle), then click and drag the label to the top center area of the form, approximately in the location shown in Figure 2-10.

Our planning sketch also shows the label as displaying a single line of text. Notice that the Label control currently displays its text on two lines. This is because the control is not large enough to accommodate the text on one line. As a result, the text wraps around to the second line. Also notice that the text appears to be partially hidden. Once again, this is because the control is not large enough to adequately display the text. These problems can be remedied by resizing the control.

A control is contained inside a bounding box. The *bounding box* is a transparent rectangular area that defines the control's size. The resizing handles are positioned along the edges of the bounding box. You can give

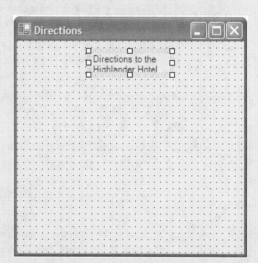

Figure 2-10 Label moved to the top center of the form

Figure 2-11 Cursor on sizing handle becomes a double-headed arrow

a control more or less room on a form by using its resizing handles to enlarge or shrink the control's bounding box. Steps 3 through 5 guide you through the process of resizing the label.

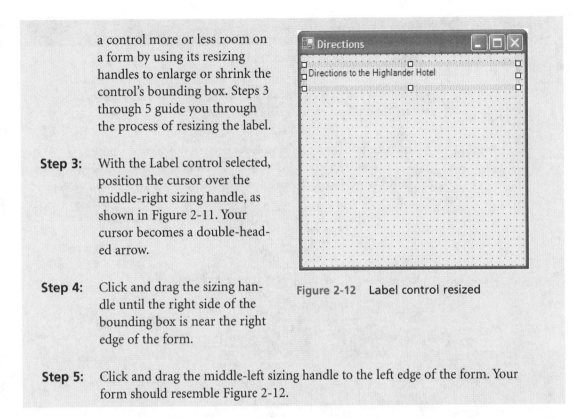

Step 3: With the Label control selected, position the cursor over the middle-right sizing handle, as shown in Figure 2-11. Your cursor becomes a double-headed arrow.

Figure 2-12   Label control resized

Step 4: Click and drag the sizing handle until the right side of the bounding box is near the right edge of the form.

Step 5: Click and drag the middle-left sizing handle to the left edge of the form. Your form should resemble Figure 2-12.

By default, a label's text is aligned with the top and left edges of the label's bounding box. The position of the text within a label's bounding box is controlled by the *TextAlign property*, which may be set to any of the following values: TopLeft, TopCenter, TopRight, MiddleLeft, MiddleCenter, MiddleRight, BottomLeft, BottomCenter, or BottomRight. Figure 2-13 shows nine Label controls, each with a different TextAlign value.

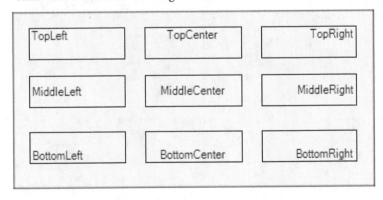

Figure 2-13   Text alignments

Tutorial 2-4 takes you through the process of aligning the label's text.

TUTORIAL 2-4:

Setting the label's TextAlign property

Step 1:   With the label selected, look at the Properties window. Notice that the value of the TextAlign property is TopLeft.

Step 2:   Click on the TextAlign property. Notice that a down-arrow button (▼) appears next to the property value. When you click on the arrow a small dialog box with nine buttons appears. Each of the buttons represents a TextAlign value, as shown in Figure 2-14.

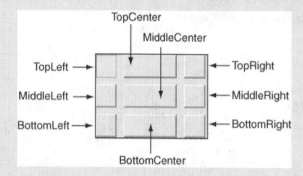

Figure 2-14   TextAlign drop-down dialog

Step 3:   Click the MiddleCenter button. Notice that the label's text is now centered in the middle of the label's bounding box, as shown in Figure 2-15.

Figure 2-15   Label text centered

In the planning phase, we indicated that the label's text should be displayed in an 18-point bold Microsoft sans serif font. These characteristics are controlled by the label's Font property. The Font property allows you to set the font, font style, and size of the label's text.

TUTORIAL 2-5:

Changing the label's font size and style

Step 1: With the label selected, click on the Font property in the Properties window. Notice that an ellipses button (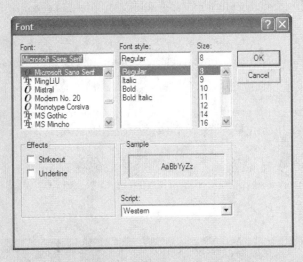) appears. Click the ellipses button and the Font dialog box appears, as shown in Figure 2-16.

Figure 2-16   Font dialog box

Step 2: Microsoft Sans Serif is already the selected font. Click on Bold under Font style, and "18" under Size. Notice that the text displayed in the Sample box changes to reflect your selections. Click the OK button.

The text displayed by the label is now in 18-point bold Microsoft sans serif. Unfortunately, not all the text can be seen because it is too large for the Label control. You must enlarge both the form and the Label control so all of the label text is visible.

Step 3: Select the form by clicking anywhere on it, except on the Label control. You will know you have selected the form when the sizing handles appear around it and the form's properties appear in the Properties window.

Figure 2-17   Resized form showing all text

Step 4: Use the form's sizing handles to widen the form, then enlarge the label so it appears similar to Figure 2-17.

To delete a control, you simply select it and press the delete key on the keyboard. In the following steps you add another Label control to the form (one that you will not need) and then delete it.

TUTORIAL 2-6:

Deleting a control

Step 1: Double-click the Label tool in the toolbox. Another Label control appears on the form.

Step 2: With the new Label control still selected, press the delete key on the keyboard. The label is deleted from the form.

> **TIP:** If you accidentally delete a control you can restore it with the Undo button ( ) on the standard toolbar.

The last step in building this application is to insert the road map. In Tutorial 2-7 you will insert a *PictureBox control*, which can be used to display an image.

TUTORIAL 2-7:

Inserting a PictureBox control

Step 1: Double-click the PictureBox tool in the toolbox. An empty PictureBox control appears on the form. Move the control to a position approximately in the center of the form, as shown in Figure 2-18.

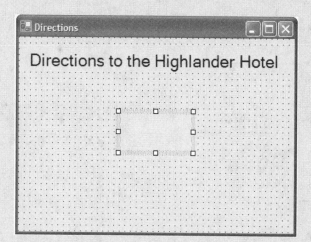

Figure 2-18 PictureBox control placed

Step 2: The PictureBox control displays an image in a variety of ways, depending on the setting of the *SizeMode property*. The SizeMode property may be set to the values listed in Table 2-3.

Table 2-3

SizeMode property values

Setting	Description
AutoSize	The size of the PictureBox control's bounding box is automatically adjusted to fit the size of the image it displays.
CenterImage	If the PictureBox control's bounding box is larger than the image, the image is displayed in the center of the control. If the image is larger than the control's bounding box, the image is displayed in the center of the control and is clipped to fit within the bounding box.
Normal	The image is aligned with the upper left corner of the PictureBox control's bounding box. If the image is larger than the control's bounding box, it is clipped.
StretchImage	The size of the image is scaled to fit within the PictureBox control's bounding box. If the image is smaller than the control, the image is stretched. If the image is larger than the control, the image is shrunk.

In the Properties window, notice that the SizeMode property is set to Normal. Click the SizeMode property and notice that a down-arrow button (▾) appears next to the property value. Click the down-arrow button and a drop-down list appears. Select StretchImage.

Step 3: Make sure your student disk is inserted in the CD-Rom drive. Notice that the Image property is currently set to (none), indicating that no image is loaded into the PictureBox control. Click the Image property and notice that an ellipses button ⌷ appears next to the property value. Click the ellipses button. The Open dialog box appears. Use the dialog box to browse to the Chap2 folder on the student disk. Click on the HotelMap.jpg file, and then click the Open button. This loads the graphic stored in HotelMap.jpg into the PictureBox control. The application's form now appears similar to Figure 2-19.

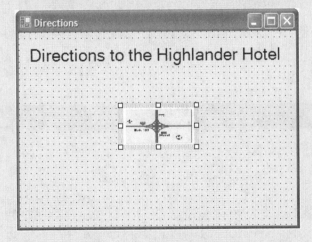

Figure 2-19   PictureBox control with image in place

Step 4: Because we set the SizeMode property to StretchImage, the image is scaled to fit the size of the PictureBox control. Use the control sizing handles to enlarge the image so its details are clearly visible, as shown in Figure 2-20.

TIP: You may want to enlarge the form again to make more room for the image.

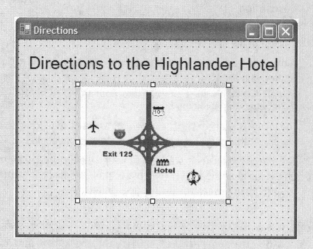

Figure 2-20 HotelMap.jpg enlarged

NOTE: *You have now seen that properties are set in the Properties window in one of three ways:*

- *Typing a value for the property*
- *By selecting a value for the property from a drop-down list by clicking the down-arrow button (▾).*
- *Establishing a value for the property with a dialog box, which appears when the ellipses button (...) is clicked.*

Recall that when you created the project you set its name to Directions and you either kept the default location on your disk drive, or you specified a location. Now it's time to save the changes you've made to your project. Tutorial 2-8 describes three different ways to save a project.

TUTORIAL 2-8:

Saving the project

Step 1: You may use any of the following methods to save a project.

- Click File on the menu bar, then click Save All on the File menu
- Press Ctrl+Shift+S on the keyboard
- Click the Save All button on the standard toolbar

Use one of these methods to save your project.

TIP: You should save your work often to prevent accidental loss of changes you have made to your project.

Now you can run the application. It doesn't have any event procedures, so it will only display the form, as you have designed it. There are three ways to run an application in Visual Basic .NET:

- By clicking the start button (▶) on the toolbar
- By clicking Debug on the menu bar, then clicking Start on the Debug menu
- By pressing the F5 key

TUTORIAL 2-9:

Running the application

Step 1:   To run the application, click the start button on the standard toolbar, click the start command on the Debug menu, or press the F5 key. If it is not already visible, you will see the Output window appear as shown in Figure 2-21.

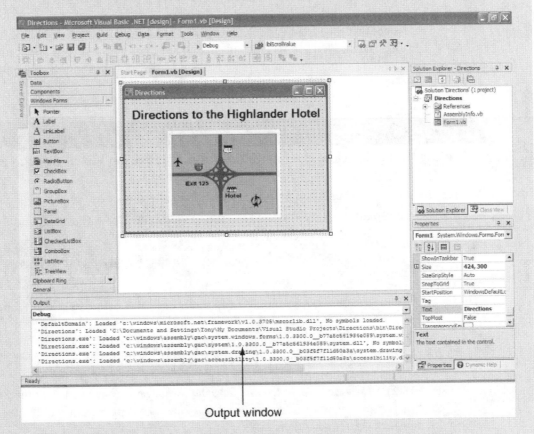

Output window

Figure 2-21   The Visual Basic .NET environment with the Output window visible

While Visual Basic .NET builds the application you will see various messages displayed in the Output window. Once the application is built, it will run and you will see the form appear as shown in Figure 2-22.

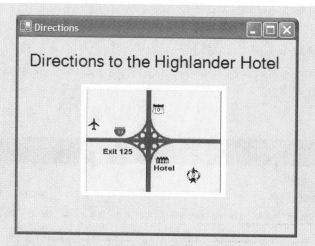

Figure 2-22 The Directions application

Notice that the Visual Basic .NET title bar now reads Directions – Microsoft Visual Basic .NET [run]. The [run] designator indicates that your application is now in run-time. *Run-time* is the mode in which you run and test an application.

TUTORIAL 2-10:

Ending the application, closing the solution, and exiting Visual Basic .NET

Step 1: To end the application, perform one of the following operations:

- ◆ Click the close button (⊠)on the application window. (Be careful not to click the Visual Studio close button.)

- ◆ Click Debug on the menu bar, then click Stop Debugging on the Debug menu.

The application stops running and Visual Basic .NET returns to design time.

Step 2: You close a Visual Basic .NET project by closing its solution. To close the solution, click File on the menu bar, then click Close Solution.

NOTE: *If you close a solution and have made changes to the project since the last time you saved it, you will see a dialog box asking you whether you want to save your changes. Click the Yes button.*

Step 3: You exit Visual Basic .NET in the same manner you exit most other Windows applications:

- ◆ Click on the File menu, then click the exit command.
- ◆ Click the close button (⊠) on the right edge of the title bar.

Use one of these methods to exit Visual Basic .NET.

✓ **Checkpoint**

2.1 You want to change what is displayed in a form's title bar. Which of its properties do you change?

2.2 How do you insert a Label control onto a form?

2.3 What is the purpose of a control's sizing handles?

2.4 What are the possible values for a label's TextAlign property?

2.5 How do you delete a control?

2.6 What happens when you set a PictureBox control's SizeMode property to StretchImage?

2.7 When you run an application from the Visual Basic .NET environment, what changes do you see in the Visual Basic .NET title bar? What does this indicate?

How Solutions and Projects are Organized on the Disk

Recall from Chapter 1 that a solution is a container that holds a Visual Basic .NET project. Every project must be part of a solution. When you create a new project, Visual Basic .NET automatically creates a solution with the same name as the project, and adds the project to the solution. For example, when you created the Directions project, Visual Basic .NET also created a solution named Directions, and added the project to the Directions solution.

Recall from Tutorial 2-1 that you must specify a disk location in the New Project dialog box. Visual Basic .NET creates a folder at this location. The folder is given the same name as the solution (which is also the name of the project). Several files, and some other folders, are created and stored in this folder.

When you created the Directions project (and the solution that contains it), Visual Basic .NET created a folder named Directions at the location specified in the New Project dialog box. All of the files related to this project are stored under this folder. Two of the files are Directions.sln and Directions.vbproj. The .sln file is the *solution file*, and contains data describing the solution. The .vbproj file is the *project file*, and contains data describing the project.

Opening an Existing Project

Visual Basic .NET gives you several ways to open an existing project. One method is to use the Visual Studio Start Page, as shown in Figure 2-23. Notice that the Start Page displays a list of the most recently opened projects. You may open any of the projects in the list by clicking its name.

You may also open an existing project by clicking the Open Project button on the Start Page, or by clicking File on the menu bar, then clicking New, then clicking Project. Either of these actions causes the Open Project dialog box to appear. Use the dialog box to browse to and open the folder containing your solution and project. For example, Figure 2-24 shows the Open Project dialog box with the Directions folder open.

The Open Project dialog box displays only solution files and project files. Select the solution file (the one that ends with .sln) or the project file (the one that ends with .vbproj), and click the Open button. Tutorial 2-12 guides you through the process of opening the Directions project after it has been closed.

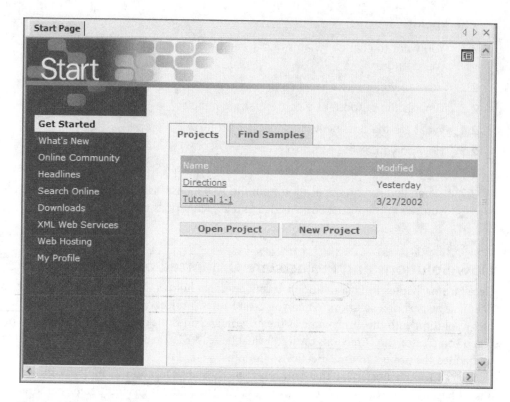

Figure 2-23   Visual Studio Start page

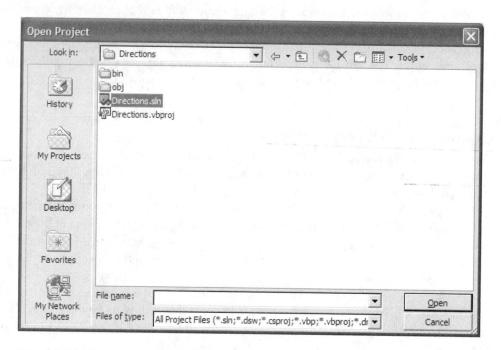

Figure 2-24   Open Project dialog box with Directions folder open

TUTORIAL 2-11:

Opening an existing project

This tutorial assumes you have the Directions project saved to your disk and Visual Basic .NET is not currently running.

Step 1:   Start Visual Studio .NET. If you see the Start Page, as previously shown in Figure 2-23, you may open the Directions project by clicking its name.

Alternatively, you can click the Open Project button on the Start Page. This causes the Open Project dialog box to appear. Browse to and open the Directions folder, then select the Directions.sln file and click the Open button.

If you do not see the Start Page, click File on the menu bar, then click New, then click Project. This also causes the Open Project dialog box to appear. Browse to and open the Directions folder, then select the Directions.sln file and click the Open button.

Step 2:   After performing one of these actions, the Directions project should be open and you should see the form with the map to the hotel displayed in the Design window. If you do not see the form displayed, look in the Solutions Explorer window and double-click Form1.vb.

More About the Properties Window

In this section you will learn about the Properties window's object box and its alphabetic and categorized buttons. Figure 2-25 shows the location of the object box. The alphabetic and categorized buttons appear just below the object box, on a small toolbar. Figure 2-26 shows the location of the buttons on this toolbar.

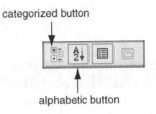

Figure 2-26   Alphabetic and categorized buttons

Figure 2-25   Object box

In addition to clicking objects in the Design window, you can also use the object box on the Properties window to select any object in the project. The *object box* provides a drop-down list of the objects in the project.

The alphabetic and categorized buttons affect the way properties are displayed in the Properties window. When the *alphabetic button* is selected, the properties are displayed in alphabetical order. When the *categorized button* is selected, related properties are displayed together in groups. For example, in categorized view, a Label control's Text and TextAlign properties are displayed in the Appearance group. Figure 2-27 shows examples of the Properties window in each view.

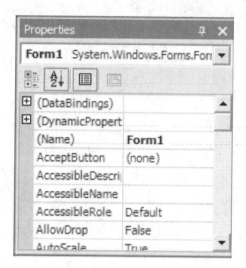
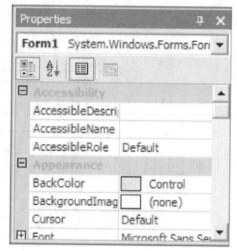

properties listed alphabetically   properties categorized

Figure 2-27   Properties window in alphabetic and categorized views

You have probably noticed that a few of the properties, including the Name property, are enclosed in parentheses. These properties are commonly accessed, and placing them in parentheses causes them to appear at the top of the alphabetic list.

In Tutorial 2-13 you practice using these components of the Properties window.

TUTORIAL 2-12:

Using the object box, alphabetic button, and categorized button

Step 1:   With the Directions project loaded, click the down-arrow button that appears at the right edge of the object box. You see the names of the `Form1`, `Label1`, and `PictureBox1` controls.

Step 2:   Click the name `Label1` in the list. Notice that the `Label1` label is now selected in the Design window. Repeat this procedure, selecting the `PictureBox1` control, and the `Form1` control. As you select these objects, notice that they also become selected in the Design window.

Step 3:   Select the `Label1` control, then click the categorized button. Scroll through the list of properties displayed in the Properties window. Notice there are several categories of properties.

✓ **Checkpoint**

2.8 Describe three ways to open an existing Visual Basic .NET project.

2.9 What are the two viewing modes for the Properties window? How do you select either of these modes? What is the difference between the two?

2.10 Start Visual Basic .NET and open the directions project. Look at Form1's properties categorized into groups. Under what category does the Text property appear? Under what category does the Name property appear?

2.11 How can you select an object in a project by only using the Properties window?

▶2.3 Focus on Problem Solving: Responding to Events

The manager of the Highlander Hotel reports that the Directions application has been quite helpful to the desk clerks. Some clerks, however, have requested that the application be modified to display written directions as well as the map. Some have also requested a more obvious way to exit the application, other than clicking the standard windows close button, located on the application's title bar.

You decide to add a button to the application form that, when clicked, causes the written directions to appear. In addition, you decide to add an Exit button that causes the application to stop when clicked.

Figure 2-28 shows the modified sketch of the form presented by this application.

CONCEPT

AN APPLICATION RESPONDS TO EVENTS, SUCH AS MOUSE CLICKS AND KEYBOARD INPUT, BY EXECUTING CODE KNOWN AS EVENT PROCEDURES. IN THIS SECTION, YOU WRITE EVENT PROCEDURES FOR THE DIRECTIONS APPLICATION.

Figure 2-28 Modified Directions application sketch

Table 2-4 lists the controls that will be added to the application. Because the Label control will be accessed in code, and the buttons will have code associated with them, you will assign them names.

Table 2-4

Controls to be added to Directions application

Control Type	Control Name	Description
Label	lblDirections	Displays written directions to the hotel.
Button	btnDisplayDirections	When clicked, causes the lblDirections control's text to appear on the form.
Button	btnExit	Stops the application when clicked.

Each control's property settings are listed in Table 2-5. The table mentions a new property, Visible, used with the lblDirections control. Visible is a *Boolean* property, which means it can only hold one of two values: true or false. When a control's *Visible* property is set to true, the control can be seen on the form. A control is hidden, however, when its Visible property is set to false. In this application, we want the lblDirections control to be hidden until the user clicks the btnDisplayDirections button, so we initially set its Visible property to false.

Table 2-5

Directions application control properties

Label Control	
Name	lblDirections
Text	"Traveling on I-89, take Exit 125 onto Highway 101 South. The hotel is on the left, just past the I-89 intersection. Traveling on Highway 101 North, the hotel is on the right, just before the I-89 intersection."
Visible	False
Button Control	
Name	btnDisplayDirections
Text	"Display Directions"
Button Control	
Name	btnExit
Text	"Exit"

There are only two event procedures needed in the Directions application. Table 2-6 lists and describes them. btnDisplayDirections_Click is the name of the procedure that is invoked when the btnDisplayDirections button is clicked, and btnExit_Click is the event procedure that executes when the btnExit button is clicked.

Table 2-6

Directions application event procedures

Method	Description
btnDisplayDirections_Click	Causes the lblDirections control to become visible on the form. This is accomplished by setting the label's Visible property to true.
btnExit_Click	Terminates the application.

Figure 2-29 shows a flowchart for the `btnDisplay Directions_Click` event procedure.

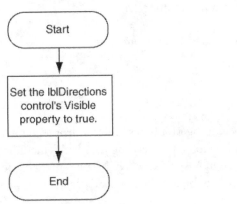

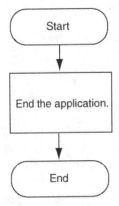

Figure 2-29 Flowchart for `btnDisplayDirections_Click`

Figure 2-30 Flowchart for `btnExit_Click`

Figure 2-30 shows a flowchart for the `btnExit_Click` event procedure.

Now that you have seen flowcharts for the event procedures, let's look at the actual code we will write. The code for the `btnDisplayDirections_Click` event procedure is as follows.

```
Private Sub btnDisplayDirections_Click(ByVal sender As System.Object, _
    ByVal e As System.EventArgs) Handles btnDisplayDirections.Click
    ' Make the directions visible
    lblDirections.Visible = True
End Sub
```

NOTE: *The first two lines of code shown here will normally appear as one very long line in the Visual Basic .NET editor. Because we can print only a limited number of characters on a line in this book, we have broken the long line into two lines.*

Event procedures are a type of Sub procedure. The word Sub is an abbreviation for the older term "subroutine." This event procedure begins with the words `Private Sub` and ends with the words `End Sub`. Among other things, the first line of the event procedure (which is printed as two lines here) identifies the control it belongs to and the event it responds to. This is illustrated in Figure 2-31.

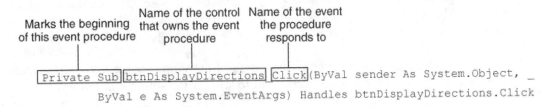

Figure 2-31 Parts of the first line of an event procedure

As you can see from Figure 2-31 the name of the control that owns the procedure appears after the words `Private Sub`. An underscore character separates the name of the owning control from the name of the event that the procedure responds to. So the code in Figure 2-31 indicates the beginning of a Sub procedure that belongs to the `btnDisplayDirections` control. The procedure responds to the `Click` event, which means it executes when the user clicks the control with the mouse.

For now, don't be concerned with anything else that appears in the first two lines of code. As you progress through the book you will learn more about it.

NOTE: *Event procedures are also known as event handlers.*

The next line reads

```
' Make the directions visible
```

The apostrophe (') marks the beginning of a remark. Recall from Chapter 1 that a *remark* is a note of explanation intended for people who may be reading your code (including yourself). Remarks are part of the program but are ignored by Visual Basic .NET. The remark "Make the directions visible" explains in ordinary terms what action the next line of code performs. A person reading the code doesn't have to guess what it does.

It is important that you develop the habit of annotating your code with descriptive remarks that explain how and why you are performing steps in your program. Imagine creating a large and complex application. Once you have tested and debugged it, you give it to its user and move on to the next project. Ten months later, the user asks you to make a modification (or worse, track down and fix an elusive bug). You start looking through several hundred lines of code and to your astonishment some of it makes no sense at all. If only you had left notes to yourself explaining the program's nuances and oddities. Of course, it's too late now. All that is left for you to do is decide what will take less time: figuring out the old code, or completely rewriting it. Writing remarks in your program might take extra time now, but it will almost certainly save time in the future.

The next line reads

```
lblDirections.Visible = True
```

This is called an *assignment statement*. The equal sign, known as the *assignment operator*, copies the value on its right into the item on its left. The item to the left of the operator is

```
lblDirections.Visible
```

This identifies the Visible property of the `lblDirections` control. The standard notation for referring to a control's properties in code is

```
ControlName.PropertyName
```

The value to the right of the equal sign, `True`, is copied into the `lblDirections.Visible` property. The effect of this statement is that the `lblDirections` control becomes visible on the form.

TIP: In an assignment statement, the name of the item receiving the value must be on the left side of the = operator. The following statement will not work:

```
True = lblDirections.Visible   ' Incorrect Code!
```

Notice that the code between the first and last lines of the event procedure is indented. Although not required, it is a common practice to indent the lines inside a procedure so they are visually set apart. As you work through this book, you will see that indention is used in other places as well.

Now, let's look at the `btnExit_Click` event procedure. Here is the code:

```
Private Sub btnExit_Click(ByVal sender As System.Object, _
        ByVal e As System.EventArgs) Handles btnExit.Click
    ' End the application
    End
End Sub
```

Other than the remark "End the application", this procedure contains only one statement: End. The End statement causes the application to terminate.

In Tutorial 2-14 you place the controls needed to complete this part of the project.

TUTORIAL 2-13:

Placing the `lblDirections`, `btnDisplayDirections`, and `btnExit` controls

Step 1: Start Visual Basic .NET and open the directions project. Select the Form1 form, if it is not already selected.

Step 2: You will place the new controls at the bottom of the form, below the graphic. Because the form is too small to accommodate them, you will need to enlarge it. Drag the bottom edge of the form down until it looks something like the one shown in Figure 2-32. (Don't worry about the exact size of the form. You can adjust it again if you need to.)

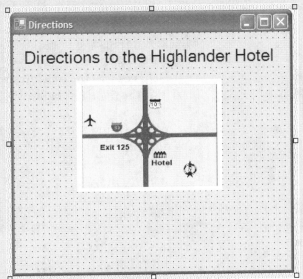

Figure 2-32 Directions application with enlarged form

Step 3: You are ready to place the new Label control on the form. Previously you learned to place a control by double-clicking its button in the toolbox. Double-clicking a control's button in the toolbox places a default-sized control on the selected form. This time you will learn to draw the control. Click the Label tool in the toolbox once.

Step 4: Move the cursor over the form. Notice the cursor is now in the shape of crosshairs. Click and hold the mouse button with the crosshairs below the image and near the left edge of the form. As you hold the mouse button down, drag the crosshairs down and to the right, as shown in Figure 2-33. Notice that the rectangle you are drawing as you drag the cursor.

Step 5: With the cursor in the approximate location shown in Figure 2-33, release the mouse button. The rectangle becomes a Label control named `Label2`.

Step 6: Change the control's Name property to `lblDirections`.

Step 7: Type the following text into the new Label control's Text property:

Figure 2-33   Drawing a Label control

Traveling on I-89, take Exit 125 onto Highway 101 South. The hotel is on the left, just past the I-89 intersection. Traveling on Highway 101 North, the hotel is on the right, just before the I-89 intersection.

TIP: When typing the directions, do not press the Enter key until you have entered all the text. When you press the Enter key, Visual Basic .NET will stop accepting input to the Text property. If you accidentally press the Enter key too early, select the Text property again and enter the rest of the text.

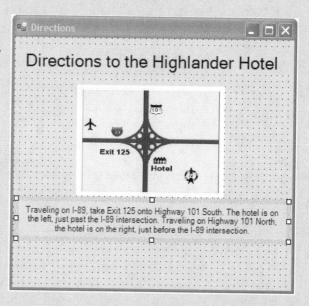

Figure 2-34   Label with directions text entered

Step 8: Set the Label control's TextAlign property to MiddleCenter. The form should now appear similar to Figure 2-34.

Step 9: Locate the Label control's Visible property in the Properties window. The property's value is currently set to true. Click the property value. A down-arrow button ([▾]) appears next to the property value. Click the down-arrow button and a drop-down list appears, showing the values True and False. Click False.

NOTE: *During design time, all controls are displayed, even if their Visible property is set to false.*

Step 10: You are now ready to place the buttons. Double-click the button tool in the toolbox. A default-sized button named `Button1` appears on the form. Drag it to the form's bottom edge.

Step 11: Double-click the button tool in the toolbox again. Another button, this one named `Button2`, appears on the form.

NOTE: *If a control is already selected when you double-click a tool in the toolbox, the new control will appear on top of the selected control. If the* `Button1` *control was still selected when you created* `Button2`, *the* `Button2` *control will appear on top of the* `Button1` *control.*

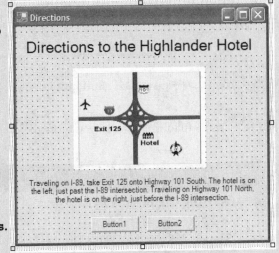

Drag the `Button2` control to the bottom edge of the form and place it to the right of the `Button1` control. Arrange the two buttons as shown in Figure 2-35.

Step 12: Select the `Button1` button.

Step 13: In the Properties window, change the button's Name to **btnDisplay Directions**.

Figure 2-35   Buttons in place

Step 14: Change the Text property to **Display Directions**. Notice that the button is not large enough to accommodate the text. Use the button's sizing handles to increase its height, as shown in Figure 2-36.

Step 15: Select the `Button2` button.

Figure 2-36   Button with increased height

Step 16: In the Properties window, change the button's name to **btnExit** and change the button's Text property to **Exit**.

Step 17: Resize the `btnExit` button so its size is the same as the `btnDisplayDirections` button. Your form should now resemble the one shown in Figure 2-37.

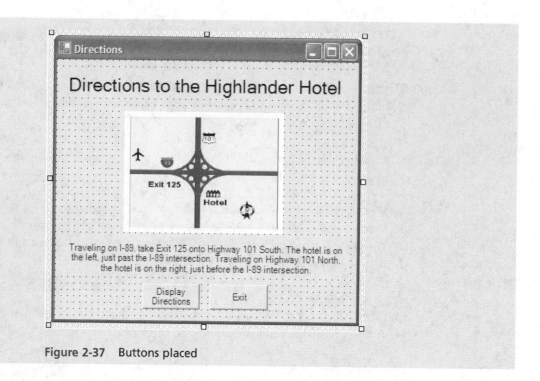

Figure 2-37 Buttons placed

In the following tutorial you write the event procedures for the buttons.

TUTORIAL 2-14:

Writing the Event Procedures

Step 1: Double-click the Display Directions button (`btnDisplayDirections`). The Code window opens, as shown in Figure 2-38.

The *Code window* is a text-editing window in which you write code. Notice that Visual Basic .NET has automatically supplied a *code template* for the `btnDisplayDirections_Click` event procedure. The template consists of the first and last lines of the procedure. You must add the code that appears between these two lines.

Step 2: Type the following code between the first and last lines of the `btnDisplayDirections_Click` procedure:

```
' Make the directions visible
lblDirections.Visible = True
```

> **TIP:** Make sure you type the code exactly as it appears here. Otherwise, you may encounter an error when you run the application.

Did you notice that as you entered the second line, `lblDirections.Visible = True`, when you typed the period the scrollable list box in Figure 2-39 appeared?

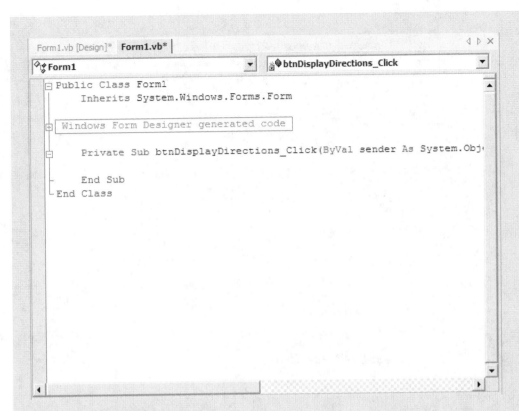

Figure 2-38   Code window

This is called an Intellisense auto list box. *Intellisense* is a feature of Visual Studio .NET that provides help and some automatic code completion while you are developing an application. The *auto list box* displays information that may be used to complete part of a statement. This auto list box contains the name of every property and method that belongs to the `lblDirections` object. When you type the letter V the selector bar in the list box automatically moves to Visible. You can continue typing, or you can press the tab key or spacebar to select Visible from the list. You may then continue typing.

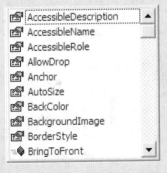

Figure 2-39   Auto list box

Another auto list box, shown in Figure 2-40, appears after you type the = operator.

This auto list box shows only two values: False and True. These are the only valid values you can assign to the Visible property. As before, you may continue typing or let the auto list box help you select the code to insert.

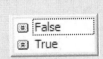

Figure 2-40   Auto list box showing valid values

> TIP: If you did not see the auto list box, you have either misspelled the object name, or that feature has been disabled. To enable it, click Tools on the menu bar, then click Options... You will see the Options dialog box, as described in step 12 of Tutorial 1-4 in Chapter 1. In the left pane, click Text Editor, then click Basic. With General selected in the left pane, make sure the auto list members box is checked.

Your code window should look like the one shown in Figure 2-41.

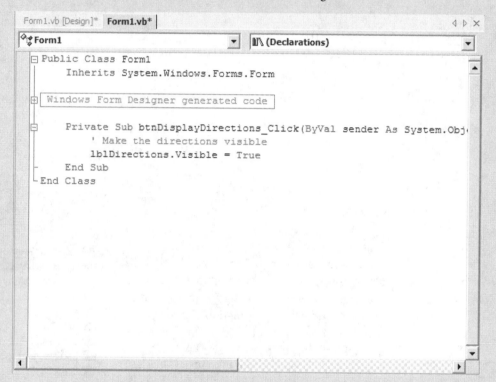

Figure 2-41   Code for making directions visible

Step 3:   Now you will switch back to the Design window. Here are four different ways to do this.

- ◆ Notice at the top of the code window the two tabs shown in Figure 2-42.

Figure 2-42   Design and code tabs

You can open the Design window by clicking the Form1.vb [Design] tab, and then you can open the code window again by clicking the Form1.vb tab.

- ◆ You can also click View on the menu bar, then click Designer on the View menu.

- ◆ Another way is to use the Solutions Explorer window. Click the view designer button (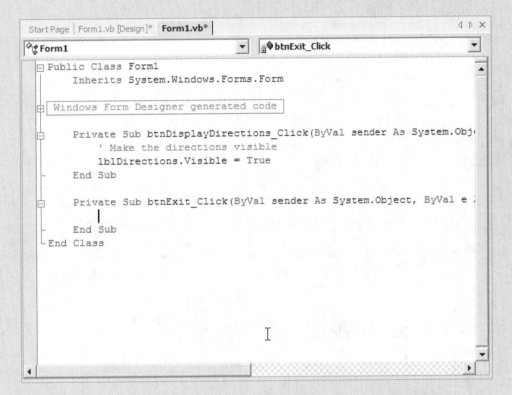) to switch to the Design window, and click the view code button ( ) to switch back to the Code window.
- ◆ You can also press Shift+F7 on the keyboard.

Use one of these techniques to open the Design window.

Step 4: Now you must write the event procedure for the other button. On the form, double-click the Exit button. The Code window reappears, as shown in Figure 2-43.

```
Start Page   Form1.vb [Design]*   Form1.vb*                         ◁ ▷ ×
Form1                              ▼    btnExit_Click              ▼

Public Class Form1
     Inherits System.Windows.Forms.Form

  Windows Form Designer generated code

     Private Sub btnDisplayDirections_Click(ByVal sender As System.Obj
          ' Make the directions visible
          lblDirections.Visible = True
     End Sub

     Private Sub btnExit_Click(ByVal sender As System.Object, ByVal e

     End Sub
End Class
```

Figure 2-43   Code window, ready for exit button code

Notice that Visual Basic .NET has now provided a code template for the `btnExit_Click` procedure.

Step 5: Between the first and last lines of the `btnExit_Click` code template, type the following code:

```
' End the application
End
```

The Code window should now look like the one shown in Figure 2-44.

Step 6: Use the Save All command on the File menu to save the project.

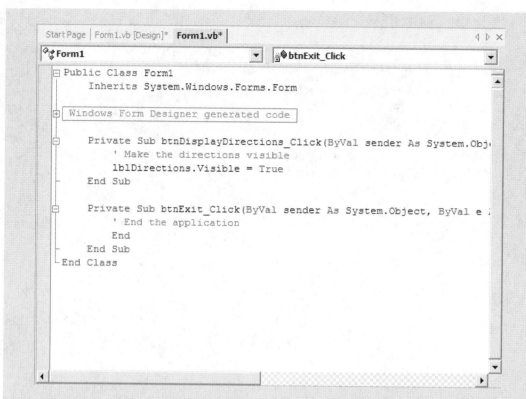

Figure 2-44   Code window with `btnExit_Click` procedure completed

Step 7:   Click the Start button (▶) on the Visual Basic .NET toolbar. The application begins executing, as shown in Figure 2-45. Notice that the `lblDirections` label is not visible.

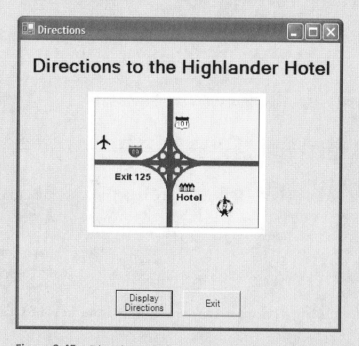

Figure 2-45   Directions application at startup

Step 8: Click the "Display Directions" button. The written directions appear on the form, as shown in Figure 2-46.

Figure 2-46   Directions application with text displayed

Step 9: Click the "Exit" button. The application terminates.

✓ Checkpoint

2.12 How do you decide whether you will keep a control's default name or assign it a name?

2.13 What is a Boolean property?

2.14 Suppose an application has a button named `btnShowName`. The button has an event procedure that executes when the user clicks it. What would the event procedure be named?

2.15 Assume the following line appears in a button's `Click` event procedure. What does the line cause the application to do?

```
' Display the word "Hello"
```

2.16 What is the purpose of a remark?

2.17 Suppose an application has a Label control named `lblSecretAnswer`. Write the Visual Basic .NET assignment statement that causes the control to be hidden. (*Hint*: Use the Visible property.)

2.18 What is the purpose of the `End` statement?

More About Code and the Code Window

In Tutorial 2-15, you learned to display the Code window by double-clicking the control that you wish to write an event procedure for. You may also display the Code window by any of the following actions:

- Click the view code button (⬛) on the Solution Explorer window.
- Click View on the menu bar, then click the Code command.
- Press the F7 key.

Collapsed Code Regions

Notice in the Code window the line that reads Windows Form Designer generated code. This line, which appears as shown in Figure 2-47, is in a box, in a light colored font, with a plus sign next to it in the left margin.

⊞ | `Windows Form Designer generated code`

Figure 2-47 Collapsed code region

This line indicates the presence of a code region. A *code region* is a section of code that may be hidden from view, or collapsed. When a code region is collapsed, the name of the region appears with a plus sign next to it. You can expand the code region by clicking the plus sign. When a code region is expanded, the plus sign becomes a minus sign. You collapse the region by clicking the minus sign.

Visual Basic .NET allows you to collapse regions of code in order to simplify the appearance of your program and make it more readable. The code that is hidden in the Windows Form Designer generated code region is necessary for your application to run, but makes your code appear cluttered and cumbersome. Because you will not modify the code in this region, it's a good idea to leave it collapsed.

TUTORIAL 2-15

Experimenting with code regions

Step 1: With the Directions project loaded, open the code window.

Step 2: Click the plus sign that appears next to the line that reads Windows Form Designer generated code. The region expands, revealing the hidden code. Scroll down in the code window and notice that the region contains a large amount of code.

Step 3: Scroll back to the top of the Code window and locate the line that reads #Region " Windows Form Designer generated code ". Click the minus sign that appears next to this line. The region should collapse.

Step 4: Notice that the event procedures you wrote in Tutorial 2-15 (btnDisplayDirections_Click and btnExit_Click) also have minus signs next their first line. Click the minus signs to collapse the event procedures. When a procedure is collapsed you only see its first line in the Code window, and the minus sign becomes a plus sign.

Step 5:   Click the plus signs that now appear next to the `btnDisplayDirections_Click` and `btnExit_Click` event procedures to expand them.

Changing Text Colors

You have already learned that the font style and size of text on a control can be easily changed through the Properties window. You can also change the text background and foreground color with the *BackColor* and *ForeColor* properties.

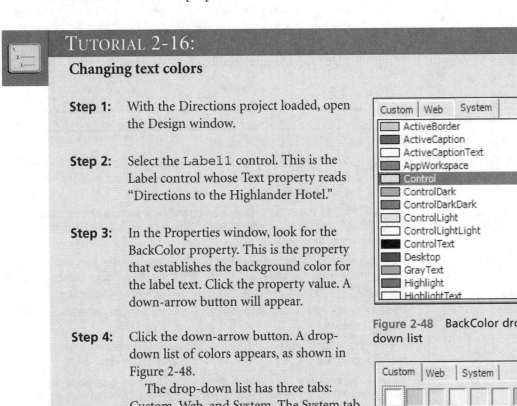

TUTORIAL 2-16:

Changing text colors

Step 1:   With the Directions project loaded, open the Design window.

Step 2:   Select the `Label1` control. This is the Label control whose Text property reads "Directions to the Highlander Hotel."

Step 3:   In the Properties window, look for the BackColor property. This is the property that establishes the background color for the label text. Click the property value. A down-arrow button will appear.

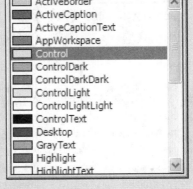

Figure 2-48   BackColor drop-down list

Step 4:   Click the down-arrow button. A drop-down list of colors appears, as shown in Figure 2-48.

The drop-down list has three tabs: Custom, Web, and System. The System tab lists colors that are defined in the current Windows configuration. The Web tab lists colors that are displayed with consistency in web browsers. The Custom tab displays a color palette, as shown in Figure 2-49.

Select a color from one of the tabs. Notice that the label text background changes to the color you selected.

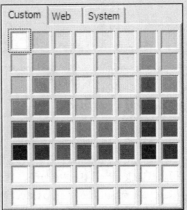

Figure 2-49   Custom color palette

Step 5:   Now look for the ForeColor property in the Properties window. When you click it, a down-arrow button appears.

Step 6: Click the down-arrow button and you see the same drop-down list as you saw in step 4. Once again, select a color from one of the tabs. Notice that the label's text foreground color changes to the color you selected.

Step 7: Start the application to test the new colors. After you close the application, save your project.

Setting the FormBorderStyle Property and Locking Controls

The FormBorderStyle Property

Sometimes you want to prevent the user from resizing, minimizing, or maximizing a window, or from closing a window using its close button (⊠). You can control all of these actions by selecting an appropriate value for the form's *FormBorderStyle property*.

Table 2-6 shows a list of the possible values for the FormBorderStyle property.

Table 2-6

Values for BorderStyle

BorderStyle Value	Description
Fixed3D	Displays a 3D border. The form's size is fixed and displayed with minimize, maximize, and close buttons on its title bar. Although the form may be maximized and minimized, it may not be resized by its edges or corners.
FixedDialog	This type of border shows minimize, maximize, and close buttons on its title bar. Although the form may be maximized and minimized, it may not be resized by its edges or corners.
FixedSingle	The form's size is fixed and uses a border that is a single line. The form is displayed with minimize, maximize, and close buttons on its title bar. Although the form may be maximized and minimized, it may not be resized by its edges or corners.
FixedToolWindow	Intended for use with floating toolbars. Only shows the title bar with a close button. May not be resized.
None	The form is displayed with no border at all. Subsequently, there is no title bar, and no minimize, maximize, or close buttons. The form may not be resized.
Sizable	This is the default value. The form is displayed with minimize, maximize, and close buttons on its title bar. The form may be resized, but the controls on the form do not change position.
SizableToolWindow	Like Fixed ToolWindow, but resizable.

Locking Controls

Once you have placed all the controls in their proper positions on a form, it is usually a good idea to lock them. When you lock the controls on a form, they cannot be accidentally moved at design time. They must be unlocked before they can be moved.

To lock all the controls on a form, place the cursor over an empty spot on the form and right-click. A small menu pops up. One of the selections on the menu is Lock Controls.

In Tutorial 2-17 we will modify the value of the form's BorderStyle property so the user cannot minimize, maximize, or resize the window.

TUTORIAL 2-17:

Setting the FormBorderStyle property and locking the controls

Step 1:   Select the form and find the FormBorderStyle property in the Properties window.

Step 2:   Click on the FormBorderStyle property. A down-arrow button appears. Click the down-arrow button to see a list of values.

Step 3:   Click on FixedSingle.

Step 4:   Start the application and test the new border style. Notice that you can move the window, but you cannot resize it by its edges or its corners.

Step 5:   Click the Exit button to end the application.

Step 6:   Now you will lock the controls. Place the cursor over an empty spot on the form and right-click. A small menu pops up.

Step 7:   Click the lock controls command.

Step 8:   Select any control on the form and try to move it. Because the controls are locked, you cannot move them.

Step 9:   Save the project.

When you are ready to move the controls, just right-click over an empty spot on the form and select the lock controls command again. This toggles the locked state of the controls.

TIP: Be careful. Visual Basic .NET still allows you to delete a locked control.

Printing Your Code

To print a project's code, open the Code window, then click File on the menu bar, then click the Print command on the File menu.

✓ Checkpoint

2.19   What is a code region?

2.20   How do you expand a code region? How do you collapse it?

2.21   What happens when you change a Label control's BackColor property?

2.22   What happens when you change a Label control's ForeColor property?

2.23   What property do you set in order to prevent a form from being resized when the application is running?

2.24   What happens when you lock the controls on a form?

2.25   How do you lock the controls on a form?

2.26   How do you unlock the controls on a form?

►2.4 Modifying the Text Property with Code

While building the directions application, you learned that an assignment statement is used to copy a value into a property while the application is running. Recall that the following statement sets the `lblDirections` control's Visible property to True.

> **CONCEPT**
>
> QUITE OFTEN, YOU WILL NEED TO CHANGE A CONTROL'S TEXT PROPERTY WITH CODE. THIS IS DONE WITH AN ASSIGNMENT STATEMENT.

```
lblDirections.Visible = True
```

You use the same technique to change the value of a control's Text property. For example, assume an application has a Label control named `lblMessage`. The following statement copies the sentence "Programming is fun!" to the control's Text property.

```
lblMessage.Text = "Programming is fun!"
```

Once the statement executes, the message displayed by the `lblMessage` control changes to

Programming is fun!

The quotation marks in the statement are not part of the message. They simply mark the beginning and end of the set of characters that are assigned to the property. In programming terms, a group of characters inside a set of quotation marks is called a string literal. You'll learn more about string literals in Chapter 3.

We usually display messages on a form by setting the value of a Label control's Text property. In the following steps, you open and examine an application on the student disk that demonstrates this technique.

TUTORIAL 2-18:

Examining an application that displays various messages at run time

Step 1:   Start Visual Basic .NET and open the KiloConverter project which is in the \Chap2\KiloConverter folder on the student disk.

Step 2:   Open the Design window, which displays `Form1` as shown in Figure 2-50.

Step 3:   Click the Start button (▶) to run the application.

Step 4:   Once the application is running, click the Inches button. The form displays the number of inches equivalent to a kilometer, as shown in Figure 2-51.

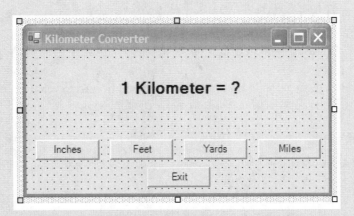

Figure 2-50   Kilometer Converter form

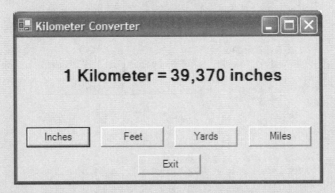

Figure 2-51   Kilometer converted to inches

Step 5:   Experiment with the other buttons and observe the messages that are displayed when each is clicked.

Step 6:   Click the Exit button to exit the application. Now we will examine the application code. Figure 2-52 shows the KiloConverter application form with its controls labeled.

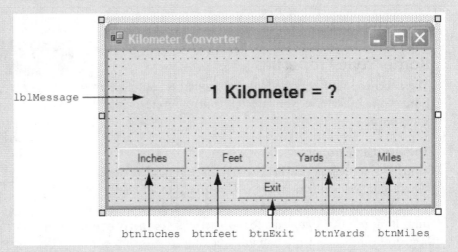

Figure 2-52   KiloConverter application controls

The buttons `btnInches`, `btnFeet`, `btnYards`, and `btnMiles` each change the `lblMessage` Text property when clicked. Use the following step to view the KiloConverter event procedures.

Step 7: Click the view code button () in the Solution Explorer window. The Code window appears. The window shows the following event procedure code:

```
Private Sub btnExit_Click(ByVal sender As System.Object, _
          ByVal e As System.EventArgs) Handles btnExit.Click
    ' End the application.
    End
End Sub

Private Sub btnFeet_Click(ByVal sender As System.Object, _
          ByVal e As System.EventArgs) Handles btnFeet.Click
    ' Display the conversion to feet.
    lblMessage.Text = "1 Kilometer = 3,281 feet"
End Sub

Private Sub btnInches_Click(ByVal sender As System.Object, _
          ByVal e As System.EventArgs) Handles btnInches.Click
    ' Display the conversion to inches.
    lblMessage.Text = "1 Kilometer = 39,370 inches"
End Sub

Private Sub btnMiles_Click(ByVal sender As System.Object, _
          ByVal e As System.EventArgs) Handles btnMiles.Click
    ' Display the conversion to miles.
    lblMessage.Text = "1 Kilometer = 0.6214 miles"
End Sub

Private Sub btnYards_Click(ByVal sender As System.Object, _
          ByVal e As System.EventArgs) Handles btnYards.Click
    ' Display the conversion to yards.
    lblMessage.Text = "1 Kilometer = 1,093.6 yards"
End Sub
```

2.5 The AutoSize, BorderStyle, and TextAlign Properties

The Label Control AutoSize and BorderStyle Properties

The Label control has two additional properties, AutoSize and BorderStyle, that give you greater control over the label's appearance.

The AutoSize Property

AutoSize is a Boolean property, which is set to false by default. When AutoSize is set to false, the bounding box of the Label control remains, at run time, the size that it was given at design time. If the text that is copied into the label's Text property is too large to fit in the control's bounding box, the text is only partially displayed. When a label's AutoSize property is set to true,

> **CONCEPT**
>
> THE LABEL CONTROL'S AUTOSIZE PROPERTY ALLOWS A LABEL TO CHANGE SIZE AUTOMATICALLY TO ACCOMMODATE THE AMOUNT OF TEXT IN ITS TEXT PROPERTY. THE BORDERSTYLE PROPERTY ALLOWS YOU TO SET A BORDER AROUND A LABEL CONTROL. YOU PREVIOUSLY LEARNED TO SET THE TEXTALIGN PROPERTY AT DESIGN TIME. THE TEXTALIGN PROPERTY CAN ALSO BE SET WITH CODE.

however, the label's bounding box will automatically resize to accommodate the text in the label's Text property.

The BorderStyle Property

The Label control's *BorderStyle property* may have one of three values: None, FixedSingle, and Fixed3D. The property is set to None by default, which means the label will have no border. If BorderStyle is set to FixedSingle, the label will be outlined with a border that is a single pixel wide. If BorderStyle is set to Fixed3D, the label will have a recessed 3D appearance. Figure 2-53 shows an example of two Label controls: one with BorderStyle set to FixedSingle, and the other with BorderStyle set to Fixed3D.

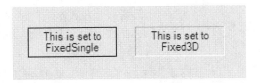

Figure 2-53 FixedSingle and Fixed3D BorderStyle

Quite often you will want to display output, such as the results of a calculation, in a Label control with a border. You will see many example applications in this book that use this approach.

Changing a Label's TextAlign Property with Code

Recall that the Label control has a property named TextAlign. The TextAlign property establishes the justification of the control's displayed text. This property may have one of the following values: TopLeft, TopCenter, TopRight, MiddleLeft, MiddleCenter, MiddleRight, BottomLeft, BottomCenter, or BottomRight.

At design time, you establish the TextAlign property's value with the Properties window. You can also set the property with code at run time. You do this by using an assignment statement to store one of the following values in the property:

```
ContentAlignment.TopLeft

ContentAlignment.TopCenter

ContentAlignment.TopRight

ContentAlignment.MiddleLeft

ContentAlignment.MiddleCenter

ContentAlignment.MiddleRight

ContentAlignment.BottomLeft

ContentAlignment.BottomCenter

ContentAlignment.BottomRight
```

For example, assume an application uses a Label control named `lblReportTitle`. The following statement aligns the control's text with the middle and center of the control's bounding box.

```
lblReportTitle.TextAlign = ContentAlignment.MiddleCenter
```

TIP: When you write an assignment statement that stores a value in the TextAlign property, an auto list box appears showing all the valid values.

✓ Checkpoint

2.27   Suppose an application has a Label control named `lblTemperature`. Write a code statement that will cause the label's Text property to display the message "48 degrees".

2.28 What results when a Label control's AutoSize property is set to false? When it is set to true?

2.29 What are the possible values for the Label control's BorderStyle property, and what does each value result in?

2.30 An application has a Label control named `lblName`. Write the programming statements described for the following:

- ◆ A statement that aligns the label's text in the top right.
- ◆ A statement that aligns the label's text in the bottom left.
- ◆ A statement that aligns the label's text in the top center

▶2.6 Clickable Images

CONCEPT

CONTROLS OTHER THAN BUTTONS HAVE CLICK EVENT PROCEDURES. IN THIS SECTION, YOU LEARN TO CREATE PICTUREBOX CONTROLS THAT RESPOND TO MOUSE CLICKS.

In this chapter, you learned that buttons have Click event procedures. A Click event procedure is executed when the user clicks the button. Other controls, such as PictureBoxes and labels, may also have Click event procedures. In the following tutorial, you write Click event procedures for a group of PictureBox controls.

TUTORIAL 2-19:

Writing Click event procedures for PictureBox controls

Step 1: Start Visual Basic .NET and open the Flags project which is stored in the \Chap2\Flags folder on the student disk.

Step 2: Open the Design window and look at Form1. Figure 2-54 shows the form and the names of the controls that are on the form.

Step 3: Select the `lblMessage` control and set its TextAlign property to MiddleCenter, and its Font property to Microsoft sans serif, bold, 10 points.

Step 4: Change the form's Text property to "Flags".

Step 5: `PictureBox1` shows the flag of the United States. Rename this control `picUSA`.

Step 6: `PictureBox2` shows the flag of Canada. Rename this control `picCanada`.

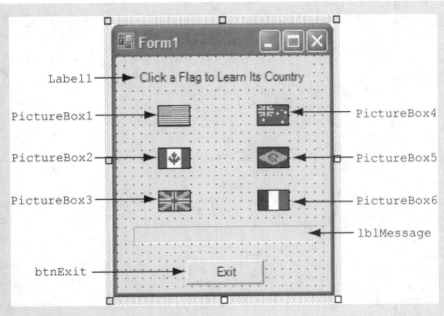

Figure 2-54   Form1 of the Flags project

Step 7:   PictureBox3 shows the flag of the United Kingdom. Rename this control picUK.

Step 8:   PictureBox4 shows the flag of Australia. Rename this control picAustralia.

Step 9:   PictureBox5 shows the flag of Brazil. Rename this control picBrazil.

Step 10:   PictureBox6 shows the flag of Italy. Rename this control picItaly.

Step 11:   Double-click the picUSA control. The Code window appears with a code template for the picUSA_Click procedure. Write the following code shown here in bold, which copies the string "United States of America" into the lblMessage Text property.

```
Private Sub picUSA_Click(ByVal sender As System.Object, _
            ByVal e As System.EventArgs) Handles picUSA.Click
    ' Display the country name
    lblMessage.Text = "United States of America"
End Sub
```

Step 12:   Repeat the process outlined in step 11 for each of the other PictureBox controls. The Click procedure for each PictureBox control should copy the name of its flag's country into the lblMessage.Text property.

Step 13:   Save the application.

Step 14: Run the application. When you click any of the flags, you should see the name of the flag's country appear in the `lblMessage` Label control. For example, when you click the flag of Australia, the form should appear similar to Figure 2-55.

Step 15: Exit the application.

Figure 2-55 Flags application identifying flag of Australia

▶2.7 Using Visual Basic .NET Help

CONCEPT

IN THIS SECTION YOU LEARN TO USE THE VISUAL BASIC .NET HELP SYSTEM.

Dynamic Help

Recall from Chapter 1 that the Dynamic Help window displays a list of help topics that changes as you perform operations. The topics that are displayed are relevant to the operation you are currently performing.

The Dynamic Help window occupies the same location as the Properties window, as shown in Figure 2-56. Notice the Properties and Dynamic Help tabs at the bottom of the window. You switch between Properties and Dynamic Help by clicking the tabs.

If you do not see the Dynamic Help tab, click Help on the menu bar, then click Dynamic Help.

The Dynamic Help window also has a small toolbar with icons to access the help contents, the help index, and to search the help topics. Tutorial 2-20 guides you through the process of using dynamic help.

Figure 2-56 Dynamic Help window

TUTORIAL 2-20:

Using Dynamic Help

Step 1: Start Visual Basic .NET and load the Directions project. Make sure the Design window is open.

Figure 2-57 Dynamic Help window with topics related to Label controls

Step 2: Click the Dynamic Help tab to display the Dynamic Help window. (If you do not see the Dynamic Help tab, click Help on the menu bar, then click Dynamic Help.)

Step 3: In the Design window, select one of the Label controls on the form. Notice that the contents of the Dynamic Help window has changed. It should look similar to Figure 2-57. The topics that are now displayed are related to Label controls.

Step 4: Click the first help topic, which should read Label Members (System.Windows.Forms). This should cause the help screen shown in Figure 2-58 to be displayed. This screen provides help on all the properties and methods of the Label control.

Form1.vb [Design]	Form1.vb	**Label Members**	
⊞ .NET Framework Class Library	
Label Members	
Label overview	
Public Constructors	
Label Constructor	Initializes a new instance of the **Label** class.
Public Properties	
AccessibilityObject (inherited from **Control**)	Gets the AccessibleObject assigned to the control.
AccessibleDefaultActionDescription (inherited from **Control**)	Gets or sets the default action description of the control for use by accessibility client applications.
AccessibleDescription (inherited from **Control**)	Gets or sets the description of the control used by accessibility client applications.
AccessibleName (inherited from **Control**)	Gets or sets the name of the control used by accessibility client applications.
AccessibleRole (inherited from **Control**)	Gets or sets the accessible role of the control
AllowDrop (inherited from **Control**)	Gets or sets a value indicating whether the control can accept data that the user drags onto it.
Anchor (inherited from **Control**)	Gets or sets which edges of the control are anchored to the edges of its

Figure 2-58 Label Members help screen

Step 5:   Click the close button (✕) that appears in the upper right corner of the Label Members help screen to close it.

Step 6:   Figure 2-59 shows the locations of the contents, index, and search buttons. When any of these buttons are clicked, another help window that provides additional functionality appears in the same location as the Solution Explorer. The *contents button* displays a table of contents in which related topics are organized into groups. The *index button* displays a searchable alphabetized index of all the help topics. The *search button* allows you to search for help using key words.

Click the search button.

Figure 2-59   The contents, index, and search buttons

Step 7:   The search window should appear, as shown in Figure 2-60.

The Filtered by drop-down list allows you to filter the results of a search. Recall from Chapter 1 that Visual Studio .NET contains multiple programming languages. When you perform a search, it is common to see many unrelated topics. Make sure Visual Basic is selected so you only see topics related to Visual Basic.

Figure 2-60   Search window

Step 8:   In the Look for text box, type **FormBorderStyle**, then click the Search button. A Search Results window, as shown in Figure 2-61, should appear. Double-click one of the items displayed in the search results window to see its help screen. When finished, close the Search Results window.

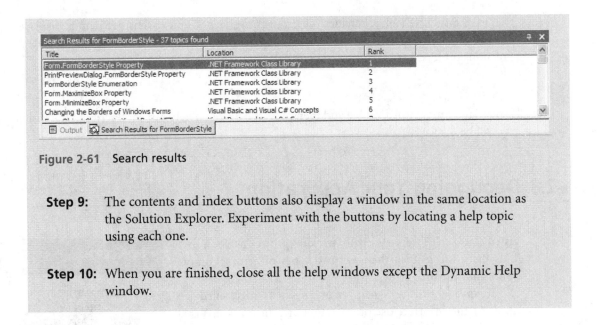

Figure 2-61   Search results

Step 9:   The contents and index buttons also display a window in the same location as the Solution Explorer. Experiment with the buttons by locating a help topic using each one.

Step 10:   When you are finished, close all the help windows except the Dynamic Help window.

The Help Menu and Context-Sensitive Help

The Visual Basic .NET Help menu is shown in Figure 2-62. As you can see, it also provides Contents, Index, and Search commands.

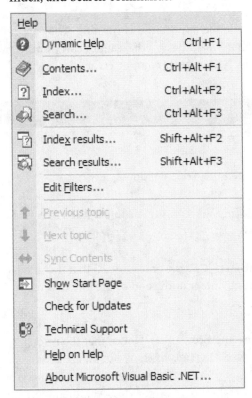

Figure 2-62   The Help menu

Visual Basic .NET also provides *context-sensitive help*. Context-sensitive help is displayed when you select an item and then press the F1 key. For example, look at the following line of code from the Directions project.

```
lblDirections.Visible = True
```

If you highlight the word Visible and then press the F1 key, a help screen describing the Visible property will be displayed.

▶2.8 Debugging Your Application

Visual Basic .NET reports errors in your project as soon as it finds them. In general, there are two types of errors, compile errors and run-time errors.

Compile errors are syntax errors, such as misspelled key words or the incorrect use of operators or punctuation. Visual Basic .NET checks each line of code for compile errors as soon as you enter it. When a compile error is found, it is underlined with a jagged blue line. A description of the error is also displayed in the Task List window. Until now we have not used the Task List window. You display it by clicking View on the menu bar, then selecting Other Windows, then clicking Task List.

CONCEPT

AT SOME POINT, MOST APPLICATIONS CONTAIN BUGS, OR ERRORS THAT PREVENT THE APPLICATION FROM OPERATING PROPERLY. IN THIS SECTION, YOU LEARN FUNDAMENTAL DEBUGGING TECHNIQUES.

Run-time errors are errors that are found while the application is running. They are not syntax errors but an attempt to perform an operation that Visual Basic .NET cannot carry out.

Tutorial 2-21 demonstrates how Visual Basic .NET reports compile errors.

TUTORIAL 2-21:

Locating a Compile Error in Design Time

Step 1: Load the Directions project and open the Code window.

Step 2: Open the Task List window by clicking View on the menu bar, then selecting Other Windows, then clicking Task List.

Step 3: You are going to modify the btnExit_Click procedure so that it contains a syntax error. Position the text editing cursor at the end of the line that reads End.

Step 4: Type a period at the end of the line and press Enter. Notice that the End statement is now underlined with a jagged blue line, as shown in Figure 2-63.

Step 5: Look at the Task List window, which should appear as shown in Figure 2-64. It shows an error message indicating that the End statement is not valid.

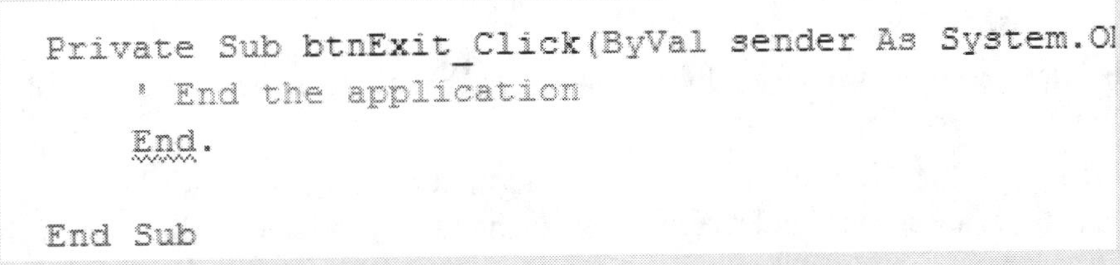

```
Private Sub btnExit_Click(ByVal sender As System.Ol
    ' End the application
    End.

End Sub
```

Figure 2-63   Error underlined

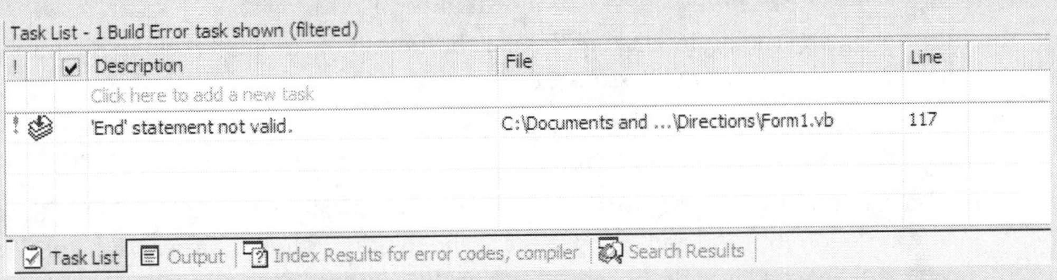

Task List - 1 Build Error task shown (filtered)

!	☑	Description	File	Line
		Click here to add a new task		
!	▨	'End' statement not valid.	C:\Documents and ...\Directions\Form1.vb	117

☑ Task List   ▤ Output   🔲 Index Results for error codes, compiler   🔍 Search Results

Figure 2-64   Task List window with error message

Step 6:   The Task List window also helps you find the statement that contains the error. Double-click the error message in the Task List window. Notice that the End statement is highlighted in the Code window.

> TIP: Sometimes you will see an error message that you do not fully understand. When this happens, look at the highlighted area of the line that contains the error and try to determine what the problem is. When you figure out what caused the error, look at how that relates to the error message.

Step 7:   Erase the period to correct the error.

✓ Checkpoint

2.31   If the Dynamic Help window is not visible, how to you display it?

2.32   Describe two ways to display a searchable alphabetized index of help topics.

2.33   How do you cause the contents, index, and search windows to only display the help topics related to Visual Basic?

2.34   What is context-sensitive help?

2.35   What are the two general types of errors in a Visual Basic .NET project?

SUMMARY

You use the Properties window at design time to set control property values.

The TextAlign property aligns text within a label.

The Font property indicates the size and style of a text font.

The Visible property causes a control to be visible on the form when set to true or hidden when set to false.

The PictureBox control's SizeMode property determines how the control will place and size its image.

When you select a control in the Design window, it appears surrounded by small squares. The squares are sizing handles. You use sizing handles to enlarge or shrink the control.

Once you place a control on a form, you can move it by clicking and dragging.

A control's bounding box is a transparent rectangular area that defines the control's size.

To delete a control, you simply select it and then press the Delete key.

You may run an application by clicking the start button on the toolbar, clicking the start command on the Debug menu, or by pressing the F5 key.

To end a running application, click the Stop Debugging command on the Debug menu, or click the close button on the application window.

When you create a new project, Visual Basic .NET automatically creates a solution with the same name as the project, and adds the project to the solution. The solution and the project are stored on the disk in a folder with the same name as the solution. The solution file ends with the .sln extension and the project file ends with the .vbproj extension.

You can open a project by clicking its name on the Start Page, or by clicking the Open Project button on the Start Page, or by clicking File on the menu bar, then New, then Project.

The Properties window's object box provides a drop-down list of the objects in the project. The alphabetic button causes the properties to be listed in alphabetical order. The categorized button causes related properties to be displayed in groups.

The apostrophe (') marks the beginning of a remark in code. A remark is a note of explanation that is ignored by Visual Basic .NET.

An assignment statement uses the assignment operator to copy a value from one object to another.

The assignment operator copies the value on its right into the item on its left.

The Code window is a text-editing window in which you write code.

Intellisense is a feature of Visual Studio .NET that provides help and some automatic code completion while you are developing an application.

The End statement causes an application to stop running.

You may display the Code window by clicking the view code button on the Solution Explorer window, or by clicking View on the menu bar, then Code, or by pressing the F7 key on the keyboard.

A code region is a section of code that may be hidden from view, or collapsed. This makes code more readable.

You may change the color of a label's text with the BackColor and ForeColor properties.

The FormBorderStyle property determines whether a form can be resized, minimized, or maximized.

Once you have placed all the controls in their proper positions on a form, it is usually a good idea to lock them.

You may change a control's Text property with code. An assignment statement copies a value into the property at run time.

The Label control's AutoSize property allows a label to change size automatically, to accommodate the amount of text in its Text property.

The Label control's BorderStyle property allows you to set a border around the label.

You can set the TextAlign property with code at run time. You do this by using an assignment statement to store a valid value in the property.

Buttons are not the only controls with `Click` event procedures. Other controls, such as PictureBoxes and Labels, also have `Click` event procedures.

The Dynamic Help window displays a list of help topics that changes as you perform operations. The window also has buttons to view the help contents, index, and to search for a help topic.

Context-sensitive help is a help screen displayed when the F1 key is pressed, for the item that is currently selected.

Compile errors are syntax errors, such as misspelled key words or the incorrect use of operators or punctuation. Visual Basic .NET checks each line of code for compile errors as soon as you enter it. When a compile error is found, it is underlined with a jagged blue line.

Run-time errors are errors that are found while the application is running. They are not syntax errors but an attempt to perform an operation that Visual Basic .NET cannot carry out.

KEY TERMS

Alphabetic button	ForeColor Property
Assignment operator	FormBorderStyle property
Assignment statement	Index button
Auto list box	Intellisense
AutoSize property	Object box
BackColor property	PictureBox control
Boolean	Project file
BorderStyle	Remark
Bounding box	Run-time
Categorized button	Run-time errors
Code region	Search button
Code template	SizeMode property
Code window	Sizing handles
Compile errors	Solution file
Contents button	String literal
Context-sensitive help	TextAlign Property
Font property	Visible property

Review Questions

Fill-in-the-blank

1. The _____ property determines how a Label control's text is aligned.
2. A PictureBox control's _____ property lists the name of the file containing the graphic image.
3. A PictureBox control's _____ property determines how the graphic image will be positioned and scaled to fit the control's bounding box.

4. When set to _____, the TextAlign property causes text to appear in the bottom right area of a Label control.

5. The contents of a form's Text property is displayed on the form's _____.

6. Anytime you select an existing control, _____ appear, which you use to resize the control.

7. A control's _____ is a transparent rectangular area that defines the control's size.

8. A Label control's _____ property establishes the font, style, and size of the label's displayed text.

9. To delete a control during design time, select it and press the _____ key.

10. The _____ control is used to display graphic images.

11. The SizeMode property is set to _____ by default.

12. When the _____ button is selected on the Solution Explorer window, it opens the Code window.

13. Clicking the _____ button in the Properties window causes related properties to be listed in groups.

14. Visible is a _____ property, which means it can only hold one of two values: true or false.

15. An apostrophe (') in code marks the beginning of a _____.

16. The equal sign (=) is known as the _____ operator. It copies the value on its right into the item on its left.

17. In an assignment statement, the name of the item receiving the value must be on the _____ side of the = operator.

18. Visual Basic .NET automatically provides a code _____, which is the first and last lines of an event procedure.

19. The _____ statement causes the application to end.

20. The _____ property establishes the background color for a Label control's text.

21. The _____ property establishes the color of the type for a Label control's text.

22. The _____ property allows you to prevent the user from resizing, minimizing, or maximizing a form, or closing a form using its close button.

23. When you _____ the controls on a form, they cannot be accidentally moved at design time.

24. You display text in a form's title bar by setting the value of the form's _____ property.

25. You commonly display messages on a form by setting the value of a Label control's _____ property.

26. The _____ property causes the Label control to resize automatically to accommodate the amount of text in the Text property.

27. _____is a help screen displayed for the item that is currently selected.

28. _____ errors are errors that are found while the application is running.

True or False

Indicate whether the following statements are true or false.

1. T F: Sizing handles appear around the control that is currently selected.

2. T F: The PictureBox control has an ImageStretch property.

3. T F: The Visible property is Boolean.

4. T F: A control is hidden at design time if its Visible property is set to False.

5. T F: You can delete a locked control.

6. T F: A control is accessed in code by its Text property.

7. T F: The TextAlign property causes a control to be aligned with other controls on the same form.
8. T F: Text is frequently the first property that the programmer changes, so it is listed in parentheses in the Properties window. This causes it to be displayed at the top of the alphabetized list of properties.
9. T F: Resizing handles are positioned along the edges of a control's bounding box.
10. T F: A label's text is MiddleCenter aligned by default.
11. T F: You can run an application in the Visual Basic .NET environment by pressing the F5 key.
12. T F: The first line of an event procedure identifies the control it belongs to, and the event it responds to.
13. T F: You should be very cautious about, and even avoid, placing remarks in your code.
14. T F: In an assignment statement, the name of the item receiving the value must be on the right side of the = operator.
15. T F: You can bring up the Code window by pressing the F7 key while the Design window is visible.
16. T F: The BackColor property establishes the color of a Label control's text.
17. T F: A form's BorderStyle property can be used to prevent the user from resizing, minimizing, or maximizing a window, or closing the window using its close button.
18. T F: When you lock the controls on a form, the user must enter a password before the application will run.
19. T F: You cannot modify a control's Text property with code.
20. T F: The Properties window only shows a control's properties that may be changed at design time.
21. T F: The AutoSize property is set to True by default.
22. T F: PictureBox controls have a `Click` event procedure.
23. T F: Context-sensitive help is a help screen displayed for the item that is currently selected.
24. T F: You access context-sensitive help by pressing the F1 key.

Short Answer

1. Explain the difference between an object's Text and its Name.
2. List three ways to run an application within the Visual Basic .NET environment.
3. List three ways to display the Code window.
4. Why is the code between the first and last lines of an event procedure usually indented?
5. In this chapter you learned two techniques for placing controls on a form. What are they?
6. How do you make a PictureBox control respond to mouse clicks?

What Do You Think?

1. Why, in the Properties window, do you change some properties with a drop-down list or a dialog box, while you change others by typing a value?
2. Why is it a good idea to equip a form with a button that terminates the application, if the form already has a standard Windows close button in the upper-right corner?
3. What is the benefit of creating PictureBox controls that respond to mouse clicks?

Find the Error

1. Open the Error1 project, which is located in the \Chap2\Error1 folder on the student disk.
    Run the application. When Visual Basic .NET reports an error, find and fix the error.

2.   Open the Error2 project, which is located in the \Chap2\Error2 folder on the student disk. Run the application. When Visual Basic .NET reports an error, find and fix the error.

PROGRAMMING CHALLENGES

1.   Welcome Screen Modification

For this exercise, you will modify an application that displays a welcome screen for the First Federal Bank. After starting Visual Basic .NET, load the First Federal project which is located in the \Chap2\First Federal1 folder on the student disk.

Figure 2-65 shows the application's form.

Figure 2-65   First Federal Bank welcome screen, `Form1`

Make the following modifications to the application:

a) Change the form's title bar text to read First Federal Bank.

b) Change the label's Font property to Microsoft sans serif, bold, 14-point.

c) Change the label's text alignment to middle center.

d) Change the button's name to `btnExit`.

e) Change the button's text to read Exit.

f) Change the label's background color to a shade of red, or another color of your choice.

g) Change the form's background color to the same color you chose for the label.

h) Write a `Click` event procedure for the button that terminates the application.

2.   Name and Address

Create an application that that displays your name and address when a button is clicked. The application's form should appear as Figure 2-66 when it first runs.

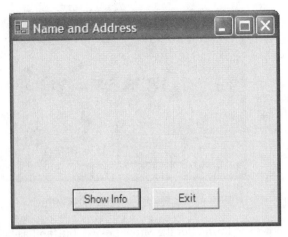

Figure 2-66   Name and Address form

Once the Show Info button is clicked, the form should appear similar to Figure 2-67.

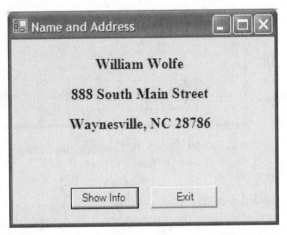

Figure 2-67   Name and Address form after
Show Info button has been clicked

Here are the detailed property specifications:

a) The button that displays the name and address should be named `btnShowInfo`. Its text should read Show Info.

b) The button that closes the application should be named `btnExit`. Its text should read Exit.

c) The form should have three Label controls. The first will hold your name, the second will hold your street address, and the third will hold your city, state, and zip code. The labels should be named `lblName`, `lblStreet`, and `lblCityStateZip` respectively. The labels' Font property should be set to Times New Roman, bold, 12 point. The labels' TextAlign property should be set to middle center.

d) The form's title bar should read Name and Address.

3.   Math Tutor Application

You are to create a math tutor application. The application should display a simple math problem in a Label control. The form should have a button that displays the answer to the math problem in a second label, when clicked. It should also have a button that closes the application. Figure 2-68 shows an example of the application's form before the button is clicked to display the answer.

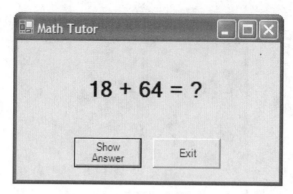

Figure 2-68   Math Tutor application

Figure 2-69 shows the form after the Show Answer button has been clicked.

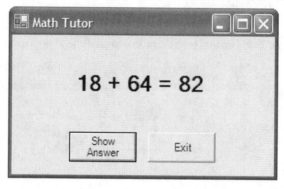

Figure 2-69   Math Tutor application after
Show Answer button has been clicked

Here are the detailed property specifications:

a) The button that displays the answer should be named `btnShowAnswer`. Its text should read Show Answer.

b) The button that closes the application should be named `btnExit`. Its text should read Exit.

c) The label that displays the answer to the math problem should be named `lblAnswer`.

d) The form's title bar should read Math Tutor.

Design Your Own Forms

4. State Abbreviations

The following table shows lists of six states and their official abbreviations.

State	Abbreviation
Virginia	VA
North Carolina	NC
South Carolina	SC
Georgia	GA
Alabama	AL
Florida	FL

Create an application that allows the user to select a state, then displays that state's official abbreviation. The form should have six buttons, one for each state. When the user clicks a button, the application displays the state's abbreviation in a Label control.

5. Latin Translator

Look at the following list of Latin words and their meanings.

Latin	English
sinister	left
dexter	right
medium	center

Create an application that "translates" the Latin words to English. The form should have three buttons, one for each Latin word. When the user clicks a button, the application should display the English translation in a Label control. When the user clicks the "sinister" button, the translation should appear with middle left alignment. When the user clicks the "dexter" button, the translation should appear middle right alignment. When the user clicks the "medium" button, the translation should appear with middle center alignment.

6. Clickable Image

Note: This exercise requires that Visual Basic .NET's graphics files be installed.

Create an application with a PictureBox control. For the Image property, use one of Visual Basic .NET's graphics files. The graphics files are normally stored in the following location on your hard drive: C:\Program Files\Microsoft Visual Studio .NET\Common7\Graphics. In this location, you will find several folders of graphics files. Explore them and select a file you want to use.

Once you have selected a graphic file, place a Label control on the form. Then, write code in the PictureBox control's `Click` event procedure that displays the name of your school in the Label control.

3

CHAPTER

Input, Variables, Constants, and Calculations

▶ 3.1 Introduction

T his chapter covers the use of text boxes to gather input from users. It also discusses the use of variables, named constants, intrinsic functions, and mathematical calculations. The GroupBox control is introduced as a way to organize an application's form. The Format menu commands, which allow you to align, size, and center controls, are also discussed. The form's `Load` procedure, which automatically executes when a form is loaded into memory, is covered. In addition, we discuss debugging techniques for locating logic errors.

▶ 3.2 Gathering Text Input

CONCEPT

IN THIS SECTION, WE USE THE TEXTBOX CONTROL TO GATHER INPUT THAT THE USER HAS TYPED ON THE KEYBOARD. WE ALSO ALTER A FORM'S TAB ORDER AND ASSIGN KEYBOARD ACCESS KEYS TO CONTROLS.

The programs you have written and examined so far perform their operations without requiring information from the user. In reality, most programs ask the user to enter values. For example, a program that calculates payroll for a small business might ask the user to enter the name of the employee, the hours worked, and the hourly pay rate. The program then uses this information to print the employee's paycheck.

MAJOR TOPICS

A *text box* is a rectangular area on a form that accepts keyboard input. As the user types, the characters are stored in the text box. In Visual Basic .NET, you create a text box with a *TextBox* control. Tutorial 3-1 examines an application that uses a TextBox control.

TUTORIAL 3-1:

Using a TextBox control

Step 1: Start Visual Basic .NET and open the Greetings project, which is stored in the Chap3\Greetings folder on the student disk.

Step 2: Click the Start button (▶) to run the application. The application's form appears, as shown in Figure 3-1. The TextBox control is the white rectangular area beneath the label that reads Enter Your Name.

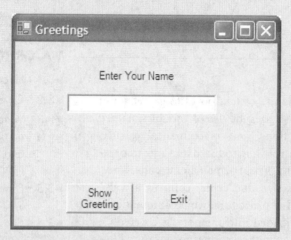

Figure 3-1 Greetings project initial form

Notice that the TextBox control shows a blinking text cursor, indicating it is ready to receive keyboard input.

Step 3: Type your name. Notice that, as you enter characters on the keyboard, they appear in the TextBox control.

Step 4: Click the Show Greeting button. The message "Hello " followed by the name you entered, appears in a label below the Text-Box control. The form now appears similar to that shown in Figure 3-2.

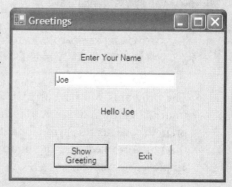

Figure 3-2 Greetings project completed form

Step 5: Click inside the TextBox control and use the delete and/or backspace key to erase the name you entered. Enter another name, then click the Show Greeting button. Notice that the greeting message changes accordingly.

Step 6: Click the Exit button to exit the application. You are now in design time in Visual Basic .NET.

Step 7: Look at the application's form in the Design window. Figure 3-3 depicts the form with its controls.

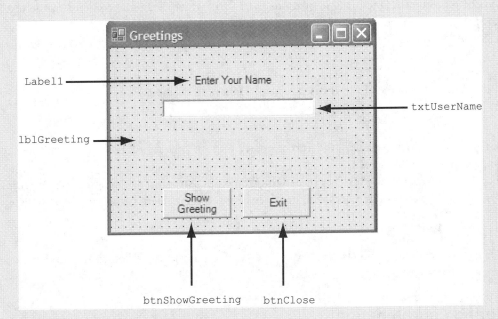

Figure 3-3   Greetings project form with controls labeled

Notice that the name of the TextBox control starts with `txt`, which is the standard prefix for TextBox controls.

Like the Label control, the TextBox control has a Text property. However, the Label control's Text property is only for displaying information—the user cannot directly alter its contents. The TextBox control's Text property is for input purposes. The user can alter it by typing characters into the TextBox control. Whatever the user types into the TextBox control is stored, as a string, in its Text property.

Using the Text Property in Code

You access a TextBox control's Text property in code in the same way you access other properties. For example, assume an application has a Label control named `lblInfo`, and a TextBox control named `txtInput`. The following assignment statement copies the contents of the TextBox control's Text property into the Label control's Text property.

```
lblInfo.Text = txtInput.Text
```

Clear a Text Box

Recall from the discussion on object-oriented programming in Chapter 1 that an object contains methods, which are actions that the object performs. To execute an object's method, you write a statement that calls the method. The general format of such as statement is:

```
Object.Method
```

Object is the name of the object and *Method* is the name of the method that is being called.

A TextBox control is an object, and has a variety of methods that perform operations on the text box or its contents. One of these methods is Clear, which clears the contents of the text box's Text property. The general format of the Clear method is

```
TextBox.Clear()
```

TextBox is the name of the TextBox control. Here is an example:

```
txtInput.Clear()
```

Once this statement executes, the Text property of txtInput will be cleared and the text box will appear empty on the screen.

You may also clear a text box by assigning an empty string to its Text property. An empty string is a set of double quotation marks with no space between them. Here is an example:

```
txtInput.Text = ""
```

Once this statement executes, the Text property of txtInput will be cleared and the text box will appear empty on the screen.

String Concatenation

Turning our attention back to the Greetings application, let's look at the code for the btnShowGreeting control's Click event:

```
Private Sub btnShowGreeting_Click(ByVal sender As System.Object, _
     ByVal e As System.EventArgs) Handles btnShowGreeting.Click
  ' Display a customized greeting to the user
  ' in the lblGreeting control
  lblGreeting.Text = "Hello " & txtUserName.Text
End Sub
```

The assignment statement in this procedure introduces a new operator: the ampersand (&). When the ampersand is used in this way, it performs a *string concatenation*. This means that one string is appended to another.

The & operator creates a string that is the combination of the string on its left and the string on its right. Specifically, it appends the string on its right to the string on its left. For example, assume an application uses a Label control named lblMessage. The following statement copies the string "Good morning Charlie" into the control's Text property:

```
lblMessage.Text = "Good morning " & "Charlie"
```

In our Greetings application, if the user types **Becky** into the `txtUserName` control, the control's Text property will be set to `"Becky"`. So the statement

```
lblGreeting.Text = "Hello " & txtUserName.Text
```

assigns the string `"Hello Becky"` into `lblGreeting`'s Text property.

Look again at the assignment statement. Notice there is a space in the string literal after the word "Hello". This prevents the two strings that are being concatenated from running together.

Now it's your turn to create an application using TextBox controls and string concatenation. Tutorial 3-2 leads you through the process.

TUTORIAL 3-2:

Building the Date String application

In this exercise, you create an application that lets the user enter the following information about today's date:

- The day of the week
- The name of the month
- The numeric day of the month
- The year

Once the user enters the information and clicks a button, the application displays a date string such as Friday, December 6, 2002.

Step 1: Start Visual Basic .NET and start a new windows application named Date String.

Step 2: Create the form shown in Figure 3-4, using the following instructions:

- Give each control the name indicated in Figure 3-4. The labels that display "Enter the day of the week:", "Enter the month:", "Enter the day of the month:", and "Enter the year:" will not be referred to in code, so they may keep their default names.

- Set the `lblDateString` label's BorderStyle property to Fixed3D and its TextAlign property to MiddleCenter.

- Set the form's Text to "Date String".

- You insert a TextBox control by double-clicking the TextBox tool in the toolbox.

- When you insert the TextBox controls, notice that they initially display their default names. For example, the first TextBox control you create will have the default name `TextBox1`. The control will appear similar to this:

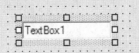

As you place the TextBox controls on your form, delete the contents of their Text properties. This will cause their contents to appear empty when the application runs.

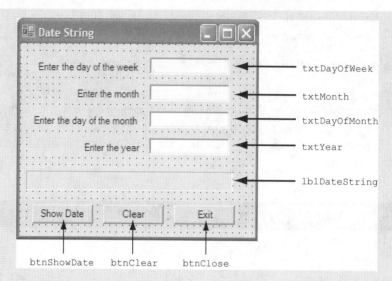

Figure 3-4   Date String form

Step 3:   The code for the btnShowDate button's Click event procedure is as follows. Double-click the button to create the code template, and then enter the lines shown in bold.

```
Private Sub btnShowDate_Click(ByVal sender As System.Object, _
        ByVal e As System.EventArgs) Handles btnShowDate.Click
    ' Concatenate the input and build the date string.
    lblDateString.Text = txtDayOfWeek.Text & ", " _
            & txtMonth.Text & " " _
            & txtDayOfMonth.Text & ", " _
            & txtYear.Text
End Sub
```

This introduces a new programming technique: breaking up long lines of code with the line-continuation character. The *line-continuation character* is actually two characters: a space, followed by an underscore or underline character.

Quite often, you will find yourself writing statements that are too long to fit entirely inside the code window. This makes your code harder to read because you have to scroll the code window to the right to view these long statements. The line-continuation character allows you to break a long statement into several lines. For example, the btnShowDate_Click procedure uses the line-continuation character in the following statement:

```
lblDateString.Text = txtDayOfWeek.Text & ", " _
            & txtMonth.Text & " " _
            & txtDayOfMonth.Text & ", " _
            & txtYear.Text
```

The line-continuation character marks the end of a line and indicates to Visual Basic .NET that the statement continues on the next line. Without this programming technique, the statement would not be entirely viewable without scrolling the Code window.

Here are some guidelines to remember about the line-continuation character:

- The space must immediately precede the underscore character.
- You cannot break up a word or name using the line-continuation character.
- You cannot break an object name from its property or method name.
- You cannot put a remark at the end of a line, after the line-continuation character. The line-continuation character must be the last thing you type on a line.

TIP: You can reduce the font size used in the code window by clicking Tools on the menu bar, and then clicking the Options... command. On the Options dialog box, click Environment in the left pane, and then click Fonts and Colors. You may then select the desired font and size.

Step 4: The btnClear button allows the user to start over with a form that is empty of previous values. The btnClear_Click event procedure will clear the contents of all the TextBox controls, and the lblDateString label. To accomplish this, the procedure calls each TextBox control's Clear method, and copies an empty string to lblDateString's Text property. Enter the following code into the btnClear_Click event procedure:

```
Private Sub btnClear_Click(ByVal sender As System.Object, _
        ByVal e As System.EventArgs) Handles btnClear.Click
    ' Clear the Text Boxes and lblDateString
    txtDayOfWeek.Clear()
    txtMonth.Clear()
    txtDayOfMonth.Clear()
    txtYear.Clear()
    lblDateString.Text = ""
End Sub
```

Step 5: Enter the following code, which terminates the application, into the btnExit_Click event procedure:

```
Private Sub btnExit_Click(ByVal sender As System.Object, _
        ByVal e As System.EventArgs) Handles btnExit.Click
    ' End the application
    End
End Sub
```

Step 6: Save the project.

Step 7: Click the Start button (▶) to run the application. With the application running, enter the requested information into the TextBox controls and click the Show Date button. Your form should appear similar to Figure 3-5.

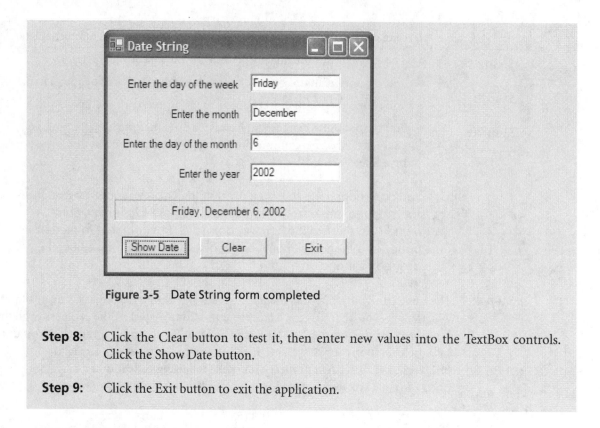

Figure 3-5   Date String form completed

Step 8:   Click the Clear button to test it, then enter new values into the TextBox controls. Click the Show Date button.

Step 9:   Click the Exit button to exit the application.

The Focus Method

When an application is running and a form is displayed, one of the form's controls always has the *focus*. The control that has the focus is the one that receives the user's keyboard input or mouse clicks. For example, when a TextBox control has the focus, it receives the characters that the user enters on the keyboard. When a button has the focus, pressing the Enter key executes the button's Click event procedure.

You can tell which control has the focus by looking at the form at run time. When a TextBox control has the focus, a blinking text cursor appears inside it, or the text inside the TextBox control appears highlighted. When a button, radio button, or check box has the focus, a thin dotted line appears around the control.

NOTE: *Only controls that are capable of receiving some sort of input, such as text boxes and buttons, may have the focus.*

Quite often, you want to make sure a particular control has the focus. Consider the Date String application, for example. When the Clear button is clicked, the focus should return to the txtDayOfWeek TextBox control. This would make it unnecessary for the user to click the TextBox control in order to start entering another set of information.

In code, you move the focus to a control with the *Focus* method. The method's general syntax is:

```
Control.Focus()
```

where *Control* is the name of the control. For instance, you move the focus to the txtDayOfWeek TextBox control with the statement txtDayOfWeek.Focus(). After the statement executes, the txtDayOfWeek control will have the focus. In the following tutorial, you add this statement to the Clear button's Click event procedure so txtDayOfWeek has the focus after the TextBox controls and the lblDateString label are cleared.

TUTORIAL 3-3:

Using the Focus Method

Step 1: Open the Date String project in Visual Basic .NET.

Step 2: Open the Code window and add the following boldface statements to the btnClear_Click event procedure.

```
Private Sub btnClear_Click(ByVal sender As System.Object, _
        ByVal e As System.EventArgs) Handles btnClear.Click
    ' Clear the Text Boxes and lblDateString
    txtDayOfWeek.Clear()
    txtMonth.Clear()
    txtDayOfMonth.Clear()
    txtYear.Clear()
    lblDateString.Text = ""
    ' Return the focus to txtDayOfWeek
    txtDayOfWeek.Focus()
End Sub
```

Step 3: Run the application. Enter some information into the TextBox controls, then click the Clear button. The focus should return to the txtDayOfWeek TextBox control.

Step 4: Save the project.

Controlling a Form's Tab Order with the TabIndex Property

In a Windows application, pressing the Tab key changes the focus from one control to another. The order in which controls receive the focus is called the *tab order*. When you place controls on a form in Visual Basic .NET, the tab order will be the same sequence in which you created the controls. Usually this is the tab order you want, but sometimes you rearrange controls on a form, delete controls, and add new ones. These modifications often lead to a disorganized tab order, which can confuse and irritate the users of your application. Users want to tab smoothly from one control to the next, in a logical sequence.

You can modify the tab order by changing a control's TabIndex property. The *TabIndex property* contains a numeric value, which indicates the control's position in the tab order. When you create a control, Visual Basic .NET automatically assigns a value to its TabIndex property. The first control you create on a form will have a TabIndex of 0, the second will have a TabIndex of 1, and so forth. The control with a TabIndex of 0 will be the first control in the tab order. The next control in the tab order will be the one with the TabIndex of 1. The tab order continues in this sequence.

You may change the tab order of a form's controls by selecting them, one-by-one, and changing their TabIndex property in the Properties window. An easier method, however, is to click View on the menu bar, then click Tab Order. This causes the form to be displayed in *tab order selection mode*. In this mode, each control's existing TabIndex value is displayed on the form. You then establish a new tab order by clicking the controls in the order you want. When finished, you exit tab order selection mode by clicking View, then Tab Order.

TUTORIAL 3-4:

Changing the tab order

In this tutorial, you rearrange the controls in the Date String application, and then change the tab order to accommodate the controls' new positions.

Step 1:   Open the Date String project in Visual Basic .NET.

Step 2:   Open the application's form in the Design window. Rearrange the controls to match Figure 3-6. (You might want to temporarily enlarge the form so you have room to move some of the controls around. Don't forget to move the labels that correspond with the TextBox controls.)

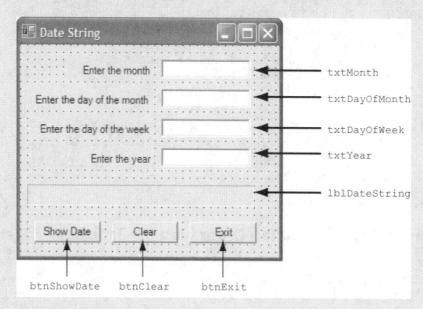

Figure 3-6   Date String form

Step 3:   Run the application. Notice which control has the focus. Press the Tab key several times and observe the tab order.

Step 4:   Stop the application and go back to design time.

Step 5:   Click View on the menu bar, then click Tab Order. The form should now be displayed in tab order selection mode, as shown in Figure 3-7. The numbers displayed in the upper left corner of each control are the existing TabIndex values.

NOTE: *Your existing TabIndex values may be different from those shown in Figure 3-7.*

Figure 3-7   Form in tab order selection mode

Step 6:   Click the following controls in the order they are listed: `txtMonth`, `txtDayOfMonth`, `txtDayOfWeek`, `txtYear`, `btnShowDate`, `btnClear`, `btnExit`.

Step 7:   The controls you clicked should now have the following TabIndex values displayed:

```
txtMonth: 0

txtDayOfMonth: 1

txtDayOfWeek: 2

txtYear: 3

btnShowDate: 4

btnClear: 5

btnExit: 6
```

NOTE: *The Label controls cannot receive the focus, so do not be concerned with the Tab-Index values displayed for them.*

Step 8:   You are now ready to exit tab order selection mode. Click View on the menu bar, then click Tab Order.

Step 9:   Don't forget to change the `btnClear_Click` event procedure so that `txtMonth` gets the focus when the form is cleared. The code for the procedure is as follows, with the modified lines in boldface.

```
Private Sub btnClear_Click(ByVal sender As System.Object, _
        ByVal e As System.EventArgs) Handles btnClear.Click
    ' Clear the Text Boxes and lblDateString
    txtDayOfWeek.Clear()
    txtMonth.Clear()
    txtDayOfMonth.Clear()
    txtYear.Clear()
    lblDateString.Text = ""
    ' Return the focus to txtMonth
    txtMonth.Focus()
End Sub
```

Step 10:   Run the application and test the new tab order.

Step 11:   End the application and save the project.

Here are a few last notes about the TabIndex property:

♦   If you do not want a control to receive the focus when the user presses the Tab key, set its *Tab-Stop property* to False.

♦   An error will occur if you assign a negative value to the TabIndex property in code.

♦   A control whose Visible property is set to False, or whose Enabled property is set to False, cannot receive the focus.

♦   GroupBox and Label controls have a TabIndex property, but they are skipped in the tab order.

Assigning Keyboard Access Keys to Buttons

An *access key*, also known as a *mnemonic*, is a key that you press in combination with the Alt key to quickly access a control such as a button. When you assign an access key to a button, the user can trigger a Click event either by clicking the button with the mouse or by using the access key. Users who are quick with the keyboard prefer to use access keys instead the mouse.

You assign an access key to a button through its Text property. For example, assume an application has a button whose Text property is set to "Exit." You wish to assign the access key Alt+X to the button, so the user may trigger the button's Click event by pressing Alt+X on the keyboard. To make the assignment, place an ampersand (&) before the letter x in the button's Text property: E&xit. Figure 3-8 shows how the Text property appears in the Property window.

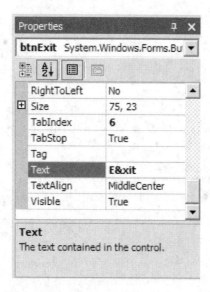

Figure 3-8   Text property E&xit

Even though the ampersand is part of the button's Text property, it is not displayed on the button. With the ampersand in front of the letter x, the button will appear as shown in Figure 3-9. Notice that the ampersand is not displayed on the button, but the letter x is underlined. This indicates that the button may be clicked by pressing Alt+X on the keyboard.

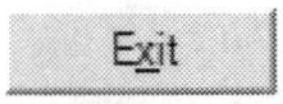

Figure 3-9   Button with `E&xit` text

NOTE: *Access keys do not distinguish between upper- and lowercase. There is no difference between Alt+X and Alt+x.*

Suppose we had stored the value `&Exit` in the button's Text property. The ampersand is in front of the letter E, so Alt+E becomes the access key. The button will appear as shown in Figure 3-10.

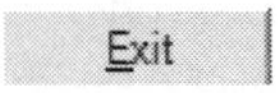

Figure 3-10   Button with `&Exit` text

Assigning the Same Access Key to Multiple Buttons

Be careful not to assign the same access key to two or more buttons on the same form. If two or more buttons share the same access key, Visual Basic .NET will trigger a `Click` event for the button that was created first when the user presses the access key.

Displaying the & Character on a Button

If you want to display an ampersand character on a button use two ampersands (`&&`) in the Text property, in the place you want one ampersand to appear. Using two ampersands causes a single ampersand to display and does not define an access key. For example, if a button has the Text property `Beans && Cream` the button will appear as shown in Figure 3-11.

Figure 3-11   Button with text `Beans && Cream`

GUI Design and User Convenience: Using Access Keys with Labels

Visual Basic .NET supports a clever programming technique that allows you to indirectly assign an access key to a TextBox control. Because the TextBox control's Text property is used to hold the user's input, you cannot use this property to assign an access key. You can, however, use a label to indirectly assign an access key a TextBox control.

Although labels cannot receive the focus, they have the following characteristics:

◆ They have a TabIndex property.
◆ You can assign them access keys through their Text properties.
◆ They have a UseMnemonic property that may be set to true or false.

When a label's *UseMnemonic property* is set to true, which is the default value, you may assign an access key to the label by preceding a character in its Text property with an ampersand. When the user uses the label's access key, the focus is set to the control that immediately follows the label in the tab order. (If the UseMnemonic property is set to False, the ampersand is displayed as part of the label's text and no access key is defined.) Follow the steps in the next exercise to apply this technique to the Date String application.

TUTORIAL 3-5:

Assigning Access Keys to Labels

In this tutorial you assign access keys to the labels that appear on the Date String application's form.

Step 1:   Open the Date String project in Visual Basic .NET.

Step 2:   Change the values of the TabIndex properties of the form's controls to match the values shown in Figure 3-12.

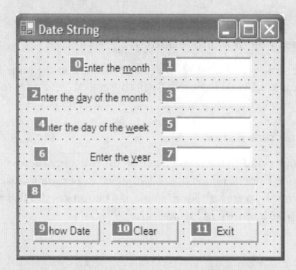

Figure 3-12   Date String TabIndex properties

Step 3:   Notice that each of the labels in Figure 3-12 is assigned an access key, as indicated by the underlined character. Change the Text properties of the labels, so each label is assigned the correct access key. Confirm that each label's UseMnemonic property is set to true.

Step 4:   Run the application.

Step 5:   Press Alt+Y. The txtYear control receives the focus.

Step 6:   Press Alt+D. The txtDayOfMonth control receives the focus.

Step 7:   Experiment with the other access keys.

Step 8:   Exit the application.

Accept Buttons and Cancel Buttons

An *accept button* is a button on a form that is clicked when the user presses the Enter key. A *cancel button* is a button on a form that is clicked when the user presses the Escape key. Forms have two properties, AcceptButton and CancelButton, that allow to designate an accept button and a cancel button. When you select these properties in the Properties window, a down-arrow button appears, which allows you to display a drop-down list. The list contains the names of all the buttons on the form. You select the button that you want to designate as the accept button or the cancel button.

Any button that is frequently clicked should probably be selected as the accept button. This will allow keyboard users to access the button quickly and easily. Buttons that read "Exit" or "Cancel" are likely candidates to become cancel buttons.

TUTORIAL 3-6:

Setting access keys, accept, and cancel buttons

In this tutorial, you assign access keys to the buttons in the Date String application, and set accept and cancel buttons

Step 1:   Open the Date String project in Visual Basic .NET.

Step 2:   Open the application's form in the Design window.

Step 3:   Select the Show Date button (`btnShowDateString`) and change its Text to read **Show &Date**. This assigns Alt+D as the button's access key.

Step 4:   Select the Clear button (`btnClear`) and change its Text to read **Clea&r**. This assigns Alt+R as the button's access key.

Step 5:   Select the Exit button (`btnExit`) and change its Text to read **E&xit**. This assigns Alt+X as the button's access key.

Step 6:   Select the form, and then select the AcceptButton property in the Properties window. Click the down-arrow button to display the drop-down list of buttons. Select `btnShowDate` from the list.

Step 7:   With the form still selected, select the CancelButton property in the Properties window. Click the down-arrow button to display the drop-down list of buttons. Select `btnExit` from the list.

Step 8:   Run the application and test the buttons' new settings. Notice that anytime you press the Enter key, the Show Date String button's `Click` procedure is executed, and any time you press the Escape key, the application exits.

NOTE: *In Windows 2000 and Windows XP, the access keys you assigned to the buttons may not be displayed as underlined characters until you press the Alt key.*

Step 9:   Save the solution.

✓ **Checkpoint**

3.1   What TextBox control property holds text entered by the user?

3.2   Assume an application has a label named `lblMessage`, and a TextBox control named `txtInput`. Write the statement that copies the text that the user entered into the TextBox control, into the label's Text property.

3.3   If the following statement is executed, what will the `lblGreeting` control display?

```
lblGreeting.Text = "Hello " & "Jonathon, " & "how are you?"
```

3.4   What is the line-continuation character, and what does it do?

3.5   What is meant when it is said that a control has the focus?

3.6   Write the statement that gives the focus to the `txtLastName` control.

3.7   What is meant by tab order?

3.8   How does the TabIndex property affect the tab order?

3.9   How does Visual Basic .NET normally assign the tab order?

3.10   What happens when a control's TabStop property is set to False?

3.11   Assume a button's Text property is set to the text `Show &Map`. What effect does the `&` character have?

3.12   What is an accept button? What is a cancel button? How do you establish these buttons on a form?

▶ 3.3   Variables

CONCEPT

AN APPLICATION USES VARIABLES TO HOLD INFORMATION SO IT MAY BE MANIPULATED, USED TO MANIPULATE OTHER INFORMATION, OR REMEMBERED FOR LATER USE.

A *variable* is a storage location in the computer's memory, used for holding information while the program is running. The information that is stored in a variable may change, hence the name "variable."

So far, you have used and written Visual Basic .NET programs that store data in control properties. You have not actually manipulated the data, however. Variables are useful for temporarily holding data so you can work with it in some way. Here are a few things you can do with variables:

◆   Copy and store values entered by the user, so they may be manipulated

◆   Perform arithmetic on values

◆   Test values to determine that they meet some criterion

◆   Temporarily hold and manipulate the value of a control property

◆   Remember information for later use in the program

Think of a variable as a name that represents a location in the computer's random-access memory (RAM). When a value is stored in a variable, it is actually stored in RAM. You use the assignment operator (=) to store a value in a variable, just as you do with a control property. For example, assume a program uses a variable named `length`. The following statement stores the value 112 in that variable:

```
length = 112
```

When this statement executes, the value 112 will be stored in the memory location that the name `length` represents. As another example, assume the following statement appears in a program that uses a variable named `greeting` and a TextBox control named `txtName`:

```
greeting = "Good morning " & txtName.Text
```

Let's say the user has already entered "Holly" into the `txtName` TextBox control. When the statement executes, the variable `greeting` will contain the string `"Good morning Holly"`.

Use the following steps to open and run a Visual Basic .NET project that uses a variable. Leave the project open so you can refer to it as you read the remainder of this section.

TUTORIAL 3-7:

Examining an application that uses a variable

Step 1:   Start Visual Basic .NET and open the Variable Demo project, which is stored in the Chap3\Variable Demo folder on the student disk.

Step 2:   Click the Start button (▶) to run the application. The application's form appears, as shown in Figure 3-13.

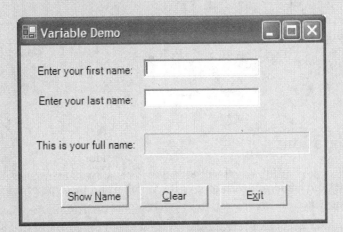

Figure 3-13   Variable Demo application

Step 3:   Enter your first and last names in the TextBox controls, as requested by the application. Click the Show Name button and your full name appears in the Label control. The Clear button clears the label and the two text boxes, and sets the focus to the first TextBox control.

Step 4: Open the Code window and examine the event procedures. You will refer to them as you read the remainder of this section. The only new feature introduced in this project is the use of a variable in the `btnShowName_Click` procedure. The project's code is as follows.

```
Private Sub btnShowName_Click(ByVal sender As System.Object, _
      ByVal e As System.EventArgs) Handles btnShowName.Click
    ' Declare a string variable to hold the full name.
    Dim fullName As String

    ' Put the first and last names together
    ' and copy the result to lblFullName
    fullName = txtFirstName.Text & " " _
          & txtLastName.Text
    lblFullName.Text = fullName
End Sub

Private Sub btnClear_Click(ByVal sender As System.Object, _
      ByVal e As System.EventArgs) Handles btnClear.Click
    'Clear the TextBox controls and the label
    txtFirstName.Clear()
    txtLastName.Clear()
    lblFullName.Text = ""
    ' Give the focus to the first TextBox control
    txtFirstName.Focus()
End Sub

Private Sub btnExit_Click(ByVal sender As System.Object, _
        ByVal e As System.EventArgs) Handles btnExit.Click
      ' End the application
    End
End Sub
```

Variable Declarations

A *variable declaration* is a statement that causes Visual Basic .NET to create a variable in memory. The declaration indicates the name you wish to give the variable and the type of information the variable will hold. Here is the general form of a variable declaration:

```
Dim VariableName As DataType
```

Here is an example of a variable declaration:

```
Dim length As Integer
```

Let's look at each part of this statement, and its purpose:

- The word `Dim` tells Visual Basic .NET that a variable is being declared. This word stands for "dimension."

- `length` is the name of the variable.

◆   `As Integer` indicates that the variable will be used to hold integer numbers.

You may also declare multiple variables with one `Dim` statement, as shown in the following statement.

```
Dim length, width, height As Integer
```

This statement declares three variables: length, width, and height. All three variables will be used to hold integers.

Now let's look at the variable declaration in the Variable Demo application. In the code window, look at the `btnShowName_Click` procedure. You see the following declaration:

```
Dim fullName As String
```

This tells Visual Basic .NET to create a variable named `fullName`, which will be used to hold a string. Look again at the code for the `btnShowName_Click` procedure:

```
Private Sub btnShowName_Click(ByVal sender As System.Object, _
        ByVal e As System.EventArgs) Handles btnShowName.Click
    ' Declare a string variable to hold the full name.
    Dim fullName As String

    ' Put the first and last names together
    ' and copy the result to lblFullName
    fullName = txtFirstName.Text & " " _
            & txtLastName.Text
    lblFullName.Text = fullName
End Sub
```

Notice the following things about the procedure:

◆   Other than the initial comment, the variable declaration appears first in the procedure. Visual Basic .NET does not require that variable declarations appear first in a procedure, but many programmers prefer to place them there. However, a variable declaration must appear before any statement in the procedure that uses the variable.

◆   A blank line separates the variable declaration and the statements that follow it. Once again, this is not a Visual Basic .NET requirement, but it makes the procedure appear more organized, especially when there are several variable declarations.

Data Types

The word that appears after `As` in a `Dim` statement indicates the variable's *data type*, which is the type of data that the variable can hold. Selecting the proper data type is important because a variable's data type determines the amount of memory the variable uses, and the way the variable formats and stores information. It is important to select a data type that is appropriate for the type of information that your program will work with. If you are writing a program to calculate the number of miles to a distant star, you will need variables that can hold very large numbers. If you are designing software to record microscopic dimensions, you will need variables that store very small and precise numbers. If you are writing a program that must perform thousands of intensive calculations, you want variables that can be processed quickly. The data type of a variable determines all of these factors.

Table 3-1 lists and describes most of the data types used in Visual Basic .NET.

Table 3-1

Visual Basic .NET Data Types

Data Type	Description	Amount of Memory Used
Boolean	Used to hold the values True or False.	2 bytes
Byte	Holds a whole number. Range: 0 through 255.	1 byte
Char	Holds a single character.	2 bytes
Date	Stores date and time information. Range: The smallest date and time that may be held is midnight (00:00:00) on January 1 of the year 1. The largest time and date that may be held is 11:59:59 on December 31 of the year 9999.	8 bytes
Decimal	Holds a real number such as 3.14159. Decimal variables may have up to 29 significant digits, and are suitable for financial and other calculations that must be very precise. Range: +/-79,228,162,514,264,337,593,543,950,335	16 bytes
Double	Holds a real number, such as 3.14159. Variables of the Double data type may hold larger numbers than Decimal variables, but with lesser precision. Range: $-1.79769313486231570 \times 10^{308}$ through $-4.94065645841246544 \times 10^{-324}$ for negative numbers, and $4.94065645841246544 \times 10^{-324}$ through $1.79769313486231570 \times 10^{308}$ for positive numbers.	8 bytes
Integer	Holds a whole number. Range: -2,147,483,648 through 2,147,483,647.	4 bytes
Long	Holds a whole number. Range: -9,223,372,036,854,775,808 through 9,223,372,036,854,775,807.	8 bytes
Object	Holds a reference (memory address) of an object.	4 bytes
Short	Holds a whole number. Range -32,768 through 32,767.	2 bytes
Single	Holds a real number, such as 3.14159. Variables of the Single data type may hold larger numbers than Decimal variables, but with lesser precision. Range: $-3.4028235 \times 10^{38}$ through $-1.401298 \times 10^{-45}$ for negative numbers and 1.401298×10^{-45} through 3.4028235×10^{38} for positive numbers.	4 bytes
String	Holds strings, which may consist of letters, numbers, punctuation symbols, etc.	Depends on the number of characters[a]

[a]Strings occupy 10 bytes, plus 2 bytes for each character in the string.

Variable Naming Rules and Conventions

Just as there are rules and conventions for naming controls, there are rules and conventions for naming variables. Naming rules are a set of guidelines that must be followed. These are part of the Visual Basic .NET syntax. If a variable name does not conform to Visual Basic .NET's naming rules, it's not a legal variable name. Here are Visual Basic .NET's naming rules for variables:

- The first character must be a letter or an underscore character.
- After the first character, you may use letters, numeric digits, and underscore characters.
- Variable names cannot contain spaces or periods.
- You cannot use a Visual Basic .NET key word, such as `Dim`, `Integer`, `Sub`, `Private`, etc., as a variable name. Key words are reserved for special uses and cannot be used for anything other than their intended purpose.

Naming conventions are a set of recommended naming practices that are not part of the Visual Basic .NET syntax but that follow a standard style of programming. Naming conventions help programmers that are reading your code understand the purpose of variables, and make variable names easy to read.

The first convention you should follow is to give variables descriptive names that indicate their purpose. For example, a variable that is used to hold the number of items that a customer has ordered might be named `itemsOrdered`. This name gives anyone reading the program an idea of what data the variable holds.

The second convention you should follow is to adopt a consistent style of using lower and uppercase characters. Notice that the variable name `itemsOrdered` consists of two words: `items` and `Ordered`. Because you cannot have a space in a variable name, the two words must be put together. The reason the `O` is capitalized is to improve readability. Sometimes you will put more than two words together to form a variable name, as in `chessTeamScore`. When this is done, the first letter of the second word and all subsequent words is capitalized. All the other characters are lowercase. This naming style is known as camel casing because the uppercase characters might remind you of a camel's humps. We will use camel casing for variable names in this book.

The following are examples of variable declarations of various data types:

```
Dim housesBuilt As Byte
Dim isEmpty As Boolean
Dim rebate As Decimal
Dim appointment As Date
Dim stars As Double
Dim count As Integer
Dim inquiries As Long
Dim salaryIncrease As Single
Dim collegeName As String
```

Variable Declarations and the Auto List Feature

When you are entering a variable declaration, the Visual Basic .NET auto list feature helps you fill in the data type. After you type `As` and press the spacebar, an auto list box appears with all the possible data types in alphabetical order. This is illustrated in Figure 3-14.

```
Dim payRate As
```

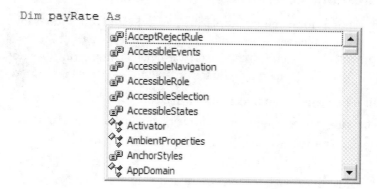

Figure 3-14   Auto list box

When the Auto List box appears, simply type the first few letters of the data type name, and the box will highlight the data type that matches what you have typed. For example, after you type si the box will highlight Single. Once the desired data type is highlighted, press Enter, the spacebar, or Tab to select it.

TIP: You can use the arrow keys or the mouse with the Auto List box's scroll bar to scroll through the list. Once you see the desired data type, you can double-click it with the mouse to select it.

Default Values and Initialization

When a variable is first created in memory, Visual Basic .NET assigns it a default value. Variables with a numeric data type (Byte, Decimal, Double, Integer, Long, and Single) are automatically assigned the value 0. Boolean variables are initially assigned the value `False`, and Date variables start with the value 12:00:00 AM, January 1 of the year 1. String variables are automatically assigned a special value known as `Nothing`.

You may also specify a starting value in the `Dim` statement. This is called *initialization*. Here is an example:

```
Dim unitsSold As Integer = 12
```

This statement declares `unitsSold` as an integer and assigns it the starting value 12. Here are other examples:

```
Dim lastName As String = "Johnson"
Dim isFinished As Boolean = True
Dim grossPay As Decimal = 2500
Dim middleInitial As Char = "E"
```

Depending on a variable's default value is not a good programming practice. Unless you are certain that a variable will be assigned a value before being used in a operation, always initialize it.

This is particularly true with string variables. Performing an operation on an uninitialized string variable often results in a run-time error, which causes the program to halt execution. This is because the value `Nothing` is invalid for many operations. To prevent such errors, always initialize string variables or make sure they are assigned a value before being used in other operations. A good practice is to initialize string variables with an empty string, as in the following statement.

```
Dim name As String = ""
```

Scope and Lifetime of Variables

Every variable has a scope and a lifetime. A variable's *scope* is the part of the program where the variable is visible and may be accessed by programming statements. A variable's *lifetime* is the time during which the variable exists in memory. Let's look at both concepts more closely.

Scope

The first rule of scope you should learn is that a variable cannot be used before it is declared. Remember, Visual Basic .NET executes the statements in a procedure in sequential order, from the first statement to the last. If a programming statement attempts to use a variable before Visual Basic .NET has seen the variable's declaration, an error will occur. For example, look at the following `Click` procedure. It is a modification of the `btnShowName_Click` procedure presented earlier.

```
' This procedure will NOT work!
Private Sub btnShowName_Click(ByVal sender As System.Object, _
        ByVal e As System.EventArgs) Handles btnShowName.Click
    ' Put the first and last names together
    ' and copy the result to lblFullName.
    fullName = txtFirstName.Text & " " _
            & txtLastName.Text
    ' Declare a string variable to hold the full name.
    Dim fullName As String
    lblFullName.Text = fullName
End Sub
```

The procedure will not work because it attempts to use the variable `fullName` before the variable was declared.

Another rule of scope is that a variable that is declared inside a procedure is only visible to statements inside the same procedure. For example, look at the following event procedures. The `btnClear_Click` procedure (which in this example has been modified from the way it appears in the project on disk) attempts to access the `fullName` variable, which is declared in another procedure. Visual Basic .NET will respond with the error message Name 'fullName' is not defined.

```
'This procedure will cause an error!

Private Sub btnClear_Click(ByVal sender As System.Object, _
        ByVal e As System.EventArgs) Handles btnClear.Click
    ' Clear the TextBox controls and the label
    fullName = ""
    txtFirstName.Clear()
    txtLastName.Clear()
    lblFullName.Text = ""
    ' Give the focus to the first TextBox control
    txtFirstName.Focus()
End Sub
```

```
Private Sub btnShowName_Click(ByVal sender As System.Object, _
        ByVal e As System.EventArgs) Handles btnShowName.Click
    ' Declare a string variable to hold the full name.
    Dim fullName As String

    ' Put the first and last names together
    ' and copy the result to lblFullName
    fullName = txtFirstName.Text & " " _
            & txtLastName.Text
    lblFullName.Text = fullName
End Sub
```

Variables declared inside a procedure are local to that procedure and are called *local variables*. Because `fullName` is local to the `btnShowName_Click` procedure, it cannot be accessed by statements outside that procedure.

The last rule of scope to remember is that you cannot have more than one variable in the same scope with the same name. For example, suppose the following statements appear together in an event procedure.

```
Dim testScore As Integer
Dim testScore As Single' ERROR! Variable names must be unique.
```

The second declaration of `testScore` will result in an error because the name is already in use.

Lifetime

As already mentioned, the lifetime of a variable is the time during which the variable exists in memory. Normally, a local variable's lifetime is the execution period of the procedure that contains the variable. When the procedure ends, its local variables are destroyed and the memory they occupied becomes free for other procedures to use.

More About the Date Data Type

Variables of the Date data type can hold both a date and a time. Internally, the date and time is stored as an 8 byte integer value. The smallest value that may be held in a Date variable is midnight (00:00:00) of January 1 of the year 1. The largest value that may be held in a Date variable is 11:59:59 PM of December 31 of the year 9999.

Date Literals

A date literal may contain the date, the time, or both, and must be enclosed in # symbols. For example, all of the following are valid date literals:

```
#12/10/2002#
#8:45 PM#
#21:15:02#
#10/20/2002 6:30:00 AM#
```

The following code segment shows a date literal representing 1:00 AM on December 3, 2002 being assigned to `startDate`, which is a Date variable.

```
startDate = #12/3/2002 1:00:00 AM#
```

You may also use the `System.Convert.ToDateTime` function to convert a string to a Date value, as shown in the following:

```
startDate = System.Convert.ToDateTime("12/3/2002 1:00:00 AM")
```

In addition, you may store a date value that has been entered by the user into a Date variable. The following statement shows how a value in a TextBox control's Text property may be converted to a Date value.

```
userDate = System.Convert.ToDateTime(txtDate.Text)
```

Getting the Current Date and Time from the System

Your computer system has an internal clock that it uses to store the current date and time. Visual Basic .NET provides the key words listed in Table 3-2 which allow you to retrieve the current date, time, or both from your computer.

Table 3-2

Date and time key words

Key Word	Description
Now	Returns the current date and time from the system.
TimeOfDay	Returns the current time from the system, without the date.
Today	Returns the current date from the system, without the time.

The following code segment demonstrates how to use the `Now` key word.

```
Dim systemDate As Date
systemDate = Now
```

After the code executes, the `systemDate` variable will contain the current date and time, as reported by the system.

The `TimeOfDay` key word retrieves only the current time from the system, and is demonstrated by the following statement.

```
systemDate = TimeOfDay
```

After the statement executes, the `systemDate` variable will contain the current time, but will not contain the current date. Instead, it will contain the date January 1 of the year 1.

The `Today` key word retrieves only the current date from the system, and is demonstrated by the following statement.

```
systemDate = Today
```

After the statement executes, the `systemDate` variable will contain the current date, but will not contain the current time. Instead, it will contain the time 00:00:00.

TIP: Later in this chapter you will see how to use the *FormatDateTime* function to extract only the date or only the time from a Date variable.

Implicit Type Conversion, the `Val` Function, and the `ToString` Method

When you assign a value of one data type to a variable of another data type, Visual Basic .NET attempts to convert the value being assigned to the data type of the variable. This is known as *implicit type conversion*. For instance, assume a procedure in an application has a variable named `number`, which is of the Single data type. The procedure also has the following statement:

```
number = 5
```

When the statement is executed, Visual Basic .NET converts the integer value 5 to the real number 5.0, which is stored in `number`. But what happens when a program attempts to store a real number in an integer variable? For example, assume a procedure has an integer variable named `count` and uses the following statement:

```
count = 12.2
```

When this statement is executed, Visual Basic .NET converts the value 12.2 to an integer by rounding it to the nearest whole number. The variable `count` will hold the integer value 12.

Visual Basic .NET will even try to convert string values to numbers. For instance, look at the following statement:

```
count = "12.2"
```

Although the value "12.2" looks like a number, it is actually a string. This is because it is enclosed in quotation marks. There is a difference between the string "12.2" and the number 12.2. The string is a sequence of characters, intended to be displayed on a screen or printed on paper. The number is intended for mathematical operations. You cannot perform mathematical operations on strings. When the statement is executed, Visual Basic .NET will convert the string "12.2" to the number 12.2. Because `count` is an integer, Visual Basic .NET rounds 12.2 to 12, which is stored in the variable.

A similar effect occurs when the user has entered a number into a TextBox control, and the contents of the Text property are assigned to a numeric variable. Although the value entered by the user is stored as a string in the Text property, Visual Basic .NET will convert it to a number when necessary. The following statement is an example.

```
count = txtInput.Text
```

Assuming the user has entered "45" into the TextBox control, the statement will assign the numeric value 45 to `count`.

Type Conversion Run-Time Errors

A problem arises when Visual Basic .NET cannot convert a string to a number, as illustrated by

```
count = "abc123"
```

Since the string "abc123" begins with characters other than numeric digits, Visual Basic .NET cannot automatically convert it to a number. When this statement executes, a run-time error known as a *type conversion* or *type mismatch* error occurs. Recall from Chapter 2 that run-time errors are errors that occur while the application is running. They are not syntax errors but an attempt to perform an operation that Visual Basic .NET cannot carry out. When a run-time error occurs, the application halts execution and an error message is displayed. Because they stop a program's execution, it is important to prevent type conversion run-time errors.

The Val Function

To help you correctly convert strings to numeric values and prevent type conversion run-time errors, Visual Basic .NET provides the Val function. The *Val function* converts a string like "34.7" to a number, such as 34.7.

Val is a *function*, which means it is a specialized routine that performs a specific operation, then returns a value back to the program. Val is also an *intrinsic function*, which means it is built into Visual Basic .NET.

Suppose you are writing an application and you use the statement

```
number = txtInput.Text
```

The statement assigns the contents of a TextBox control's Text property to number, which is an integer variable. You want to prevent the possibility of a type conversion error, however, so you rewrite the statement to use the Val function:

```
number = Val(txtInput.Text)
```

The statement now contains a *function call* which causes the Val function to execute. The general form of a Val function call is:

```
Val(string)
```

The value inside the parentheses is an argument. An *argument* is the information being sent to the function. The Val function expects its argument to be a string. Val converts the string argument to a numeric value and returns the numeric value to the statement that called the function. In Figure 3-15 the number that Val returns is assigned to the number variable. So, if "45" is stored in txtInput's Text property, the Val function will return the number 45, which is assigned to the number variable.

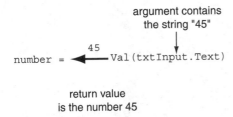

Figure 3-15 Val function

It might be helpful to think of Val as a box that you put a string value into, and it sends a number out. The number that comes out of the box is the converted value of the string that was sent in, as illustrated in Figure 3-16.

Figure 3-16 Val function as string argument converter

The `Val` function does not cause a run-time error if it cannot convert the string argument to a number. `Val` reads its string argument one character at a time, from left to right. When it finds a character that it cannot convert, it stops and returns the value it has converted so far. If the first character in the string cannot be converted, `Val` returns 0. Table 3-3 shows various strings, and how they are converted by the `Val` function.

Table 3-3

`Val` function string conversions

String	Is Converted To
"34.90"	34.9
"86abc"	86
"$24.95"	0
"3,789"	3
" "	0
"x29"	0
"47%"	47
"Geraldine"	0

NOTE: *The `Val` function ignores any leading or trailing spaces or tabs in its argument. For example, the strings " 56" and "78.9 " would both be properly converted.*

The `ToString` Method

Each of the Visual Basic .NET data types has a *`ToString` method*, which returns a string representation of the variable calling the method. You call the `ToString` method using the following general format.

```
VariableName.ToString
```

The following code segment shows an example of the method's use.

```
Dim number As Integer = 123
lblNumber.Text = number.ToString
```

In the code, the `number` variable's `ToString` method is called. The method returns the string "123" which is assigned to the Text property of `lblNumber`.

The `ToString` method is a member of all the data types, including Date. The following code demonstrates.

```
systemDate = Now
lblDateAndTime.Text = systemDate.ToString
```

In the first statement, the current date and time is retrieved from the system and stored in the `systemDate` variable. In the second statement, the `ToString` method returns a string representing the value stored in `systemDate`, which is assigned to the Text property of `lblDateAndTime`. The string will contain both the date and the time in the format `"10/27/2003 11:09:22 AM"`.

If You Want to Know More: The `Option Strict On` Statement

The `Option Strict On` statement prevents Visual Basic .NET from performing most implicit data type conversions. Some programmers prefer to use this statement because it reduces the errors that can result from implicit data type conversions. If you use the statement, it must appear at the very top of the Code window, before any other statements.

When you place the `Option Strict On` statement in your code, Visual Basic .NET will not implicitly convert values between strings and numbers. This forces you to use the `Val` function or the `ToString` method. In fact, when the `Option Strict On` statement is in use, Visual Basic .NET will perform only widening conversions. A widening conversion takes place when a value of a smaller data type is converted to a larger data type. For example, storing an Integer value in a Single variable causes a widening conversion. Statements that cause any other type of implicit conversion will generate a compile error.

✓ Checkpoint

3.13 What is a variable?

3.14 What is a variable declaration?

3.15 Which of the following variable names are written in camel casing?

  a. `InterestRate`
  b. `interestrate`
  c. `interestRate`

3.16 Indicate whether each of the following is a legal variable name. If it is not, explain why.

  a. `count`
  b. `rate*Pay`
  c. `deposit.amount`
  d. `down_payment`

3.17 What is a local variable?

3.18 What is the difference between a variable's scope and its lifetime?

3.19 What are variables of each of the following data types initially assigned when created in memory?

  a. Integer
  b. Single
  c. Boolean
  d. Byte
  e. Date

3.20 Assuming that `number` is an integer variable, what value will each of the following statements assign to `number`?

  a. `number = "27"`
  b. `number = 12.8`
  c. `number = "12.8"`

3.21 When does a type conversion run-time error occur? (Assume the `Option Strict On` Statement is not used.)

3.22 Why should you use the `Val` function when assigning a string to a numeric variable or property?

3.23 How would the following strings be converted by the `Val` function?

  a. `"48.5000"`
  b. `"$34.95"`
  c. `"99%"`
  d. `"Twelve"`

3.24 Write a Date literal for the following date and time: 5:35:00 PM on February 20, 2003.

3.25 Assume `myDate` is a Date variable. Write a statement that retrieves the current date and time from the system and stores it in `myDate`.

▶ 3.4 Performing Calculations and Working with Numbers

CONCEPT

VISUAL BASIC .NET PROVIDES SEVERAL OPERATORS FOR PERFORMING MATHEMATICAL OPERATIONS. YOU MAY ALSO USE PARENTHESES TO GROUP OPERATIONS AND BUILD MORE COMPLEX MATHEMATICAL STATEMENTS.

Arithmetic operations are very common in programming. Table 3-4 shows Visual Basic .NET's most commonly used arithmetic operators.

Table 3-4

Common arithmetic operators

Arithmetic Operator	Operation
+	Addition
-	Subtraction
*	Multiplication
/	Division
^	Exponentiation

Each of these operators works as you probably expect. For example, the addition operator returns the sum of its two operands. In the following assignment statement, the variable amount is assigned the value 12:

```
amount = 4 + 8
```

The exponentiation operator returns the value of its left operand raised to the power of its right operand. For example, the following statement assigns 8 to result:

```
result = 2 ^ 3
```

Of course, variables can be operands as well. All of the following are examples of valid statements.

```
total = price + tax
area = length * width
average = total / items
salePrice = retail / 2
cube = side ^ 3
```

You can also use the return value of the Val function in a mathematical statement. For example, assume an application has a TextBox control named txtInput. The following statement calls the Val function to convert txtInput's Text property, then multiplies the Val function's return value by 5. The result is stored in result.

```
result = Val(txtInput.Text) * 5
```

The following statement is another example. Here, the `Val` function is called to convert the Text properties of the TextBox controls `txtItem` and `txtTax`. The two converted values are added together and the result is stored in `total`.

```
total = Val(txtItem.Text) + Val(txtTax.Text)
```

WARNING:

When performing division, be careful that the operand to the right of the / operator is not 0. If you attempt to divide a number by 0 an error will occur.

If you want to know more about math operators: Integer division and the modulus operator

Visual Basic .NET provides two specialized arithmetic operators: \ and MOD. You will not use these operators as much as the +, −, *, /, and ^ operators, but it is still important that you know about them.

The \ Operator

The \ operator performs *integer division*. As its name implies, it performs a division operation, but the result is always an integer value. If there is any fractional portion, it is discarded. For example, the following statement assigns the value 5 to `parts`.

```
parts = 17 \ 3
```

The following statement assigns 2 to `num`.

```
num = 5 \ 2
```

TIP: If the integer division operator's operands are floating-point numbers, they are rounded to the nearest whole number before the division takes place.

WARNING:

Try not to confuse the regular division operator, which is a forward slash (/), with the integer division operator, which is a back slash (\). Inadvertently using one where you intended to use the other, could cause a serious, but hard-to-find error.

WARNING:

If the operand to the right of the / operator is 0, an error will occur.

The MOD Operator

The modulus operator, which is the word MOD, also performs division. Instead of returning the quotient, however, it returns only the remainder. For example, the following statement assigns 2 to the variable `leftOver`.

```
leftOver = 17 MOD 3
```

This statement assigns 2 to `leftOver` because 17 divided by 3 is 5 with a remainder of 2.

TIP: If the MOD operator's operands are floating-point numbers, they are rounded to the nearest whole number before the division takes place.

Operator Precedence

It is possible to build mathematical expressions with several operators. The following statement assigns the sum of 17, x, 21, and y to the variable answer.

```
answer = 17 + x + 21 + y
```

Some expressions are not that straightforward, however. Consider the following statement:

```
outcome = 12 + 6 / 3
```

What value will be stored in outcome? The number 6 is used as an operand for both the addition and division operators. If the addition takes place before the division, then outcome will be assigned 6. If the division takes place first, outcome will be assigned 14. The correct answer is 14 because the division operator has higher *precedence* than the addition operator.

Mathematical expressions are evaluated from left to right. When two operators share an operand, the operator with the highest precedence works first. Multiplication and division have higher precedence than addition and subtraction, so the statement works like this:

```
outcome = 12 + 6 / 3

outcome = 12 + 2

outcome =     14
```

Figure 3-17   outcome = 12 + 6 / 3

- ◆ 6 is divided by 3, yielding a result of 2.

- ◆ 12 is added to 2, yielding a result of 14.

It could be diagrammed as shown in Figure 3-17.

The precedence of the arithmetic operators, from highest to lowest, is as follows:

1. Exponentiation (the ^ operator)
2. Multiplication and division (the * and / operators)
3. Integer division (the \ operator)
4. Modulus (the MOD operator)
5. Addition and subtraction (the + and – operators)

The multiplication and division operators have the same precedence. This is also true of the addition and subtraction operators. When two operators with the same precedence share an operand, the operator on the left works first, then the operator on the right.

Table 3-5 shows some example math expressions with their values.

Table 3-5

Math expressions and their values

Expression	Value
5 + 2 * 4	13
2^3 * 4 + 3	35
10 / 2 - 3	2
8 + 12 * 2 - 4	28
6 - 3 * 2 + 7 - 1	6

Grouping with Parentheses

Parts of a mathematical expression may be grouped with parentheses to force some operations to be performed before others. In the following statement, the sum of x, y, and z is divided by 3. The result is assigned to average.

```
average = (x + y + z) / 3
```

Without the parentheses, however, z would be divided by 3, and the result added to the sum of x and y. Table 3-6 shows more expressions and their values.

Table 3-6

Math expressions and their value

Expression	Value
(5 + 2) * 4	28
10 / (5 - 3)	5
8 + 12 * (6 - 2)	56
(6 - 3) * (2 + 7) / 3	9

If you want to know more about mathematical operations: Converting mathematical expressions to programming statements

You probably learned in an algebra class that the expression $2xy$ is understood to mean 2 times x times y. Visual Basic .NET, however, requires an operator for any mathematical operation. Table 3-7 shows some mathematical expressions that perform multiplication and the equivalent Visual Basic .NET expression.

Table 3-7

Visual Basic .NET equivalents of mathematical expressions

Mathematical Expression	Operation	Visual Basic .NET Equivalent
6B	6 times B	6 * B
(3)(12)	3 times 12	3 * 12
4xy	4 times x times y	4 * x * y

TIP: If you need to convert more complex mathematical expressions, see Appendix D.

TUTORIAL 3-8:

Examining the Simple Calculator application

This tutorial examines an application that functions as a simple calculator. The application has two TextBox controls, in which you enter numbers. There are buttons for addition, subtraction, multiplication, division, exponentiation, integer division, and modulus. When you click one of these buttons, the application performs a math operation using the two numbers entered into the TextBox controls and displays the result in a label.

Step 1: Start Visual Basic .NET and open the Simple Calculator project, which is stored in the Chap3\Simple Calculator folder on the student disk.

Step 2: Click the Start button to run the application. The application's form appears, as shown in Figure 3-18.

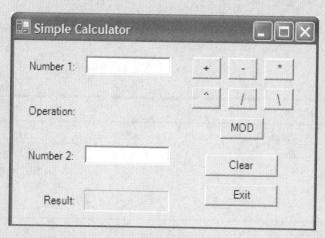

Figure 3-18 Simple Calculator form

Step 3: Enter **10** into the Number 1 TextBox control. (In the code, this TextBox control is named txtNumber1.)

Step 4: Enter **3** into the Number 2 TextBox control. (In the code, this TextBox control is named txtNumber2.)

Step 5: Click the + button. Notice that next to the word "Operation:" a large + sign appears on the form. This indicates that an addition operation has taken place. (The plus sign is displayed in a label named lblOperation.) The result of 10 + 3 displays in the Result label, which is named lblResult. The form appears as shown in Figure 3-19.

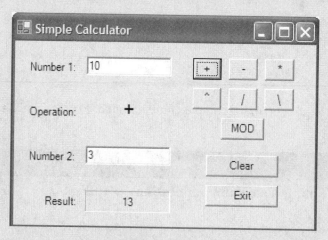

Figure 3-19 Result of 10 + 3

Step 6:   Click the − button. Notice that the `lblOperation` label changes to a minus sign and the result of 10 minus 3 displays in the `lblResult` label.

Step 7:   Click the *, ^, /, \, and MOD buttons. Each performs math operation using 10 and 3 as its operands, and displays the result in the `lblResult` label.

Step 8:   If you wish to experiment with other numbers, click the Clear button and continue.

Step 9:   When you are finished, click the Exit button.

Step 10:   In the Visual Basic .NET environment, open the Design window, if it is not already open. Double-click the + button on the application form. This opens the Code window, with the text cursor positioned in the `btnPlus_Click` event procedure. The code is as follows.

```
Private Sub btnPlus_Click(ByVal sender As System.Object, _
        ByVal e As System.EventArgs) Handles btnPlus.Click
    ' Perform addition
    Dim result As Single

    lblOperation.Text = "+"
    result = Val(txtNumber1.Text) + Val(txtNumber2.Text)
    lblResult.Text = result.ToString
End Sub
```

Looking at the procedure more closely, the first statement after the remark is a variable declaration:

```
Dim result As Single
```

The next statement copies the + character to the `lblOperation` label's Text property:

```
lblOperation.Text = "+"
```

The next statement in the procedure is

```
result = Val(txtNumber1.Text) + Val(txtNumber2.Text)
```

This statement uses the `Val` function to convert the values in `txtNumber1.Text` and `txtNumber2.Text` to numbers. The values are added together and the result is stored in the `result` variable.

The next statement uses the `ToString` method to convert the number in `result` to a string. The string is copied into the `lblResult` label's Text property:

```
lblResult.Text = result.ToString
```

NOTE: *We could have assigned* `result` *to* `lblResult.Text` *whithout calling the* `ToString` *method because Visual Basic .NET will automatically convert* `result` *to a string. Calling the* `ToString` *method in such a statement, however, makes it evident that a conversion is taking place.*

Step 11: Examine the other event procedures in this application. Notice that the arithmetic operator buttons are all very similar.

Combined Assignment Operators

Quite often, programs have assignment statements of the following form:

```
number = number + 1
```

On the right-hand side of the assignment operator, 1 is added to `number`. The result is then assigned to `number`, replacing the value that was previously stored there. Effectively, this statement adds 1 to `number`. In a similar fashion, the following statement subtracts 5 from `number`.

```
number = number - 5
```

Table 3-8 shows examples of similar statements. Assume that the variable `x` is set to 6 prior to each statement executing.

Table 3-8

Assignment statements (Assume x = 6 prior to each statement executing)

Statement	Operation performed	Value of x after the statement executes
x = x + 4	Adds 4 to x	10
x = x - 3	Subtracts 3 from x	3
x = x * 10	Multiplies x by 10	60
x = x / 2	Divides x by 2	3

These types of operations are very common in programming. For convenience, Visual Basic .NET offers a special set of operators designed specifically for these jobs. Table 3-9 shows the *combined assignment operators*, or *compound operators*.

Table 3-9

Combined assignment operators

Operator	Example usage	Equivalent to
+=	x += 2	x = x + 2
-=	x -= 5	x = x - 5
*=	x *= 10	x = x * 10
/=	x /= y	x = x / y
\=	x \= y	x = x \ y
&=	name &= lastName	name = name & lastName

Note that the last operator shown in the table, `&=`, combines the assignment operator with the string concatenation operator.

If You Want To Know More About Type Conversion: The Type Conversion Functions

In the previous section you learned about the `Val` function, which converts a string expression to a number. Visual Basic .NET also provides several functions that allow you to convert an expression to a specific data type.

For example, the `CInt` function converts an expression to an Integer number. Here is an example of how the function can convert a string.

```
number = CInt("47")
```

In this statement the `CInt` function returns the integer value 47, which is stored in `number`. If the string expression contains a number with a fractional part, the number is rounded up. For example, in the following statement `number` is assigned the value 48.

```
number = CInt("47.5")
```

The `CInt` function can also convert string expressions of numbers with comma separators, as shown in this statement:

```
number = CInt("1,240,567")
```

In this statement the `CInt` function converts the string "1,240,567" to the integer value 1240567.

The `CInt` function can also accept a numeric expression as its argument. For example, the following statement converts the real number 123.67.

```
number = CInt(123.67)
```

Table 3-10 lists all of the type conversion functions. Note that the type conversion functions cause a run-time error if the argument expression cannot be converted.

Table 3-10

Type conversion functions

Type Conversion Function	Description
CBool	Converts an expression to a Boolean value. The expression must be a number, a string that represents a number, or the strings "True" or "False". Otherwise a run-time error is generated.
	If the expression is nonzero, the function returns `True`. Otherwise it returns `False`. For example, `CBool(10)` and `CBool("7")` return `True`, while `CBool(0)` and `CBool("0")` return `False`. If the argument is the string "True", the function returns `True`, and if the expression is the string "False" the function returns `False`.
CByte	Converts an expression to a Byte, which can hold the values 0 through 255. If the argument is a fractional number it is rounded. If the expression cannot be converted to a value in the range of 0 – 255 a run-time error is generated.
CChar	Converts a string expression to a Char. If the string contains more than one character, only the first character is returned. For example, `CChar("xyz")` returns the character "x".
CDate	Converts an expression to a Date. String expressions must be valid Date literals. For example, `CDate("#10/14/2002 1:30 PM#")` returns a Date with the value 1:30 PM, October 14th, 2002.
	If the expression cannot be converted to a Date value, a run-time error is generated.
CDbl	Converts a numeric or string expression to a Double. If the expression converts to a value outside the range of a Double, or is not a numeric value, a run-time error is generated.
CDec	Converts a numeric or string expression to a Decimal. The `CDec` function can even convert strings with a $ character, such as $1,200.00. If the expression converts to a value outside the range of a Decimal, or is not a numeric value, a run-time error is generated.

Table 3-10 *continued*

Type conversion functions

Type Conversion Function	Description
CInt	Converts a numeric or string expression to an Integer. If the expression converts to a value outside the range of an Integer, or is not a numeric value, a run-time error is generated.
CLng	Converts a numeric or string expression to a Long. If the expression converts to a value outside the range of a Long, or is not a numeric value, a run-time error is generated.
CObj	Converts an expression to an object.
CShort	Converts a numeric or string expression to a Short. If the expression converts to a value outside the range of a Short, or is not a numeric value, a run-time error is generated.
CSng	Converts a numeric or string expression to a Single. If the expression converts to a value outside the range of a Single, or is not a numeric value, a run-time error is generated.
CStr	Converts a numeric, Boolean, Date, or string expression to a string.

Named Constants

You have seen several programs and examples where numbers and strings are expressed as literal values. For example, the following statement contains the literal numeric value 0.129:

```
amount2 = amount1 * 0.129
```

Let's assume this statement appears in a banking program that calculates loan information. In such a program, two potential problems arise. First, it is not clearly evident to anyone other than the original programmer what 0.129 is. It appears to be an interest rate, but in some situations there are other fees associated with loan payments. How can you determine the purpose of this statement without painstakingly checking the rest of the program?

The second problem occurs if this number is used in other calculations throughout the program and must be changed periodically. Assuming the number is an interest rate, if the rate changes from 12.9% to 13.2% the programmer will have to search through the source code for every occurrence of the number.

Both of these problems can be addressed by using named constants. A *named constant* is like a variable whose content is read-only, and cannot be changed by a programming statement while the program is running. The general form of a named constant declaration is

```
Const ConstantName as DataType = Value
```

Here is an example of a named constant declaration:

```
Const interestRate as Single = 0.129
```

It looks like a regular variable declaration except for these two differences:

- ◆ The word Const is used instead of Dim.
- ◆ An initialization value is required.

The word `Const` tells Visual Basic .NET you are declaring a named constant instead of a variable. The value given after the = sign is the value of the constant throughout the program's execution.

A value must be given when a named constant is declared or an error will result. An error will also result if there are any statements in the program that attempt to change the contents of a named constant.

One advantage of using named constants is that they help make programs self-documenting. The statement

```
amount2 = amount1 * 0.129
```

can be changed to read

```
amount2 = amount1 * interestRate
```

A new programmer can read the second statement and know what is happening. It is evident that `amount1` is being multiplied by the interest rate.

Another advantage to using named constants is that widespread changes can easily be made to the program. Let's say the interest rate appears in a dozen different statements throughout the program. When the rate changes, the value assigned to the named constant in its declaration is the only value that needs to be modified. If the rate increases to 13.2% the declaration is changed to the following:

```
Const interestRate as Single = 0.132
```

Every statement that uses `interestRate` will use the new value.

It is also useful to declare named constants for common values that are difficult to remember. For example, any program that calculates the area of a circle must use the value pi, which is 3.14159. This value could easily be declared as a named constant, as shown in the following statement:

```
Const pi as Single = 3.14159
```

✓ Checkpoint

3.26 After the statement result = 10 \ 3 executes, what value will be stored in result?

3.27 After each of the following statements executes, what value will be stored in result?

    a. result = 6 + 3 * 5
    b. result = 12 / 2 - 4
    c. result = 2 + 7 * 3 - 6
    d. result = (2 + 4) * 3

3.28 What value will be stored in result after the following statement executes?

```
result = CInt("28.5")
```

3.29 Will the following statement execute or cause a run-time error?

```
result = CDbl("186,478.39")
```

3.30 What is a named constant?

▶ 3.5 Formatting Numbers for Output

CONCEPT

NUMBERS MAY BE FORMATTED IN VARIOUS WAYS FOR OUTPUT. VISUAL BASIC .NET PROVIDES A NUMBER OF FORMAT FUNCTIONS THAT ALLOW YOU TO CONVERT VALUES TO STRINGS AND FORMAT THEIR APPEARANCE.

A number can be displayed in several ways. For example, the number 7250 can be displayed as

7250
7250.0
7250.00
$7,250.00

The way a value is printed or displayed is called its *formatting*. Visual Basic .NET provides several intrinsic functions that format numbers in various ways. Table 3-11 lists the functions we will cover.

Table 3-11

Visual Basic .NET Number Formats

Function	Description
FormatNumber	Formats a number to include commas and a specified number of decimal points.
FormatCurrency	Formats a number as currency, such as dollars and cents. The number will also include a dollar sign or other currency symbol.
FormatPercent	Formats a number as a percent.
FormatDateTime	Formats an expression as a date, time, or both.

Let's look at each function more closely.

NOTE: *By default, each of these functions formats numbers to the specifications of your computer's regional settings. Regional settings are configured in your operating system and establish the way that numbers, dates, times, and currency are displayed.*

FormatNumber

By default, the FormatNumber function formats a number to two decimal places. Commas are included. For example, the number 4572 would be formatted as 4,572.00. The number 4676341.89712 would be formatted as 4,676,341.90. The following code is an example of the function's usage.

```
Dim numPoints as Single
numPoints = 7823.279
lblPoints.Text = FormatNumber(numPoints)
```

The last statement passes the variable numPoints to the FormatNumber function. The function returns the string "7,823.28" which is assigned to the lblPoints Text property.

The FormatNumber function takes an optional second argument, which specifies the number of decimal places. Here is an example of the function's usage, with the optional second argument.

```
lblTemperature.Text = FormatNumber(number, 4)
```

In this statement the number in `number` is rounded to four decimal places. Table 3-12 shows various calls to `FormatNumber`, using numeric literal values as arguments, and shows the return value of each.

Table 3-12

Calls to `FormatNumber` and return values

Function Call	Return Value
FormatNumber(87321.784)	"87,321.78"
FormatNumber(76)	"76.00"
FormatNumber(76, 0)	"76"
FormatNumber(3921.387, 1)	"3,921.4"
FormatNumber(.75)	"0.75"

If you want to know more about the **FormatNumber** *function*

The `FormatNumber` function takes other optional, more advanced, arguments as well. Here is the general form of the function call:

```
FormatNumber(NumericExpression[,DecimalPoints
            [,IncludeLeadingDigit
            [,UseParensForNegativeNumbers
            [,GroupDigits]]]])
```

The arguments in brackets are optional. In this book, we use only the `FormatNumber` function with its first and second arguments. However, here are brief descriptions of the third, fourth, and fifth arguments:

- The *IncludeLeadingDigit* argument can be one of the following values: `TriState.True`, `TriState.False`, or `TriState.UseDefault`. If `TriState.True` is passed as the argument, the number is formatted to include a leading zero if it is fractional. For example, the number .27 would be formatted as 0.27. If `TriState.False` is passed as this argument, no leading zero is used. If `TriState.UseDefault` is passed, or if no argument is passed in this position, the function uses the regional settings. Here is an example statement that calls the `FormatNumber` function, and uses this argument:

  ```
  lblMeasurement.Text = FormatNumber(number, 5, TriState.True)
  ```

  In this statement, `FormatNumber` rounds number to five decimal points and places a leading 0 to the left of the decimal point if the number is fractional.

- The *UseParensForNegativeNumbers* argument can also be one of the values `TriState.True`, `TriState.False`, or `TriState.UseDefault`. If `TriState.True` is passed as the argument, the formatted number is placed inside parentheses if it is negative. If `TriState.False` is passed as this argument, negative numbers are not placed inside parentheses. If `TriState.UseDefault` is passed, or if no argument is passed in this position, the function uses the regional settings. Here is an example statement that calls the `FormatNumber` function, and uses this argument:

  ```
  lblTotal.Text = FormatNumber(number, 1, TriState.True, _
              TriState.True)
  ```

◆ The *GroupDigits* argument can also be one of the values `TriState.True`, `TriState.False`, or `TriState.UseDefault`. If `TriState.True` is passed as the argument, the function inserts commas into the formatted number, according to the regional settings specifications. If `TriState.False` is passed as this argument, no commas are inserted. If `TriState.UseDefault` is passed, or if no argument is passed in this position, the function uses the regional settings. Here is an example statement that calls the `Format Number` function, and uses this argument:

```
lblPopulation.Text = FormatNumber(number, 0, TriState.True, _
                     TriState.True, TriState.True)
```

FormatCurrency

The `FormatCurrency` function formats a number as currency, such as dollars and cents. The number will also include a dollar sign or other currency symbol. (The currency symbol that is configured in your operating system will be used.) Normally, the number is rounded to two decimal places. Commas are inserted as needed.

For example, the number 24687.23 would be formatted as $24,687.23. The number 45861741.62112 would be formatted as $45,861,741.62. The following code is an example of the function's usage.

```
Dim salary as Decimal
salary = 87500.0
lblSalary.Text = FormatCurrency(salary)
```

The last statement passes the variable `salary` to the `FormatCurrency` function. The function returns the string `"$87,500.00"` which is assigned to `lblSalary`'s Text property. Table 3-13 shows various calls to `FormatCurrency`, using numeric literal values as arguments, and shows the return value of each.

Table 3-13

Calls to `FormatCurrency` and return values

Function Call	Return Value
FormatCurrency(87321.784)	"$87,321.78"
FormatCurrency(76)	"$76.00"
FormatCurrency(.82)	"$0.82"
FormatCurrency(2348921.387)	"$2,384,921.39"

The `FormatCurrency` function takes the same optional arguments as the `FormatNumber` function. Here is the general form of the function call:

```
FormatCurrency(NumericExpression[,DecimalPoints
              [,IncludeLeadingDigit
              [,UseParensForNegativeNumbers
              [,GroupDigits]]]])
```

In this book we only use the function in its simplest form, as shown in the following code and Table 3-13. For more information on the optional arguments, see the description of `FormatNumber`.

FormatPercent

The FormatPercent function formats its numeric argument as a percent. It does this by multiplying the argument by 100, then rounding it two decimal places and adding a percent sign.

For example, the number .80 would be formatted as 80.00%. The number .05 would be formatted as 5.00%. The following code is an example of the function's usage.

```
Dim ratio as Single
ratio = 0.89
lblCorrect.Text = FormatPercent(ratio)
```

The last statement passes the variable ratio to the FormatPercent function. The function returns the string "89.00%" which is assigned to lblCorrect's Text property.

Like FormatNumber and FormatCurrency, the FormatPercent function takes an optional second argument, which specifies the number of decimal places. Here is an example of the function's usage, with the optional second argument.

```
lblPercent.Text = FormatPercent(ratio, 1)
```

This statement multiplies the number in ratio by 100, then rounds the result to one decimal place. Table 3-14 shows various calls to FormatPercent, using numeric literal values as arguments, and shows the return value of each.

Table 3-14

Calls to FormatPercent and return values

Function Call	Return Value
FormatPercent(.784)	"78.40%"
FormatPercent(.48129)	"48.13%"
FormatPercent(8.2)	"820.00%"
FormatPercent(.387, 1)	"38.7%"

The FormatPercent function takes the same, optional third, fourth, and fifth arguments as the FormatNumber and FormatCurrency functions. Here is the general form of the function call:

```
FormatPercent(NumericExpression[,DecimalPoints
             [,IncludeLeadingDigit
             [,UseParensForNegativeNumbers
             [,GroupDigits]]]])
```

In this book we only use the function with the first two arguments, as shown in the code and in Table 3-14. For more information on the optional arguments, see the description of FormatNumber.

FormatDateTime

The FormatDateTime function takes a Date data type argument and formats it in various ways. The general form of the function call is

```
FormatDateTime(DateExpression [, Format])
```

The first argument is the date expression that is to be formatted. The second argument, which is optional, is a value that tells Visual Basic .NET how to format the date. Table 3-15 lists and describes the values that may be used as the second argument. The description and example is based upon the typical result. Note, however, that these constants rely on the system's regional settings, and their output may vary.

Table 3-15

`FormatDateTime` format values

Format Value	Description
`DateFormat.GeneralDate`	If the date argument contains a date, it formats it the same way as `DateFormat.ShortDate`. If the Date argument contains a time, it formats it the same way as `DateFormat.LongTime`. (If you omit the second argument, the `FormatDateTime` function defaults to `DateFormat.GeneralDate`.)
	Example: `"08/10/2002 3:22:18 PM"`
`DateFormat.LongDate`	Formats a date in long format, which contains the day of the week, month, day, and year. The time is not reported.
	Example: `"Saturday, August 10, 2002"`
`DateFormat.ShortDate`	Formats a date in short format, which contains the month, day, and year. The time is not reported.
	Example: `"8/10/02"`
`DateFormat.LongTime`	Formats a time in long format, which contains the hour, minutes, seconds, and an AM/PM indicator. The date is not reported.
	Example: `"03:22:18 PM"`
`DateFormat.ShortTime`	Formats a time in short format, which contains two digits for the hour and two digits for the minutes. The time is given in 24 hour format. The date is not reported.
	Example: `"15:22"`

The following code is an example of the function's usage.

```
Dim systemDate as Date
systemDate = Today
lblDate.Text = FormatDateTime(systemDate, DateFormat.LongDate)
```

The second line uses the `Today` key word to retrieve the current date from the system and stores it in `systemDate`. (Recall that `Today` only retrieves the date, not the time.) The third line formats the value in `systemDate` in long date format (which will be a string such as `"Wednesday, January 1, 2003"`), and assigns the result to the `lblDate` label's Text property. Because long date format only includes the date, it doesn't matter that `systemDate` contains no time data.

In the following tutorial, you examine an application that demonstrates many of the format function calls discussed in this section.

TUTORIAL 3-9:

Examining the Format Demo application

Step 1:   Start Visual Basic .NET and load the Format Demo project, which is stored in the Chap3\Format Demo folder on the student disk.

Step 2:   Click the Start button (▶) to run the application. The application's form appears, as shown in Figure 3-20.

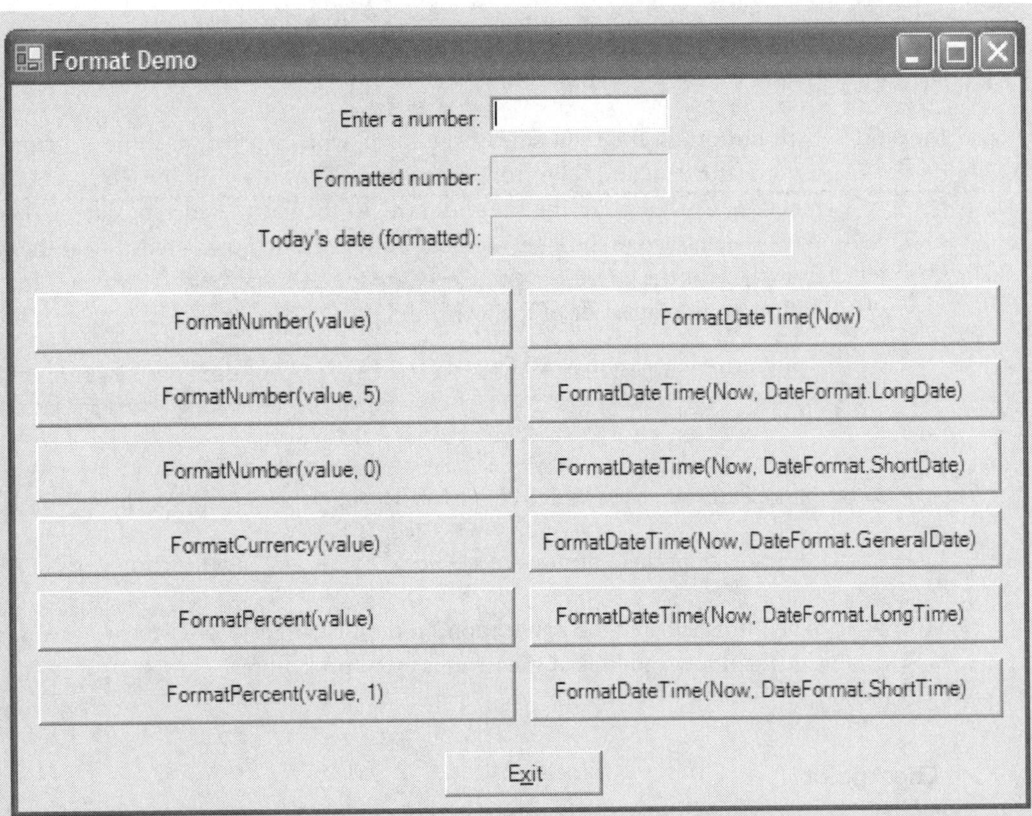

Figure 3-20   **Format Demo form**

The application has 12 buttons that demonstrate various formatting functions. The six buttons on the left side of the form demonstrate the `FormatNumber`, `FormatCurrency`, and `FormatPercent` functions. The six buttons on the right side of the form demonstrate the `FormatDateTime` function. The face of each button shows the function that it calls when clicked.

Step 3:   Enter a value such as **67895.34926** into the TextBox control at the top of the form.

Step 4:   Each button on the left side of the form, when clicked, copies the value from the Text-Box control into a variable named `value`. The `value` variable is then passed to the formatting function shown on the face of the button. The result of the function call is then displayed in the label below the text box. For example, here is the `Click` event procedure for `btnFmtNum1`, which is the topmost button on the left side of the form.

```
Private Sub btnFmtNum1_Click(ByVal sender As System.Object, _
      ByVal e As System.EventArgs) Handles btnFmtNum1.Click
   ' Uses the FormatNumber function
   Dim value As Single

   value = Val(txtNumber.Text)
   lblFormatted.Text = FormatNumber(value)
End Sub
```

Click each of the `FormatNumber` buttons, and the `FormatCurrency` button, to see how the various formatting functions work.

Step 5:   Enter the value **0.24** into the text box. Click the buttons that call the `FormatPercent` function to see how they format the value as a percentage.

Step 6:   Each button on the right side of the form, when clicked, uses the `Now` key word to retrieve the date and time from the system. They also call the `FormatDateTime` function, as shown on the button's face, to format the current date and time. The value is displayed in the label marked "Today's Date (Formatted):" near the top of the form. Here is the `Click` event procedure for `btnFmtDate1`, which is the topmost button on the right side of the form.

```
Private Sub btnFmtDate1_Click(ByVal sender As System.Object, _
        ByVal e As System.EventArgs) Handles btnFmtDate1.Click
    ' Uses the FormatDateTime function
    lblTodayDate.Text = FormatDateTime(Now)
End Sub
```

Click each of these buttons to see `FormatDateTime` function works.

Step 7:   When finished, exit the application. In the Visual Basic .NET environment, open the Code window and look at the various event procedures.

✓ Checkpoint

3.31   By default, to how many decimal places does the `FormatNumber` function format a number?

3.32   How are the `FormatNumber` function and the `FormatCurrency` functions similar? How are they different?

3.33   What would the function call `FormatPercent(0.07)` return?

3.34   Which format argument would you use with the `FormatDateTime` function to format a date in the form `"Monday, January 20, 2003"`

▶ 3.6   Group Boxes, Form Formatting, and the `Load` Event Procedure

CONCEPT

IN THIS SECTION WE DISCUSS THE GROUPBOX CONTROL, WHICH IS USED TO GROUP OTHER CONTROLS, AND HOW TO ALIGN AND CENTER CONTROLS ON A FORM.

Group Boxes

A *group box* is a rectangular border with an optional title that appears in the upper-left corner. Other controls may be placed inside a group box. You can give forms a more organized look by grouping related controls together inside group boxes.

In Visual Basic .NET you use the *GroupBox control* to create a group box with an optional title. The title is stored in the GroupBox control's Text property. Figure 3-21 shows a GroupBox control. The control's Text property is set to "Personal Data", and a group of other controls are inside the group box.

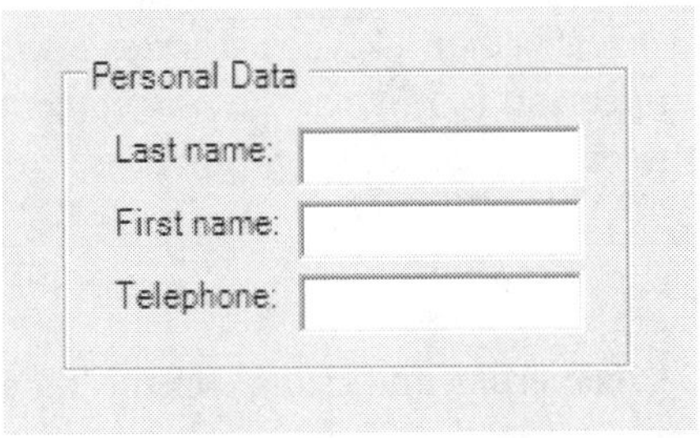

Figure 3-21   GroupBox containing other controls

Creating a Group Box and Adding Controls to It

To create a group box you select the GroupBox tool from the toolbox and then draw the group box at the desired size on the form. When you create a group box to hold other controls, you must create the GroupBox control first, then follow one of these procedures to place a control inside the GroupBox:

- ◆ Select the existing GroupBox control, then double-click the desired tool in the toolbox to place another control inside the GroupBox.

- ◆ Select the existing GroupBox control, then click the desired tool in the toolbox and draw the control inside the GroupBox.

Note that with either procedure, the existing GroupBox control must be selected before you create the control that is to be placed inside the GroupBox control.

The controls inside a group box become part of a group. When you move a group box, the objects inside it move as well. When you delete a group box, the objects that belong to it are also deleted.

Moving an Existing Control to a Group Box

If an existing control is not inside a group box, but you want to move it to the group box, follow this procedure:

1. Select the control you wish to add to the group box.
2. Cut the control to the clipboard.
3. Select the group box.
4. Paste the control.

Group Box Tab Order

The value of a control's TabIndex property is handled differently when the control is placed inside a GroupBox control. GroupBox controls have their own TabIndex property, and the TabIndex value of the controls inside the Group-Box are relative to the GroupBox control's TabIndex property. For example, Figure 3-22 shows a GroupBox control displayed in tab order selection mode. As you can see, the GroupBox control's TabIndex is set to 2. The TabIndex of the controls inside the group box are displayed as 2.0, 2.1, 2.2, and so forth.

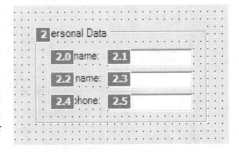

Figure 3-22   Group box TabIndex values

NOTE: *The TabIndex properties of the controls inside the group box will not appear this way in the Properties window. They will appear as 0, 1, 2, and so forth.*

Assigning an Access Key to a GroupBox Control

Although GroupBox controls cannot receive the focus, you can assign a keyboard access key to them by preceding a character in their Text property with an ampersand (&). When the user enters the access key, the focus moves to the control with the lowest TabIndex value inside the group box.

Form Formatting

Visual Basic .NET provides numerous tools for aligning, centering, and sizing controls on a form. In this section we discuss the form grid and the Format menu commands.

The Form Grid

You have probably noticed that forms in the Design window are displayed with a grid of dots, as shown in Figure 3-23. The grid is a useful tool for aligning and sizing controls, and is only displayed at design time.

By default, the grid dots are positioned with 8 pixels between them. You can change this and other grid settings by clicking Tools on the menu bar, then clicking the Options command. The Options dialog box should appear. Click Windows Forms Designer in the left pane. The Options dialog box should appear as shown in Figure 3-24.

Figure 3-23   Form grid dots

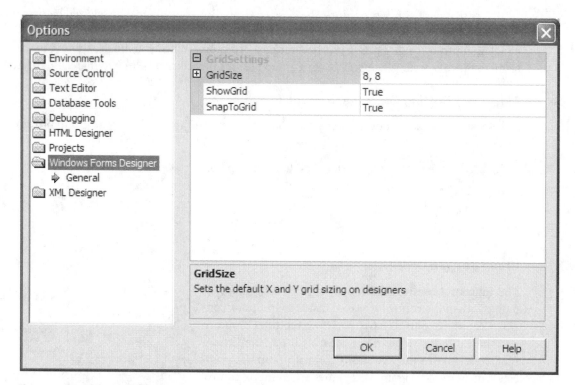

Figure 3-24   Figure 3-24 Options dialog box showing grid settings

The GridSize option controls the default width and height of the space between the grid dots. When the ShowGrid option is set to true (the default setting), the grid is displayed. The grid is hidden when ShowGrid is set to false. When the SnapToGrid option is set to true (the default setting) controls can only be positioned along the grid dots. In addition, the sizing of controls is constrained to the grid dots. When SnapToGrid is set to false, controls may be placed at any position and drawn to any size. In most cases, it is best to leave SnapToGrid set to true.

These Option dialog box values only establish the Visual Basic .NET default grid settings. Each form has properties that may override these settings. The properties are GridSize, DrawGrid, and SnapToGrid. For example, setting a form's DrawGrid property to false will hide the grid on that form, regardless of how the ShowGrid option is set in the Options dialog box.

Selecting and Moving Multiple Controls

It is possible to select multiple controls and work with them all at once. For example, you can select a group of controls and move them all to a different location on the form. You can also select a group of controls and change some of their properties all at once.

You select multiple controls by using one of the following techniques:

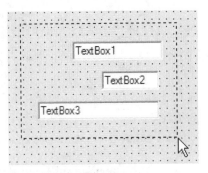

Figure 3-25 Click-and-drag selection of multiple controls

- ◆ Position the cursor over an empty part of the form that is near the controls you wish to select. Click and drag a selection box around the controls. This is illustrated in Figure 3-25. When you release the mouse button, all the controls that were partially or completely enclosed in the selection box will be selected.

- ◆ Hold the Ctrl key down while clicking each control you wish to select.

After using either of these techniques, all the controls you have selected will appear with sizing handles. You may now move them, delete them, or use the Properties window to set many of their properties to the same value.

TIP: It's easy to deselect a control that you have accidentally selected. Simply hold down the Ctrl key and click the control you wish to deselect.

The Format Menu

The Format menu, shown in Figure 3-26, provides several submenus for aligning, centering, and sizing controls.

Figure 3-26   The Format menu

The Align Submenu

The Align SubMenu contains the following vertical alignment commands:

- Lefts—Aligns the selected controls vertically by their left edges
- Centers—Aligns the selected controls vertically by their center points
- Rights—Aligns the selected controls vertically by their right edges

Figure 3-27 shows a group of TextBox controls aligned by their lefts, centers, and rights.

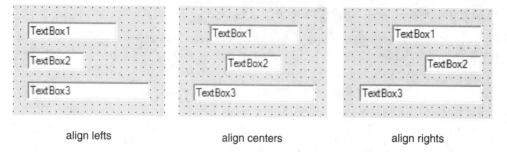

align lefts   align centers   align rights

Figure 3-27   Left, center, and right alignment

The Align submenu also contains the following horizontal alignment commands:

- Tops—Aligns the selected controls horizontally by their top edges
- Middles—Aligns the selected controls horizontally by their middle points
- Bottoms—Aligns the selected controls horizontally by their bottom edges

Figure 3-28 shows a group of differently sized buttons aligned by their tops, middles, and bottoms.

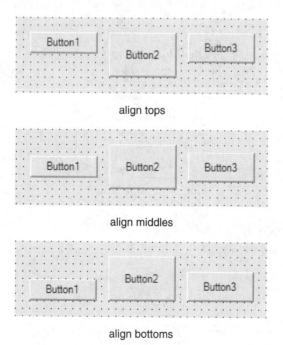

align tops

align middles

align bottoms

Figure 3-28   Top, middle, and bottom alignment

The Align submenu also provides the To Grid command. This command aligns the selected controls to the grid points. This is useful if you have drawn controls with the SnapToGrid option set to false and wish to align them to the grid.

The Make Same Size Submenu

The Make Same Size submenu provides commands for making a group of selected controls the same size. The commands are Width (makes all selected controls the same width), Size to Grid (adjusts the size of the selected controls to the grid points), Height (makes all selected controls the same height), and Both (makes both the width and height of all selected controls the same).

NOTE: *The form's SnapToGrid property must be set to true for the Size To Grid command to work.*

The Horizontal and Vertical Spacing Submenus

These submenus provide commands to control the horizontal and vertical space between selected commands. Both submenus contain the following commands: Make Equal, Increase, Decrease, and Remove.

The Center in Form Submenu

This submenu provides the following useful commands: Horizontally (horizontally centers the selected controls on the form) and Vertically (vertically centers the selected controls on the form).

The Order Submenu

It is possible to place controls on top of each other on a form. The control on top is said to be at the front, while the control on the bottom is said to be at the back. This submenu provides the following commands for rearranging the order of controls that are placed on top of each other: Bring to Front (moves the selected control to the top) and Send to Back (moves the selected control to the bottom).

The Load Event Procedure

Every form has a *Load event procedure*, which is executed each time the form loads into memory. If you need to execute code automatically when a form is displayed, you can place the code in the form's Load event procedure. For example, in the next section you will develop an application that displays the current date and time on the application's form. You will accomplish this by writing code in the form's Load event procedure that retrieves the date and time from the system.

To write code in a form's Load event procedure, double-click any area of the form where there is no other control. The code window will appear with a code template similar to the following.

```
Private Sub Form1_Load(ByVal sender As System.Object, _
        ByVal e As System.EventArgs) Handles MyBase.Load

End Sub
```

Between the first and last lines of the template, simply write the statements you wish the procedure to execute.

✓ Checkpoint

3.35 How is a group box helpful when you are designing a form with a large number of controls?

3.36   What is the result of setting a form's SnapToGrid property to true?

3.37   How do you align a group of controls along their right edges?

3.38   How do you make a group of controls the same size in both width and height?

3.39   When does a form's Load event procedure execute?

▶ 3.7   Focus on Program Design and Problem Solving: Building the Room Charge Calculator Application

A customer staying at the Highlander Hotel may incur the following types of charges:

- ◆ Room charges, based on a per-night rate
- ◆ Room service charges
- ◆ Telephone charges
- ◆ Miscellaneous charges

The manager of the Highlander Hotel has asked you to create an application that calculates the customer's total charges. Figure 3-29 shows a sketch of the application's form.

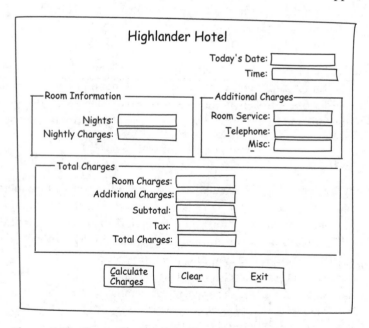

Figure 3-29   Room Charge Calculator form sketch

Notice that some of the labels in Figure 3-29 will be assigned access keys (evidenced by the underlined characters). This application will use the technique, described earlier, of assigning an access key to a label so the user can quickly access the TextBox control that is next in the tab order.

Figure 3-30 shows the names of all the named controls.

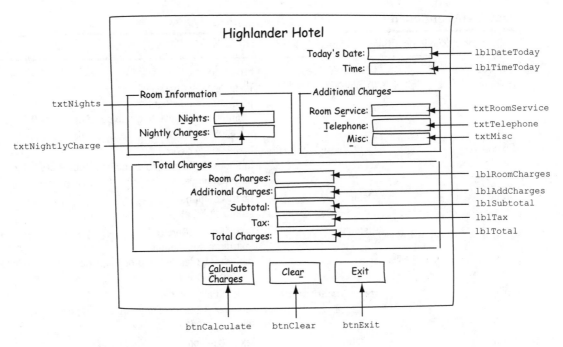

Figure 3-30 **Named controls**

Table 3-16 lists each control, along with any relevant property values.

Table 3-16

Named controls in Room Charge Calculator form

Control Type	Control Name	Properties
Label	(Default)	Text: "Highlander Hotel" Font: MS sans serif, bold, 18 point TextAlign: MiddleCenter
Label	(Default)	Text: "Today's Date:" TextAlign: MiddleRight
Label	lblDateToday	Text: Initially cleared BorderStyle: Fixed3D TextAlign: MiddleCenter
Label	(Default)	Text: "Time:" TextAlign: MiddleRight
Label	lblTimeToday	Text: Initially cleared BorderStyle: Fixed3D TextAlign: MiddleCenter
Group box	(Default)	Text: "Room Information" TabIndex: 0
Label	(Default)	Text: "&Nights:" TextAlign: MiddleRight TabIndex: 0 (Relative to group box. Appears as 0.0 in tab order selection mode.)
TextBox	txtNights	Text: Initially cleared TabIndex: 1 (relative to group box. Appears as 0.1 in tab order selection mode.)

Table 3-16 *continued*

Named controls in Room Charge Calculator form

Control Type	Control Name	Properties
Label	(Default)	Text: "Nightly Char&ge:" TextAlign: MiddleRight TabIndex: 2 (Relative to group box. Appears as 0.2 in tab order selection mode.)
TextBox	txtNightlyCharge	Text: Initially cleared TabIndex: 3 (Relative to group box. Appears as 0.3 in tab order selection mode.)
Group box	(Default)	Text: "Additional Charges" TabIndex: 1
Label	(Default)	Text: "Room S&ervice:" TextAlign: MiddleRight TabIndex: 0 (Relative to group box. Appears as 1.0 in tab order selection mode.)
TextBox	txtRoomService	Text: Initially cleared TabIndex: 1 (Relative to group box. Appears as 1.1 in tab order selection mode.)
Label	(Default)	Text: "&Telephone:" TextAlign: MiddleRight TabIndex: 2 (Relative to group box. Appears as 1.2 in tab order selection mode.)
TextBox	txtTelephone	Text: Initially cleared TabIndex: 3 (Relative to group box. Appears as 1.3 in tab order selection mode.)
Label	(Default)	Text: "&Misc:" TextAlign: MiddleRight TabIndex: 4 (Relative to group box. Appears as 1.4 in tab order selection mode.)
TextBox	txtMisc	Text: Initially cleared TabIndex: 5 (Relative to group box. Appears as 1.5 in tab order selection mode.)
Group box	(Default)	Text: "Total Charges"
Label	(Default)	Text: "Room Charges:" TextAlign: MiddleRight
Label	lblRoomCharges	Text: Initially cleared BorderStyle: Fixed3D
Label	(Default)	Text: "Additional Charges:" TextAlign: MiddleRight
Label	lblAddCharges	Text: Initially cleared BorderStyle: Fixed3D
Label	(Default)	Text: "Subtotal:" TextAlign: MiddleRight
Label	lblSubtotal	Text: Initially cleared BorderStyle: Fixed3D
Label	(Default)	Text: "Tax:" TextAlign: MiddleRight
Label	lblTax	Text: Initially cleared BorderStyle: Fixed3D
Label	(Default)	Text: "Total Charges:" TextAlign: MiddleRight

Table 3-16 *continued*

Named controls in Room Charge Calculator form

Control Type	Control Name	Properties
Label	lblTotal	Text: Initially cleared BorderStyle: Fixed3D
Button	btnCalculate	Text: "C&alculate Charges" TabIndex: 2
Button	btnClear	Text: "Clea&r" TabIndex: 3
Button	btnExit	Text: "E&xit" TabIndex: 4

NOTE: *Do not be concerned with the TabIndex property of the controls that have no TabIndex value listed in the table.*

Table 3-17 lists and describes the methods (event procedures) needed for this application. Notice that a Load event procedure is needed for the form.

Table 3-17

Methods in Room Charge Calculator application

Method	Description
btnCalculate_Click	Calculates the room charges, additional charges, subtotal (room charges plus additional charges), 8% tax, and the total charges. These values are copied to the Text properties of the appropriate labels.
btnClear_Click	Clears the TextBox controls, and the labels that are used to display summary charge information. This procedure also resets the values displayed in the lblDateToday and lblTimeToday labels.
btnExit_Click	Ends the application.
Form1_Load	Initializes the lblDateToday and lblTimeToday labels to the current system date and time.

Figure 3-31 shows the flowchart for the btnCalculate_Click procedure. The procedure uses the following Decimal variables:

```
roomCharges
addCharges
subtotal
tax
total
```

The procedure also uses a named constant, taxRate, to hold the tax rate.

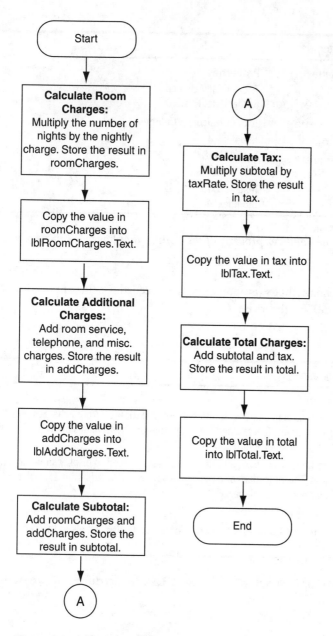

Figure 3-31 Flowchart for `btnCalculate_Click`

Notice that the flowchart in Figure 3-31 uses a new symbol:

This is called the *connector symbol* and is used when a flowchart is broken into two or more smaller flowcharts. This is necessary when a flowchart does not fit on a single page or must be divided into sections. A connector symbol, which is a small circle with a letter or number inside it, allows you to connect two flowcharts. In the flowchart in Figure 3-31, the A connector indicates that the second flowchart segment begins where the first flowchart segment ends.

The flowchart for the `btnClear_Click` procedure is shown in Figure 3-32.

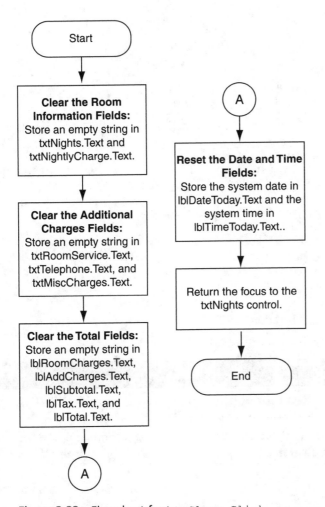

Figure 3-32 Flowchart for `btnClear_Click`

Figure 3-33 shows the flowchart for the `btnExit_Click` procedure.

Figure 3-34 shows the flowchart for the `Form1_Load` procedure. Recall that the form's `Load` procedure executes each time the form loads into memory.

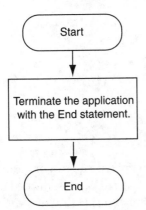

Figure 3-33 Flowchart for `btnExit_Click`

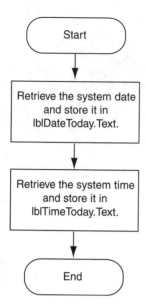

Figure 3-34 Flowchart for `Form1_Load` Procedure

TUTORIAL 3-10:

Beginning the Room Charge Calculator application

Step 1: Start Visual Basic .NET and begin a new Windows application project. Name the project **Room Charge Calculator**.

Step 2: Figure 3-29 shows a sketch of the application's form, and Figure 3-30 shows the names of the named controls. Refer back to these figures as you set up the form and create the controls. Once you have completed the form, it should appear as shown in Figure 3-35. Use the form grid and the Format menu to properly align the controls.

Figure 3-35 Room Charge Calculator form

TIP: Notice that most of the controls are contained inside group boxes. Refer to section 3.6 for instructions on creating controls inside a group box.

TIP: Notice that the TextBox controls are all the same size. In addition, all the Label controls that display output are also the same size. If you are creating many similar instances of a control, it is easier to create the first one, set its size and properties as needed, copy it to the clipboard, and then paste it onto the form to create another one.

Step 3:   Table 3-16 lists the relevant property settings of all the controls on the form. Refer back to this table and make the necessary property settings.

Step 4:   Now you will write the application's event procedures, beginning with the form's `Load` procedure. Double-click any area of the form that is occupied by another control. The Code window should open with a code template for the `Form1_Load` procedure. Complete the procedure by typing the following code shown in bold.

```
Private Sub Form1_Load(ByVal sender As System.Object, _
        ByVal e As System.EventArgs) Handles MyBase.Load
    ' Get today's date from the system and display it.
    lblDateToday.Text = FormatDateTime(Now, DateFormat.ShortDate)
    ' Get the current time from the system and display it.
    lblTimeToday.Text = FormatDateTime(Now, DateFormat.LongTime)
End Sub
```

Step 5:   Open the Design window and double-click the Calculate Charges button. The Code window should open with a code template for the `btnCalculate_Click` procedure. Complete the procedure by typing the following code shown in bold.

```
Private Sub btnCalculate_Click(ByVal sender As System.Object, _
        ByVal e As System.EventArgs) Handles btnCalculate.Click
    ' Declare variables for the calculations.
    Dim roomCharges As Decimal    ' Room charges total
    Dim addCharges As Decimal     ' Additional charges
    Dim subtotal As Decimal       ' Subtotal
    Dim tax As Decimal            ' Tax
    Dim total As Decimal          ' Total of all charges
    Const taxRate As Single = 0.08  ' Tax rate

    ' Calculate and display the room charges.
    roomCharges = Val(txtNights.Text) * Val(txtNightlyCharge.Text)
    lblRoomCharges.Text = FormatCurrency(roomCharges)

    ' Calculate and display the additional charges.
    addCharges = Val(txtRoomService.Text) + _
                 Val(txtTelephone.Text) + _
                 Val(txtMisc.Text)
    lblAddCharges.Text = FormatCurrency(addCharges)
```

```
    ' Calculate and display the subtotal.
    subtotal = roomCharges + addCharges
    lblSubtotal.Text = FormatCurrency(subtotal)

    ' Calculate and display the tax.
    tax = subtotal * taxRate
    lblTax.Text = FormatCurrency(tax)

    ' Calculate and display the total charges.
    total = subtotal + tax
    lblTotal.Text = FormatCurrency(total)
End Sub
```

TIP: When you type the name of an intrinsic function or a method in the code window, an Intellisense box appears showing help on the function or method's arguments. If you do not want to see the Intellisense box, press the Escape key.

Step 6:   Open the Design window and double-click the Clear button. The Code window should open with a code template for the `btnClear_Click` procedure. Complete the procedure by typing the following code shown in bold.

```
Private Sub btnClear_Click(ByVal sender As System.Object, _
    ByVal e As System.EventArgs) Handles btnClear.Click

    ' Clear the room info fields.
    txtNights.Clear()
    txtNightlyCharge.Clear()

    ' Clear the additional charges fields.
    txtRoomService.Clear()
    txtTelephone.Clear()
    txtMisc.Clear()

    ' Clear the total fields.
    lblRoomCharges.Text = ""
    lblAddCharges.Text = ""
    lblSubtotal.Text = ""
    lblTax.Text = ""
    lblTotal.Text = ""

    ' Get today's date from the operating system and display it.
    lblDateToday.Text = FormatDateTime(Now, DateFormat.LongDate)
    ' Get the current time from the operating system and display it.
    lblTimeToday.Text = FormatDateTime(Now, DateFormat.LongTime)

    ' Reset the focus to the first field.
    txtNights.Focus()
End Sub
```

Step 7: Open the Design window and double-click the Exit button. The Code window should open with a code template for the `btnExit_Click` procedure. Complete the procedure by typing the following code shown in bold.

```
Private Sub btnExit_Click(ByVal sender As System.Object, _
        ByVal e As System.EventArgs) Handles btnExit.Click
    ' End the application
    End
End Sub
```

Step 8: Use the Save All command on the File menu (or the save all button) to save the project.

Step 9: Attempt to run the application. If there are errors, compare your code with that shown, and correct them. Once the application runs, enter test values for the charges and confirm that it displays the correct output.

Changing Colors with Code

Chapter 2 discussed how to change the foreground and background colors of a control's text with the ForeColor and BackColor properties. In addition to using the Properties window, you can also store values in these properties with code. Visual Basic .NET provides numerous values that represent colors, and can be assigned to the ForeColor and BackColor properties in code. Here are just a few of the values:

```
Color.Black
Color.Blue
Color.Cyan
Color.Green
Color.Magenta
Color.Red
Color.White
Color.Yellow
```

For example, assume an application has a Label control named `lblMessage`. The following code sets the label's background color to black and foreground color to yellow.

```
lblMessage.BackColor = Color.Black
lblMessage.ForeColor = Color.Yellow
```

Visual Basic .NET also provides values that represent default colors on your system. For example, the value `SystemColors.Control` represents the default control background color and `SystemColors.ControlText` represents the default control text color. The following statements set the `lblMessage` control's background and foreground to the default colors.

```
lblMessage.BackColor = SystemColors.Control
lblMessage.ForeColor = SystemColors.ControlText
```

In the Tutorial 3-11 you modify the room charge calculator application so the total charges are displayed in white characters on a blue background. This will make the total charges stand out visually from the rest of the information on the form.

TUTORIAL 3-11:

Changing a label's colors

In this tutorial you will modify two of the application's event procedures: `btnCalculate_Click` and `btnClear_Click`. In the `btnCalculate_Click` procedure, you will add code that changes the `lblTotal` control's color settings just before the total charges are displayed. In the `btnClear_Click` procedure, you will add code that reverts `lblTotal`'s colors back to their normal state.

Step 1: With the room charge calculator project open, open the Code window and scroll to the `btnCalculate_Click` event procedure.

Step 2: The modified event procedure code is as follows. Type the new lines that appear in boldface.

```
Private Sub btnCalculate_Click(ByVal sender As System.Object, _
     ByVal e As System.EventArgs) Handles btnCalculate.Click
   ' Declare variables for the calculations.
   Dim roomCharges As Decimal    ' Room charges total
   Dim addCharges As Decimal     ' Additional charges
   Dim subtotal As Decimal       ' Subtotal
   Dim tax As Decimal            ' Tax
   Dim total As Decimal          ' Total of all charges
   Const taxRate As Single = 0.08  ' Tax rate

   ' Calculate and display the room charges.
   roomCharges = Val(txtNights.Text) * Val(txtNightlyCharge.Text)
   lblRoomCharges.Text = FormatCurrency(roomCharges)

   ' Calculate and display the additional charges.
   addCharges = Val(txtRoomService.Text) + _
       Val(txtTelephone.Text) + _
       Val(txtMisc.Text)
   lblAddCharges.Text = FormatCurrency(addCharges)

   ' Calculate and display the subtotal.
   subtotal = roomCharges + addCharges
   lblSubtotal.Text = FormatCurrency(subtotal)

   ' Calculate and display the tax.
   tax = subtotal * taxRate
   lblTax.Text = FormatCurrency(tax)

   ' Calculate and display the total charges.
   total = subtotal + tax
   lblTotal.Text = FormatCurrency(total)

   ' Change the background and foreground colors
   ' for the total charges.
   lblTotal.BackColor = Color.Blue
   lblTotal.ForeColor = Color.White
End Sub
```

TIP: When you type `Color.` in the code window, an auto list box appears showing all the color values that are available to you.

Step 3:   Scroll to the `btnClear_Click` procedure. The modified event procedure code is as follows. Type the new lines that appear in boldface.

```
Private Sub btnClear_Click(ByVal sender As System.Object, _
        ByVal e As System.EventArgs) Handles btnClear.Click

    ' Clear the room info fields.
    txtNights.Clear()
    txtNightlyCharge.Clear()

    ' Clear the additional charges fields.
    txtRoomService.Clear()
    txtTelephone.Clear()
    txtMisc.Clear()

    ' Clear the total fields.
    lblRoomCharges.Text = ""
    lblAddCharges.Text = ""
    lblSubtotal.Text = ""
    lblTax.Text = ""
    lblTotal.Text = ""

    ' Get today's date from the operating system and display it.
    lblDateToday.Text = FormatDateTime(Now, DateFormat.ShortDate)
    ' Get the current time from the operating system and display it.
    lblTimeToday.Text = FormatDateTime(Now, DateFormat.LongTime)

    ' Reset the lblTotal control's colors.
    lblTotal.BackColor = SystemColors.Control
    lblTotal.ForeColor = SystemColors.ControlText

    ' Reset the focus to the first field.
    txtNights.Focus()
End Sub
```

Step 4:   Save the application.

Step 5:   Run and test the application. When you click the Calculate Charges button, the value displayed in the `lblTotal` label should appear in white text on a blue background. When you click the Clear button, the color of the `lblTotal` label should return to normal.

▶ 3.8   More About Debugging: Locating Logic Errors

A *logic error* is a mistake that does not prevent an application from running, but does cause the application to produce incorrect results. Mathematical mistakes, copying a value to the wrong variable, or copying the wrong value to a variable are all examples of logic errors. Logic errors can be difficult to find. Fortunately, Visual Basic .NET provides you with debugging tools that make locating logic errors easier.

CONCEPT

VISUAL BASIC .NET ALLOWS YOU TO PAUSE A PROGRAM, THEN EXECUTE ITS STATEMENTS ONE AT A TIME. AFTER EACH STATEMENT EXECUTES, YOU MAY EXAMINE VARIABLE CONTENTS AND PROPERTY VALUES.

First, Visual Basic .NET allows you to set breakpoints in your program code. A *breakpoint* is a line that you select in your code. When the application is running and it reaches a breakpoint, it pauses and Visual Basic .NET enters break mode. While the application is paused, you may examine variable contents and the values stored in certain control properties.

Second, Visual Basic .NET allows you to *single-step* through an application's code once its execution has been paused by a breakpoint. This means that the application's statements execute one at a time, under your control. After each statement executes, you can re-examine variable and property contents. This process allows you to identify the line or lines of code causing the error.

TUTORIAL 3-12:

Single-stepping through an application's execution

In this tutorial, you set a breakpoint in an application's code, then single-step through the application's code to find a logic error.

Step 1:   Start Visual Basic .NET and open the Average Race Time project, which is stored in the Chap3\Average Race Time folder on the student disk.

Step 2:   Run the application. The application's form appears, as shown in Figure 3-36.

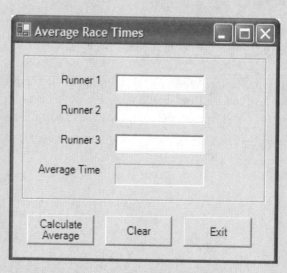

Figure 3-36   Average Race Times form

Step 3: This application allows you to enter the finishing times of three runners in a race, then see their average time. Enter **25** as the time for all three runners.

Step 4: Click the Calculate Average button. The application displays the incorrect value 58.3 as the average time. (The correct value is 25.)

Step 5: Click the Exit button to stop the application.

Step 6: Open the Code window and locate the following line of code, which appears in the `btnCalculate_Click` event procedure:

```
runner1 = Val(txtRunner1.Text)
```

This line of code is where we want to pause the execution of the application. We must make this line a breakpoint.

Step 7: Place the cursor in the left margin of the Code window, next to the line of code, as shown in Figure 3-37.

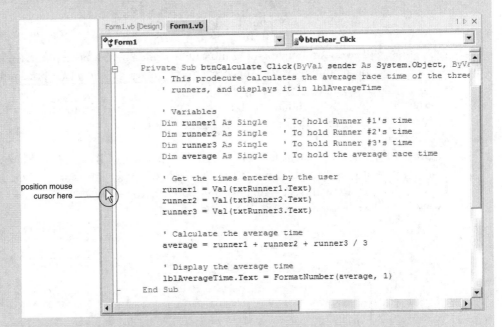

Figure 3-37 Cursor positioned in left margin of Code window

Step 8: With the cursor in position, click the mouse button. The line of code is now highlighted, and a dot appears next to the line in the left margin. This is shown in Figure 3-38.

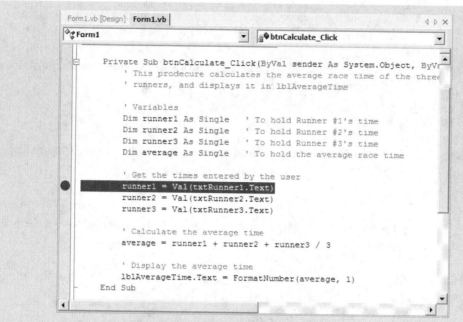

Figure 3-38 Breakpoint code highlighted

The dot and highlighting indicate that the line is a breakpoint. Another way to set a breakpoint is to move the cursor to the line you wish to set as a breakpoint, then press F9.

Step 9: Now that you have set the breakpoint, run the application. When the form appears, enter **25** as the time for each runner.

Step 10: Click the Calculate Average button. When Visual Basic .NET reaches the breakpoint, it goes into break mode and the Code window will reappear. The breakpoint line is shown with yellow highlighting, and a small yellow arrow appears in the left margin, as shown in Figure 3-39.

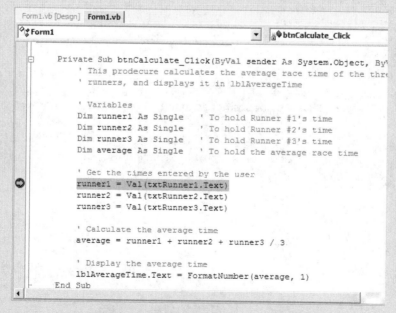

Figure 3-39 Breakpoint during break mode

The yellow highlighting and small arrow indicate the application's current execution point. The *execution point* is the next line of code that will execute. (The line has not yet executed.)

NOTE: *If the highlighting and arrow appear in a color other than yellow, the color options on your system have been changed.*

Step 11: To examine the contents of a variable or control property, simply hold the cursor over the variable or the property's name in the Code window. A small box will appear showing the variable or property's contents. For example, Figure 3-40 shows the result of holding the mouse cursor over the expression `txtRunner1.Text` in the highlighted line. The box indicates that the property is currently set to 25.

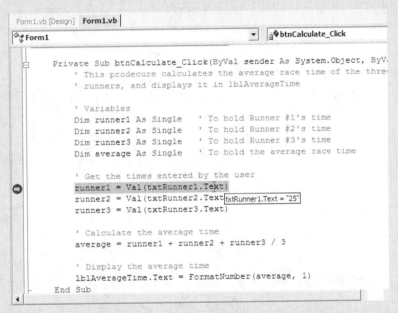

Figure 3-40 `txtRunner1.Text` **property contents revealed**

Step 12: Now hold the cursor over the variable name `runner1`. A box appears indicating the variable is set to 0.0. Because the highlighted statement has not yet executed, no value has been assigned to `runner1`.

Step 13: You may also examine the contents of variables with the Autos, Locals, and Watch windows. Figure 3-41 shows the Autos window with tabs to select the Locals and Watch windows. This window should appear near the bottom of your screen.

Autos			
Name	Value		Type
average	0.0		Single
runner1	0.0		Single
runner2	0.0		Single
runner3	0.0		Single
txtRunner1.Text	"25"		String

Autos   Locals   Watch 1

Build succeeded

Figure 3-41 The Autos window

Here is a description of each window:

- The *Autos window* displays a list of the variables that appear in the current statement, the three statements before, and the three statements after the current statement. The current value and the data type of each variable are also displayed.

- The *Locals window* displays a list of all the variables in the current procedure. The current value and the data type of each variable are also displayed.

- The *Watch window* allows you to add the names of variables that you want to watch. This window displays only the variables that you have added. You may have up to four Watch windows.

If you do not see these windows displayed, click Debug on the menu bar, then click Windows. On the Windows menu you may select Autos, Locals, or Watch. (When you select Watch a submenu appears allowing you to select Watch 1 through Watch 4. Select Watch 1.)

Step 14: With the Autos, Locals, and Watch 1 windows displayed, click the Watch 1 window tab to bring it to the front. The window should appear similar to Figure 3-42.

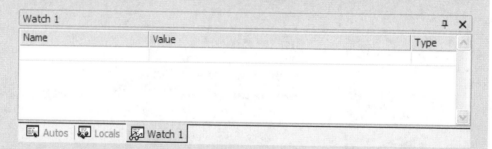

Figure 3-42 Watch 1 window displayed

Step 15: The window is ready for you to enter a variable name. Click the blank line that appears in the window. Type **runner1** and press Enter. Type **runner2**, and press Enter. Type **runner3** and press Enter. Type **average** and press Enter. You have added the variables `runner1`, `runner2`, `runner3`, and `average` to the Watch 1 window. Notice that all the variables are currently set to 0.0.

Step 16: Now you are ready to single-step through each statement in the event procedure. To do this you need to use the *Step Into command*. (The *Step Over* command, which is similar to Step Into, is covered in Chapter 6.) You activate the Step Into command by one of these methods:

- Press the F8 key.

- Select Debug from the menu bar, then select Step Into from the Debug menu.

NOTE: *This text assumes that your profile is set to Visual Basic Developer. If your profile is set to Visual Studio Developer, the Step Into command is executed by the F11 key instead of the F8 key.*

When you activate the Step Into command, Visual Basic .NET executes the statement that is highlighted. Press the F8 key now. Look at the Watch 1 window and notice that the `runner1` variable is now set to 25.0. Also notice that the next line of code is now highlighted.

Step 17: Press the F8 key two more times. All three variables, `runner1`, `runner2`, and `runner3`, should now have the value 25 stored in them.

Step 18: The following mathematical statement, which is intended to calculate the average of `runner1`, `runner2`, and `runner3`, is now highlighted:

```
average = runner1 + runner2 + runner3 / 3
```

You have confirmed that `runner1`, `runner2`, and `runner3` each hold the value 25. After this statement executes, the average of the three numbers, which is also 25, should be stored in `average`. Press F8 to execute the statement.

Step 19: Notice that the Watch 1 window now reports that `average` holds the value 58.3333321. Because this is not the correct value, there must be a problem with the math statement that just executed. Can you find it? The math statement does not calculate the correct value because the division operation takes place before any of the addition operations. You must correct the statement by inserting a set of parentheses.

Click Debug, then click Stop Debugging to halt the applicaton. In the Code window insert a set of parentheses into the math statement so it appears as:

```
average = (runner1 + runner2 + runner3) / 3
```

Step 20: Now you should clear the breakpoint so the application will not pause again when it reaches that line of code. To clear the breakpoint, use one of these methods:

- Position the cursor over the breakpoint dot in the left margin of the Code window, then click the left mouse button.

- Press Ctrl+Shift+F9.

- Select Debug from the menu bar, and then select Clear All Breakpoints from the Debug menu.

Any of these procedures will remove the breakpoint from the code.

Step 21: Run the application again. Enter 25 as each runner's time, then click the Calculate Average button. This time the correct average, 25.0, is displayed.

Step 22: Click the Exit button to stop the application.

If you want to know more: The debug toolbar

Visual Basic .NET provides a toolbar that contains only debugging commands. This toolbar can be used as an alternative to the Debug menu commands. To display the toolbar, select View on the menu bar, then select Toolbars. A submenu appears. Select Debug from the submenu. The Debug toolbar appears, which is shown in Figure 3-43.

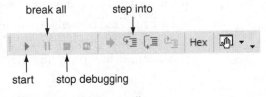

Figure 3-43 Debug toolbar

✓ **Checkpoint**

3.40 What is the difference between a compile error (or syntax error) and a logic error?

3.41 What is a breakpoint?

3.42 What is the purpose of single-stepping through an application?

SUMMARY

The TextBox control allows you to capture input that the user has typed on the keyboard. Whatever the user types into a TextBox control is stored in the control's Text property.

The standard prefix for TextBox control names is `txt`.

String concatenation means that one string is appended to another. The & operator is used to perform string concatenation.

The line-continuation character, which is a space followed by an underscore, allows you to break a long programming statement into two or more lines.

The control that has the focus is the one that receives the user's keyboard input or mouse clicks.

You move the focus to a control in code with the `Focus` method.

The order in which controls receive the focus is called the tab order. When you place controls on a form in Visual Basic .NET, the tab order will be the same sequence in which you created the controls.

You can modify the tab order by changing a control's TabIndex property.

Tab order selection mode allows you to easily view the TabIndex property values of all the controls on a form.

If you do not want a control to receive the focus when the user presses the Tab key, set its TabStop property to False.

An access key, or mnemonic, is a key that you press in combination with the Alt key to quickly access a control such as a button.

You assign an access key to a button by placing an ampersand (&) in its Text property. The letter that immediately follows the ampersand becomes the access key, and that letter will appear underlined on the button.

An accept button is a button on a form that is clicked when the user presses the Enter key. A cancel button is a button on a form that is clicked when the user presses the Escape key. Forms have two properties, AcceptButton and CancelButton, that allow you to designate an accept button and a cancel button.

A variable is a named storage location in the computer's memory, used for holding information while the program is running.

You use the assignment operator (=) to store a value in a variable, just as you do with a control property.

A variable declaration is a statement that causes Visual Basic .NET to create a variable in memory.

A variable's data type is the type of information that the variable can hold.

There are rules and conventions for naming variables. Rules are mandatory, while conventions are recommended naming practices that are not part of the Visual Basic .NET syntax but follow a standard style of programming.

When a variable is first created in memory, Visual Basic .NET assigns it an initial value. A variable's initial value depends on its data type. You may also initialize a variable, which means to specify the variable's starting value.

A variable's scope is the part of the program where the variable is visible, and may be accessed by programming statements. A variable's lifetime is the time during which the variable exists in memory.

A variable that is declared inside a procedure is called a local variable, and is visible only to statements inside the same procedure.

Variables of the Date data type can hold both a date and a time. You may store values in a Date variable with date literals, strings, or user input.

The `Now` keyword retrieves the current date and time from the computer system. The `TimeOfDay` keyword retrieves the current time. The `Today` keyword retrieves the current date.

When you assign a value of one data type to a variable of another data type, Visual Basic .NET attempts to convert the value being assigned to the data type of the variable.

A type conversion or type mismatch error is generated anytime a nonnumeric value that cannot be automatically converted to a numeric value is assigned to a numeric variable or property.

A function is a specialized routine that performs a specific operation, then returns or produces a value.

An intrinsic function is a function that is built into Visual Basic .NET.

An argument is information being sent to a function.

The `Val` function, which is intrinsic to Visual Basic .NET, takes a string argument, which it converts to a number.

Each of the Visual Basic .NET data types has a method named `ToString`, which returns a string representation of the variable calling the method.

When two operators share an operand, the operator with the highest precedence works first.

Parts of a mathematical expression may be grouped with parentheses to force some operations to be performed before others.

A combined assignment operator combines the assignment operator with another operator.

Visual Basic .NET provides several intrinsic type conversion functions, such as `CInt` and `CDbl`, which convert expressions to other data types.

A named constant is like a variable whose content is read-only: It cannot be changed by a programming statement while the program is running.

The way a value is printed or displayed is called its formatting. Visual Basic .NET provides several intrinsic functions that format numbers in various ways.

A group box, which is used to group other controls, appears as a rectangular border with an optional title. When you create a group box to hold other controls, you must create the group box first, then draw the other controls inside the group box.

A grid may be displayed on forms in the Design window. This grid is used to align controls.

You can select and work with multiple controls simultaneously.

Visual Basic .NET provides a Format menu with several commands for aligning, sizing, and centering controls on a form.

Every form has a `Load` event procedure, which is executed each time the form loads into memory. If you need to execute code automatically when a form is displayed, you can place the code in the form's `Load` event procedure.

Visual Basic .NET provides numerous values that represent colors. These values may be used in code to change a control's foreground and background color.

A logic error is a programming mistake that does not prevent an application from running but that does cause the application to produce incorrect results.

A breakpoint is a line of code that causes a running application to pause execution and enter break mode. While the application is paused, you may perform debugging operations, such as examining variable contents and the values stored in control properties.

Single-stepping is the debugging technique of executing an application's programming statements one at a time. After each statement executes, you can examine variable and property contents.

KEY TERMS

Accept button	Local variable
Access key	Locals window
Argument	Logic error
Autos window	Mnemonic
Breakpoint	Named constant
Cancel button	Precedence
Combined assignment operators	Scope
Compound operators	Single-step
Connector symbol	Step Into command
Data type	String concatenation
Execution point	Tab order
Focus	Tab order selection mode
Focus method	TabIndex property
Formatting	TabStop property
Function	Text box
Function call	TextBox control
Group box	ToString method
GroupBox control	Twip
Implicit type conversion	Type conversion error
Initialization	Type mismatch error
Integer division	UseMnemonic property
Intrinsic function	Val function
Lifetime	Variable
Line-continuation character	Variable declaration
Load event procedure	Watch window

Review Questions

Fill-in-the-Blank

1. The _____ control allows you to capture input that the user has typed on the keyboard.

2. _____ is the standard prefix for TextBox control names.

3. _____ means that one string is appended to another.

4. The _____ character allows you to break a long statement into two or more lines of code.

5. The _____ character is actually two characters: a space followed by an underscore.

6. The control that has the _____ is the one that receives the user's keyboard input or mouse clicks.

7. The order in which controls receive the focus is called the _____.

8. You can modify the tab order by changing a control's _____ property.

9. If you do not want a control to receive the focus when the user presses the Tab key, set its _____ property to False.

10. An access key is a key that you press in combination with the _____ key to quickly access a control such as a button.

11. You define a button's access key through its _____ property.

12. A(n) _____ is a storage location in the computer's memory, used for holding information while the program is running.

13. A(n) _____ is a statement that causes Visual Basic .NET to create a variable in memory.

14. A variable's _____ is the type of information that the variable can hold.

15. A(n) _____ variable is declared inside a procedure.

16. A(n) _____ error is generated anytime a nonnumeric value that cannot be automatically converted to a numeric value is assigned to a numeric variable or property.

17. A(n) _____ is a specialized routine that performs a specific operation, and then returns a value.

18. The _____ function converts a string to a number.

19. A(n) _____ function is built into Visual Basic .NET.

20. A(n) _____ is information being sent to a function.

21. When two operators share an operand, the operator with the highest _____ works first.

22. A(n) _____ is like a variable whose content is read-only: it cannot be changed while the program is running.

23. A(n) _____ appears as a rectangular border with an optional title.

24. A form's _____ procedure executes each time a form loads into memory.

25. A(n) _____ is a line of code that causes a running application to pause execution, and enter break mode.

True or False

1. T F: The TextBox control's Text property holds the text entered by the user into the TextBox control at run time.

2. T F: You can access a TextBox control's Text property in code.

3. T F: The string concatenation operator automatically inserts a space between the joined strings.

4. T F: You cannot break up a word with the line-continuation character.

5. T F: You can put a remark at the end of a line, after the line-continuation character.

6. T F: Only controls that are capable of receiving input, such as TextBox controls and buttons, may have the focus.

7. T F: You can cause a control to be skipped in the tab order by setting its TabPosition property to False.

8.   T F: An error will occur if you assign a negative value to the TabIndex property in code.

9.   T F: A control whose Visible property is set to False still receives the focus.

10. T F: GroupBox and Label controls have a TabIndex property, but they are skipped in the tab order.

11. T F: When you assign an access key to a button, the user can trigger a `Click` event by typing Alt+ the access key character.

12. T F: A local variable may be accessed by any event procedure in an application.

13. T F: When a string variable is created in memory, Visual Basic .NET assigns it the initial value 0.

14. T F: A variable's scope is the time during which the variable exists in memory.

15. T F: A variable that is declared inside a procedure is only visible to statements inside the same procedure.

16. T F: The `Val` function converts a number to a string.

17. T F: If the `Val` function cannot convert its argument, it causes a type conversion run-time error.

18. T F: The multiplication operator has higher precedence than the addition operator.

19. T F: A named constant's value can be changed by a programming statement, while the program is running.

20. T F: The statement `lblMessage.BackColor = Green` will set `lblMessage` control's background color to green.

21. T F: You can select multiple controls simultaneously with the mouse.

22. T F: You can change the same property for multiple controls simultaneously.

23. T F: To group controls in a group box, draw the controls first, then draw the group box around them.

24. T F: While single-stepping through an application's code in break mode, the highlighted execution point is the line of code that has already executed.

Multiple Choice

1. When the user types input into a TextBox control, it is stored in what property?
   a. Input
   b. Text
   c. Value
   d. Keyboard

2. What character is the string concatenation operator?
   a. &
   b. +
   c. %
   d. @

3. In code, you move the focus to a control with what method?
   a. `MoveFocus`
   b. `SetFocus`
   c. `ResetFocus`
   d. `Focus`

4. What form property allows you to select a button that is to be clicked anytime the user presses the Enter key while the form is active?
   a. DefaultButton
   b. AcceptButton
   c. CancelButton
   d. EnterButton

5. What form property allows you to select a button that is to be clicked anytime the user presses the Escape key while the form is active?
   a. DefaultButton
   b. AcceptButton
   c. CancelButton
   d. EnterButton

6. You can modify a control's position in the tab order by changing what property?
   a. TabIndex
   b. TabOrder
   c. TabPosition
   d. TabStop

7. You assign an access key to a button through what property?
   a. AccessKey
   b. AccessButton
   c. Mnemonic
   d. Text

8. A group box's title is stored in what property?
   a. Title
   b. Caption
   c. Text
   d. Heading

9. You declare a named constant with what key word?
   a. `Constant`
   b. `Const`
   c. `NamedConstant`
   d. `Dim`

10. The part of a program in which a variable is visible and may be accessed by programming statements is the variable's
    a. segment
    b. lifetime
    c. scope
    d. module

11. The time during which a variable exists in memory is the variable's
    a. segment
    b. lifetime
    c. scope
    d. module

12. What string is returned from the function call `FormatPercent(0.25)`?
    a. "0.25%"
    b. "2.50%"
    c. "25.00%"
    d. "0.25"

Short Answer

1. Describe the difference between the Label control's Text property and the TextBox control's Text property.

2. How do you clear the contents of a text box?

3. What is the focus?

4. Write a statement that gives the focus to the `txtPassword` control.

5. How does Visual Basic .NET automatically assign the tab order to controls as you create them?

6. How does a control's TabIndex property affect the tab order?

7. How do you assign an access key to a button?

8. How does assigning an access key to a button change the button's appearance?

9. What is the difference between the Single and Integer data types?

10. Make up variable names that would be appropriate for holding each of the following information items.
    a. The number of backpacks sold this week.
    b. The number of pounds of dog food in storage.
    c. Today's date.
    d. An item's wholesale price.
    e. A customer's name.
    f. The distance between two galaxies.
    g. The number of the month (1=January, 2=February, etc.)

11. Why should you always make sure that a string variable is initialized or assigned a value before it is used in an operation?

12. When is a local variable destroyed?

13. How would the following strings be converted by the `Val` function?
    a. "22.9000"
    b. "1xfc47uvy"
    c. "$19.99"
    d. "0.05%"
    e. ""

14. Briefly describe how the `Val` function converts its string argument to a number.

15. Complete the following table by providing the value of each mathematical expression.

Expression	Value
`5 + 2 * 8`	
`20 / 5 - 2`	
`4 + 10 * 3 - 2`	
`(4 + 10) * 3 - 2`	

16. Complete the following table by indicating the format functions return value.

Function Call	Return Value
`FormatNumber(67521.584)`	
`FormatCurrency(67521.584)`	
`FormatNumber(46, 0)`	
`FormatPercent(.284)`	

17. Describe one way to select multiple controls.

18. Describe three ways to set a breakpoint in an application's code.

What Do You Think?

1. Why doesn't Visual Basic .NET automatically insert a space between strings that are concatenated with the & operator?

2. Why would you want to use the line-continuation character to cause a statement to span multiple lines?

3. Why are Label controls not capable of receiving the focus?

4. Why should you be concerned that the tab order of the controls in your application is not disorganized?

5. Why do you want to assign access keys to buttons?

6. What is the significance of showing an underlined character on a button?

7. Generally speaking, what button should be set as a form's default button?

8. Why can't you perform math operations on strings, such as "28.9"?

9. A number is used in calculations throughout a program and must be changed periodically. What benefit is there to using a named constant to represent the number?

10. How can you get your application to execute a group of statements each time a form is loaded into memory?

11. How can you place an existing control in a group box?

12. Visual Basic .NET automatically reports compile errors. Why doesn't it automatically report logic errors?

Find the Error

1. Insert your student disk, start Visual Basic .NET, and load the \Chap3\Error1\Error1 project. Run the application. Type 2, 4, and 6 into the three TextBox controls, and then click the Show Sum button. The application reports the sum as 246. Fix the application so it correctly displays the sum of the numbers.

2. Insert your student disk, start Visual Basic .NET, and load the \Chap3\Error2\Error2 project. The application has an error. Find the error and fix it.

3. Insert your student disk, start Visual Basic .NET, and load the \Chap3\Error3\Error3 project. The btnCalculate_Click procedure contains an error. Find the error and fix it.

Algorithm Workbench

1. Create a flowchart that depicts the steps necessary for making the cookies in the following recipe.
   Ingredients

   > 1/2 cup butter
   > 1 egg
   > 1 cup sifted all-purpose flour
   > 1/2 cup brown sugar
   > 1/2 cup sugar
   > 1/2 teaspoon vanilla
   > 1/2 teaspoon salt
   > 1/2 teaspoon baking soda

> 1/2 cup chopped nuts
> 1/2 cup semisweet chocolate chips
>
> Steps:
> Preheat oven to 375 degrees.
> Cream the butter.
> Add the sugar and the brown sugar to the butter and beat until creamy.
> Beat the egg and vanilla into the mixture.
> Sift and stir the flour, salt, and baking soda into the mixture.
> Stir the nuts and chocolate chips into the mixture.
> Shape the mixture into 1/2-inch balls.
> Place the balls about an inch apart on a greased cookie sheet.
> Bake for 10 minutes.

2. A hot dog, which is still in its package, should be heated for 40 seconds in a microwave. Draw a flowchart depicting the steps necessary to cook the hot dog.

3. The following pseudocode algorithm, for the event procedure `btnCalcArea`, has an error. The event procedure is supposed to calculate the area of a room's floor. The area is calculated as the room's width (entered by the user into `txtWidth`), multiplied by the room's length (entered by the user into in `txtLength`). The result is displayed with the label `lblArea`. Find the error and correct the algorithm.

   Multiply the `width` variable by the `length` variable, and store the result in the `area` variable.
   Copy the value in `txtWidth.Text` into the `width` variable.
   Copy the value in `txtLength.Text` into the `length` variable.
   Copy the value in the `area` variable into `lblArea.Text`.

4. The following steps should be followed in the event procedure `btnCalcAvailCredit_Click`, which calculates a customer's available credit. Construct a flowchart that depicts the steps listed above.
   a. Copy the value in the TextBox control `txtMaxCredit` into the variable `maxCredit`.
   b. Copy the value in the TextBox control `txtUsedCredit` into the variable `usedCredit`.
   c. Subtract the value in `usedCredit` from `maxCredit`. Store the result in `availableCredit`.
   d. Copy the value in `availableCredit` into the label `lblAvailableCredit`.

5. Convert the flowchart you constructed in exercise 4 into Visual Basic .NET code.

6. Design a flowchart or pseudocode for the event procedure `btnCalcSale_Click`, which calculates the total of a retail sale. Assume the program uses `txtRetailPrice`, a TextBox control that holds the retail price of the item being purchased, and `taxRate`, a constant that holds the sales tax rate. The event procedure use the items above to calculate and display the sales tax for the purchase and the total of the sale

7. Convert the flowchart or pseudocode you constructed in exercise 6 into Visual Basic .NET code.

PROGRAMMING CHALLENGES

1. Miles-Per-Gallon Calculator

Create an application that calculates a car's gas mileage. The application's form should have TextBox controls that let the user enter the number of gallons of gas the tank holds, and the number of miles it can be driven on a full tank. When a Calculate MPG button is clicked, the application should display the number of miles that the car may be driven per gallon of gas. The form should also have a

Clear button that clears the input and results, as well as an Exit button that ends the application. The application's form should appear as in Figure 3-44.

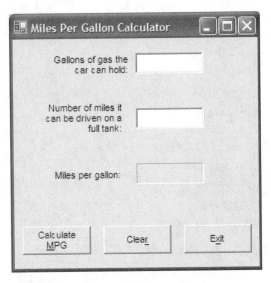

Figure 3-44 Miles Per Gallon calculator

Use the following set of test data to determine if the application is calculating properly:

Gallons	Miles	Miles Per Gallon
10	375	37.50
12	289	24.08
15	190	12.67

2. Stadium Seating

There are three seating categories at an athletic stadium. For a baseball game, Class A seats cost $15 each, Class B seats cost $12 each, and Class C seats cost $9 each. Create an application that allows the user to enter the number of tickets sold for each class. The application should be able to display the amount of income generated from each class of ticket sales and the total revenue generated. The application's form should resemble the one shown in Figure 3-45.

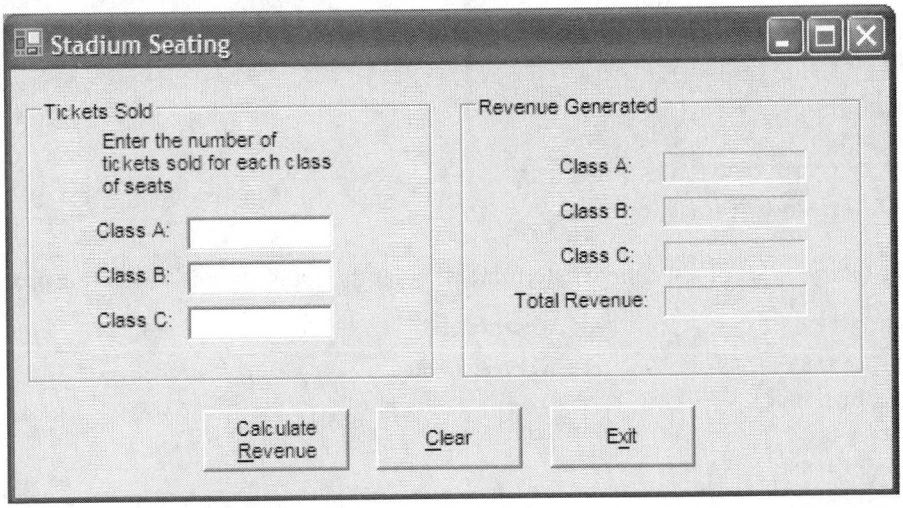

Figure 3-45 Stadium Seating form

Use the following set of test data to determine whether the application is calculating properly:

Ticket sales

Class A: 320
Class B: 570
Class C: 890

Revenue

Class A: $4,800.00
Class B: $6,840.00
Class C: $8, 010.00
Total Revenue: $19,650.00

Class A: 500
Class B: 750
Class C: 1,200

Class A: $7,500.00
Class B: $9,000.00
Class C: $10,800.00
Total Revenue: $27,300.00

Class A: 100
Class B: 300
Class C: 500

Class A: $1,500.00
Class B: $3,600.00
Class C: $4,500.00
Total Revenue: $9,600.00

3. **Test Average**

Create an application that allows the user to enter five test scores. It should be able to calculate and display the average score. The application's form should resemble Figure 3-46. Notice that the labels next to each TextBox control have been assigned an access key. As described in this chapter, use a label to indirectly assign an access key to a TextBox control.

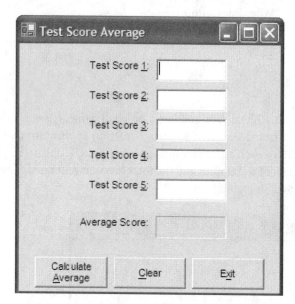

Figure 3-46   Test Score Average form

Use the following set of test data to determine whether the application is calculating properly:

Test Scores

Test Score 1: 85
Test Score 2: 90
Test Score 3: 78
Test Score 4: 88
Test Score 5: 92

Averages

Average: 86.60

Test Score 1: 90	Average: 70.00
Test Score 2: 80	
Test Score 3: 70	
Test Score 4: 60	
Test Score 5: 50	
Test Score 1: 100	Average: 82.2
Test Score 2: 92	
Test Score 3: 56	
Test Score 4: 89	
Test Score 5: 740	

4. Theater Revenue

A movie theater only keeps a percentage of the revenue earned from ticket sales. The remainder goes to the movie company. Create an application that calculates and displays the following figures for one night's box office business at a theater:

◆   Gross revenue for adult tickets sold. This is the amount of money taken in for all adult tickets sold.

◆   Net revenue for adult tickets sold. This is the amount of money from adult ticket sales left over after the payment to the movie company has been deducted.

◆   Gross revenue for child tickets sold. This is the amount of money taken in for all child tickets sold.

◆   Net revenue for child tickets sold. This is the amount of money from child ticket sales left over after the payment to the movie company has been deducted.

◆   Total gross revenue. This is the sum of gross revenue for adult and child tickets sold.

◆   Total net revenue. This is the sum of net revenue for adult and child tickets sold.

The application's form should resemble Figure 3-47

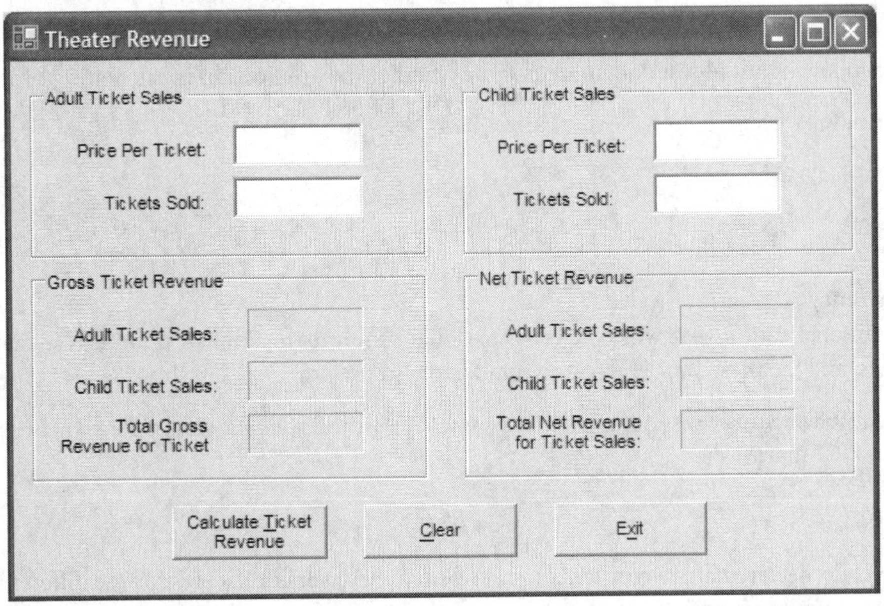

Figure 3-47   Theater Revenue form

Assume the theater keeps 20% of its box office receipts. Use a named constant in your code to represent this percentage.

Use the following set of test data to determine wheter the application is calculating properly:

Ticket Sales

Price per Adult Ticket: $6.00
Adult Tickets Sold: 120
Price per Child Ticket: $4.00
Child Tickets Sold: 72

Revenue

Gross Adult Ticket Sales: $720.00
Gross Child Ticket Sales: $288.00
Total Gross Revenue: $1,008.00
Net Adult Ticket Sales: $144.00
Net Child Ticket Sales: $57.60
Total Net Revenue: $201.60

Design Your Own Forms

5. How Many Widgets?

The Yukon Widget Company manufactures widgets that weigh 9.2 pounds each. Create an application that calculates how many widgets are stacked on a pallet, based on the total weight of the pallet. The user should be able to enter how much the pallet weighs by itself and how much it weighs with the widgets stacked on it. The user should click a button to calculate and display the number of widgets stacked on the pallet. Use the following set of test data to determine whether the application is calculating properly.

Pallet	Pallet and Widgets	Number of Widgets
100	5620	600
75	1915	200
200	9400	1,000

6. Centigrade to Fahrenheit

Create an application that converts centigrade to Fahrenheit. The formula is

$$F = \frac{9}{5}C + 32$$

where F is the Fahrenheit temperature and C is the centigrade temperature.

Use the following set of test data to determine whether the application is calculating properly:

Centigrade	Fahrenheit
100	212
0	32
56	132.8

7. Currency

Create an application that will convert U.S. dollar amounts to English pounds, German marks, French francs, and Japanese yen. The conversion factors to use are

1 dollar = .68 pounds
1 dollar = 1.7 marks
1 dollar = 5.82 francs
1 dollar = 108.36 yen

In your code, declare named constants to represent the conversion factors for the different types of currency. For example, you might declare the conversion factor for yen as:

```
Const yenFactor As Single = 108.36
```

Then use the named constants in the mathematical conversion statements. Use the following set of test data to determine whether the application is calculating properly:

Dollars	Conversion Values
$100	Pounds: 68 Marks: 170 Francs: 582 Yen: 10,836
$25	Pounds: 17 Marks: 42.5 Francs: 145.5 Yen: 2,709
$1	Pounds: 0.68 Marks: 1.70 Francs: 5.82 Yen: 108.36

8. Monthly Sales Tax

A retail company must file a monthly sales tax report listing the total sales for the month, and the amount of state and county sales tax collected. The state sales tax rate is 4%, and the county sales tax rate is 2%. Create an application that allows the user to enter the total sales for the month. From this figure, the application should calculate and display

◆ The amount of county sales tax

◆ The amount of state sales tax

◆ The total sales tax (county plus state)

In the application's code, represent the county tax rate (0.02) and the state tax rate (0.04) as named constants. Use the named constants in the mathematical statements. Use the following set of test data to determine whether the application is calculating properly:

Total Sales	Tax Amounts
9,500	County sales tax: $190.00 State sales tax: $380.00 Total sales tax: $570.00
5,000	County sales tax: $100.00 State sales tax: $200.00 Total sales tax: $300.00
15,000	County sales tax: $300.00 State sales tax: $600.00 Total sales tax: $900.00

9. Property Tax

A county collects property taxes on the assessment value of property, which is 60% of the property's actual value. If an acre of land is valued at $10,000, its assessment value is $6,000. The property tax is then $0.64 for each $100 of the assessment value. The tax for the acre assessed at $6,000 will be $38.40. Create an application that displays the assessment value and property tax when a user enters the actual value of a property. Use the following set of test data to determine whether the application is calculating properly:

Actual Property Value	Assessment and Tax
100,000	Assessment value: $60,000.00
	Property tax: $384.00
75,000	Assessment value: $45,000.00
	Property tax: $288.00
250,000	Assessment value: $150,000.00
	Property tax: $960.00

10. Pizza Pi

Joe's Pizza Palace needs an application to calculate the number of slices a pizza of any size can be divided into. The application should do the following

- Allow the user to enter the diameter of the pizza, in inches.
- Calculate the number of slices that may be taken from a pizza of that size.
- Display a message telling the number of slices.

To calculate the number of slices that may be taken from the pizza, you must know the following facts:

- Each slice should have an area of 14.125 inches.
- To calculate the number of slices, divide the area of the pizza by 14.125.
- The area of the pizza is calculated with the formula:

$$\text{Area} = \pi r^2$$

NOTE: *π is the Greek letter pi. 3.14159 can be used as its value. The variable r is the radius of the pizza. Divide the diameter by 2 to get the radius.*

Use the following set of test data to determine whether the application is calculating properly:

Diameter of Pizza	Number of Slices
22"	27
15"	13
12"	8

Making Decisions and Working with Strings

►4.1 Introduction

This chapter covers using If...Then, If...Then...Else and If...Then...ElseIf statements to make decisions. It discusses how you can compare values using relational operators and build complex comparisons using logical operators. It also covers the Select Case statement. Radio buttons, which allow the user to select one choice from many possible choices, and check boxes, which allow the user to make on/off or yes/no types of selections, are discussed. Message boxes, which allow you to conveniently display messages to the user, are covered. In addition, class-level variables, and the process of input validation, are introduced.

►4.2 The Decision Structure

CONCEPT

THE DECISION STRUCTURE ALLOWS A PROGRAM TO HAVE MORE THAN ONE PATH OF EXECUTION.

In all the programs you have written so far, the event procedures execute their statements sequentially. This means that the statements are executed one after the other, in the order they appear in the procedure.

You might think of sequentially executed statements as the steps you take as you walk down a road. To complete the journey, you must start at the beginning and take each step, one after the other, until you reach your destination. This is illustrated in Figure 4-1.

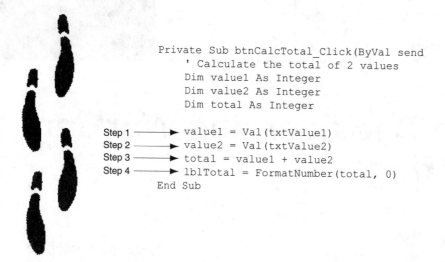

```
Private Sub btnCalcTotal_Click(ByVal send
    ' Calculate the total of 2 values
    Dim value1 As Integer
    Dim value2 As Integer
    Dim total As Integer

    value1 = Val(txtValue1)
    value2 = Val(txtValue2)
    total = value1 + value2
    lblTotal = FormatNumber(total, 0)
End Sub
```

Step 1 ⟶ `value1 = Val(txtValue1)`
Step 2 ⟶ `value2 = Val(txtValue2)`
Step 3 ⟶ `total = value1 + value2`
Step 4 ⟶ `lblTotal = FormatNumber(total, 0)`

Figure 4-1   Sequence instruction

This type of code is called a *sequence structure*, because the statements are executed in sequence, without branching off in another direction. Programs often need more than one path of execution, however. Many algorithms require a program to execute some statements only under certain circumstances. This can be accomplished with a *decision structure*.

Decision Structures in Flowcharts and Pseudocode

In a decision structure's simplest form, an action is taken only when a condition exists. If the condition does not exist, the action is not performed. Figure 4-2 shows a flowchart segment for a decision structure. A new symbol, the diamond, represents a yes/no question, or a true/false condition. If the answer to the question is yes (or if the condition is true), the program flow follows one path. If the answer to the question is no (or the condition is false), the program flow follows another path.

In the flowchart, the action "Wear a coat" is only performed when it is cold outside. If it is not cold outside, the action is skipped. The action is *conditionally executed* because it is only performed when a certain condition (cold outside) exists. Figure 4-3 shows a more elaborate flowchart, where three actions are taken, only when it is cold outside.

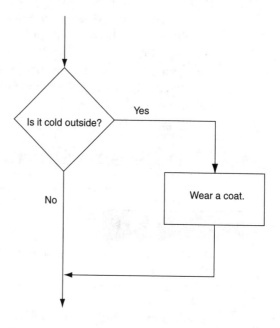

Figure 4-2   Simple decision structure flowchart

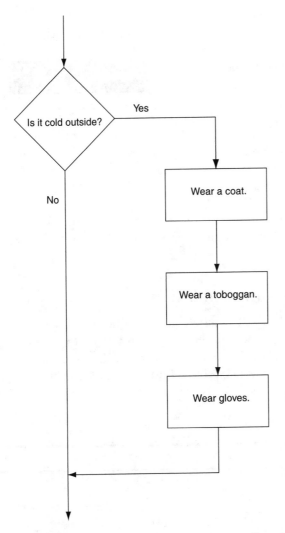

Figure 4-3   Three-action decision structure flowchart

Decision structures can also be expressed as pseudocode. For example, the decision structure depicted in Figure 4-2 can be expressed as

If it is cold outside Then
    Wear a coat.
End If

Notice that the End If statement marks the end of the decision structure in pseudocode. The statements that appear between *If...Then* and *End If* are executed only when the condition that is being tested is met. The decision structure shown in Figure 4-3, which conditionally executes three actions, can be expressed as

If it is cold outside Then
    Wear a coat.
    Wear a toboggan.
    Wear gloves.
End If

► 4.3 The If...Then Statement

One way to code a decision structure in Visual Basic .NET is with the If...Then statement. Here is the general form of the If...Then statement.

```
If condition Then
     statement
       (more statements may follow)
End If
```

The If...Then statement is really very simple: if the condition is true, the statement or statements that appear between the If...Then and the End If are executed. Otherwise, the statements are skipped.

Using Relational Operators to Form Conditions

Typically, the condition that is tested by an If...Then statement is formed with relational operator. A *relational operator* determines whether a specific relationship exists between two values. For example, the greater than operator (>) determines whether one value is greater than another. The equal to operator (=) determines whether two values are equal. Table 4-1 lists all of the Visual Basic .NET relational operators.

Table 4-1

Visual Basic .NET relational operators

Relational Operator	Meaning
>	Greater than
<	Less than
=	Equal to
<>	Not equal to
>=	Greater than or equal to
<=	Less than or equal to

All of the relational operators are binary, which means they use two operands. Here is an example of an expression using the greater than operator:

```
length > width
```

This expression is called a relational expression. A *relational expression* consists of a relational operator and its operands. This one is used to determine whether length is greater than width. The following expression determines whether length is less than width:

```
length < width
```

Table 4-2 shows examples of several relational expressions that compare the variables x and y.

Table 4-2

Relational expressions

Relational Expression	Meaning
x > y	Is x greater than y?
x < y	Is x less than y?
x >= y	Is x greater than or equal to y?
x <= y	Is x less than or equal to y?
x = y	Is x equal to y?
x <> y	Is x not equal to y?

Relational expressions can only be evaluated as true or false. If x is greater than y, the expression x > y is true, while the expression x < y is false.

The = operator, when used in a relational expression, determines whether the operand on its left is equal to the operand on its right. If both operands have the same value, the expression is true. Assuming that a is 4, the expression a = 4 is true and the expression a = 2 is false.

A couple of the relational operators actually test for two relationships. The >= operator determines whether the operand on its left is greater than or equal to the operand on the right. Assuming that a is 4, b is 6, and c is 4, both of the expressions b >= a and a >= c are true and a >= 5 is false. When using this operator, the > symbol must precede the = symbol, and there is no space between them.

The <= operator determines whether the operand on its left is less than or equal to the operand on its right. Once again, assuming that a is 4, b is 6, and c is 4, both a <= c and b <= 10 are true, but b <= a is false. When using this operator, the < symbol must precede the = symbol, and there is no space between them.

The <> operator is the not equal operator. It determines whether the operand on its left is not equal to the operand on its right, which is the opposite of the = operator. As before, assuming a is 4, b is 6, and c is 4, both a <> b and b <> c are true because a is not equal to b and b is not equal to c. However, a <> c is false because a is equal to c.

Putting It All Together

The following If...Then statement

```
If sales > 50000 Then
    getsBonus = True
End If
```

uses the > operator to determine whether sales is greater than 50000. If that condition is true, the Boolean variable getsBonus is set to true. The following example conditionally executes multiple statements.

```
If sales > 50000 Then
    getsBonus = True
    commissionRate = 0.12
    daysOff = daysOff + 1
End If
```

Here are some specific rules to remember about the If...Then statement:

- The words If and Then must appear on the same line.
- Nothing other than a remark can appear after the Then key word, on the same line.

◆ The `End If` statement must be on a line by itself. Only a remark may follow it on the same line.

TUTORIAL 4-1:

Examining an application that uses the `If...Then` statement

Step 1: Start Visual Basic .NET and open the Test Score Average 1 project, which is stored in the \Chap4\Test Score Average 1 folder on the student disk.

Step 2: Run the application. The form appears, as shown in Figure 4-4.

Step 3: Enter the following test scores in the three text boxes: 80, 90, 75.

Step 4: Click the Calculate Average button. The average test score is displayed.

Step 5: Click the Clear button, and then enter the following test scores in the three text boxes: **100, 97, 99**.

Step 6: Click the Calculate Average button. This time, in addition to the average test score being displayed, a congratulatory message appears. The form appears, as shown in Figure 4-5.

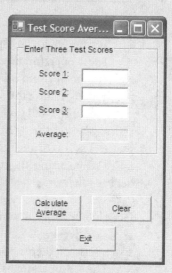

Figure 4-4 Test Score Average form

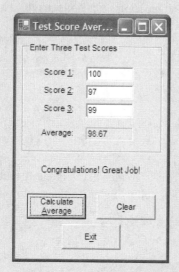

Figure 4-5 Average and message displayed

Step 7: Click the Exit button to terminate the application.

Step 8:   In the Visual Basic .NET environment, open the Code window and find the `btnCalculate_ Click` event procedure. The code is as follows.

```
Private Sub btnCalculate_Click(ByVal sender As System.Object, _
        ByVal e As System.EventArgs) Handles btnCalculate.Click
    ' This procedure calculates and displays the
    ' average test score. If the score is high, it
    ' displays a congratulatory message.
    Dim score1 As Single
    Dim score2 As Single
    Dim score3 As Single
    Dim average As Single
    ' Copy the scores into the variables
    score1 = Val(txtScore1.Text)
    score2 = Val(txtScore2.Text)
    score3 = Val(txtScore3.Text)
    ' Calculate and display the average
    average = (score1 + score2 + score3) / 3
    lblAverage.Text = FormatNumber(average)
    ' If the score is high, give the student a
    ' pat on the back!
    If average > 95 Then
        lblMessage.Text = "Congratulations! Great Job!"
    End If
End Sub
```

Near the bottom of the procedure, the following statement causes the congratulatory message to be displayed only if `average` is greater than 95.

```
If average > 95 Then
        lblMessage.Text = "Congratulations! Great Job!"
End If
```

Programming Style and the `If...Then` Statement

Notice that in each `If...Then` statement we have looked at, the conditionally executed statements are indented. This is not a syntax requirement but a programming style convention. For example, compare the following statements.

```
If sales > 50000 Then
    getsBonus = True
    commissionRate = 0.12
    daysOff = daysOff + 1
End If
```

```
If sales > 50000 Then
getsBonus = True
commissionRate = 0.12
daysOff = daysOff + 1
End If
```

Both of the `If...Then` statements will execute and both do the same thing. The first example, however, is more readable than the second because the conditionally executed statements are indented.

NOTE: *Visual Basic .NET automatically indents the conditionally-executed statements as you type an* If...Then *statement. If this feature has been turned off, you can turn it on by clicking Tools on the menu bar, then clicking Options. On the Options dialog box, perform the following:*

- *Click Text Editor in the left pane, then click Basic, then click Tabs. Make sure "Smart" is checked on the dialog box under Indenting.*

- *In the left pane click VB Specific. Make sure "Pretty listing (reformatting) of code" and "Automatic insertion of end constructs" are both checked.*

Using Relational Operators with Math Operators

It is possible to use a relational operator and math operators in the same expression. Here is an example:

```
If x + y > 20 Then
    lblMessage.Text = "It is true!"
End If
```

When a relational operator appears in the same expression as one or more math operators, the math operators always perform first. In this statement, the + operator adds x and y. The result is compared to 20 with the > operator. Here is another example:

```
If x + y > a - b Then
    lblMessage.Text = "It is true!"
End If
```

In this statement, the result of x + y is compared, with the > operator, to the result of a - b.

Using Function Calls with Relational Operators

It is possible to compare the return value of a function call with another value, using a relational operator. Here is an example:

```
If Val(txtInput.Text) < 100 Then
    lblMessage.Text = "It is true!"
End If
```

This If...Then statement calls the intrinsic Val function to get the numeric value of txtInput.Text. The function's return value is compared to 100 with the < operator. If the result of Val(txtInput.Text) is less than 100, the assignment statement is executed.

Using Boolean Variables as Flags

A *flag* is a Boolean variable that signals when some condition exists in the program. When the flag is set to false, it indicates the condition does not yet exist. When the flag is set to true, it means the condition does exist. Look at the following code, which uses a Boolean variable named quotaMet.

```
If quotaMet Then
    lblMessage.Text = "You have met your sales quota"
End If
```

This statement assigns the string "You have met your sales quota" to lblMessage.Text if the Boolean variable quotaMet is set to true. If quotaMet is false, the assignment statement will not be executed. It is not necessary to use the = operator to compare the variable to true. The statement is equivalent to:

```
If quotaMet = True Then
    lblMessage.Text = "You have met your sales quota"
End If
```

If You Want to Know More about Truth

You have seen that an If...Then statement can test a relational expression or a Boolean variable for a true or false value. In reality, an If...Then statement can test any variable or expression, and determine whether its value is true or false. A variable or expression is considered false if its value is 0. If its value is anything other than 0, it is considered true.

For example, look at the following code segment:

```
Dim value As Integer = 5
If value Then
    lblMessage.Text = "It is true!"
End If
```

The If...Then statement does not test a relational expression or a Boolean variable, but rather the contents of an integer variable. Because value is set to 5 (a nonzero value), the string "It is true!" will be copied to lblMessage.Text. If value had been set to 0, however, the assignment statement would have been skipped. Here is another example:

```
If x + y Then
    lblMessage.Text = "It is True!"
End If
```

In this statement the sum of x and y is tested like any other value in an If statement: 0 is false and all other values are true. If the sum of the two variables is 0, the assignment statement will be skipped. Otherwise, the statement is executed.

You may also use the return value of function calls as conditional expressions. Here is an example that uses the intrinsic Val function:

```
If Val(txtInput.Text) Then
    lblMessage.Text = "It is True!"
End If
```

This If...Then statement uses the Val function to get the numeric equivalent of txtInput.Text. If this value is anything other than 0, the assignment statement is executed. Otherwise, the statement is skipped.

✓ Checkpoint

4.1 Assuming X is 5, Y is 6, and Z is 8, indicate whether each of the following relational expressions is true or false:

```
a. x = 5           T  F
b. 7 <= (x + 2)    T  F
c. z > 4           T  F
d. (2 + x) <> y    T  F
```

```
e. Z <> 4          T    F
f. x >= 0          T    F
g. x <= (y * 2)    T    F
```

4.2   In the following If statement, assume that isInvalid is a Boolean variable. Exactly what condition is being tested?

```
If isInvalid Then
    ' Do something
End If
```

4.3   Do both of the following If...Then statements perform the same operation?

```
If sales > 10000 Then
    commissionRate = 0.15
End If
If sales > 10000 Then
commissionRate = 0.15
End If
```

4.4   Of the two If...Then statements shown in Checkpoint 4.3, one is preferred over the other. Which is preferred, and why?

▶ 4.4   The If...Then...Else Statement

CONCEPT

THE IF...THE...NELSE STATEMENT EXECUTES ONE GROUP OF STATEMENTS IF THE CONDITION IS TRUE AND ANOTHER GROUP OF STATEMENTS IF THE CONDITION IS FALSE.

The If...Then...Else statement is an expansion of the If...Then statement. Here is its format:

```
If condition Then
      statement
      (more statements may follow)
Else
      statement
      (more statements may follow)
End If
```

As in an If...Then statement, an expression is evaluated to determine whether a condition exists. If the expression is true, a statement or group of statements is executed. If the expression is false, a separate group of statements is executed, as in the following.

```
If temperature < 40 Then
   lblMessage.Text = "A little cold, isn't it?"
Else
   lblMessage.Text = "Nice weather we're having!"
End If
```

The `Else` statement specifies a statement or group of statements to be executed when the expression is false. In the preceding example, when the expression `temperature < 40` is not true, the statement appearing after the `Else` is executed. Note that the conditionally executed statement(s) in the `Else` part are indented.

The code in the `If...Then...Else` statement will take only one of the two paths. If you think of the statements in a computer program as steps taken down a road, consider the `If...Then...Else` statement as a fork in the road. Instead of being a momentary detour, like an `If...Then` statement, the `If...Then...Else` statement causes program execution to follow one of two exclusive paths. Figure 4-6 shows a flowchart for this type of decision structure.

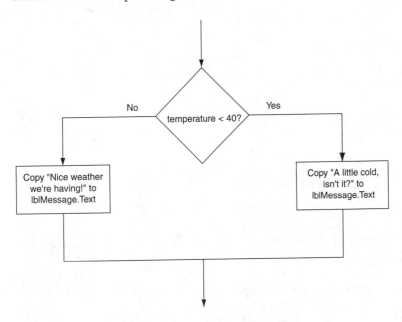

Figure 4-6   Flowchart for `If...Then...Else` **statement**

The logic shown in the flowchart in Figure 4-6 can also be expressed in pseudocode:

> *If temperature < 40 Then*
>   *lblMesage.Text = "A little cold, isn't it?"*
> *Else*
>   *lblMesage.Text = "Nice weather we're having!"*
> *End If*

TUTORIAL 4-2:

Examining an application that uses the `If...Then...Else` statement

Step 1:   Start Visual Basic .NET and open the Test Score Average 2 project, which is stored in the \Chap4\Test Score Average 2 folder on the student disk. (This is a modification of the Test Score Average 1 application you ran in Tutorial 4-1.)

Step 2:   Run the application. When the form appears, enter the following test scores in the three text boxes: 80, 90, 75.

Step 3: Click the Calculate Average button. As shown in Figure 4-7, the average test score is displayed, and the message "Keep trying!" appears.

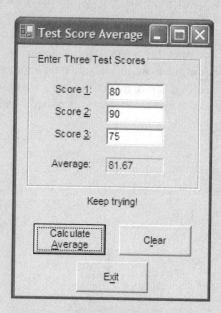

Figure 4-7 Test Score Average form with message displayed

Step 4: Click the Clear button, then enter the following test scores in the three text boxes: **100, 97, 99.**

Step 5: Click the Calculate Average button. This time, the message "Congratulations! Great job!" appears.

Step 6: Click the Exit button to terminate the application.

Step 7: In the Visual Basic .NET environment, open the Code window and find the btnCalculate_Click event procedure. The code is as follows.

```
Private Sub btnCalculate_Click(ByVal sender As System.Object, _
    ByVal e As System.EventArgs) Handles btnCalculate.Click
    ' This procedure calculates and displays the
    ' average test score. If the score is high, it
    ' displays a congratulatory message.
    Dim score1 As Single
    Dim score2 As Single
    Dim score3 As Single
    Dim average As Single

    ' Copy the scores into the variables
    score1 = Val(txtScore1.Text)
    score2 = Val(txtScore2.Text)
    score3 = Val(txtScore3.Text)
    ' Calculate and display the average
    average = (score1 + score2 + score3) / 3
    lblAverage.Text = FormatNumber(average)
```

```
        ' If the score is high, give the student a
        ' pat on the back. Otherwise, give some encouragement.
        If average > 95 Then

            lblMessage.Text = "Congratulations! Great Job!"
        Else
            lblMessage.Text = "Keep trying!"
        End If
    End Sub
```

The `If...Then...Else` statement causes one of two messages to be displayed, depending upon the value stored in `average`.

Notice the programming style used with the `If...Then...Else` statement. The word `Else` is at the same level of indention as `If`. The statement whose execution is controlled by `Else`, however, is indented. This visually depicts the two paths of execution that may be followed. The statement could have been written as

```
If average > 95 Then
lblMessage.Text = "Congratulations! Great job!"
Else
lblMessage.Text = "Keep trying!"
End If
```

The code, however, would lose an important part of its visual clarity.

✓ Checkpoint

4.5 Look at each of the following code segments. What value will the `If...Then...Else` statements store in the variable `y`?

a.
```
x = 0
If x < 1 Then
    y = 99
Else
    y = 0
End If
```

b.
```
x = 100
If x <= 1 Then
    y = 99
Else
    y = 0
End If
```

c.
```
x = 0
If x <> 1 Then
    y = 99
Else
    y = 0
End If
```

▶ 4.5 The If...Then...ElseIf Statement

We make certain mental decisions by using sets of different but related rules. For example, we might decide which type of coat or jacket to wear by consulting the following rules:

CONCEPT

THE IF...THEN...ELSEIF STATEMENT IS LIKE A CHAIN OF IF...THEN...ELSE STATEMENTS. THEY PERFORM THEIR TESTS, ONE AFTER THE OTHER, UNTIL ONE OF THEM IS FOUND TO BE TRUE.

- ◆ If it is very cold, wear a heavy coat,
- ◆ Else, if it is chilly, wear a light jacket,
- ◆ Else, if it is windy wear a windbreaker,
- ◆ Else, if it is hot, wear no jacket.

The purpose of these rules is to decide on one type of outer garment to wear. If it is cold, the first rule dictates that a heavy coat must be worn. All the other rules are then ignored. If the first rule doesn't apply (if it isn't cold) the second rule is consulted. If that rule doesn't apply, the third rule is consulted, and so forth.

The way these rules are connected is very important. If they were consulted individually, we might go out of the house wearing the wrong jacket or, possibly, more than one jacket. For instance, if it is windy, the third rule says to wear a windbreaker. What if it is both windy and very cold? Will we wear a windbreaker? A heavy coat? Both? Because of the order in which the rules are consulted, the first rule will determine that a heavy coat is needed. The remaining rules will not be consulted, and we will go outside wearing the most appropriate garment.

This type of decision making is also common in programming. In Visual Basic .NET, it is accomplished with the If...Then...ElseIf statement. Here is its general format:

```
If condition Then
      statement
      (more statements may follow)
ElseIf condition
      statement
      (more statements may follow)

(put as many ElseIf statements as necessary)
End If
```

This construction is like a chain of If...Then...Else statements. The Else part of one statement is linked to the If part of another. The chain of If...Then...Else statements becomes one long statement.

TUTORIAL 4-3:

Examining an application that uses the If...Then...ElseIf statement

Step 1: Start Visual Basic .NET and open the Test Score Average 3 project, which is stored in the \Chap4\Test Score Average 3 folder on the student disk. (This is a modification of the Test Score Average 2 application you ran in Tutorial 4-2.)

Step 2: Run the application. When the form appears, enter the following test scores in the three text boxes: **80, 90, 75**.

Step 3:   Click the Calculate Average button. As shown in Figure 4-8, the average test score, a letter grade, and the message "Keep up the hard work" are displayed.

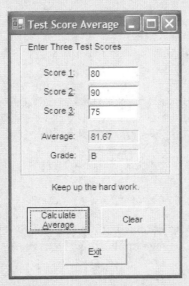

Figure 4-8   Test Score Average form with average, grade, and message displayed

Step 4:   Experiment with the application by entering other test scores and observing the letter grades displayed.

Step 5:   When you are finished, click the Exit button to terminate the application.

Step 6:   In the Visual Basic .NET environment, open the Code window and find the `btnCalculate_Click` event procedure. The code is as follows.

```
Private Sub btnCalculate_Click(ByVal sender As System.Object, _
        ByVal e As System.EventArgs) Handles btnCalculate.Click
    ' This procedure calculates and displays the
    ' average test score. If the score is high, it
    ' displays a congratulatory message.
    Dim score1 As Single
    Dim score2 As Single
    Dim score3 As Single
    Dim average As Single

    ' Copy the scores into the variables
    score1 = Val(txtScore1.Text)
    score2 = Val(txtScore2.Text)
    score3 = Val(txtScore3.Text)
    ' Calculate and display the average
    average = (score1 + score2 + score3) / 3
    lblAverage.Text = FormatNumber(average)
    ' Calculate and display the letter grade.
    If average < 60 Then
        lblGrade.Text = "F"
    ElseIf average < 70 Then
```

```
            lblGrade.Text = "D"
        ElseIf average < 80 Then
            lblGrade.Text = "C"
        ElseIf average < 90 Then
            lblGrade.Text = "B"
        ElseIf average <= 100 Then
            lblGrade.Text = "A"
        End If
        ' If the score is high, give the student a
        ' pat on the back. Otherwise, give some encouragement.
        If average > 95 Then
            lblMessage.Text = "Congratulations! Great Job!"
        Else
            lblMessage.Text = "Keep up the hard work."
        End If
    End Sub
```

The If...Then...ElseIf statement has a number of notable characteristics. Let's analyze how it works in the Test Average application. First, the relational expression average < 60 is tested.

```
    → If average < 60 Then
            lblGrade.Text = "F"
```

If average is less than 60, "F" is assigned to lblGrade.Text, and the rest of the ElseIf statements are ignored. If average is not less than 60, the next ElseIf statement executes.

```
        If average < 60 Then
            lblGrade.Text = "F"
    → ElseIf average < 70 Then
            lblGrade.Text = "D"
```

The first If...Then statement filtered out all of the grades less than 60, so when this ElseIf statement executes, average will have a value of 60 or greater. If average is less than 70, "D" is assigned to lblGrade.Text, and the rest of the ElseIf statements are ignored. This chain of events continues until one of the expressions is found true, or the End If statement is encountered. Figure 4-9 shows how this statement might appear in a flowchart.

The logic in the flowchart in Figure 4-9 can be expressed in the following pseudocode:

If average < 60 Then
    Copy "F" to lblGrade.Text
ElseIf average < 70 Then
    Copy "D" to lblGrade.Text
ElseIf average < 80 Then
    Copy "C" to lblGrade.Text
ElseIf average < 90 Then
    Copy "B" to lblGrade.Text
ElseIf average <= 100 Then
    Copy "A" to lblGrade.Text
End If

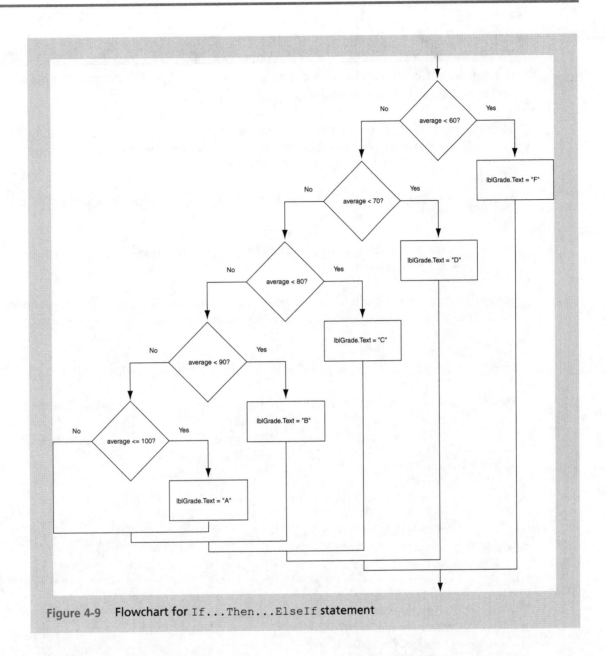

Figure 4-9   Flowchart for `If...Then...ElseIf` statement

The Difference Between the `If...Then...ElseIf` Statement and a Series of `If...Then` Statements

The execution of each `ElseIf` statement in the structure depends on all the conditions tested before it being false. The conditionally-executed statements following an `ElseIf` are executed when the conditional expression following the `ElseIf` is true and all previous expressions are false. To demonstrate how this interconnection works, let's look at a version of the program that uses independent `If...Then` statements instead of an `If...Then...ElseIf` statement.

TUTORIAL 4-4:

Seeing the difference between an `If...Then...ElseIf` statement and a series of `If...Then` statements

Step 1:   Start Visual Basic .NET and open the Test Score Average 4 project, which is stored in the \Chap4\Test Score Average 4 folder on the student disk. (This is a modification of the Test Score Average 3 application you ran in Tutorial 4-3.)

Step 2:   Run the application. When the form appears, enter the following test scores in the three text boxes: **40, 40, 40**.

Step 3:   Click the Calculate Average button. Despite the low scores, the grade A is displayed. Click the Clear button.

Step 4:   Experiment by entering more test scores and clicking the Calculate Average button. Notice that regardless of the scores you enter, the application always reports a grade of A.

Step 5:   When finished, click the Exit button to terminate the application.

Step 6:   In the Visual Basic .NET environment, open the Code window and find the `btnCalculate_Click` event procedure. Notice that instead of an `If...Then...ElseIf` statement, this procedure uses a series of `If...Then` statements to assign a letter grade. The code is as follows.

```
If average < 60 Then
    lblGrade.Text = "F"
End If
If average < 70 Then
    lblGrade.Text = "D"
End If
If average < 80 Then
    lblGrade.Text = "C"
End If
If average < 90 Then
    lblGrade.Text = "B"
End If
If average <= 100 Then
    lblGrade.Text = "A"
End If
```

In this procedure, all the `If...Then` statements execute because they are individual statements. When you ran the tutorial, you entered three scores of 40, which give an average of 40. Because this is less than 60, the first `If...Then` statement causes "F" to be assigned to `lblGrade.Text`.

```
→ If average < 60 Then
    lblGrade.Text = "F"
End If
```

Because the next statement is `If...Then` instead of `ElseIf`, it executes. `average` is also less than 70, so it causes "D" to be assigned to `lblGrade.Text`. "D" overwrites the "F" that was previously stored there.

```
If average < 60 Then
    lblGrade.Text = "F"
End If
→ If average < 70 Then
    lblGrade.Text = "D"
End If
```

This will continue until all the `If...Then` statements have executed. The last one will assign "A" to `lblGrade.Text`. (Most students prefer this method since "A" is the only grade it gives out!)

Using a Trailing Else

There is one minor problem with the test averaging applications shown so far: What if the user enters a test score greater than 100? The `If...Then...ElseIf` statement in the Test Score Average 3 project handles all scores through 100, but none greater. Figure 4-10 shows the form when the user enters values greater than 100.

The program does not give a letter grade because there is no code to handle a score greater than 100. Assuming that any grade over 100 is invalid, we can fix the program by placing an `Else` at the end of the `If...Then...ElseIf` statement, as follows:

Figure 4-10 Test Score Average 3 application showing values greater than 100

```
' Calculate and display the letter grade.
If average < 60 Then
    lblGrade.Text = "F"
ElseIf average < 70 Then
    lblGrade.Text = "D"
ElseIf average < 80 Then
    lblGrade.Text = "C"
ElseIf average < 90 Then
    lblGrade.Text = "B"
ElseIf average <= 100 Then
    lblGrade.Text = "A"
Else
    lblGrade.Text = "Invalid"
End If
```

The trailing `Else` catches any value that falls through the cracks. It provides a default response when the `If...Then` or none of the `ElseIf` statements find a true condition.

TIP: When writing an `If...Then...ElseIf` statement, it is sometimes helpful to code the structure of the statement first, identifying all the conditions that must be tested. You then insert the conditionally executed statements. For example, the code in our example could initially be written as:

```
If average < 60 Then

ElseIf average < 70 Then

ElseIf average < 80 Then

ElseIf average < 90 Then

ElseIf average <= 100 Then

Else

End If
```

This creates the framework of the statement. Notice that a blank line has been left after the `If`, `ElseIf` and `Else` parts. Once you have coded the structure, you can insert the conditionally executed statements:

```
If average < 60 Then
     lblGrade.Text = "F"
ElseIf average < 70 Then
     lblGrade.Text = "D"
ElseIf average < 80 Then
     lblGrade.Text = "C"
ElseIf average < 90 Then
     lblGrade.Text = "B"
ElseIf average <= 100 Then
     lblGrade.Text = "A"
Else
     lblGrade.Text = "Invalid"
End If
```

Sometimes it is easier to think about all the conditions that must be tested first, then decide what actions must be taken for each condition. This technique enforces that design approach.

✓ Checkpoint

4.6   The following `If...Then...ElseIf` statement has several conditions that test the variable x. Assuming x is set to the value 20, how many times will the following statement compare x before it finds a condition that is true?

```
If x < 10 Then
    y = 0
ElseIf x < 20 Then
    y = 1
ElseIf x < 30 Then
    y = 2
ElseIf x < 40 Then
    y = 3
Else
    y = -1
End If
```

4.7   In the following If...Then...ElseIf statement, if the variable x is set to 5, how many times will the code assign a value to y?

```
If x < 10 Then
    y = 0
ElseIf x < 20 Then
    y = 1
ElseIf x < 30 Then
    y = 2
ElseIf x < 40 Then
    y = 3
End If
```

In the following set of If...Then statements, if the variable x is set to 5, how many times will the code assign a value to y?

```
If x < 10 Then
    y = 0
End If
If x < 20 Then
    y = 1
End If
If x < 30 Then
    y = 2
End If
If x < 40 Then
    y = 3
End If
```

▶ 4.6   Nested If Statements

CONCEPT

A NESTED IF STATEMENT IS AN IF STATEMENT IN THE CONDITIONALLY EXECUTED CODE OF ANOTHER IF STATEMENT. (IN THIS SECTION, WE USE THE TERM IF STATEMENT TO REFER TO AN IF...THEN, IF...THEN...ELSE, OR IF...THEN...ELSEIF STATEMENT.)

A *nested* If statement is an If statement that appears inside another If statement. In Tutorial 4-5, you examine an application that uses nested If statements. The application determines whether a bank customer qualifies for a special loan. The customer must meet one or the other of the following qualifications.

◆   Earn $30,000 per year or more and have worked in his or her current job for more than two years.

◆   Have worked at his or her current job for more than five years.

TUTORIAL 4-5:

Examining an application with a nested If statement

Step 1:   Start Visual Basic .NET and open the Loan Qualifier project, which is stored in the Chap4\Loan Qualifier folder on the student disk.

Step 2: Run the application. The form shown in Figure 4-11 appears.

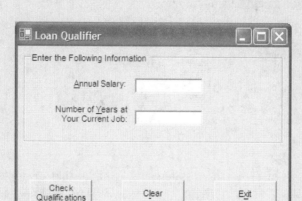

Figure 4-11 Loan Qualifier form

Step 3: Enter **45000** for salary and **3** for years at current job. Click the Check Qualifications button. The message "The applicant qualifies" appears on the form.

Step 4: Enter **15000** for salary and **3** for years at current job. Click the Check Qualifications button. The message "The applicant does not qualify" appears on the form.

Step 5: Experiment with other values. When you are finished, click the Exit button to terminate the application.

Step 6: In the Visual Basic .NET environment, open the Code window and find the btnCheckQual_Click event procedure. The code is as follows.

```
Private Sub btnCheckQual_Click(ByVal sender As System.Object, _
        ByVal e As System.EventArgs) Handles btnCheckQual.Click
    ' Determine whether the applicant qualifies
    ' for the special loan.
    If Val(txtSalary.Text) > 30000 Then
        If Val(txtYearsOnJob.Text) > 2 Then
            lblMessage.Text = "The applicant qualifies."
        Else
            lblMessage.Text = "The applicant does not qualify."
        End If
    Else
        If Val(txtYearsOnJob.Text) > 5 Then
            lblMessage.Text = "The applicant qualifies."
        Else
            lblMessage.Text = "The applicant does not qualify."
        End If
    End If
End Sub
```

The outermost If statement tests the following condition:

```
Val(txtSalary.Text) > 30000
```

If this condition is true, the nested If statement shown in boldface is executed.

```
If Val(txtSalary.Text) > 30000 Then
    If Val(txtYearsOnJob.Text) > 2 Then
        lblMessage.Text = "The applicant qualifies."
    Else
            lblMessage.Text = "The applicant does not qualify."
    End If
Else
    If Val(txtYearsOnJob.Text) > 5 Then
        lblMessage.Text = "The applicant qualifies."
    Else
        lblMessage.Text = "The applicant does not qualify."
    End If
End If
```

However, if the condition `Val(txtSalary.Text) > 30000` is not true, the `Else` part of the outermost `If` statement causes its nested `If` statement, shown in boldface, to execute:

```
If Val(txtSalary.Text) > 30000 Then
    If Val(txtYearsOnJob.Text) > 2 Then
        lblMessage.Text = "The applicant qualifies."
    Else
        lblMessage.Text = "The applicant does not qualify."
    End If
Else
    If Val(txtYearsOnJob.Text) > 5 Then
        lblMessage.Text = "The applicant qualifies."
    Else
        lblMessage.Text = "The applicant does not qualify."
    End If
End If
```

Figure 4-12 shows a flowchart for these nested `If` statements.

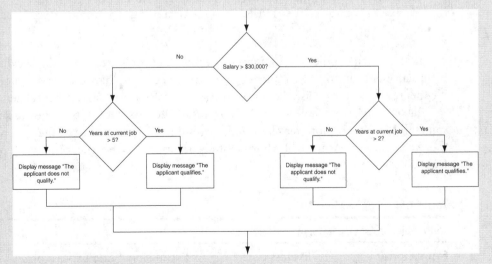

Figure 4-12   Flowchart of nested `If` statements

► 4.7 Logical Operators

CONCEPT

LOGICAL OPERATORS CONNECT TWO OR MORE RELATIONAL EXPRESSIONS INTO ONE, OR REVERSE THE LOGIC OF AN EXPRESSION.

Logical operators combine two or more relational expressions into one, or reverses the logic of an expression. Table 4-3 lists Visual Basic .NET's logical operators.

Table 4-3

Visual Basic .NET Logical Operators

Operator	Effect
And	Combines two expressions into one. Both expressions must be true for the overall expression to be true.
Or	Combines two expressions into one. One or both expressions must be true for the overall expression to be true. It is only necessary for one to be true, and it does not matter which.
Xor	Combines two expressions into one. One expression (not both) must be true for the overall expression to be true. If both expressions are true, or both expressions are false, the overall expression is false.
Not	Reverses the logical value of an expression: makes a true expression false and a false expression true.

The And Operator

The *And operator* combines two expressions into one. Both expressions must be true for the overall expression to be true. The following If statement uses the And operator:

```
If temperature < 20 And minutes > 12 Then
    lblMessage.Text = "The temperature is in the danger zone."
End If
```

In this statement the two relational expressions are combined into a single expression. The assignment statement will only be executed if temperature is less than 20 and minutes is greater than 12. If either relational test is false, the entire expression is false and the assignment statement is not executed.

Table 4-4 is a truth table for the And operator. The truth table lists all the possible combinations of values that two expressions may have and the resulting value returned by the And operator connecting the two conditions. As the table shows, both conditions must be true for the And operator to return a true value.

Table 4-4

Truth Table for And Operator

Expression 1	Expression 2	Expression 1 **And** Expression 2
True	False	False

Table 4-4 *continued*

Truth Table for And Operator

Expression 1	Expression 2	Expression 1 **And** Expression 2
False	True	False
False	False	False
True	True	True

TIP: You must provide complete expressions on both sides of the And operator. For example, the following is not correct because the condition on the right side of the And operator is not a complete expression.

```
temperature > 0 And < 100
```

The expression must be rewritten as

```
temperature > 0 And temperature < 100
```

NOTE: *If the subexpression on the left side of an* And *operator is false, the expression on the right side will not be checked. Because the entire expression is false if only one of the subexpressions is false, it would be a waste of CPU time to check the remaining expression.*

The Or Operator

The *Or operator* combines two expressions into one. One or both expressions must be true for the overall expression to be true. It is only necessary for one to be true, and it does not matter which. The following If statement uses the Or operator:

```
If temperature < 20 Or temperature > 100 Then
    lblMessage.Text = "The temperature is in the danger zone."
End If
```

The assignment statement will be executed if temperature is less than 20 or temperature is greater than 100. If either relational test is true, the entire expression is true and the assignment statement is executed.

Table 4-5 is a truth table for the Or operator.

Table 4-5

Truth table for Or operator

Expression 1	Expression 2	Expression 1 **Or** Expression 2
True	False	True
False	True	True
False	False	False
True	True	True

All it takes for an Or expression to be true is for one of the subexpressions to be true. It doesn't matter if the other subexpression is false or true.

TIP: You must provide complete expressions on both sides of the Or operator. For example, the following is not correct because the condition on the right side of the Or operator is not a complete expression.

```
temperature < 0 Or > 100
```

The expression must be rewritten as

```
temperature < 0 Or temperature > 100
```

NOTE: *If the subexpression on the left side of an Or operator is true, the expression on the right side will not be checked. Because the entire expression is true if only one of the subexpressions is true, it would be a waste of CPU time to check the remaining expression.*

The Xor Operator

Xor stands for "exclusive Or". The *Xor operator* takes two expressions as operands and creates an expression that is true when one, but not both, of the subexpressions is true. The following If statement that uses the Xor operator:

```
If total > 1000 Xor average > 120 Then
    lblMessage.Text = "You may try again."
End If
```

The assignment statement will be executed if total is greater than 1000 or average is greater than 120, but not both. If both relational tests are true, or neither is true, the entire expression is false. Table 4-6 is a truth table for the Xor operator.

Table 4-6

Truth table for Xor operator

Expression 1	Expression 2	Expression 1 **Or** Expression 2
True	False	True
False	True	True
False	False	False
True	True	False

TIP: You must provide complete expressions on both sides of the Xor operator. For example, the following is not correct because the condition on the right side of the Xor operator is not a complete expression.

```
value < 0 Xor > 100
```

The expression must be rewritten as

```
value < 0 Or value > 100
```

The Not Operator

The *Not operator* takes an operand and reverses its logical value. In other words, if the expression is true, the Not operator returns false, and if the expression is false, it returns true. The following If statement uses the Not operator:

```
If Not temperature > 100 Then
    lblMessage.Text = "You are below the maximum temperature."
End If
```

First, the expression `temperature > 100` is tested to be true or false. Then the `Not` operator is applied to that value. If the expression `temperature > 100` is true, the `Not` operator returns false. If it is false, the `Not` operator returns true. This example is equivalent to asking "Is the temperature not greater than 100?"

Table 4-7 is a truth table for the `Not` operator.

Table 4-7

Truth Table for `Not` operator

Expression	**Not** Expression
True	False
False	True

Checking Numeric Ranges with Logical Operators

When your program is determining whether a number is inside a numeric range, it's best to use the `And` operator. For example, the following `If` statement checks the value in x to determine whether it is in the range of 20 through 40:

```
If x >= 20 And x <= 40 Then
    lblMessage.Text = "The value is in the acceptable range."
End If
```

The expression in the `If` statement will be true only when x is greater than or equal to 20 *and* less than or equal to 40. The value in x must be within the range of 20 through 40 for this expression to be true.

When your program is determining whether a number is outside a range, it's best to use the `Or` operator. The following statement determines whether x is outside the range of 20 through 40:

```
If x < 20 Or x > 40 Then
    lblMessage.Text = "The value is outside the acceptable range."
End If
```

It's important not to get the logic of these logical operators confused. For example, the following `If` statement would never test true:

```
If x < 20 And x > 40 Then
    lblMessage.Text = "The value is outside the acceptable range."
End If
```

Obviously, x cannot be less than 20 and at the same time greater than 40.

If You Want to Know More about Using Not, And, Or, and Xor Together

It is possible to write an expression that contains more than one logical operator. For example, examine the following `If` statement.

```
If x < 0 And y > 100 Or z = 50 Then
    ' Perform some statement.
End If
```

Like the math operators, the logical operators have an order of precedence. The Not operator has the highest precedence, followed by the And operator, followed by the Or operator, followed by the Xor operator. So, in the example statement, the following expression is evaluated first:

```
x < 0 And y > 100
```

The result of this expression will then be used with the Or operator to carry out the rest of the condition. For example, if the expression is true, then the remainder of the condition will be tested as

```
True Or z = 50
```

If the first expression is false, however, the remainder of the condition will be tested as

```
False Or z = 50
```

Placing parentheses around the And expressions might help you visualize how this condition is tested. The following If statement works exactly like the preceding one. The parentheses emphasize the fact that the And expressions are tested first.

```
If (x < 0 And y > 100) Or z = 50 Then
    ' Perform some statement.
End If
```

You can use parentheses to force one expression to be tested before others. For example, look at the following If statement:

```
If x < 0 And (y > 100 Or z = 50) Then
    ' Perform some statement.
End If
```

In the statement, the expression (y > 100 Or z = 50) is tested first.

If You Want to Know More About Using Math Operators with Relational and Logical Operators

It is possible to write expressions that contain math, relational, and logical operators. For example, look at the following code segment.

```
a = 5
b = 7
x = 100
y = 30
If x > a * 10 And y < b + 20 Then
    ' Perform some statement.
End If
```

In statements such as this that contain complex conditions, math operators always perform first. After the math operators, relational operators perform. The logical operators perform last. Let's use this order to step through the evaluation of the condition shown in the If statement. First, the math operators perform, causing the statement to become

```
If x > 50 And y < 27 Then
```

Next, the relational operators perform, causing the statement to become

```
If True And False Then
```

Since `True And False` is false, the condition is false.

✓ **Checkpoint**

4.8   The following truth table shows various combinations of the values `True` and `False` connected by a logical operator. Complete the table by indicating whether the result of such a combination is `True` or `False`.

Logical Expression	Result
True And False	
True And True	
False And True	
False And False	
True Or False	
True Or True	
False Or True	
False Or False	
True Xor False	
True Xor True	
Not True	
Not False	

▶ 4.8   Comparing, Testing, and Working with Strings

CONCEPT

VISUAL BASIC .NET PROVIDES VARIOUS MEANS TO WORK WITH STRINGS. THIS SECTION SHOWS YOU HOW TO USE RELATIONAL OPERATORS TO COMPARE STRINGS, AND DISCUSSES SEVERAL INTRINSIC FUNCTIONS THAT PERFORM TESTS AND MANIPULATIONS ON STRINGS.

You saw in the preceding examples how numbers can be compared using the relational operators. You may also use the relational operators to compare strings. For example, look at the following code segment, in which `name1` and `name2` are string variables.

```
name1 = "Mary"
name2 = "Mark"
If name1 = name2 Then
    lblMessage.Text = "The names are the same"
Else
    lblMessage.Text = "The names are NOT the same"
End If
```

The = operator tests `name1` and `name2` to determine if they are equal. Since the strings "Mary" and "Mark" are not equal, the `Else` part of the `If` statement will cause the message "The names are NOT the same" to be copied to `lblMessage.Text`.

You can compare string variables with string literals as well. The following code sample uses the <> operator to determine if `month` is not equal to "October."

```
If month <> "October" Then
   ' statement
End If
```

You can also use the >, <, >=, and <= operators to compare strings. Before we look at these operators, though, we must understand how characters are stored in memory.

Computers do not actually store characters, such as A, B, C, and so forth, in memory. Instead, they store numeric codes that represent the characters. Visual Basic .NET uses *Unicode*, which is a set of numbers that represents all the letters of the alphabet (both lower- and uppercase), the printable digits 0 through 9, punctuation symbols, and special characters. When a character is stored in memory, it is actually the Unicode number that is stored. When the computer is instructed to print the value on the screen, it displays the character that corresponds with the numeric code.

NOTE: *Unicode is an international encoding system that is extensive enough to represent all the characters of all the world's alphabets.*

In Unicode, letters are arranged in alphabetic order. Because "A" comes before "B", the numeric code for the letter "A" is less than the code for the letter "B". In the following `If` statement, the relational expression `"A" < "B"` is true.

```
If "A" < "B" Then
    ' Do something
End If
```

Also, the uppercase letters come before the lowercase letters, so the numeric code for "A" is less than the numeric code for "a". In addition, the space character comes before all the alphabetic characters.

When you use relational operators to compare strings, the strings are compared character-by-character. For example, look at the following code segment.

```
name1 = "Mary"
name2 = "Mark"
If name1 > name2 Then
    lblMessage.Text = "Mary is greater than Mark"
Else
    lblMessage.Text = "Mary is not greater than Mark"
End If
```

The > operator compares each character in the strings "Mary" and "Mark," beginning with the first, or leftmost, characters. This is illustrated in Figure 4-13.

Figure 4-13 String comparison

Here is how the comparison takes place:

1. The "M" in "Mary" is compared with the "M" in "Mark." Since these are the same, the next characters are compared.

2. The "a" in "Mary" is compared with the "a" in "Mark." Since these are the same, the next characters are compared.

3. The "r" in "Mary" is compared with the "r" in "Mark." Since these are the same, the next characters are compared.

4. The "y" in "Mary" is compared with the "k" in "Mark." Since these are not the same, the two strings are not equal. The character "y" is greater than "k", so it is determined that "Mary" is greater than "Mark."

NOTE: *If one of the strings in a relational comparison is shorter in length than the other, Visual Basic .NET treats the shorter character as if it were padded with blank spaces. For example, suppose the strings "High" and "Hi" were being compared. The string "Hi" would be treated as if it were four characters in length, with the last two characters being spaces. Because the space character comes before the letters of the alphabet in Unicode, "Hi" would be less than "High".*

Testing for No Input

You can determine whether the user has entered a value into a text box by comparing the text box's Text property to an empty string. An *empty string* is represented by two quotation marks, with no space between them, as in this example:

```
If txtInput.Text = "" Then
    lblMessage.Text = "Please enter a value"
Else
    ' The txtInput control contains input, so
    ' perform an operation with it here.
End If
```

The If statement copies the string "Please enter a value" to lblMessage if the txtInput control contains no input. The statements following Else are only executed if txtInput contains a value. You can use this technique to determine whether the user has provided input for a required field before performing operations on that field.

NOTE: *This technique will not detect a string that contains only spaces. A space is a character, just as the letter "A" is a character. If the user types only spaces into a text box, you will have to trim away the spaces to determine if any other characters were typed. Later, this chapter will discuss functions for trimming spaces from strings.*

The ToUpper and ToLower methods

The ToUpper and ToLower methods are both members of the String data type, so they may be called with any string variable or expression. The *ToUpper method* returns the uppercase equivalent of a string. Here is the method's general format:

```
StringExpression.ToUpper
```

StringExpression can be any string variable or string expression. In the following example, littleWord and bigWord are String variables:

```
littleWord = "Hello"
bigWord = littleWord.ToUpper
```

After the statement executes, `bigWord` will contain "HELLO" in all uppercase letters. Notice that the original string, "Hello", had one uppercase letter—the beginning H. The `ToUpper` method only converts lowercase characters. Characters that are already uppercase, and characters that are not alphabet letters, are not converted.

TIP: The `ToUpper` method does not modify the value of the string, but returns a string that is its uppercase equivalent. For example, after the statements in the previous example execute, `littleWord` will still contain the original string "Hello".

The *ToLower method* works just like the `ToUpper` method, except it returns a lowercase version of a string. Here is the method's general format:

```
StringExpression.ToLower
```

In the following example, `bigTown` and `littleTown` are String variables:

```
bigTown = "NEW YORK"
littleTown = bigTown.ToLower
```

After the statements execute, the variable `littleTown` will contain the string "new york." `ToLower` only converts uppercase characters. Characters that are already lowercase, and characters that are not alphabet letters, are not converted.

TIP: Like `ToUpper`, the `ToLower` method does not modify the original string.

You may also use the `ToUpper` and `ToLower` methods with a control's Text property. In the following example `lastName` is a string variable:

```
lastName = txtLastName.Text.ToUpper
```

TIP: Visual Basic .NET also provides the `UCase` and `LCase` intrinsic functions, which converts strings to upper- and lowercase. See Appendix B for more information.

The `ToUpper` and `ToLower` methods are helpful in performing string comparisons. String comparisons in Visual Basic .NET are case sensitive, which means that uppercase letters are not considered to be the same as their lowercase counterparts. In other words, "A" is not the same as "a." This can lead to problems when you are constructing `If` statements that compare strings. Tutorial 4-6 leads you through such an example.

TUTORIAL 4-6:

Examining an application that performs a case sensitive string comparison

Step 1: Start Visual Basic .NET and open the Secret Word 1 project, which is stored in the \Chap4\Secret Word 1 folder on the student disk.

Step 2:   Run the application. The form shown in Figure 4-14 appears.

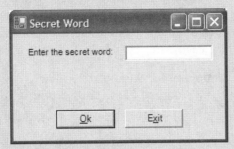

Figure 4-14   Secret Word form

This application asks you to enter the secret word, which might be similar to a password in some programs. The secret word is "PROSPERO".

Step 3:   Enter **prospero** in all lowercase letters, and click the Ok button. You will see the message "Wrong! That is NOT the secret word!"

Step 4:   Enter **Prospero** with an uppercase P, followed by all lowercase letters. Click the Ok button. Once again, you see the message "Wrong! That is NOT the secret word!"

Step 5:   Enter **PROSPERO** in all uppercase letters and click the Ok button. This time you see the message "Congratulations! That is the secret word!"

Step 6:   Click the Exit button to close the application.

Step 7:   In the Visual Basic .NET environment, open the Code window and find the btnOk_Click event procedure. The code is as follows.

```
Private Sub btnOk_Click(ByVal sender As System.Object, _
        ByVal e As System.EventArgs) Handles btnOk.Click
    ' Compare the word entered with
    ' the secret word.
    If txtInput.Text = "PROSPERO" Then
        lblMessage.Text = "Congratulations! That " & _
        "is the secret word!"
    Else
        lblMessage.Text = "Wrong! That is NOT the secret word!"
    End If
End Sub
```

As you can see, the If...Then...Else statement only compares the string entered by the user with "PROSPERO" in all uppercase letters. But what if the programmer intended to accept the word without regard to case? What if "prospero" in all lowercase letters is valid as well? One solution would be to modify the If statement to test for all the other possible values. However, to test for all the possible combination of lower- and uppercase letters would require a large amount of code.

A better approach is to convert the text entered by the user to all uppercase letters, and then compare the converted text to "PROSPERO". When the user enters the word "prospero" in any combination of upper or lowercase characters, this test will return true. Modify the code by adding a call to the ToUpper method, as shown in the following code.

```
If txtInput.Text.ToUpper = "PROSPERO" Then
    lblMessage.Text = "Congratulations! That " & _
    "is the secret word!"
Else
    lblMessage.Text = "Wrong! That is NOT the secret word!"
End If
```

Step 8:   Run the application. When the form appears, Enter **prospero** in all lowercase letters and click the Ok button. This time you see the message "Congratulations! That is the secret word!" You can experiment with various combinations of upper- and lowercase letters. As long as you type the word "prospero" the application will recognize it as the secret word.

Step 9:   Exit the application.

The ToLower method can also be used in Tutorial 4-6 to accomplish the same result, as shown in the following code. Just make sure you compare the return value of the ToLower method to an all lowercase string.

```
If txtInput.Text.ToLower = "prospero" Then
    lblMessage.Text = "Congratulations! That " & _
    "is the secret word!"
Else
    lblMessage.Text = "Wrong! That is NOT the secret word!"
End If
```

The IsNumeric Function

The intrinsic *IsNumeric function* accepts a string as its argument and returns true if the string contains a number. The function returns false if the string's contents cannot be recognized as a number. Here is the function's general use:

```
IsNumeric(StringExpression)
```

Here is an example:

```
stringNumber = "576"
If IsNumeric(stringNumber) Then
    lblMessage.Text = "It is a number"
Else
    lblMessage.Text = "It is NOT a number"
End If
```

In this statement, the expression IsNumeric(stringNumber) will return true because the contents of stringNumber can be recognized as a number. In the following code segment, however, the expression will return false.

```
stringNumber = "123abc"
If IsNumeric(stringNumber) Then
    lblMessage.Text = "It is a number"
Else
    lblMessage.Text = "It is NOT a number"
End If
```

In some applications, you want the user to enter numeric data only. The `IsNumeric` function is very useful for checking user input and confirming that it is valid.

Determining the Length of a String

The `Length` *method*, which is a member of the String data type, allows you to determine the length of a string. The general format of the method is:

```
StringExpression.Length
```

The method returns the number of characters in the string stored in `StringExpression`. Here is an example:

```
Dim name As String = "Herman"
Dim numChars As Integer
numChars = name.Length
```

The code stores 6 in `numChars` because the length of the string "Herman" is 6.

You can also determine the length of a control's Text property with the `Length` method, as shown in the following code.

```
If txtInput.Text.Length > 20 Then
    lblMessage.Text = "Please enter no more than 20 characters."
End If
```

There are many situations in which the `Length` method is useful. One example is when you must display or print a string and have only a limited amount of space.

WARNING:

If you attempt to use the `Length` method with an uninitialized string variable a run-time error will occur. You can prevent this error from occurring by initializing string variables with an empty string, as shown in the following statement:

```
Dim str As String = ""
```

TIP: Visual Basic .NET also provides the Len intrinsic function, which may be used to determine the length of a string. See Appendix B for more information.

Trimming Spaces from Strings

Sometimes it is necessary to trim leading and/or trailing spaces from a string before performing other operations on the string, such as a comparison. A *leading space* is a space that appears at the beginning, or left side, of a string. For instance, the following string has three leading spaces:

```
"   Hello"
```

A *trailing space* is a space that appears at the end, or right side, of a string, after the nonspace characters. The following string has three trailing spaces:

```
"Hello   "
```

The String data type has three methods for removing spaces: TrimStart, TrimEnd, and Trim. Here is the general format of each method.

```
StringExpression.TrimStart
StringExpression.TrimEnd
StringExpression.Trim
```

The *TrimStart method* returns a copy of the string expression with all leading spaces removed. The *TrimEnd method* returns a copy of the string expression with all trailing spaces removed. The *Trim method* returns a copy of the string expression with all leading and trailing spaces removed. Here is an example:

```
greeting = "   Hello   "
lblMessage1.Text = greeting.TrimStart
lblMessage2.Text = greeting.TrimEnd
lblMessage3.Text = greeting.Trim
```

In this code, the first statement assigns the string "   Hello   " (with three leading spaces and three trailing spaces) to the string variable greeting. In the second statement the TrimStart method is called. Its return value, which is "Hello   ", is assigned to lblMessage1.Text. In the third statement the TrimEnd method is called. Its return value, which is "   Hello", is assigned to lblMessage2.Text. In the fourth statement the Trim method is called. Its return value, which is "Hello", is assigned to lblMessage3.Text.

Note that these methods do not modify the string variable, but return a modified copy of the variable. To actually modify the string variable you must use a statement such as

```
greeting = greeting.Trim
```

After this statement executes, the greeting variable will no longer contain leading or trailing spaces.

Like the Length method, these methods may also be used with a control's Text property. Here is an example.

```
Dim name As String
name = txtName.Text.Trim
```

TIP: Visual Basic .NET also provides the LTrim, RTrim, and Trim intrinsic functions, which perform the same operations as the TrimStart, TrimEnd, and Trim methods. See Appendix B for more information.

The Substring Method

The *Substring method* returns a substring, or a string within a string. There are two different formats for the method, which are:

```
StringExpression.Substring(Start)
StringExpression.Substring(Start, Length)
```

The positions of the characters in *StringExpression* are numbered, with the first character at position 0. In the first format shown for the method, an integer argument, *Start*, indicates the starting position of the string that is to be extracted from *StringExpression*. The method returns a string containing all the characters from the *Start* position to the end of *StringExpression*. For example, look at the following code.

```
Dim lastName As String
Dim fullName As String = "George Washington"
lastName = fullName.Substring(7)
```

After this code executes, the variable `lastName` will contain the string "Washington". This is because "Washington" begins at position 7 in `fullName`, and continues to the end of the string.

In the second format shown for the method, a second integer argument, *Length*, is given. The *Length* argument indicates the number of characters to extract, including the starting character. For example, look at the following code:

```
Dim firstName As String
Dim fullName As String = "George Washington"
firstName = fullName.Substring(0, 6)
```

In this code, the `Substring` method returns the 6 characters that begin at position 0 in `fullName`. After the code executes, the variable `firstName` will contain the string "George".

TIP: Visual Basic .NET also provides the `Left`, `Right`, and `Mid` intrinsic functions which extract substrings. See Appendix B for more information.

The `IndexOf` Method

The `IndexOf` method is used to search for a character or a string within a string. The method has three general formats, which are:

```
StringExpression.IndexOf(SearchString)
StringExpression.IndexOf(SearchString, Start)
StringExpression.IndexOf(SearchString, Start, Count)
```

In the first format, *SearchString* is the string or character to search for within *String Expression*. The method returns the character position, or index, of the first occurrence of *SearchString* if it is found within *StringExpression*. If *SearchString* is not found, the method returns -1. For example, look at the following code.

```
Dim name As String = "Angelina Adams"
Dim position As Integer
position = name.IndexOf("e")
```

After this code executes, the variable `position` will contain the value 3. This is because the character "e" is found at character position 3. (With the `IndexOf` method, the first character position is 0.)

In the second format shown for the method, a second argument, *Start*, is an integer that specifies a starting position within *StringExpression* for the search to begin. Here is an example:

```
Dim name As String = "Angelina Adams"
Dim position As Integer
position = name.IndexOf("A", 1)
```

After the code executes, the variable `position` will contain 9. The `IndexOf` method begins its search at character position 1 (the second character), so the first "A" is skipped.

NOTE: *The `IndexOf` method performs a case-sensitive search. When searching for "A" it does not return the position of "a".*

In the third format shown for the method, a third argument, *Count*, is an integer that specifies the number of characters within *StringExpression* to search. Here is an example:

```
Dim name As String = "Angelina Adams"
Dim position As Integer
position = name.IndexOf("A", 1, 7)
```

After the code executes, the variable `position` will contain -1. The `IndexOf` method searches only 7 characters, beginning at character 1. Because "A" is not found in the characters searched, the method returns -1.

WARNING:

A run-time error will occur if the starting position argument is negative or specifies a non-existent position.

The following code shows how to use the `IndexOf` method to determine if a search string exists within a string.

```
Dim name As String = "Angelina Adams"
If name.IndexOf("Adams") = -1 Then
    lblMessage.Text = "Adams is not found"
End If
```

TUTORIAL 4-7:

Examining an application that works with strings

In this tutorial, you examine an application that uses string methods to determine if a software serial number, which is entered by the user, is valid. Valid serial numbers are 10 characters long, and in the following format:

```
NNNNAAAAAA
```

In this format, each N represents a numeric digit and each A represents an alphabetic character. For example, 5714ASDFQZ is a valid serial number, but 47QR61ZDBH is not. If the serial number entered by the user is not in the correct format, it is invalid.

Step 1: Start Visual Basic .NET and open the Serial Number project, which is stored in the \Chap4\Serial Number folder on the student disk.

Step 2:   Run the application. The form shown in Figure 4-15 appears.

Step 3:   Enter **5714ASDFQZ** as the serial number and click the Ok button. You see the message "The serial number is valid".

Step 4:   Enter **47QR61ZDBH** as the serial number and click the Ok button. You see the message "The serial number is invalid".

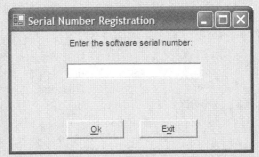

Figure 4-15   Serial Number Registration form

Step 5:   Click the Exit button to end the application.

Step 6:   In the Visual Basic .NET environment, open the Code window and find the btnOk_Click event procedure. The code is as follows.

```
Private Sub btnOk_Click(ByVal sender As System.Object, _
        ByVal e As System.EventArgs) Handles btnOk.Click
   ' This procedure tests the serial number entered by the user.
   ' A message is displayed indicating the validity of the serial
   ' number.

   ' Local Variable Declarations
   Dim serial As String ' To hold the entered serial number
   Dim group1 As String ' To hold the 1st group of characters
   Dim group2 As String ' To hold the 2nd group of characters
   Dim isValid As Boolean ' To signal the input's validity

   ' Initialize the flag to True
   isValid = True
   ' Get the serial number with spaces trimmed
   serial = txtSerialNumber.Text.Trim
   ' Check the length
   If serial.Length = 10 Then
       ' Extract the first four characters
       group1 = serial.Substring(0, 4)
       ' Extract the rest of the characters
       group2 = serial.Substring(4)
        ' Test group1
       If Not IsNumeric(group1) Then
           isValid = False
       End If
       ' Test group2
       If IsNumeric(group2) Then
           isValid = False
       End If
   Else
       ' This executes if serial is not 10 characters long.
       isValid = False
   End If
```

```
        ' Display a message indicating that the serial number
        ' is valid or invalid.
        If isValid Then
            lblMessage.Text = "The serial number is valid"
    Else
            lblMessage.Text = "The serial number is invalid"
        End If
End Sub
```

Let's look at each part of the function, beginning with the variable declarations:

```
Dim serial As String ' To hold the entered serial number
Dim group1 As String ' To hold the 1st group of characters
Dim group2 As String ' To hold the 2nd group of characters
Dim isValid As Boolean ' To signal the input's validity
```

The `serial` string variable will hold the serial number. The variables `group1` and `group2` will be used to hold groups of characters, copied from the `serial` variable. The Boolean `isValid` variable will be used as a flag to indicate whether the serial number is valid.

The following statements appear next:

```
' Initialize the flag to True
isValid = True
' Get the serial number with spaces trimmed
serial = txtSerialNumber.Text.Trim
```

First the `isValid` variable is set to true. Then the contents of the `txtSerial-Number` control's Text property, with leading and trailing spaced trimmed, is copied to the `serial` variable.

The following `If...Then...Else` statement appears next.

```
' Check the length
If serial.Length = 10 Then
    ' Extract the first four characters
    group1 = serial.Substring(0, 4)
    ' Extract the rest of the characters
    group2 = serial.Substring(4)
     ' Test group1
    If Not IsNumeric(group1) Then
        isValid = False
    End If
     ' Test group2
    If IsNumeric(group2) Then
        isValid = False
    End If
Else
    ' This executes if serial is not 10 characters long.
    isValid = False
End If
```

Here's a summary of what this code does: If the length of `serial` is equal to 10, the first four characters in `serial` are copied to `group1`, and the remaining characters are copied to `group2`. The following `If...Then` statement tests `group1` to determine if its contents are not numeric. If the group of characters is not numeric, `isValid` is set to false.

```
' Test group1
If Not IsNumeric(group1) Then
    isValid = False
End If
```

The following `If...Then` statement then tests `group2` to determine if its contents are numeric. If the group of characters is numeric, `isValid` is set to false.

```
' Test group2
If IsNumeric(group2) Then
    isValid = False
End If
```

The following `Else` statement executes if the length of `serial` is not 10:

```
Else
    ' This executes if serial is not 10 characters long.
    isValid = False
End If
```

After this code executes, `isValid` will be still be set to true if the serial number is valid. Otherwise, `isValid` will be set to false. The following code then displays a message in the `lblMessage` control indicating whether the serial number is valid or invalid.

```
' Display a message indicating that the serial number
' is valid or invalid.
If isValid Then
    lblMessage.Text = "The serial number is valid"
Else
    lblMessage.Text = "The serial number is invalid"
End If
```

✓ Checkpoint

4.9 Are each of the following relational expressions true or false?

a. `"ABC" > "XYZ"`

b. `"AAA" = "AA"`

c. `"ABC123" < "abc123"`

4.10 Match the description in the right column with the method or function in the left column.

_____ `IsNumeric`   a. Returns the uppercase equivalent of a string.

_____ `ToLower`   b. Returns the number of characters in a string.

_____ `ToUpper`   c. Returns a copy of a string without trailing spaces.

_____ Length	d.	Returns a copy of a string without leading or trailing spaces.
_____ TrimStart	e.	Searches for the first occurrence of a character or string within a string.
_____ Substring	f.	Accepts a string as its argument and returns true if the string contains a number.
_____ IndexOf	g.	Returns the lowercase equivalent of a string.
_____ TrimEnd	h.	extracts a string from within a string.
_____ Trim	i.	Returns a copy of a string without leading spaces.

▶ 4.9 Focus on GUI Design: The Message Box

CONCEPT

SOMETIMES YOU NEED A CONVENIENT WAY TO DISPLAY A MESSAGE TO THE USER. THIS SECTION INTRODUCES THE MESSAGEBOX.SHOW METHOD, WHICH ALLOWS YOU TO DISPLAY A MESSAGE IN A DIALOG BOX.

A *message box* is a dialog box that displays a message to the user. You display message boxes with the *MessageBox.Show* method. We will discuss five general formats of the method, which are:

```
MessageBox.Show(Message)
MessageBox.Show(Message, Caption)
MessageBox.Show(Message, Caption, Buttons)
MessageBox.Show(Message, Caption, Buttons, Icon)
MessageBox.Show(Message, Caption, Buttons, Icon, _ DefaultButton)
```

When MessageBox.Show is executed, a message box (which is a Windows dialog box) appears on the screen. In the first format shown, *Message* is a string that is displayed in the message box. For example, the following statement causes the message box shown in Figure 4-16 to appear.

```
MessageBox.Show("Operation complete.")
```

Figure 4-16 Message box

In the second format, *Caption* is a string to be displayed in the message box's title bar. The following statement causes the message box shown in figure 4-17 to appear.

```
MessageBox.Show("Operation complete.", "Status")
```

Figure 4-17 Message box with caption

In both of these formats, the message box has only an OK button. In the third format, *Buttons* is a value that specifies which buttons to display in the message box. Table 4-8 lists the available values for *Buttons* and describes each.

Table 4-8

Message box button values

Value	Description
MessageBoxButtons.AbortRetryIgnore	Displays Abort, Retry, and Ignore buttons.
MessageBoxButtons.OK	Displays only an OK button.
MessageBoxButtons.OKCancel	Displays OK and Cancel buttons.
MessageBoxButtons.RetryCancel	Display Retry and Cancel buttons.
MessageBoxButtons.YesNo	Displays Yes and No buttons.
MessageBoxButtons.YesNoCancel	Displays Yes, No, and Cancel buttons.

For example, the following statement causes the message box shown in Figure 4-18 to appear.

```
MessageBox.Show("Do you wish to continue?", "Please Confirm", _
        MessageBoxButtons.YesNo)
```

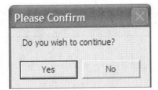

Figure 4-18   **Message box with caption and Yes/No buttons**

In the fourth format, *Icon* is a value that specifies an icon to display in the message box. The available values for *Icon* are MessageBoxIcon.Asterisk, MessageBoxIcon.Error, MessageBoxIcon.Exclamation, MessageBoxIcon.Hand, MessageBoxIcon.Information, MessageBoxIcon.Question, MessageBoxIcon.Stop, and MessageBoxIcon.Warning. Figure 4-19 shows the icons that are displayed for each value. Note that some values display the same icon as others.

For example, the following statement causes the message box shown in Figure 4-20 to appear.

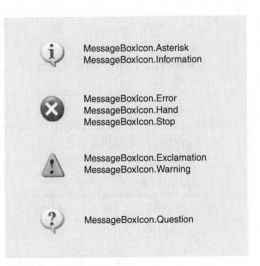

Figure 4-19   **Message box icons**

```
MessageBox.Show("Do you wish to continue?", "Please Confirm", _
        MessageBoxButtons.YesNo , MessageBoxIcon.Question)
```

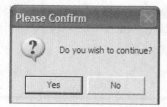

Figure 4-20 Message box with caption, Yes/No buttons, and Question icon

In the fifth format, the *DefaultButton* argument is a value that specifies which button to select as the default button. The default button is the button that is clicked when the user presses the Enter key. Table 4-9 lists the available values for this argument.

Table 4-9

`DefaultButton` values

Value	Description
MessageBoxDefaultButton.Button1	Selects the leftmost button on the message box as the default button.
MessageBoxDefaultButton.Button2	Selects the second button from the left edge of the message box as the default button.
MessageBoxDefaultButton.Button3	Selects the third button from the left edge of the message box as the default button.

For example, the following statement displays a message box and selects button 2 (the No button) as the default button.

```
MessageBox.Show("Do you wish to continue?", "Please Confirm", _
        MessageBoxButtons.YesNo , MessageBoxIcon.Question, _
        MessageBoxDefaultButton.Button2)
```

Determining Which Button the User Clicked

When the user clicks any button on a message box, the message box is dismissed. In code, the `MessageBox.Show` method returns an integer value that indicates which button the user clicked. You can compare the integer returned from the method with the values listed in Table 4-10 to determine which button was clicked.

Table 4-10

`MessageBox.Show` return values

Value	Meaning
DialogResult.Abort	The user clicked the Abort button.
DialogResult.Cancel	The user clicked the Cancel button.
DialogResult.Ignore	The user clicked the Ignore button.
DialogResult.No	The user clicked the No button.
DialogResult.OK	The user clicked the OK button.
DialogResult.Retry	The user clicked the Retry button.
DialogResult.Yes	The user clicked the Yes button.

The following code shows how an `If` statement may be used to take actions based on which message box button the user clicked.

```
Dim result As Integer
result = MessageBox.Show("Do you wish to continue?", "Please Confirm", _
              MessageBoxButtons.YesNo)
If result = DialogResult.Yes Then
    ' Perform an action here
ElseIf result = DialogResult.No Then
    ' Perform another action here
End If
```

Using `ControlChars.CrLf` to Display Multiple Lines

Sometimes you want to display multiple lines of information in a message box. This can be accomplished with the constant `ControlChars.CrLf`. (CrLf stands for "carriage return line feed.") To use `ControlChars.CrLf`, you concatenate it with the string you wish to display, at the position you wish to begin a new line, as shown in this example:

```
MessageBox.Show("This is line 1" & ControlChars.CrLf & _
              "This is line 2")
```

This statement causes the message box in Figure 4-21 to appear. As Visual Basic .NET is displaying the string `"This is line 1" & ControlChars.CrLf & "This is line 2"`, it interprets `ControlChars.CrLf` as a command to begin a new line of output.

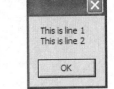

TIP: In code, you can use `ControlChars.CrLf` to create multiple lines in label text too.

Figure 4-21 Message box displaying two lines

✓ **Checkpoint**

4.11 Match each of the message boxes in Figure 4-22 with the statement that displays it.

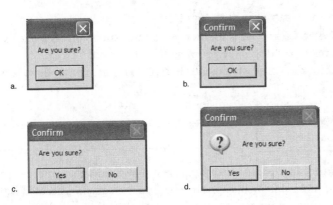

Figure 4-22 Message boxes

```
_____ MessageBox.Show("Are you sure?", "Confirm", MessageBoxButtons.YesNo)
_____ MessageBox.Show("Are you sure?")
_____ MessageBox.Show("Are you sure?", "Confirm", _
                MessageBoxButtons.YesNo, MessageBoxIcon.Question)
_____ MessageBox.Show("Are you sure?", "Confirm")
```

4.12   What value can you compare with the `MessageBox.Show` method's return value to determine if the user has clicked the Abort button?

4.13   The following statement displays William Joseph Smith in a message box. How would you modify the statement so William, Joseph, and Smith appear on three separate lines?

```
MessageBox.Show("William Joseph Smith")
```

▶ 4.10   The Select Case Statement

CONCEPT

IN A SELECT CASE STATEMENT, ONE OF SEVERAL POSSIBLE ACTIONS IS TAKEN, DEPENDING ON THE VALUE OF AN EXPRESSION.

The `If...Then...ElseIf` statement allows your program to branch into one of several possible paths. It performs a series of tests and branches when one of these tests is true. The *Select Case statement*, which is a similar mechanism, tests the value of an expression only once, then uses that value to determine which set of statements to branch to. Following is the general format of the `Select Case` statement. The items inside the brackets are optional.

```
Select Case TestExpression
      [Case ExpressionList
            [one or more statements]]
      [Case ExpressionList
            [one or more statements]]
      ' Case statements may be repeated
      ' as many times as necessary.
      [Case Else
            [one or more statements]]
End Select
```

The first line starts with `Select Case` and is followed by a test expression. The test expression may be any numeric or string expression whose value you wish to test.

Starting on the next line is a block of `Case` statements. Each `Case` statement follows this general form:

```
Case ExpressionList
      one or more statements
```

After the word `Case` is an expression list, so called because it may hold one or more expressions. Beginning on the next line, one or more statements appear. These statements are executed if the value of the test expression matches any of the expressions in the `Case` statement's expression list.

A `Case Else` comes after all the `Case` statements. This section is branched to if none of the `Case` expression lists holds a value matching the test expression. The entire `Select Case` construct is terminated with an `End Select` statement.

WARNING:

The `Case Else` section is optional. If you leave it out, however, your program will have nowhere to branch to if the test expression doesn't match any of the expressions in the `Case` expression lists.

Here is an example of the `Select Case` statement:

```
Select Case Val(txtInput.Text)
    Case 1
        MessageBox.Show("Day 1 is Monday.")
    Case 2
        MessageBox.Show("Day 2 is Tuesday.")
    Case 3
        MessageBox.Show("Day 3 is Wednesday.")
    Case 4
        MessageBox.Show("Day 4 is Thursday.")
    Case 5
        MessageBox.Show("Day 5 is Friday.")
    Case 6
        MessageBox.Show("Day 6 is Saturday.")
    Case 7
        MessageBox.Show("Day 7 is Sunday.")
    Case Else
        MessageBox.Show("That value is invalid.")
End Select
```

Let's look at this example more closely. The test expression is `Val(txtInput.Text)`. The `Case` statements `Case 1`, `Case 2`, `Case 3`, `Case 4`, `Case 5`, `Case 6`, and `Case 7` mark where the program is to branch to if the test expression is equal to the values 1, 2, 3, 4, 5, 6, or 7. The `Case Else` section is branched to if the test expression is not equal to any of these values.

For instance, let's assume the user has entered 3 into the `txtInput` text box, so the expression `Val(txtInput.Text)` is equal to 3. Visual Basic .NET compares this value with the first `Case` statement's expression list:

```
Select Case Val(txtInput.Text)
→   Case 1
        MessageBox.Show("Day 1 is Monday.")
```

The only value in the expression list is 1, and this is not equal to 3, so Visual Basic .NET goes to the next `Case` statement.

```
Select Case Val(txtInput.Text)
    Case 1
        MessageBox.Show "Day 1 is Monday."
→   Case 2
        MessageBox.Show "Day 2 is Tuesday."
```

Once again, the value in the expression list does not equal 3, so Visual Basic .NET goes to the next `Case` statement.

```
Select Case Val(txtInput.Text)
    Case 1
        MessageBox.Show("Day 1 is Monday.")
```

```
     Case 2
          MessageBox.Show("Day 2 is Tuesday.")
→    Case 3
          MessageBox.Show("Day 3 is Wednesday.")
```

This time, the value in the `Case` statement's expression list matches the value of the test expression, so Visual Basic .NET executes the `MessageBox.Show` statement on the next line. (If there had been multiple statements appearing between the `Case 3` and `Case 4` statements, Visual Basic .NET would have executed all of them.) After the `MessageBox.Show` statement is executed, Visual Basic .NET jumps to the statement immediately following the `End Select` statement.

The `Select Case` Structure in Flowcharts and Pseudocode

The flowchart segment in Figure 4-23 shows the general form of a `Case` structure. The diamond represents the test expression, which is compared against a series of values. The path of execution follows the value matching that of the test expression. If none of the values match the test expression, the default path is followed. The default path represents the `Case Else` statement.

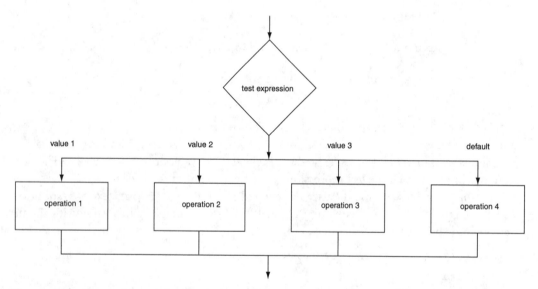

Figure 4-23   General form of a case structure

As with the `If` statement, the pseudocode for the `Select Case` statement looks very similar to the actual programming statements. Here is an example:

Select Input
    Case 1
        Display Message "Day 1 is Monday."
    Case 2
        Display Message "Day 2 is Tuesday."
    Case 3
        Display Message "Day 3 is Wednesday."
    Case 4
        Display Message "Day 4 is Thursday."
    Case 5
        Display Message "Day 5 is Friday."

```
Case 6
     Display Message "Day 6 is Saturday."
Case 7
     Display Message "Day 7 is Sunday."
Case Else
     Display Message "That value is invalid."
End Select
```

More About the Expression List

The `Case` statement's expression list can contain multiple expressions, separated by commas. For example, the first `Case` statement in the following code compares `number` to 1, 3, 5, 7, and 9, and the second `Case` statement compares it to 2, 4, 6, 8, and 10. Assume that `status` is a string variable.

```
Select Case number
    Case 1, 3, 5, 7, 9
        status = "Odd"
    Case 2, 4, 6, 8, 10
        status = "Even"
    Case Else
        status = "Out of Range"
End Select
```

The `Case` statement can also test string values. In the following code assume that `animal` is a string variable:

```
Select Case animal
    Case "Dogs", "Cats"
        MessageBox.Show ("House Pets")
    Case "Cows", "Pigs", "Goats"
        MessageBox.Show ("Farm Animals")
    Case "Lions", "Tigers", "Bears"
            MessageBox.Show ("Oh My!")
End Select
```

You may also use relational operators in the `Case` statement. However, the `Is` key word is required. In the following example assume that `temperature` is a Single variable and `tooCold`, `tooHot`, and `justRight` are Boolean variables:

```
Select Case temperature
    Case Is <= 75
        tooCold = True
    Case Is >= 100
        tooHot = True
    Case Else
        justRight = True
End Select
```

The `Is` key word represents the test expression in the relational comparison.

Finally, you may determine whether the test expression falls within a range of values with the `Case` statement. This requires the `To` key word, as shown in the following code. Assume that `score` is an integer variable and `grade` is a string variable:

```
Select Case score
    Case Is >= 90
        grade = "A"
    Case 80 To 89
        grade = "B"
    Case 70 To 79
        grade = "C"
    Case 60 To 69
        grade = "D"
    Case 0 To 59
        grade = "F"
    Case Else
        MessageBox.Show("Invalid Score")
End Select
```

The numbers used on each side of the `To` key word are included in the range. So, the statement `Case 80 To 89` will match the values 80, 89, or any number between.

TIP: The `To` key word only works properly when the smaller number appears on its left and the larger number appears on its right. You can write an expression such as `10 To 0`, but it will not function properly at run time.

TUTORIAL 4-8:

Examining Crazy Al's sales commission calculator application

Crazy Al's Computer Emporium is a retail seller of personal computers. The sales staff at Crazy Al's work strictly on commission. At the end of the month, each salesperson's commission is calculated according to Table 4-11.

Table 4-11

Sales commission rates

Sales This Month	Commission Rate
Less than $10,000	5%
$10,000 - $14,999	10%
$15,000 - $17,999	12%
$18,000 - $21,999	14%
$22,000 or more	16%

For example, a salesperson with $16,000 in monthly sales would earn a 12% commission ($1,920.00). A salesperson with $20,000 in monthly sales would earn a 14% commission ($2,800.00)

Because the staff is paid once per month, Crazy Al's allows each employee to take up to $1,500 per month in advance. When sales commissions are calculated, the amount of each employee's advance pay is subtracted from the commission. If any salesperson's commissions are less than the amount of the advance, he or she must reimburse Crazy Al's for the difference.

Here are two examples: Beverly and John have $21,400 and $12,600 in sales, respectively. Beverly's commission is $2,996 and John's commission is $1,260. Both Beverly and John took $1,500 in advance pay. At the end of the month, Beverly gets a check for $1,496, but John must pay $240 back to Crazy Al's.

In this tutorial, you examine the sales commission calculator application that Crazy Al uses to determine a salesperson's commission.

Step 1: Start Visual Basic .NET and open the Crazy Al project, which is stored in the \Chap4\Crazy Al folder on the student disk.

Step 2: Run the application. The form shown in Figure 4-24 appears.

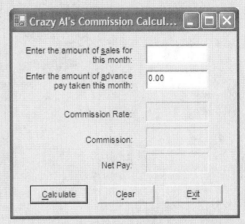

Figure 4-24   Crazy Al's Commission Calculator form

Step 3: Enter **16000** as the amount of sales for this month (first text box).

Step 4: Enter **1000** as the amount of advance pay taken (second text box). Click the Calculate button. You should see the commission rate, commission, and net pay information shown in Figure 4-25.

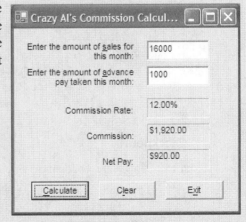

Figure 4-25   Calculations filled in

Step 5: Click the Clear button to reset the contents of the input and display fields. Experiment with other values for sales and advance.

Step 6: When you are finished, click the Exit button to end the application.

Step 7: In the Visual Basic .NET environment, open the Code window and find the `btnCalculate_Click` event procedure. The code is as follows.

```
Private Sub btnCalculate_Click(ByVal sender As System.Object, _
        ByVal e As System.EventArgs) Handles btnCalculate.Click
    ' This procedure determines the sales commission.
    Dim sales As Decimal      ' Monthly sales amount
    Dim advance As Decimal     ' Advance pay taken
    Dim rate As Single        ' Commission rate
    Dim commission As Decimal' Commission
    Dim netPay As Decimal      ' Net pay

    ' Get the values for sales and advance pay.
    sales = Val(txtSales.Text)
    advance = Val(txtAdvance.Text)

    ' Determine the rate of commission.
    Select Case sales
        Case Is < 10000
            rate = 0.05
        Case 10000 To 14999
            rate = 0.1
        Case 15000 To 17999
            rate = 0.12
        Case 18000 To 21999
            rate = 0.14
        Case Is >= 22000
            rate = 0.15
    End Select
    ' Calculate the amount of commission and net pay.
    commission = sales * rate
    netPay = commission - advance
    ' Display the rate, commission, and net pay.
    lblRate.Text = FormatPercent(rate)
    lblCommission.Text = FormatCurrency(commission)
    lblNetPay.Text = FormatCurrency(netPay)
End Sub
```

As you can see, the `Select Case` construct has a `Case` statement for each level of sales in the commission table.

✓ Checkpoint

4.14 Convert the following `If...Then...ElseIf` statement into a `Select Case` statement.

```
If quantity >= 0 And quantity <= 9 Then
    discount = 0.1
Else If quantity >= 10 And quantity <= 19 Then
    discount = 0.2
```

```
Else If quantity >= 20 And quantity <= 29 Then
    discount = 0.3
ElseIf quantity >= 30 Then
    discount = 0.4
Else
    MessageBox.Show("Invalid Data")
End If
```

▶ 4.11 Introduction to Input Validation

The accuracy of a program's output is only as good as the accuracy of its input. For this reason it is important that your applications perform input validation on the values entered by the user. *Input validation* is the process of inspecting input values and determining whether they are valid.

CONCEPT

INPUT VALIDATION IS THE PROCESS OF INSPECTING INPUT VALUES AND DETERMINING WHETHER THEY ARE VALID.

Now that you have learned about decision structures, you can begin to equip your applications with input validation. For example, consider the Crazy Al's commission calculator application previously discussed. The `btnCalculate_Click` procedure gets the amount of a salesperson's sales and advance pay taken (values entered by the user) and calculates the sales commission. Any numbers entered by the user, even negative numbers, are used in the calculation because the procedure does not validate the values. The following code shows part of the procedure after it has been modified to validate the user's input. (The new lines of code are shown in bold.)

```
' Get the values for sales and advance pay.
sales = Val(txtSales.Text)
advance = Val(txtAdvance.Text)
' Validate the input to ensure that
' no negative numbers were entered.
If sales < 0 Or advance < 0 Then
        MessageBox.Show("Please enter positive numbers for " & _
                " sales and/or advance pay.")
Else
    ' Determine the rate of commission.
    Select Case sales
        Case Is < 10000
            rate = 0.05
        Case 10000 To 14999
            rate = 0.1
    (Code continues)
EndIf
```

The `If...Then...Else` statement displays an error message if `sales` or `advance` contain negative numbers. The commission calculations are only performed when these variables contain nonnegative numbers. This code could be further modified to use the `IsNumeric` function to determine if the user has entered nonnumeric data.

▶ 4.12   Focus on GUI Design: Radio Buttons and Check Boxes

CONCEPT

RADIO BUTTONS APPEAR IN GROUPS OF TWO OR MORE, AND ALLOW THE USER TO SELECT ONE OF SEVERAL POSSIBLE OPTIONS. CHECK BOXES, WHICH MAY APPEAR ALONE OR IN GROUPS, ALLOW THE USER TO MAKE YES/NO OR ON/OFF SELECTIONS.

Radio Buttons

Radio buttons are useful when you want the user to select one choice from several possible choices. Figure 4-26 shows a group of radio buttons.

Figure 4-26   Radio buttons

A radio button may be selected or deselected. Each radio button has a small circle that appears filled-in when the radio button is selected, and appears empty when the radio button is deselected.

Visual Basic .NET provides the *RadioButton control* which allows you to create radio buttons. Radio buttons are normally part of a group, and are grouped together in one of the following ways.

◆   All the radio buttons that are inside a group box are members of the same group.

◆   All the radio buttons on a form that are not inside a group box are members of the same group.

Figure 4-27 shows two forms. The left form has three radio buttons that are part of the same group. The right form has two groups of radio buttons.

 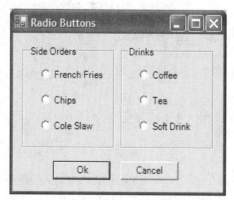

Figure 4-27   Forms with radio buttons

Only one radio button in a group may be selected at any time. Clicking on a radio button selects it, and automatically deselects any other radio button in the same group. Because only one radio button in a group can be selected at any given time, they are said to be mutually exclusive.

NOTE: *The name "radio button" refers to the old car radios that had push buttons for selecting stations. Only one of the buttons could be pushed in at a time. When you pushed a button in, it automatically popped out the currently selected button.*

Radio Button Properties

Like labels and text boxes, radio buttons have a Text property. The Text property holds the text that is displayed next to the radio button's circle. For example, the radio buttons in the leftmost form in Figure 4-27 have their Text properties set to "Coffee", "Tea", and "Soft Drink".

Radio buttons also have a Boolean property named Checked. The *Checked property* is set to true when the radio button is selected and false when the radio button is deselected.

Working with Radio Buttons in Code

The standard prefix for radio button control names is `rad`. You determine if a radio button is selected by testing its Checked property. The following code shows an example. Assume that `radChoice1`, `radChoice2`, and `radChoice3` are radio buttons in the same group.

```
If radChoice1.Checked = True Then
    MessageBox.Show("You selected Choice 1")
ElseIf radChoice2.Checked = True Then
    MessageBox.Show("You selected Choice 2")
ElseIf radChoice3.Checked = True Then
    MessageBox.Show("You selected Choice 3")
End If
```

Assigning a TabIndex Value and an Access Key to a Radio Button

RadioButton controls have a position in the form's tab order which may be changed with the TabIndex property. As with other controls, you may assign an access key to a radio button by placing an ampersand (&) in the Text property, just before the character that you wish to serve as the access key. The character will appear underlined on the form. At run time, when the user presses the Alt+Access key combination, the focus will shift to the radio button, and the radio button will be selected.

Selecting a Radio Button in Code

You can use code to select a radio button. Simply use an assignment statement to set the desired radio button's Checked property to true. Here is an example:

```
radChoice1.Checked = True
```

Setting a Default Radio Button

If you set a radio button's Checked property to true at design time (with the Properties window), it will become the default radio button for that group. It will initially be selected when the application starts up and will remain selected until the user or application code selects another radio button.

The Radio Button's CheckChanged Event

Radio buttons have a *CheckChanged event* that is triggered whenever the user selects or deselects a radio button. If you double-click a radio button in the Design window, a code template for the `CheckChanged` event procedure will be created in the Code window. If you have written a `CheckChanged` event procedure for the radio button, it will execute whenever the user selects or deselects the radio button.

Check Boxes

A *check box* appears as a small box, labeled with a caption. An example is shown in Figure 4-28.

Figure 4-28   Check box

Visual Basic provides the *CheckBox control* which allows you to create check boxes. Like radio buttons, check boxes may be selected or deselected at run time. When a check box is selected, a small check mark appears inside the box. Unlike radio buttons, check boxes are not mutually exclusive. You may have one or more check boxes on a form or in a group box, and any number of them can be selected at any given time.

The standard prefix for a CheckBox control's name is chk. Like radio buttons, check boxes have a Checked property. When a check box is selected, or checked, its Checked property is set to true. When a check box is deselected, or unchecked, its Checked property is set to false.

Here is a summary of other characteristics of the check box.

- ◆ A check box's caption is stored in the Text property.
- ◆ A check box's place in the tab order may be modified with the TabIndex property. When a check box has the focus, a thin dotted line appears around its text. You can check or uncheck it by pressing the spacebar.
- ◆ You may assign an access key to a check box. By placing an ampersand (&) in the Text property, just before the character that you wish to serve as the access key.
- ◆ You can use code to select or deselect a check box. Simply use an assignment statement to set the desired check box's Value property. Here is an example:

```
chkChoice4.Checked = True
```

- ◆ You may set a check box's Checked property at design time.
- ◆ Like radio buttons, check boxes have a CheckChanged event which is triggered whenever the user changes the state of the check box. If you have written a CheckChanged event procedure for the check box, it will execute whenever the user checks or unchecks the check box.

In Tutorial 4-9 you examine an application that demonstrates radio buttons and checkboxes.

TUTORIAL 4-9:

Examining an application with check boxes

Step 1:   Start Visual Basic .NET and open the Radio Button Check Box Demo project, which is stored in the \Chap4\Radio Button Check Box Demo folder on the student disk.

Step 2:   Run the application. The form shown in Figure 4-29 appears.

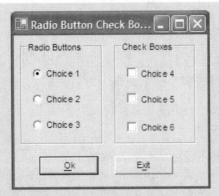

Figure 4-29   Radio Button Check Box Demo form

Step 3:   Click the Choice 3 radio button. Also click the Choice 4 and the Choice 6 check boxes.

Step 4:   Click the Ok button. The message box in Figure 4-30 appears.

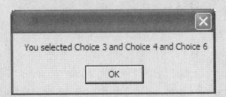

Figure 4-30   Message box

Step 5:   Click the OK button to dismiss the message box. Experiment by selecting the other combinations of radio buttons and check boxes, and clicking the OK button. Notice that each time, a message box appears indicating which choices were made.

Step 6:   Click the Exit button to terminate the application.

Step 7:   The RadioButton controls are named `radChoice1`, `radChoice2` and `radChoice3`. The CheckBox controls are named `chkChoice4`, `chkChoice5` and `chkChoice6`. Open the Code window and find the `btnOk_Click` event procedure. The code is as follows.

```
Private Sub btnOk_Click(ByVal sender As System.Object, _
        ByVal e As System.EventArgs) Handles btnOk.Click
    'Declare a string variable to hold a message.
    Dim message As String

    ' The following If...ElseIf statement tests the
    ' group of radio buttons and copies the
    ' first part of the message to message.
    If radChoice1.Checked = True Then
        message = "You selected Choice 1"
    ElseIf radChoice2.Checked = True Then
        message = "You selected Choice 2"
    ElseIf radChoice3.Checked = True Then
        message = "You selected Choice 3"
    End If
```

```
' The following If...Then statements test the
' check boxes and concatenates another part
' of the message to message.
If chkChoice4.Checked = True Then
    message = message & " and Choice 4"
End If
If chkChoice5.Checked = True Then
    message = message & " and Choice 5"
End If
If chkChoice6.Checked = True Then
    message = message & " and Choice 6"
End If

' Now display the message.
MessageBox.Show(message)
End Sub
```

Notice that the check boxes are tested by a set of If...Then statements, not an If...Then...ElseIf statement. Since all or none of the check boxes may be selected, the code must test each one individually.

✓ **Checkpoint**

4.15   In code, how do you determine whether a radio button has been selected?

4.16   If several radio buttons are placed on a form, not inside group boxes, how many of them may be selected at any given time?

4.17   In code, how do you determine whether a check box has been selected?

4.18   If several check boxes appear on a form, how many of them may be selected at any given time?

4.19   How can the user check or uncheck a check box that has the focus by using the keyboard?

▶ 4.13   Class-Level Variables

CONCEPT

CLASS-LEVEL VARIABLES ARE NOT LOCAL TO ANY PROCEDURE. IN A FORM FILE THEY ARE DECLARED OUTSIDE OF ANY PROCEDURE, AND MAY BE ACCESSED BY STATEMENTS IN ANY PROCEDURE IN THE SAME FORM.

The variables you have worked with so far are local variables. A local variable is declared inside a procedure and can only be accessed by statements in the same procedure. Sometimes, however, you want to access a variable from multiple procedures. This can be accomplished with *class-level variables*.

A class-level variable's Dim statement must appear outside of any procedure. Normally you place the Dim statement for a class-level variable near the top of a form's code, prior to the first procedure. Figure 4-31 shows an example.

```
Public Class Form1
        Inherits System.Windows.Forms.Form

    Windows Form Designer generated code

        ' Class-level variables
        Dim itemCount As Integer         ' Number of items purchased
        Const taxRate As Single = 0.06   ' Sales tax rate

        Private Sub btnCalculate_Click(ByVal sender As System.Object, ByVa
            ' This procedure calculates the total
            ' of the sale.
            Dim subtotal As Decimal
            Dim salesTax As Decimal
            Dim total As Decimal
```

class-level variables ——

Figure 4-31   Declaration of class-level variables

In addition to being outside any procedure, the `Dim` statements for class-level variables must appear somewhere between the `Public Class` statement that appears at the top of the file and the `End Class` statement that appears at the bottom.

NOTE: *Recall that a variable's scope is the part of the program where the variable is visible and may be accessed by programming statements. A class-level variable's scope is the entire form file in which the variable is declared.*

Overuse of Class-Level Variables

Overuse of class-level variables can lead to problems as programs become larger and more complex. While debugging your program, if you find that the wrong value is being stored in a class-level variable, you'll have to track down every statement that accesses it to determine where the bad value is coming from. In a large program, this can be a tedious and time-consuming process.

Also, when two or more procedures modify the same variable, you must be careful that what one procedure does will not upset the accuracy or correctness of another procedure. Although class-level variables make it easy to share information, they require responsibility of the programmer.

✓ Checkpoint

4.20   What is the difference between a class-level variable and a local variable?

4.21   Where do you declare class-level variables?

► 4.14   Focus on Program Design and Problem Solving: Building the Health Club Membership Application

CONCEPT

IN THIS SECTION YOU BUILD THE HEALTH CLUB MEMBERSHIP APPLICATION. THE APPLICATION WILL USE MANY OF THE VISUAL BASIC .NET FEATURES DISCUSSED IN THIS CHAPTER, INCLUDING IF STATEMENTS, A SELECT CASE STATEMENT, RADIO BUTTONS, AND CHECK BOXES.

The Bay City Health and Fitness Club charges the following monthly membership rates:

Standard adult membership: $40/month
Child (age 12 and under): $20/month
Student: $25/month
Senior citizen (age 65 and over): $30/month

The club also offers the following optional services, which increase the base monthly fee:

Yoga lessons: add $10 to the monthly fee
Karate lessons: add $30 to the monthly fee
Personal trainer: add $50 to the monthly fee

Discounts are available, depending on the length of membership:

1 - 3 months: No discount
4 - 6 months: 5% discount
7 - 9 months: 8% discount
10 or more months: 10% discount

The manager of the club has asked you to create a membership fee calculator application. The application should allow the user to select a membership rate, select optional services, and enter the number of months of the membership. It should calculate the member's monthly and total charges for the specified number of months. The application should also validate the number of months entered by the user. An error message should be displayed if the user enters a number less than one or greater than 24. (Membership fees tend to increase every two years, so there is a club policy that no membership package can be purchased for more than 24 months at a time.)

Figure 4-32 shows a sketch of the application's form. The figure also shows the name of each control with a programmer-defined name.

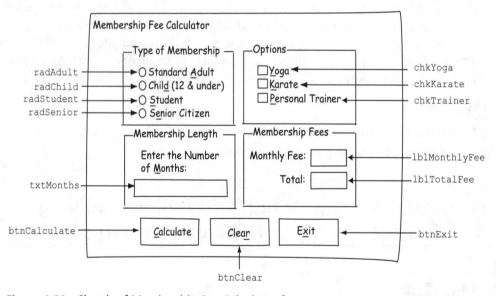

Figure 4-32   Sketch of Membership Fee Calculator form

Table 4-12 lists each control, along with any relevant property settings.

Table 4-12

Health Club Membership Fee Calculator controls

Control Type	Control Name	Properties
Form	(Default)	Text: "Membership Fee Calculator"
Group box	(Default)	Text: "Type of Membership" TabIndex: 0
Radio button	optAdult	Text: "Standard &Adult" TabIndex: 0 (relative to group box)
Radio button	radChild	Text: "Chil&d (12 && under)" TabIndex: 1 (relative to group box)
Radio button	radStudent	Text: "&Student" TabIndex: 2 (relative to group box)
Radio button	radSenior	Text: "S&enior Citizen" TabIndex: 3 (relative to group box)
Group box	(Default)	Text: "Options" TabIndex: 1
Check box	chkYoga	Text: "&Yoga" TabIndex: 0 (relative to group box)
Check box	chkKarate	Text: "&Karate" TabIndex: 1 (relative to group box)
Check box	chkTrainer	Text: "&Personal Trainer" TabIndex: 2 (relative to group box)
Group box	(Default)	Text: "Membership Length" TabIndex: 2
Label	(Default)	Text: "Enter the Number of &Months:" TabIndex: 0 (relative to group box)
Text box	txtMonths	Text: " " TabIndex: 1 (relative to group box)
Group box	(Default)	Text: "Membership Fees"
Label	(Default)	BorderStyle: Fixed3D Text: "Monthly Fee:"
Label	(Default)	BorderStyle: Fixed3D Text: "Total:"
Button	btnCalculate	Text: "&Calculate" TabIndex: 3
Button	btnClear	Text: "Clea&r" TabIndex: 4
Button	btnExit	Text: "E&xit" TabIndex: 5

Table 4-13 lists and describes the event procedures needed for this application.

Table 4-13

Health Club Membership Fee Calculator event procedures

Method	Description
btnCalculate_Click	First this procedure validates the number of months entered by the user. If the input is valid it calculates the monthly fees and the total fee for the time period. Charges for optional services and discounts are included. If the input is not valid, it displays an error message.

Table 4-13 *continued*

Health Club Membership Fee Calculator event procedures

Method	Description
btnClear_Click	Clears the text box, output labels, and check boxes, and resets the radio buttons so radAdult is selected.
btnExit_Click	Ends the application.

Figure 4-33 shows a flowchart for the btnCalculate_Click event procedure.

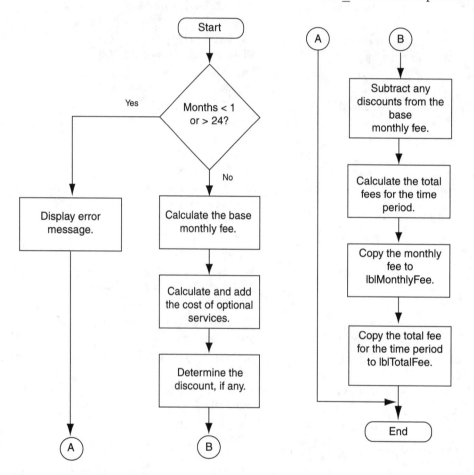

Figure 4-33 Flowchart for btnCalculate_Click

First, the number of months entered by the user is tested to determine if it is valid. If the value is less than 1 or greater than 24, an error message is displayed. If the number of months is valid, the fees are calculated.

The first three processes in the calculation are (1) Calculate the base monthly fee, (2) Calculate and add the cost of optional services, and (3) Determine the discount, if any. Each of these processes can be expanded into more detailed flowcharts. Figure 4-34 shows a more detailed view of the Calculate the base monthly fee process.

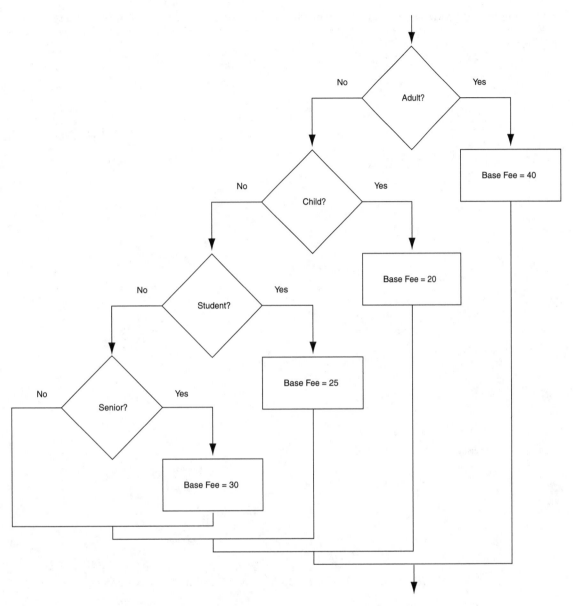

Figure 4-34   Flowchart of calculate the base monthly fee process

The logic in the flowchart can be expressed by the following pseudocode:

If Member is an Adult Then
    Monthly Base Fee = 40.
ElseIf Member is a Child Then
    Montlhy Base Fee = 20.
ElseIf Member is a Student Then
    Monthly Base Fee = 25.
ElseIf Member is a Senior Citizen Then
    Monthly Base Fee = 30.
End If

Figure 4-35 shows a more detailed view of the calculate and add the cost of optional services process.

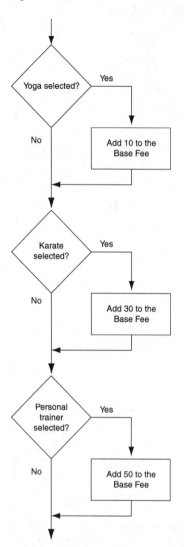

Figure 4-35 Flowchart of calculate and add the cost of optional services process

The logic in the flowchart can be expressed with the following pseudocode:

> *If Yoga is selected Then*
>   *Add 10 to the monthly base fee.*
> *End If*
> *If Karate is selected Then*
>   *Add 30 to the monthly base fee.*
> *End If*
> *If Personal Trainer is selected Then*
>   *Add 50 to the monthly base fee.*
> *End If*

Figure 4-36 shows a more detailed view of the determine the discount, if any process.

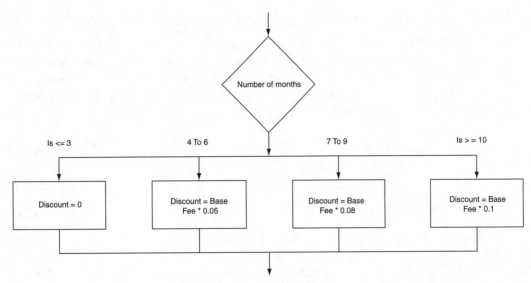

Figure 4-36   Flowchart of determine the discount process

The logic in the flowchart may be expressed with the following pseudocode:

Select number of months
    Case Is <= 3
        Discount = 0% of monthly base fee.
    Case 4 To 6
        Discount = 5% of monthly base fee.
    Case 7 To 9
        Discount = 8% of monthly base fee.
    Case Is >= 10
        Discount = 10% of monthly base fee.
End Select

TUTORIAL 4-10:

Building the Health Club Membership Fee Calculator application

Step 1:   Start Visual Basic .NET and begin a new Windows application project. Name the project Health Club Membership Calculator.

Step 2:   Set the form up as shown in Figure 4-37. Create the group boxes, radio buttons, and check boxes. Refer to the sketch in Figure 4-32 for the control names and Table 4-12 for the relevant property settings of each control.

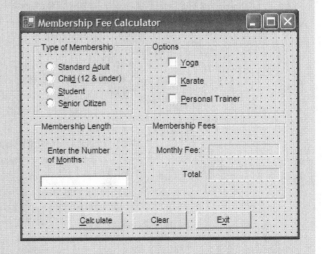

Figure 4-37   Membership Fee Calculator form

Step 3: Once you have placed all the controls on the form and set their properties, you can write the application's code. First you will write the Dim statements for class-level named constants that are used to calculate the discounts. Click the view code button (⊞) on the Solutions Explorer window to open the Code window. Write the following remarks and declarations. (Because these named constants are class-level, they will not be declared inside any procedure.)

```
' The following class-level constants are used
' to calculate discounts.
Const discount4to6 As Decimal = 0.05     ' 4 to 6 months
Const discount7to9 As Decimal = 0.08     ' 7 to 9 months
Const discount10orMore As Single = 0.1   ' 10 or more mo.
```

Step 4: Open the Design window and double-click the btnCalculate button to create the code template for the control's Click event procedure. Complete the event procedure by typing the lines shown in bold as follows.

```
Private Sub btnCalculate_Click(ByVal sender As System.Object, _
        ByVal e As System.EventArgs) Handles btnCalculate.Click
    'Calculate and display the membership fees.

    ' Declare the local variables
    Dim baseFee As Decimal ' Base Monthly Fee
    Dim discount As Decimal ' Discount
    Dim totalFee As Decimal ' Total Membership Fee

    ' Validate the number of months.
    If Val(txtMonths.Text) < 1 Or Val(txtMonths.Text) > 24 Then
    MessageBox.Show("Enter a value in the range of 1 - 24 for " & _
                    "months.", "Input Error")
    Else
        ' Calculate the base monthly fee.
        If radAdult.Checked = True Then
            baseFee = 40
        ElseIf radChild.Checked = True Then
            baseFee = 20
        ElseIf radStudent.Checked = True Then
            baseFee = 25
        ElseIf radSenior.Checked = True Then
            baseFee = 30

        End If
        ' Add any additional services.
        If chkYoga.Checked = True Then
            baseFee = baseFee + 10
        End If
        If chkKarate.Checked = True Then
            baseFee = baseFee + 30
        End If
        If chkTrainer.Checked = True Then
            baseFee = baseFee + 50
        End If
```

```
        ' Determine the discount.
        Select Case Val(txtMonths.Text)
            Case Is <= 3
                discount = 0
            Case 4 To 6
                discount = baseFee * discount4to6
            Case 7 To 9
                discount = baseFee * discount7to9
            Case Is >= 10
                discount = baseFee * discount10orMore
        End Select

        ' Adjust the base fee for any discounts.
        baseFee = baseFee - discount
        ' Calculate the total membership fee.
        totalFee = baseFee * Val(txtMonths.Text)

        ' Display the fees.
        lblMonthlyFee.Text = FormatCurrency(baseFee)
        lblTotalFee.Text = FormatCurrency(totalFee)
        End if
    End Sub
```

Step 5: Return to the Design window and double-click the `btnClear` button to create the code template for the control's `Click` event procedure. Complete the event procedure by typing the lines shown in bold as follows.

```
Private Sub btnClear_Click(ByVal sender As System.Object, _
        ByVal e As System.EventArgs) Handles btnClear.Click
    ' Clear the form and reset the radio buttons
    ' and check boxes
    radAdult.Checked = True
    chkYoga.Checked = False
    chkKarate.Checked = False
    chkTrainer.Checked = False
    txtMonths.Clear()
    lblMonthlyFee.Text = ""
    lblTotalFee.Text = ""
End Sub
```

Step 6: Return to the Design window and double-click the `btnExit` button to create the code template for the control's `Click` event procedure. Complete the event procedure by typing the lines shown in bold as follows.

```
Private Sub btnExit_Click(ByVal sender As System.Object, _
        ByVal e As System.EventArgs) Handles btnExit.Click
        ' End the application.
    End
End Sub
```

Step 7: Save the project.

Step 8:   Attempt to run the application. If there are errors, refer to the code previously shown and correct them. If you make corrections, be sure to save the project again. Once the application runs, enter the following test data and confirm that it displays the correct output.

Type of Membership	Monthly Fee	Total
Standard adult with yoga, karate, and personal trainer for six months.	$123.50	$741.00
Child with karate for 3 months.	$50.00	$150.00
Student with yoga for 12 months.	$31.50	$378.00
Senior citizen with karate and personal trainer for 8 months.	$101.20	$809.60

Step 9:   End the application.

SUMMARY

The decision structure allows a program to have more than one path of execution.

The `If...Then` statement can cause other statements to execute under certain conditions.

A relational operator determines whether a specific relationship exists between two values.

Relational expressions can only be evaluated as true or false.

You can use math operators and function calls with relational operators.

A flag is a Boolean variable that signals when some condition exists in the program.

A non-Boolean variable or expression is considered false if its value is 0. If its value is anything other than 0, it is considered true.

The `If...Then...Else` statement will execute one group of statements if a condition is true, and another group of statements if the condition is false.

The `If...Then...ElseIf` statement is like a chain of `If...Then...Else` statements. They perform their tests, one after the other, until one of them is found to be true.

A nested `If` statement is an `If` statement in the conditionally executed code of another `If` statement.

Logical operators connect two or more relational expressions into one (using `And`, `Or`, or `Xor`), or reverse the logic of an expression (using `Not`).

The `And` logical operator connects two expressions into one. Both expressions must be true for the overall expression to be true.

The `Or` logical operator connects two expressions into one. One or both expressions must be true for the overall expression to be true. It is only necessary for one to be true, and it does not matter which.

The `Xor` operator takes two expressions as operands and creates an expression that is true when one, but not both, of the subexpressions is true.

The `Not` operator reverses the logical value of an expression. It makes a true expression false, and a false expression true.

When determining whether a number is inside a numeric range, it's best to use the `And` operator.

When determining whether a number is outside a range, it's best to use the `Or` operator.

You may use relational operators to compare strings.

An empty string is represented by two quotation marks, with no space between them.

The `ToUpper` method returns the uppercase equivalent of a string. The `ToLower` method returns the lowercase equivalent of a string.

The intrinsic `IsNumeric` function accepts a string as its argument and returns true if the string contains a number. The function returns false if the string's contents cannot be recognized as a number.

The `Length` method returns the number of characters in a string.

The `TrimStart` method returns a copy of a string without leading spaces. The `TrimEnd` method returns a copy of a string without leading spaces. The `Trim` method returns a copy of a string without leading or trailing spaces.

The `Substring` method extracts a specified number of characters from within a specified position in a string.

The `IndexOf` method is used to search for a character or a string within a string.

You display message boxes with the `MessageBox.Show` method. You may specify the types of buttons and an icon to display in the message box.

You can test the return value of the `MessageBox.Show` method to determine which button the user clicked to dismiss the message box.

The value `ControlChars.CrLf` can be concatenated with a string to produce multiple line displays.

In a `Select Case` statement, one of several possible actions is taken, depending on the value of an expression.

Radio buttons appear in groups and allow the user to select one of several possible options. Radio buttons that are placed inside a group box are treated as one group, separate and distinct from any other groups of radio buttons. Only one radio button in a group can be selected at any time.

Clicking on a radio button selects it and automatically deselects any other radio button that is currently selected in the same group.

Check boxes, which may appear alone or in groups, allow the user to make yes/no or on/off selections. Unlike radio buttons, check boxes are not mutually exclusive. You may have one or more check boxes on a form, and any number of them can be selected at any given time.

Class-Level variables are available to statements in all the procedures in a form file.

TERMS

And operator	MessageBox.Show
CheckBox control	Nested If statement
CheckChanged event	Not
Checked property	Or operator
Conditionally executed statement	RadioButton control
ControlChars.CrLf	Relational expression
Decision structure	Relational operator
Empty string	Select Case
Flag	Sequence structure
If...Then	ToLower method
If...Then...Else	ToUpper method
If...Then...ElseIf	Trailing space
Input validation	Trim
IsNumeric function	TrimEnd
Leading space	TrimStart
Length	Unicode
Logical operator	Xor operator
Message box	

Review Questions

Fill-in-the-blank

1. The _____ statement can cause other statements to execute under certain conditions.

2. A(n) _____ operator determines if a specific relationship exists between two values.

3. Relational expressions can only be evaluated as _____ or _____.

4. A(n) _____ is a Boolean variable that signals when some condition exists in the program.

5. A non-Boolean variable or expression is considered _____ if its value is 0. If its value is anything other than 0, it is considered _____.

6. The _____ statement will execute one group of statements if the condition is true, and another group of statements if the condition is false.

7. The _____ statement is like a chain of If...Then...Else statements. They perform their tests, one after the other, until one of them is found to be true.

8. A _____ If statement is an If statement in the conditionally executed code of another If statement.

9. _____ operators connect two or more relational expressions into one or reverse the logic of an expression.

10. The _____ method returns the uppercase equivalent of a string.

11. The _____ method returns a lowercase version of a string.

12. The _____ intrinsic function accepts a string as its argument and returns true if the string contains a number, or false if the string's contents cannot be recognized as a number.

13. The _____ method returns the number of characters in a string.

14. The _____ method returns a copy of a string without leading spaces.

15. The _____ method returns a copy of a string without trailing spaces.

16. The _____ method returns a copy of the string without leading or trailing spaces.

17. The _____ method extracts a specified number of characters from within a specified position in a string.

18. You can display message boxes with the _____ method.

19. The value _____ can be concatenated with a string to produce multiple line displays.

20. In a(n) _____ statement, one of several possible actions is taken, depending on the value of an expression.

21. _____ is the process of inspecting input values and determining whether they are valid.

22. _____ usually appear in groups and allow the user to select one of several possible options.

23. _____ may appear alone or in groups and allow the user to make yes/no, or on/off, selections.

24. A _____ variable may be accessed by statements in any procedure in the same file as the variable's declaration.

Multiple Choice

1. Relational operators allow you to _____ numbers.
   a. Add
   b. Multiply
   c. Compare
   d. Average

2. This statement can cause other program statements to execute only under certain conditions.
   a. `MessageBox.Show`
   b. `Decide`
   c. `If`
   d. `Execute`

3. This is a variable, usually a Boolean, that signals when a condition exists.
   a. Relational operator
   b. Flag
   c. Arithmetic operator
   d. Float

4. This statement is like a chain of `If` statements. They perform their tests, one after the other, until one of them is found to be true.
   a. `If...Then`
   b. `If...Then...ElseIf`
   c. `Chain...If`
   d. `Relational`

5. A trailing _____ placed at the end of an `If...Then...ElseIf` statement provides default action when none of the `ElseIf` statements have true expressions.

   a. `If`

   b. `Select`

   c. `Otherwise`

   d. `Else`

6. When an `If` statement is placed within the conditionally executed code of another `If` statement, this is known as:

   a. A nested `If` statement

   b. A complex `If` statement

   c. A compound `If` statement

   d. An invalid `If` statement

7. This operator connects two expressions into one. One or both expressions must be true for the overall expression to be true. It is only necessary for one to be true, and it does not matter which.

   a. `And`

   b. `Or`

   c. `Xor`

   d. `Not`

8. This operator connects two expressions into one. Both expressions must be true for the overall expression to be true.

   a. `And`

   b. `Or`

   c. `Xor`

   d. `Not`

9. This operator reverses the logical value of an expression. It makes a true expression false, and a false expression true.

   a. `And`

   b. `Or`

   c. `Xor`

   d. `Not`

10. This operator connects two expressions into one. One, and only one, of the expressions must be true for the overall expression to be true. If both expressions are true, or if both expressions are false, the overall expression is false.

    a. `And`

    b. `Or`

    c. `Xor`

    d. `Not`

11. When determining whether a number is inside a numeric range, it's best to use this logical operator.

    a. `And`

    b. `Or`

    c. `Xor`

    d. `Not`

12. When determining whether a number is outside a range, it's best to use this logical operator.
    a. And
    b. Or
    c. Xor
    d. Not

13. In code you should test this property of a radio button or a check box to determine whether it is selected.
    a. Selected
    b. Checked
    c. On
    d. Toggle

14. `str` is a string variable. This statement returns the length of the string stored in `str`.
    a. `Length(str)`
    b. `str.Length`
    c. `str.StringSize`
    d. `CharCount(str)`

15. Use this method to display a message box and determine which button the user clicked to dismiss the message box.
    a. `MessageBox.Show`
    b. `MessageBox.Button`
    c. `Message.Box`
    d. `MessageBox.UserClicked`

True or False

Indicate whether each of the following statements is true or false.

1. T F: It is not possible to write an expression that contains more than one logical operator.
2. T F: It is not possible to write expressions that contain math, relational, and logical operators.
3. T F: You may use the relational operators to compare strings.
4. T F: Clicking on a radio button selects it, and leaves any other selected radio button in the same group selected as well.
5. T F: Radio buttons that are placed inside a group box are treated as one group, separate and distinct from any other groups of radio buttons.
6. T F: When a group of radio buttons appears on a form (outside of a group box), any number of them can be selected at any time.
7. T F: You may have one or more check boxes on a form, and any number of them can be selected at any given time.
8. T F: The `If...Then` statement is an example of a sequence structure.
9. T F: The `Dim` statement for a class-level variable appears inside a procedure.
10. T F: The `Substring` method returns a lowercase copy of a string.

Short Answer

1. Describe the difference between the `If...Then...ElseIf` statement and a series of `If...Then` statements.

2. In an `If...Then...ElseIf` statement, what is the purpose of a trailing `Else`?

3. What is a flag and how does it work?

4. Can an `If` statement test expressions other than relational expressions? Explain.

5. Briefly describe how the `And` operator works.

6. Briefly describe how the `Or` operator works.

7. How is the `Xor` operator different from the `Or` operator?

What Do You Think?

1. Why are the relational operators called relational?

2. Answer the following questions about relational expressions with a yes or no.
   a. If it is true that `X > Y` and it is also true that

      `X < Z`, does that mean `Y < Z` is true?

      If it is true that `X >= Y` and it is also true that

      `Z = X`, does that mean that `Z = Y` is true?

      If it is true that `X <> Y` and it is also true that

      `X <> Z`, does that mean that `Z <> Y` is true?

3. Why do most programmers indent the conditionally executed statements in a decision structure?

4. Explain why you cannot convert the following `If...Then...ElseIf` statement into a `Select Case` statement.

```
If temperature = 100 Then
    x = 0
ElseIf population > 1000 Then
    X = 1
ElseIf rate < .1 Then
    X = -1
End If
```

Find the Errors

1. What is syntactically incorrect with each of the following statements?
   a.
   ```
   If x > 100
       MessageBox.Show("Invalid Data")
   End If
   ```
   b.
   ```
   Dim str As String = "Hello"
   Dim stringLength As Integer
   stringLength = Length(str)
   ```
   c.
   ```
   If z < 10 Then
       MessageBox.Show("Invalid Data")
   ```
   d.
   ```
   Dim str As String = "123"
   If str.IsNumeric Then
       MessageBox.Show("It is a number.")
   End If
   ```
   e.
   ```
   Select Case x
       Case < 0
           MessageBox.Show("Value too low.")
   ```

```
      Case > 100
          MessageBox.Show("Value too high.")
      Case Else
          MessageBox.Show("Value just right.")
   End Select
```

Algorithm Workbench

1. Read the following instructions for cooking a pizza, then design a flowchart with a decision structure that depicts the steps necessary to cook the pizza with either thin and crispy or thick and chewy crust.

   ◆ For thin and crispy crust, do not preheat oven. Bake pizza at 450 degrees for 15 minutes.

   ◆ For thick and chewy crust, preheat oven to 400 degrees. Bake pizza for 20 minutes.

      Design a flowchart with a decision structure that depicts the steps necessary to cook the pizza with either thin and crispy or thick and chewy crust.

2. Write an If statement that assigns 0 to x when y is equal to 20.

3. Write an If statement that multiplies payRate by 1.5 when hours is greater than 40.

4. Write an If statement that assigns 0.2 to commissionRate when sales is greater than or equal to $10,000.00.

5. Write an If statement that sets the variable fees to 50 when the Boolean flag variable isMax is set to true.

6. Write an If...Then...Else statement that assigns 1 to x when y is equal to 100. Otherwise it should assign 0 to x.

7. The string variable people contains a list of names, such as "Bill Jim Susan Randy Wilma" and so forth. Write code that searches people for "Gene". If "Gene" is found in people, display a message box indicating that Gene was found.

8. Write an If...Then statement that prints the message "The number is valid" if the variable speed is within the range 0 through 200.

9. Write an If...Then statement that prints the message "The number is not valid" if the variable speed is outside the range 0 through 200.

10. Convert the following If...Then...ElseIf statement into a Select Case statement.

```
If selection = 1 Then
   MessageBox.Show("Pi times radius squared")
ElseIf selection = 2 Then
   MessageBox.Show("Length times width")
ElseIf selection = 3 Then
   MessageBox.Show("Pi times radius squared times height")
ElseIf selection = 4 Then
   MessageBox.Show("Well okay then, good bye!")
Else
   MessageBox.Show("Not good with numbers, eh?")
End If
```

PROGRAMMING CHALLENGES

1. Minimum/Maximum

Create an application that allows the user to enter two numbers on a form similar to one shown in Figure 4-38. The application should determine which number is the smaller and which is the larger, and display a message to the user indicating this. (Display the message in a label or in a message box.)

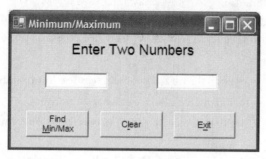

Figure 4-38   Minimum/Maximum form

2. Roman Numeral Converter

Create an application that allows the user to enter a number on a form similar to one shown in Figure 4-39. The number entered by the user should be within the range of 1 through 10. Use either an `If...Then...ElseIf` statement or a `Select Case` statement to display the Roman numeral version of that number. (Display the message in a label or in a message box.)

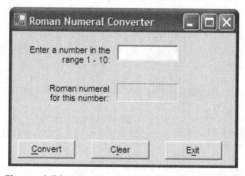

Figure 4-39   Roman Numeral Converter form

The following table lists the Roman numerals for the numbers 1 through 10.

Number	Roman Numeral
1	I
2	II
3	III
4	IV
5	V
6	VI
7	VII
8	VIII
9	IX
10	X

Input validation: Do not accept a number less than 1 or greater than 10. If the user enters a number outside this range, display an error message.

3. Fat Gram Calculator

Create an application that allows the user to enter the number of calories and fat grams in a food. The application should display the percentage of the calories that come from fat. If the calories from fat are less than 30% of the total calories of the food, it should also display a message indicating the food is low in fat. (Display the message in a label or a message box.) The application's form should appear similar to Figure 4-40.

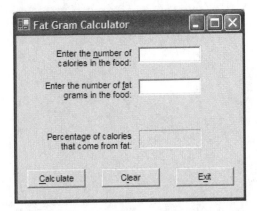

Figure 4-40 Fat Gram Calculator form

One gram of fat has 9 Calories, so:

Calories from fat = fat grams * 9

The percentage of calories from fat can be calculated as:

Percentage of calories from fat = Calories from fat total calories

Input validation: Make sure the number of calories and fat grams are not less than 0. Also, the number of calories from fat cannot be greater than the total number of calories. If that happens, display an error message indicating that either the calories or fat grams were incorrectly entered.

Use the following set of test data to determine if your application is calculating properly:

Calories and Fat	Percentage Fat
200 calories, 8 fat grams	Percentage of calories from fat: 36%
150 calories 2 fat grams	Percentage of calories from fat: 12% (a low-fat food)
500 calories, 30 fat grams	Percentage of calories from fat: 54%

4. Running the Race

Create an application that allows the user to enter the names of three runners and the time it took each of them to finish a race. The application should display who came in first, second, and third place. The application's form should appear similar to Figure 4-41.

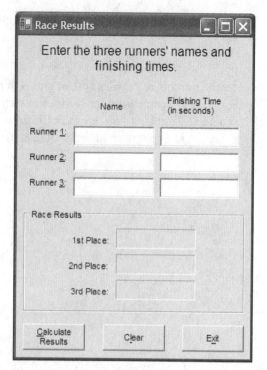

Figure 4-41   Race Results form

Use the following set of test data to determine whether your application is calculating properly:

Names and Times	Results
John, 87 seconds	First place: Carol
Carol, 74 seconds	Second place: John
Shelly, 94 seconds	Third place: Shelly

5. Software Sales

A software company sells three packages, Package A, Package B, and Package C, which retail for $99, $199, and $299, respectively. Quantity discounts are given according to the following table:

Quantity	Discount
10 through 19	20%
20 through 49	30%
50 through 99	40%
100 or more	50%

Create an application that allows the user to enter the number of units sold for each package. The application's form should resemble Figure 4-42. The application should calculate and display the total of the software order in a message box, as shown in Figure 4-43.

Figure 4-42   Software Sales form

Figure 4-43   Amount of Order message box

Notice that the application's main form (Figure 4-42) has a check box captioned "Display Grand Total Only". If this check box is selected, the message box should only display the grand total of the order, as shown in Figure 4-44.

Figure 4-44   Message box showing grand total only

Input validation: Make sure the number of units for each package is not negative.

Use the following set of test data to determine whether your application is calculating properly:

Units Sold	Amount of Order
Package A: 15 units	Package A: $1,188.00
Package B: 75 units	Package B: $8,955.00
Package C: 120 units	Package C: $21,528.00
	Grand Total: $31,671.00

Design Your Own Forms

6. Bank Charges
A bank charges $10 per month, plus the following check fees for a commercial checking account:

$0.10 each for less than 20 checks
$0.08 each for 20 through 39 checks
$0.06 each for 40 through 59 checks
$0.04 each for 60 or more checks

Create an application that allows the user to enter the number of checks written. The application should compute and display the bank's service fees for the month.

Input validation: Do not accept a negative value for the number of checks written.

Use the following set of test data to determine whether your application is calculating properly:

Number of Checks	Total Fees
15	$ 11.50
25	$ 12.00
45	$ 12.70
75	$ 13.00

7. Shipping Charges

The Fast Freight Shipping Company charges the rates listed in the following table.

Weight of the Package (in kilograms)	Shipping Rate per Mile
2 kg or less	$0.01
Over 2 kg, but not more than 6 kg	$0.015
Over 6 kg, but not more than 10 kg	$0.02
Over 10 kg, but not more than 20 kg	$0.025

Create an application that allows the user to enter the weight of the package and the distance it is to be shipped, and then displays the charges.

Input validation: Do not accept values of 0 or less for the weight of the package. Do not accept weights of more than 20 kg (this is the maximum weight the company will ship). Do not accept distances of less than 10 miles or more than 3000 miles. These are the company's minimum and maximum shipping distances.

Use the following set of test data to determine whether your application is calculating properly.

Weight and Distance	Shipping Cost
1.5 Kg, 100 miles	$ 1.00
5 Kg, 200 miles	$ 3.00
8 Kg, 750 miles	$ 15.00
15 Kg, 2000 miles	$ 50.00

8. The Speed of Sound

The following table shows the approximate speed of sound in air, water, and steel.

Medium	Speed
Air	1,100 feet per second
Water	4,900 feet per second
Steel	16,400 feet per second

Create an application that displays a set of radio buttons allowing the user to select air, water, or steel. After the user has made a selection, he or she should be asked to enter the distance a sound wave will travel in the selected medium. The program will then display the amount of time it will take.

Input validation: Do not accept distances less than 0.

Use the following set of test data to determine whether your application is calculating properly

Medium and Distance	Speed of Sound
Air, 10,000 feet	9.09 seconds
Water, 10,000 feet	2.04 seconds
Steel, 10,000 feet	0.61 seconds

9. Freezing and Boiling Points

The following table lists, in degrees Fahrenheit, the freezing and boiling points of several substances. Create an application that allows the user to enter a temperature, then shows all the substances that will freeze at that temperature and all that will boil at that temperature. For example, if the user enters -20, the program should report that water will freeze and oxygen will boil at that temperature.

Substance	Freezing Point	Boiling Point
Ethyl alcohol	-173°	172°
Mercury	-38°	676°
Oxygen	-362°	-306°
Water	32°	212°

Use the following set of test data to determine whether your application is calculating properly:

Temperature	Results
-20	Water will freeze, and oxygen will boil.
-50	Mercury and water will freeze, and oxygen will boil.
-200	Ethyl alcohol, mercury, and water will freeze, and oxygen will boil.
-400	Ethyl alcohol, mercury, oxygen, and water will freeze.

10. Long-Distance Calls

A long-distance provider charges the following rates for telephone calls:

Rate Category	Rate per Minute
Daytime (6:00 a.m. through 5:59 p.m.)	$0.07
Evening (6:00 p.m. through 11:59 p.m.)	$0.12
Off-Peak (12:00 a.m. through 5:59 a.m.)	$0.05

Create an application that allows the user to select a rate category (from a set of radio buttons), and enter the number of minutes of the call, then displays the charges.

Use the following set of test data to determine whether your application is calculating properly.

Rate Category and Minutes	Charge
Daytime, 20 minutes	$ 1.40
Evening, 20 minutes	$ 2.40
Off-peak, 20 minutes	$ 1.00

11. Internet Service Provider

An Internet service provider offers three subscription packages to its customers, plus a discount for nonprofit organizations:

Package A:	10 hours of access for $9.95 per month. Additional hours are $2.00 per hour.
Package B:	20 hours of access for $14.95 per month. Additional hours are $1.00 per hour.
Package C:	Unlimited access for $19.95 per month.
Nonprofit Organizations:	The service provider gives all nonprofit organizations a 20% discount on all packages.

The user should select the package the customer has purchased (from a set of radio buttons) and enter the number of hours used. A check box captioned "Nonprofit Organization" should also appear on the form. The application should calculate and display the total amount due. If the user selects the "Nonprofit Organization" check box, a 20% discount should be deducted.

Input validation: The number of hours used in a month cannot exceed 744.

Use the following set of test data to determine whether your application is calculating properly.

Package and Hours	The Monthly Charge
Package A, 5 hours, nonprofit	$7.96
Package A, 25 hours	$39.95
Package B, 10 hours, nonprofit	$11.96
Package B, 25 hours	$19.95
Package C, 18 hours, nonprofit	$15.96
Package C, 25 hours	$19.95

12. Internet Service Provider, Part 2

Modify the program in problem 11 so the form has a check box captioned "Display Potential Savings". When this check box is selected, the application should also display the amount of money that Package A customers would save if they purchased packages B or C, or the amount that Package B customers would save if they purchased Package C. If there would be no savings, the message should indicate that.

Use the following set of test data to determine whether your application is calculating properly:

Package and Hours	Total Monthly Savings
Package A, 5 hours, nonprofit	$7.96, no savings with packages B or C
Package A, 25 hours	$39.95, save $20.00 with package B, and save $20.00 with package C
Package B, 10 hours, nonprofit	$11.96, no savings with package C
Package B, 25 hours	$19.95, no savings with package C

13. Internet Service Provider, Part 3

Months with 30 days have 720 hours, and months with 31 days have 744 hours. February, with 28 days, has 672 hours. Enhance the input validation of the Internet service provider application by allowing the user to select the month (from a set of radio buttons) and validating that the number of hours entered is not more than the maximum for the entire month. Following is a table of the months, their days, and number of hours in each.

Month	Days	Hours
January	31	744
February	28	672

March	31	744
April	30	720
May	31	744
June	30	720
July	31	744
August	31	744
September	30	720
October	31	744
November	30	720
December	31	744

5

Lists, Loops, Validation, and More

▶ 5.1 Introduction

This chapter begins by showing you how to use input boxes, which provide a quick and simple way to ask the user to enter data. List boxes and combo boxes are also introduced. Next, you write loops, which cause programming statements to repeat. Visual Basic has three types of loops: the Do While loop, the Do Until loop, and the For...Next loop. This chapter also shows you how to use the CausesValidation property and the Validating event to ensure that the user has entered acceptable data as input. Finally, the ToolTip control is covered, which allows you to add tool tips to the other controls on a form.

▶ 5.2 Input Boxes

CONCEPT

INPUT BOXES PROVIDE A SIMPLE WAY TO GATHER INPUT WITHOUT PLACING A TEXT BOX ON A FORM.

An input box is a quick and simple way to ask the user to enter data. Figure 5-1 shows an example.

As you can see from the figure, an input box displays a message to the user and provides a text box for the user to enter input. The input box also has an OK and a Cancel button.

You display input boxes with the intrinsic InputBox function. When the InputBox function is called, an input box such as the one shown in Figure 5-1 appears on the screen. Here is the general format:

```
InputBox(Prompt [, Title] [, Default] [, Xpos] [, Ypos])
```

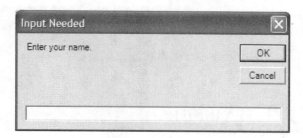

Figure 5-1 Input box

The brackets are drawn around the *Title*, *Default*, *Xpos*, and *Ypos* arguments to indicate that they are optional. The first argument, *Prompt*, is a string that is displayed to the user in the input box. Normally, this string is a prompt requesting the user to enter a value. The optional arguments, *Title*, *Default*, *Xpos*, and *Ypos*, are described as follows.

- *Title* is a string that appears in the input box's title bar. If you do not provide a value for *Title*, the name of the project appears.

- *Default* is a string value that is initially displayed in the input box's text box. This value serves as the default input. If you do not provide a value for *Default*, the input box's text box will initially appear empty.

- *Xpos* and *Ypos* specify the input box's location on the screen. *Xpos* is an integer that specifies the distance of the input box's leftmost edge from the left edge of the screen. *Ypos* is an integer that specifies the distance of the topmost edge of the input box from the top of the screen. *Xpos* and *Ypos* are both measured in twips. (A *twip* is 1/1440th of an inch.) If *Xpos* is omitted, Visual Basic centers the input box horizontally on the screen. If *Ypos* is omitted, Visual Basic places the input box near the top of the screen, approximately one third the distance down.

If the user clicks the input box's OK button or presses the Enter key, the function returns the value that is in the input box's text box. The value is returned as a string. If the user clicks the Cancel button, the function returns an empty string (" "). To retrieve the value returned by the InputBox function, use the assignment operator to assign it to a variable. For example, the following statement will display the input box shown in Figure 5-2. Assume that userInput is a string variable.

```
userInput = InputBox("Enter your age.", "Input Needed")
```

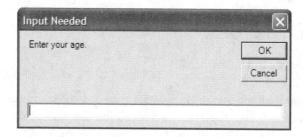

Figure 5-2 Input box

After this statement executes, the value that the user entered in the input box is stored as a string in userInput. As another example, the following statement will display the input box shown in Figure 5-3.

```
userInput = InputBox("Enter the distance.", "Provide a Value", "150")
```

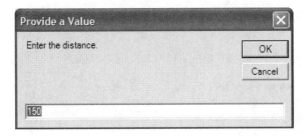

Figure 5-3 Input box with default user input

If the user simply clicks the OK button, without entering a value in the text box, the input box function will return " 150".

✓ Checkpoint

Carefully examine the input box in Figure 5-4 and answer questions 5.1 and 5.2.

Figure 5-4 Input box

5.1 Write a statement that will display the input box at the default location on the screen.

5.2 Write the statement that will display the input box, with its leftmost edge at 100 twips from the left edge of the screen, and its topmost edge 300 twips from the top edge of the screen.

▶ 5.3   List Boxes

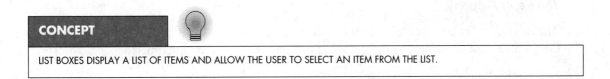

CONCEPT

LIST BOXES DISPLAY A LIST OF ITEMS AND ALLOW THE USER TO SELECT AN ITEM FROM THE LIST.

The ListBox Control

A list box is a control that displays a list of items and also allows the user to select one or more items from the list. Visual Basic .NET provides the *ListBox control* for creating list boxes. Figure 5-5 shows a form with two examples of a list box.

At run time, the user may select one of the items in a list box, which causes the item to appear highlighted.

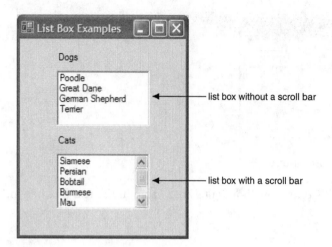

Figure 5-5   List box examples

Notice that one of the list boxes in Figure 5-5 does not have a scroll bar but the other does. Visual Basic automatically adds a scroll bar to a list box when it contains more items than can be displayed. In the figure, the top list box has four items (Poodle, Great Dane, German Shepherd, and Terrier), and all of those items are displayed. The bottom list box shows five items (Siamese, Persian, Bobtail, Burmese, and Mau), but because it has a scroll bar, we know that there are more items in the list box than those five.

Creating a ListBox Control

You create a ListBox control by either of the following methods.

◆ Double-click the ListBox tool in the toolbox, A default-sized ListBox control appears on the form. Move the control to the desired location and resize it, if necessary.

◆ Click the ListBox tool in the toolbox, and then draw the ListBox control on the form at the desired location and size.

At design time, a list box appears as a rectangle on the form. The size you draw the rectangle becomes the size of the list box. The standard prefix for a list box control's name is `lst`. Let's discuss some of the list box's important properties and methods.

The Items Property

The items in a list box are stored in the *Items property*. You can store items in the Items property at design time or at run time. To store items in the Items property at design time, follow these steps:

1. Make sure the list box control is selected in the Design window.
2. In the Properties window, the setting for the Items property is displayed as "(Collection)". Select the Items property and an ellipses button (**...**) appears.
3. Click the ellipses button. The String Collection Editor dialog box, shown in Figure 5-6, appears.
4. Type the items that are to appear in the list box into the String Collection Editor dialog box. Type each item on a separate line.
5. When you have entered all the items, click the OK button.

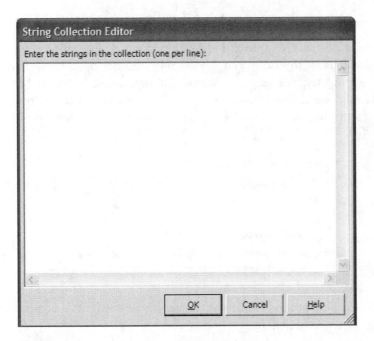

Figure 5-6   The String Collection Editor dialog box

The Items.Count Property

You can use the *Items.Count property* to determine the number of items that are stored in the Items property. When there are no items in the Items property, Items.Count will hold 0. For example, assume an application has a list box named lstEmployees. The following If...Then statement displays a message box when there are no items in the list box.

```
If lstEmployees.Items.Count = 0 Then
        MessageBox.Show("There are no items in the list!")
End If
```

And the following statement assigns the number of items in the list box to the variable numEmployees.

```
numEmployees = lstEmployees.Items.Count
```

Item Indexing

Internally, the items that are stored in a list box are numbered. Each item's number is called its index. The first item (which is the item stored at the top of the list) has the index 0, the second item has the index 1, and so forth.

You can use an index value with the Items property to retrieve a specific item from a list box. For example, the following statement copies the third item from lstCustomers to the string variable name.

```
name = lstCustomers.Items(2)
```

WARNING:

In a statement such as this, a run-time error will occur if the index value is out of range. Because the indices start at 0, the largest index in a list box will be 1 less than the number of items in the list.

The SelectedIndex Property

When the user selects an item in a list box, that item's index is stored in the SelectedIndex property. If no item is selected, SelectedIndex is set to -1. You can use the SelectedIndex property to retrieve the selected item from the Items property. For example, assume an application has a list box named lstLocations. The following code segment uses an If...Then statement to determine if the user has selected an item in the list box. If so, it copies the item from the Items property to the string variable location.

```
If lstLocations.SelectedIndex <> -1 Then
        location = lstLocations.Items(lstLocations.SelectedIndex)
End If
```

WARNING:

 To prevent a run-time error from occurring, always test the SelectedIndex property to make sure it is not set to -1 before using it with the Items property to retrieve an item, as shown in this statement.

You can also use the SelectedIndex property to deselect an item by setting it to -1. For example, the following statement deselects any selected item in lstLocations.

```
lstLocations.SelectedIndex = -1
```

The SelectedItem Property

Where the SelectedIndex property contains the index of the currently selected item, the SelectedItem property contains the item itself. For example, suppose the list box lstFruit contains the strings "Apples", "Pears", and "Bananas". If the user has selected "Pears", the following statement copies the string "Pears" to the variable selectedFruit.

```
selectedFruit = lstFruit.SelectedItem
```

The Sorted Property

You can use the list box's *Sorted property* to cause the items in the Items property to be displayed in alphabetical order. The property, which is Boolean, is set to false by default. This causes the items to be displayed in the order they were entered or inserted into the list. When set to true, the items are alphabetically sorted.

The Items.Add Method

To store items in the Items property with code at run time, you must use the *Items.Add method*. Here is the general format:

```
ListBox.Items.Add(Item)
```

ListBox is the name of the list box control. *Item* is the item that is to be added to the Items property. For example, suppose an application uses a list box named lstStudents. The following statement adds the string "Sharon" to the list box. The item is added to the end of the list.

```
lstStudents.Items.Add("Sharon")
```

This statement adds a string to a list box. However, you can add virtually any type of item to a list box. For example, the following statements add values of the Integer, Decimal, and Date data types to list boxes.

```
Dim num As Integer = 5
Dim grossPay As Decimal = 1200.00
Dim startDate As Date = #1/18/2003#
lstNumbers.Items.Add(num)
lstWages.Items.Add(grossPay)
lstDates.Items.Add(startDate)
```

When you add an object other than a string to a list box, the text that is displayed in the list box is the text returned from the object's `ToString` method.

The `Items.Insert` Method

To insert an item at a specific position, you must use the `Items.Insert` method. Here is the general format of the `Items.Insert` method:

```
ListBox.Items.Insert(Index, Item)
```

`ListBox` is the name of the list box control. `Index` is an integer argument that specifies the position where `Item` is to be placed in the Items property. `Item` is the item to add to the list.

For example, suppose the list box `lstStudents` contains the following items, in the order they appear: "Bill", "Joe", "Geri", and "Sharon". Since the string "Bill" is the first item, its index is 0. The index for "Joe" is 1, for "Geri" is 2, and for "Sharon" is 3. Now, suppose the following statement executes:

```
lstStudents.Items.Insert(2, "Jean")
```

This statement inserts "Jean" at index 2. The string that was previously at index 2 ("Geri") is moved to index 3, and the string previously at index 3 ("Sharon") is moved to index 4. The items in the Items property are now Bill, Joe, Jean, Geri, and Sharon.

The `Items.Remove` and `Items.RemoveAt` Methods

The `Items.Remove` and `Items.RemoveAt` methods both erase one item from a list box's Items property. Here is the general format of both methods:

```
ListBox.Items.Remove(Item)
ListBox.Items.RemoveAt(Index)
```

With both methods, `ListBox` is the name of the list box control. With the `Items.Remove` method, `Item` is the item you wish to remove. For example, the following statement erases the item "Industrial Widget" from the `lstInventory` list box.

```
lstInventory.Items.Remove("Industrial Widget")
```

If you specify an item that is not in the list box, nothing is removed.

The `Items.RemoveAt` method removes the item at a specific index. For example, the following statement removes the item at index 4 from the `lstInventory` list box:

```
lstInventory.Items.RemoveAt(4)
```

WARNING:

If you specify an invalid index with the `Items.RemoveAt` method, a run-time error will occur.

The `Items.Clear` Method

The *`Items.Clear` method* erases all the items in the Items property. Here is the method's general format:

```
ListBox.Items.Clear()
```

For example, assume an application has a list box named `lstCars`. The following statement erases its contents:

```
lstCars.Items.Clear()
```

In the following tutorial, you create an application with two list boxes.

TUTORIAL 5-1:

Creating list boxes

Step 1:   Start Visual Basic and begin a new Windows application project. Name the project List Boxes.

Step 2:   On the form, draw a list box as shown in Figure 5-7. Notice that the default name of the list box is `ListBox1`. Also notice that the name of the list box is displayed in the list box at design time. It will not appear there at run time.

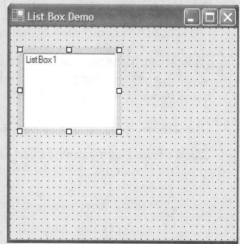

Step 3:   Change the name of the list box to `lstMonths`.

Step 4:   With the list box selected, click the Items property in the Property window. Then click the ellipses button (...) that appears.

Figure 5-7   A list box

Step 5:   The String Collection Editor dialog box should appear. Type the following names of the months, with one name per line: **January, February, March, April, May, June, July, August, September, October, November,** and **December**. When you are finished, the dialog box should appear as shown in Figure 5-8. Click the OK button.

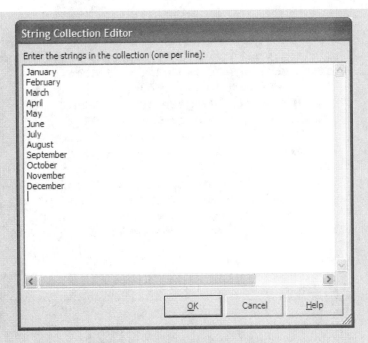

Figure 5-8   String Collection Editor with months filled in

Step 6:   Draw another list box and make it the same size as the first one. Change its name to lstYears. Enter the following items in its Items property: **2002, 2003, 2004,** and **2005**. Your form should look like that in Figure 5-9.

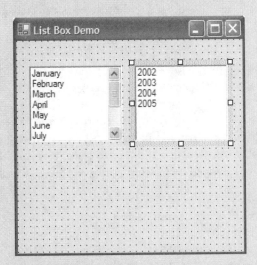

Figure 5-9   The form with two list boxes

Step 7:   Draw a button on the form, name it btnOk, and change its caption to "OK".

Step 8:   Double-click the btnOk button to add a Click event procedure code template. Write the following code, shown in bold.

```
Private Sub btnOk_Click(ByVal sender As System.Object, _
        ByVal e As System.EventArgs) Handles btnOk.Click
    Dim input As String ' To hold the selected month
    If lstMonths.SelectedIndex = -1 Then
        ' No month is selected
        MessageBox.Show("Select a month.")
    ElseIf lstYears.SelectedIndex = -1 Then
        ' No year is selected
        MessageBox.Show("Select a year.")
    Else
        ' Get the selected month and year
        input = lstMonths.SelectedItem & " " & _
            lstYears.SelectedItem
        MessageBox.Show("You selected " & input)
    End If
End Sub
```

Let's take a closer look at the code. Here is the beginning of the `If...Then` statement:

```
If lstMonths.SelectedIndex = -1 Then
    ' No month is selected
    MessageBox.Show("Select a month.")
```

It first tests `lstMonths.SelectedIndex` to determine whether it is set to -1. If it is, the user has not selected an item from `lstMonths`, so a message box is displayed instructing the user to do so. If the user has selected an item from `lst Months`, the `ElseIf` portion executes:

```
ElseIf lstYears.SelectedIndex = -1 Then
    ' No year is selected
    MessageBox.Show("Select a year.")
```

This tests `lstYears.SelectedIndex` to determine whether the user has selected an item from `lstYears`. If `lstYears.SelectedIndex` is set to -1, a message box is displayed instructing the user to select a year. The `Else` portion is executed if the user has selected items from both `lstMonths` and `lstYears`:

```
Else
    ' Get the selected month and year
    input = lstMonths.SelectedItem & " " & _
        lstYears.SelectedItem
    MessageBox.Show("You selected " & input)
End If
```

In that case, the selected items from both list boxes are concatenated and stored in the variable `input`. A message box is then displayed showing the contents of `input`.

Step 9: Draw another button on the form. Name it `btnReset` and change its text to "Reset".

Step 10: Double-click the `btnReset` button to add a `Click` event procedure code template. Write the following code shown in bold.

```
Private Sub btnReset_Click(ByVal sender As System.Object,
            ByVal e As System.EventArgs) Handles btnReset.Click
    ' Reset the list boxes by deselecting the currently
    ' selected items
    lstMonths.SelectedIndex = -1
    lstYears.SelectedIndex = -1
End Sub
```

When this button is clicked, the SelectedIndex property of both list boxes is set to -1. This deselects any selected items.

Step 11: Run the application. Without selecting any item in either list box, click the OK button. A message box appears instructing you to "Select a month."

Step 12: Select March in `lstMonths`, but do not select an item from `lstYears`. Click the OK button. This time a message box appears instructing you to "Select a year."

Step 13: With March still selected in `lstMonths`, select 2004 in `lstYears`. Click the OK button. Now a message box appears with the message "You selected March 2004." Click the message box's OK button to dismiss it.

Step 14: Click the Reset button. The items you previously selected in `lstMonths` and `lstYears` are deselected.

Step 15: Close the application and save it to your disk.

✓ Checkpoint

5.3 What is the index of the first item stored in a list box's Items property?

5.4 Which list box property holds the number of items stored in the Items property?

5.5 If a list box has 12 items stored in it, what is the index of the twelfth item?

5.6 Which list box property holds the item that has been selected from the list?

5.7 Which list box property holds the index of the item that has been selected from the list?

5.8 Assume `lstNames` is a list box with 15 items and `selectedName` is a string variable. Write a statement that stores the second item in `lstNames` in `selectedName`.

▶ 5.4   Introduction to Loops: The Do While Loop

CONCEPT

A LOOP IS PART OF A PROGRAM THAT REPEATS.

Chapter 4 introduced the concept of decision structures, which direct the flow of a program along two or more paths. A *repetition structure*, or *loop* causes one or more statements to repeat. Visual Basic has three types of loops: the Do While loop, the Do Until loop, and the For...Next loop. The difference between each of these is in how they control the repetition.

The Do While Loop

The *Do While loop* has two important parts: (1) an expression that is tested for a true or false value, and (2) a statement or group of statements that is repeated as long as the expression is true. Figure 5-10 shows a flowchart of a Do While loop.

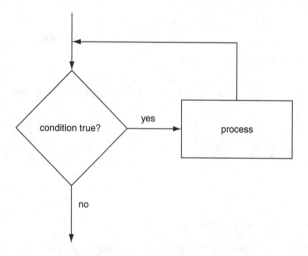

Figure 5-10   Flowchart of a Do While Loop

Notice the use of the diamond symbol for testing a condition. If the condition is true, the structure performs a process. Then it tests the condition again; if the condition is still true, the process is repeated. This continues as long as the condition is true when it is tested.

Here is the general format of the Do While loop in code:

```
Do While expression
        statement
        (more statements may follow)
Loop
```

The Do While statement marks the beginning of the loop, and the Loop statement marks the end. The statements between these are known as the body of the loop.

When the code runs, the expression in the Do While statement is tested. If it is true, the statements in the body of the loop are executed. (Because these statements are only executed under the condition that the expression is true, they are called *conditionally executed* statements.) This cycle repeats until the expression is false.

The Do While loop works like an If statement that executes over and over. As long as the expression is true, the conditionally executed statements will repeat. Each repetition of the loop is called an *iteration*. In Tutorial 5-2, you examine an application that demonstrates the Do While loop.

TUTORIAL 5-2:

Examining an application that uses the Do While loop

Step 1:   Start Visual Basic and open the Do While Demo project, which is stored in the \Chap5\Do While Demo folder on the student disk.

Step 2:   Run the application. The form appears, as shown in Figure 5-11.

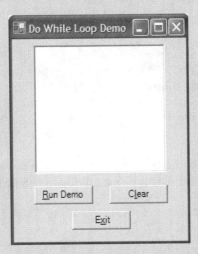

Figure 5-11   Do While **Loop Demo form**

Step 3:   Click the Run Demo button. The form now appears as shown in Figure 5-12.

Figure 5-12   **Results of** Do While **Loop Demo**

Notice that the word "Hello" is displayed 10 times in the list box.

Step 4: Click the Exit button to terminate the application.

Step 5: In the Visual Basic environment, open the Code window and find the btnRunDemo _Click event procedure. The code is as follows.

```
Private Sub btnRunDemo_Click(ByVal sender As System.Object, _
        ByVal e As System.EventArgs) Handles btnRunDemo.Click
    ' Demonstrate the Do While loop
    Dim count As Integer = 0
    Do While count < 10
        lstOutput.Items.Add("Hello")
        count += 1
    Loop
End Sub
```

Let's examine this procedure. An integer variable, count, is declared and initialized to the value 0. The Do While loop begins with this statement:

```
Do While count < 10
```

The statement tests the variable count to determine whether it is less than 10. If it is, the statements in the body of the loop are performed:

```
lstOutput.Items.Add("Hello")
count += 1
```

The first statement in the body of the loop adds the word "Hello" to the lstOutput listbox. The second statement uses the += combined assignment operator to add 1 to count.

The next line reads

```
Loop
```

This marks the end of the body of the loop, so Visual Basic repeats these steps, beginning with the Do While statement. When the test expression count < 10 is no longer true, the loop will terminate and the program will resume with the line that appears immediately after the Loop statement.

NOTE: *You might be wondering why we initialized the count variable to 0, when Visual Basic .NET automatically initializes numeric variables to 0. In this code, it is critical that count starts at 0 in order for the loop to execute 10 times. Because of this, we have explicitly given 0 as the initialization value so that anyone reading the program is aware that count starts at 0.*

Infinite Loops

In all but rare cases, loops must contain within themselves a way to terminate. This means that something inside the loop must eventually make the test expression false. The loop in the `Do While Loop` Demo program stops when the variable `count` is no longer less than 10.

If a loop does not have a way of stopping, it is called an *infinite loop*. Infinite loops keep repeating until the program is interrupted. Here is an example:

```
count = 0
Do While count < 10
    lstOutput.Items.Add("Hello")
Loop
```

This loop above will execute forever because it does not contain a statement that changes `count`. Each time the test expression is evaluated, `count` will still be equal to 0.

Programming Style and Loops

Traditionally, the conditionally executed statements (which are those in the body of a loop) should be indented. This sets them apart visually from the surrounding statements and makes it clear which statements are being repeated. For example, compare the two loops shown in the following code. The loop on the left is not properly indented, but the loop on the right is.

```
Do While count < 10             Do While count < 10
lstOutput.Items.Add("Hello")        lstOutput.Items.Add("Hello")
count += 1                          count += 1
Loop                            Loop
```

You will find that a similar style of indentation is used with the other types of loops presented in this chapter.

NOTE: *As with* `If...Then` *statements, Visual Basic .NET automatically indents the conditionally-executed statements in a loop. If this feature has been turned off, you can turn it on by clicking Tools on the menu bar, then clicking Options. On the Options dialog box, perform the following:*

◆ *Click Text Editor in the left pane, then click Basic, then click Tabs. Make sure "Smart" is checked on the dialog box under Indenting.*

◆ *In the left pane click VB Specific. Make sure "Pretty listing (reformatting) of code" and "Automatic insertion of end constructs" are both checked.*

Counters

A *counter* is a variable that is regularly incremented or decremented each time a loop iterates. To increment a variable means to add 1 to its value. For example, both of the following statements increment the variable x.

```
x = x + 1
x += 1
```

To decrement a variable means to subtract 1 from its value. Both of the following statements decrement the variable x.

```
x = x - 1
x -= 1
```

Often, it is important for a program to control or keep track of the number of iterations a loop performs. For example, the loop in the Do While Loop Demo program adds "Hello" to the list box 10 times. Let's look at part of the code again:

```
Do While count < 10
   lstOutput.Items.Add("Hello")
   count += 1
Loop
```

In the code, the variable count, which starts at 0, is incremented each time through the loop. When count reaches 10 the loop stops. count is used as a counter variable, which means it is regularly incremented in each iteration of the loop. In essence, count keeps track of the number of iterations the loop has performed.

TIP: It's important that count be properly initialized. If count is initialized at 1 instead of 0, the loop will only iterate 9 times.

Pretest and Posttest Do While Loops

A *pretest loop* evaluates its test expression before each iteration. A posttest loop evaluates its test expression after each iteration. The Do While loop may be written as either a pretest or posttest loop. Here is the general format of the posttest Do While loop:

```
Do
        statement
        (more statements may follow)
Loop While expression
```

The Do While Loop Demo program uses a pretest Do While loop. The code is as follows.

```
Do While count < 10
        lstOutput.Items.Add("Hello")
    count += 1
Loop
```

Figure 5-13 shows a flowchart for this loop.

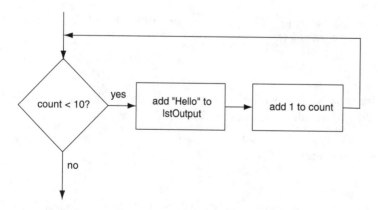

Figure 5-13   Flowchart for pretest Do While loop

As you can see, the test expression `count < 10` is tested before each iteration of the loop. The code may be modified to create a posttest loop:

```
Do
    lstOutput.Items.Add("Hello")
    count += 1
Loop While count < 10
```

When the word `While` and the test expression are moved so that they appear after the word `Loop`, the code becomes a posttest loop. Figure 5-14 shows a flowchart for this loop.

A posttest loop always performs at least one iteration, even if the test expression is false from the start. For example, the following loop will iterate once because the `Do While` loop does not evaluate the expression `x < 0` until the end of the iteration.

```
x = 1
Do
    MessageBox.Show(x.ToString)
    x += 1
Loop While x < 0
```

In the following tutorial, you modify the `Do While Loop Demo` program to use a posttest loop.

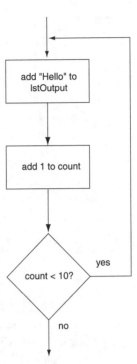

Figure 5-14 Flowchart for posttest `Do While` loop

TUTORIAL 5-3:

Modifying the `Do While Loop Demo` program to use a posttest loop

Step 1: Start Visual Basic .NET and open the Do While Demo project, which is stored in the \Chap5\Do While Demo folder on the student disk.

Step 2: Open the Code window and find the `btnRunDemo_Click` event procedure. The procedure uses a pretest `Do While` loop. Modify the loop so the procedure appears as follows. The modified lines of code are shown in bold.

```
Private Sub btnRunDemo_Click(ByVal sender As System.Object, _
        ByVal e As System.EventArgs) Handles btnRunDemo.Click
    ' Demonstrate the Do While loop
    Dim count As Integer = 0

    Do

        lstOutput.Items.Add("Hello")
        count += 1
    Loop While count < 10
End Sub
```

Step 3: Run the application and click the Run Demo button. The loop should display "Hello" 10 times in the list box.

Step 4: Click the Exit button to end the application. In the code window, modify the loop as shown in the following lines.

```
Do
    lstOutput.Items.Add("Hello")
    count += 1
Loop While count > 10
```

Although the expression count > 10 will be false, the loop will still iterate once.

Step 5: Run the application and click the Run Demo button. The loop should display "Hello" one time in the list box.

Step 6: Click the Exit button to end the application.

Keeping a Running Total

Some programming tasks require a running total to be kept. A *running total* is a sum of numbers that accumulates with each iteration of a loop. The variable used to keep the running total is called an *accumulator*.

The application in Tutorial 5-4, for example, calculates a company's total sales for five days by taking daily sales figures as input and keeping a running total of them as they are gathered.

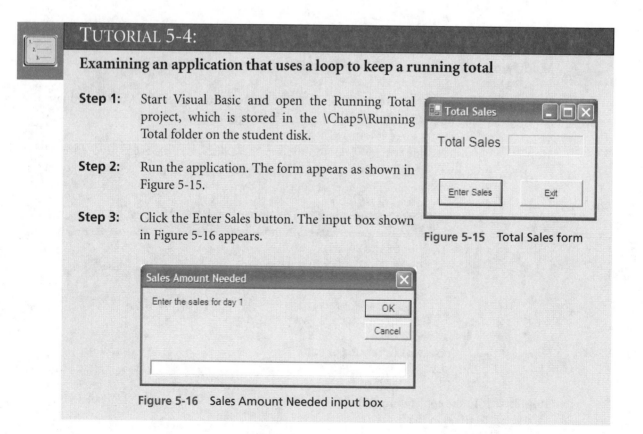

TUTORIAL 5-4:

Examining an application that uses a loop to keep a running total

Step 1: Start Visual Basic and open the Running Total project, which is stored in the \Chap5\Running Total folder on the student disk.

Step 2: Run the application. The form appears as shown in Figure 5-15.

Step 3: Click the Enter Sales button. The input box shown in Figure 5-16 appears.

Figure 5-15 Total Sales form

Figure 5-16 Sales Amount Needed input box

Step 4: The input box is asking for the sales for day 1. Enter **2000**, and click the OK button. (If you prefer, you many press the **Enter** key.)

Step 5: The application will present input boxes asking for the sales for days 2, 3, 4, and 5. Enter the following amounts:

Day 2: **1800**
Day 3: **1950**
Day 4: **2500**
Day 5: **1780**

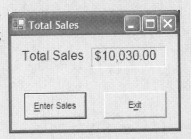

Figure 5-17 Total sales displayed

Step 6: After you enter the sales amount for day 5, the application will display the total sales in the main form, as shown in Figure 5-17.

Step 7: Click the Exit button to end the application.

Step 8: In the Visual Basic .NET environment, open the Code window and find the btnEnterSales_Click event procedure. The code is as follows.

```
Private Sub btnEnterSales_Click(ByVal sender As System.Object, _
        ByVal e As System.EventArgs) Handles btnEnterSales.Click
    ' Get the daily sales from the user
    ' and calculate the total.

    Dim count As Integer ' Loop counter
    Dim sales As Decimal ' To hold the daily sales
    Dim total As Decimal ' Use as an accumulator.
    Dim input As String  ' To get the user input

    ' Store the correct starting values in the counter
    ' and the accumulator.
    count = 1
    total = 0
    ' The loop below gets the sales for each day.
    Do While count <= 5
        input = InputBox("Enter the sales for day " & _
            count.ToString, "Sales Amount Needed")
        If input <> "" Then
        sales = CDec(input)    ' store converted input in sales
        total += sales         ' Add sales to total
        count += 1             ' Increment the counter
        End If
    Loop

    ' Now display the running total.
    lblTotal.Text = FormatCurrency(total)
End Sub
```

After the variable declarations, the procedure stores the correct starting values in the count and total variables:

```
count = 1
total = 0
```

It is very important that these variables be properly initialized. `count` is used as a counter, to determine the number of times the Do While loop will iterate. `total` is used as an accumulator in the loop, so it must start with the value 0. If it starts with any other value, the sum of the sales figures will not be correct.

The `Do While` loop uses an input box to ask for the daily sales figures. Notice the use of the following `If...Then` statement:

```
If input <> "" Then
    sales = CDec(input)     ' store converted input in sales
    total += sales          ' Add sales to total
    count += 1              ' Increment the counter
End If
```

If `input` is equal to an empty string (`""`), the user either clicked the Cancel button or did not enter a value. The `If...Then` statement only processes the return value of the `InputBox` function if the user entered a value and clicked the OK button or pressed the Enter key.

Inside the `If...Then` statement, the following statement converts the value entered by the user to a Decimal value and stores it in the `sales`.

```
sales = CDec(input) ' store converted input in sales
```

The next statement adds the contents of `sales` to `total`.

```
total += sales ' Add sales to total
```

`total` was initialized to 0, so the first time through the loop it is set to the same value as `sales`. In each iteration after the first, `total` is increased by the amount in `sales`. After the loop has finished, `total` will contain the total of all the daily sales figures entered.

Letting the User Control the Loop

Sometimes the user must decide how many times a loop should iterate. In Tutorial 5-5 you examine a modification of the Running Total application. This version of the program asks the user how many days he or she has sales figures for. The application then uses that value to control the number of times the `Do While` loop repeats.

TUTORIAL 5-5:

Examining an application that uses a user-controlled loop

Step 1: Start Visual Basic .NET and open the User Controlled project, which is stored in the \Chap5\User Controlled folder on the student disk.

Step 2: Run the application. When the form appears, click the Enter Sales button. The input box shown in Figure 5-18 appears.

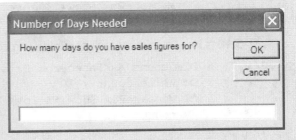

Step 3: The input box asks you to enter the number of days you have sales figures for. Enter **3** and click the OK button (or press Enter).

Figure 5-18   Number of Days Needed input box

Step 4: Because you entered "3" for the number of days, the application presents three input boxes asking for the sales for days 1, 2, and 3. Enter the following values when asked:

Day 1:   **1800**
Day 2:   **2700**
Day 3:   **2400**

Step 5: After you enter the sales figure for day 3, the application's form displays $6,900.00 as the total sales.

Step 6: Click the Exit button to terminate the application.

Step 7: In the Visual Basic environment, open the Code window and find the `btnEnterSales_Click` event procedure. Notice that a new variable has been added:

```
Dim days As Integer ' Number of days
```

The `days` variable is used in the following lines which ask the user to enter the number of days for which there are sales figures. The value entered by the user is stored in `days`.

```
' Get the number of days from the user.
input = InputBox("How many days do you have sales figures for?", _
        "Number of Days Needed")
days = Val(input)
```

Now, look at the first line of the `Do While` loop:

```
Do While count <= days
```

The loop now repeats while `count` is less than or equal to `days`. This limits the number of iterations to no more than the value entered by the user.

✓ **Checkpoint**

5.9   How many times will the following code display the message box?

```
Dim count As Integer = 0
Do While count < 10
```

```
        MessageBox.Show("I love Visual Basic .NET!")
    Loop
```

5.10 How many times will the following code segment display the message box?

```
Dim count As Integer = 0
Do While count < 10
    MessageBox.Show("I love Visual Basic .NET!")
    count += 1
Loop
```

5.11 How many times will the following code segment display the message box?

```
Dim count As Integer = 100
Do
    MessageBox.Show("I love Visual Basic .NET!")
    count += 1
Loop While count < 10
```

5.12 In the following code segment, which variable is the counter and which is the accumulator?

```
Dim a As Integer
Dim x As Integer
Dim y As Integer
Dim z As Integer
Dim input As String
x = 0
y = 0
input = InputBox("How many numbers do you wish to enter?")
z = Val(input)
Do While x < z
    input = InputBox( "Enter a number.")
    a = Val(input)
    y += a
    x += 1
Loop
MessageBox.Show("The sum of those numbers is " & y.ToString)
```

5.13 The following loop adds the numbers 1 through 5 to the lstOutput list box. Modify the loop so that, instead of starting at 1 and counting to 5, it starts at 5 and counts backward to 1.

```
Dim count As Integer = 1
Do While count <= 5
    lstOutput.Items.Add(count)
    count += 1
Loop
```

5.14 Write a Do While loop that uses an input box to ask the user to enter a number. The loop should keep a running total of the numbers entered and stop when the total is greater than 300.

5.15 If you want a Do While loop always to iterate at least once, which form should you use, pretest or posttest?

▶ 5.5 The Do Until and For...Next Loops

The Do Until Loop

The Do While loop, repeats while its test expression is true. The Do Until loop repeats until its test expression is true. Here is the general format of the Do Until loop.

```
Do Until expression
      statement
      (more statements may follow)
Loop
```

Like the Do While loop, the Do Until loop may be written in pretest or posttest form. The syntax shown is for a pretest Do Until loop. Here is the general format of the posttest Do Until loop:

```
Do
      statement
      (more statements may follow)
Loop Until expression
```

In Tutorial 5-6, you examine an application that uses the Do Until loop. The application asks the user to enter test scores, then displays the average of the scores.

TUTORIAL 5-6:

Examining an application that uses a Do Until loop

Step 1: Start Visual Basic and open the Test Scores 1 project, which is stored in the \Chap5\Test Scores 1 folder on the student disk.

Step 2: Run the application. The form appears, as shown in Figure 5-19.

Step 3: Click the Calculate Average button. The input box shown in Figure 5-20 appears.

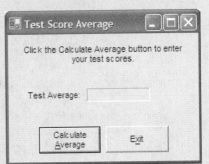

Figure 5-19 Test Score Average form

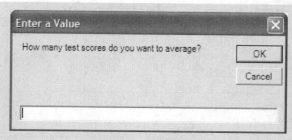

Figure 5-20   Input box

Step 4:   Enter **5** for the number of test scores and click the OK button (or press Enter).

Step 5:   Because you entered "5" for the number of test scores, the application presents five input boxes asking for scores 1, 2, 3, 4, and 5. Enter the following values when asked:

Test Score 1:   **98**
Test Score 2:   **87**
Test Score 3:   **100**
Test Score 4:   **74**
Test Score 5:   **92**

Step 6:   After you enter the fifth test score, the test score average 90.2 is displayed on the application form. Click the Exit button to end the application.

Step 7:   In the Visual Basic .NET environment, open the Code window and look at the btnCalcAverage_Click event procedure. The code is as follows.

```
Private Sub btnCalcAverage_Click(ByVal sender As System.Object, _
        ByVal e As System.EventArgs) Handles btnCalcAverage.Click
    ' This procedure gets the test scores, then calculates and
    ' displays the average.
    Dim total As Single      ' Holds the running total of test scores
    Dim numScores As Integer ' The number of test scores
    Dim average As Single    ' The average of the test scores
    Dim input As String      ' To hold user input
    Dim count As Integer     ' Counter variable for the loop
    ' Get the number of test scores
    input = InputBox("How many test scores do you want " & _
                     to average?", "Enter a Value")
    numScores = Val(input)
    ' Store the starting values in total and count
    total = 0
    count = 1
    Get the test scores
    Do Until count > numScores
        input = InputBox("Enter the value for test score " & _
            count.ToString, "Test Score Needed")
        total = total + Val(input)
        count = count + 1
    Loop
```

```
             ' Calculate and display the average
             average = total / numScores
             lblAverage.Text = average.ToString
        End Sub
```

The number of test scores entered by the user is stored in the variable num Scores. The procedure uses a Do Until loop, which begins with the following line:

```
    Do Until count > numScores
```

The loop iterates until count is greater than numScores. This loop asks the user to enter a test score, keeps a running total of the test scores, and increments count.

The For...Next Loop

The *For...Next loop* is ideal for situations that require a counter because it is specifically designed to initialize, test, and increment a counter variable. Here is the format of the For...Next loop:

```
For CounterVariable = StartValue To EndValue [Step Increment]
        statement
        (more statements may follow)
Next [CounterVariable]
```

As usual, the brackets are not part of the syntax, but indicate the optional parts. Let's look closer at the syntax:

◆ *CounterVariable* is the variable to be used as a counter. It must be a numeric variable.

◆ *StartValue* is the value the counter variable will be initially set to. This value must be numeric.

◆ *EndValue* is the value the counter variable is tested against just prior to each iteration of the loop. This value must be numeric.

◆ The Step *Increment* part of the statement is optional. If it is present, *Increment* (which must be a numeric expression) is the amount added to the counter variable at the end of each iteration. If the Step Increment part of the statement is omitted, the counter variable is incremented by 1 at the end of each iteration.

◆ The Next [*CounterVariable*] statement marks the end of the loop and causes the counter variable to be incremented. Notice that the name of the counter variable is optional. For readability, it is recommended that you always list the name of the counter variable after the Next statement.

Here is an example of the For...Next loop:

```
For count = 1 To 10
    lstOutput.Items.Add("Hello")
Next count
```

This loop executes the lstOutput.Items.Add("Hello") statement 10 times. Here are the steps that take place when the loop executes:

1. count is set to 1 (the start value).

2. count is compared to 10 (the end value). If count is less than or equal to 10, continue to step 3. Otherwise the loop is exited.

3. The lstOutput.Items.Add("Hello") statement in the body of the loop is executed.

4. count is incremented by 1.

5. Go back to step 2 and repeat this sequence.

Figure 5-21 shows a flowchart depicting the loop's actions.

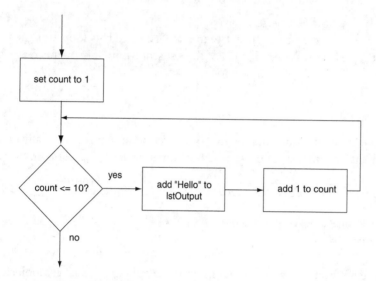

Figure 5-21 Flowchart of For...Next loop

NOTE: *Because the* For...Next *loop performs its test prior to each iteration, it is a pretest loop. Unlike the* Do While *and* Do Until *loops, this is the only form that the* For...Next *loop may be written in.*

WARNING:

 Be careful not to place a statement in the body of the For...Next loop that changes the counter variable's value. For example, the following loop increments x twice for each iteration:

```
' Warning!
For x = 1 To 10
    Print "Hello"
    x += 1
Next x
```

In Tutorial 5-7, you examine an application that demonstrates the For...Next loop.

TUTORIAL 5-7:

Examining an application that uses the For...Next loop

Step 1: Start Visual Basic and open the For Next Demo 1 project, which is stored in the \Chap5\For Next Demo 1 folder on the student disk.

Step 2: Run the application. The form appears, as shown in Figure 5-22.

Figure 5-22 For...Next Demo 1 form

Step 3: Click the Run Demo button. The form now appears as shown in Figure 5-23.

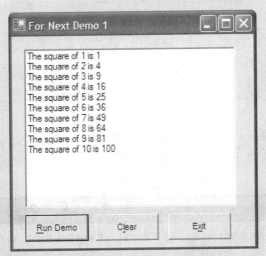

Figure 5-23 Results of For...Next loop

Step 4: Click the Exit button to terminate the application.

Step 5: In the Visual Basic environment, open the Code window and find the btnRunDemo_Click event procedure. The code is as follows.

```
Private Sub btnRunDemo_Click(ByVal sender As System.Object, _
        ByVal e As System.EventArgs) Handles btnRunDemo.Click
    ' Demonstrate the For...Next loop.
    Dim count As Integer ' Loop counter
    Dim square As Integer' To hold squares
    Dim str As String    ' To hold output
```

```
        For count = 1 To 10
            square = count ^ 2
            str = "The square of " & count.ToString & " is " & _
            square.ToString
            lstOutput.Items.Add(str)
        Next count
    End Sub
```

Figure 5-24 illustrates the order of the steps taken by the For...Next loop in this program.

Step 2: Compare count to 10. If count is greater than 10, terminate the loop. Otherwise, go to step 3.

Step 1: Initialize count to 1.

```
        For count = 1 To 10
            square = count ^ 2
            str = "The square of " & count.ToString & " is " & _
                square.ToString
            lstOutput.Items.Add(str)
        Next count
```

Step 3: Execute the body of the loop.

Step 4: Increment count by 1. Go back to step 2.

Figure 5-24   Steps in For...Next **loop**

In Tutorial 5-8, you complete a partially written application, which is on the student disk. The application will use a graphic image and a For...Next loop to perform a simple animation.

TUTORIAL 5-8:

Completing an application that uses the For...Next loop

Step 1:   Start Visual Basic and open the For Next Demo 2 project, which is stored in the \Chap5\For Next Demo 2 folder on the student disk.

Step 2:   Open the application's form. It appears as shown in Figure 5-25.

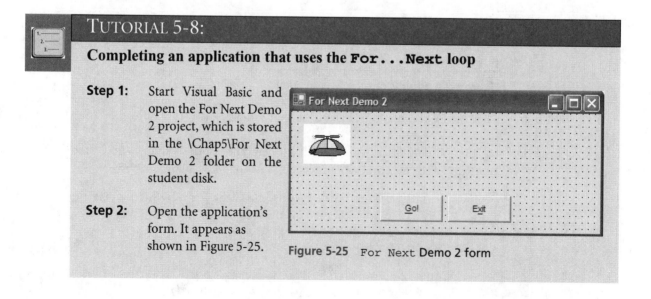

Figure 5-25   For Next Demo 2 form

The propeller cap graphic is displayed by a PictureBox control. The PictureBox control has a Left property that specifies the distance from the left edge of the form to the left edge of the PictureBox control. (The distance is measured in pixels.) In this tutorial, you write a `For...Next` loop that makes the image move across the form by increasing the value of the PictureBox control's Left property.

Step 3: Double-click the Go! button. Complete the code template for the `btnGo_Click` event procedure, as follows.

```
Private Sub btnGo_Click(ByVal sender As System.Object, _
        ByVal e As System.EventArgs) Handles btnGo.Click
    ' Run the animation
    Dim count As Integer

    For count = 16 To 328
        picPropellerCap.Left = count
    Next count
End Sub
```

Look at the first line of the `For...Next` loop:

```
For count = 16 To 328
```

The start value for `count` is 16, and its end value is 328. Inside the loop, the following statement stores the value of `count` in the PictureBox control's Left property.

```
picPropellerCap.Left = count
```

As the loop iterates, the value in the Left property grows larger, which causes the PictureBox control to move across the form.

Step 4: Run the application. Each time you click the Go! button, the propeller cap image should move from the form's left edge to its right edge.

Step 5: Click the Exit button to end the application. If you wish, open the Code window and experiment with different start and end values for the `For...Next` loop.

Specifying a Step Value

The *step value* is the value added to the counter variable at the end of each iteration of the `For...Next` loop. By default, the step value is one. You can specify a different step value with the `Step` key word. For example, look at the following code.

```
For x = 0 To 100 Step 10
    MessageBox.Show("x is now " & x.ToString)
Next x
```

In this loop the starting value of `x` is 0 and the ending value of `x` is 100. The step value is 10, which means that 10 is added to `x` at the end of each iteration. During the first iteration `x` is 0, during the second iteration `x` is 10, during the third iteration `x` is 20, and so forth.

You may also specify a negative step value if you want to decrement the counter variable. For example, look at the following loop.

```
For x = 10 To 1 Step -1
    MessageBox.Show("x is now " & x.ToString)
Next x
```

In this loop the starting value of x is 10 and the ending value of x is 1. The step value is negative 1, which means that 1 is subtracted from x at the end of each iteration. During the first iteration x is 10, during the second iteration x is 9, and so forth.

Summing a Series of Numbers with the For...Next Loop

The For...Next loop can be used to calculate the sum of a series of numbers, as shown in the following code.

```
Dim x, total As Integer
total = 0
For x = 1 to 100
    total += x
Next x
MessageBox.Show("The sum of 1 through 100 is " & total.ToString)
```

This code uses the variable total as an accumulator, and calculates the sum of the numbers from 1 through 100. The counter variable, x, has a starting value of 1 and an ending value of 100. During each iteration, the value of x is added to total.

You may also let the user specify how many numbers to sum, and the value of each number. For example, look at the following code.

```
Dim x, maxNumbers As Integer
Dim total, num As Double
maxNumbers = CInt(InputBox("How many numbers do " & _
                            "you wish to sum?"))
total = 0
For x = 1 to maxNumbers
    num = CDbl(InputBox("Enter a number."))
    total += num
Next x
MessageBox.Show("The sum of the numbers is " & total.ToString)
```

This code asks the user for the number of numbers to sum. The number entered by the user is stored in maxNumbers. In the loop, the counter variable x has a starting value of 1 and an ending value of maxNumbers. This causes the loop to iterate maxNumber times.

An input box is used in the loop to ask the user to enter a number. The value entered by the user is stored in the num variable. The value in num is then added to the accumulator variable, total.

If You Want to Know More About Loops: Breaking Out of a Loop

Sometimes it is necessary to stop a Do While, Do Until, or For...Next loop before it goes through all its iterations. The Exit Do and Exit For statements, when placed inside the body of a loop, stop the execution of the loop and cause the program to jump to the statement immediately following the loop.

For example, the following code is a modification of the code for summing a user-specified series of numbers shown in the previous section.

```
Dim x, maxNumbers As Integer
Dim total, num As Double
Dim input As String
maxNumbers = CInt(InputBox("How many numbers do " & _
                          "you wish to sum?"))
total = 0
For x = 1 to maxNumbers
    input = InputBox("Enter a number.")
    If input = "" Then
        Exit For
    Else
        num = CDbl(input)
        total += num
    End If
Next x
MessageBox.Show("The sum of the numbers is " & total.ToString)
```

In the loop, the user is asked to enter a number in an input box. The value entered by the user is stored, as a string, in the variable `input`. Recall that the `InputBox` function returns an empty string if the user clicks the Cancel button. An `If...Then...Else` statement tests the variable `input` to determine whether it contains an empty string. If so, the `Exit For` statement causes the loop to terminate.

WARNING:

Use the `Exit Do` and `Exit For` statements with caution. Because they bypass the loop's normal termination, they can make your code more difficult to debug.

Deciding Which Loop to Use

Although most repetitive algorithms can be written with any of the three types of loops, each works best in different situations.

- The `Do While` Loop

    Use the `Do While` loop when you wish the loop to repeat as long as the test expression is true. You can write the `Do While` loop as a pretest or posttest loop. Pretest `Do While` loops are ideal when you do not want the loop to iterate if the test expression is false from the beginning. Posttest loops are ideal when you always want the loop to iterate at least once.

- The `Do Until` Loop

    Use the `Do Until` loop when you wish the loop to repeat until the test expression is true. You can write the `Do Until` loop as a pretest or posttest loop. Pretest `Do Until` loops are ideal when you do not want the loop to iterate if the test expression is true from the beginning. Posttest loops are ideal when you always want the loop to iterate at least once.

- The `For...Next` Loop

    The `For...Next` loop is a pretest loop that first initializes a counter variable to a starting value. It automatically increments the counter variable at the end of each iteration. The loop repeats as long as the counter variable is not greater than an end value. The `For...Next` loop is primarily used when the number of required iterations is known.

✓ Checkpoint

5.16 How many times will the following loop iterate? What will be displayed in the message box?

```
x = 0
Do Until x = 10
    x += 2
Loop
MessageBox.Show(x.ToString)
```

5.17 Write a `For...Next` loop that adds every fifth number, starting at zero, through 100, to the list box `lstOutput`.

5.18 Write a `For...Next` loop that repeats seven times, each time displaying an input box that asks the user to enter a number. The loop should also calculate and display the sum of the numbers entered.

5.19 Which type of loop is best to use when you know exactly how many times the loop should repeat?

5.20 Which type of loop is best to use when you want the loop to repeat as long as a condition exists?

5.21 Which type of loop is best to use when you want the loop to repeat until a condition exists?

▶ 5.6   Nested Loops

A *nested loop* is a loop that is inside another loop. A clock is a good example of something that works like a nested loop. The second hand, minute hand, and hour hand all spin around the face of the clock. The hour hand, however, only makes one revolution for every 60 of the minute hand's revolutions. And it takes 60 revolutions of the second hand for the minute hand to make one revolution. This means that for every complete revolution of the hour hand, the second hand has revolved 3,600 times!

CONCEPT

NESTED LOOPS ARE NECESSARY WHEN A TASK PERFORMS A REPETITIVE OPERATION AND THAT TASK ITSELF MUST BE REPEATED.

Here is a code segment with a `For...Next` loop that partially simulates a digital clock. It displays the seconds from 0 through 59 in a label named `lblSeconds`:

```
For seconds = 0 To 59
        lblSeconds.Text = seconds.ToString
Next seconds
```

We can add a `minutes` variable and another label, and nest the loop inside another loop that cycles through 60 minutes:

```
For minutes = 0 To 59
    lblMinutes.Text = minutes.ToString
    For seconds = 0 To 59
        lblSeconds.Text = seconds.ToString
```

```
        Next seconds
    Next minutes
```

To make the simulated clock complete, another variable, label, and loop can be added to count the hours:

```
For hours = 0 To 24
        lblHours.Text = hours.ToString
    For minutes = 0 To 59
        lblMinutes.Text = minutes.ToString
        For seconds = 0 To 59
            lblSeconds.Text = seconds.ToString
        Next seconds
    Next minutes
Next hours
```

The innermost loop will iterate 60 times for each iteration of the middle loop. The middle loop will iterate 60 times for each iteration of the outermost loop. When the outermost loop has iterated 24 times, the middle loop will have iterated 1440 times and the innermost loop will have iterated 86,400 times.

The simulated clock example brings up a few points about nested loops:

- An inner loop goes through all of its iterations for each iteration of an outer loop.
- Inner loops complete their iterations before outer loops do.
- To get the total number of iterations of a nested loop, multiply the number of iterations of all the loops.

✓ Checkpoint

5.22   What values will the following code segment add to the lstNumbers list box?

```
For x = 1 to 3
    lstNumbers.Items.Add(x)
    For y = 1 to 2
        lstNumbers.Items.Add(y)
    Next y
Next x
```

5.23   How many times will the value in y be displayed in the following code segment?

```
For x = 1 to 20
    For y = 1 to 30
        MessageBox.Show(y.ToString)
    Next y
Next x
```

▶ 5.7 Multicolumn List Boxes, Checked List Boxes and Combo Boxes

CONCEPT

A MULTICOLUMN LIST BOX DISPLAYS ITEMS IN COLUMNS WITH A HORIZONTAL SCROLL BAR, IF NECESSARY. A CHECKED LIST BOX DISPLAYS A CHECK BOX NEXT TO EACH ITEM IN THE LIST. A COMBO BOX IS LIKE A LIST BOX COMBINED WITH A TEXT BOX.

Multicolumn List Boxes

The ListBox control has a Multicolumn property that may be set to true or false. By default it set to false. When set to true, it causes the list box to display its list in columns. You set the size of the columns, in pixels, with the ColumnWidth property. For example, suppose a form has list box named lstNumbers, which is shown in Figure 5-26.

Figure 5-26   List box

The list box's Multicolumn property is set to true, and its ColumnWidth property is set to 30. The following code executes, which adds the numbers 0 through 100 to the list box.

```
For number = 0 To 100
    lstNumbers.Items.Add(number)
Next
```

After the code executes, the list box appears as shown in Figure 5-27.

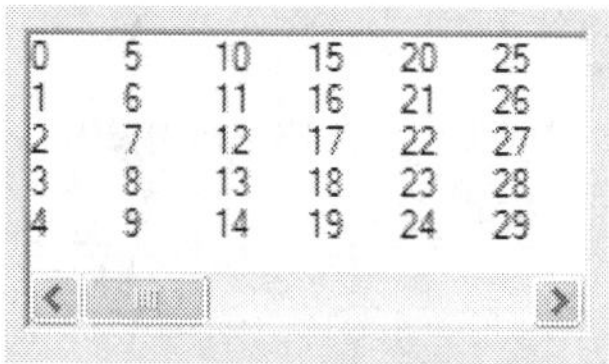

Figure 5-27   List box with multicolumn display

Notice that a horizontal scroll bar automatically appears in the list box. The user may scroll through the list, and select a number.

Checked List Boxes

The CheckedListBox control is a variation of the ListBox control. It supports all the ListBox properties and methods we discussed in section 5-2. Each of the items in a CheckedListBox control, however, is displayed with a check box next to it. Figure 5-28 shows an example.

Figure 5-28 Checked list box

An item in a checked list box may be selected and/or checked. Only one item in a checked list box may be selected at a given time, but multiple items may be checked. The CheckOnClick property determines how items become checked:

- ◆ When set to false, the user clicks an item once to select it, and then clicks it again to check it (or uncheck it, if it is already checked).

- ◆ When set to true, the user clicks an item only once to both select it and check it (or uncheck it, if it is already checked).

The CheckOnClick property is set to false by default. Because this setting makes working with the control a bit complicated, you may prefer setting it to true for most applications.

You access the selected item in a checked list box exactly as you do with a regular list box: through the SelectedIndex and SelectedItem properties. These properties only indicate which item is selected, however, and do not report which items are checked. You access the checked items through the GetItemChecked method, which has the following general format.

```
CheckedListBox.GetItemChecked(Index)
```

CheckedListBox is the name of the CheckedListBox control. *Index* is the index of an item in the list. If the item is checked, the method returns true. Otherwise, it returns false. For example, assume an application has a checked list box name clbCities. (Note that clb is the prefix for checked list boxes.) The following code counts the number of items in the control that are checked.

```
Dim i As Integer                    ' Loop counter
Dim checkedCities As Integer = 0 ' Keeps count of checked cities

For i = 0 To clbCities.Items.Count - 1
   If clbCities.GetItemChecked(i) = True Then
       checkedCities += 1
   End If
Next i
MessageBox.Show("You checked " & checkedCities.ToString & _
             " cities.")
```

As another example, assume an application uses the controls shown in Figure 5-29. The checked list box on the left is clbCities and the list box on the right is lstChecked. The OK button, btnOk, uses the following Click event procedure.

```
Private Sub btnOk_Click(ByVal sender As System.Object, _
      ByVal e As System.EventArgs) Handles btnOk.Click
   Dim i As Integer' Loop counter

   For i = 0 To clbCities.Items.Count - 1
       If clbCities.GetItemChecked(i) = True Then
```

```
                lstChecked.Items.Add(clbCities.Items(i))
            End If
        Next i
    End Sub
```

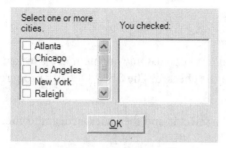

Figure 5-29   Checked list box and a list box

The `btnOk_Click` event procedure adds the items that are checked in the `clbCities` control to the `lstChecked` control. Figure 5-30 shows how the controls will appear after the user has checked three cities and clicked the OK button.

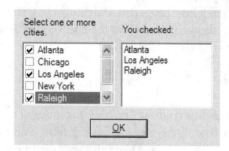

Figure 5-30   Cities checked

Combo Boxes

Combo boxes and list boxes are similar in the following ways:

* They both display a list of items to the user.
* They both have Items, Items.Count, SelectedIndex, SelectedItem, and Sorted properties.
* They both have `Items.Add`, `Items.Clear`, `Items.Remove`, and `Items.RemoveAt` methods.
* All of these properties and methods work the same with combo boxes and list boxes.

In addition, a combo box also has a rectangular area that functions like a text box. The user may either select an item from the combo box's list or type text into the combo box's text input area.

Like a text box, the combo box has a Text property. If the user types text into the combo box, the text is stored in the Text property. Also, when the user selects an item from the combo box's list, the item is copied to the Text property.

The standard prefix for combo box names is `cbo`.

Combo Box Styles

There are three different styles of combo box: the drop-down combo box, the simple combo box, and the drop-down list combo box. You select a combo box's style with its *DropDownStyle property*. Let's look at the differences between each style.

The Drop-Down Combo Box

This is the default setting for the combo box DropDownStyle property. At run time, a drop-down combo box appears like the one shown in Figure 5-31.

Figure 5-31   A drop-down combo box

This style of combo box behaves like either a text box or a list box. The user may either type text into the box (like a text box) or click the down arrow. If the user clicks the down arrow, a list of items drops down, as shown in Figure 5-32.

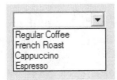

Figure 5-32   A list drops down when the user clicks the down arrow

Now the user may select an item from the list. When the user selects an item, it appears in the text input area at the top of the box, and is copied to the combo box's Text property.

NOTE: *When typing text into the combo box, the user may enter a string that does not appear in the drop-down list.*

TIP: When the combo box has the focus, the user may also press Alt+down arrow to drop the list down. This is also true for the drop-down list combo box.

The Simple Combo Box

With this style of combo box, the list of items does not drop-down but is always displayed. Figure 5-33 shows an example.

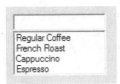

Figure 5-33   The simple combo box

As with the drop-down combo box, this style allows the user to type text directly into the combo box or select from the list. When typing, the user is not restricted to the items that appear in the list. When an item is selected from the list, it is copied to the text input area and to the combo box's Text property.

Drop-Down List Combo Box

With this style, the user may not type text directly into the combo box. An item must be selected from the list. Figure 5-34 shows a drop-down list combo box.

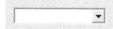

Figure 5-34 The drop-down list combo box

When the user clicks the down arrow, a list of items appears as shown in Figure 5-35.

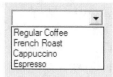

Figure 5-35 A list drops down when the user clicks the down arrow

When the user selects an item from the list, it is copied to the text area at the top of the combo box and to the Text property. Because the user can only select items from the list, it is not possible to enter text that does not appear in the list.

Getting the User's Input from a Combo Box

As with the list box, you can determine which item has been selected from a combo box's list by retrieving the value in the SelectedIndex or SelectedItem properties. If the user has typed text into the combo box's text area, however, you cannot use the SelectedIndex or SelectedItem properties to get the text. The best way to get the user's input is with the Text property, which will contain either the user's text input or the item selected from the list.

NOTE: *The drop-down list combo box's Text property is read-only. You cannot change its value with code.*

List Boxes versus Combo Boxes

Here are some guidelines to help you decide when to use a list box and when to use a combo box.

- ◆ Use a drop-down or simple combo box when you want to provide the user a list of items to select from but do not want to limit the user's input to the items on the list.

- ◆ Use a list box or a drop-down list combo box when you want to limit the user's selection to a list of items. The drop-down list combo box generally takes less space than a list box (because the list doesn't appear until the user clicks the down arrow), so use it when you want to conserve space on the form.

TUTORIAL 5-9:

Creating combo boxes

In this tutorial you will create each of the three styles of combo box.

Step 1: Start Visual Basic .NET and begin a new Windows application project. Name the project Combo Box Demo.

Step 2: Set the form up like the one shown in Figure 5-36. Note that you are to draw three combo boxes: `cboCountries` (drop-down combo box), `cboPlays` (a simple combo box), and `cboArtists` (a drop-down list combo box).

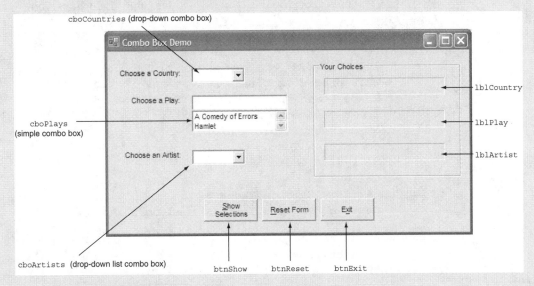

Figure 5-36   Combo Box Practice form

Step 3: Enter the following items into the Items property of the `cboCountries` combo box: **England**, **Ireland**, **Scotland**, and **Wales**.

Step 4: Enter the following items into the Items property of the `cboPlays` combo box: **Hamlet**, **Much Ado About Nothing**, **Romeo and Juliet**, **A Comedy of Errors**, and **The Merchant of Venice**.

Step 5: Enter the following items into the Items property of the `cboArtists` combo box: **Michelangelo**, **Raphael**, and **da Vinci**.

Step 6: The `btnShow_Click` event procedure should perform the following tasks:

- Copy the selected item or typed text from the `cboCountries` combo box to the `lblCountry` Text property.

- Copy the selected item or typed text from the `cboPlays` combo box to the `lblPlay` Text property.

- Copy the selected item from the `cboArtists` combo box to the `lblArtist` Text property.

Enter the following code shown in bold for the `btnShow_Click` event procedure.

```
Private Sub btnShow_Click(ByVal sender As System.Object, _
        ByVal e As System.EventArgs) Handles btnShow.Click
    ' This procedure displays the combo box selections.
    lblCountry.Text = cboCountries.Text
    lblPlay.Text = cboPlays.Text
    lblArtist.Text = cboArtists.Text
End Sub
```

Step 7: The btnReset_Click event procedure should deselect any items that are selected in the combo boxes. As with list boxes, this is accomplished by setting the SelectedIndex property to -1. The procedure should also set the Text property of lblCountry, lblPlay, and lblArtist to "". Enter the following code for the btnReset_Click event procedure.

```
Private Sub btnReset_Click(ByVal sender As System.Object, _
        ByVal e As System.EventArgs) Handles btnReset.Click
    ' This procedure clears selections in the
    ' Combo Boxes and resets the labels to "".
    ' Reset the combo boxes.
    cboCountries.SelectedIndex = -1
    cboCountries.Text = ""
    cboPlays.SelectedIndex = -1
    cboPlays.Text = ""
    cboArtists.SelectedIndex = -1
    ' Note: cboArtists.Text is read-only.

    ' Reset the labels.
    lblCountry.Text = ""
    lblPlay.Text = ""
    lblArtist.Text = ""
End Sub
```

NOTE: *If the user types characters into a combo box's text input area, those characters are not cleared by setting the SelectedIndex to -1. You must set the Text property to "" to accomplish that.*

Step 8: The btnExit_Click event procedure should end the application. Write the code for that event procedure.

Step 9: Run the application. Experiment with the combo boxes by trying a combination of text input and item selection. For example, select an item from the cboCountries list and type text into the cboPlays' text input area. Click the btnShow button to see what you have entered.

Step 10: End the application when you are finished experimenting with it.

✓ Checkpoint

5.24 What is the index of the first item stored in a list box or combo box's Items property?

5.25 Which list box or combo box property holds the number of items stored in the Items property?

5.26 Which list box or combo box property holds the index of the item that has been selected from the list?

5.27 What is the difference between a drop-down and drop-down list combo box?

5.28 What is the best method of getting the user's input from a combo box?

5.29 You have created a form and want to place a list box on it. The list box takes up too much space, however. What other control can you use?

▶ 5.8   Input Validation

Perhaps the most famous saying of the computer world is "garbage in, garbage out." The integrity of an application's output is only as good as its input, so you should try to make sure garbage does not go into your applications as input. *Input validation* is the process of inspecting information given to an application by the user and determining whether it is valid. A properly designed application should give clear instructions about the kind of input that is acceptable and should not assume the user has followed those instructions. Here are just a few examples of input validations performed by programs:

CONCEPT

AS LONG AS THE USER OF AN APPLICATION ENTERS BAD INPUT, THE APPLICATION WILL PRODUCE BAD OUTPUT. APPLICATIONS SHOULD BE WRITTEN TO FILTER OUT BAD INPUT. THIS SECTION SHOWS YOU HOW TO USE THE CAUSESVALIDATION PROPERTY AS WELL AS THE VALIDATING AND VALIDATED EVENTS TO ENSURE THE USER HAS ENTERED ACCEPTABLE DATA AS INPUT.

◆ Numbers are checked to ensure they are within a range of possible values. For example, there are 168 hours in a week. It is not possible for a person to work more than 168 hours in one week.

◆ Values are checked for their "reasonableness." Although it might be possible for a person to work 168 hours in a week, it is not probable.

◆ Items selected from a menu or other sets of choices are checked to ensure they are available options.

◆ Variables are checked for values that might cause problems, such as division by zero.

Most controls in Visual Basic have a Boolean property named *CausesValidation*. In addition, most controls are capable of triggering a `Validating` event. A control's `Validating` event is triggered just before the focus is shifts to another control whose CausesValidation property is set to true. The following scenario describes how the CausesValidation property and the `Validating` event work in harmony.

Suppose an application has two text box controls: `txtFirst` and `txtSecond`. The user has just entered a value into `txtFirst` and pressed the Tab key, which should shift the focus from `txt First` to `txtSecond`. But `txtSecond`'s CausesValidation property is set to true, so `txtFirst`'s Validating event is triggered before the focus shifts. The `txtFirst` control has a `Validating` event procedure which is executed as a result of the `Validating` event being triggered. The `Validating` event procedure contains code that checks the value in `txtFirst`. If the value is invalid the event procedure displays an error message instructing the user to re-enter the data. Furthermore, the code prevents the focus from shifting if the value is not valid.

NOTE: *By default, a control's CausesValidation property is set to true.*

In Tutorial 5-10, you examine an application that demonstrates this.

TUTORIAL 5-10:

Examining an application that demonstrates the `Validating` event and the CausesValidation property

Step 1:   Start Visual Basic and open the Validation Demo project, which is stored in the \Chap5\Validation Demo folder on the student disk.

Step 2: Open the Form window. The application's form is shown in Figure 5-37.

The form instructs the user to enter two numbers in the range 1 to 10. However, the application contains no input validation code.

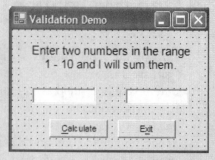

Figure 5-37 Validation Demo form

Step 3: Select the two text boxes and the two command buttons, one after another. As you select each one, notice that its CausesValidation property is set to true. This is the CausesValidation property's default value.

Step 4: Now you will write the code for two text boxes' Validating event procedures. Open the Code window. From the class name drop-down list, select txtNum1, as shown in Figure 5-38.

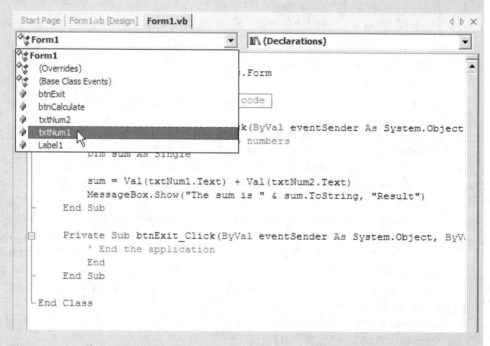

Figure 5-38 Class name drop-down list with txtNum1 selected

Step 5: From the method name drop-down list, select Validating, as shown in Figure 5-39.

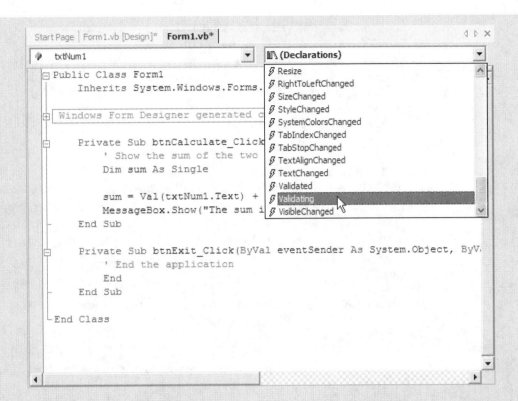

Figure 5-39   Method name drop-down list with `Validating` selected

Step 6:   When you selected `Validating` from the method name drop-down list, Visual Basic .NET created a code template for the `txtNum1_Validating` event procedure, which follows.

```
Private Sub txtNum1_Validating(ByVal sender As Object, _
    ByVal e As System.ComponentModel.CancelEventArgs)
    Handles txtNum1.Validating

End Sub
```

You might notice that this code template is slightly different from the code templates for `Click` event procedures. The difference is in the following code, which appears inside the parentheses:

```
ByVal e As System.ComponentModel.CancelEventArgs
```

This code declares an object named e, which is a parameter. A *parameter* is a special object that holds a value being passed into a procedure. As you will soon see, this event procedure uses the e object as part of the input validation process.

Write the following code, shown in bold, to complete the procedure.

```
Private Sub txtNum1_Validating(ByVal sender As Object, _
        ByVal e As System.ComponentModel.CancelEventArgs)
        Handles txtNum1.Validating
    ' Validate the number entered by the user.
    Dim value As Single
```

```
        value = Val(txtNum1.Text)
        If value < 1 Or value > 10 Then
            MessageBox.Show("Enter a value in the range 1 - 10.", _
                        "Input Error")
            e.Cancel = True
        Else
            e.Cancel = False
        End If
    End Sub
```

At run time, this event procedure will be executed when the focus is about to leave the txtNum1 control and shift to a control whose CausesValidation property is set to true. As you can see, the procedure tests the value stored in txtNum1 to determine whether it is less than 1 or greater than 10. Let's look at the If statement's conditionally executed statements to see what happens when either of these conditions is true:

```
    MessageBox.Show("Enter a value in the range 1 - 10.", _
                "Input Error")
    e.Cancel = True
```

The first statement displays a message box reporting the error. After that, the Cancel property of the e object is set to true. By setting the e object's Cancel property to true, the procedure is indicating that the event should be canceled and the focus should remain with txtNum1. If the e object's Cancel property is set to false, the focus will shift to the next control when the event procedure terminates.

The Else part if the If statement executes the following statement:

```
    e.Cancel = False
```

This statement is executed if the input is valid. Setting the e object's Cancel property to false causes the focus to shift to the next control when the event procedure terminates.

Step 7: Write the following Validating event procedure for txtNum2.

```
    Private Sub txtNum2_Validating(ByVal sender As Object, _
            ByVal e As System.ComponentModel.CancelEventArgs) _
            Handles txtNum2.Validating
        ' Validate the number entered by the user.
        Dim value As Single

        value = Val(txtNum2.Text)
        If value < 1 Or value > 10 Then
            MessageBox.Show("Enter a value in the range 1 - 10.", _
                        "Input Error")
            e.Cancel = True
        Else
            e.Cancel = False
        End If
    End Sub
```

Step 8:   Save the project.

Step 9:   Run the application and enter a value that is outside the range 1 through10 for `txtNum1`. Press the Tab key to shift the focus to `txtNum2`. A message box appears reporting the input error.

Step 10:   Click the OK button to dismiss the message box. Notice that the focus returns to the `txtNum1` control. This is because the event procedure sets `e.Cancel` to true before the procedure terminates. Change the value in `txtNum1` to a number from 1 to 10, and then press Tab to change the focus to `txtNum2`.

Step 11:   With the focus in `txtNum2`, enter a number outside the range from 1 to 10. Click the Calculate button. Once again, a message box appears reporting the input error. Click the OK button to dismiss the message box. The focus returns to the `txtNum2` control. Change the value to a number in the 1 to 10 range, then click the Calculate button again. This time, the application displays the sum of the two numbers.

Step 12:   Although it effectively validates the numbers entered into `txtNum1` and `txtNum2`, the application has a problem. To see the problem, erase the number in `txtNum1` or `txtNum2`. Now click the Exit button. A message box appears reporting the input error. This is because the Exit button's CausesValidation property is set to true. It is a good idea to have a control such as an Exit or Cancel button whose CausesValidaion property is set to false. This gives the user a way to exit the form, even in an error condition.

Step 13:   Terminate the application by clicking Debug on the menu bar, then clicking Stop Debugging. With the form open, select the Exit button. Notice its CausesValidation property is set to true. Change it to false.

Step 14:   Run the application again. Enter a number outside the 1 to 10 range for `txtNum1`. Click the Exit button. This time the application terminates without displaying an error message.

The `Validated` Event

After the `Validating` event has been triggered and the focus has shifted to another control, the *Validated event* is triggered. If you need to perform an operation on the user's input after it has been validated, such as copying it to a variable, you can write a `Validated` event procedure to do so.

To create a `Validated` event procedure, follow similar steps as when you create a `Validating` event procedure. First, select the name of the control in the class name drop-down list, then select `Validated` in the method name drop-down list. A code template will be created.

Using the SelectionStart and SelectionLength Properties to Select Text

Text boxes have two properties, *SelectionStart* and *SelectionLength*, that you can use to make the process of correcting invalid input more convenient for the user. To understand how correcting invalid input can be inconvenient, follow the instructions in Tutorial 5-11.

TUTORIAL 5-11:

An example of inconvenient data input correction

Step 1:   Run the Validation Demo project again. This time, enter a long series of digits, such as **777777777777**, in the txtNum1 text box. Press the Tab key.

Step 2:   A message box appears reporting the input error. Click the OK button to dismiss the message box. Notice that the focus returns to the txtNum1 control.

Step 3:   Press the Backspace key several times to erase the invalid number. Now you have observed the inconvenience that this application causes when the user must correct invalid input. There is no quick method of replacing long entries in the text boxes.

Step 4:   Click the Exit button to end the application.

The SelectionStart and SelectionLength properties can be used in code to automatically select the text in a text box. The SelectionStart property holds the position of the first selected character in the text box. The SelectionLength property holds the number of characters that are selected. For example, assume that txtName is a text box and look at the following code.

```
txtName.SelectionStart = 0
txtName.SelectionLength = 5
```

The first statement establishes that the first character in txtName (which is at position 0), is the first selected character. The next statement establishes that five characters will be selected. Together, the statements cause the first five characters in txtName to be selected. So, how do you use similar code to select all the text in a text box? You use the Text.Length property to get the length of the text, and assign that value to the text box's SelectionLength property. Here is an example:

```
txtName.SelectionStart = 0
txtName.SelectionLength = txtName.Text.Length
```

Follow the instructions in Tutorial 5-12 to modify the Validation Demo project so it uses the SelectionStart and SelectionLength properties to make data correction easier.

TUTORIAL 5-12:

Modifying the Validation Demo project to use the SelectionStart and SelectionLength properties

Step 1:   With the Validation Demo project open in Visual Basic .NET, open the Code window.

Step 2:   Scroll to the txtNum1_Validating event procedure, which is shown here. Add the statements shown in bold.

```
Private Sub txtNum1_Validating(ByVal sender As Object, _
        ByVal e As System.ComponentModel.CancelEventArgs) _
        Handles txtNum1.Validating
    ' Validate the number entered by the user.
    Dim value As Single

    value = Val(txtNum1.Text)
    If value < 1 Or value > 10 Then
        MessageBox.Show("Enter a value in the range 1 - 10.", _
                    "Input Error")
        txtNum1.SelectionStart = 0
        txtNum1.SelectionLength = txtNum1.Text.Length
        e.Cancel = True
    Else
        e.Cancel = False
    End If
End Sub
```

Step 3: Scroll to the txtNum2_Validating event procedure, which is shown here. Add the statements shown in bold.

```
Private Sub txtNum2_Validating(ByVal sender As Object, _
        ByVal e As System.ComponentModel.CancelEventArgs) _
        Handles txtNum2.Validating
    ' Validate the number entered by the user.
    Dim value As Single

    value = Val(txtNum2.Text)
    If value < 1 Or value > 10 Then
        MessageBox.Show("Enter a value in the range 1 - 10.", _
                    "Input Error")
        txtNum2.SelectionStart = 0
        txtNum2.SelectionLength = txtNum2.Text.Length
        e.Cancel = True
    Else
        e.Cancel = False
    End If
End Sub
```

Step 4: Run the application. In the txtNum1 text box, enter a long series of digits, such as **2222222222222222**, and press the Tab key.

Step 5: A message box appears reporting the input error. Click the OK button to dismiss the message box. Notice that the focus returns to the txtNum1 control and the series of digits is automatically selected. The code you added to txtNum1_Validating caused this to happen.

Step 6: Because the invalid input is already selected, you may simply type the correct number and it will automatically replace the selected value. Type a number such as **5** to see this happen.

Step 7: Repeat the process in step 6 to confirm that the code you added to `txtNum2`
`_Validating` works as well.

Step 8: Click the Exit button to end the application.

TIP: You can also use the SelectionStart and SelectionLength properties to find the starting position and length of text that is already selected. In addition, the SelectedText property gets the text that is selected. For example, assume `txtName` is a text box in the following code:

```
startPosition = txtName.SelectionStart
textLength = txtName.SelectionLength
selection = txtName.SelectedText
```

The first statement assigns the starting position of the text that is selected in `txtName` to the `startPosition` variable. The second statement assigns the length of the text that is selected in `txtName` to the `textLength` variable. The third statement assigns the text that is selected to the string variable `selection`.

Using the `With...End With` Statement

Sometimes you must write statements that perform several operations on the same object. For example, look at the following code segment from the Validation Demo project's `txtNum1_Validating` procedure.

```
txtNum1.SelectionStart = 0
txtNum1.SelectionLength = txtNum1.Text.Length
```

Notice that the name `txtNum1` appears three times in the code. You can use the `With...End With` *statement* to simplify the code. Here is the general format of the `With...EndWith` statement:

```
With ObjectName
     statement
     (more statements may follow)
End With
```

As a whole, these statements are called a *With block*. Here is the same code, rewritten as a `With` block.

```
With txtNum1
   .SelectionStart = 0
   .SelectionLength = .Text.Length
End With
```

Notice that statements inside the `With` block do not have to explicitly use the `txtNum1` object's name in order to refer to its properties.

✓ Checkpoint

5.30 When the focus is shifting to a control, what happens if that control's CausesValidation property is set to true?

5.31   When is a control's Validating event triggered?

5.32   By default, what value is a control's CausesValidation property set to?

5.33   Explain the purpose of the text box's SelectionStart and SelectionLength properties.

5.34   Write code that causes the text in the `txtSerialNumber` text box to be selected.

5.35   Use the `With...End With` statement to rewrite the statements you wrote for Checkpoint 5.34.

▶ 5.9   Tool Tips

CONCEPT

TOOL TIPS ARE A STANDARD AND CONVENIENT WAY OF PROVIDING HELP TO THE USERS OF AN APPLICATION. VISUAL BASIC .NET PROVIDES THE TOOLTIP CONTROL, WHICH ALLOWS YOU TO ASSIGN TOOL TIPS TO THE OTHER CONTROLS ON A FORM.

A *tool tip* is a small box that is displayed when the user holds the mouse cursor over a control. The box gives a short description of what the control does. Most Windows applications use tool tips as a way of providing immediate and concise help to the user.

Visual Basic .NET provides the *ToolTip control* which allows you to create tool tips for the other controls on a form. You place a ToolTip control in your application just as you place other controls: double-click the ToolTip tool in the tool box. When you do so, a ToolTip control appears in the Design window as shown in Figure 5-40.

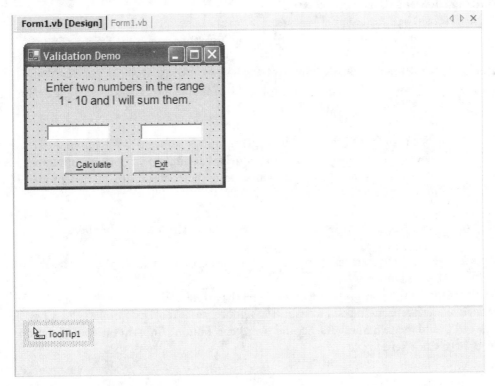

Figure 5-40   ToolTip control placed

Because the ToolTip control is invisible at run-time, it does not appear on the form at design time. Instead, it appears in an area known as the component tray. The *component tray* is a resizable region at the bottom of the Design window that holds invisible controls.

When you add a ToolTip control to a form, a new property is added to all the other controls. The new property is named ToolTip on *ToolTipControl*, where *ToolTipControl* is the name of the ToolTip control. For example, suppose you add a tool tip control to a form and keep the default name ToolTip1. The new property that is added to the other controls will be named ToolTip on ToolTip1. This new property holds the string that is displayed as the control's tool tip.

ToolTip Properties

You can select the ToolTip control in the component tray and then examine its properties in the Properties window. The InitialDelay property determines the amount of time, in milliseconds, that elapses between the user pointing the mouse at a control and the tool tip appearing. The default setting is 500. (One *millisecond* is $1/1000^{th}$ of a second, so 500 milliseconds are half of a second.)

The AutoPopDelay property is also a measure of time in milliseconds. It determines how long a tool tip remains on the screen once it is displayed. The default setting is 5000. The ReshowDelay property holds the number of milliseconds that will elapse between the displaying of different tool tips as the user moves the mouse from control to control. The default setting is 100.

You can set these properties individually, or set them all at once with the AutomaticDelay property. When you store a value in the AutomaticDelay property, InitialDelay is set to the same value, AutoPopDelay is set to 10 times the value, and ReshowDelay is set to 1/5 the value.

TUTORIAL 5-13:

Adding tool tips to an application

Step 1:   Load the Validation Demo project and open the form in the Design window.

Step 2:   Scroll down in the toolbox until you find the ToolTip tool (ToolTip). Double-click the tool to add a ToolTip control to the component tray. Notice that the default name of the ToolTip control is `ToolTip1`.

Step 3:   When you added the `ToolTip1` control, Visual Basic .NET automatically added a new property named ToolTip on ToolTip1 to the other controls on the form. Select the `txtNum1` text box control and locate the ToolTip on ToolTip1 property in the Properties window.

Step 4:   Set the ToolTip on ToolTip1 property to **Enter the first number here**.

Step 5:   Select the `txtNum2` property and set its ToolTip on Tooltip1 property to **Enter the second number here**.

Step 6:   Set the `btnCalculate` button's ToolTip on ToolTip1 property to **Click here to add the two numbers**. Set the `btnExit` button's ToolTip on ToolTip1 property to **Click here to exit**.

Step 7: Save the project and then run it. When the form appears, hold the mouse cursor over the txtNum1 control. The tool tip shown in Figure 5-41 should appear.

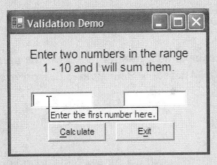

Figure 5-41   Tool tip for txtNum1 **displayed**

Step 8: Experiment with the other tool tips. When you are finished, exit the application.

▶ 5.10   Focus on Program Design and Problem Solving: Building the Vehicle Loan Calculator Application

CONCEPT

IN THIS SECTION, YOU BUILD THE VEHICLE LOAN CALCULATOR APPLICATION. THE APPLICATION USES A LOOP, INPUT VALIDATION, AND TOOL TIPS. THIS SECTION ALSO COVERS SOME OF THE VISUAL BASIC .NET INTRINSIC FINANCIAL FUNCTIONS.

Visual Basic .NET has a number of intrinsic functions for performing financial calculations. In creating the vehicle loan calculator application, you use the following functions: Pmt, IPmt, and PPmt. Let's look at each function in detail before continuing with the case study.

The Pmt Function

The *Pmt function* returns the periodic payment amount for a loan. It assumes the loan has a fixed interest rate. Here is the general form of the Pmt function call:

```
Pmt(PeriodicInterestRate, NumberOfPeriods, -LoanAmount)
```

Here is a description of each argument:

1. *PeriodicInterestRate*: You usually know what a loan's annual interest rate is; however, this function needs to know the loan's periodic interest rate. A loan is divided into periods, and you make a payment each period. The periodic interest rate is the rate of interest per period of the loan. For example, if you make monthly payments on a loan, the period is each month. If the annual interest rate is 9%, then the periodic interest rate is .09 divided by 12, which is .0075.

2. *NumberOfPeriods*: For a loan that requires monthly payments, this is the total number of months of the loan. For example, a three-year loan is given for 36 months.

3. *LoanAmount*: This is the amount being borrowed. Notice that it must be specified as a negative number.[*]

Here is an example of the function call:

```
payment = Pmt(annInt / 12, 24, -5000)
```

In this statement, `annInt` contains the annual interest rate, 24 is the number of months of the loan, and the amount of the loan is $5,000. After the statement executes, `payment` will hold the fixed monthly payment amount.

The **IPmt** Function

The *IPmt function* returns the required interest payment for a specific period on a loan. It assumes the loan has a fixed interest rate, with fixed monthly payments. Here is the general format of the `IPmt` function call:

```
IPmt(PeriodicInterestRate, Period, NumberOfPeriods, - LoanAmount)
```

Here is a description of each argument:

1. *PeriodicInterestRate*: As with the `Pmt` function, this function must know the periodic interest rate. (See the description of argument 1 for the `Pmt` function.)
2. *Period*: This argument specifies which period you wish to calculate the interest payment for. The argument must be at least 1, and no more than the total number of periods of the loan.
3. *NumberofPeriods*: The total number of periods of the loan. (See the description of argument 2 for the `Pmt` function.)
4. *LoanAmount*: As with the `Pmt` function, the loan amount must be expressed as a negative number.

Here is an example of the function call:

```
interest = IPmt(annInt / 12, 6, 24, -5000)
```

In this statement, `annInt` contains the annual interest rate, 6 is the number of the month we wish to calculate the interest payment for, 24 is the number of months of the loan, and the amount of the loan is $5,000. After the statement executes, `interest` will hold the amount of interest that must be paid in month 6 of the loan.

The **PPmt** Function

The *PPmt function* returns the principal payment for a specific period on a loan. It assumes the loan has a fixed interest rate, with fixed monthly payments. Here is the general format of the `PPmt` function call:

```
PPmt(PeriodicInterestRate, Period, NumberOfPeriods, -LoanAmount)
```

Here is a description of each argument:

---

[*] The `Pmt` function can also be used to calculate payments on a savings plan. When using it for that purpose, you specify the desired value of the savings as a positive number.

1. *PeriodicInterestRate*: As with the `Pmt` function, this function must know the periodic interest rate. (See the description of argument 1 for the `Pmt` function.)

2. *Period*: This argument specifies which period you wish to calculate the interest payment for. The argument must be at least 1, and no more than the total number of periods of the loan.

3. *NumberOfPeriods*: The total number of periods of the loan. (See the description of argument 2 for the `Pmt` function.)

4. *LoanAmount*: As with the `Pmt` function, the loan amount must be expressed as a negative number.

Here is an example of the function call:

```
principal = PPmt(annInt / 12, 6, 24, -5000)
```

In this statement, `annInt` contains the annual interest rate, 6 is the number of the month we wish to calculate the interest payment for, 24 is the number of months of the loan, and the amount of the loan is $5,000. After the statement executes, `principal` will hold the amount of principal that is to be paid in month 6 of the loan.

The Case Study

The Central Mountain Credit Union finances new and used vehicles for its members. A credit union branch manager has asked you to write a loan calculator application that displays the following information for a loan:

♦ The monthly payment amount

♦ The amount of the monthly payment that is applied toward interest

♦ The amount of the monthly payment that is applied toward the principal

The credit union currently charges 8.9% annual interest for new vehicle loans, and 9.5% annual interest on used vehicle loans. The credit union does not finance a vehicle for less than 6 months or more than 48 months.

Figure 5-42 shows a sketch of the application's form.

Table 5-1 lists each control, along with any relevant property settings. Note that you will add a ToolTip control to the form.

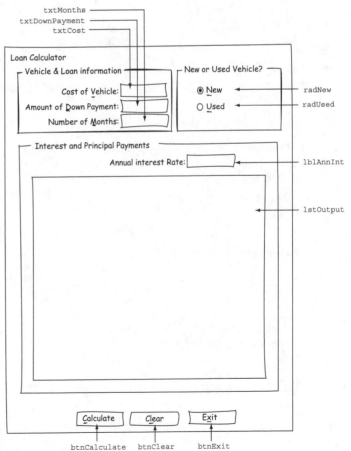

Figure 5-42   Sketch of Loan Calculator form

Table 5-1

Controls for loan calculator

Control Type	Control Name	Properties
Form	(Default)	Text: "Loan Calculator"
ToolTip	(Default)	(Retain all default property settings)
GroupBox	(Default)	Text: "Vehicle && Loan Information" TabIndex: 0
Label	(Default)	Text: "Cost of &Vehicle:" TabIndex: 0 (relative to group box)
Text box	txtCost	CausesValidation: True TabIndex: 1 (relative to group box) Text: " " ToolTip on ToolTip1: "Enter the cost of the vehicle here."
Label	(Default)	Text: "Amount of &Down Payment:" TabIndex: 2 (relative to group box)
Text box	txtDownPayment	CausesValidation: True TabIndex: 3 (relative to group box) Text: " " ToolTip on ToolTip1: "Enter the amount of the down payment here."
Label	(Default)	Text: "Number of &Months:" TabIndex: 4 (relative to group box)
Text box	txtMonths	CausesValidation: True TabIndex: 5 (relative to group box) Text: " " ToolTip on ToolTip1: "Enter the number of months of the loan here."
GroupBox	(Default)	Text: "New or Used Vehicle?" TabIndex: 1
RadioButton	radNew	Text: "&New" CausesValidation: True TabIndex: 0 (relative to group box) ToolTip on ToolTip1: "Click here if the vehicle is new."
RadioButton	radUsed	Text: "&Used" CausesValidation: True TabIndex: 1 (relative to group box) ToolTip on ToolTip1: "Click here if the vehicle is used."
GroupBox	(Default)	Text: "Interest and Principal Payments" TabIndex: 2
Label	(Default)	Text: "Annual Interest Rate:" TabIndex: 0 (relative to group box)
Label	lblAnnInt	Text: " " BorderStyle: Fixed3D TabIndex: 1 (relative to group box) ToolTip on ToolTip1: "Annual interest rate"
ListBox	lstOutput	TabIndex: 2 (relative to group box)

Table 5-1 *continued*

Controls for loan calculator

Control Type	Control Name	Properties
Button	`btnCalculate`	Text: "&Calculate" CausesValidation: True TabIndex: 3 ToolTip on ToolTip1: "Click here to calculate the payment data."
Button	`btnClear`	Text: "C&lear" CausesValidation: False TabIndex: 4 ToolTip on ToolTip1: "Click here to clear the form."
Button	`btnExit`	Text: E&xit" CausesValidation: False TabIndex: 5 ToolTip on ToolTip1: "Click here to exit."

Table 5-2 lists and describes the event procedures needed in this application.

Table 5-2

Event procedures for loan calculator

Method	Description
`btnCalculate_Click`	Calculates and displays a table in the list box showing interest and principal payments for the loan.
`btnClear_Click`	Resets the interest rate, clears the text boxes, and clears the list box.
`btnExit_Click`	Ends the application.
`radNew_CheckedChanged`	Updates the annual interest rate if the user selects a new vehicle loan.
`radUsed_CheckedChanged`	Updates the annual interest rate if the user selects a used vehicle loan.
`txtCost_Validating`	Validates that a numeric value has been entered int `txtCost`.
`txtDownPayment_Validating`	Validates that a numeric value has been entered int `txtDownPayment`.
`txtMonths_Validating`	Validates that a numeric value of 6 or greater has been entered int `txtMonths`.

Figure 5-43 shows a flowchart for the `btnCalculate_Click` event procedure.

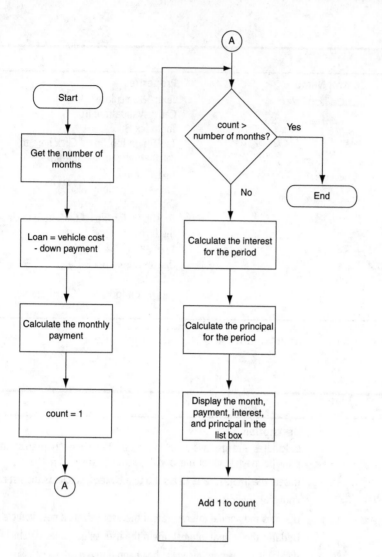

Figure 5-43 Flowchart for `btnCalculate_Click` event procedure

Pseudocode for the `btnCalculate_Click` event procedure is as follows. Note that the actual arguments needed for the `Pmt`, `IPmt`, and `PPmt` functions are not shown.

Loan = Cost - DownPayment
Payment = Pmt()
For Count = 0 To Months
    Interest = IPmt()
    Principal = PPmt()
    Display Month, Payment, Interest, and Principal in list box
Next Count

Figure 5-44 shows flowcharts for the `radNew_CheckedChanged` and `radUsed_Checked Changed` event procedures.

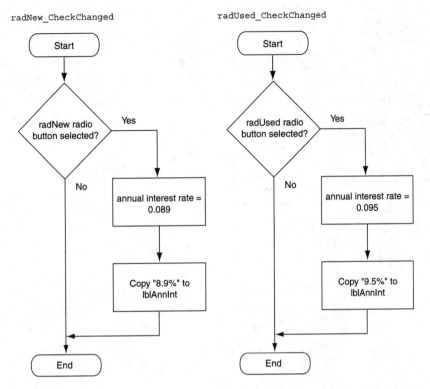

Figure 5-44 Flowcharts for `radNew_CheckedChanged` and `radUsed_CheckedChanged` event procedures

The purposes of these event procedures is to change the annual interest rate when the user clicks either of the `radNew` or `radUsed` radio buttons. Pseudocode for the `radNew_CheckedChanged` event procedure is as follows.

If `radNew` is selected Then
 Annual Interest Rate = 0.089
 Display Annual Interest Rate in `lblAnnInt`
End If

Pseudocode for the `radUsed_CheckedChanged` event procedure is as follows.

If `radUsed` is selected Then
 Annual Interest Rate = 0.095
 Display Annual Interest Rate in `lblAnnInt`
End If

Figure 5-45 shows a flowchart for the `txtCost_Validating` event procedure. This procedure displays an error message when a nonnumeric value is entered in `txtCost`. If this happens, the value in `txtCost` is selected and the focus remains on the control.

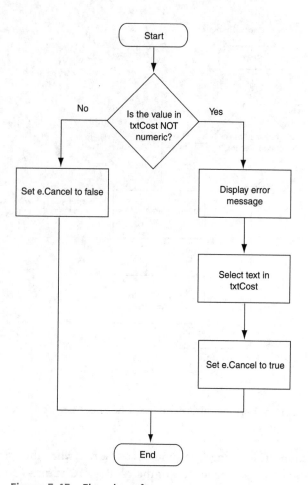

Figure 5-45   Flowchart for `txtCost_Validating` **event procedure**

Pseudocode for the `txtCost_Validating` event procedure is as follows.

> *If Cost is not numeric Then*
> > *Display "Cost must be a number."*
> > *Select existing text in the text box.*
> > *e.Cancel = True*
> *Else*
> > *e.Cancel = False*
> *End If*

Figure 5-46 shows a flowchart for the `txtDownPayment_Validating` event procedure. This procedure displays an error message when a nonnumeric value is entered in `txtDownPayment`. If this happens, the value in `txtDownPayment` is selected, and the focus remains on the control.

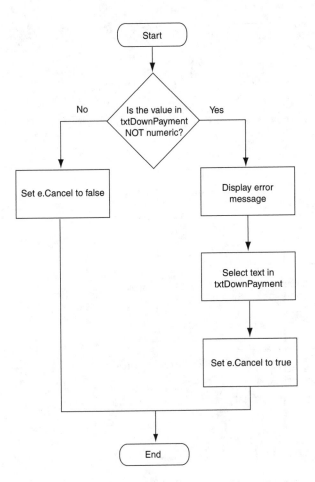

Figure 5-46 Flowchart for `txtDownPayment_Validating` **event procedure**

Pseudocode for the `txtDownPayment_Validate` event procedure is as follows.

> *If Down payment is not numeric Then*
> > *Display "Down payment must be a number."*
> > *Select existing text in the text box*
> > *e.Cancel = True*
> *Else*
> > *e.Cancel = False*
> *End If*

Figure 5-47 shows a flowchart for the `txtMonths_Validating` event procedure. This procedure uses an `If...Then...ElseIf` statement to validate the value in `txtMonths`. It displays an error message when a nonnumeric value, or a value less than 6 or greater than 48, is entered in `txtMonths`. If this happens, the value in `txtCost` is selected, and the focus remains on the control.

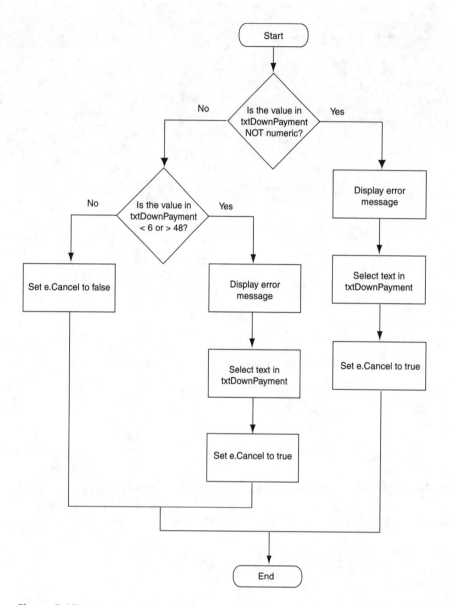

Figure 5-47 Flowchart for `txtMonth_Validating` Event Procedure

Pseudocode for the `txtMonths_Validating` event procedure is as follows.

> *If Months is not numeric Then*
>> *Display "Cost must be a number."*
>> *Select existing text in the text box*
>> *e.Cancel = True*
> *Else If Months < 6 Or Months > 48 Then*
>> *Display "Months must be in the range 6 - 48."*
>> *Select existing text in the text box.*
>> *e.Cancel = True*
> *Else*
>> *e.Cancel = False*
> *End If*

TUTORIAL 5-14:

Building the loan calculator application

Step 1:   Start Visual Basic .NET and begin a new Windows application project. Name the project Loan Calculator.

Step 2:   Set the form up as shown in Figure 5-48.

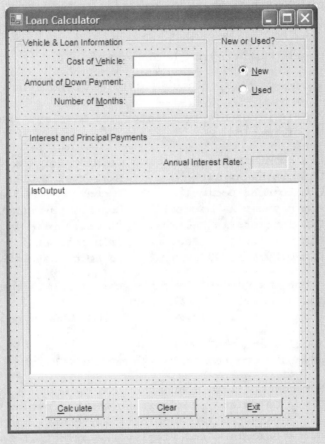

Figure 5-48   Loan Calculator form

Refer to Figure 5-42 for the names of the programmer-defined control names, and Table 5-1 for the important property settings.

Step 3:   Add a ToolTip control to the form. The ToolTip control will appear in the component tray.

Step 4:   Once you have placed all the controls on the form and set their properties, you can write the application's code. Open the code window and write the following remark and class-level variable declaration. This code should not appear inside of any event procedure.

```
' This application calculates the monthly payment for a vehicle loan
' and displays monthly payments, the interest payments, and
' the principal payments.

' Class-level variable
Dim annInt As Single = 0.089 ' Annual interest rate
```

The variable, annInt, will be used to hold the annual interest rate. It is declared as a class-level variable because it will be accessed by multiple procedures. It is initialized to 0.089 because a new vehicle loan will be selected by default.

Step 5:   Create the code template for the btnCalculate_Click event procedure. Complete the procedure by entering the code shown in bold.

```
Private Sub btnCalculate_Click(ByVal sender As System.Object, _
    ByVal e As System.EventArgs) Handles btnCalculate.Click
    ' This procedure calculates and displays the loan payment
    ' information.

    Dim count As Integer      ' Counter for the loop
    Dim months As Integer     ' Number of months for the loan
    Dim loan As Decimal       ' Amount of the loan
    Dim payment As Decimal    ' Monthly payment
    Dim interest As Decimal   ' Interest paid for the period
    Dim principal As Decimal  ' Principal paid for the period
    Dim output As String      ' To hold list box output

    ' Get the number of months and calculate the loan amount
    months = Val(txtMonths.Text)
    loan = Val(txtCost.Text) - Val(txtDownPayment.Text)

    ' Calculate the monthly payment
    payment = Pmt(annInt / 12, months, -loan)

    For count = 1 To months
        ' Calculate the interest for the period
        interest = IPmt(annInt / 12, count, months, -loan)
        ' Calculate and display the principal for the period
        principal = PPmt(annInt / 12, count, months, -loan)

        ' Add the month to the output string
        output = "Month: " & count.ToString
        ' Add the payment amount to the output string
        output &= " Payment: " & FormatCurrency(payment)
        ' Add the interest amount to the output string
        output &= " Interest: " & FormatCurrency(interest)
        ' Add the principal for the period
        output &= " Principal: " & FormatCurrency(principal)

        ' Add the output string to the list box
        lstOutput.Items.Add(output)
    Next count
End Sub
```

Step 6: Create the code template for the `btnClear_Click` event procedure. Complete the procedure by entering the code shown in bold.

```
Private Sub btnClear_Click(ByVal sender As System.Object, _
        ByVal e As System.EventArgs) Handles btnClear.Click
    ' Reset the interest rate, clear the text boxes
    ' and clear the list box.
    radNew.Checked = True
    annInt = 0.089
    lblAnnInt.Text = "8.9%"
    txtCost.Clear()
    txtDownPayment.Clear()
    txtMonths.Clear()
    lstOutput.Items.Clear()

    ' Reset the focus
    txtCost.Focus()
End Sub
```

Step 7: Create the code template for the `btnExit_Click` event procedure. Complete the procedure by entering the code shown in bold.

```
Private Sub btnExit_Click(ByVal sender As System.Object, _
        ByVal e As System.EventArgs) Handles btnExit.Click
    ' End the application
    End
End Sub
```

Step 8: Create the code template for the `radNew_CheckedChanged` event procedure. (You can easily create the code template by opening the Design window and double-clicking the `radNew` control.) Complete the procedure by entering the code shown in bold.

```
Private Sub radNew_CheckedChanged(ByVal sender As System.Object, _
        ByVal e As System.EventArgs) Handles radNew.CheckedChanged
    ' If the New radio button is checked, then
    ' the user has selected a new car loan.
    If radNew.Checked = True Then
        annInt = 0.089
        lblAnnInt.Text = "8.9%"
    End If
End Sub
```

Step 9: Create the code template for the `radUsed_CheckedChanged` event procedure. Complete the procedure by entering the code shown in bold.

```
Private Sub radUsed_CheckedChanged(ByVal sender As System.Object, _
        ByVal e As System.EventArgs) Handles radUsed.CheckedChanged
    ' If the Used radio button is checked, then
    ' the user has selected a used car loan.
    If radUsed.Checked = True Then
```

```
                        annInt = 0.095
                        lblAnnInt.Text = "9.5%"
                    End If
                End Sub
```

Step 10: Create the code template for the txtCost_Validating event procedure. (You create the code template by opening the Code window, selecting txtCost from the class name drop-down list, then selecting Validating from the method name drop-down list.) Complete the procedure by entering the code shown in bold.

```
Private Sub txtCost_Validating(ByVal sender As Object, _
        ByVal e As System.ComponentModel.CancelEventArgs) _
        Handles txtCost.Validating
    ' Validates that a number has been entered into txtCost.
    If Not IsNumeric(txtCost.Text) Then
        MessageBox.Show("Cost must be a number.", _
            "Invalid Vehicle Cost")
        ' Select the existing text in the text box.
        txtCost.SelectionStart = 0
        txtCost.SelectionLength = txtCost.Text.Length
        ' Set e.Cancel to true so the focus will stay
        ' in this control.
        e.Cancel = True
    Else
        e.Cancel = False
    End If
End Sub
```

Step 11: Create the code template for the txtDownPayment_Validating event procedure. Complete the procedure by entering the code shown in bold.

```
Private Sub txtDownPayment_Validating(ByVal sender As Object, _
        ByVal e As System.ComponentModel.CancelEventArgs) _
        Handles txtDownPayment.Validating
    ' Validates that a number has been entered into txtDownPayment.
    If Not IsNumeric(txtDownPayment.Text) Then
        MessageBox.Show("Down payment must be a number.", _
            "Invalid Vehicle Cost")
        ' Select the existing text in the text box.
        txtDownPayment.SelectionStart = 0
        txtDownPayment.SelectionLength = txtDownPayment.Text.Length
        ' Set e.Cancel to true so the focus will stay
        ' in this control.
        e.Cancel = True
    Else
        e.Cancel = False
    End If
End Sub
```

Step 12: Create the code template for the txtMonths_Validating event procedure. Complete the procedure by entering the code shown in bold.

```
Private Sub txtMonths_Validating(ByVal sender As Object, _
        ByVal e As System.ComponentModel.CancelEventArgs) _
        Handles txtMonths.Validating
    ' Validates that a number in the range of 6 or greater
    ' has been entered into txtMonths.
    If Not IsNumeric(txtMonths.Text) Then
        MessageBox.Show("Months must be a number.", _
            "Invalid Number of Months")
        ' Select the existing text in the text box.
        txtMonths.SelectionStart = 0
        txtMonths.SelectionLength = txtMonths.Text.Length
        ' Set e.Cancel to true so the focus will stay
        ' in this control.
        e.Cancel = True
    ElseIf Val(txtMonths.Text) < 6 Or Val(txtMonths.Text) > 48 Then
        MessageBox.Show("Months must be in the range 6 - 48.", _
            "Invalid Number of Months")
        ' Select the existing text in the text box.
        txtMonths.SelectionStart = 0
        txtMonths.SelectionLength = txtMonths.Text.Length
        ' Set e.Cancel to true so the focus will stay
        ' in this control.
        e.Cancel = True
    Else
        e.Cancel = False
    End If
End Sub
```

Step 13: Attempt to run the application. If there are errors, compare your code and property settings with those listed to locate them.

Step 14: Save the project.

SUMMARY

Input boxes provide a simple way to gather input without placing a text box on a form.

A list box is a control that displays a list of items and also allows the user to select one or more items from the list.

A repetition structure, or loop, causes one or more statements to repeat.

Each repetition of a loop is called an iteration.

The Do While loop causes one or more statements to repeat as long as an expression is true.

The Do Until loop causes one or more statements to repeat until its test expression is true.

The For...Next loop is specifically designed to initialize, test, and increment a counter variable.

If a loop does not have a way of stopping, it is called an infinite loop.

A counter is a variable that is regularly incremented or decremented each time a loop iterates.

A pretest loop evaluates its test expression before each iteration.

A posttest loop evaluates its test expression after each iteration.

The `Do While` and `Do Until` loops may be written as either pretest or posttest loops.

The `For...Next` loop is a pretest loop.

A running total is a sum of numbers that accumulates with each iteration of a loop. The variable used to keep the running total is called an accumulator.

The `Exit Do` and `Exit For` statements, when placed inside the body of a loop, stop the execution of the loop and cause the program to jump to the statement immediately following the loop.

A loop that is inside another loop is called a nested loop.

A multicolumn list box displays items in columns with a horizontal scroll bar, if necessary.

A checked list box displays a check box next to each item in the list.

A combo box is like a list box combined with a text box. There are three different styles of combo box: the drop-down combo box, the simple combo box, and the drop-down list combo box. You select a combo box's style with its DropDownStyle property.

Input validation is the process of inspecting information given to an application by the user and determining whether it is valid.

Most controls in Visual Basic have a Boolean CausesValidation property and a `Validating` event procedure. The two work in harmony to provide a way of performing input validation.

After the `Validating` event has been triggered and the focus has shifted to another control, the `Validated` event is triggered. If you need to perform an operation on the user's input after it has been validated, such as copying it to a variable, you can write a `Validated` event procedure to do so.

The SelectionStart and SelectionLength properties can be used in code to automatically select the text in a text box.

The `With...End With` statement allows you to create a `With` block. The statements inside a `With` block may perform several operations on the same object without specifying the name of the object each time.

A tool tip is a small box that is displayed when the user holds the mouse cursor over a control. The box gives a short description of what the control does. Visual Basic .NET provides the ToolTip control which allows you to create tool tips for the other controls on a form.

Because the ToolTip control is invisible at run-time, it appears in the component tray during design time.

The `Pmt` function returns the periodic payment amount for a loan. The `IPmt` function returns the required interest payment for a specific period on a loan. The `PPmt` function returns the principal payment for a specific period on a loan.

KEY TERMS

Accumulator	Loop
CausesValidation	Millisecond
Component tray	Nested loop
Conditionally-executed statements	Pmt function
Counter	Posttest loop
Do Until loop	PPmt function
Do While loop	Pretest loop
Exit Do	Prompt
Exit For	Repetition structure
For...Next loop	Running total
Infinite loop	SelectedIndex property
Input Box	SelectedItem property
Input validation	SelectionLength
IPmt function	SelectionStart
Items property	Step value
Items.Add method	Tool tip
Items.Count property	ToolTip control
Items.Insert method	Twip
Items.Remove method	Validating event
Items.RemoveAt method	With block
Iteration	With...End With
ListBox control	

Review Questions

Fill-in-the-blank

1. A(n) _____ provides a simple way to gather input without placing a text box on a form.

2. A(n) _____ displays a list of items and allow the user to select an item from the list.

3. A _____ causes one or more statements to repeat.

4. If a loop does not have a way of stopping, it is called an _____ loop.

5. A _____ is a variable that is regularly incremented or decremented each time a loop iterates.

6. A _____ loop evaluates its test expression after each iteration.

7. Each repetition of the loop is called a(n) _____.

8. The _____ statement, when placed inside the body of a Do While loop, stops the execution of the loop and causes the program to jump to the statement immediately following the loop.

9. A loop that is inside another loop is called a _____ loop.

10. _____ is the process of inspecting information given to an application by the user and determining whether it is valid.

11. You can use the _____ property to get or set the starting position of the selected text in a text box.

12. You can use the _____ property to get or set the length of the selected text in a text box.

13. The _____ function returns the periodic payment amount for a loan.

14. The _____ function returns the principal payment for a specific period on a loan.

15. The _____ function returns the required interest payment for a specific period on a loan.

Multiple Choice

1. You display input boxes with the intrinsic _____ function.
   a. `InBox`
   b. `Input`
   c. `InputBox`
   d. `GetInput`

2. An input box returns the value entered by the user as a _____.
   a. String
   b. Integer
   c. Single
   d. Boolean

3. Visual Basic .NET automatically adds a _____ to a list box when it contains more items than can be displayed.
   a. Larger list box
   b. Scroll bar
   c. Second form
   d. Message box

4. A list box or combo box's index numbering starts at
   a. 0
   b. 1
   c. -1
   d. any value you specify.

5. This property holds the index of the selected item in a list box.
   a. Index
   b. SelectedItem
   c. SelectedIndex
   d. Items.SelectedIndex

6. The _____ method erases one item from a list box.
   a. `Erase`
   b. `Items.Remove`
   c. `Items.RemoveItem`
   d. `Clear`

7. The `Do While` statement marks the beginning of a Do While loop, and the `Loop` statement marks the end. The statements between these are known as the _____ of the loop.
   a. Processes

b. Functions

c. Substance

d. Body

8. A(n) _____ loop evaluates its test expression before each iteration.
    a. Out-test

    b. Pretest

    c. Posttest

    d. In-test

9. A(n) _____ is a sum of numbers that accumulates with each iteration of a loop
    a. Counter

    b. Running total

    c. Summation function

    d. Iteration count

10. The _____ loop is ideal for situations that require a counter because it is specifically designed to initialize, test, and increment a counter variable.
    a. Do While

    b. Do Until

    c. For...Next

    d. Posttest Do Until

11. To get the total number of iterations of a nested loop
    a. Add the number of iterations of all the loops.

    b. Multiply the number of iterations of all the loops.

    c. Average the number of iterations of all the loops.

    d. Get the number of iterations of the outermost loop.

12. When the ListBox control's _____ property is set to true, it causes the ListBox control to display its list in multiple columns.
    a. Columns

    b. Multicolumn

    c. ColumnList

    d. TableDisplay

13. A _____ has a rectangular area that functions like a text box.
    a. List box

    b. Drop-down list box

    c. Combo box

    d. Input label

14. The standard prefix for combo box names is
    a. cbo

    b. com

    c. cbx

    d. cob

15. With this style of combo box, the list of items does not drop down, but is always displayed.
    a. Drop-down combo box
    b. Simple combo box
    c. Drop-down list combo box
    d. Simple drop-down combo list box

16. The combo box's _____ property will contain the user's text input or the item selected from the list.
    a. Input
    b. Caption
    c. List
    d. Text

17. A control's _____ property can be set to true or false. If it is set to true, the _____ event of the control that focus is shifting from will fire.
    a. Validating, `CausesValidation`
    b. CausesValidation, `Validating`
    c. Validated, `PerformValidation`
    d. PerformValidation, `Validating`

18. You may use the _____ and _____ properties to set the selected text in a text box.
    a. Text, SetSelection
    b. SetSelection, GetSelection
    c. SelectionStart, SelectionLength
    d. SelectionStart, SelectionText

19. The statements inside a _____ may perform several operations on the same object without specifying the name of the object each time.
    a. Validating procedure
    b. `With` block
    c. Set of parentheses
    d. `Use Object` block

20. At design time, the _____ holds controls that are invisible at run time, such as the ToolTip control.
    a. Component tray
    b. Control container
    c. Invisible control box
    d. Invisible property

True or False

Indicate whether each of the following statements is true or false.
1. T F: If you do not provide a value for an input box's title, an error will occur.
2. T F: If the user clicks an input box's Cancel button, the function returns the number -1.
3. T F: The `Items.RemoveAt` method always removes the last item in a list box (the item with the highest index value).

4. T F: Infinite loops keep repeating until the program is interrupted.

5. T F: A loop's conditionally executed statements should be indented.

6. T F: A pretest loop always performs at least one iteration, even if the test expression is false from the start.

7. T F: The Do While loop may be written as either a pretest or posttest loop.

8. T F: In a For...Next loop, the *CounterVariable* must be numeric.

9. T F: The Step *Increment* part of the For...Next statement is optional

10. T F: The For...Next loop is a posttest loop.

11. T F: In a nested loop, the inner loop goes through all of its iterations for each iteration of an outer loop.

12. T F: To create a checked list box, you draw a regular list box and set its Checked property to true.

13. T F: A drop-down list combo box allows the user to either select an item from a list or type text into a text input area.

14. T F: By default, a control's CausesValidation property is set to true.

15. T F: The Validated event is triggered before the Validating event.

Short Answer

1. What buttons automatically appear on an input box?

2. Where is an input box positioned if you leave out the *Xpos* and *Ypos* arguments?

3. Write a statement that adds "Spinach" to the list box lstVeggies at index 2.

4. Write a statement that removes the item at index 12 of the combo box cboCourses.

5. Describe the two important parts of a Do While loop.

6. In general terms, describe how a Do While loop works.

7. Why should you indent the statements in the body of a loop?

8. Describe the difference between pretest loops and posttest loops.

9. Why are the statements in the body of a loop called conditionally-executed statements?

10. What is the difference between the Do While loop and the Do Until loop?

11. Which loop should you use in situations where you wish the loop to repeat as long as the test expression is true?

12. Which loop should you use in situations where you wish the loop to repeat until the test expression is true?

13. Which loop should you use when you know the number of required iterations?

14. What feature do combo boxes have that list boxes do not have?

15. With one style of combo box the user may not type text directly into the combo box, but must select an item from the list. Which style does this describe?

16. With one style of combo box the Text property is read-only. Which style?

17. Describe the interaction between the CausesValidation property and the Validating event.

18. Why would you want to use the SelectionStart and SelectionLength properties in a Validating event procedure?

What Do You Think?

1. Why is it critical that counter variables be properly initialized?

2. Why should you be careful not to place a statement in the body of a `For...Next` loop that changes the value of the loop's counter variable?

3. You need to write a loop that iterates until the user enters a specific value into an input box. Which type of loop should you choose? Why?

4. You need to write a loop that will repeat 224 times. Which type of loop will you choose? Why?

5. You need to write a loop that iterates as long as a variable has a specific value stored in it. Which type of loop will you choose? Why?

6. Why should a Cancel button's CausesValidation property be set to false?

7. You use the statement `lstNames.Items.RemoveAt(6)` to remove an item from a list box. Does the statement remove the sixth or seventh item in the list? Why?

8. What kind of control(s) do you use when you want to provide the user a list of items to select from, but do not want to limit the user's input to the items on the list?

9. What kind of control(s) do you use when you want to limit the user's selection to a list of items?

Find the Errors

Identify the syntactically incorrect statements in the following:

```
1.  Loop
        x = x + 1
    Do While x < 100
2.  Do
        lstOutput.Items.Add("Hello")
    While count < 10
3.  Loop Until x = 99
        x = x + 1
    Do
4.  For x = 1
        lstOutput.Items.Add(x)
    Next x
```

Algorithm Workbench

1. An event procedure named `btnShow_Click` must add the numbers 1 through 20 to a list box named `lstNumbers`. Design a flowchart for this event procedure.

2. Write the code that you would insert into the code template for the event procedure described in question 1.

3. Write a `Do While` loop that uses an input box to get a number from the user. The number should be multiplied by 10 and the result stored in the variable `product`. The loop should iterate as long as `product` contains a value less than 100.

4. Write a `Do While` loop that uses input boxes to get two numbers from the user. The numbers should be added and the sum displayed message box. An input box should ask the user whether he or she wishes to perform the operation again. If so, the loop should repeat; otherwise it should terminate.

5. Write a `For...Next` loop that adds the following set of numbers to the list box `lstNumbers`.

```
0, 10, 20, 30, 40, 50 . . . 1000
```

6. Write a loop that uses an input box to get a number from the user. The loop should iterate 10 times and keep a running total of the numbers entered.

7. Convert the following pretest Do While loop to a posttest Do While loop:

```
x = 1
Do While x > 0
    input = InputBox("Enter a number")
    x = Val(input)
Loop
```

8. Convert the following Do While loop to a Do Until loop.

```
input = ""
Do While input.ToUpper <> "Y"
    input = InputBox("Are you sure you want to quit?"
Loop
```

9. Convert the following Do While loop to a For...Next loop:

```
count = 0
Do While count < 50
    lstOutput.Items.Add(count)
    count += 1
Loop
```

10. Convert the following For...Next loop to a Do While loop.

```
For x = 50 To 0 Step -1
        lstOutput.Items.Add(x)
Next x
```

11. Rewrite the following statements so they appear inside a With block.

```
txtName.SelectionStart = 0
txtName.SelectionLength = txtName.Text.Length
```

PROGRAMMING CHALLENGES

1. Sum of Numbers
Create an application that displays a form similar to Figure 5-49.

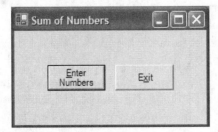

Figure 5-49 Sum of Numbers form

When the Enter Numbers button is clicked, the application should display the input box shown in Figure 5-50.

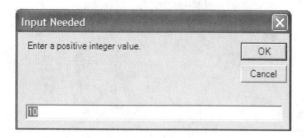

Figure 5-50   Sum of Numbers input box

The input box asks the user to enter a positive integer value. Notice that the default input value is 10. When the OK button is clicked, the application should display a message box with the sum of all the integers from 1 through the value entered by the user, as shown in Figure 5-51.

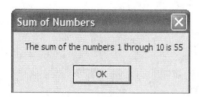

Figure 5-51   Sum of Numbers message box

If the user enters a negative value, the application should display an error message.
Use the following set of test data to determine whether your application is calculating correctly.

Value	Sum
5	15
10	55
20	210
100	5050

2. **Distance Calculator**

If you know a vehicle's speed and the amount of time it has traveled, you can calculate the distance it has traveled as follows:

Distance = Speed * Time

For example, if a train travels 40 miles per hour for 3 hours, the distance traveled is 120 miles. Create an application with a form similar to Figure 5-52.

When the user clicks the Calculate button, the application should display an input box asking the user for the speed of the vehicle in miles-per-hour, followed by another input box asking for the amount of time, in hours, that the vehicle has traveled. It should then use a loop to display in a list box the distance the vehicle has

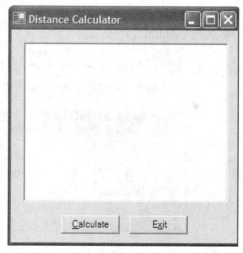

Figure 5-52   Distance Calculator

traveled for each hour of that time period. Figure 5-53 shows an example of what the application's form should look like.

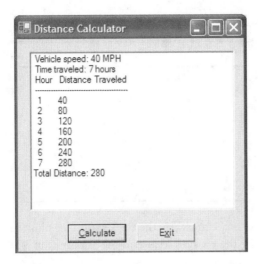

Figure 5-53   Distance Calculator completed

Input validation: Do not accept a value less than one for the vehicle's speed or the number of hours traveled.

Use the following set of test data to determine if your application is calculating correctly.

Vehicle Speed: **60**
Hours Traveled: **7**

Hour	Distance Traveled
1	60
2	120
3	180
4	240
5	300
6	360
7	420

3. Workshop Selector

Table 5-3 shows a training company's workshops, the number of days of each, and their registration fees.

Table 5-3

Workshops and registration fees

Workshop	Number of Days	Registration Fee
Handling Stress	3	$595
Time Management	3	$695
Supervision Skills	3	$995
Negotiation	5	$1,295
How to Interview	1	$395

The training company conducts its workshops in the six locations shown in Table 5-4. The table also shows the lodging fees per day at each location.

Table 5-4

Training locations and lodging fees

Location	Lodging Fees per Day
Austin	$95
Chicago	$125
Dallas	$110
Orlando	$100
Phoenix	$92
Raleigh	$90

When a customer registers for a workshop, he or she must pay the registration fee plus the lodging fees for the selected location. For example, here are the charges to attend the Supervision Skills workshop in Orlando:

Registration:	$995
Lodging:	$100 × 3 days = $300
Total:	$1,295

Design an application with a form that resembles Figure 5-54.

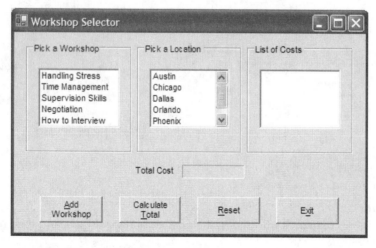

Figure 5-54 Workshop Selector form

The application should allow the user to select a workshop from one list box and a location from another list box. When the user clicks the Add Workshop button, the application should add the total cost of the selected workshop at the selected location in the third list box. When the user clicks the Calculate Total button, the total cost of all the selected workshops should be calculated and displayed in the label. The Reset button should deselect the workshop and location from the first two list boxes, clear the third list box, and clear the total cost label.

Be sure to add appropriate tool tips for the list boxes and the buttons.

4. Hotel Occupancy

The ElGrande Hotel has eight floors and 30 rooms on each floor. Create an application that calculates the occupancy rate for each floor, and the overall occupancy rate for the hotel. The occupancy rate is the percentage of rooms occupied, and may be calculated by dividing the number of rooms occupied by the number of rooms. For example, if 18 rooms on the first floor are occupied, the occupancy rate is:

```
18 / 30 = .6 or 60%
```

The application's form should appear similar to Figure 5-55.

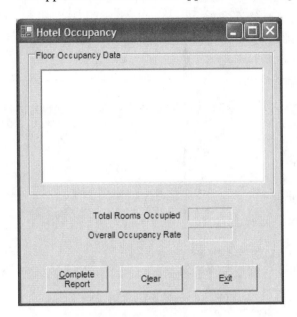

Figure 5-55 Hotel Occupancy form

When the user clicks the Complete Report button, a loop should execute and iterate eight times. Each time the loop iterates, it should display an input box for one of the hotel's floors. The input box should ask the user to enter the number of rooms occupied on that floor. As the user enters a value for each floor the loop should calculate the occupancy rate for that floor, and display the information for that floor in the list box. When the number of occupied rooms has been entered for all the floors, the application should display the total number of rooms occupied and the overall occupancy rate for the hotel. (The hotel has a total of 240 rooms.)

Figure 5-56 shows an example of the form after occupancy information has been provided for all the floors.

The Clear button should clear all the appropriate controls on the form. The Exit button should

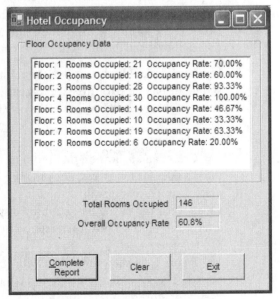

Figure 5-56 Completed Hotel Occupancy form

end the application. Use the values shown in Figure 5-56 to confirm that your application is performing the correct calculations. Be sure to add appropriate tool tips for the button controls.

Input validation: Do not accept a number less than 0 or greater than 30 for the number of occupied rooms on each floor.

5. Rainfall Statistics

Create an application that allows the user to enter each month's amount of rainfall (in inches) and calculates the total and average rainfall for a year. Figure 5-57 shows the application's form.

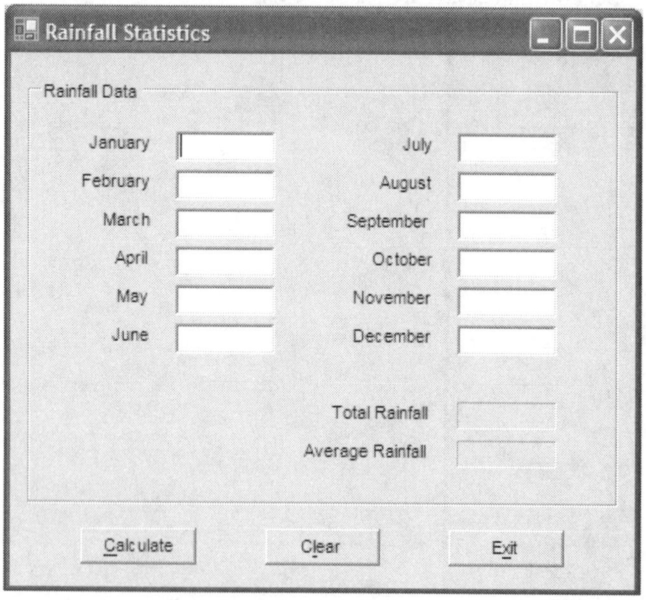

Figure 5-57   Rainfall Statistics form

Once the user has entered the amount of rainfall for each month, he or she may click the Calculate button to display the total and average rainfall. The Clear button should clear all the text boxes and labels on the form. The Exit button should end the application. Be sure to add appropriate tool tips for the text boxes and the buttons.

Input validation: Each text box should have a `Validating` event procedure. The event procedure should display an error message if the user has entered a nonnumeric value or a number less than 0. If either of these conditions exists, the invalid value should be selected so the user can re-enter it.

6. Bar Chart

Create an application that prompts the user to enter today's sales for five stores. The program should then display a simple bar graph comparing each store's sales. Create each bar in the bar graph by displaying a row of asterisks (*) in a list box. Each asterisk in a bar represents $100 of sales.

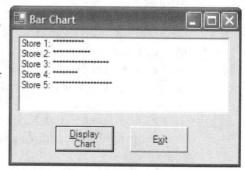

Figure 5-58   Bar Chart form

Figure 5-58 shows the form with the bar chart displayed. The sales data entered was $1000 for store #1, $1200 for store #2, $1800 for store #3, $800 for store #4, and $1900 for store #5.

7. Grade Report

Create an application that allows a teacher to enter three test scores each for three students. The application should calculate each student's average test score and assign a letter grade based on the following grading scale:

Average Test Score	Letter Grade
90 or greater	A
80 through 89	B
70 through 79	C
60 through 69	D
Below 60	F

The application should prompt the user for each student's name and three test scores. Figure 5-59 shows an example of how the application's form might appear after all the data has been entered.

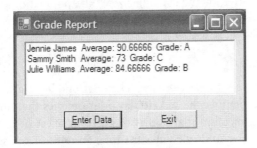

Figure 5-59   Grade Report Form

Design Your Own Forms

8. Centigrade to Fahrenheit Table

In Programming Challenge 6 of Chapter 3, you created an application that converts centigrade temperatures to Fahrenheit. Recall that the formula for performing this conversion is

$$F = \frac{9}{5}C + 32$$

In the formula, F is the Fahrenheit temperature and C is the centigrade temperature.

For this exercise, create an application that displays a table of the centigrade temperatures 0 through 20 and their Fahrenheit equivalents. The application should use a loop to display the temperatures in a list box.

9. Population

Create an application that will predict the approximate size of a population of organisms. The user should select or enter the starting number of organisms in a combo box, enter the average daily population increase (as a percentage), in a text box, and select or enter the number of days the organisms will be left to multiply in another combo box. For example, assume the user enters the following values:

Starting number of organisms: 2

Average daily increase: 30%

Number of days to multiply: 10

The application should display the following table of data:

Day	Approximate Population
1	2
2	2.6
3	3.38
4	4.394
5	5.7122
6	7.42586
7	9.653619
8	12.5497
9	16.31462
10	21.209

Be sure to add appropriate tool tips for each control on the form.

Input validation: Do not accept a number less than 2 for the starting size of the population. Do not accept a negative number for the average daily population increase. Do not accept a number less than 1 for the number of days the organisms will multiply.

10. Pennies for Pay

Susan is hired for a job, and her employer agrees to pay her every day. Her employer also agrees that Susan's salary is one penny the first day, two pennies the second day, four pennies the third day, and continuing to double each day. Create an application that allows the user to select or enter the number of days that Susan will work in a combo box, and calculates the total amount of pay she will receive over that period of time.

Be sure to add appropriate tool tips for each control on the form.

Input validation: Do not accept a number less than 1 for the number of days worked.

11. Payroll

Create an application that displays payroll information. The application should prompt the user to enter the following data for four employees:

- Number of hours worked
- Hourly pay rate
- Percentage to be withheld for state income tax
- Percentage to be withheld for federal income tax
- Percentage to be withheld for FICA

The application should calculate and display the following data for each employee in a list box:

- Gross pay (the number of hours worked multiplied by the hourly pay rate)
- State income tax withholdings (gross pay multiplied by state income tax percentage)
- Federal income tax withholdings (gross pay multiplied by federal income tax percentage)
- FICA withholdings (gross pay multiplied by FICA percentage)
- Net pay (the gross pay minus state income tax, federal income tax, and FICA)

When the calculations are performed, be sure to check for the following error:

- If any employee's state income tax plus federal tax plus FICA is greater than the employee's gross pay, display an error message stating that the withholdings are too great.

Be sure to add appropriate tool tips for each control on the form.

6

Sub Procedures and Functions

▶ 6.1 Introduction

In Visual Basic .NET there are two broad categories of procedures: Sub procedures and function procedures. A Sub procedure is a collection of statements that performs a task. The word Sub is an abbreviation for the older term "subroutine." Event procedures belong to this category. A function procedure is a collection of statements that performs a task and then returns a value to the part of the program that executed it. Function procedures work like intrinsic functions, such as `Val` and `IsNumeric`.

This chapter discusses how to write general purpose Sub procedures and function procedures. These procedures do not respond to events, but execute when they are called by statements. The chapter shows you how to create, call, and pass arguments to these procedures as well as various techniques for debugging applications that use them.

▶ 6.2 Sub Procedures

CONCEPT

YOU CAN WRITE YOUR OWN GENERAL PURPOSE SUB PROCEDURES THAT PERFORM SPECIFIC TASKS. GENERAL PURPOSE SUB PROCEDURES ARE NOT TRIGGERED BY EVENTS BUT CALLED FROM STATEMENTS IN OTHER PROCEDURES.

A *Sub procedure* is a collection of statements that performs a task. The word Sub is an abbreviation for the older term "subroutine." An event procedure is a type of Sub procedure that is executed when an event, such as a mouse click, occurs while the program is running. This section discusses general purpose Sub procedures that are not triggered by events, but executed by statements in other procedures.

By writing Sub procedures, you can *modularize* an application's code, that is, break it into small, manageable procedures. Imagine a book that has a thousand pages but isn't divided into chapters or sections. Trying to find a single topic in the book would be very difficult. Real-world applications can easily have thousands of lines of code, and unless they are modularized, they can be very difficult to modify and maintain.

Sub procedures also simplify a program's code. If a specific task is performed in several places in a program, a Sub procedure for performing that task can be written once then executed anytime it is needed.

Tutorial 6-1 walks you through an example application that uses a Sub procedure.

TUTORIAL 6-1:

Examining an application with a Sub procedure

Step 1: Start Visual Basic .NET and open the Sub Procedure Demo project, which is stored in the \Chap6\Sub Procedure Demo folder on the student disk. The application's form is shown in Figure 6-1. The form has a list box named `lstOutput` and two buttons: `btnGo` and `btnExit`.

Figure 6-1 Sub Procedure Demo form

Step 2: Open the Code window and find the Sub procedure named `DisplayMessage`. The code for the procedure is as follows:

```
Sub DisplayMessage()
    ' A Sub procedure that displays a message.
    lstOutput.Items.Add("")
    lstOutput.Items.Add("Hello from the DisplayMessage procedure.")
    lstOutput.Items.Add("")
End Sub
```

The code for a procedure, such as this, is called a *procedure declaration*. The declaration for a Sub procedure begins with a `Sub` statement and ends with an `End Sub` statement. The code that appears between these two statements is the body of the procedure. When the `DisplayMessage` Sub procedure executes, it displays a blank line in the list box, followed by the string "Hello from the DisplayMessage procedure.", followed by another blank line.

Figure 6-2 shows the parts of the Sub statement.

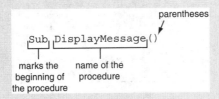

Figure 6-2   First Line of `DisplayMessage` Procedure

The first line of the Sub procedure begins with the word Sub, followed by the name of the procedure, followed by a set of parentheses. In this procedure the parentheses are empty. Later you will see procedures that have items written inside the parentheses.

NOTE: *An event procedure is associated with a control, so its name is prefixed with the control's name. For example, the btnGo button's Click event procedure is named btnGo_Click. Since a general purpose Sub procedure is not associated with a control, its name is not prefixed by a control name.*

Step 3:   General purpose Sub procedures are not executed by an event. Instead, a general purpose Sub procedure must be called. Look at the following code for the btnGo_Click event procedure. The statement that is printed in bold calls the DisplayMessage procedure.

```
Private Sub btnGo_Click(ByVal sender As System.Object, _
    ByVal e As System.EventArgs) Handles btnGo.Click
    ' This procedure calls the DisplayMessage procedure.
    lstOutput.Items.Add("Hello from the btnGo_Click procedure.")
    lstOutput.Items.Add("Now I am calling the DisplayMessage " & _
                    "procedure.")
    DisplayMessage()
    lstOutput.Items.Add("Now I am back in the btnGo_Click
                    procedure.")

End Sub
```

This type of statement, which is known as a *procedure call*, causes the procedure to execute. A procedure call is simply the name of the procedure that is to be executed. Notice that parentheses follow the name of the procedure. You can also use the Call key word, as

```
Call DisplayMessage()
```

The Call key word is optional, and is not used in this text.

When the application is running and a procedure call is encountered, the application branches to that procedure and executes its statements. When the procedure has finished, the application branches back to the procedure call and resumes executing at the next statement. Figure 6-3 illustrates how this application branches from the btnGo_Click procedure to the DisplayMessage procedure call, then back to the btnGo_Click procedure.

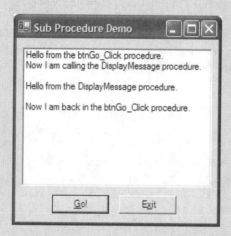

```
Private Sub btnGo_Click(ByVal sender As System.Object, _
       ByVal e As System.EventArgs) Handles btnGo.Click
    ' This procedure calls the DisplayMessage procedure.
    lstOutput.Items.Add("Hello from the btnGo_Click procedure.")
    lstOutput.Items.Add("Now I am calling the DisplayMessage " & _
                        "procedure.")
    DisplayMessage()
    lstOutput.Items.Add("Now I am back in the btnGo_Click procedure.")
End Sub

Sub DisplayMessage()
    ' A general procedure that displays a message.
    lstOutput.Items.Add("")
    lstOutput.Items.Add("Hello from the DisplayMessage procedure.")
    lstOutput.Items.Add("")
End Sub
```

(Diagram annotations: "procedure is called", "branch back")

Figure 6-3 Procedure call

Step 4: Run the application. Click the Go button. The form should appear as shown in Figure 6-4.

Figure 6-4 Results of Sub Procedure Demo

As you can see, the statements in the btnGo_Click event procedure executed up to the DisplayMessage procedure call. At that point, the application branched to the DisplayMessage procedure and executed all of its statements. When the DisplayMessage procedure finished, the application branched back to the btnGo_Click procedure and resumed executing at the line following the DisplayMessage call.

Step 5: Click the Exit button to end the application.

Declaring a Sub Procedure

The general format of a Sub procedure declaration is:

```
[AccessSpecifier] Sub ProcedureName ([ParameterList])
      [Statements]
End Sub
```

The items shown in brackets are optional. *AccessSpecifier* specifies the accessibility of the procedure. This is an important issue because some applications have more than one form. If you want a procedure that is declared in form A to be called from statements in form B, the procedure must be accessible to the statements in form B. Likewise, if you want to prevent statements outside form A from accessing the procedure, you must limit the accessibility of the procedure. Valid access specifiers are the key words `Private`, `Public`, `Protected`, `Friend`, and `Protected Friend`. When you use the `Private` access specifier, the procedure may only be accessed by other procedures declared in the same form. When a Sub procedure begins with `Public`, it may also be accessed by procedures that are declared in other forms. If you do not provide an access specifier, the Sub procedure becomes `Public`. We will not use access specifers in this chapter, but you will learn more about them in later chapters.

Following the key word `Sub` is the name of the procedure. You should always give the procedure a name that reflects its purpose. You should also adopt a consistent style of using upper- and lowercase letters. Recall from Chapter 3 that this text uses camel casing for variable names. For procedure names, we use *Pascal casing*, which capitalizes the first character and the first character of each subsequent word in the procedure name. All other characters are lowercase. Using different styles of capitalization for variables and procedures lets the reader of your code know what type of entity a name belongs to.

Inside the parentheses is an optional *ParameterList*. A parameter is a special variable that receives a value being passed into a procedure. Later in this chapter you will see procedures that use parameters to accept data that is passed into them.

The last line of a Sub procedure declaration is the `End Sub` statement. Between the `Sub` statement and the `End Sub` statement, you write the statements that are to execute each time the procedure is called.

Tutorial 6-2 guides you through this process of writing a Sub procedure. In the tutorial, you add two Sub procedures to an existing application on the student disk.

TUTORIAL 6-2:

Creating a Sub procedure

The student disk contains a partially completed test averaging application that should calculate and display a grade based on three test scores. The application gives the user two methods of determining the grade:

- ◆ Calculate the average of the three test scores and assign a letter grade.
- ◆ Drop the lowest of the three scores, calculate the average, and assign a letter grade.

Step 1:   Start Visual Basic .NET and open the Test Average project, which is stored in the \Chap6\Test Average folder on the student disk.

Step 2: Open the Design window and examine the application's form, which is shown in Figure 6-5.

The form has three text boxes in which the user will enter three test scores. The text boxes are named `txtTestScore1`, `txtTestScore2`, and `txtTestScore3`. The form has the labels `lblAverage` (to display the average test score) and `lblLetterGrade` (to display the assigned letter grade). The buttons are named `btnShow-Grade`, `btnDropLowest`, `btnClear`, and `btnExit`.

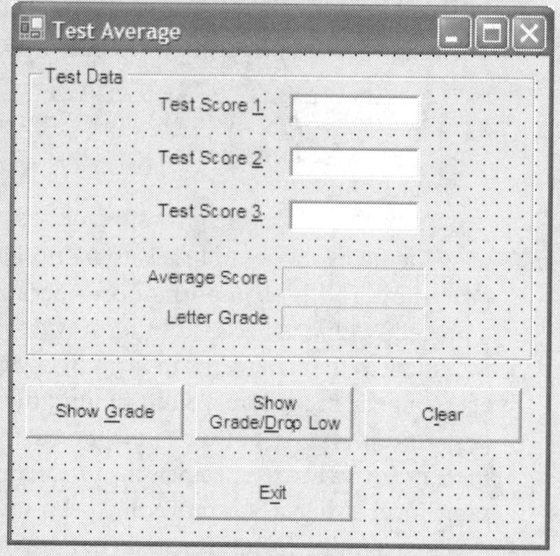

Figure 6-5 Test Average form

When the user clicks the Show Grade button (`btnShow Grade`), the application should simply calculate the average of the three test scores and determine the letter grade. The average and letter grade should be displayed in the appropriate labels. If the user clicks the Show Grade/Drop Low button (`btnDropLowest`), the application should calculate the average of the two highest scores (in effect, dropping the lowest score) and determine the letter grade. The average and letter grade should be displayed in the appropriate labels. Both buttons should calculate the average rounded to the nearest whole number.

Step 3: Open the Code window and look at the following class-level variable declarations.

```
' Class-level variables
Dim testScore1 As Integer ' To hold test score 1
Dim testScore2 As Integer ' To hold test score 2
Dim testScore3 As Integer ' To hold test score 3
Dim average As Integer     ' To hold average test score
```

The application has class-level variables to hold the three test scores and the average test score. By scrolling down in the Code window, you can see that the following event procedures have already been written:

```
btnClear_Click
btnExit_Click
btnDropLowest_Click
btnShowGrade_Click
```

In this tutorial, you will write the following Sub procedures:

- `GetScores` will copy the values in the `txtTestScore1`, `txtTestScore2`, and `txtTestScore3` text boxes into the `testScore1`, `testScore2`, and `testScore3` variables, respectively.

- ◆ `DisplayGrade` will display the student's grade based on the following scale:

90 through 100	A
80 through 89	B
70 through79	C
60 through 69	D
Below 60	F

Step 4: Scroll down to the bottom of the Code window and find the following comment:

```
' Write the declaration for the GetScores procedure here.
```

Delete the comment and in its place write the `GetScores` procedure, as follows.

```
Sub GetScores()
    ' Retrieve the test scores from the form and store
    ' them in variables.
    testScore1 = Val(txtTestScore1.Text)
    testScore2 = Val(txtTestScore2.Text)
    testScore3 = Val(txtTestScore3.Text)
End Sub
```

Step 5: Now you are ready to create the `DisplayGrade` procedure, which should perform the following steps:

- ◆ Assign the average test score to the `lblAverage` control's Text property.

- ◆ Determine the student's letter grade and assign it to the `lblLetterGrade` control's Text property.

Find the following comment, which appears near the bottom of the Code window.

```
' Write the declaration for the DisplayGrade procedure here.
```

Delete the comment and in its place write the `DisplayGrade` procedure, as follows.

```
Sub DisplayGrade()
    ' Determine the letter grade and display it.

    ' Display the average score.
    lblAverage.Text = average.ToString

    ' Determine and display the letter grade.
    Select Case average
        Case 90 To 100
            lblLetterGrade.Text = "A"
        Case 80 To 89
            lblLetterGrade.Text = "B"
        Case 70 To 79
            lblLetterGrade.Text = "C"
        Case 60 To 69
            lblLetterGrade.Text = "D"
        Case Else
            lblLetterGrade.Text = "F"
    End Select
End Sub
```

Step 6:   Now that you have created the Sub procedures, you must place appropriate procedure calls in the existing event procedures. First, locate the `btnShowGrade_Click` event procedure. Find the line in the procedure that reads

```
' Place a call to the GetScores procedure here.
```

Replace it with the following lines:

```
' Call the GetScores procedure
GetScores()
```

Step 7:   Still in the `btnShowGrade_Click` event procedure, locate the following line:

```
' Place a call to the DisplayGrade procedure here.
```

Replace it with the following lines:

```
' Call the DisplayGrade procedure
DisplayGrade()
```

The event procedure should now appear as the following code. The lines you added are shown in bold.

```
Private Sub btnShowGrade_Click(ByVal sender As System.Object, _
        ByVal e As System.EventArgs) Handles
btnShowGrade.Click
    ' Calculate the average test score and grade WITHOUT
    ' dropping the lowest score.

    ' Call the GetScores procedure
    GetScores()

    ' Calculate the average test score
    average = (testScore1 + testScore2 + testScore3) / 3
    ' Call the DisplayGrade procedure
    DisplayGrade()
End Sub
```

NOTE: *Because* average *is an integer variable, Visual Basic .NET will round its contents to the nearest whole number.*

Step 8:   Now locate the `btnDropLowest_Click` event procedure in the Code window. Find the line in the procedure that reads

```
' Place a call to the GetScores procedure here.
```

Replace it with the following lines:

```
' Call the GetScores procedure.
GetScores()
```

Step 9:   Still in the `btnDropLowest_Click` event procedure, locate the following line:

```
' Place a call to the DisplayGrade procedure here.
```

Replace it with the following lines:

```
' Call the DisplayGrade procedure
DisplayGrade()
```

The event procedure should now appear as the following code. The lines you added are shown in bold.

```
Private Sub btnDropLowest_Click(ByVal sender As System.Object, _
        ByVal e As System.EventArgs) Handles btnDropLowest.Click
    ' Drop the lowest test score and calculate
    ' the average score and grade.

    ' Call the GetScores procedure.
    GetScores()

    ' Determine the lowest score
    If testScore1 <= testScore2 And testScore1 <= testScore3 Then
        average = (testScore2 + testScore3) / 2
    ElseIf testScore2 <= testScore1 And testScore2 <= testScore3 Then
        average = (testScore1 + testScore3) / 2
    ElseIf testScore3 <= testScore1 And testScore3 <= testScore2 Then
        average = (testScore1 + testScore2) / 2
    End If

    ' Call the DisplayGrade procedure
    DisplayGrade()

End Sub
```

Step 10: Run the application. On the form, enter the following test scores: **90, 92,** and **77.** Click the Show Grade button. If you typed everything exactly as shown in this tutorial, the form should appear as in Figure 6-6.

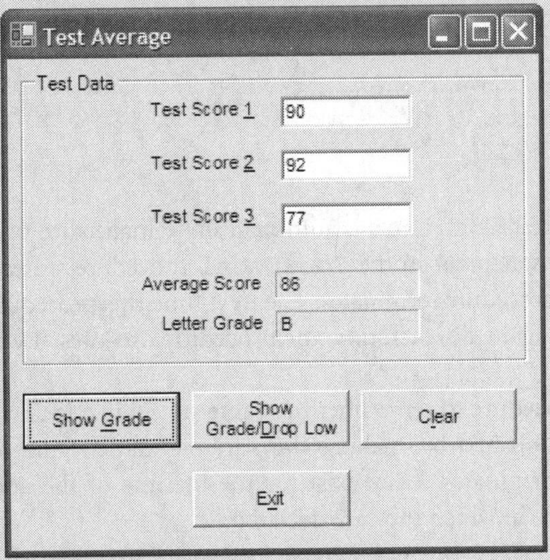

Figure 6-6   Completed Test Average form after Show Grade button is clicked

Step 11:   Click the Show Grade/Drop Low button. The form should appear as in Figure 6-7.

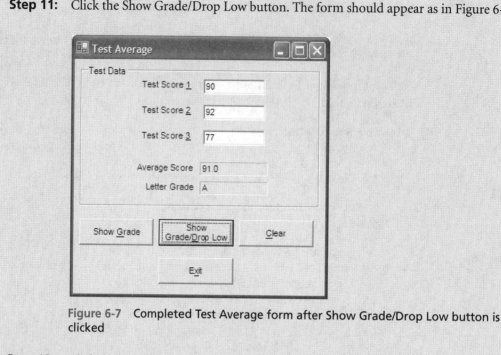

Figure 6-7   Completed Test Average form after Show Grade/Drop Low button is clicked

Step 12:   Click the Exit button to end the application.

If You Want to Know More: Static Local Variables

If a procedure is called more than once in a program, the values stored in the procedure's local variables do not persist between procedure calls. This is because the local variables are destroyed when the procedure terminates, and are then re-created when the procedure starts again. For example, look at the following Sub procedure:

```
Sub ShowLocal()
   Dim localNum As Integer

   MessageBox.Show(localNum.ToString)
   localNum = 99
End Sub
```

When this procedure is called, `localNum` is automatically initialized to 0, so the message box will display 0. Even though the last statement in the `ShowLocal` procedure stores 99 in `localNum`, the variable is destroyed when the procedure terminates. The next time this procedure is called, `localNum` is recreated and initialized to 0 again. So, each time the procedure executes, it will display 0 in the message box.

Sometimes you want a procedure to remember the value stored in a local variable between procedure calls. This can be accomplished by making the variable static. *Static local variables* are not destroyed when a procedure terminates. They exist for the lifetime of the application, even though their scope is only the procedure in which they are declared.

To declare a static local variable, simply use the word `Static` instead of `Dim`. Here is the general format of a static variable declaration:

```
Static VariableName As DataType
```

For example, look at the following Sub procedure.

```
Sub ShowStatic()
    Static staticNum As Integer

    MessageBox.Show(staticNum.ToString)
    staticNum += 1
End Sub
```

Notice that `staticNum` is declared `Static`. When the procedure is called, `staticNum` is automatically initialized to 0 and its value is displayed in the a message box. The last statement adds 1 to `staticNum`. Because the variable is static, it retains its value between procedure calls. The second time the procedure is called, `staticNum` will hold 1. Likewise, the third time the procedure is called, `staticNum` will hold 2, and so forth.

NOTE: *You cannot declare a class-level variable as* `Static`. *Only variables that are declared inside a procedure may be declared as* `Static`.

✓ **Checkpoint**

6.1 Figure 6-8 shows an application's form.

Figure 6-8 Form for Checkpoint 6.1 application

The list box is named `lstOutput`. The buttons are named `btnGo` and `btnExit`. The application's procedures are as follows:

```
Private Sub btnGo_Click(ByVal sender As System.Object, _
        ByVal e As System.EventArgs) Handles btnGo.Click
    Dim number As Integer

    number = Val(InputBox("Enter a number"))
    If number < 10 Then
        Message1()
```

```
                    Message2()
            Else
                Message2()
                Message1()
            End If

        End Sub

        Private Sub btnExit_Click(ByVal sender As System.Object, _
                ByVal e As System.EventArgs) Handles btnExit.Click
            ' End the application
            End
        End Sub

        Sub Message1()
            lstOutput.Items.Add("Able was I")
        End Sub

        Sub Message2()
            lstOutput.Items.Add("I saw Elba")
        End Sub
```

Suppose you run this application and click the `btnGo` button. What will the application display in the list box if you enter 10 into the input box? What if you enter 5?

6.2 What is the difference between a regular local variable and a static local variable?

▶ 6.3   Passing Values to a Sub Procedure

CONCEPT

WHEN A PROCEDURE IS CALLED, VALUES MAY BE PASSED TO IT.

Values that are sent into a procedure are called arguments. You are already familiar with how to use arguments. In the following statement the `Val` function is being called and an argument, `txtInput.Text`, is passed to it.

```
value = Val(txtInput.Text)
```

There are two ways to pass an argument to a procedure: by value, or by reference. Passing an argument *by value* means that only a copy of the argument is passed to the procedure. Because the procedure has only a copy, it cannot make changes to the original argument. When an argument is passed *by reference*, however, the procedure has access to the original argument and can make changes to it.

In order for a procedure to accept an argument, it must be equipped with a parameter. A *parameter* is a special variable that receives an argument being passed into a procedure. Here is an example Sub procedure that uses a parameter:

```
Sub DisplayValue(ByVal number As Integer)
    ' This procedure displays a value in a message box.
```

```
        MessageBox.Show(number.ToString)
    End Sub
```

Notice the statement inside the parentheses:

```
    ByVal number As Integer
```

This statement declares the variable number as an integer parameter. The key word ByVal indicates that arguments passed into the variable are passed by value. This parameter variable enables the DisplayValue procedure to accept an integer argument.

TIP: The declaration of the parameter variable looks like a regular variable declaration, except the word ByVal is used instead of Dim.

Here is an example of how you would call the procedure and pass an argument to it:

```
    DisplayValue(5)
```

The argument, 5, is listed inside the parentheses. This value is passed into the procedure's parameter variable, number. This is illustrated in Figure 6-9.

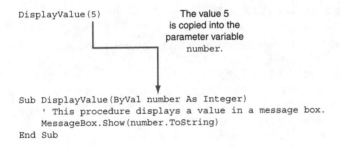

Figure 6-9   Passing 5 to DisplayValue

You may also pass variables and the values of expressions as arguments. For example, the following statements call the DisplayValue procedure with various arguments passed.

```
    DisplayValue(x)
    DisplayValue(x * 4)
    DisplayValue(CInt(txtInput.Text))
```

The first statement passes the value in the variable x as the argument. The second statement passes the result of x * 4 as the argument. The third statement passes the value returned from CInt (txtInput.Text) as the argument.

Tutorial 6-3 guides you through an application that demonstrates argument passing.

TUTORIAL 6-3:

Examining an application that demonstrates argument passing to a procedure

Step 1:   Start Visual Basic .NET and open the Argument Demo project, which is stored in the \Chap6\Argument Demo folder on the student disk. The application's form is shown in Figure 6-10. The application's form has four buttons: btnDemo1, btnDemo2, btnDemo3, and btnExit.

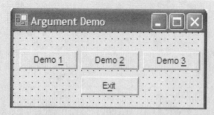

Figure 6-10   Argument Demo form

Step 2:   In addition to the event procedures for each of the form's buttons, the application uses the DisplayValue procedure described earlier. Open the Code window and locate the btnDemo1_Click event procedure. The code is as follows:

```
Private Sub btnDemo1_Click(ByVal sender As System.Object, _
        ByVal e As System.EventArgs) Handles btnDemo1.Click
    ' This procedure passes an argument to the
    ' DisplayValue procedure.
    DisplayValue(5)
End Sub
```

This event procedure calls DisplayValue with 5 as the argument.

Step 3:   Locate the btnDemo2_Click event procedure. The code is as follows:

```
Private Sub btnDemo2_Click(ByVal sender As System.Object, _
        ByVal e As System.EventArgs) Handles btnDemo2.Click
    ' This procedure calls the DisplayValue procedure
    ' several times, passing different arguments.
    DisplayValue(5)
    DisplayValue(10)
    DisplayValue(2)
    DisplayValue(16)
    ' Now, the value of an expression is passed to the
    ' DisplayValue procedure.
    DisplayValue(3 + 5)
End Sub
```

This event procedure calls the DisplayValue procedure five times. Each procedure call is given a different argument. Notice the last procedure call:

```
DisplayValue(3 + 5)
```

This statement passes the value of an expression as the argument. When this statement executes, the value 8 will be passed to DisplayValue.

Step 4:   Locate the btnDemo3_Click event procedure. The code is as follows:

```
Private Sub btnDemo3_Click(ByVal sender As System.Object, _
        ByVal e As System.EventArgs) Handles btnDemo3.Click
    ' This procedure uses a loop to call the DisplayValue
    ' procedure, passing a variable as the argument.
```

```
        Dim count As Integer

        For count = 1 To 10
            DisplayValue(count)
        Next count
    End Sub
```

This event procedure has a local variable named count. It uses a For...Next loop to call the DisplayValue procedure ten times, each time passing the count variable as the argument.

Step 5: Run the application and click the Demo 1 button. A message box appears displaying the value 5.

Step 6: Click the Demo 2 button. Five successive message boxes are displayed, showing the values 5, 10, 2, 16, and 8.

Step 7: Click the Demo 3 button. Ten successive message boxes are displayed, showing the values 1 through 10.

Step 8: Exit the application.

Passing Multiple Arguments

Often, it is useful to pass more than one argument to a procedure. For example, here is a procedure that accepts two arguments.

```
Sub ShowSum(ByVal num1 As Integer, ByVal num2 As Integer)
    ' This procedure accepts two arguments, and prints
    ' their sum on the form.
    Dim sum As Integer

    sum = num1 + num2
    MessageBox.Show("The sum is " & sum.ToString)
End Sub
```

Assuming that value1 and value2 are integer variables, here is an example call to the ShowSum procedure.

```
ShowSum(value1, value2)
```

When a procedure with multiple parameters is called, the arguments are passed to the parameters in the order they appear in. This is illustrated in Figure 6-11.
The following procedure call will cause 5 to be passed into the num1 parameter and 10 to be passed into num2:

```
ShowSum(5, 10)
```

However, the following procedure call will cause 10 to be passed into the num1 parameter and 5 to be passed into num2:

```
ShowSum(10, 5)
```

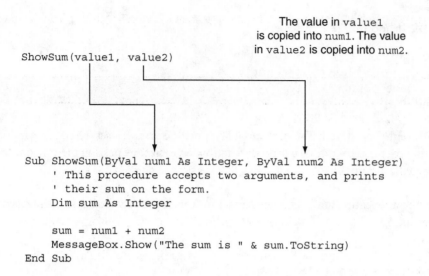

```
ShowSum(value1, value2)
```

The value in value1 is copied into num1. The value in value2 is copied into num2.

```
Sub ShowSum(ByVal num1 As Integer, ByVal num2 As Integer)
    ' This procedure accepts two arguments, and prints
    ' their sum on the form.
    Dim sum As Integer

    sum = num1 + num2
    MessageBox.Show("The sum is " & sum.ToString)
End Sub
```

Figure 6-11 Multiple arguments passed to multiple parameters

More About Passing Arguments by Value or by Reference

You have learned that when the ByVal key word is used in the declaration of a parameter variable, an argument is passed by value to the parameter. This means that only a copy of the argument is passed to the parameter variable. If the parameter's value is changed inside the procedure, it has no affect on the original argument.

When an argument is passed by reference, however, the procedure has access to the original argument. Any changes made to the parameter variable are actually performed on the original argument. You use the ByRef key word in the declaration of a parameter variable to cause arguments to be passed by reference to the parameter. Here is an example of a procedure that uses ByRef:

```
Sub GetName(ByRef name as String)
    ' Get the user's name
    name = InputBox("Enter your name.")
End Sub
```

This procedure uses ByRef to declare the name parameter. Any argument passed into the parameter is passed by reference, and any changes made to name are actually made to the argument passed into it. For example, assume the following code is used to call the procedure.

```
' Declare a string variable
Dim userName As String
' Get the user's name
GetName(userName)
' Display the user's name
MessageBox.Show("Your name is " & userName)
```

This code calls the GetName procedure and passes the string variable userName, by reference, into the name parameter. The GetName procedure displays an input box instructing the user to enter his or her name. The user's input is stored in the name variable. Because userName was passed by reference, the value stored in name is actually stored in userName. When the message box is displayed, it will show the name entered by the user.

Tutorial 6-4 further demonstrates how passing an argument by reference differs from passing it by value.

TUTORIAL 6-4:

Working with **ByVal** and **ByRef**

In this tutorial you examine a procedure that accepts a `ByVal` argument. You then change `ByVal` to `ByRef`, to see how the procedure behaves differently.

Step 1:   Start Visual Basic .NET and open the ByVal ByRef Demo project, which is stored in the \Chap6\ByVal ByRef Demo folder on the student disk. The application's form is shown in Figure 6-12.

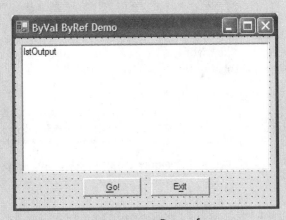

Figure 6-12 `ByVal ByRef` **Demo form**

The form has a list box named `lstOutput` and two buttons named `btnGo` and `btnExit`.

Step 2:   Open the Code window and look at the `btnGo_Click` event procedure. The code is as follows:

```
Private Sub btnGo_Click(ByVal sender As System.Object, _
       ByVal e As System.EventArgs) Handles btnGo.Click
   Dim number As Integer

   number = 100
   lstOutput.Items.Add("Inside btnGo_Click the value of " & _
                       "number is " & number.ToString)
   lstOutput.Items.Add("Now I am calling ChangeArg.")
   ChangeArg(number)
   lstOutput.Items.Add("Now back in btnGo_Click, the value of " & _
                       "number is " & number.ToString)
End Sub
```

Notice the variable `number` is set to 100. This procedure calls the `ChangeArg` procedure and passes `number` as the argument.

Step 3:   Now look at the `ChangeArg` procedure. The code is as follows:

```
Sub ChangeArg(ByVal arg As Integer)
    lstOutput.Items.Add("Inside the ChangeArg procedure, I will " & _
                     "change the value of arg.")
    arg = 0
    lstOutput.Items.Add("arg is now " & arg)
End Sub
```

Notice that the parameter variable, `arg`, is declared `ByVal`.

Step 4:   Run the application and click the Go! button. The form should appear as shown in Figure 6-13. Even though the `ChangeArg` procedure set `arg` to 0, the value of `number` did not change. This is because the `ByVal` key word was used in the declaration of `arg`.

Step 5:   Click the Exit button to end the application.

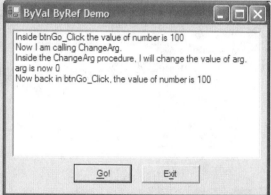

Figure 6-13   Results with argument passed by value

Step 6:   Open the Code window. Change the `ByVal` key word in the `ChangeArg` procedure to `ByRef`. The first line of the procedure should now look like this:

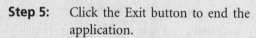

```
Sub ChangeArg(ByRef arg As Integer)
```

Step 7:   Run the application again and click the Go! button. The form should appear as Figure 6-14. This time, when `ChangeArg` set `arg` to 0, it changed the value of `number` to 0. This is because the `ByRef` key word was used in the declaration of `arg`.

Step 8:   Exit the application.

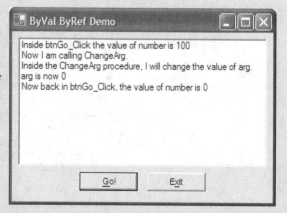

Figure 6-14   Results with argument passed by reference

NOTE: *As you have learned, it is possible to pass variables as arguments to procedures. It is also possible to pass non-variables, such as constants and expressions, as arguments to procedures. Although you can pass both variable and non-variable arguments by reference, only variable arguments can be changed by the procedure receiving the arguments. If you pass a non-variable argument by reference to a procedure, the procedure cannot change the argument.*

If You Want to Know More: The Event Procedure Parameters

When you create a code template for an event procedure, two parameters are always listed inside the event procedure's parentheses. Here is an example of the first line of a button's `Click` event procedure.

```
Private Sub btnClear_Click(ByVal sender As System.Object,
            ByVal e As System.EventArgs) Handles btnClear.Click
```

As you can see, the event procedure has two parameters: `sender` and `e`. The `sender` parameter references the object that triggered the event, and can be used to get information about that object. The use of the `sender` parameter is beyond the scope of this book.

The `e` parameter can contain values passed by the object that triggered the event. These values differ from one type of event to another. You do not use the `e` parameter in a `Click` event procedure, but in Chapter 5 you saw how it is used in the `Validating` event procedure. Other uses of the `e` parameter are determined by the type of event procedure being called. The only time we use the `e` parameter in this text is in the `Validating` event procedure.

✓ Checkpoint

6.3   On paper, write the code for a Sub procedure named `TimesTen`. The procedure should have an integer parameter variable named `value`. The procedure should multiply the parameter by 10 and display the result in a message box.

6.4   Write a statement that calls the `TimesTen` procedure you wrote in Checkpoint 6.3. Pass the number 25 as the argument.

6.5   On paper, write the code for a Sub procedure named `PrintTotal`. The procedure should have the following three parameters:

```
num1, a Single
num2, an Integer
num3, a Long
```

The procedure should calculate the total of the three numbers and display the result in a message box.

6.6   Write a statement that calls the `PrintTotal` procedure you wrote in Checkpoint 6.5. Pass the variables `units`, `weight`, and `count` as the arguments. The variable `weight` should be passed into the `num1` parameter, the variable `count` should be passed into the `num2` parameter, and the variable `units` should be passed into the `num3` parameter.

6.7   You need to write a procedure that accepts an argument, and uses the argument in a mathematical operation. You want to make sure that the original argument is not altered. Do you declare the parameter `ByRef` or `ByVal`?

▶ 6.4 Function Procedures

CONCEPT

A FUNCTION PROCEDURE RETURNS A VALUE TO THE PART OF THE PROGRAM THAT CALLED THE FUNCTION PROCEDURE.

This section shows you how to write your own function procedures (which are usually just called *functions*). Like a Sub procedure, a *function procedure* is a set of statements that perform a task when the function is called. A function, however, returns a value that can be used in an expression.

You are already experienced at using functions. For instance, you have used the intrinsic `Val` function to convert strings to numbers. You have also seen the intrinsic functions `FormatNumber` and `FormatCurrency`, which convert numbers to strings. Now you will learn to write your own functions that return values in the same way that the intrinsic functions do.

Declaring a Function

The general format of a function procedure declaration is:

```
[AccessSpecifier] Function FunctionName ([ParameterList])
As DataType
        [Statements]
End Function
```

A function declaration is very much like a Sub procedure declaration. *AccessSpecifier* is optional, and specifies the accessibility of the function. As with Sub procedures, you may use the key words `Private`, `Public`, `Protected`, `Friend`, and `Protected Friend` as access specifiers. Next is the key word `Function`, followed by the name of the function. Inside the parentheses is an optional *ParameterList*. Following the parentheses is `As DataType`, where *DataType* is any Visual Basic .NET data type. The data type listed in this part of the declaration is the data type of the value returned by the function.

The last line of a function declaration is the `End Function` statement. Between the `Function` statement and the `End Function` statement, you write the statements that are to execute each time the function is called. Here is an example of a completed function:

```
Function Sum(ByVal num1 As Single, ByVal num2 As Single) As Single
    Dim result As Single

    result = num1 + num2
    Return result
End Function
```

This code shows a function named `Sum` that accepts two arguments, adds them, and returns their sum. (Everything you have learned about passing arguments to Sub procedures applies to functions as well.) The `Sum` function has two parameter variables, `num1` and `num2`, both of the Single data type. Notice that the words `As Single` appear after the parentheses. This indicates that the value returned by the function will be of the `Single` data type.

Inside the function, the following lines appear:

```
Dim result As Single
```

```
result = num1 + num2
Return result
```

The first line declares a local variable, `result`. The second line adds the parameter variables num1 and num2 and stores the result in `result`. The last line reads `Return result`. The Return statement causes the function to end execution and returns a value to the part of the program that called the function. The general format of the `Return` statement, when used to return a value from a function, is:

```
Return Expression
```

Expression is the value that is to be returned. It can be any expression that has a value, such as a variable, a constant, or a mathematical expression. In this case, the Sum function returns the value in the `result` variable. However, we could have eliminated the `result` variable, and returned the expression num1 + num2, as shown in the following code.

```
Function Sum(ByVal num1 As Single, ByVal num2 As Single) As Single
    Return num1 + num2
End Function
```

The value of the `Return` statement's expression should be the same as the function's return type. For example, the Sum function returns a Single, so the value of the `Return` statement's expression should be of the Single data type. If the return value cannot be converted to the function's return data type, a run-time error will occur.

Calling a Function

Assuming that `total`, `value1`, and `value2` are variables of the Single data type, here is an example of how you might call the Sum function:

```
total = Sum(value1, value2)
```

This statement passes the variables `value1` and `value2` as arguments. It assigns the value returned by the Sum function to the variable `total`. So, if `value1` is 20.0 and `value2` is 40.0, the statement will assign 60.0 to `total`.

Figure 6-15 illustrates how the arguments are passed into the function and how a value is passed back from the function.

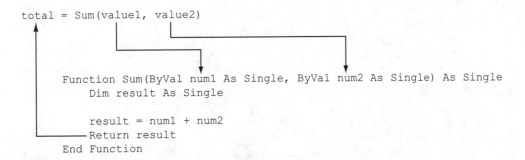

Figure 6-15   Arguments passed and a value returned

In Tutorial 6-5, you examine an application that has several functions.

TUTORIAL 6-5:

Examining the GPA Calculator application

In this tutorial you examine the grade point average (GPA) calculator application, which allows a student to enter his or her grades and number of credit hours for four courses, then calculates the student's GPA. The GPA is calculated in the following manner: The student receives a grade of A, B, C, D, or F for each course. Each course is then assigned a number of grade points, based on the grade. Table 6-1 shows the number of grade points assigned for each grade.

Table 6-1

Grade points assigned for each grade

Course Grade	Grade Points
A	4
B	3
C	2
D	1
F	0

Each course's grade points are then multiplied by the course's credit hours. This gives the course's quality points. The quality points for all the courses are then totaled and divided by the total number of credit hours. The result is the grade point average. Table 6-2 gives an example.

Table 6-2

Sample grade point average

Course Grade Points	Credit Hours	Grade Points	Course Quality
B	3	3	9
A	3	4	12
C	4	2	8
D	2	1	2
Total Credit Hours →	12	Total Quality Points →	31

GPA = Total Quality Points / Total Credit Hours
= 31 / 12
= 2.58

The GPA calculator application uses functions to perform the necessary calculations.

Step 1: Start Visual Basic .NET and open the GPA Calculator project, which is stored in the \Chap6\GPA Calculator folder on the student disk. The application's form is shown in Figure 6-16.

The letter grades are entered into four text boxes named txtGrade1, txtGrade2, txtGrade3, and txtGrade4. The course credit hours are entered into four text boxes named txtCreditHours1, txtCreditHours2, txtCreditHours3, and txtCreditHours4. All of these controls have Validating event procedures that ensure the user has entered valid data.

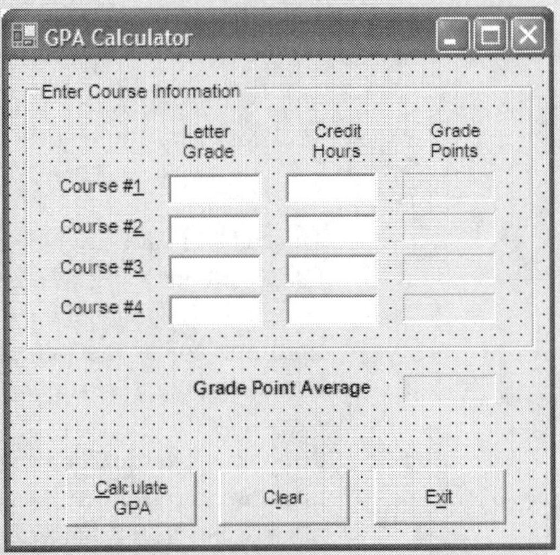

Figure 6-16   GPA Calculator form

When the Calculate GPA button (btnCalculate) is clicked, the application displays the grade points for each course in the labels lblGradePoints1, lblGradePoints2, lblGradePoints3, and lblGradePoints4. The grade point average is displayed in a label named lblGPA.

Step 2: Open the Code window and look at the btnCalculate_Click event procedure. The code is as follows:

```
Private Sub btnCalculate_Click(ByVal sender As System.Object, _
       ByVal e As System.EventArgs) Handles btnCalculate.Click
    ' This event procedure displays the quality points for
    ' each course and the GPA.
    Dim gradePointAverage As Single ' To hold the GPA
    Dim gradePoints As Integer      ' To hold the grade points

    ' Display the quality points for course 1.
    gradePoints = CalcGradePoints(txtGrade1.Text)
    lblGradePoints1.Text = gradePoints.ToString

    ' Display the quality points for course 2.
    gradePoints = CalcGradePoints(txtGrade2.Text)
    lblGradePoints2.Text = gradePoints.ToString

    ' Display the quality points for course 3.
    gradePoints = CalcGradePoints(txtGrade3.Text)
    lblGradePoints3.Text = gradePoints.ToString

    ' Display the quality points for course 4.
    gradePoints = CalcGradePoints(txtGrade4.Text)
    lblGradePoints4.Text = gradePoints.ToString

    ' Get the GPA and display it with 2 decimal places
    gradePointAverage = CalcGPA()
    lblGPA.Text = FormatNumber(gradePointAverage, 2)
End Sub
```

Look at the first section of code following the variable declarations:

```
' Display the quality points for course 1.
gradePoints = CalcGradePoints(txtGrade1.Text)
lblGradePoints1.Text = gradePoints.ToString
```

This code displays the grade points for course 1. Notice that the second line shown here calls a function named CalcGradePoints, and passes txtGrade1.Text as the argument. The function's return value is assigned to the variable gradePoints. The third line copies the value in gradePoints to the lblGradePoints1 label. Notice that there are similar sections of code for course 2, course 3, and course 4.

Step 3:   Scroll down in the Code window and find the CalcGradePoints function. This function accepts a string argument which holds a letter grade. It returns the number of grade points for that letter grade. Here is the code for the function:

```
Function CalcGradePoints(ByVal grade As String) As Integer
    ' This function accepts a letter grade as an argument
    ' and returns the number of grade points for that grade.
    Dim points As Integer     ' To hold the grade points

    Select Case grade.ToUpper
        Case "A"
            points = 4
        Case "B"
            points = 3
        Case "C"
            points = 2
        Case "D"
            points = 1
        Case "F"
            points = 0
    End Select

    ' Return the number of grade points
    Return points
End Function
```

This function uses a Select Case statement to determine the number of grade points, which is assigned to the points variable. The Return statement returns the value in points.

Step 4:   Scroll back to the btnCalculate_Click event procedure. Look at the following line, which appears near the bottom of the procedure, after the grade points have been calculated and displayed for all four courses.

```
gradePointAverage = CalcGPA()
```

The statement calls the CalcGPA function and assigns its return value to the gradePointAverage variable. Notice that no argument is passed to the CalcGPA function.

Step 5:   Scroll down in the Code window and find the CalcGPA function. Here is the code for the function:

```
Function CalcGPA()
    ' This Function calculates the student's GPA and
    ' returns that value.
    Dim totalCH As Integer  ' To hold total credit hours
    Dim totalQP As Integer  ' To hold total quality points
    Dim gpa As Single       ' To hold grade point average

    ' Get the total credit hours.
    totalCH = Val(txtCreditHours1.Text) + _
              Val(txtCreditHours2.Text) + _
              Val(txtCreditHours3.Text) + _
              Val(txtCreditHours4.Text)
' Caculate the quality points
totalQP = (Val(txtCreditHours1.Text) * Val(lblGradePoints1.Text)) + _
          (Val(txtCreditHours2.Text) * Val(lblGradePoints2.Text)) + _
          (Val(txtCreditHours3.Text) * Val(lblGradePoints3.Text)) + _
          (Val(txtCreditHours4.Text) * Val(lblGradePoints4.Text))
    ' Divide the total quality points by the total credit hours
    ' to get the GPA.
    gpa = totalQP / totalCH
    ' Return the GPA
    Return gpa
End Function
```

Look at the first section of code after the variable declarations.

```
    ' Get the total credit hours.
    totalCH = Val(txtCreditHours1.Text) + _
              Val(txtCreditHours2.Text) + _
              Val(txtCreditHours3.Text) + _
              Val(txtCreditHours4.Text)
```

This code adds the credit hours for each of the four courses and stores the total in totalCH. Now look at the next section of code:

```
 ' Caculate the quality points
totalQP = (Val(txtCreditHours1.Text) * Val(lblGradePoints1.Text)) + _
          (Val(txtCreditHours2.Text) * Val(lblGradePoints2.Text)) + _
          (Val(txtCreditHours3.Text) * Val(lblGradePoints3.Text)) + _
          (Val(txtCreditHours4.Text) * Val(lblGradePoints4.Text))
```

Recall that a course's quality points are calculated as the course's credit hours multiplied by the course's grade points. This code adds all of the quality points for all of the courses and stores the total in totalQP. Here is the next section of code:

```
 ' Divide the total quality points by the total credit hours
 ' to get the GPA.
 gpa = totalQP / totalCH
 ' Return the GPA
 Return gpa
```

This code calculates the GPA and stores it in the variable gpa. The `Return` statement ends the function's execution and returns the value in gpa.

Step 6: Scroll back to the `btnCalculate_Click` procedure and look at the last line inside the procedure:

```
lblGPA.Text = FormatNumber(gradePointAverage, 2)
```

This line formats the value in `gradePointAverage` (which now holds the value returned from the `CalcGPA` function) and assigns it to `lblGPA.Text`.

Step 7: Run the application, and enter the following values:

Course Grade	Credit Hours
B	3
A	3
C	4
D	2

Step 8: Click the Calculate GPA button. The form should look like Figure 6-17.

Step 9: Click the Exit button to end the application.

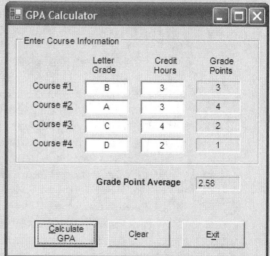

Figure 6-17 Completed GPA Calculator form

If You Want to Know More About Functions: Returning Nonnumeric Values

When writing functions, you are not limited to returning numeric values. You can also return nonnumeric values, such as strings and Boolean values. For example, here is the code for a function that returns a string value.

```
Function FullName(ByVal first As String, ByVal last As String) As String
    Dim name As String
    name = last & ", " & first
    Return name
End Function
```

Here is an example of a call to this function:

```
customer = FullName("John", "Martin")
```

After this call, the string variable `customer` will hold "Martin, John".
Here is an example of a function that returns a Boolean value:

```
Function IsValid(num As Integer) As Boolean
    Dim status As Boolean
```

```
        If num >= 0 And num <= 100 Then
            status = True
        Else
            status = False
        End If
        Return status
    End Function
```

This function returns true if its argument is within the range 0 to 100. Otherwise, it returns false. The following code segment has an If...Then statement with an example call to the function:

```
value = 20
If IsValid(value) Then
    MessageBox.Show("The value is within range.")
Else
    MessageBox.Show("The value is out of range.")
End If
```

When this code executes, it will display "The value is within range." in a message box. Here is another example:

```
value = 200
If IsValid(value) Then
    MessageBox.Show("The value is within range.")
Else
    MessageBox.Show("The value is out of range.")
End If
```

When this code executes, it will display "The value is out of range." in a message box.

✓ Checkpoint

6.8   Look at the following line, which is the first line of a function, then answer the questions.

```
Function Distance(ByVal rate As Single, ByVal time As Single) As Single
```

a. What is the name of the function?
b. When you call this function, how many arguments do you pass to it?
c. What are the names of the parameter variables and what are their data types?
d. This function returns a value of what data type?

6.9   Write the first line of a function named Days. The function should return an integer value. It should have three integer parameters: years, months, and weeks. All arguments should be passed by value.

6.10   Write an example function call statement for the function described in Checkpoint 6.9.

6.11   Write the first line of a function named LightYears. The function should return a value of the Single data type. It should have one parameter variable, miles, of the Long data type. The parameter should declared so that the argument is passed by value.

6.12   Write an example function call statement for the function described in Checkpoint 6.11.

6.13   Write the entire code for a function named TimesTwo. The function should accept an integer argument and return the value of that argument multiplied by two.

▶ 6.5 More About Debugging: Stepping Into, Over, and Out of Procedures and Functions

CONCEPT

VISUAL BASIC .NET'S DEBUGGING COMMANDS ALLOW YOU TO SINGLE-STEP THROUGH APPLICATIONS WITH PROCEDURE AND FUNCTION CALLS. THE STEP INTO COMMAND ALLOWS YOU TO SINGLE-STEP THROUGH A CALLED PROCEDURE OR FUNCTION. THE STEP OVER COMMAND ALLOWS YOU TO EXECUTE A PROCEDURE OR FUNCTION CALL WITHOUT SINGLE-STEPPING THROUGH ITS LINES. THE STEP OUT COMMAND ALLOWS YOU TO EXECUTE ALL THE REMAINING LINES OF A PROCEDURE OR FUNCTION THAT YOU ARE SINGLE-STEPPING THROUGH.

In Chapter 3, you learned to set a breakpoint in your application's code, and to single-step through the code's execution. This section shows you how to step into or step over a procedure or function, and step out of a procedure or function.

Recall that when an application is in break mode, the Step Into command causes the currently highlighted line (the execution point) to execute. If that line contains a call to a procedure or a function, the next line that is highlighted is the first line in that procedure or function. In other words, the *Step Into command* allows you to single-step through a procedure or function when that procedure or function is called. Recall that you activate the Step Into command by using one of these methods:

- ◆ Pressing the F8 key
- ◆ Selecting Debug from the menu bar, then selecting Step Into from the Debug menu
- ◆ Clicking the Step Into button ( ) on the Debug Toolbar, if the Toolbar is visible

Like the Step Into command, the *Step Over command* causes the currently highlighted line to execute. If the line contains a procedure or function call, however, the procedure or function is executed and you are not given an opportunity to single-step through its statements. The entire procedure or function is executed, and the next line in the current procedure is highlighted. You activate the Step Over command by using one of these methods:

- ◆ Pressing Shift+F8
- ◆ Selecting Debug from the menu bar, then selecting Step Over from the Debug menu
- ◆ Clicking the Step Over button ( ) on the Debug Toolbar, if the Toolbar is visible

You use the *Step Out command* when you are single-stepping through a procedure or function and you want the remainder of the procedure or function to complete execution without single-stepping. After the procedure or function has completed, the line following the procedure or function call is highlighted, and you may resume single-stepping. You activate the Step Out command by using one of these methods:

- ◆ Pressing Ctrl+Shift+F8
- ◆ Selecting Debug from the menu bar, then selecting Step Out from the Debug menu
- ◆ Clicking the Step Out button ( ) on the Debug Toolbar, if the Toolbar is visible

In Tutorial 6-6 you practice using each of these commands.

TUTORIAL 6-6:

Practicing the Step Into, Step Over, and Step Out Commands

In this tutorial, you use the GPA calculator application to practice single-stepping through procedures and functions.

Step 1:   Start Visual Basic .NET and open the GPA calculator project, which is stored in the \Chap6\GPA Calculator folder on the student disk.

Step 2:   Open the Code window and set a breakpoint at the line in the btnCalculate _Click event procedure shown in Figure 6-18.

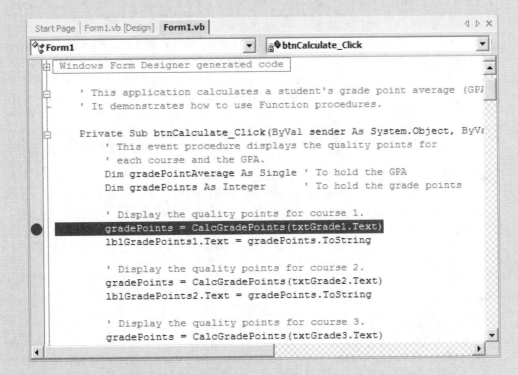

Figure 6-18   Location of breakpoint

TIP: Recall that you set a breakpoint by clicking the mouse while the pointer is positioned in the left margin, next to the line of code. You can also move the text cursor to the line you wish to set as a breakpoint, then press F9.

Step 3:   Run the application, and enter some grade and credit hour values on the form. (Which values you enter is unimportant, as long as they are valid.)

Step 4:   Click the Calculate GPA button. The application enters break mode with the breakpoint line highlighted.

Step 5:   Notice that the highlighted line contains a call to the CalcGradePoints function. Press F8 to execute the Step Into command.

Step 6: Because you pressed F8, the first line of the CalcGradePoints function is highlighted next. Continue pressing the F8 key to single-step though the CalcGradePoints function. When the End Function line is highlighted, press F8 once more to return to the line containing the function call.

Step 7: Press the F8 key two more times. The execution point should be positioned at the line shown in Figure 6-19. Notice that this line also contains a call to the CalcGradePoints function.

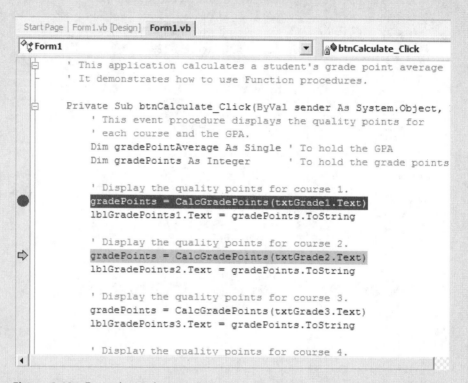

Figure 6-19 Execution point

Step 8: Now execute the Step Over command by pressing Shift+F8. The line executes and the function is called, but you did not single-step through it. The next line is now highlighted.

> **TIP:** When the current execution point does not contain a procedure or function call, both the Step Into and Step Over commands perform identically.

Step 9: Press F8 one time. The line that is now highlighted should also contain a call to the CalcGradePoints function. Press F8 again to step into the function.

Step 10: Because you pressed F8, the first line of the CalcGradePoints function should be highlighted. Press the F8 key once more to advance to the next line in the function.

Step 11: Instead of continuing to step through the function, you will now step out of the function. Now press Ctrl+Shift+F8 to execute the Step Out command. Single-stepping is suspended while the remaining statements in the `CalcGPA` function execute. You are returned back to the `btnCalculate_Click` procedure, at the line containing the function call.

Step 12: Press F5 or click Debug on the menu bar and then click Continue to exit break mode, and resume run mode.

Step 13: Click the Exit button to end the application.

✓ Checkpoint

6.14 You are debugging an application in break mode, and are single-stepping through a function that has been called. If you want to execute the remaining lines of the function and return to the line that called the function, what command do you use? What key(s) do you press to execute this command?

6.15 You are debugging an application in break mode and the current execution point contains a procedure call. If you want to single-step through the procedure that is being called, what command do you use? What key(s) do you press to execute this command?

6.16 You are debugging an application in break mode, and the current execution point contains a function call. If you want to execute the line, but not single-step through the function, what command do you use? What key(s) do you press to execute this command?

▶ 6.6 Focus on Program Design and Problem Solving: Building the Bagel and Coffee Price Calculator Application

CONCEPT

IN THIS SECTION YOU BUILD THE BAGEL AND COFFEE PRICE CALCULATOR APPLICATION. THE APPLICATION USES SUB PROCEDURES AND FUNCTIONS TO CALCULATE THE TOTAL OF A CUSTOMER ORDER.

Brandi's Bagel House has a bagel and coffee delivery service for the businesses in her neighborhood. Customers may call in and order white and whole wheat bagels with a variety of toppings. In addition, customers may order three different types of coffee. Here is a complete price list:

Bagels:
White bagel	$1.25
Whole wheat bagel	$1.50

Toppings:
Cream cheese	$0.50
Butter	$0.25
Blueberry jam	$0.75

| Raspberry jam | $0.75 |
| Peach jelly | $0.75 |

Coffee:

Regular coffee	$1.25
Cappuccino	$2.00
Café au lait	$1.75

(Note: Delivery for coffee alone is not offered.)

Brandi, the owner, has asked you to write an application that her staff can use to record an order as it is called in. The application should display the total of the order, including 6% sales tax. Figure 6-20 shows a sketch of the application's form and identifies all the controls with programmer-defined names.

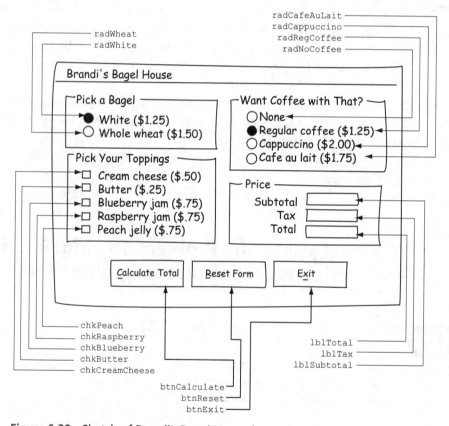

Figure 6-20   Sketch of Brandi's Bagel House form

Table 6-3 lists each control, along with any relevant property settings.

Table 6-3

Bagel and Coffee Calculator controls

Control Type	Control Name	Properties
Form	(Default)	Text: "Brandi's Bagel House"
ToolTip	(Default)	Retain all default property settings.
GroupBox	(Default)	Text: "Pick a Bagel"

Table 6-3 *continued*

Bagel and Coffee Calculator controls

Control Type	Control Name	Properties
RadioButton	radWhite	Text: "White" Checked: True ToolTip on ToolTip1: "Click here to choose a white bagel."
RadioButton	radWheat	Text: "Whole Wheat" Checked: False ToolTip on ToolTip1: "Click here to choose a whole wheat bagel."
GroupBox	(Default)	Text: "Pick Your Toppings"
CheckBox	chkCreamCheese	Text: "Cream Cheese ($.50)" Checked: False ToolTip on ToolTip1: "Click here to choose a cream cheese."
CheckBox	chkButter	Text: "Butter ($.25)" Checked: False ToolTip on ToolTip1: "Click here to choose butter."
CheckBox	chkBlueberry	Text: "Blueberry Jam ($.75)" Checked: False ToolTip on ToolTip1: "Click here to choose blueberry jam."
CheckBox	chkRaspBerry	Text: "Raspberry Jam ($.75)" Checked: False ToolTip on ToolTip1: "Click here to choose raspberry jam."
CheckBox	chkPeach	Text: "Peach Jelly ($.75)" Checked: False ToolTip on ToolTip1: "Click here to choose peach jelly."
GroupBox	(Default)	Text: "Want coffee with that?"
RadioButton	radNoCoffee	Text: "None" Checked: False ToolTip on ToolTip1: "Click here to choose no coffee."
RadioButton	radRegCoffee	Text: "Regular Coffee ($1.25)" Checked: True ToolTip on ToolTip1: "Click here to choose regular coffee."
RadioButton	radCappuccino	Text: "Cappuccino ($2.00)" Checked: False ToolTip on ToolTip1: "Click here to choose cappuccino."
RadioButton	radCafeAuLait	Text: "Cafe au lait ($1.75)" Checked: True ToolTip on ToolTip1: "Click here to choose cafe au lait."
GroupBox	(Default)	Text: "Price"
Label	(Default)	Text: "Subtotal"
Label	lblSubtotal	Text: "" BorderStyle: Fixed3D
Label	(Default)	Text: "Tax"
Label	lblTax	Text: "" BorderStyle: Fixed3D
Label	(Default)	Text: "Total"
Label	lblTotal	Text: "" BorderStyle: Fixed3D

Table 6-3 *continued*

Bagel and Coffee Calculator controls

Control Type	Control Name	Properties
Button	btnCalculate	Text: "Calculate &Total" ToolTip on ToolTip1: "Click here to calculate the total of the order."
Button	btnReset	Text: "&Reset Form" ToolTip on ToolTip1: "Click here to clear the form and start over."
Button	btnExit	Text: "&Close" ToolTip on ToolTip1: "Click here to exit."

Table 6-4 lists and describes the methods (event procedures, Sub procedures, and functions) used in this application.

Table 6-4

Methods for Bagel and Coffee Calculator

Method	Type of Method	Description
btnCalculate_Click	Event procedure	Calculates and displays the total of an order. Calls the following functions: BagelCost, CoffeeCost, ToppingCost, and CalcTax.
btnExit_Click	Event procedure	Ends the application.
btnReset_Click	Event procedure	Resets the controls on the form to their initial values. Calls the following Sub procedures: ResetBagels, ResetToppings, ResetCoffee, ResetPrice.
BagelCost	Function	Returns the price of the selected bagel.
ToppingCost	Function	Returns the total price of the selected toppings.
CoffeeCost	Function	Returns the price of the selected coffee.
CalcTax	Function	Accepts an argument, amount, which is the amount of a sale. Returns the amount of sales tax on that amount. The tax rate is stored in a class-level constant, taxRate.
ResetBagels	Sub procedure	Resets the bagel type radio buttons to their initial value.
ResetToppings	Sub procedure	Resets the topping check boxes to unchecked.
ResetCoffee	Sub procedure	Resets the coffee radio buttons to their initial values.
ResetPrice	Sub procedure	Sets the lblSubtotal, lblTax, and lblTotal labels to "".

Figure 6-21 shows a flowchart for the btnCalculate_Click event procedure. This procedure calculates the total of an order and displays its price. Notice that very little math is actually performed in this procedure, however. It calls the BagelCost, ToppingCost, CoffeeCost, and CalcTax functions to get the values it needs.

Notice that a new flowchart symbol, which represents a call to a procedure or function, is introduced:

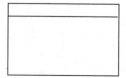

Pseudocode for the btnCalculate_Click procedure is as follows:

subtotal = BagelCost() + ToppingCost() + CoffeeCost()
tax = CalcTax(subtotal)
total = subtotal + tax

lblSubtotal.Text = subtotal
lblTax.Text = tax
lblTotal.Text = total

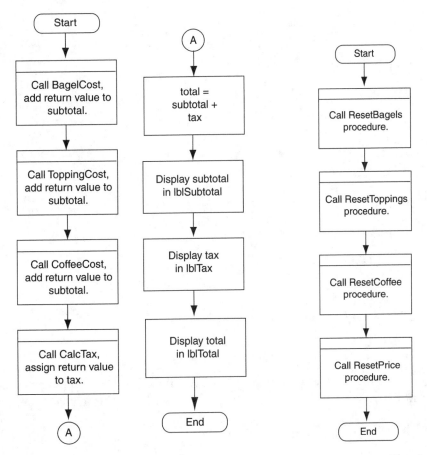

Figure 6-21 Flowchart for
`btnCalculate_Click` **event procedure**

Figure 6-22 Flowchart for
`btnReset_Click` **event procedure**

Figure 6-22 shows a flowchart for the `btnReset_Click` event procedure. The purpose of this procedure is to reset all the radio buttons, check boxes, and labels on the form to their initial values. This operation has been broken into the following Sub procedures: `ResetBagels`, `ResetToppings`, `ResetCoffee`, `ResetPrice`. When `btnReset_Click` executes, it simply calls these procedures.

Pseudocode for the `btnReset_Click` procedure is as follows:

ResetBagels()
ResetToppings()
ResetCoffee()
ResetPrice()

Figure 6-23 shows a flowchart for the `BagelCost` function. This function determines whether the user has selected white or whole wheat, and returns the price of that selection.

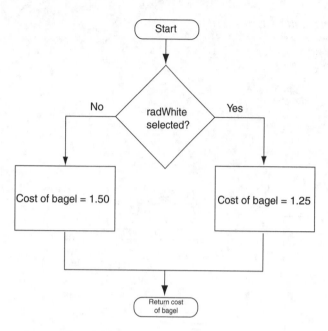

Figure 6-23   Flowchart for `BagelCost` function

Pseudocode for the `BagelCost` function is as follows:

If radWhite Is Selected Then
    costOfBagel = 1.25
Else
    costOfBagel = 1.5
End If
Return costOfBagel

Figure 6-24 shows a flowchart for the `ToppingCost` function. This function examines the topping check boxes to determine which toppings the user has selected. The total topping price is returned.

Pseudocode for the `ToppingCost` function is as follows:

cost of topping = 0.0
If chkCreamCheese Is Checked Then
    cost of topping += 0.5
End If
If chkButter Is Checked Then
    cost of topping += 0.25
End If
If chkBlueberry Is Checked Then
    cost of topping += 0.75
End If
If chkRaspberry Is Checked Then
    cost of topping += 0.75
End If
If chkPeach Is Checked Then
    cost of topping += 0.75
End If
Return cost of topping

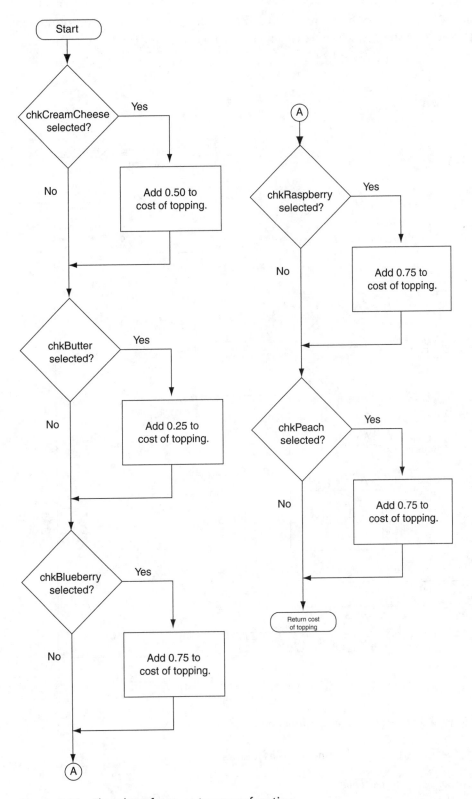

Figure 6-24   Flowchart for ToppingCost function

Figure 6-25 shows a flowchart for the CoffeeCost function. This function examines the coffee radio buttons to determine which coffee (if any) the user has selected. The price is returned.

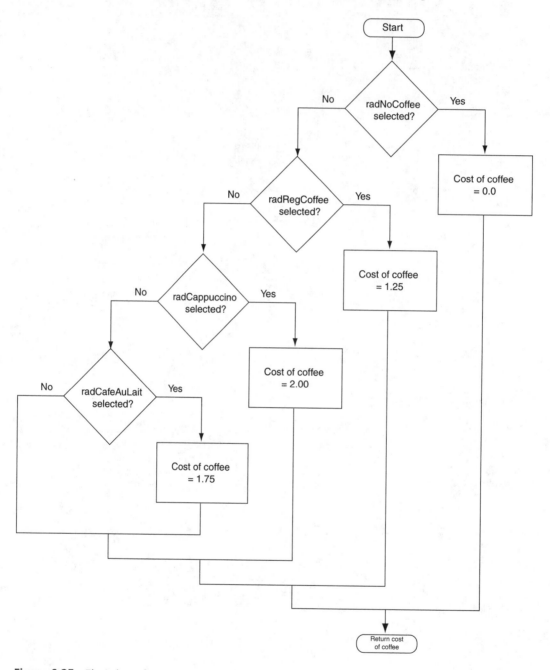

Figure 6-25   Flowchart for CoffeeCost function

Pseudocode for the CoffeeCost function is as follows:

If radNoCoffee Is Selected Then
    cost of coffee = 0
ElseIf radRegCoffee Is Selected Then
    cost of coffee = 1.25
ElseIf radCappuccino Is Selected Then
    cost of coffee = 2

ElseIf radCafeAuLait Is Selected Then
    cost of coffee = 1.75
End If
Return cost of coffee

Figure 6-26 shows a flowchart for the `CalcTax` function. Note that `CalcTax` accepts an argument, which is passed into the `amount` parameter variable. The function uses the class-level variable, `taxRate`, which holds the sales tax rate. The amount of sales tax on the amount in `amount` is returned.

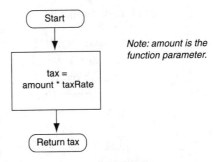

Figure 6-26 Flowchart for `CalcTax` Function

Pseudocode for the `CalcTax` function is as follows:

*sales tax = amount * taxRate*
Return sales tax

Figure 6-27 shows a flowchart for the `ResetBagels` Sub procedure. This procedure resets the bagel radio buttons to their initial values.
Pseudocode for the `ResetBagels` Sub procedure is as follows:

radWhite = Selected
radWheat = Deselected

Figure 6-28 shows a flowchart for the `ResetToppings` Sub procedure. This procedure unchecks all the topping check boxes.

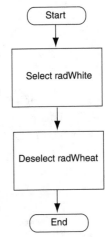

Figure 6-27 Flow chart for `ResetBagels` Sub procedure

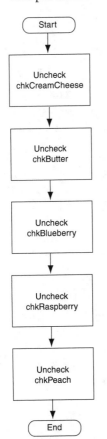

Figure 6-28 Flowchart for `ResetToppings` Sub procedure

Pseudocode for the `ResetToppings` Sub procedure is as follows:

chkCreamCheese= Unchecked
chkButter = Unchecked
chkBlueberry= Unchecked
chkRaspberry= Unchecked
chkPeach = Unchecked

Figure 6-29 shows a flowchart for the `ResetCoffee` Sub procedure. This procedure resets the coffee radio buttons to their initial values. Pseudocode for the `ResetCoffee` Sub procedure is as follows:

radNoCoffee = Deselected
radRegCoffee = Selected
radCappuccino = Deselected
radCafeAuLait = Deselected

Figure 6-30 shows a flowchart for the `ResetPrice` Sub procedure. This procedure copies an empty string to `lblSubtotal`, `lblTax`, and `lblTotal`.

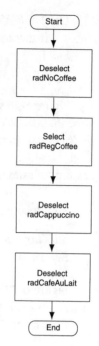

Figure 6-29 Flowchart for `ResetCoffee` Sub procedure

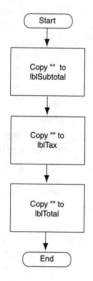

Figure 6-30 Flowchart for `ResetPrice` Sub procedure

Pseudocode for the `ResetPrice` Sub procedure is as follows:

lblSubtotal.Text = ""
lblTax.Text = ""
lblTotal.Text = ""

TUTORIAL 6-7:

Building the Bagel application

Step 1:   Start Visual Basic .NET and begin a new Windows application.

Step 2:   Set the form up as shown in Figure 6-31. Refer to Figure 6-20 and Table 6-3 for specific details about the controls and their properties.

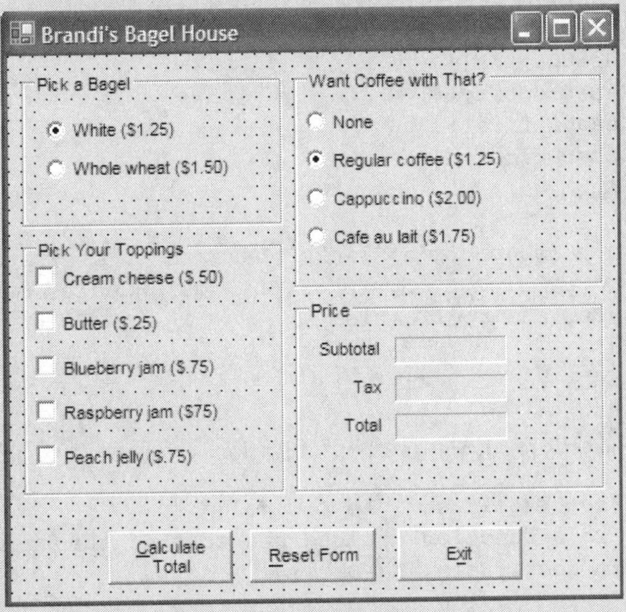

Figure 6-31   Brandi's Bagel House form

Step 3:   Once you have placed all the controls on the form and set their properties, you can begin writing the code. Start by opening the Code window and writing the following comments and class-level variable declaration.

```
' This application calculates the total order for a bagel and coffee
' at Brandi's Bagel house. The application uses several functions
' to calculate the total cost.
Const taxRate As Single = 0.06 ' Sales tax rate
```

Step 4:   Now write the `btnCalculate_Click`, `btnReset_Click`, and `btnExit_Click` event procedures, as follows.

```
Private Sub btnCalculate_Click(ByVal sender As System.Object, _
        ByVal e As System.EventArgs) Handles btnCalculate.Click
    ' This procedure calculates the total of an order.
    Dim subtotal As Decimal ' To hold the order subtotal
    Dim tax As Decimal      ' To hold the sales tax
    Dim total As Decimal    ' To hold the order total

    subtotal = BagelCost() + ToppingCost() + CoffeeCost()
    tax = CalcTax(subtotal)
    total = subtotal + tax
```

```
                lblSubtotal.Text = FormatCurrency(subtotal)
                lblTax.Text = FormatCurrency(tax)
                lblTotal.Text = FormatCurrency(total)
        End Sub


        Private Sub btnReset_Click(ByVal sender As System.Object, _
                ByVal e As System.EventArgs) Handles btnReset.Click
            ' This procedure resets the controls to
            ' their default values.

            ' Reset the bagel type.
            ResetBagels()
            ResetToppings()
            ResetCoffee()
            ResetPrice()
        End Sub


        Private Sub btnExit_Click(ByVal sender As System.Object, _
                ByVal e As System.EventArgs) Handles btnExit.Click
            ' End the application
            End
        End Sub
```

Step 5: Write the code for the `BagelCost` function, as follows.

```
        Function BagelCost() As Decimal
            ' This function returns the cost of the bagel.
            Dim costOfBagel As Decimal

            If radWhite.Checked = True Then
                costOfBagel = 1.25
            Else
                costOfBagel = 1.5
            End If

            Return costOfBagel
        End Function
```

Step 6: Write the code for the `ToppingCost` function, as follows.

```
        Function ToppingCost() As Decimal
            ' This function returns the cost of the toppings.
            Dim costOfTopping As Decimal = 0

            If chkCreamCheese.Checked = True Then
                costOfTopping += 0.5
            End If
            If chkButter.Checked = True Then
                costOfTopping += 0.25
            End If
            If chkBlueberry.Checked = True Then
                costOfTopping += 0.75
            End If
            If chkRaspberry.Checked = True Then
```

```
                    costOfTopping += 0.75
            End If
            If chkPeach.Checked = True Then
                    costOfTopping += 0.75
            End If
            Return costOfTopping
    End Function
```

Step 7:   Write the code for the CoffeeCost function, as follows.

```
Function CoffeeCost() As Decimal
    ' This function returns the cost of the selected coffee.
    Dim costOfCoffee As Decimal

    If radNoCoffee.Checked = True Then
        costOfCoffee = 0
    ElseIf radRegCoffee.Checked = True Then
        costOfCoffee = 1.25
    ElseIf radCappuccino.Checked = True Then
        costOfCoffee = 2
    ElseIf radCafeAuLait.Checked = True Then
        costOfCoffee = 1.75
    End If

    Return costOfCoffee
End Function
```

Step 8:   Write the code for the CalcTax function, as follows.

```
Function CalcTax(ByVal amount As Decimal) As Decimal
    ' This function accepts an argument which is the amount of
    ' a sale. It returns the amount of sales tax
    ' on that amount. The sales tax rate is stored in taxRate.
    Dim salesTax As Decimal

    salesTax = amount * taxRate
    Return salesTax
End Function
```

Step 9:   Write the code for the ResetBagels, ResetToppings, ResetCoffee, and ResetPrice Sub procedures, as follows.

```
Private Sub ResetBagels()
    ' This procedure resets the bagel selection.
    radWhite.Checked = True
    radWheat.Checked = False
End Sub

Sub ResetToppings()
    ' This procedure resets the topping selection.
    chkCreamCheese.Checked = False
    chkButter.Checked = False
    chkBlueberry.Checked = False
    chkRaspberry.Checked = False
```

```
                    chkPeach.Checked = False
             End Sub

             Sub ResetCoffee()
                ' This procedure resets the coffee selection.
                radNoCoffee.Checked = False
                radRegCoffee.Checked = True
                radCappuccino.Checked = False
                radCafeAuLait.Checked = False
             End Sub

             Sub ResetPrice()
                ' This procedure resets the price.
                lblSubtotal.Text = ""
                lblTax.Text = ""
                lblTotal.Text = ""
             End Sub
```

Step 10: Save the project.

Step 11: Run the application. If there are errors, use the debugging techniques you have learned to find and correct them.

Step 12: Once the application is running correctly, save it.

SUMMARY

A Sub procedure is a collection of statements that performs a specific task. For a Sub procedure to execute, it must be called.

Modularizing an application's code involves breaking it into small, manageable procedures.

The declaration for a Sub procedure begins with a `Sub` statement and ends with an `End Sub` statement. The code that appears between these two statements is the body of the procedure.

A procedure call is simply the name of the procedure that is to be executed. The `Call` key word can also be used.

When the application is running and a procedure call is encountered, the application branches to that procedure and executes its statements. When the procedure has finished, the application branches back to the procedure call and resumes executing at the next statement.

Static local variables are not destroyed when a procedure returns. They exist for the lifetime of the application, even though their scope is only the procedure in which they are declared.

To declare a static local variable, simply use the word `Static` instead of `Dim`.

Like a Sub procedure, a function procedure is a set of statements that perform a task when the function is called. A function, however, returns a value that can be used in an expression.

You return a value from a function with the `Return` statement.

Values that are sent into a procedure or function are called arguments.

A parameter is a special variable that receives an argument being passed into a procedure or function. If you write a procedure or function with a parameter variable, you must supply an argument when you call that procedure or function.

When a procedure or function with multiple parameters is called, the arguments are passed to the parameters in the order in which they appear.

There are two ways to pass an argument to a procedure: by value, or by reference. Passing an argument by value means that only a copy of the argument is passed to the procedure. Because the procedure has only a copy, it cannot make changes to the original argument. When an argument is passed by reference, however, the procedure has access to the original argument and can make changes to it.

The `ByVal` key word in a parameter declaration specifies that the argument is to be passed by value. The `ByRef` key word specifies that the argument is to be passed by reference.

The Step Into command allows you to single-step through a procedure or function when that procedure or function is called.

Like the Step Into command, the Step Over command causes the currently highlighted line to execute. If the line contains a procedure or function call, however, the procedure or function is executed and you are not given an opportunity to single-step through its statements. The entire procedure or function is executed and the next line in the current procedure is highlighted.

The Step Out command causes the remainder of the current procedure or function to complete execution without single-stepping. After the procedure or function has completed, the line following the procedure or function call is highlighted and single-stepping may resume.

KEY TERMS

Argument	Procedure declaration
ByRef	Reference, pass by
ByVal	Static
Call	Static local variable
Function procedure	Step Into command
Modularize	Step Out command
Parameter	Step Over command
Pascal casing	Sub procedure
Procedure call	Value, pass by

Review Questions

Fill-in-the-blank

1. A(n) _____ is a collection of code that performs a specific task and does not return a value.

2. A(n) _____ is a statement that causes a procedure to be executed.

3. A(n) _____ is a set of statements that execute and returns a value.

4. You return a value from a function by variables are not destroyed when a procedure returns.

5. _____ local variables are not destroyed when a procedure returns.

6. Values that are sent into a procedure or function are called _____.

7. A(n) _____ is a special variable that receives an argument being passed into a procedure or function.

8. When an argument is passed by _____, it means that only a copy of the argument is passed to the parameter variable.

9. When an argument is passed by_____ the procedure has access to the original argument.

10. The _____ debugging command allows you to single-step through a called procedure or function.

Multiple Choice

1. This term means to break an application's code into small, manageable procedures.
   a. Break
   b. Modularize
   c. Parameterize
   d. Bind

2. This type of statement causes a procedure to execute
   a. Procedure declaration
   b. Access specifier
   c. Procedure call
   d. Step-into

3. When a Sub procedure has finished executing,
   a. the application branches back to the procedure call, and resumes executing at the next line.
   b. the application terminates.
   c. the application waits for the user to trigger the next event.
   d. the application enters break mode.

4. In what way is a function procedure different from a Sub procedure?
   a. A Sub procedure returns a value and a function does not.
   b. A function returns a value and a Sub procedure does not.
   c. A function must be executed in response to an event.
   d. There is no difference.

5. What type of local variable retains its value between calls to the procedure or function in which it is declared?
   a. Private
   b. Persistent
   c. Permanent
   d. Static

6. What is an argument?
   a. A variable that a parameter is passed into.
   b. A value passed to a procedure or function when it is called.
   c. A local variable that retains its value between procedure calls.
   d. A reason not to create a procedure or function.

7. What key word is used in a parameter declaration to specify that the argument is to be passed by value?

    a. `ByVal`

    b. `Val`

    c. `Value`

    d. `AsValue`

8. When an argument is passed to a procedure this way, the procedure has access to the original argument and may make changes to it.

    a. By value

    b. By address

    c. By reference

    d. By default

9. This is a debugging command that causes a Sub procedure or function to execute without single-stepping through the procedure's or function's code.

    a. Step-into

    b. Step-through

    c. Jump-over

    d. Step-over

10. This debugging command is used when you are stepping through a procedure's code and you wish to execute the remaining statements in the procedure without single-stepping through them.

    a. Jump-out

    b. Step-through

    c. Step-out

    d. Step-over

True or False

Indicate whether each of the following statements is true or false.

1. T F: A general purpose Sub procedure is associated with a specific control.

2. T F: You must use the `Call` key word to execute a procedure.

3. T F: The declaration of a parameter variable looks like a regular variable declaration, except `ByVal` or `ByRef` is used instead of `Dim`.

4. T F: You can pass more than one argument to a procedure or function.

5. T F: If you write a procedure or function with a parameter variable, it is not required that you supply an argument when you call that procedure.

6. T F: If you are debugging an application in break mode, and you want to single-step through a procedure that will be called in the highlighted statement, use the Step Over command.

Short Answer

1. Why do regular local variables loose their values between calls to the procedure or function in which they are declared?

2. What is the difference between an argument and a parameter variable?

3. Where do you declare parameter variables?

4. If you are writing a procedure that accepts an argument and you want to make sure the procedure cannot change the value of the argument, what do you do?

5. When a procedure or function accepts multiple arguments, does it matter what order the arguments are passed in?

6. How do you return a value from a function?

What Do You Think?

1. What is the advantage of breaking your application's code into several small procedures?

2. How would a `Static` local variable be useful?

3. Give an example where passing an argument by reference would be useful.

4. You want to write a procedure to perform an operation. How do you decide if the procedure should be a Sub procedure or a function procedure?

5. When debugging an application, why would you not want to single-step through each procedure or function?

Find the Errors

Locate the errors in the following code segments.

1.
```
Sub DisplayValue(Dim number As Integer)
    ' This displays a value.
    MessageBox.Show(number.ToString)
End Sub
```

2. The following is a procedure.

```
Sub Greeting(ByVal name As String)
    ' This procedure displays a greeting.
    MessageBox.Show("Hello " & name)
End Sub
```

And the following is a call to the procedure.

```
Greeting()
```

3. The following is a function:

```
Function Product(ByVal num1 As Integer, ByVal num2 As _
                 Integer) As Integer
    Dim result As Integer
    result = num1 * num2
End Function
```

4. The following is a function:

```
Sub Sum(ByVal num1 As Single, ByVal num2 As Single) As Single
    Dim result As Single
    result = num1 + num2
    Return result
End Sub
```

Algorithm Workbench

1. The following statement calls a function named `Half`. The `Half` function returns a value that is half that of the argument. Write the function.

```
result = Half(number)
```

2. An application contains the following function:

```
Function Square(ByVal value As Integer) As Integer
      Return value ^ 2
End Function
```

Write a statement that passes the value 4 to this function and assigns its return value to the variable `result`.

3. Write a Sub procedure, named `TimesTen`, that accepts an argument. When the procedure is called, it should display the product of its argument multiplied times 10 in a message box.

4. An application contains the following procedure:

```
Sub Display(ByVal arg1 As Integer, ByVal arg2 As String, _
          ByVal arg3 As Single)
   MessageBox.Show("Here are the values: " & _
                arg1.ToString & " " & _
                arg2 & " " & arg3.ToString)
End Sub
```

Write a statement that calls the procedure and passes the following variables to it:

```
Dim name As String
Dim age As Integer
Dim income As Single
```

PROGRAMMING CHALLENGES

1. Retail Price Calculator

Write an application that accepts from the user the wholesale cost of an item and its markup percentage. (For example, if an item's wholesale cost is $5 and its retail price is $10, then the markup is 100%.)

The program should contain a function, named `CalculateRetail`, that receives the wholesale cost and markup percentage as arguments, and returns the retail price of the item. The application's form should look something like the one shown in Figure 6-32.

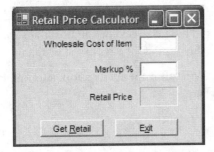

Figure 6-32   Retail Price Calculator form

When the user clicks the Get Retail button, the program should do the following:

- Verify that the values entered by the user for the wholesale cost and the markup percent are numeric and not negative.
- Call the `CalculateRetail` function.
- Display the retail cost as returned from the function.

2.   Hospital Charges

Create an application that calculates the total cost of a stay in the hospital. The application should accept the following input:

- The number of days spent in the hospital
- The amount of medication charges
- The amount of surgical charges
- The amount of lab fees
- The amount of physical rehabilitation charges

The hospital charges $350 per day. The application's form should resemble Figure 6-33.

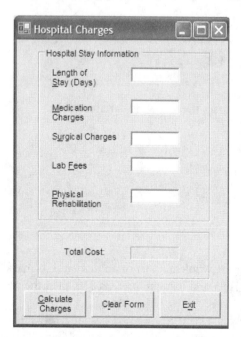

Figure 6-33   Hospital Charges form

The application should use the following functions.

`CalcStayCharges`	Calculates and returns the base charges for the hospital stay. This is computed as $350 times the number of days in the hospital.
`CalcMiscCharges`	Calculates and returns the total of the medication, surgical, lab, and physical rehabilitation charges.
`CalcTotalCharges`	Calculates and returns the total charges.

Input Validation: Do not accept a negative value for length of stay, medication charges, surgical charges, lab fees, or physical rehabilitation charges.

3. Order Status

The Middletown Wire Company sells spools of cooper wiring for $100 each. The normal delivery charge is $10 per spool. Rush delivery costs $15 per spool. Create an application that displays the status of an order. The status should include the following.

◆ The number of spools ready to ship

◆ The number of spools on back order

◆ The shipping and handling charges

◆ The total amount due

The application's form should resemble Figure 6-34.

The user should enter the number of spools ordered into the text box, and check the Rush Delivery check box if rush delivery is desired. When the Calculate Total button is clicked, an input box should appear asking the user to enter the number of spools that are currently in stock. If the user has ordered more spools than are in stock, then a portion of the order will be back ordered. For example, if the user orders 200 spools and there are only 150 spools in stock, then 150 spools will be ready to ship and 50 spools will be back ordered.

The application should have the following functions, which should be called from the Calculate Total button's Click event procedure:

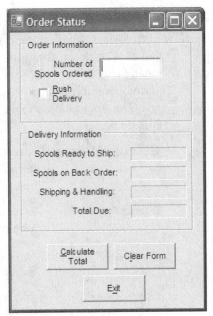

Figure 6-34 Order Status form

GetInStock	Displays an input box asking the user to enter the number of spools in stock. The function should return the value entered by the user.
ReadyToShip	Accepts the following arguments: the number of spools in stock, and the number of spools ordered. The function returns the number of spools ready to ship.
BackOrdered	Accepts the following arguments: the number of spools in stock and the number of spools ordered. The function returns the number of spools on back order. If no spools are on back order, it returns 0.
ShippingCharges	Accepts the following arguments: the number of spools ready to ship and the per-spool shipping charges. The function returns the total shipping and handling charges.

The application should have the following Sub procedures, which are called from the "Clear Form" button's Click event procedure:

ResetSpools	Clears the text box and the check box.
ResetDelivery	Clears the labels that display the delivery information.

Input Validation: Do not accept orders for less than one spool.

4. Joe's Automotive

Joe's Automotive performs the following routine maintenance services:

- Oil change—$26.00
- Lube job—$18.00
- Radiator flush—$30.00
- Transmission flush—$80.00
- Inspection—$15.00
- Muffler replacement—$100.00
- Tire rotation—$20.00

Joe also performs other nonroutine services and charges for parts and for labor ($20 per hour). Create an application that displays the total for a customer's visit to Joe's. The form should resemble Figure 6-35.

The application should have the following functions.

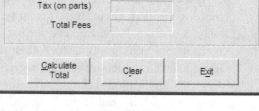

Figure 6-35   Joe's Automotive Calculator form

OilLubeCharges	Returns the total charges for an oil change and/or a lube job, if any.
FlushCharges	Returns the total charges for a radiator flush and/or a transmission flush, if any.
MiscCharges	Returns the total charges for an inspection, muffler replacement, and/or a tire rotation, if any.
OtherCharges	Returns the total charges for other services (parts and labor), if any.
TaxCharges	Returns the amount of sales tax, if any. Sales tax is 6%, and is *only* charged on parts. If the customer purchased services only, no sales tax will be charged
TotalCharges	Returns the total charges.

In addition, the application should have the following Sub procedures, which should be called when the user clicks the Clear button.

ClearOilLube	Clears the check boxes for oil change and lube job.
ClearFlushes	Clears the check boxes for radiator flush and transmission flush.
ClearMisc	Clears the check boxes for inspection, muffler replacement, and tire rotation.
ClearOther	Clears the text boxes for parts and labor.
ClearFees	Clears the labels that display the total charges and tax.

Input validation: Do not accept negative amounts for parts and labor charges.

Design Your Own Forms

5. Password Verifier

You are developing a software package that requires users to enter their own passwords. Your software requires that users' passwords meet the following criteria:

- The password should be at least six characters long.
- The password should contain at least one numeric digit and at least one alphabetic character.

Create an application that asks the user to enter a password. The application should use a function named `IsValid` to verify that the password meets the criteria. It should display a message indicating whether the password is valid or invalid.

The `IsValid` function should accept a string as its argument and return a Boolean value. The string argument is the password that is to be checked. If the password is valid, the function should return true. Otherwise, it should return false.

TIP: Refer to Chapter 4 for more information about working with strings.

6. Travel Expenses

Create an application that calculates and displays the total travel expenses of a business person on a trip. Here is the information that the user must provide:

- Number of days on the trip
- Amount of airfare, if any
- Amount of car rental fees, if any
- Number of miles driven, if a private vehicle was used
- Amount of parking fees, if any
- Amount of taxi charges, if any
- Conference or seminar registration fees, if any
- Lodging charges, per night

The company reimburses travel expenses according to the following policy:

- $37 given per day for meals
- Parking fees, up to $10.00 per day
- Taxi charges up to $20.00 per day
- Lodging charges up to $95.00 per day
- If a private vehicle is used, $0.27 per mile driven

The application should calculate and display the following:

- Total expenses incurred by the business person
- The total allowable expenses for the trip
- The excess that must be paid by the business person, if any
- The amount saved by the business person if the expenses were under the total allowed

The application should have the following functions:

`CalcMeals`   Calculates and returns the amount reimbursed for meals.

`CalcMileage`	Calculates and returns the amount reimbursed for mileage driven in a private vehicle.
`CalcParkingFees`	Calculates and returns the amount reimbursed for parking fees.
`CalcTaxiFees`	Calculates and returns the amount reimbursed for taxi charges.
`CalcLodging`	Calculates and returns the amount reimbursed for lodging.
`CalcTotalReimbursement`	Calculates and returns the total amount reimbursed.
`CalcUnallowed`	Calculates and returns the total amount of expenses that are not allowable, if any. These are any parking fees that exceed $10.00 per day, any taxi charges that exceed $20.00 per day, and any lodging charges that exceed $95.00 per day.
`CalcSaved`	Calculates and returns the total amount of expenses that are under the allowable amount, if any. For example, the allowable amount for lodging is $95.00 per day. If a business person stayed in a hotel for $85.00 per day for five days, the savings would $25.00.

Input validation: Do not accept negative numbers for any dollar amount or for miles driven in a private vehicle. Do not accept numbers less than one for the number of days.

7. Paint Job Estimator

A painting company has determined that for every 115 square feet of wall space, one gallon of paint and eight hours of labor will be required. The company charges $18.00 per hour for labor. Create an application that allows the user to enter the number of rooms that are to be painted and the price of the paint per gallon. The application should use input boxes to ask the user for the square feet of wall space in each room. It should then display the following information:

◆ The number of gallons of paint required

◆ The hours of labor required

◆ The cost of the paint

◆ The labor charges

◆ The total cost of the paint job

Input validation: Do not accept a value less than one for the number of rooms. Do not accept a value less than $10.00 for the price of paint. Do not accept a negative value for square footage of wall space.

Multiple Forms, Standard Modules, and Menus

▶ 7.1 Introduction

This chapter shows you how to add multiple forms to a project and how to create a standard module to hold procedures and functions that are not associated with a specific form. It also covers creating a menu system, as well as context menus, with commands and submenus that the user may select from.

▶ 7.2 Multiple Forms

CONCEPT

VISUAL BASIC .NET PROJECTS MAY HAVE MULTIPLE FORMS. IF ONE OF THE FORMS IS THE STARTUP OBJECT, IT IS DISPLAYED WHEN THE PROJECT EXECUTES. THE OTHER FORMS ARE DISPLAYED BY PROGRAMMING STATEMENTS.

The applications you have created so far display information and gather input with a single form. Visual Basic .NET does not limit you to one form in an application, however. You may add other forms to create dialog boxes, display information in a separate window, and so on.

A Windows application must have a startup object. The *startup object* may be a form or a Sub procedure named `Main`, which you will learn about later in this chapter. When a form is the startup object, it is automatically displayed when your application starts up. By default, the first form you create is the startup object. You will learn how to change the startup object later in this section.

Form Names and File Names

Each form has two names that you must be aware of. First, there is the name of the form, which is stored in the form's Name property. Second, there is the name of the file that the form's code is stored in. In this section we will discuss these names, how they relate to each other, and how they are used in a project.

The Form's Name Property

Like other controls, forms have a name property. You assign a name to a form by setting its Name property. Because the applications you have created so far only use one form, you have kept the default name, `Form1`, for the application's form. When your application has multiple forms, however, you should give each one a descriptive name.

The standard prefix for form names is `frm`. For example, you might name a form that displays an error message `frmError`. A common name for a project's main form, the one that is first displayed when the application runs, is `frmMain`.

Form Files

When you create a form in Visual Basic .NET, the code associated with that form is stored in a file that ends with the .vb extension. Normally, the name of the file is the same as the name of the form. For example, assume that a project has a form named `Form1` (the form's Name property is set to `Form1`). The code for that form will be stored in a file named Form1.vb. The Solution Explorer shows an entry for each form file that is part of a project. Figure 7-1 shows the Solution Explorer window with an entry for the form file Form1.vb.

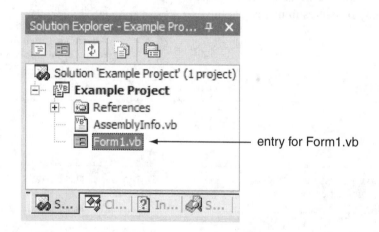

Figure 7-1 Solution Explorer window with entry for Form1.vb

NOTE: *The code that is stored in a form file is the same code you see when you open the form in the Code window.*

Renaming an Existing Form File

If you change a form's Name property, the name of the form's file does not automatically change. To maintain consistency, you should also rename the form's file to match the name of the form. For example, if a form's Name property is set to `Form1` and you change it to `frmMain`, you should change the name of the form file to frmMain.vb. You change the name of an existing form file with the following steps.

1. Right-click the form file's entry in the Solution Explorer window.

2. A pop-up menu should appear. Select Rename from the pop-up menu.

3. The name of the form file should be highlighted in the Solution Explorer window. Type the new name for the form file. Be sure to keep the .vb extension.

Adding a New Form to a Project

Follow these steps to add a new form to a project:

1. Click the add new item button (⊞) on the tool bar, or click Project on the menu bar, then click Add Windows Form on the Project menu. After performing either of these steps, the Add New Item dialog box, shown in Figure 7-2, should appear. Notice that in the figure, the name Form2.vb appears in the Name text box. In this example, Form2.vb is the default name for the new file that the form will be stored in, and Form2 is the default name for the form.

NOTE: *The default name may be different, depending on the number of forms already in the project.*

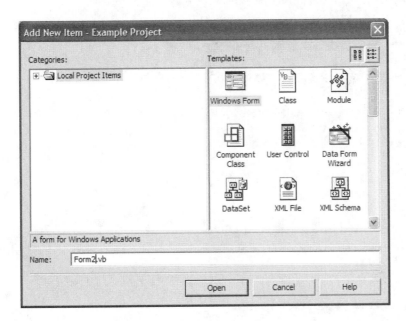

Figure 7-2   The Add New Item dialog box

2. Under Templates, make sure Windows Form is selected.

3. Change the default name that is displayed in the Name text box to the name you wish to give the new form. For example, if you wish to name the new form frmError, enter frmError.vb in the Name text box.

NOTE: *Be sure to keep the .vb extension.*

4. Click the Open button.

After completing these steps, a new blank form will be added to your project. The new form will be displayed in the Design window and an entry for the new form will appear in the Solution Explorer window. The Solution Explorer window in Figure 7-3 shows two forms: frmError and frmMain.

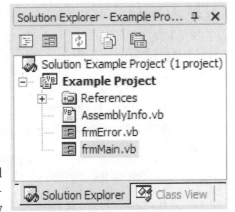

Figure 7-3   The Solution Explorer window showing multiple forms

Switching Between Forms and Form Code

At design time, you can easily switch to another form by double-clicking the form's entry in the Solution Explorer window. The form will be then displayed in the Design window. You can also use the tabs that appear at the top of the Design window to display different forms or their code. For example, look at Figure 7-4. It shows the tabs that appear for a project with two forms: frmMain and frmError. The tabs that display the [Design] designator cause a form to be displayed in the Design window. The tabs that appear without the designator cause a form's code to be displayed in the code window.

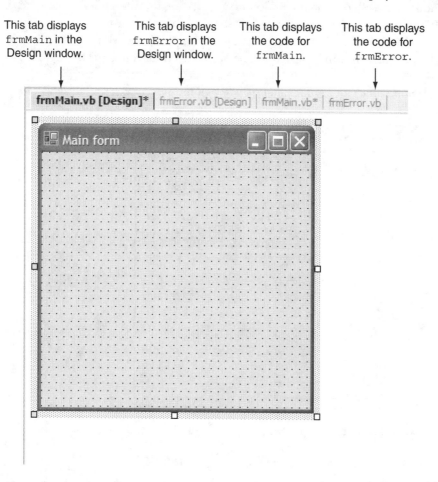

Figure 7-4   Design window tabs

Removing a Form

If you wish to remove a form from a project and delete its file from the disk, follow these steps.

1. Right-click the form's entry in the Solution Explorer window.
2. On the pop-up menu, click Delete.

If you wish to remove a form from a project but you do not want to delete its file from the disk, follow one of these sets of steps.

1. Right-click the form's entry in the Solution Explorer window.
2. On the pop-up menu, click Exclude From Project.

OR

1. Select the form's entry in the Solution Explorer window.

2. Click Project on the menu bar, then click Exclude From Project.

Changing the Startup Object to Another Form

As previously mentioned, the first form you create is, by default, the startup object. This is the form that is automatically displayed when the application runs. If you want another form to be the startup object, follow these steps:

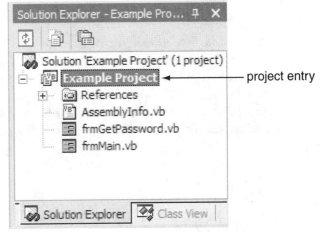

1. In the Solution Explorer window, right click the project's entry. Figure 7-5 shows the location of the project's entry in the window.

2. On the popup menu, click Properties. The project's Property Pages dialog box should appear, as shown in Figure 7-6.

Figure 7-5   Project entry location in Solution Explorer window

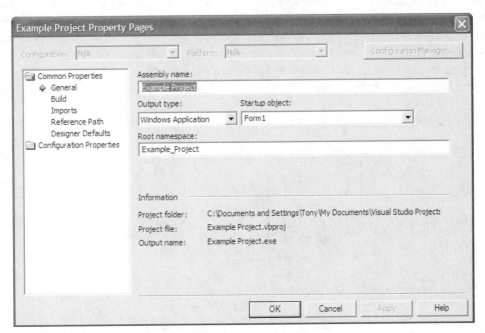

Figure 7-6   Project's Property Pages dialog box

TIP: Be sure to right-click the project's entry in the Solution Explorer window, as shown in Figure 7-5. If you right-click the solution's entry, you will see a different dialog box.

3. To change the startup object, click the down arrow in the Startup Object drop-down list. A list of all the forms in the project, as well as Sub Main, appears. Select the form you want to designate as the startup object.

4. Click the OK button.

When the application runs, the form you selected as the startup object will be displayed.

Creating an Instance of a Form

Now that we have covered adding a new form to a project, we must discuss how to write code that displays the form. Before plunging into the details, let's briefly revisit the topic of form files. When you create a form, Visual Basic .NET stores the code for the form in a form file. The form file contains a class declaration. A *class* is a program structure that describes an object's properties and methods. Recall that when you open a form in the Code window, the first and last lines of code look like the following, which mark the beginning and end of a class declaration:

```
Public Class FormName
End Class
```

FormName is the name that is stored in the form's Name property. This name is also called the form's class name. The code that appears between these two statements belongs to the form's class declaration.

A form's class declaration by itself does not create a specific form, but is merely the description of a form. It is similar to the blueprint for a house. The blueprint itself is not a house, but is a detailed description of a house. When we use the blueprint to build an actual house, we could say we are building an instance of the house described by the blueprint. If we so desire, we can build several identical houses from the same blueprint. Each house is a separate instance of the house described by the blueprint. This idea is illustrated in Figure 7-7.

blueprint that describes a house

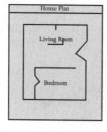

instances of the house described by the blueprint

Figure 7-7 Blueprints and instances of the blueprints

A form's class declaration serves a similar purpose. We can use it to create one or more instances of the form described by the class declaration, and then use the instance(s) to display the form on the screen.

Creating an Instance of a Form

The first step in displaying a form is to create an instance of the form. You create an instance of a form with a Dim statement. The general format is:

```
Dim ObjectVariable As New ClassName()
```

ObjectVariable is the name of an object variable that will reference an instance of the form. An *object variable* is a variable that holds the memory address of an object and allows you to work with the object. *ClassName* is the form's class name. This is the same name that is stored in the form's Name property. For example, assume that you have added a form to your project and named it frmError. The following statement creates an instance of the form.

```
Dim errorForm As New frmError()
```

Let's examine what happens as a result of this statement. First, an object variable named error Form is created. This variable will reference the instance of the form. The part of the statement that reads New frmError() causes an instance of the frmError form to be created in memory. Its memory address is then assigned to the errorForm variable. (When an object variable holds the memory address of an object, we say that it references the object.) You may now use the errorForm variable to perform operations with the form.

We must point out that this statement does not cause the form to be displayed on the screen. It only creates an instance of the form in memory and assigns its address to the object variable. To display the form on the screen, you must use the object variable to invoke one of the form's methods.

The ShowDialog and Show Methods

A form can be either modal or modeless. When a *modal form* is displayed, no other form in the application can receive the focus until the modal form is closed. The user must dismiss the modal form before he or she can work with any other form in the application. A *modeless form*, on the other hand, allows the user to switch focus to another form while it is displayed. The *ShowDialog method* causes a form to be displayed as a modal form. When this method is called, the form is displayed and it receives the focus. The general format of the method call is:

```
ObjectVariable.ShowDialog()
```

ObjectVariable is the name of an object variable that references an instance of a form. For example, the following code creates an instance of the frmError form and displays it.

```
Dim errorForm As New frmError()
errorForm.ShowDialog()
```

To display a modeless form, use the *Show method*. The general format of the Show method is:

```
ObjectVariable.Show()
```

ObjectVariable is the name of an object variable that references an instance of a form. For example, the following code creates an instance of the `frmError` form and displays it as a modeless form.

```
Dim errorForm As New frmError()
errorForm.Show()
```

TIP: Most of the time you want forms to be modal. It is common for a procedure to display a form and then perform operations that are dependent on input gathered by the form. Therefore, you will normally use the `ShowDialog` method to display a form.

Closing a Form with the `Close` method

Forms commonly have a button, such as Close or Cancel, that the user clicks to close the form. When the user clicks such a button, the form must call the `Close` method. The *Close method* closes a form and releases the memory it is using. This means that the form, its properties, and variables, are removed from memory.

The `Close` method is a member of the form class, so, when a form closes itself, it must call its own `Close` method. This is done with the Me keyword, as shown in the following general format.

```
Me.Close()
```

In this statement, the *Me keyword* references the current instance of the form. A form executing the `Me.Close()` statement is calling its own `Close` method.

For example, assume that an application has a form with a Close button named `btnClose`. When the user clicks the button, the form is closed. Here is the code for the `btnClose_Click` event procedure.

```
Private Sub btnClose_Click(ByVal sender As System.Object, _
        ByVal e As System.EventArgs) Handles btnClose.Click
    Me.Close()
End Sub
```

The `Hide` Method

The *Hide method* removes a form from the screen, but does not remove it from memory. It has the same effect as setting the form's Visible property to false. As with the `Close` method, a form uses the Me keyword to call its own Hide method, such as `Me.Hide()`. Use the `Hide` method when, instead of closing a form, you want to temporarily remove it from the screen. After hiding a form, you may redisplay it with the `ShowDialog` or `Show` methods.

More About Modal and Modeless Forms

You have already learned that when a modal form is displayed, no other form in the application can receive the focus until the modal form is closed. There is also another important aspect of modal forms. When a procedure calls the `ShowDialog` method to display a modal form, no other statements in that procedure will execute until the modal form is closed. This concept is illustrated in Figure 7-8.

```
statement
statement
messageForm.ShowDialog()
statement
statement
statement
```

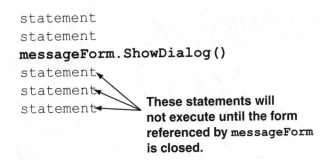

These statements will not execute until the form referenced by `messageForm` is closed.

Figure 7-8   Execution of statements after displaying a modal form

When a procedure calls the `Show` method to display a *modeless form*, however, the statements that follow the method call will continue to execute after the modeless form is displayed. Visual Basic .NET will not wait until the modeless form is closed to execute these statements. This concept is illustrated in Figure 7-9.

```
statement
statement
messageForm.Show()
statement
statement
statement
```

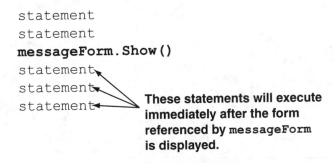

These statements will execute immediately after the form referenced by `messageForm` is displayed.

Figure 7-9   Execution of statements after displaying a modeless form

Tutorial 7-1 clearly demonstrates this difference between modal and modeless forms.

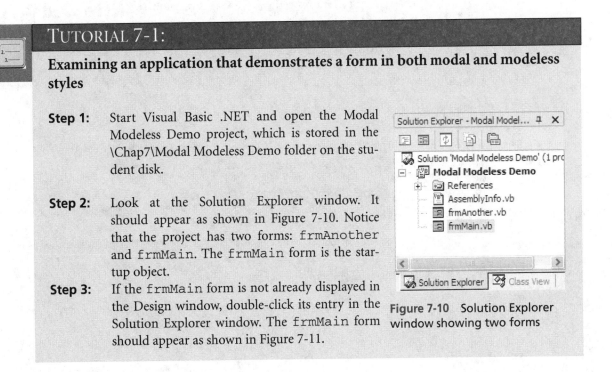

TUTORIAL 7-1:

Examining an application that demonstrates a form in both modal and modeless styles

Step 1:   Start Visual Basic .NET and open the Modal Modeless Demo project, which is stored in the \Chap7\Modal Modeless Demo folder on the student disk.

Step 2:   Look at the Solution Explorer window. It should appear as shown in Figure 7-10. Notice that the project has two forms: `frmAnother` and `frmMain`. The `frmMain` form is the startup object.

Step 3:   If the `frmMain` form is not already displayed in the Design window, double-click its entry in the Solution Explorer window. The `frmMain` form should appear as shown in Figure 7-11.

Figure 7-10   Solution Explorer window showing two forms

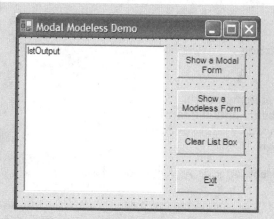

Figure 7-11 The `frmMain` form

Step 4: To look at the `frmAnother` form, double-click its entry in the Solution Explorer window. The form is shown in Figure 7-12. The Close button is named `btnClose`.

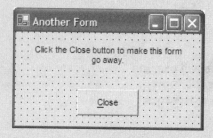

Figure 7-12 The `frmAnother` form

Step 5: Open the Code window to view the code for the `frmAnother` form. Look at the `btnClose_Click` event procedure. Its code is as follows:

```
Private Sub btnClose_Click(ByVal sender As System.Object, _
        ByVal e As System.EventArgs) Handles btnClose.Click
    ' Close the form
    Me.Close()
End Sub
```

Step 6: When this procedure executes, it closes the form.
Now open the `frmMain` form's code in the Code window. Look at the `btnShowModal_Click` event procedure. Its code is as follows:

```
Private Sub btnShowModal_Click(ByVal sender As System.Object, _
        ByVal e As System.EventArgs) Handles btnShowModal.Click
    Dim count As Integer                    ' Counter
    Dim anotherForm As New frmAnother()     ' Form instance
    ' Show the other form in modal style.
    anotherForm.ShowDialog()
```

```
        ' Display some numbers in the list box
        ' on the main form. Because the other form
        ' is displayed in modal style, this code
        ' will not execute until the user closes
        ' the other form.
        For count = 1 To 10
            lstOutput.Items.Add(count.ToString)
        Next count
    End Sub
```

The following statement in this procedure creates an instance of the `frmAnother` form and assigns its address to an object variable named `anotherForm`.

```
Dim anotherForm As New frmAnother()           ' Form instance
```

Using the `anotherForm` variable, the `ShowDialog` method is called to display the form in modal style:

```
' Show the other form in modal style.
anotherForm.ShowDialog()
```

After the `ShowDialog` method is called, this procedure has a `For...Next` loop that displays the numbers 1 through 10 in the `lstOutput` list box. Because the `frmAnother` form is displayed in modal style, the `For...Next` loop will not execute until the user closes `frmAnother`.

Step 7: Now look at the `btnShowModeless_Click` event procedure. Its code is as follows:

```
Private Sub btnShowModeless_Click(ByVal sender As System.Object, _
        ByVal e As System.EventArgs) Handles btnShowModeless.Click
    Dim count As Integer'                    ' Counter
    Dim anotherForm As New frmAnother()'  ' Form instance

    ' Show the other form in modeless style.
    anotherForm.Show()

    ' Display some numbers in the list box
    ' on the main form. Because the other form
    ' is displayed in modeless style, this code
    ' will execute while the other form is on
    ' the screen.
    For count = 1 To 10
        lstOutput.Items.Add(count.ToString)
    Next count
End Sub
```

This procedure basically performs the same operation as the `btnShowModal_Click` procedure: It displays the `frmAnother` form and then displays the numbers 1 through 10 in the `lstOutput` list box. The only difference is that `frmAnother` is displayed in modeless style, with the `Show` method. This means that the `For...Next` loop will execute immediately after the `frmAnother` form is displayed. Visual Basic .NET will not wait for the user to close the `frmAnother` form to execute the loop.

Step 8: Run the application. On the main form, click the Show a Modal Form button. The `frmAnother` form is displayed. Figure 7-13 shows the forms, positioned so you can see both of them. Notice that the `For...Next` loop has not executed, because you do not see the numbers 1 through 10 printed on the main form.

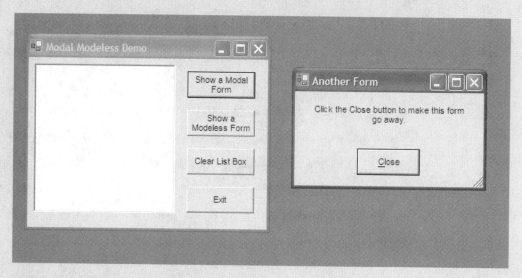

Figure 7-13 The `frmMain` form and the modal `frmAnother` form

Step 9: Click the Close button on `frmAnother` to close the form. Now look at the `frmMain` form. As shown in Figure 7-14, the `For...Next` loop executed as soon as `frmAnother` was closed.

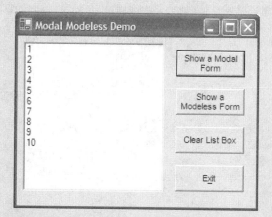

Figure 7-14 `frmMain` after the modal `frmAnother` form is closed

Step 10: Click the Clear List Box button to clear the numbers from the list box.

Step 11: Click the Show a Modeless Form button to display `frmAnother` in modeless style. As shown in Figure 7-15, notice that the `For...Next` loop executed immediately after the form was displayed; it did not wait for you to click the `frmAnother` Close button.

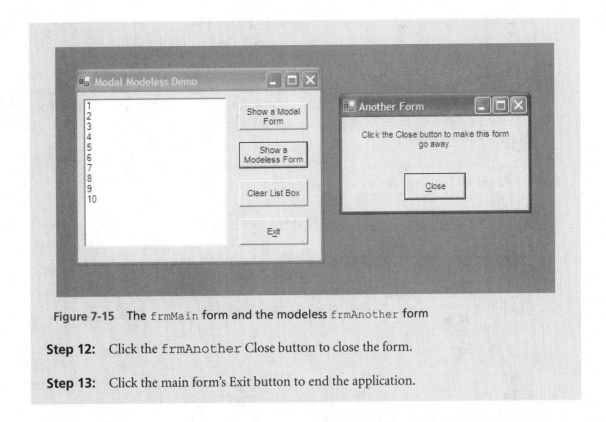

Figure 7-15 The `frmMain` form and the modeless `frmAnother` form

Step 12: Click the `frmAnother` Close button to close the form.

Step 13: Click the main form's Exit button to end the application.

The `Load`, `Activated`, `Closing`, and `Closed` Events

There are several events associated with forms. In this section we will discuss the `Load`, `Activated`, `Closing`, and `Closed` Events.

The `Load` Event

The `Load` event was introduced in Chapter 3, but a quick review is in order. Just before a form is initially displayed, a *Load event* is triggered. If you need to execute code automatically just before a form is displayed, you can create a *Load event procedure*, which is executed in response to the `Load` event. To write code in a form's `Load` event procedure, double-click any area of the form where there is no other control. The code window will appear with a code template similar to the following.

```
Private Sub frmMain_Load(ByVal sender As System.Object, _
        ByVal e As System.EventArgs) Handles MyBase.Load

End Sub
```

Complete the template with the statements you wish the procedure to execute.

The `Activated` Event

A form's `Activated` event is triggered when the user switches to the form from another form or another application. Here are two examples of how the `Activated` event is triggered:

◆ Application A and application B are both running, and a form in application A has the focus. The user clicks application B's form. When this happens, the `Activated` event is triggered for application B's form.

◆ An application has a main form and a second form. The second form is displayed in modeless style. Each time the user clicks a form that does not have the focus, an Activated event is triggered for that form.

The `Activated` event is also triggered when a form is initially displayed, after the `Load` event is triggered. If you need to execute code in any of these situations, you can create an *Activated event procedure*, which is executed in response to the `Activated` event. To create an `Activated` event procedure, follow these steps.

1. Open the Code window and click the class name drop-down list. In the drop-down list select (Base Class Events). This is shown in Figure 7-16.

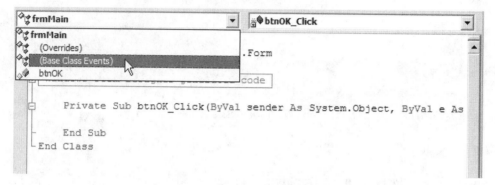

Figure 7-16 Select (Base Class Events) in the class name drop-down list

2. Click the method name drop-down list. In the drop-down list select Activated, as shown in Figure 7-17.

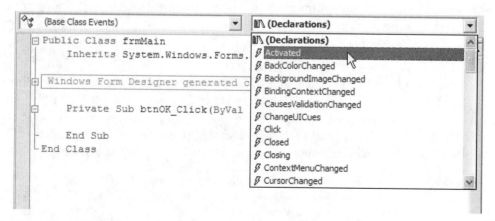

Figure 7-17 Select Activated in the method name drop-down list

After completing these steps, a code template for the `Activated` event procedure will be created in the Code window.

The `Closing` Event

The `Closing` event is triggered as a form is in the process of closing, but before it has closed. This might be in response to the `Close` method being executed, or the user clicking the standard Windows close button (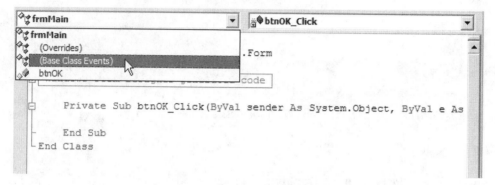) in the form's upper-right corner. If you need to execute code in response to a form closing, such as asking the user if he or she really wants to close the form, you can create a *Closing event procedure*. To create a `Closing` event procedure follow these steps.

1. Open the Code window and click the class name drop-down list. In the drop-down list select (Base Class Events).

2. Click the method name drop-down list. In the drop-down list select Closing.

After completing these steps, a code template for the `Closing` event procedure will be created in the Code window. An example of the code template follows.

```
Private Sub frmMain_Closing(ByVal sender As Object, _
        ByVal e As System.ComponentModel.CancelEventArgs) _
        Handles MyBase.Closing
End Sub
```

Notice that one of the procedure parameters is named `e`. The `e` parameter has a Boolean property named Cancel. If you set the `e` parameter's Cancel property to true, the form will not close. Code showing an example of this technique follows.

```
Private Sub frmMain_Closing(ByVal sender As Object, _
        ByVal e As System.ComponentModel.CancelEventArgs) _
        Handles MyBase.Closing
    If MessageBox.Show("Are you Sure?", "Confirm", _
        MessageBoxButtons.YesNo) = DialogResult.Yes Then
            e.Cancel = False   ' Continue to close the form.
    Else
            e.Cancel = True    ' Do not close the form.
    End If
End Sub
```

The *Closed* Event

The `Closed` event is triggered after a form has closed. If you need to execute code immediately after a form has closed, you can create a *Closed event procedure* by following these steps.

1. Open the Code window and click the class name drop-down list. In the drop-down list select (Base Class Events).

2. Click the method name drop-down list. In the drop-down list select Closed.

After completing these steps, a code template for the `Closed` event procedure will be created in the Code window.

TIP: You cannot prevent a form from closing with the `Closed` event procedure. You must use the `Closing` event procedure to prevent a form from closing.

Using Me.Close() to End an Application

When you use the `Me.Close()` method to close the form that is the startup object, the application will end. Use this approach instead of the `End` statement when you want to execute a `Closing` or `Closed` event procedure for the startup form. When you use the `End` statement, the `Closing` and `Closed` events are not triggered.

Accessing Objects on a Different Form

When you write a statement to access a control, Visual Basic .NET assumes the control is in the same form as the statement that is accessing it. For example, consider a project with a form named `frmMain`. In one of the form's procedures, the following statement appears.

```
lblName.Text = name
```

It is assumed that `lblName` is a control on `frmMain`.

Visual Basic .NET also allows you to write code to access objects on a different form. When doing so, you must fully qualify the name of the object by preceding it with the object variable name. Here is an example of such a statement:

```
Dim resultsForm As New frmResults()
resultsForm.lblAverage.Text = average.ToString
```

In this statement, Visual Basic .NET knows that `lblAverage` is on the form referenced by `resultsForm`. Here is another example. Suppose an application has two forms: `frmMain` and `frmGreeting`. A procedure in the `frmMain` form contains the following code:

```
Dim greetingForm As New frmGreeting()
greetingForm.lblMessage.Text = "Hello!"
greetingForm.ShowDialog()
```

The second statement stores a value in the `lblMessage` control, which is on the form referenced by `greetingForm`. The third statement displays the form.

Class-Level Variables in a Form

Although a form's class-level variables are accessible to all statements in the form file, they are not accessible by default to statements outside the form file. For example, assume a project has a form named `frmAmounts`, which has the following class-level variable declaration.

```
Dim total As Single        ' Class-level variable
```

The same project has another form that uses the following statements.

```
Dim amountsForm As New frmAmounts()
amountsForm.total = 100
```

Even though the assignment statement has fully qualified the name of the variable by preceding it with the object variable name, the statement still cannot access it because class-level variables are private by default. This statement will cause an error when the project is compiled.

If you wish to make a class-level variable available to statements outside the file containing the class, you must declare it with the `Public` key word. Here is an example:

```
Public total As Single      ' Class-level variable
```

Although class-level variables are automatically declared as private with a regular `Dim` statement, you may explicitly declare them as private with the `Private` key word. Here is an example:

```
Private total As Single
```

By explicitly declaring private class-level variables with the `Private` key word, you make your source code more self-documenting.

Using Private and Public Procedures in a Form

Recall from Chapter 6 that the declaration of a Sub procedure or function may begin with an optional access specifier, such as `Public` or `Private`. When a procedure declaration begins with `Private`, the procedure may only be executed by statements in the same form. When a procedure begins with `Public`, it may also be executed by statements that are outside the form. If you do not provide an access specifier, the procedure becomes `Public`. In projects that use multiple forms, you should always make the procedures in a form private unless you specifically want statements outside the form to execute the procedure.

TUTORIAL 7-2:

Examining an application with multiple forms

In this tutorial you examine the Schedule Builder application, which allows a student to select from a list of courses and professors to build a class schedule. The application uses two forms.

Step 1: Start Visual Basic .NET and open the Schedule Builder project, which is stored in the \Chap7\Schedule Builder folder on the student disk.

Step 2: Looking at the Solution Explorer window, you will see the application has two forms: `frmMain` and `frmSchedule`. Open `frmMain` in the Design window. The form is shown in Figure 7-18 with the names of its controls labeled.

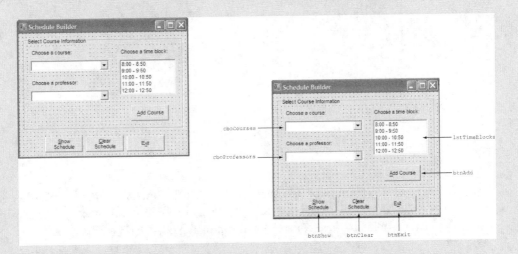

Figure 7-18 The `frmMain` form

Table 7-1 gives a brief description of each control's purpose.

Table 7-1

Schedule Builder controls

Control	Purpose
cboCourses	A combo box with a list of courses to choose from.
cboProfessors	A combo box with a list of professors to choose from.
lstTimeBlocks	A list box with five time blocks to choose from.
btnAdd	Adds the course selected in cboCourses and the professor selected in cboProfessor to the student's schedule for the time block chosen in lstTimeBlocks.
btnShow	Displays an instance of the frmSchedule form showing the student's schedule.
btnClear:	Clears all the courses, professors, and time blocks from the student's schedule.
btnClose	Ends the application.

Step 3: Open the frmSchedule form in the Design window. The form is shown in Figure 7-19 with the names of its controls labeled.

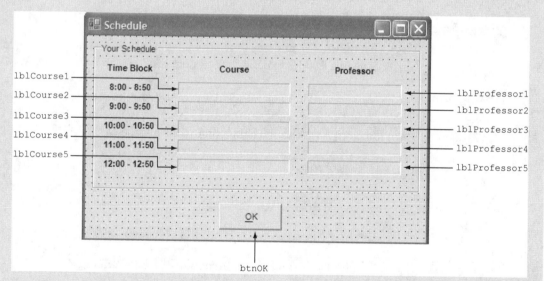

Figure 7-19 The frmSchedule Form

The form has a set of Label controls named lblCourse1, lblCourse2, and so forth, and another set of Label controls named lblProfessor1, lblProfessor2, etc. When the btnShow button on frmMain is clicked, values are copied to these controls as shown in Table 7-2.

Table 7-2

How time blocks, course labels, and professor labels correspond

Time Block	Course Stored In	Professor Stored In
8:00–8:50	lblCourse1	lblProfessor1
9:00–9:50	lblCourse2	lblProfessor2

Table 7-2 *continued*

How time blocks, course labels, and professor labels correspond

Time Block	Course Stored in	Professor Stored in
10:00–10:50	lblCourse3	lblProfessor3
11:00–11:50	lblCourse4	lblProfessor4
12:00–12:50	lblCourse5	lblProfessor5

The btnOk button closes the form.

Step 4: Open the frmMain form in the Code window. Look at the btnAdd_Click event procedure, as follows.

```
Private Sub btnAdd_Click(ByVal sender As System.Object, _
        ByVal e As System.EventArgs) Handles btnAdd.Click
    ' This procedure adds the selected course
    ' to the schedule, which is kept in the
    ' class-level variables.

    ' Determine the time block selected and then add
    ' the course and professor.
    Select Case lstTimeBlocks.SelectedItem
        Case "8:00 - 8:50"
            course1 = cboCourses.Text
            professor1 = cboProfessors.Text
        Case "9:00 - 9:50"
            course2 = cboCourses.Text
            professor2 = cboProfessors.Text
        Case "10:00 - 10:50"
            course3 = cboCourses.Text
            professor3 = cboProfessors.Text
        Case "11:00 - 11:50"
            course4 = cboCourses.Text
            professor4 = cboProfessors.Text
        Case "12:00 - 12:50"
            course5 = cboCourses.Text
            professor5 = cboProfessors.Text
    End Select

    ' Let the user know the course has been added.
    MessageBox.Show("Course added for the ", _
            lstTimeBlocks.SelectedItem & _
            " time block.", "Course Added")
    ' Clear the selected course and professor.
    cboCourses.Text = ""
    cboProfessors.Text = ""
End Sub
```

The btnAdd_Click procedure uses a Select Case statement to determine which time block was selected. It then copies the course and professor that was selected in cboCourses and cboProfessors to the proper class-level variables.

Step 5: Look at the btnShow_Click event procedure, as follows.

```
Private Sub btnShow_Click(ByVal sender As System.Object, _
      ByVal e As System.EventArgs) Handles btnShow.Click
   ' This procedure displays the schedule on an
   ' instance of the frmSchedule form.
   Dim scheduleForm As New frmSchedule()

   ' Copy the course and professor for the
   ' 8:00 - 8:50 time block to scheduleForm.
   scheduleForm.lblCourse1.Text = course1
   scheduleForm.lblProfessor1.Text = professor1

   ' Copy the course and professor for the
   ' 9:00 - 9:50 time block to scheduleForm.
   scheduleForm.lblCourse2.Text = course2
   scheduleForm.lblProfessor2.Text = professor2

   ' Copy the course and professor for the
   ' 10:00 - 10:50 time block to scheduleForm.
   scheduleForm.lblCourse3.Text = course3
   scheduleForm.lblProfessor3.Text = professor3

   ' Copy the course and professor for the
   ' 11:00 - 11:50 time block to scheduleForm.
   scheduleForm.lblCourse4.Text = course4
   scheduleForm.lblProfessor4.Text = professor4

   ' Copy the course and professor for the
   ' 12:00 - 12:50 time block to scheduleForm.
   scheduleForm.lblCourse5.Text = course5
   scheduleForm.lblProfessor5.Text = professor5

   ' Display the schedule form.
   scheduleForm.ShowDialog()
End Sub
```

This procedure creates an instance of the frmSchedule form, and then copies the course and professor names stored in the class-level variables into the appropriate Label controls on the form. It then displays the form.

Step 6: Look at the btnClear_Click procedure. The code follows.

```
Private Sub btnClear_Click(ByVal sender As System.Object, _
      ByVal e As System.EventArgs) Handles btnClear.Click
   ' This procedure clears the items in the schedule.

   ' Clear the course names.
   course1 = ""
   course2 = ""
   course3 = ""
   course4 = ""
   course5 = ""
```

```
                          ' Clear the professor names.
                          professor1 = ""
                          professor2 = ""
                          professor3 = ""
                          professor4 = ""
                          professor5 = ""
                          ' Reset the list box and combo boxes.
                          lstTimeBlocks.SelectedIndex = -1
                          cboCourses.Text = ""
                          cboProfessors.Text = ""
                      End Sub
```

The procedure copies an empty string to each of the class-level variables, deselects any selected value in lstTimeBlocks, and clears the Text properties of cboCourses and cboProfessors.

Step 7:   Look at the btnExit_Click and the frmMain_Closing event procedures. The code follows.

```
Private Sub btnExit_Click(ByVal sender As System.Object, _
        ByVal e As System.EventArgs) Handles btnExit.Click
    ' End the application with the Close method.
    ' This allows the Closing event procedure to execute.
    Me.Close()
End Sub

Private Sub frmMain_Closing(ByVal sender As Object, _
        ByVal e As System.ComponentModel.CancelEventArgs) _
        Handles MyBase.Closing
    ' Confirm that the user wants to quit.
    If MessageBox.Show("Are you sure you want to quit?", "Confirm", _
        MessageBoxButtons.YesNo) = DialogResult.No Then
        e.Cancel = True ' Do not quit
    Else
        e.Cancel = False ' Go ahead and quit
    End If
End Sub
```

The btnExit_Click event procedure calls Me.Close() to close the form. Because frmMain is the startup object, this will end the application. The frmMain_Closing event procedure displays a message box asking the user to confirm that he or she wishes to quit.

Step 8:   Run the application. Select the 8:00 – 8:50 time block in the list box, and then select a course and a professor from the combo boxes. Click the Add Course button to add the selections to the schedule. Repeat this process for the remaining time blocks.

Step 9:   After selecting a course and professor for each of the time blocks, click the Show Schedule button. The frmSchedule form, similar to Figure 7-20, should be displayed with the courses and professors you selected.

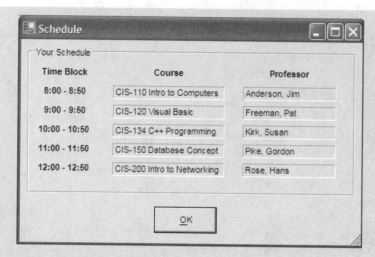

Figure 7-20 Schedule form

Step 10: Click the OK button to close the form.

Step 11: On the main form, click the Exit button. This calls the Me.Close() method, which causes the form's Closing event procedure to execute. A message box appears asking "Are you sure you want to quit?" Click the Yes button.

If You Want to Know More: Using a Form in More than One Project

Once you create a form, you do not have to recreate it to use it in another project. After a form has been saved to a file, it may be used in other projects. Follow these steps to add an existing form to a project:

1. Click Project on the menu bar, and then click Add Existing Item.
2. The Add Existing Item dialog box appears. Use the dialog box to locate the form file that you want to add to the project. (Remember that form files end with the .vb extension.) When you locate the file, select it and click the Open button. The form is now added to the project.

✓ Checkpoint

7.1 How do you cause a form to be displayed automatically when your application executes?

7.2 What is the standard prefix for form names?

7.3 Describe the process of adding a new form to a project.

7.4 Describe the process of exluding a form from a project.

7.5 What is a form file? What file extension does a form file have?

7.6 What is the difference between a modal form and a modeless form?

7.7 A project has an object variable named resultsForm, which references an instance of a form. Write the statement that uses the resultsForm variable to display the form in modal style.

7.8 Write a statement that displays the form referenced by resultsForm in modeless style.

7.9 Where do you write code if you want it to execute when the user switches to a form from another form or from another application?

7.10   A project has a form named `frmInfo`, which has a label named `lblCustomer`. The following declaration statement appears in `frmMain`:

```
Dim infoForm As New frmInfo()
```

The `infoForm` variable references an instance of `frmInfo`. Write a statement that uses the `infoForm` variable to copy "Jim Jones" to the `lblCustomer` Label control on the `frmInfo` form.

7.11   What is the `Me` key word used for?

7.12   You want to declare a class-level variable of the Single data type named `average` in a form. You want code in other forms to access it. Write the variable declaration.

▶ 7.3   Standard Modules

CONCEPT

A STANDARD MODULE CONTAINS CODE—DECLARATIONS AND PROCEDURES—THAT ARE USED BY OTHER FILES IN A PROJECT.

This section shows you how to create standard modules. A *standard module* is a file that contains code such as variable declarations, procedures, and functions. Standard modules are not associated with a form and contain no event procedures. Like forms, standard modules are saved on disk as files that end with the .vb extension.

Standard modules are useful for organizing code in projects that have multiple forms. You should store in a form module the procedures and variables that are used only by that form. If a procedure or variable is used by more than one form, store it in a standard module.

Module Names and Module Files

The contents of a standard module begins with a `Module` statement and ends with an `End Module` statement. The general format is:

```
Module ModuleName
        [Module Contents]
End Module
```

ModuleName is the name of the standard module. This can be any valid Visual Basic .NET identifier. If you have only one standard module in your project then you should give it a name that clearly relates to the project. For example, if a project is named Order Entry, then its standard module might be named `OrderEntryModule`. It is possible to have multiple standard modules in a project. For example, you might have one standard module containing math procedures and another standard module containing procedures for retrieving information from a database. If your project has multiple standard modules, give each standard module a name that describes its purpose.

When you create a standard module in Visual Basic .NET, the code for the module is stored in a file that ends with the .vb extension. Normally, the name of the file is the same as the name of the module. So, a module named `OrderEntryModule` should be saved to the file OrderEntryModule.vb.

Adding a Standard Module

Follow these steps to add a standard module to a project.

1.   Click the Add New Item button (🔳) on the toolbar, or click Project on the menu bar, then click Add Module. The Add New Item dialog box shown in Figure 7-21 should appear. Notice that in the figure, the name Module1.vb appears in the Name text box. In this example, Module1.vb is the default name for the file that the module will be stored in, and Module1 is the default name for the module.

NOTE: *The default name may be different, depending on the number of modules already in the project.*

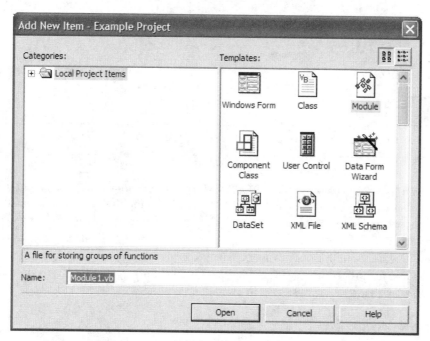

Figure 7-21   The Add New Item dialog box

2.   Under Templates, make sure Module is selected.

3.   Change the default name that is displayed in the Name text box to the name you wish to give the new module file. For example, if you wish to name the new module OrderEntryModule, enter OrderEntryModule.vb in the Name text box.

4.   Click the Open button.

NOTE: *When you rename the module file, be sure to keep the .vb extension.*

A new, empty module will be added to your project. The module will be displayed in the Code window and an entry for the new module will appear in the Solution Explorer window. The Solution Explorer window in Figure 7-22 shows two forms and one module: frmError, frmMain, and ExampleProjectModule.

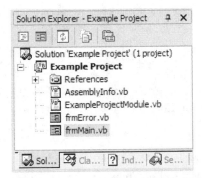

Figure 7-22   The Solution Explorer window showing two forms and one module

Once you have added a standard module to your project, you write the code for Sub procedures and functions in it, just as you would in a form module.

Using Private and Public Procedures in a Module

When a procedure declaration in a module begins with `Private`, it may only be accessed by statements in the same module. When a procedure declaration in a module begins with `Public`, it may be accessed by statements that are outside the module. If you do not provide an access specifier, a procedure becomes `Public`. For example, look at the following functions which appear in the same module.

```
Private Function calcArea(ByVal length As Single, _
                          ByVal width As Single) As Single
    ' Calculates and returns the area of a rectangle.
    Dim area As Single

    area = length * width
    Return area
End Function

Public Function getArea() As Single
    ' Asks the user for a rectangle's length and width,
    ' and then returns the area.
    Dim length, width, area As Single

    length = Val(InputBox("Enter the length of the rectangle."))
    width = Val(InputBox("Enter the width of the rectangle."))
    area = calcArea(length, width)
    Return area
End Function
```

The first function, `calcArea`, is private. It can only be called from statements in the same module as the function. The second function, `getArea`, is public. It can be called from statements outside the module. Notice that the `getArea` function calls the `calcArea` function.

Module-Level Variables

A variable that is declared inside a module (between the `Module` and the `End Module` statements), but not inside a Sub procedure or function, is a module-level variable. The same rules that you have already learned about the scope of class-level variables in a form apply to module-level variables in a standard module.

◆ A module-level variable in a standard module is accessible to any Sub procedure or function in the standard module.

◆ If a module-level variable is declared with either the `Dim` or `Private` key words, the variable is not accessible to statements outside the standard module. Such a variable has *module scope*.

◆ If a module-level variable is declared with the `Public` key word, it is accessible to statements outside the standard module. Such a variable has *global scope*.

A module-level variable that is declared as `Public` is also known as a *global variable* because it can be accessed globally, by any statement in the project. Many programmers prefix the names of global variables with the characters `g_`. This documents the variable's scope. For example, a global variable that holds the tax rate might be names `g_taxRate`.

WARNING:

Although global variables provide an easy way to share data among procedures, forms, and modules, you should be careful not to overuse them. While debugging an application, if you find that the wrong value is being stored in a global variable, you will have to track down every statement that accesses it to determine where the bad value is coming from. Also, when two or more procedures modify the same variable, you must be careful that what one procedure does will not upset the accuracy or correctness of another procedure. Although global variables make it easy to share data, they require great responsibility from the programmer.

TUTORIAL 7-3:

Examining an application that uses a standard module

In this tutorial you examine the University Concert Hall application, which calculates the prices of tickets for performances in the concert hall. The hall has three sections of seats for the general public. Section A tickets cost $20 each, section B tickets cost $15 each, and section C tickets cost $10 each. In addition there is a student section where tickets cost $7 each. This application has three form modules and a standard module.

Step 1: Start Visual Basic .NET and open Ticket Sales project, which is stored in the \Chap7\Ticket Sales folder on the student disk.

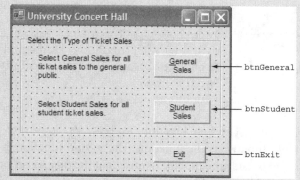

Figure 7-23   University Concert Hall main form

Step 2: Look at the Solution Explorer window: the project has three forms: `frmMain`, `frmGeneral`, and `frmStudent`. The project also has a standard code module named `TicketSalesModule`. Open `frmMain` in the Design window. The form is shown in Figure 7-23 with the names of its Button controls labeled.

The btnGeneral button displays an instance of the frmGeneral form, which processes ticket sales to the general public. The btnStudent button displays an instance of the frmStudent form, which processes student ticket sales. The btnExit button ends the application.

Step 3:   Open the frmGeneral form, which is shown in Figure 7-24 with the names of its controls labeled.

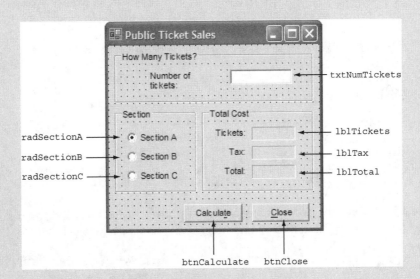

Figure 7-24   Public Ticket Sales form

Step 4:   Open the Code window and look at the btnCalculate_Click event procedure, which is as follows. Notice the line that is shown here in bold.

```
Private Sub btnCalculate_Click(ByVal sender As System.Object, _
        ByVal e As System.EventArgs) Handles btnCalculate.Click
    ' Calculate and display the ticket costs.
    Dim numTickets As Integer ' The number of tickets purchased
    Dim ticketCost As Decimal ' The price of tickets
    Dim tax As Decimal        ' The sales tax
    Dim total As Decimal      ' The total cost

    ' Calculate the cost.
    numTickets = Val(txtNumTickets.Text)
    ticketCost = numTickets * PriceEachTicket()
    tax = CalcTax(ticketCost)
    total = ticketCost + tax
    ' Display the cost.
    lblTickets.Text = FormatCurrency(ticketCost)
    lblTax.Text = FormatCurrency(tax)
    lblTotal.Text = FormatCurrency(total)
End Sub
```

The bold line calls a function named CalcTax, which returns the amount of sales tax on the value passed as an argument to the function.

Step 5:   Open the `frmStudent` form, which is shown in Figure 7-25 with the names of its controls labeled.

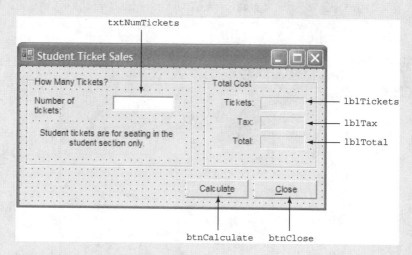

Figure 7-25   Student Ticket Sales form

Step 6:   Open the Code window and look at the `btnCalculate_Click` event procedure, which is as follows. Notice the line that is shown here in bold.

```
Private Sub btnCalculate_Click(ByVal sender As System.Object, _
        ByVal e As System.EventArgs) Handles btnCalculate.Click
    ' Calculate and display the ticket costs.
    Dim numTickets As Integer ' The number of tickets purchased
    Dim ticketCost As Decimal ' The price of tickets
    Dim tax As Decimal        ' The sales tax
    Dim total As Decimal      ' The total cost

    ' Calculate the cost.
    numTickets = Val(txtNumTickets.Text)
    ticketCost = numTickets * studentPrice
    tax = CalcTax(ticketCost)
    total = ticketCost + tax
    ' Display the cost.
    lblTickets.Text = FormatCurrency(ticketCost)
    lblTax.Text = FormatCurrency(tax)
    lblTotal.Text = FormatCurrency(total)
End Sub
```

The bold line in this event procedure also calls the `CalcTax` function. Because the function is called by statements in both forms, it is stored in a standard module.

Step 7:   Open the standard module by double-clicking the entry for TicketSalesModule.vb in the Solution Explorer window. The module's contents are shown here.

```
Module TicketSalesModule
```

```
                    ' This module contains the CalcTax function.

                    Const taxRate As Single = 0.06 ' Sales Tax Rate

                    Public Function CalcTax(ByVal cost As Decimal) As Decimal
                        ' This function calculates and returns the
                        ' sales tax on ticket sales. The ticket cost is
                        ' passed as an argument.
                        Return cost * taxRate
                    End Function
                End Module
```

Step 8:   Run the application and test various values on the frmGeneral form and the frmStudent form. When you have finished, close the application.

Creating an Application with No Startup Form

Visual Basic .NET allows you to designate either a form or a public Sub procedure named Main as an application's startup object. If a Sub procedure named Main is designated as the startup object, it must reside in a standard module. When the application runs, no form is initially displayed. Instead, the Sub procedure Main is executed. This allows your application to perform operations before the user sees a form displayed on the screen.

To designate the Sub procedure Main as the startup object, follow these steps.

1. In the Solution Explorer window, right click the project's entry.

2. On the popup menu, click Properties. The project's Property Pages dialog box should appear.

3. To change the startup object, click the down arrow in the Startup Object drop-down list. A list of all the forms in the project, as well as Sub Main, appears. Select Sub Main.

4. Click the OK button.

When you run the application, the Sub procedure Main will execute. Because you have designated Main as the startup object, Visual Basic .NET will not display a form automatically. Instead, you will have to write code in Main that displays a form. For example, imagine an application that has a form named frmMain and Sub procedure named CalcInitValues. The CalcInitValues Sub procedure calculates some initial values and displays them on frmMain. Here is a Main Sub procedure that calls CalcInitValues and then displays frmMain:

```
Public Sub Main()
    ' This procedure calculates the startup values
    ' for the main form.
    Dim mainForm as New frmMain()' Declare an instance of frmMain
    CalcInitValues()               ' Call CalcInitValues.
    mainform.ShowDialog()          ' Display frmMain.
End Sub
```

If You Want to Know More: Using a Standard Module in More Than One Project

It is possible to use a standard module in more than one project. For example, suppose you have created a project with a standard module that contains several generic math functions. Later, you find yourself working on a new project that needs many of the same functions. Instead of rewriting the functions, you can simply add the standard module to the new project.

Follow these steps to add an existing standard module to a project.

1. Click Project on the menu bar, and then click Add Existing Item.

2. The Add Existing Item dialog box appears. Use the dialog box to locate the module file that you want to add to the project. When you locate the file, select it and click the Open button. The module is now added to the project.

✓ Checkpoint

7.13 What do standard modules contain?

7.14 With what file extension are standard modules saved?

7.15 Describe the steps you take to add a new standard module to a project.

7.16 An application's project file is named Customers. The application has one standard module. What name would give the standard module?

7.17 You want to designate a Sub procedure as an application's startup object. What name must the Sub procedure have?

▶ 7.4 Menus

CONCEPT

VISUAL BASIC .NET ALLOWS YOU TO CREATE A SYSTEM OF DROP-DOWN MENUS FOR ANY FORM IN YOUR APPLICATION. YOU USE THE MENU DESIGNER TO CREATE A MENU SYSTEM.

In the applications you have studied so far, the user performs tasks by clicking command buttons. When an application has several operations for the user to choose from, a menu system is more commonly used than command buttons. A *menu system* is a collection of commands organized in one or more drop-down menus. The *menu designer* allows you to visually create a custom menu system for any form in an application.

Before you learn how to use the menu designer, you must learn about the typical components of a menu system. Look at the example menu system in Figure 7-26.

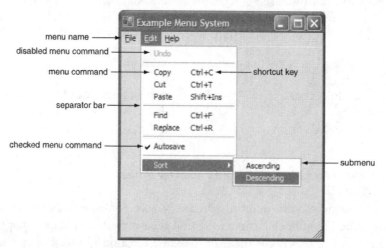

Figure 7-26 Example Menu System

The menu system in the figure consists of the following items.

- Menu names—Each drop-down menu has a name. The menu names are listed on a menu bar that appears just below the form's title bar. The menu names in Figure 7-26 are File, Edit, and Help. The user may activate a menu by clicking the menu name. In the figure, the Edit menu has been activated. Notice that the menu names have access keys (F for File, E for Edit, and H for Help). The user may also activate a menu by entering Alt + its access key.

- Menu command—Menus have commands. The user selects a command by clicking it, entering its access key, or entering its shortcut key.

- Shortcut key—A *shortcut key* is a key or combination of keys that cause a menu command to execute. Shortcut keys are shown on a menu to the right of their corresponding commands. For example, in Figure 7-26, Ctrl+C is the shortcut key for the Copy command. Here is the primary difference between a shortcut key and an access key: a menu command's access key only works while the menu is open, but a shortcut key may be executed at any time while the form is active.

- Disabled menu command—You can cause a menu command to be disabled when you do not want the user to select it. A disabled menu command appears in dim lettering (grayed out) and cannot be selected. In Figure 7-26 the Undo command is disabled.

- Checked menu command—A checked menu command is usually one that turns an option on or off. A check mark appears to the left of the command, indicating the option is turned on. When no check mark appears to the left of the command, the option is turned off. The user toggles a checked menu command each time he or she selects it. In Figure 7-26 Auto Save is a checked menu command.

- Submenu—Some of the commands on a menu are actually the names of submenus. You can tell when a command is the name of a submenu because a right arrow (▶) appears to its right. Activating the name of a submenu causes the submenu to appear. For example, in Figure 7-26, clicking the Sort command causes a submenu to appear.

- Separator bar—A separator bar is a horizontal bar used to separate groups of commands on a menu. In Figure 7-26, separator bars are used to separate the Copy, Cut, and Paste commands into one group, the Find and Replace commands into another group, and the Sort command in a box by itself. Separator bars are only used as a visual aid and cannot be selected by the user.

The MainMenu Control

An application's menu system is constructed with a *MainMenu control*. You place a MainMenu control in your application just as you place other controls: double-click the MainMenu tool in the tool box. When you do so, a MainMenu control appears in the component tray at the bottom of the Design window. The default name of the MainMenu control is `MainMenu1`.

A MainMenu control is composed of *MenuItem objects*. Each item in a menu, including separator bars, is a separate MenuItem object. When you create MenuItem objects, you name them with the `mnu` prefix. You place the text you want displayed by a MenuItem object in its Text property. As with controls, access keys are assigned by placing an ampersand (&) in the Text property before the character that is to become the access key. For example, look at the menu system sketch in Figure 7-27. Table 7-3 lists the MenuItem objects in the menu system shown in Figure 7-27, with the contents of their Text properties.

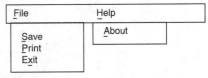

Figure 7-27   Example menu system sketch

Table 7-3

MenuItem objects and their Text properties

MenuItem Object Name	Text Property
mnuFile	&File
mnuFileSave	&Save
mnuFilePrint	&Print
mnuFileExit	E&xit
mnuHelp	&Help
mnuHelpAbout	&About

Notice that the MenuItem object names listed in Table 7-3 indicate where in the menu hierarchy each control belongs. The names of the objects that are commands on the File menu all begin with mnuFile. For example, the object for the Save command on the File menu is named mnuFile Save. Likewise, the object for the About command on the Help menu is named mnuHelpAbout.

MenuItem objects have properties and respond to events. You make a menu functional by writing Click event procedures for its MenuItem objects.

The Menu Designer

Once you have placed a MainMenu control in a form's component tray, you create MenuItem objects with the menu designer. You start the menu designer by selecting the MainMenu control. Figure 7-28 shows a form with a MainMenu control selected in the component tray, and the menu designer started. The menu designer appears on the form in the location that the menu system will appear.

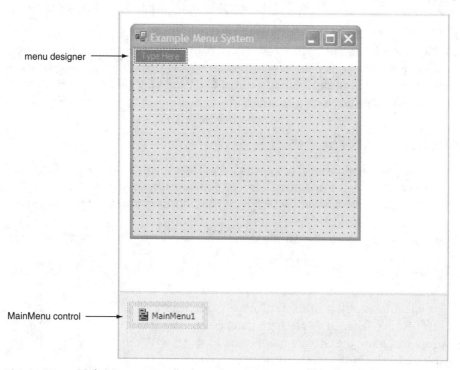

Figure 7-28   MainMenu control selected and menu designer started

Notice in Figure 7-28 that the words "Type Here" appear in a small box in the menu designer. This marks the position of the first MenuItem object. The MenuItem object is automatically created when you type text into the box. The text that you type is stored in the Menu Item's Text property, and will be displayed on the menu bar. Figure 7-29 shows the menu designer after the word "File" has been typed as the text for the first MenuItem object. Notice that the menu designer now shows two new "Type Here" boxes, one below and one to the right of the first object. Press the down-arrow key to move down, and the right-arrow key to move to the right.

You continue to type in the "Type Here" boxes the text that you wish your menu system to display. Figure 7-30 shows the menu designer with a more complete menu system. The menu system has a File, Edit, and Help menu. The Edit menu is displayed.

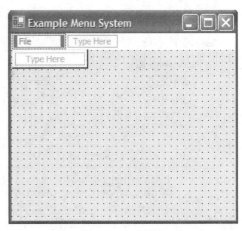

Figure 7-29 MenuItem object with "File" as its text

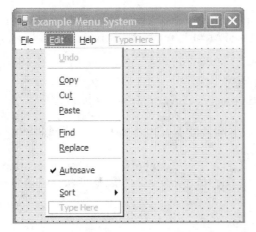

Figure 7-30 Menu designer with many MenuItem objects

MenuItem Object Names

The menu designer assigns default names to the MenuItem objects as you create them. The first object is named `MenuItem1`, the second object is named `MenuItem2`, and so forth. You can change a MenuItem object's name by changing its Name property in the Properties window. In Figure 7-31, the Properties window shows the properties of a MenuItem object. Notice that the Name property has been changed to `mnuEditCopy`.

Shortcut Keys

As previously stated, a shortcut key is a key or combination of keys that cause a menu command to execute. Table 7-4 lists some commonly used shortcut keys in Windows applications.

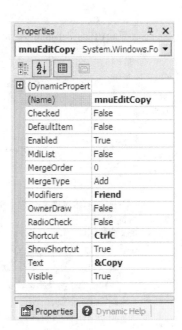

Figure 7-31 Properties Window showing a MenuItem object's properties

Table 7-4

Some commonly used Windows application shortcut keys

Shortcut Key	Command
Ctrl+S	Save
Ctrl+P	Print
Ctrl+C	Copy
Ctrl+X	Cut
Ctrl+V or Shift+Insert	Paste

Shortcut keys are shown on a menu to the right of their corresponding commands. To create a shortcut key for a MenuItem object, select the *Shortcut property* in the Properties window. A list appears with all the available shortcut keys. Select the one you wish to assign to the MenuItem object. You must also make sure that the *ShowShortcut property* is set to true. When set to false, the MenuItem object's shortcut key will not be displayed.

Checked MenuItem Objects

A checked MenuItem object appears with a checkmark to its left. When the user selects the menu item, the check mark is turned on or off. To make a checked MenuItem object, do one of the following:

- ◆ In the menu designer, click the area to the left of a menu item's text. A check mark will appear indicating that the item is now a checked menu item.
- ◆ In the Properties window set the MenuItem object's *Checked property* to true.

If the *RadioChecked property* is set to true, the menu item will appear with a radio button next to it instead of a check mark.

You may work with the Checked property in code. For example, assume an application uses a MenuItem object named `mnuSettingsAlarm`. The following code displays a message box if the menu item is checked.

```
If mnuSettingsAlarm.Checked = True Then
    MessageBox.Show("WAKE UP!")
End If
```

NOTE: *A menu control's Checked property is only available if the control does not cause a menu or sub-menu to appear.*

Disabled MenuItem Objects

A disabled menu item appears dimmed, or "grayed out," and may not be selected by the user. You may disable a MenuItem object by setting its Enabled property to false. For example, applications that provide Cut, Copy, and Paste commands usually disable the Paste command until something is Cut or Copied. So, the Paste MenuItem object's Enabled property can be set to false at design time (in the Properties window), and then set to true in code after the Cut or Copy commands have been used. Assuming that the Paste MenuItem object is named `mnuEditPaste`, the following code enables it.

```
mnuEditPaste.Enabled = True
```

Separator Bars

You can insert a separator bar into a menu in either of the following ways.

◆ Right-click an existing menu item. On the pop-up menu that appears, select Insert Separator. A separator bar will be inserted above the menu item.

◆ Type a hyphen ("-") as a MenuItem object's Text property.

Submenus

When a menu item is selected in the menu designer, a "Type Here" box is displayed to its right. Figure 7-32 shows an example. This box allows you to create a submenu item. When you create a submenu, a right-arrow (▶) will automatically be displayed next to the menu item that is the parent of the submenu.

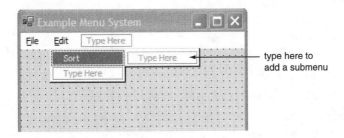

Figure 7-32   Creating a submenu

Inserting MenuItem Objects in an Existing Menu

If you need to insert a new menu item above an existing menu item, start the menu designer by selecting the existing name. Then right-click the existing menu item. On the pop-up menu that appears, select Insert New. A new menu item will be inserted above the existing menu item.

If you need to insert a new menu item at the bottom of an existing menu, start the menu designer and simply select the desired menu or submenu. A "Type Here" box automatically appears at the bottom.

Deleting MenuItem Objects

To delete a menu item, start the menu designer and perform one of the following procedures.

◆ Right-click the menu item you wish to delete. On the pop-up menu, select Delete.

◆ Select the menu item you wish to delete, then press the Delete key on the keyboard.

Rearranging Menu Items

You can move a MenuItem object by clicking and dragging. Simply select it in the menu designer and drag it to the desired location.

MenuItem Object `Click` Event Procedures

You do not have to write code to display a menu or a submenu. When the user clicks a MenuItem object that displays a menu or a submenu, Visual Basic .NET automatically causes the menu or submenu to appear.

If a MenuItem object does not have a menu or submenu to display, you make it functional by providing a `Click` event procedure for it. For example, assume a menu system has a File menu with an Exit command, which causes the application to end. The MenuItem object for the Exit command is named `mnuFileExit`. Here is the code for the object's `Click` event procedure:

```
Private Sub mnuFileExit_Click(ByVal sender As System.Object, _
        ByVal e As System.EventArgs) Handles mnuFileExit.Click
    ' End the application
    End
End Sub
```

To write a `Click` event procedure for a MenuItem object, start the menu designer, then double-click the desired menu item. A code template for the `Click` event procedure will be created.

Standard Menu Items

Although all applications do not have identical menu systems, it is standard for most applications to have the following menu items.

- A File menu as the leftmost item on the menu bar, with the access key Alt+F.
- An Exit command on the File menu, with the access key Alt+X and optionally the shortcut key Alt+Q. This command ends the application.
- A Help menu as the rightmost item on the menu bar, with the access key Alt+H.
- An About command on the Help menu with the access key Alt+A. This command displays an About box.

You should always add these items to your menu systems because most Windows users expect to see them. You should also assign shortcut keys to the most commonly used commands. Study the menu system in an application such as Microsoft Word or Microsoft Excel to become familiar with a typical menu design.

In Tutorial 7-4 you will learn to use the menu designer by building a simple menu system.

TUTORIAL 7-4:

Building a menu

In this tutorial you create an application that demonstrates how a label appears in different colors. You build a menu system that allows the user to select a color, which is then applied to a Label control. Figure 7-33 shows a sketch of the menu system.

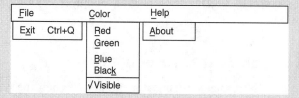

Figure 7-33   Sketch of menu system

Step 1:   Start Visual Basic .NET and begin a new Windows application project named **Menu Demo**.

Step 2:   Change the form's Text property to **Menu Demo**. Place a label named `lblMessage`, with the Text property **Hello World!**, on the form, as shown in Figure 7-34.

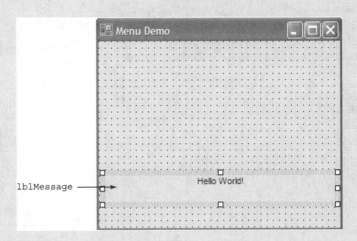

lblMessage

Figure 7-34   Menu Demo form

Step 3:   Double-click the MainMenu tool in the toolbox to add a MainMenu control to the form. The control, which will appear in the component tray, should be selected. If it is not, select it. The menu designer should now be running, as shown in Figure 7-35.

Figure 7-35   Form with menu designer running

Step 4:   First you will create the File MenuItem object. In the "Type Here" box, type **&File**. Press the Enter key to create the object. The text "File" should now appear on the menu bar.

Step 5:   Now you will set the Name property for the MenuItem object you just created. Use the mouse or the keyboard up-arrow key to select the word File on the menu. The MenuItem object's properties should be displayed in the Properties window. Change the Name property to **mnuFile**.

Step 6: Now you will create the Exit MenuItem object on the File menu. Use the mouse or the keyboard down-arrow key to select the "Type Here" box below the File menu item. Type **E&xit** and press Enter to create the object. The text "Exit" should now appear on the File menu, as shown in Figure 7-36.

Figure 7-36 Exit menu item created

Step 7: Now you will set the properties for the MenuItem object you just created. Use the mouse or the keyboard up-arrow key to select the word Exit. The MenuItem object's properties should be displayed in the Properties window. Change the Name property to **mnuFileExit**. In the Shortcut property select CtrlQ.

Step 8: Now you are ready to add the Color MenuItem object. In the "Type Here" box shown in Figure 7-37 type **&Color** and press Enter.

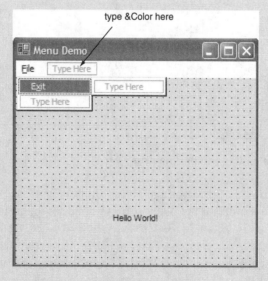

Figure 7-37 Where to type &Color

Step 9:   Now set the Name property for the MenuItem object you just created. Use the mouse or the keyboard up-arrow key to select the word Color on the menu. The MenuItem object's properties should be displayed in the Properties window. Change the Name property to **mnuColor**.

Step 10:   Now you will add the first four menu items to the Color menu. Below the mnu Color MenuItem object, add an object whose Text reads **&Red**, and whose Name property is **mnuColorRed**.

Below the mnuColorRed object, add an object whose Text reads **&Green**, and whose Name property is **mnuColorGreen**.

Below the mnuColorGreen object, add an object whose Text reads **&Blue**, and whose Name property is **mnuColorBlue**.

Below the mnuColorBlue object, add an object whose Text reads **Blac&k**, and whose Name property is **mnuColorBlack**.

Step 11:   The menu sketch in Figure 7-33 shows a separator bar just below the work Black on the Color menu. Create the separator bar by typing a hypen ("-") in the "Type Here" box below the mnuColorBlack object.

Step 12:   Below the separator bar, add an object whose Text reads **Visible**, and whose Name property is **mnuColorVisible**. The object's Checked property should be set to true. The Color menu should now appear as shown in Figure 7-38.

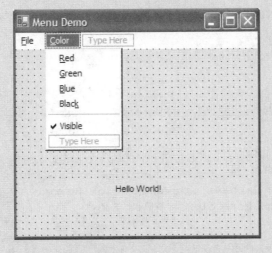

Figure 7-38   Completed Color menu

Step 13:   To the right of the Color menu item, add the Help menu item with the text **&Help** and the name **mnuHelp**.

Step 14: Below the word Help, add a MenuItem object with the text **&About** and the name **mnuHelpAbout**. When finished, the Help menu should appear as shown in Figure 7-39.

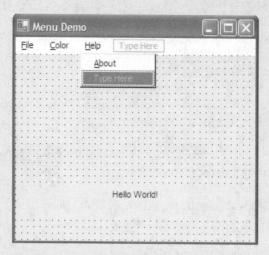

Figure 7-39 Completed Help menu

Step 15: Now you will write the `Click` event procedures for the appropriate MenuItem objects, starting with `mnuFileExit`. In the menu designer, double-click the word Exit, which is on the File menu. The Code window opens with a code template for the `mnuFileExit_Click` event procedure. Complete the procedure by typing the code shown in bold, as follows.

```
Private Sub mnuFileExit_Click(ByVal sender As System.Object, _
        ByVal e As System.EventArgs) Handles mnuFileExit.Click
    ' End the application
    End
End Sub
```

Step 16: Follow this same procedure to write the event procedures for the commands on the Color menu. The code for the event procedures is as follows.

```
Private Sub mnuColorRed_Click(ByVal sender As System.Object, _
        ByVal e As System.EventArgs) Handles mnuColorRed.Click
    ' Set the label's forground color to red
    lblMessage.ForeColor = Color.Red
End Sub

Private Sub mnuColorGreen_Click(ByVal sender As System.Object, _
        ByVal e As System.EventArgs) Handles mnuColorGreen.Click
    ' Set the label's forground color to green
    lblMessage.ForeColor = Color.Green
End Sub

Private Sub mnuColorBlue_Click(ByVal sender As System.Object, _
        ByVal e As System.EventArgs) Handles mnuColorBlue.Click
    ' Set the label's forground color to blue
    lblMessage.ForeColor = Color.Blue
End Sub
```

```
Private Sub mnuColorBlack_Click(ByVal sender As System.Object, _
        ByVal e As System.EventArgs) Handles mnuColorBlack.Click
    ' Set the label's forground color to black
    lblMessage.ForeColor = Color.Black
End Sub

Private Sub mnuColorVisible_Click(ByVal sender As System.Object, _
        ByVal e As System.EventArgs) Handles mnuColorVisible.Click
    ' Make the label visible or invisible
    If mnuColorVisible.Checked = True Then
        lblMessage.Visible = False
        mnuColorVisible.Checked = False
    Else
        lblMessage.Visible = True
        mnuColorVisible.Checked = True
    End If
End Sub
```

Let's take a closer look at the mnuColorVisible_Click procedure. When this procedure executes, it tests the mnuColorVisible object's Checked property. If the property is true, it means that the Visible item was already checked when the user clicked it. In this case, the user wants to uncheck the Visible item, thus making the label invisible. So, we set lblMessage's Visible property to false and we remove the checkmark from the Visible item by setting mnuColorVisible's Checked property to false.

If mnuColorVisible's Checked property is false when this procedure executes, it means that the Visible item was not checked when the user clicked it. In this case, the user wants to check the Visible item, thus making the label visible. So, we set lblMessage's Visible property to true and we place the checkmark next to the Visible item by setting mnuColorVisible's Checked property to true.

Step 17: The Help menu has one item: About. Most applications have this command, which displays a dialog box known as an About box. An *About box* usually shows some brief information about the application. Write the following code for the mnuHelp About MenuItem object's Click event procedure.

```
Private Sub mnuHelpAbout_Click(ByVal sender As System.Object, _
        ByVal e As System.EventArgs) Handles mnuHelpAbout.Click
    ' Display a simple About window.
    MessageBox.Show("Menu System Demo" & vbCrLf & _
            "Designed for Starting Out with Visual Basic .NET", _
            "About Menu Demo")
End Sub
```

Step 18: Save the project and run it. Try selecting different colors to see how they make the label appear. Also test the Visible command, and the About command. When finished, type Ctrl+Q to exit the application.

If the Menu Does Not Display

When you add a MainMenu control to a form, Visual Basic .NET also adds a property named Menu to the form, which is set to the name of the MainMenu control. If you add a menu to a form and it does not display when you run the application, make sure that the form's Menu property is set to the name of the MainMenu control.

Context Menus

A *context menu* is a pop-up menu that is displayed when the user right-clicks a form or control. To create a context menu, you must add a ContextMenu control to a form. You do this just as you add other controls: double-click the ContextMenu tool in the toolbox. A ContextMenu control is then created in the form's component tray. The first such control will have the default name ContextMenu1, the second will have the default name ContextMenu2, and so forth.

Once you have added a ContextMenu control to a form, you add items to it with the menu designer, just as you do with a regular menu. After you have built the context menu, you add Click event procedures for its MenuItem object. Then, you associate the context menu with a control by setting the control's ContextMenu property to the name of the context menu control. At run time, the context menu will pop-up when the user right-clicks the control. For example, Figure 7-40 shows a context menu that is displayed when the user right-clicked a Label control.

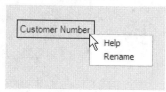

Figure 7-40 Context menu

✓ **Checkpoint**

7.18 Briefly describe each of the following menu system components.

    a. Menu name

    b. Menu command

    c. Disabled menu command

    d. Checked menu command

    e. Shortcut key

    f. Submenu

    g. Separator bar

7.19 What is the difference between a menu item's access key and its shortcut key?

7.20 What is the standard prefix for MenuItem objects?

7.21 An application has a File menu with the following commands: Save, Save As, Print, and Exit. What name would you give each of the controls?

7.22 How do you assign an access key to a menu control?

7.23 What happens if you set a MenuItem object's Checked property to true?

7.24 How do you disable a menu control in code?

7.25 How do you display a check mark next to a menu item in code?

7.26 What event procedure executes when the user clicks on a menu item?

7.27 How does the user display a context menu?

7.28 How do you associate a context menu with a control?

▶ 7.5 Focus on Problem Solving: Building the High Adventure Travel Agency Price Quote Application

CONCEPT

IN THIS SECTION YOU BUILD AN APPLICATION FOR THE HIGH ADVENTURE TRAVEL AGENCY. THE APPLICATION USES MULTIPLE FORMS, A STANDARD MODULE, AND A MENU SYSTEM.

The High Adventure Travel Agency offers three vacation packages for thrill-seeking customers. The rates and options vary for each package. You've been asked to create an application to calculate and itemize the charges for each package.

- ◆ **Scuba Bahama:** A weeklong cruise to the Bahamas with three days of scuba diving. Those with advanced experience may dive right in, while beginners should choose to take optional, but very affordable lessons.

  Rates:

Base Charge:	$1,000 per person
Scuba Instruction:	$300 per person

- ◆ **Sky Dive Colorado:** Four thrilling days with expert sky diving instructors in Colorado Springs, Colorado. For lodging, you may choose either the Wilderness Lodge or the Luxury Inn. Sky diving instruction is included for all members of the party.

  Rates:

Base Charge:	$400 per person
Lodging at Wilderness Lodge:	$80/day per person
Lodging at Luxury Inn:	$150/day per person

- ◆ **Barron Cliff Spelunk:** Seven days spent hiking and exploring caves in the Barron Cliff Wilderness Area, Tennessee. Camping equipment rental is available.

  Rates:

Base Charge:	$700 per person
Equipment Rental:	$50/day per person

A 10% discount is given on the total charges for any package when a party has five or more.

The application will have four forms: `frmMain`, `frmScuba`, `frmSkyDive`, and `frmSpelunk`. A standard module will also be used.

The Standard Module

The standard module declares module-level variables and functions that are accessible to code in the other modules. These variables are listed in Table 7-5. The variables that have global scope (are accessible to all statements in the project) have the `g_` prefix.

Table 7-5

Module-level variables

Name	Description
discountRate	A constant, which is set to 0.1. This constant holds the discount rate for packages with five or more in the party.
depositRate	A constant, which is set to 0.5. This constant holds the percentage of the total package price that must be deposited.
g_package	A global string variable for holding the name of the vacation package.
g_partyMembers	A global integer variable for holding the total number of party members.
g_subtotal	A global decimal variable for holding the subtotal (before any discount) of the vacation package.

Table 7-6 describes the functions in the standard module.

Table 7-6

Functions in the standard module

Function	Description
IsPositiveNumber	This function accepts a string argument and returns true if the string contains a positive numeric value. Otherwise it returns false. The function is used in validation procedures.
CalcDiscount	This function returns the discount, if any, on a package. It accepts two arguments. The first argument is the number of party members, and the second argument is the subtotal of the package.
CalcDeposit	This function returns the amount of the required deposit. It accepts one argument, the total of the package charges.

The `frmMain` Form

Figure 7-41 shows a sketch of `frmMain` with the form's controls labeled.

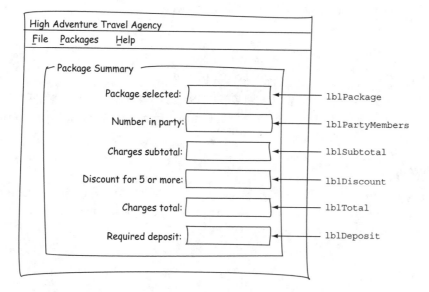

Figure 7-41 Sketch of `frmMain` form

Table 7-7 lists each of the form's controls (excluding the MenuItem objects) along with any relevant property setting.

Table 7-7

`frmMain` Controls and Property Settings

Control Type	Control Name	Properties
Form	`frmMain`	Text: "High Adventure Travel Agency"
GroupBox	(Default)	Text: "Package Summary"
Label	(Default)	Text: "Package selected:"
Label	`lblPackage`	Text: "" BorderStyle: Fixed3D
Label	(Default)	Text: "Number in party:"
Label	`lblPartyMembers`	Text: "" BorderStyle: Fixed3D
Label	(Default)	Text: "Charges subtotal:"
Label	`lblSubtotal`	Text: "" BorderStyle: Fixed3D
Label	(Default)	Text: "Discount for 5 or more:"
Label	`lblDiscount`	Text: "" BorderStyle: Fixed3D
Label	(Default)	Text: "Charges subtotal:"
Label	`lbltotal`	Text: "" BorderStyle: Fixed3D
Label	(Default)	Text: "Required deposit:"
Label	`lblDeposit`	Text: "" BorderStyle: Fixed3D

Figure 7-42 shows a sketch of the menu system on `frmMain`. Table 7-8 lists the menu controls and their shortcut keys.

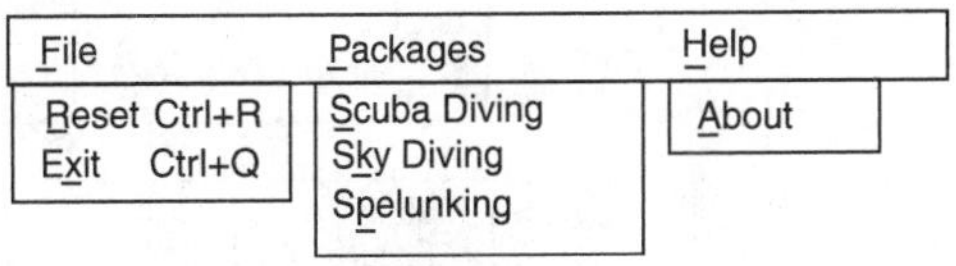

Figure 7-42 Menu System on `frmMain`

Table 7-8

`frmMain` MenuItem objects and shortcut keys

Name	Caption	Shortcut Key
`mnuFile`	&File	(none)
`mnuFileReset`	&Reset	Ctrl+R
`mnuFileExit`	E&xit	Ctrl+Q
`mnuPackages`	&Packages	(none)
`mnuPackagesScubaDiving`	&Scuba Diving	(none)
`mnuPackagesSkyDiving`	S&ky Diving	(none)
`mnuPackagesSpelunking`	S&pelunking	(none)
`mnuHelp`	&Help	(none)
`mnuHelpAbout`	&About	(none)

Table 7-9 lists and describes the methods in `frmMain`.

Table 7-9

frmMain methods

Method	Description
mnuFileExit_Click	Ends the application.
mnuFileReset_Click	Clears the lblPackage, lblPartyMembers, lblSubtotal, lblDiscount, lblTotal, and lblDeposit labels.
mnuPackagesScubaDiving_Click	Displays the frmScuba form.
mnuPackagesSkyDiving_Click	Displays the frmSkyDive form.
mnuPackagesSpelunking_Click	Displays the frmSpelunk form.
mnuHelpAbout_Click	Displays an About box.
DisplayCharges	Calculates and displays the discount, total charges, and required deposit for the selected package.

The *frmScuba* Form

Figure 7-43 shows a sketch of frmScuba with the form's controls labeled.

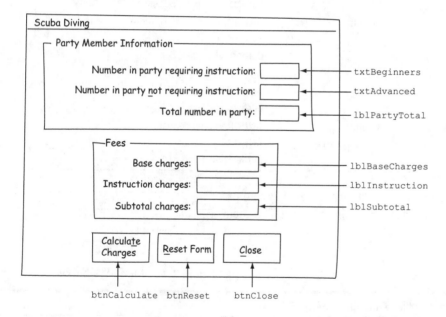

Figure 7-43 Sketch of frmScuba form

Table 7-10 lists each of the form's controls along with any relevant property setting.

Table 7-10

frmScuba controls and property settings

Control Type	Control Name	Properites
Form	frmScuba	Text: "Scuba Diving"
GroupBox	(Default)	Text: "Party Member Information" TabIndex: 0
Label	(Default)	Text: "Number in party requiring &instruction:" TabIndex: 0 (relative to GroupBox control)

Table 7-10 *continued*

`frmScuba` controls and property settings

Control Type	Control Name	Properites
Text box	`txtBeginners`	CausesValidation: True TabIndex: 1 (relative to GroupBox control) Text: " "
Label	(Default)	Text: "Number in party &not requiring instruction:" TabIndex: 2 (relative to GroupBox control)
TextBox	`txtAdvanced`	CausesValidation: True Text: " "
Label	(Default)	Text: "Total number in party:"
Label	`lblPartyTotal`	Text: " " BorderStyle: Fixed3D
GroupBox	(Default)	Text: "Fees"
Label	(Default)	Text: "Base charges:"
Label	`lblBaseCharges`	Text: " " BorderStyle: Fixed3D
Label	(Default)	Text: "Instruction charges:"
Label	`lblInstruction`	Text: " " BorderStyle: Fixed3D
Label	(Default)	Text: "Subtotal charges:"
Label	`lblSubtotal`	Text: " " BorderStyle: Fixed3D
Button	`btnCalculate`	Text: "Calcula&te" CausesValidation: True TabIndex: 1
Button	`btnReset`	Text: "&Reset Form" CausesValidation: False TabIndex: 2
Button	`btnClose`	Text: "&Close" CausesValidation: False TabIndex: 3

Table 7-11 lists and describes the methods in `frmScuba`.

Table 7-11

`frmScuba` Methods

Method	Description
`btnCalculate_Click`	Calculates and displays the total charge information for the scuba package.
`btnClose_Click`	Closes the form.
`btnReset_Click`	Clears the `txtBeginners` and `txtAdvanced` text boxes, and the `lblPartyTotal`, `lblBaseCharges`, `lblInstruction`, and `lblSubtotal` labels. Three global variables declared in the standard module are also cleared, as follows: `g_package` is set to " ", `g_partyMembers` is set to 0, and `g_subtotal` is set to 0.
`txtAdvanced_Validating`	Validates that the `txtAdvanced` text box contains positive number. If not, the user is prompted to re-enter a value for the text box. This procedure calls the `IsPositiveNumber` function, which is declared in the standard module.

Table 7-11 continued

`frmScuba` Methods

Method	Description
`txtBeginners_Validating`	Validates that the `txtBeginners` text box contains positive number. If not, the user is prompted to re-enter a value for the text box. This procedure calls the IsPositiveNumber function, which is declared in the standard module.

The `frmSkyDive` Form

Figure 7-44 shows a sketch of `frmSkyDive` with the form's controls labeled.

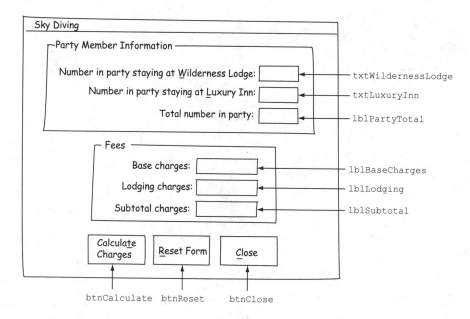

Figure 7-44 Sketch of `frmSkyDive` form

Table 7-12 lists each of the form's controls along with any relevant property setting.

Table 7-12

`frmSkyDive` Controls and Property Settings

Control Type	Control Name	Properites
Form	`frmSkyDive`	Text: "Sky Diving"
GroupBox	(Default)	Text: "Party Member Information" TabIndex: 0
Label	(Default)	Text: "Number in party staying at &Wilderness Lodge:" TabIndex: 0 (relative to GroupBox control)
TextBox	`txtWildernessLodge`	CausesValidation: True TabIndex: 1 (relative to GroupBox control) Text: ""
Label	(Default)	Text: "Number in party staying at &Luxury Inn:" TabIndex: 2 (relative to GroupBox control)
TextBox	`txtLuxuryInn`	CausesValidation: True TabIndex: 3 (relative to GroupBox control) Text: ""

Table 7-12 *continued*

frmSkyDive Controls and Property Settings

Control Type	Control Name	Properites
Label	(Default)	Text: "Total number in party:"
Label	lblPartyTotal	Text: " " BorderStyle: Fixed3D
GroupBox	(Default)	Text: "Fees"
Label	(Default)	Text: "Base charges:"
Label	lblBaseCharges	Text: " " BorderStyle: Fixed3D
Label	(Default)	Text: "Lodging charges:"
Label	lblLodging	Text: " " BorderStyle: Fixed3D
Label	(Default)	Text: "Subtotal charges:"
Label	lblSubtotal	Text: " " BorderStyle: Fixed3D
Button	btnCalculate	Text: "Calcula&te" CausesValidation: True TabIndex: 1
Button	btnReset	Text: "&Reset Form" CausesValidation: False TabIndex: 2
Button	btnClose	Text: "&Close" CausesValidation: False TabIndex: 3

Table 7-13 lists and describes the methods in frmSkyDive.

Table 7-13

frmSkyDive Methods

Method	Description
btnCalculate_Click	Calculates and displays the total charge information for the sky diving package.
btnClose_Click	Closes the form.
btnReset_Click	Clears the txtWildernessLodge and txtLuxuryInn text boxes, and the lblPartyTotal, lblBaseCharges, lblLodging, and lblSubtotal labels. Three global variables declared in the standard module, are also cleared, as follows: g_package is set to " ", g_partyMembers is set to 0, and g_subtotal is set to 0.
txtLuxuryInn_Validating	Validates that the txtLuxuryInn text box contains positive number. If not, the user is prompted to re-enter a value for the text box. This procedure calls the IsPositiveNumber function, which is declared in the standard module.
txtWildernessLodge_Validating	Validates that the txtWildernessLodge text box contains positive number. If not, the user is prompted to re-enter a value for the text box. This procedure calls the IsPositiveNumber function, which is declared in the standard module.

The `frmSpelunk` Form

Figure 7-45 shows a sketch of `frmSpelunk` with the form's controls labeled.

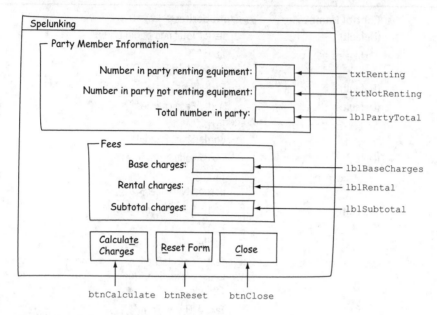

Figure 7-45 Sketch of `frmSpelunk` form

Table 7-14 lists each of the form's controls along with any relevant property setting.

Table 7-14

`frmSpelunk` controls and property settings

Control Type	Control Name	Properites
Form	`frmSpelunk`	Text: "Spelunking"
GroupBox	(Default)	Text: "Party Member Information" TabIndex: 0
Label	(Default)	Text: "Number in party renting &equipment:" TabIndex: 0 (relative to GroupBox control)
TextBox	`txtRenting`	CausesValidation: True TabIndex: 1 (relative to GroupBox control) Text: " "
Label	(Default)	Text: "Number in party &not renting equipment:" TabIndex: 2 (relative to GroupBox control)
TextBox	`txtNotRenting`	CausesValidation: True TabIndex: 3 (relative to GroupBox control) Text: " "
Label	(Default)	Text: "Total number in party:"
Label	`lblPartyTotal`	Text: " " BorderStyle: Fixed3D
GroupBox	(Default)	Text: "Fees"
Label	(Default)	Text: "Base charges:"
Label	`lblBaseCharges`	Text: " " BorderStyle: Fixed3D

Table 7-14 *continued*

`frmSpelunk` controls and property settings

Control Type	Control Name	Properites
Label	(Default)	Text: "Rental charges:"
Label	`lblRental`	Text: "" BorderStyle: Fixed3D
Label	(Default)	Text: "Subtotal charges:"
Label	`lblSubtotal`	Text: "" BorderStyle: Fixed3D
Button	`btnCalculate`	Text: "Calcula&te" CausesValidation: True TabIndex: 1
Button	`btnReset`	Text: "&Reset Form" CausesValidation: False TabIndex: 2
Button	`btnClose`	Text: "&Close" CausesValidation: False TabIndex: 3

Table 7-15 lists and describes the methods in `frmSpelunk`.

Table 7-15

frmSpelunk methods

Method	Description
`btnCalculate_Click`	Calculates and displays the total charge information for the spelunking `g_package`.
`btnClose_Click`	Closes the form.
`btnReset_Click`	Clears the `txtRenting` and `txtNotRenting` text boxes, and the `lblPartyTotal`, `lblBaseCharges`, `lblLodging`, and `lblSubtotal` labels. Three global variables declared in the standard module, are also cleared, as follows: `g_package` is set to "", `g_partyMembers` is set to 0, and `g_subtotal` is set to 0.
`txtRenting_Validating`	Validates that the `txtRenting` text box contains positive number. If not, the user is prompted to reenter a value for the text box. This procedure calls the `IsPositiveNumber` function, which is declared in the standard module.
`txtNotRenting_Validating`	Validates that the `txtNotRenting` text box contains positive number. If not, the user is prompted to re-enter a value for the text box. This procedure calls the `IsPositiveNumber` function, which is declared in the standard module.

TUTORIAL 7-5:

Building the High Adventure Travel Agency price quote application

Step 1:   Start Visual Basic .NET and begin a new Windows application project named High Adventure.

Step 2: Name the initial form frmMain. Set the form up as shown in Figure 7-46. Refer to Table 7-6 for the control names and their property settings.

Figure 7-46 frmMain

Step 3: Add a MainMenu control to the form. Refer to Figure 7-42 for the menu's layout, and to Table 7-8 for the MenuItem object properties. Figure 7-47 shows how frmMain should appear after you have added the menu system.

Figure 7-47 frmMain with the menu control in place

Step 4: Write the procedures for the frmMain form, which follows. The code consists of event procedures for the menu controls and a Sub procedure named DisplayCharges.

```
Private Sub mnuFileReset_Click(ByVal sender As System.Object, _
     ByVal e As System.EventArgs) Handles mnuFileReset.Click
   ' Reset the form.
   lblPackage.Text = ""
   lblPartyMembers.Text = ""
   lblSubtotal.Text = ""
   lblDiscount.Text = ""
   lblTotal.Text = ""
   lblDeposit.Text = ""
```

```
    ' Reset the global variables.
    g_package = ""
    g_PartyMembers = 0
    g_subtotal = 0
End Sub

Private Sub mnuFileExit_Click(ByVal sender As System.Object, _
            ByVal e As System.EventArgs) Handles mnuFileExit.Click
    ' End the application
    End
End Sub

Private Sub mnuPackagesScubaDiving_Click(ByVal sender As _
        System.Object, ByVal e As System.EventArgs) Handles _
        mnuPackagesScubaDiving.Click
    ' Calculate and display the charges for a
    ' scuba diving package.
    Dim scubaForm As New frmScuba()

    ' Display the scuba package form.
    scubaForm.ShowDialog()
    ' Display the charges less any discount and
    ' the required deposit.
    DisplayCharges()
End Sub

Private Sub mnuPackagesSkyDiving_Click(ByVal sender As _
        System.Object, ByVal e As System.EventArgs) Handles _
        mnuPackagesSkyDiving.Click
    ' Calculate and display the charges for a
    ' sky diving package.
    Dim skyDivingForm As New frmSkyDive()
    ' Display the sky diving package form.
    skyDivingForm.ShowDialog()
    ' Display the charges less any discount and
    ' the required deposit.
    DisplayCharges()
End Sub

Private Sub mnuPackagesSpelunking_Click(ByVal sender As _
        System.Object, ByVal e As System.EventArgs) Handles _
        mnuPackagesSpelunking.Click
    ' Calculate and display the charges for a
    ' spelunking package.
    Dim spelunkForm As New frmSpelunk()
    ' Display the spelunking package form.
    spelunkForm.ShowDialog()
    ' Display the charges less any discount and
    ' the required deposit.
    DisplayCharges()
End Sub
```

```
Private Sub mnuHelpAbout_Click(ByVal sender As System.Object, _
        ByVal e As System.EventArgs) Handles mnuHelpAbout.Click
    ' Display an About box.
    MessageBox.Show("Price Quote System for " & _
                    "High Adventure Travel Agency", _
                    "About")
End Sub

Private Sub DisplayCharges()
    ' This procedure calculates and displays the amount
    ' of the discount (if any), the total charges less any
    ' discount, and the required deposit.
    Dim partyMembers As Integer    ' Number in the party
    Dim subtotal As Decimal        ' Subtotal of charges
    Dim discount As Decimal        ' Package discount
    Dim total As Decimal           ' Total charges
    Dim deposit As Decimal         ' Required deposit

    ' Calculate the discount, if any.
    discount = CalcDiscount(g_partyMembers, g_subtotal)
    ' Calculate the total charges, less any discount.
    total = g_subtotal - discount
    ' Calculate the required deposit.
    deposit = CalcDeposit(total)
    ' Display the data.
    lblPackage.Text = g_package
    lblPartyMembers.Text = g_partyMembers.ToString
    lblSubtotal.Text = FormatCurrency(g_subtotal)
    lblDiscount.Text = FormatCurrency(discount)
    lblTotal.Text = FormatCurrency(total)
    lblDeposit.Text = FormatCurrency(deposit)
End Sub
```

Let's take a closer look at the event procedures that display the other forms. For example, look at mnuPackagesScubaDiving_Click. First the procedure creates an instance of the frmScuba form and displays it in modal style:

```
Dim scubaForm As New frmScuba()

' Display the scuba package form.
scubaForm.ShowDialog()
```

Once the user closes the frmScuba form, the procedure calls the DisplayCharges procedure. DisplayCharges is a Sub procedure that is stored in the frmMain module. It is stored there instead of in the standard module because it works specifically with controls on the frmMain form. DisplayCharges calculates and displays the amount of the discount (if any), the total charges less any discount, and the required deposit.

The event procedures that display the other forms work in this same way.

Step 5:   Add a new form to the project. Name the form `frmScuba`. Set the form up as shown in Figure 7-48. Refer to Figure 7-43 and Table 7-10 for the control names and their property settings.

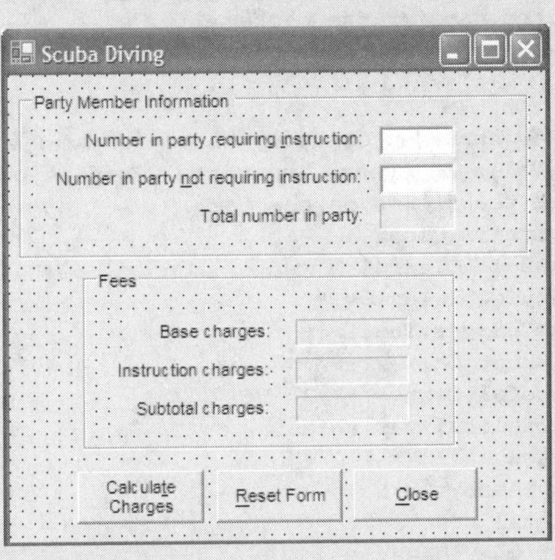

Figure 7-48   `frmScuba` form

Step 6:   Write the class-level declarations and procedures for the `frmScuba` form, as follows.

```
' This form calculates the charges (before any discount)
' for a scuba diving package.
' Declare class-level constants.
Const scubaRate As Decimal = 1000    ' Base rate.
Const scubaInstruct As Decimal = 300 ' Instruction rate.

Private Sub btnCalculate_Click(ByVal sender As System.Object, _
        ByVal e As System.EventArgs) Handles btnCalculate.Click
   ' Calculate and display total charge information.
   Dim beginners As Integer        ' Number of beginners
   Dim advanced As Integer         ' Number of advanced divers
   Dim baseCharges As Decimal      ' Base charges
   Dim instruction As Decimal      ' Instruction charges

   ' Get the number of beginners and advanced divers.
   beginners = Val(txtBeginners.Text)
   advanced = Val(txtAdvanced.Text)
   ' Calculate number in party.
   g_partyMembers = beginners + advanced
   ' Calculate base charges.
   baseCharges = scubaRate * g_partyMembers
   ' Calculate instruction charges.
   instruction = beginners * scubaInstruct
   ' Calculate total charges.
   g_subtotal = baseCharges + instruction
   ' Display data on this form.
```

```
        lblPartyTotal.Text = g_partyMembers.ToString
        lblBaseCharges.Text = FormatCurrency(baseCharges)
        lblInstruction.Text = FormatCurrency(instruction)
        lblSubtotal.Text = FormatCurrency(g_subtotal)
        ' Set the name of the package.
        g_package = "Scuba diving"
    End Sub

    Private Sub btnReset_Click(ByVal sender As System.Object, _
            ByVal e As System.EventArgs) Handles btnReset.Click
        ' Reset the fields on the form.
        txtBeginners.Clear()
        txtAdvanced.Clear()
        lblPartyTotal.Text = ""
        lblBaseCharges.Text = ""
        lblInstruction.Text = ""
        lblSubtotal.Text = ""
        ' Reset global variables.
        g_package = ""
        g_partyMembers = 0
        g_subtotal = 0
        ' Reset the focus.
        txtBeginners.Focus()
    End Sub

    Private Sub btnClose_Click(ByVal sender As System.Object, _
            ByVal e As System.EventArgs) Handles btnClose.Click
        ' Close this form
        Me.Close()
    End Sub

    Private Sub txtAdvanced_Validating(ByVal sender As Object, _
            ByVal e As System.ComponentModel.CancelEventArgs) _
            Handles txtAdvanced.Validating
        ' Validate that txtAdvanced contains a positive
        ' numeric value.
        If Not IsPositiveNumber(txtAdvanced.Text) Then
            ' Display error message.
            MessageBox.Show("Please enter a positive numeric " & _
                    "value.", "Error")
            ' Select contents of txtBeginners and set the focus.
            txtAdvanced.SelectionStart = 0
            txtAdvanced.SelectionLength = txtAdvanced.Text.Length
            txtAdvanced.Focus()
            e.Cancel = True
        Else
            e.Cancel = False
        End If
    End Sub

    Private Sub txtBeginners_Validating(ByVal sender As Object, _
            ByVal e As System.ComponentModel.CancelEventArgs) _
```

```
                    Handles txtBeginners.Validating
              ' Validate that txtBeginners contains a positive
              ' numeric value.
              If Not IsPositiveNumber(txtBeginners.Text) Then
                  ' Display error message.
                  MessageBox.Show("Please enter a positive numeric " & _
                          "value.", "Error")
                  ' Select contents of txtBeginners and set the focus.
                  txtBeginners.SelectionStart = 0
                  txtBeginners.SelectionLength = txtBeginners.Text.Length
                  txtBeginners.Focus()
                  e.Cancel = True
              Else
                  e.Cancel = False
              End If
          End Sub
```

Step 7:   Add a new form to the project. Name the form `frmSkyDive`. Set the form up as shown in Figure 7-49. Refer to Figure 7-44 and Table 7-12 for the control names and their property settings.

Figure 7-49   `frmSkyDive` form

Step 8:   Write the class-level declarations and procedures for the `frmSkyDive` form, as follows.

```
    ' This form calculates the charges (before any discount)
    ' for a sky diving package.

    ' Declare class-level constants.
    ' Base rate
    Const skyDiveRate As Decimal = 800
    ' Wilderness Lodge daily rate
```

```
    Const wildernessLodgeRate As Decimal = 80
    ' Luxury Inn daily rate
    Const luxuryInnRate As Decimal = 150

Private Sub btnCalculate_Click(ByVal sender As System.Object, _
        ByVal e As System.EventArgs) Handles btnCalculate.Click
    ' Calculate and display total charge information.
    Dim wildernessLodge As Integer' # staying at Wilderness Lodge
    Dim luxuryInn As Integer        ' # staying at Luxury Inn
    Dim baseCharges As Decimal      ' Base charges
    Dim Lodging As Decimal          ' Lodging charges

    ' Get the numbers staying at each location.
    wildernessLodge = Val(txtWildernessLodge.Text)
    luxuryInn = Val(txtLuxuryInn.Text)
    ' Calculate number in party.
    g_partyMembers = wildernessLodge + luxuryInn
    ' Calculate base charges.
    baseCharges = skyDiveRate * g_partyMembers
    ' Calculate lodging charges.
    Lodging = (wildernessLodge * wildernessLodgeRate) _
            + (luxuryInn * luxuryInnRate)
    ' Calculate total charges.
    g_subtotal = baseCharges + Lodging
    ' Display data on this form.
    lblPartyTotal.Text = g_partyMembers.ToString
    lblBaseCharges.Text = FormatCurrency(baseCharges)
    lblLodging.Text = FormatCurrency(Lodging)
    lblSubtotal.Text = FormatCurrency(g_subtotal)
    ' Set the name of the package.
    g_package = "Sky diving"
End Sub

Private Sub btnReset_Click(ByVal sender As System.Object, _
        ByVal e As System.EventArgs) Handles btnReset.Click
    ' Reset the fields on the form.
    txtWildernessLodge.Clear()
    txtLuxuryInn.Clear()
    lblPartyTotal.Text = ""
    lblBaseCharges.Text = ""
    lblLodging.Text = ""
    lblSubtotal.Text = ""
    ' Reset global variables.
    g_package = ""
    g_partyMembers = 0
    g_subtotal = 0
    ' Reset the focus.
    txtWildernessLodge.Focus()
End Sub
```

```
      Private Sub btnClose_Click(ByVal sender As System.Object, _
            ByVal e As System.EventArgs) Handles btnClose.Click
            ' Close this form
        Me.Close()
    End Sub

      Private Sub txtLuxuryInn_Validating(ByVal sender As Object, _
            ByVal e As System.ComponentModel.CancelEventArgs) _
            Handles txtLuxuryInn.Validating
        ' Validate that txtLuxuryInn contains a positive
        ' numeric value.
    If Not IsPositiveNumber(txtLuxuryInn.Text) Then
            ' Display error message.
            MessageBox.Show("Please enter a positive numeric " & _
                    "value.", "Error")
            ' Select contents of txtBeginners and set the focus.
            txtLuxuryInn.SelectionStart = 0
            txtLuxuryInn.SelectionLength = txtLuxuryInn.Text.Length
            txtLuxuryInn.Focus()
            e.Cancel = True
        Else
            e.Cancel = False
        End If
    End Sub

      Private Sub txtWildernessLodge_Validating(ByVal sender As Object, _
            ByVal e As System.ComponentModel.CancelEventArgs) _
            Handles txtWildernessLodge.Validating
        ' Validate that txtWildernessLodge contains a positive
        ' numeric value.
    If Not IsPositiveNumber(txtWildernessLodge.Text) Then
            ' Display error message.
            MessageBox.Show("Please enter a positive numeric " & _
                    "value.", "Error")
            ' Select contents of txtWildernessLodge and set the focus.
            txtWildernessLodge.SelectionStart = 0
            txtWildernessLodge.SelectionLength = _
                    txtWildernessLodge.Text.Length
            txtWildernessLodge.Focus()
            e.Cancel = True
        Else
            e.Cancel = False
        End If
    End Sub
```

Step 9:   Add a new form to the project. Name the form frmSpelunk. Set the form up as shown in Figure 7-50. Refer to Figure 7-45 and Table 7-14 for the control names and their property settings.

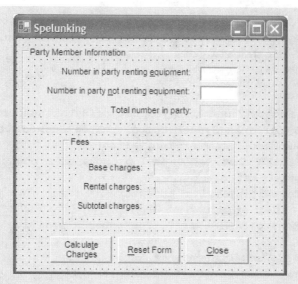

Figure 7-50 `frmSpelunk` form

Step 10: Write the class-level variable declarations and procedures for the `frmSpelunk` form, as follows.

```
' This form calculates the charges (before any discount)
' for a spelunking package.

' Declare class-level constants.
Const spelunkRate As Decimal = 700 ' Base rate.
Const rentalRate As Decimal = 50 ' Daily equipment rental rate.

Private Sub btnCalculate_Click(ByVal sender As System.Object, _
        ByVal e As System.EventArgs) Handles btnCalculate.Click
    ' Calculate and display total charge information.
    Dim renting As Integer          ' Number renting equipment
    Dim notRenting As Integer       ' Number not renting
    Dim baseCharges As Decimal      ' Base charges
    Dim Rental As Decimal           ' Rental charges

    ' Get the number renting and not renting.
    renting = Val(txtRenting.Text)
    notRenting = Val(txtNotRenting.Text)
    ' Calculate number in party.
    g_partyMembers = renting + notRenting
    ' Calculate base charges.
    baseCharges = spelunkRate * g_partyMembers
    ' Calculate rental charges.
    Rental = renting * rentalRate
    ' Calculate total charges.
    g_subtotal = baseCharges + Rental
    ' Display data on this form.
    lblPartyTotal.Text = g_partyMembers.ToString
    lblBaseCharges.Text = FormatCurrency(baseCharges)
```

```
        lblRental.Text = FormatCurrency(Rental)
        lblSubtotal.Text = FormatCurrency(g_subtotal)
        ' Set the name of the package.
        g_package = "Spelunking"
    End Sub

    Private Sub btnReset_Click(ByVal sender As System.Object, _
            ByVal e As System.EventArgs) Handles btnReset.Click
        ' Reset the fields on the form.
        txtRenting.Clear()
        txtNotRenting.Clear()
        lblPartyTotal.Text = ""
        lblBaseCharges.Text = ""
        lblRental.Text = ""
        lblSubtotal.Text = ""
        ' Reset global variables.
        g_package = ""
        g_partyMembers = 0
        g_subtotal = 0
        ' Reset the focus
        txtRenting.Focus()
    End Sub

    Private Sub btnClose_Click(ByVal sender As System.Object, _
            ByVal e As System.EventArgs) Handles btnClose.Click
        ' Close this form
        Me.Close()
    End Sub

    Private Sub txtNotRenting_Validating(ByVal sender As Object, _
            ByVal e As System.ComponentModel.CancelEventArgs) _
            Handles txtNotRenting.Validating
        ' Validate that txtNotRenting contains a positive
        ' numeric value.
        If Not IsPositiveNumber(txtNotRenting.Text) Then
            ' Display error message.
            MessageBox.Show("Please enter a positive numeric " & _
                    "value.", "Error")
            ' Select contents of txtNotRenting and set the focus.
            txtNotRenting.SelectionStart = 0
            txtNotRenting.SelectionLength = txtNotRenting.Text.Length
            txtNotRenting.Focus()
            e.Cancel = True
        Else
            e.Cancel = False
        End If
    End Sub

    Private Sub txtRenting_Validating(ByVal sender As Object, _
            ByVal e As System.ComponentModel.CancelEventArgs) _
            Handles txtRenting.Validating
        ' Validate that txtRenting contains a positive
```

```
        ' numeric value.
        If Not IsPositiveNumber(txtRenting.Text) Then
            ' Display error message.
            MessageBox.Show("Please enter a positive numeric " & _
                    "value.", "Error")
            ' Select contents of txtBeginners and set the focus.
            txtRenting.SelectionStart = 0
            txtRenting.SelectionLength = txtRenting.Text.Length
            txtRenting.Focus()
            e.Cancel = True
        Else
            e.Cancel = False
        End If
    End Sub
```

Step 11: Add a standard module named HighAdventure.vb to the project, which will hold the functions described in Table 7-6. Write the following code.

```
Module HighAdventure

    ' Standard module for the High Adventure Travel Agency
    ' vacation price quote package
    ' Declare module-level constants.
    Const discountRate As Single = 0.1   ' 10% discount for 5 or more.
    Const depositRate As Single = 0.5' Required 50% deposit
    ' Declare global variables.
    Public g_package As String          ' Name of package
    Public g_partyMembers As Integer ' Number in party
    Public g_subtotal As Decimal        ' Subtotal of charges

    Public Function IsPositiveNumber(ByVal value As String) As Boolean
        ' This function accepts a string argument and returns
        ' true if the string contains a positive numeric value.
        ' Otherwise it returns false.
        Dim status As Boolean

        If Not IsNumeric(value) Then
            status = False
        ElseIf Val(value) < 0 Then
            status = False
        Else
            status = True
        End If
        Return status
    End Function

    Public Function CalcDiscount(ByVal partyMembers As Integer, _
                    ByVal subtotal As Decimal) As Decimal
        ' This function returns the discount, if any, on a package.
        ' The first argument is the number of party members, and
        ' the second argument is the subtotal of the package.
        Dim discount As Decimal

        If partyMembers >= 5 Then
            discount = subtotal * discountRate
```

```
        Else
            discount = 0
        End If
        Return discount
    End Function

    Public Function CalcDeposit(ByVal total As Decimal) As Decimal
        ' This function returns the amount of the required deposit.
        ' The argument is the total of the package charges.
        Return total * depositRate
    End Function

End Module
```

Step 12:   Save the project.

Step 13:   Run the application. If there are errors, refer to the code listings shown earlier to debug the application.

SUMMARY

Visual Basic .NET projects may have multiple forms.

One of the forms in a project is the startup object. It is displayed when the project executes. The other forms are displayed by programming statements.

The standard prefix for form names is `frm`.

When you create a form in Visual Basic .NET, the code for that form is stored in a file that ends with the .vb extension. Normally, the name of the file is the same as the name of the form. The form file contains the form class declaration, which is code that describes the form's properties and methods.

The Project Property Pages dialog box allows you to designate a project's startup object.

Before a form can be displayed on the screen, an instance of the form must be created. The address of the form instance is assigned to an object variable.

When a form's `ShowDialog` method or `Show` method is called, the form is displayed and receives the focus. The `ShowDialog` method displays a form in modal style, and the `Show` method displays a form in modeless style.

When a modal form is displayed, no other form in the application can receive the focus until the modal form is closed. Also, no other statements in the procedure that displayed the modal form will execute until the modal form is closed.

A modeless form allows the user to switch focus to another form while it is displayed. The statements that follow the modeless `Show` method call will continue to execute after the modeless form is displayed. Visual Basic .NET will not wait until the modeless form is closed to execute these statements.

A form's `Close` method removes it from the screen, and removes the form from memory. A form must use the `Me` key word to call its own `Close` method, as in `Me.Close()`.

A form's `Hide` method removes the form from the screen but does not remove it from memory.

When a form is initially displayed, the `Load` event occurs. A form's `Activated` event is triggered when the user switches to the form from another form or another application. The `Closing` event is triggered as a form is in the process of closing, but before it has closed. The `Closed` event is triggered after a form has closed. You may write event procedures that execute in response to any of these events.

Visual Basic .NET allows you to write code to access objects on a different form. When doing so, you must fully qualify the name of the object by preceding it with the form name, followed by a period.

If you wish to make a form's class-level variable available to statements outside the form, you must declare it with the `Public` key word.

After a form has been saved to a form file, it may be used in other projects.

A standard module contains code—declarations and procedures—that is used by other files in a project. Standard modules are not associated with a form and contain no event procedures.

Visual Basic .NET allows you to designate a Sub procedure named `Main` as an application's startup object. The Sub procedure `Main` must reside in a standard module. When the application runs, no form is initially displayed. Instead, the Sub procedure `Main` is executed.

A variable that is declared inside a module (between the `Module` and the `End Module` statements), but not inside a Sub procedure or function, is a module-level variable. A module-level variable that is declared as `Public` is also known as a global variable because it can be accessed globally, by any statement in the project.

Visual Basic .NET allows you to use a standard module in more than one project.

Visual Basic .NET allows you to create a system of drop-down menus for any form in your application. You place a MainMenu control on the form, and then use the menu designer to create a menu system.

An application's menu system is constructed from MenuItem objects. When you create MenuItem objects, you name them with the `mnu` prefix.

If you do not want the user to be able to select a menu item at run time, you can disable its control in code by setting its Enabled property to false. When a menu control's Checked property is set to true, a check mark appears on the menu next to the control's caption text.

You make a MenuItem object respond to clicks by providing a `Click` event procedure for it.

KEY TERMS

About box	MenuItem object
`Activated` event procedure	mnu
Checked property	Modal form
Class	Modeless form
`Closed` event procedure	Module scope
`Closing` event procedure	Object variable
Context menu	`Public`
`frm`	RadioChecked property
Global scope	Shortcut key
Global variable	Shortcut property
`Hide` method	`Show` method
Main	`ShowDialog` method
MainMenu control	ShowShortcut property
`Me`	Standard module
Menu designer	Startup object
Menu system	

Review Questions

Fill-in-the-blank

1. If a form is the _____, it is displayed when the project executes.

2. When a _____ form is displayed, no other form in the application can receive the focus until the form is closed.

3. A _____ is a variable that holds the memory address of an object and allows you to work with the object.

4. The _____ method removes a form from the screen but does not remove it from memory.

5. The _____ method removes a form from the screen and releases the memory it is using.

6. The _____ method displays a form in modal style.

7. The _____ method displays a form in modeless style.

8. Standard modules contain no _____ procedures.

9. When a procedure declaration in a form file begins with _____, the procedure may only be accessed by statements in the same form.

10. If you wish to make a class-level variable available to statements outside the module, you must declare it with the _____ key word.

11. A module-level variable that is declared as `Public` is also known as a _____ variable.

12. Visual Basic .NET allows you to designate a Sub procedure named _____ as an application's startup object.

13. You can disable a menu control in code by setting its _____ property to false.

14. When a menu control's _____ property is set to true, a check mark appears on the menu next to the control's caption text.

15. A _____ is a pop-up menu that is displayed when the user right-clicks a form or control.

Multiple Choice

1. The standard prefix for form names is
    a. `fr`
    b. `frm`
    c. `for`
    d. `fm`

2. When a(n) _____ form is displayed, no other form in the application can receive the focus until the modal form is closed.
    a. Modal
    b. Modeless
    c. Startup
    d. Unloaded

3. When a(n) _____ form is displayed, the statements that follow the method call will continue to execute after the form is displayed.
    a. Modal
    b. Modeless
    c. Startup
    d. Unloaded

4.   What does the `Hide` method do?

   a.   Removes a form from the screen and removes it from memory

   b.   Removes a form from the screen but does not remove it from memory

   c.   Positions one form behind another one

   d.   Removes a form from memory but does not remove it from the screen

5.   The _____ method removes a form from memory and the screen.

   a.   `Remove`

   b.   `Delete`

   c.   `Close`

   d.   `Hide`

6.   If `total` is a class-level variable, which of the following declaration statements makes it accessible to statements outside the module?

   a.   `Dim total As Integer`

   b.   `Public total As Integer`

   c.   `Global total As Integer`

   d.   `Private total As Integer`

7.   Just before a form is initially displayed, this event is triggered.

   a.   `InitialDisplay`

   b.   `Load`

   c.   `Display`

   d.   `Create`

8.   This event is triggered when the user switches to the form from another form or another application.

   a.   `Activated`

   b.   `Load`

   c.   `Switch`

   d.   `Close`

9.   This event is triggered as a form is in the process of closing, but before it has closed.

   a.   `Closed`

   b.   `StartClose`

   c.   `ShutingDown`

   d.   `Closing`

10.   This event is triggered after a form has closed.

   a.   `Closed`

   b.   `EndClose`

   c.   `ShutDown`

   d.   `Closing`

11.   A form uses this statement to call its own `Close` method.

   a.   `Form.Close()`

   b.   `Me.Close()`

   c.   `Close(Me)`

   d.   `ThisForm.Close()`

12. If a procedure or variable is used by more than one form, where should it be declared?
    a. Standard module
    b. Form file
    c. Multiprocess module
    d. Project module

13. If you designate the Sub procedure `Main` as the startup object, where must it reside?
    a. In the form that is also designated as the startup object
    b. In the form's `Load` event procedure
    c. In a standard module.
    d. In the `frmMain` form.

14. If an application's menu system has a Cut command on the Edit menu, what should the menu control for the command be named?
    a. `mnuCut`
    b. `mnuEdit`
    c. `mnuCutEdit`
    d. `mnuEditCut`

15. A menu command's _____ only works while the menu is open, while a(n) _____ may be executed at any time while the form is active.
    a. Shortcut key, access key
    b. Access key, shortcut key
    c. Function key, control key
    d. Alternate key, control key

16. Which of the following statements disables the `mnuFilePrint` object?
    a. `mnuFilePrint.Disabled = True`
    b. `mnuFilePrint.Enabled = False`
    c. `mnuFilePrint.Available = False`
    d. `Disable mnuFilePrint`

True or False

Indicate whether each of the following statements is true or false.
1. T F: By default, the first form you create is the startup object.
2. T F: The `Show` method displays a form in modeless style.
3. T F: Although the `Hide` method removes a form from the screen, it does not remove it from memory.
4. T F: If you have code that you want to execute every time a form displays, the form's `Load` event procedure is the best place to write it.
5. T F: The `Activated` event only executes once: when the form is initially displayed.
6. T F: The `Closing` event executes before a form has completely closed.
7. T F: It is not possible to access a control on another form in code.
8. T F: A menu command's shortcut key only works while the menu is open.
9. T F: If a menu control does not display a menu or submenu, you make it functional by providing a `Click` event procedure for it.

10.   T   F: A context menu displays when the user double-clicks a control.

Short Answer

1. Describe the process of adding a new form to a project.

2. Describe the process of removing a form from a project, but not deleting the form file.

3. Describe the process of removing a form from a project, and deleting the form file.

4. Describe the process of changing the startup object to another form.

5. What does the statement `Me.Close()` do?

6. What is the difference between the `Load` event and the `Activated` event?

7. You want to execute code when a form is about to close, but has not fully closed. Where should you place the code?

8. You want to execute code when a form has fully closed. Where should you place the code?

9. You wish to make a form's class-level variable available to statements outside the file containing the class declaration. How should you declare the variable?

10. Describe the steps for adding a standard module to a project.

11. If you wish to execute code when an application starts, before the user sees a form displayed on the screen, what must you do?

12. What is the difference between a menu control's access key and its shortcut key?

13. How do you make a checked menu item?

14. What happens to a menu item when its RadioChecked property is set to true?

15. What is a disabled menu item? How do you make a menu item disabled?

What Do You Think?

1. If you want to display multiple forms on the screen at one time and be able to interact with any of them at any time, do you display them as modal or modeless forms?

2. You want to write code that removes a form from the screen, but you still want to access controls on the form in code. How do you accomplish this?

3. A form is named `frmStatus`, and it has a Label control named `lblArrivalGate`. Write the statement that stores the string "D West" in the label's Text property from another form.

4. You have written a function, named `CircleArea`, that returns the area of a circle. You call the function from numerous procedures in different form modules. Do you store the function in a form or a standard module?

5. You have written a function, named `InRange`, that determines whether a value is within a range of numbers. You only call the function from code in one form. Do you store the function in the form module or a standard module?

6. You have written a Sub procedure in a standard module named `Main` and designated it as the project's startup object. You also have a form that is to be displayed once `Main` has executed. When you run the application, the form does not appear on the screen. Most likely, why does the form not appear?

7. The following code creates three instances of the form `frmBannerAd`. Will all three of the forms be displayed at the same time? Why or why not?

```
Dim adForm1 As New frmBannerAd()
Dim adForm2 As New frmBannerAd()
Dim adForm3 As New frmBannerAd()
adForm1.Show()
adForm2.Show()
adForm3.Show()
```

Find the Errors

What is wrong with the following statements?

1. `Hide Me`

2. *Class-level declaration in* `frmResults`

    ```
    Dim number as Integer
    ```

    Statements in another form

    ```
    Dim resultsForm as New frmResults()
    resultsForm.number = 100
    ```

3. ```
   Dim errorForm as frmError
   errorForm.ShowDialog()
   ```

4. ```
   Dim messageForm as New frmMessage
   frmMessage.ShowDialog()
   ```

5. ```
   ' Module declaration
   Module
   ```

    Statements inside the module

    ```
    End Module
    ```

Algorithm Workbench

1. An application has three forms: `frmFirst`, `frmSecond`, and `frmThird`. The `frmSecond` form has a public class-level integer variable named `reading`. The `frmThird` form has a text box named `txtInput`. The following statements exist in the `frmFirst` form:

    ```
    Dim secondForm As New frmSecond()
    Dim thirdForm As New frmSecond()
    ```

    Assume that the user has entered a value into the `txtInput` control on the `frmThird` form. Write a statement that will execute after these statements, which stores the value entered in `txtInput` into the `reading` variable, which is in the `frmSecond` form.

2. Here is the code template for a form's `Closing` event procedure.

    ```
    Private Sub frmMain_Closing(ByVal sender As Object, _
                ByVal e As System.ComponentModel.CancelEventArgs) _
                Handles MyBase.Closing
    End Sub
    ```
    ```

You only want the form to close if the user knows the secret word, which is "water". Write the statements that should be coded in this procedure to ask the user to enter the secret word. If the user enters the correct secret word, the form can close. If the user doesn't enter the correct secret word, the form should not close. (Perform a case-insensitive test for the secret word.)

PROGRAMMING CHALLENGES

1. Conference Registration System

Create an application that calculates the registration fees for a conference. The general conference registration fee is $895 per person. There is also an optional opening night dinner with a keynote address for $30 per person. In addition, the optional preconference workshops listed in Table 7-16 are available.

Table 7-16

Optional preconference workshops

Workshop	Fee
Introduction to E-commerce	$295
The Future of the Web	$295
Advanced Visual Basic .NET	$395
Network Security	$395

The application should have two forms. The main form should appear similar to Figure 7-51.

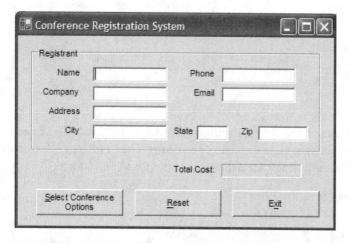

Figure 7-51   Conference registration system main form

When the user clicks the Select Conference Options button, the form shown in Figure 7-52 should appear.

The Conference Options form allows the user to select the regular conference registration, the optional opening night dinner, and an optional preconference workshop. (The user cannot register for the optional events, however, without selecting the conference registration of $895.) When the Close button is clicked, this form should be removed from the screen and the total registration fee should appear on the main form.

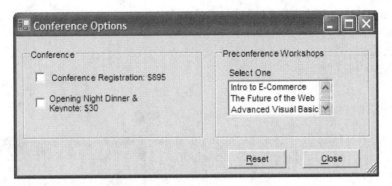

Figure 7-52   Conference Options form

2. Shopping Cart System

Design an application that works as a shopping cart system. The user should be able to add any of the following items to his or her shopping cart:

Print Books (books on paper):

I Did It Your Way	$11.95
The History of Scotland	$14.50
Learn Calculus in One Day	$29.95
Feel the Stress	$18.50

Audio Books (books on tape):

Learn Calculus in One Day	$29.95
The History of Scotland	$14.50
The Science of Body Language	$12.95
Relaxation Techniques	$11.50

The application's main form should appear similar to Figure 7-53.

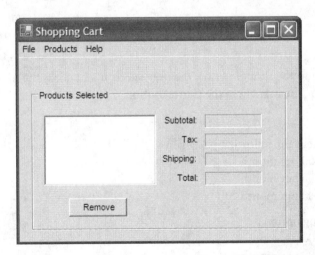

Figure 7-53   Shopping Cart main form

The list box shows all the items in the shopping cart. There is a 6% sales tax on the total cost of the items in the shopping cart. Also, for each item in the shopping cart there is a $2.00 shipping charge.

To remove an item from the shopping cart, the user selects it in the list box and clicks the Remove button. The subtotal, tax, shipping, and total fields should be adjusted accordingly.

The main form's menu system is sketched in Figure 7-54.

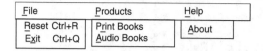

Figure 7-54   Shopping Cart menu system

When the user selects Reset from the File menu, all items in the shopping cart should be removed, and the subtotal, tax, shipping, and total fields should be cleared. When the user selects Exit from the File menu, the application should end. When the user selects About from the Help menu, a simple about box should appear.

When the user selects Print Books from the Products menu, the form in Figure 7-55 should appear.

To add one of the items in the list to the shopping cart, the user selects it and clicks the Add Book to Cart button. To cancel the operation, the user clicks the Cancel button.

On the main form, when the user selects Audio Books from the Products menu, the form in Figure 7-56 should appear.

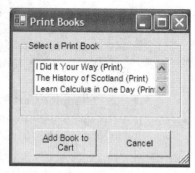

Figure 7-55   Print Books form

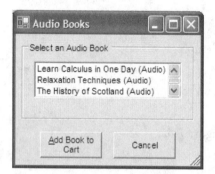

Figure 7-56   Audio Books form

To add one of the items in the list to the shopping cart, the user selects it and clicks the Add Book to Cart button. To cancel the operation, the user clicks the Cancel button.

3.   Cell Phone Packages

Cell Solutions, a cell phone provider, sells the following packages:

300 minutes per month	$45.00 per month
800 minutes per month	$65.00 per month
1500 minutes per month	$99.00 per month

Customers may also select the following options:

Voice mail	$5.00 per month
Text messaging	$10.00 per month

The provider sells the following phones:

Model 100:	$ 29.95
Model 110:	$49.95
Model 200:	$99.95

(A 6% sales tax applies to the sale of a phone.)

Additionally, the provider offers individual plans and family plans. With the Individual plan, the customer gets one phone. With the Family plan, the customer gets as many phones of the same model as he or she desires, and all the phones share the same minutes. Voice mail and text messaging fees are charged for each phone purchased under the Family plan.

Create an application that calculates a customer's plan cost. The application's main form should appear similar to Figure 7-57.

When the user clicks the Individual button, the form shown in Figure 7-58 should appear.

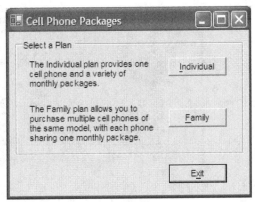

Figure 7-57   Cell Phone Packages form

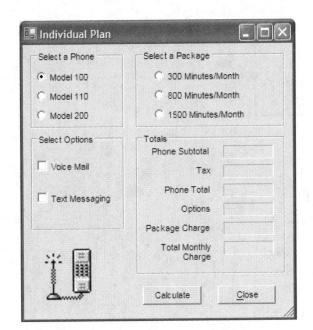

Figure 7-58   Individual Plan form

(If the graphics are installed on your system, the icon displayed in the image control can be found in the Program Files\Microsoft Visual Studio .NET\Common7\Graphics\Icons\Comm folder. If there are no graphics files in that location on your computer, substitute any graphic of your choice, or leave the image control off of the form.)

The user selects the phone model, options, and package. When the Calculate button is clicked, the charges are calculated and displayed.

When the user clicks the Family button on the main form, the form shown in Figure 7-59 should appear.

The user enters the number of phones, selects the phone model, options, and package. When the Calculate button is clicked, the charges are calculated and displayed.

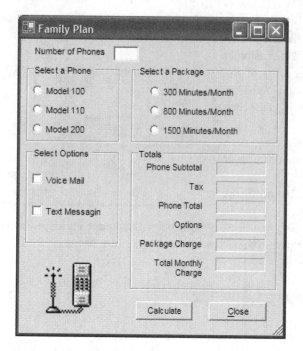

Figure 7-59   Family Plan Form

Design Your Own Forms

4. Dorm and Meal Plan Calculator

A university has the following dormitories:

Allen Hall	$1,500 per semester
Pike Hall	$1,600 per semester
Farthing Hall	$1,200 per semester
University Suites	$1,800 per semester

The university also offers the following meal plans:

7 meals per week	$560 per semester
14 meals per week	$1,095 per semester
Unlimited meals	$1,500 per semester

Create an application with two forms. One form holds the names of the dormitories, and the other holds the meal plans. The user should select a dormitory and a meal plan, and the application should show the total charges for the semester.

5. Shade Designer

A custom window shade designer charges a base fee of $50 per shade. In addition, charges are added for certain styles, sizes, and colors as follows.

Styles:

Regular shades	Add $0
Folding shades	Add $10
Roman shades	Add $15

Sizes:

25 inches wide	Add $0
27 inches wide	Add $2
32 inches wide	Add $4
40 inches wide	Add $6

Colors:

Natural	Add $5
Blue	Add $0
Teal	Add $0
Red	Add $0
Green	Add $0

Create an application that allows the user to select the style, size, color, and number of shades from list or combo boxes on a form. The total charges should be displayed on a second form.

6. Skateboard Designer

The Skate Shop sells the following skateboard products.

Decks:

The Master Thrasher	$60
The Dictator of Grind	$45
The Street King	$50

Truck assemblies:

7.75″ axle	$35
8″ axle	$40
8.5″ axle	$45

Wheel sets:

51 mm	$20
55 mm	$22
58 mm	$24
61 mm	$28

In addition, the Skate Shop sells the following miscellaneous products and services:

Grip tape	$10
Bearings	$30
Riser pads	$2
Nuts & bolts kit	$3
Assembly	$10

Create an application that allows the user to select one deck from a form, one truck assembly from a form, and one wheel set from a form. The application should also have a form that allows the user to select any miscellaneous product, using check boxes. The application should display the subtotal, the amount of sales tax (at 6%), and the total of the order. Do not apply sales tax to assembly.

7. Astronomy Helper

Create an application that displays the following data about the planets of the solar system.

Mercury

Type	Terrestrial
Average distance from the Sun	0.387 AU

Mass	3.31×10^{23} kg
Surface Temperature	-173°C to 430°C

Venus

Type	Terrestrial
Average distance from the Sun	0.7233 AU
Mass	4.87×10^{24} kg
Surface Temperature	472°C

Earth

Type	Terrestrial
Average distance from the Sun	1 AU
Mass	5.967×10^{24} kg
Surface Temperature	-50°C to 50°C

Mars

Type	Terrestrial
Average distance from the Sun	1.5237 AU
Mass	0.6424×10^{24} kg
Surface Temperature	-140°C to 20°C

Jupiter

Type	Jovian
Average distance from the Sun	5.2028 AU
Mass	1.899×10^{27} kg
Temperature at cloud tops	-110°C

Saturn

Type	Jovian
Average distance from the Sun	9.5388 AU
Mass	5.69×10^{26} kg
Temperature at cloud tops	-180°C

Uranus

Type	Jovian
Average distance from the Sun	19.18 AU
Mass	8.69×10^{25} kg
Temperature above cloud tops	-220°C

Neptune

Type	Jovian
Average distance from the Sun	30.0611 AU
Mass	1.03×10^{26} kg
Temperature at cloud tops	-216°C

Pluto

Type	Low density
Average distance from the Sun	39.44 AU
Mass	1.2×10^{22} kg
Surface Temperature	-230°C

The application should have a separate form for each planet. On the main form, create a menu system that allows the user to select the planet he or she wishes to know more about.

CHAPTER 8

Arrays, Timers, and More

▶ 8.1 Introduction

This chapter discusses arrays, which are like groups of variables that allow you to store sets of data. A single dimension array is useful for storing and working with a single set of data, while a multidimensional array can be used to store and work with multiple sets of data. This chapter presents many array programming techniques, such as summing and averaging all the elements in an array, summing all the columns in a two-dimensional array, searching an array for a specific value, and using parallel arrays. The Enabled, Anchor, and Dock properties, Timer controls, and splash screens are covered, as well as programming techniques for generating random numbers.

▶ 8.2 Arrays

CONCEPT

AN ARRAY IS LIKE A GROUP OF VARIABLES WITH ONE NAME. YOU STORE AND WORK WITH VALUES IN AN ARRAY BY USING A SUBSCRIPT.

Sometimes it is necessary for an application to store multiple values of the same type. Often it is better to create an array than several individual variables. An array is a like group of variables with a single name. All of the variables within an array are called *elements* and are of the same data type. You access the individual variables in an array through a subscript. A *subscript*, also known as an *index*, is a number that identifies a specific element within an array.

Subscript numbering begins at 0, so the subscript of the first element in an array is 0 and the subscript of the last element in an array is one less than the total number of elements. For example, consider an array of seven integers. The subscript of the first element in the array is 0 and the subscript of the last element in the array is 6.

Declaring a Array

You declare an array much like you declare a regular variable. Here is the general format of an array declaration:

```
Dim ArrayName(UpperSubscript) As DataType
```

Let's take a closer look at the syntax.

- ◆ *ArrayName* is the name of the array.
- ◆ *UpperSubscript* is the value of the array's highest subscript. This must be a positive whole number.
- ◆ *DataType* is a Visual Basic .NET data type.

Let's look at some examples.

```
Dim hours(6) As Integer
```

This statement declares `hours` as an array of integers. The number inside the parentheses, 6, indicates that the array's highest subscript is 6. Figure 8-1 illustrates that this array consists of seven elements with the subscripts 0 through 6. The figure shows each element contains the value 0 because numeric array elements are initialized to the value 0.

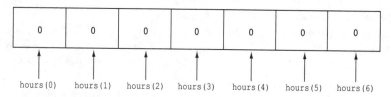

Figure 8-1 The `hours` array

NOTE: *Like regular string variables, string array elements are initialized to the special value* `Nothing`. *Before doing any work with the elements of a string array, you must store values in them. Later you will see how to initialize arrays.*

Here is another example of an array declaration:

```
Dim pay(4) As Decimal
```

This statement declares `pay` as an array of decimal variables. Figure 8-2 illustrates that this array consists of five elements with the subscripts 0 through 4.

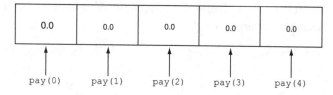

Figure 8-2 The `pay` array

Implicit Array Sizing and Initialization

Visual Basic .NET allows you to implicitly size an array by omitting the upper subscript in the declaration and providing an initialization list. An array initialization list is a set of numbers enclosed in a set of braces, with the numbers separated by commas. Here is an example of an array declaration that uses an initialization list.

```
Dim numbers() As Integer = { 2, 4, 6, 8, 10, 12 }
```

This statement declares `numbers` as an array of integers. The numbers 2, 4, 6, 8, 10, and 12 will be stored in the array. 2 will be stored in element zero, 4 will be stored in element one, and so forth. Notice that no upper subscript is provided inside the parentheses. Visual Basic .NET will automatically make the array large enough to hold the values in the initialization list. In this case, the array numbers will have six elements. Figure 8-3 illustrates the array.

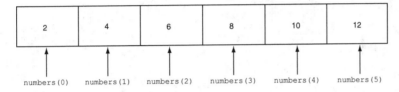

Figure 8-3   The `numbers` array

The following code declares an implicitly-sized array of strings.

```
Dim myFriends As String() = { "Joe", "Geri", _
                "Bill", "Rose" }
```

You can also initialize an array of strings with empty strings, as shown here.

```
Dim names As String() = { "", "","", "" }
```

It is a good idea to initialize a string array, especially if there is a chance that your program will access its elements before any data has been stored there. Performing an operation on a string array element will often result in a run-time error if no data has been stored in the element.

NOTE: *If you provide both an initialization list and an upper subscript in an array declaration, an error will occur.*

Using Named Constants as Subscripts in Array Declarations

You may also use a named constant as the upper subscript in an array declaration, as shown in the following code:

```
Const upperSub As Integer = 100
Dim array(upperSub) As Integer
```

This code declares `array` with the upper subscript 100.

Working with Array Elements

You can store a value in an array element with an assignment statement. On the left of the = operator, you must use the name of the array with the subscript of the element where you wish to store the value.

For example, assume that `numbers` is an array of integers with the subscripts 0 through 5. The following set of statements stores values in each element of the array:

```
numbers(0) = 100
numbers(1) = 200
numbers(2) = 300
numbers(3) = 400
numbers(4) = 500
numbers(5) = 600
```

TIP: The expression `numbers(0)` is pronounced "numbers sub zero".

Figure 8-4 shows the values assigned to the elements of the array after these statements execute.

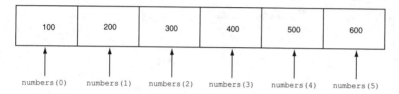

Figure 8-4   The `numbers` array with values assigned

Processing array elements is no different than processing other variables. For example, the following statement multiplies `hours(3)` by the variable `rate` and stores the result in `pay`.

```
pay = hours(3) * rate
```

The following statement adds 1 to the value in `tallies(0)`.

```
tallies(0) += 1
```

And the following statement displays the contents of `grossPay(5)` in a message box.

```
MessageBox.Show(grossPay(5).ToString)
```

Accessing Array Elements with a Loop

Visual Basic .NET allows you to store a number in a variable and then use the variable as a subscript. This makes it possible to use a loop to cycle through an entire array, performing the same operation on each element. This can be helpful if you want to process the elements in a large array, because writing individual statements would require a lot of typing.

For example, assume `series` is an array of 10 integers with the subscripts 0 through 9. The following `For...Next` loop stores the value 100 in each of its elements, beginning at subscript 0.

```
Dim count As Integer = 0
For count = 0 To 9
    series(count) = 100
Next count
```

The variable `count`, which is used as the loop counter, takes on the values 0 through 9 while the loop is executing. The first time the loop iterates, `count` is set to 0, so the statement `series(count) = 100` assigns the value 100 to `series(0)`. The second time the loop iterates, the statement stores 100 in `series(1)`, and so on.

Another example using the same array follows, this time using a Do While loop.

```
Dim count As Integer

Do While count < 10
    series(count) = 100
    count += 1
Loop
```

Yet another example shows a For...Next loop being used to get numbers from the user, which are stored in the array.

```
Dim count As Integer
For count = 0 To 9
    series(count) = Val(InputBox("Enter a number."))
Next count
```

We mentioned earlier that it is a good idea to initialize a string array if there is a chance that the program will access its elements before data has been stored there. It might be cumbersome, however, to provide an initialization list for a large array. Instead, you can use a loop to initialize the array's elements. For example, the following code stores an empty string in each element of names, a 1000-element array of strings.

```
Dim count As Integer
For count = 0 To 999
    names(count) = ""
Next count
```

Array Bounds Checking

Visual Basic .NET performs *array bounds checking*, which means it does not allow a statement to use a subscript that is outside the range of subscripts for an array. For example, in the following declaration, the array values has a subscript range of 0 through 10.

```
Dim values(10) As Integer
```

Visual Basic .NET will not allow a statement to use a subscript that is less than 0 or greater than 10 with this array.

Bounds checking occurs at run time. Visual Basic .NET does not display an error message at design time when you write a statement that uses an invalid subscript. For example, you can write the loop in the following code at design time even though it uses subscripts outside the range of subscripts for values:

```
Dim values(10) As Integer
Dim i As Integer
For i = 0 To 20
    values(i) = 99
Next i
```

At run time, this loop will execute until i has the value 11. At that point, when the assignment statement tries to use i as a subscript, Visual Basic .NET will display the dialog box and error message shown in Figure 8-5.

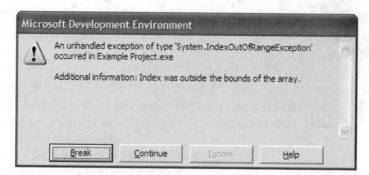

Figure 8-5 Dialog box reporting index outside the bounds of the array

When this dialog box appears, click the Break button to enter debug mode, or the Continue button to stop the application.

The `For Each...Next` Statement

The *For Each...Next loop* is a special loop designed specifically to access values from arrays and array-like structures. The general format of the loop is

```
For Each ElementVar In Array
      Statement
        (More statements may follow)
Next [ElementVar]
```

Let's look at the syntax more closely.

- ◆ `ElementVar` is the name of a variable. This variable is used to represent an element of the array during a loop iteration. During the first loop iteration, it represents the first element; during the second iteration it represents the second element, and so on. This variable must be of the same data type as the array elements, or a data type that the elements can be automatically converted to.

- ◆ `Array` is the name of an array that you wish the loop to operate on.

- ◆ `Statement` is one or more statements that are to execute during a loop iteration. When a statement accesses the `ElementVar` variable, it is actually accessing the array element that the `ElementVar` variable references during that loop iteration.

- ◆ `Next [ElementVar]` marks the end of the loop and causes the `ElementVar` variable to represent the next element in the array, if there is one. The brackets indicate that the variable name is optional. For readability it is recommended that you always list the name of the variable.

For example, the following code displays each string in the `employees` array in a message box.

```
Dim employees As String() = {"Jim", "Sally", _
      "Henry", "Jean", "Renee" }
Dim name As String
For Each name In employees
   MessageBox.Show(name)
Next name
```

TUTORIAL 8-1:

Examining an application that uses an array

JJ's House of Pizza has six employees, each paid $6 per hour. In this tutorial you examine an application that stores the number of hours worked by each employee in an array. The application uses the values in the array to calculate each employee's gross pay.

Step 1: Start Visual Basic .NET and open the Simple Payroll project which is stored in the \Chap8\Simple Payroll folder of the student disk.

Step 2: Run the application. The form shown in Figure 8-6 appears.

Figure 8-6 The Simple Payroll form

Step 3: Click the Calculate Payroll button. A series of input boxes will appear asking you to enter the number of hours worked for employees 1 through 6. Enter the following numbers:

Employee 1: **10**
Employee 2: **40**
Employee 3: **20**
Employee 4: **15**
Employee 5: **10**
Employee 6: **30**

After you enter the hours for employee 6, the form should appear as shown in Figure 8-7.

Figure 8-7 Completed Simple Payroll form

Step 4: Click the Exit button to end the application.

Step 5: Open the Code window and look at the `btnCalcPay_Click` event procedure. The code is shown as follows.

```
Private Sub btnCalcPay_Click(ByVal sender As System.Object, _
        ByVal e As System.EventArgs) Handles btnCalcPay.Click
    ' Calculate and display the gross pay earned by six employees.
    Dim hours(5) As Integer      ' Array to hold hours worked
    Dim count As Integer         ' Loop counter
    Dim empHours As Integer      ' Employee hours
    Dim empPay As Decimal        ' Employee gross pay

    ' Get the hours worked by six employees.
    For count = 0 To 5
        empHours = Val(InputBox("Enter the hours worked by " & _
                "employee number " & (count + 1).ToString, _
                "Need Hours Worked"))
        hours(count) = Val(empHours)
    Next count

    ' Calculate and display each employee's gross pay.
    lstOutput.Items.Clear()
    For count = 0 To 5
        empPay = hours(count) * payRate
        lstOutput.Items.Add("Employee " & (count + 1).ToString & _
                " earned " & FormatCurrency(empPay))
    Next count
End Sub
```

The first variable declaration in the procedure is

```
Dim hours(5) As Integer ' Array to hold hours worked.
```

This statement declares hours as an array of six integers with the subscripts 0 through 5. After the variable declarations, the following loop appears.

```
    ' Get the hours worked by six employees.
    For count = 0 To 5
    empHours = Val(InputBox("Enter the hours worked by " & _
                "employee number" & (count + 1).ToString, _
                "Need Hours Worked"))
    hours(count) = Val(empHours)
    Next count
```

The loop iterates six times, using count as its counter variable. Each iteration of the loop displays an input box asking the user to enter the number of hours worked by an employee.

Look closer at the following statement:

```
empHours = Val(InputBox("Enter the hours worked by " & _
                "employee number" & (count + 1).ToString, _
                "Need Hours Worked"))
```

This statement uses the expression `(count + 1).ToString` to print the employee number. If the expression `count.ToString` was used, the first input box would ask for the hours worked for employee number 0, and the last input box would ask for the hours worked by employee number 5. It makes more sense to refer to the first employee as number 1, so the statement uses the expression `(count + 1).ToString` instead.

The `count` variable, which takes on the values 0 through 5, is also used as the array subscript in the following assignment statement.

```
hours(count) = Val(empHours)
```

The first time the loop iterates, `count` will be set to 0. The assignment statement stores the value entered by the user in `hours(0)`. During the loop's second iteration this statement stores the value entered by the user in `hours(1)`, and so on. Once this loop finishes, another loop calculates each employee's gross pay.

```
For count = 0 To 5
    empPay = hours(count) * payRate
    lstOutput.Items.Add("Employee " & (count + 1).ToString & _
        " earned " & FormatCurrency(empPay))
Next count
```

This loop also uses `count` as a counter, taking on the values 0 through 5. The first statement in the loop multiplies the value in `hours(count)` by `payRate`, a class-level constant. The result is displayed in the `lstOutput` list box.

✓ Checkpoint

8.1 Write declaration statements for the following arrays.

  a. `empNums`, an array of 100 integers
  b. `payRate`, an array of 24 decimal variables
  c. `miles`, an array of integers initialized to the values 10, 20, 30, 40, and 50
  d. `names`, an array of strings with an upper subscript of 12
  e. `divisions`, an array of 4 strings initialized to the values "North", "South", "East", and "West".

8.2 Identify the error in the following declaration:

```
Dim numberSet(4) As Integer = { 25, 37, 45, 60 }
```

8.3 Look at the following array declarations and indicate the number of elements in each array.

  a. `Dim nums(100) As Double`
  b. `Dim values() As Integer = { 99, 99, 99 }`
  c. `Dim array(0) As Integer`

8.4 What is bounds checking?

8.5 A procedure has the following array declaration.

```
Dim points(25) As Integer
```

Write a `For...Next` loop that displays each of the array's elements in message boxes.

8.6 Rewrite your answer to Checkpoint 8.5 to use a `For Each...Next` loop.

8.7   What values will be displayed in the message boxes by the following code segment? (Use a calculator if you need to.)

```
Const rate As Single = 0.1
Dim balance(3) As Integer
Dim count As Integer
Dim result As Single
balance(0) = 100
balance(1) = 250
balance(2) = 325
balance(3) = 500
For count = 0 To 3
    result = balance(count) * rate
    MessageBox.Show(result.ToString)
Next count
```

▶ 8.3   More About Array Processing

CONCEPT

THERE ARE MANY USES OF ARRAYS AND MANY PROGRAMMING TECHNIQUES THAT INVOLVE THEM. ARRAYS MAY BE USED TO TOTAL VALUES AND SEARCH FOR DATA. RELATED INFORMATION MAY BE STORED IN MULTIPLE PARALLEL ARRAYS. IN ADDITION, ARRAYS MAY BE RESIZED AT RUN TIME.

Determining the Number of Elements in an Array

Arrays in Visual Basic .NET have a Length property that holds the number of elements in the array. For example, assume that the following declaration exists in an application:

```
Dim values(25) As Integer
```

The values array has a total of 26 elements, with an upper subscript of 25. The array's Length property will hold the value 26. Here is an example of code that uses the Length property.

```
For count = 0 to (values.Length - 1)
    MessageBox.Show(values(count).ToString)
Next count
```

Notice that the code uses the expression values.Length - 1 as the loop's upper limit. This is because the value in the Length property is 1 greater than the array's upper subscript.

As you will learn later, the size of an array can change while an application is running. The Length property can be used in code where you are unsure of an array's size.

How to Total the Values in a Numeric Array

To total the values in an array, you must use a loop with an accumulator variable. The loop adds the value in each array element to the accumulator. For example, assume that the following array declaration exists in an application, and that values have been stored in the array.

```
Dim units(24) As Integer
```

The following loop adds the values of each element in the array to the `total` variable.

```
Dim total As Integer = 0 ' Initialize accumulator
For count = 0 To (units.Length - 1)
    total += units(count)
Next count
```

NOTE: *The first statement in the code segment sets `total` to 0. Recall from Chapter 5 that an accumulator variable must be set to 0 before it is used to keep a running total or the sum will not be correct. Although Visual Basic .NET automatically initializes numeric variables to 0, this statement is shown to emphasize that `total` must equal 0 prior to the loop execution.*

Getting the Average of the Values in a Numeric Array

The first step in calculating the average of all the values in an array is to sum the values. The second step is to divide the sum by the number of elements in the array. Once again, assume that the following declaration exists in an application, and that values have been stored in the array.

```
Dim units(24) As Integer
```

The following code calculates the average of the values in the `units` array. When the code completes, the average will be stored in the `average` variable.

```
Dim total As Integer = 0 ' Initialize accumulator
Dim average As Single
For count = 0 To (units.Length - 1)
    total += units(count)
Next count
average = total / units.Length
```

Notice that the last statement, which divides `total` by `units.Length`, is not inside the loop. This statement should only execute once, after the loop has finished its iterations.

Finding the Highest and Lowest Values in a Numeric Array

The algorithms for finding the highest and lowest values in an array are very similar. First, let's look at code for finding the highest value in an array. Assume that the following array declaration exists in an application, and that values have been stored in the array.

```
Dim numbers(50) As Integer
```

The code to find the highest value in the array is as follows.

```
Dim count As Integer
Dim highest As Integer

highest = numbers(0)
For count = 1 To (numbers.Length - 1)
    If numbers(count) > highest Then
        highest = numbers(count)
    End If
Next count
```

First we copy the value in the first array element to the variable `highest`. Then the loop compares all of the remaining array elements, beginning at subscript 1, to the value in `highest`. Each time it finds a value in the array that is greater than `highest`, it copies that value to `highest`. When the loop has finished, `highest` will contain the highest value in the array.

The following code finds the lowest value in the array. As you can see, it is nearly identical to the code for finding the highest value.

```
Dim count As Integer
Dim lowest As Integer

lowest = numbers(0)
For count = 1 To (numbers.Length - 1)
    If numbers(count) < lowest Then
        lowest = numbers(count)
    End If
Next count
```

Copying One Array's Contents to Another

Suppose an application has the following statements.

```
Dim oldValues(2) As Integer
Dim newValues(2) As Integer

oldValues(0) = 10
oldValues(1) = 100
oldValues(2) = 200
```

Let's say you want to copy the contents of the `oldValues` array to the `newValues` array. You might be tempted to use a single assignment statement, such as:

```
newValues = oldValues    'Be careful!
```

Although this is a valid statement, it does not copy the `oldValues` array to the `newValues` array. Instead it causes the names `newValues` and `oldValues` to refer to the same array in memory!

Arrays in Visual Basic .NET are actually object variables. Recall from Chapter 7 that an object variable is a variable that holds the memory address of an object and allows you to work with the object. When you use the assignment operator to assign one array to another, you are causing the two array object variables to refer to the same array. Going back to the example, after the statement `newValues = oldValues` executes, the `newValues` variable will refer to the same array that the `oldValues` variable refers to. This is illustrated in Figure 8-8.

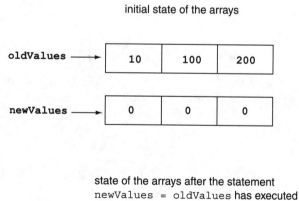

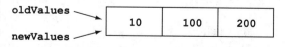

Figure 8-8 State of the arrays before and after the assignment statement

The danger of assigning `newValues` to `oldValues` is that we are no longer working with two arrays, but one. If we set all of the elements in `newValues` to 0, we will see all 0s when we display the elements of `oldValues`.

Instead of using a single assignment statement, you should use a loop to copy the individual elements from `oldValues` to `newValues`, as shown in the following code.

```
For count = 0 To 2
    newValues(count) = oldValues(count)
Next count
```

This loop will simply copy the values in `oldValue`'s elements to the `newValue` array. When finished, we will still have two separate arrays.

Parallel Arrays

Sometimes it is useful to store related data in two or more arrays. For example, assume an application has the following array declarations.

```
Dim names(4) As String
Dim addresses(4) As String
```

The `names` array is used to store the names of five persons, and the `addresses` array is used to store the addresses of the same five persons. The information for one person is stored in the same relative location in each array. For instance, the first person's name is stored at `names(0)`, and that same person's address is stored at `addresses(0)`. This is illustrated in Figure 8-9.

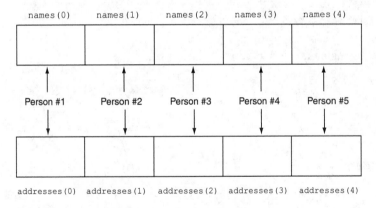

Figure 8-9   `names` and `addresses` parallel arrays

To access the information, use the same subscript with both arrays. For example, the following loop displays each person's name and address in a list box named `lstPeople`.

```
For count = 0 To 4
    lstPeople.Items.Add( "Name: " & names(count) & _
        " Address: " & addresses(count))
Next count
```

The arrays `names` and `addresses` are examples of parallel arrays. *Parallel arrays* are two or more arrays that hold related data, and the related elements in each array are accessed with a common subscript. Parallel arrays are especially useful when the related data is of unlike types. For example, an application could store the names and ages of five people in the following arrays.

```
Dim names(5) As String
Dim ages(5) As Integer
```

TUTORIAL 8-2:

Examining an application that uses parallel arrays

In this tutorial you examine a new version of the payroll application you examined in Tutorial 8-1. The new version uses parallel arrays.

Step 1:   Start Visual Basic .NET and open the Pizza Payroll project which is stored in the \Chap8\Pizza Payroll folder on the student disk.

Step 2:   Run the application. The form shown in Figure 8-10 appears.

Step 3:   Click the Calculate button. The application uses input boxes to ask for the names of six employees and the number of hours each has worked.

Figure 8-10   The Pizza Payroll form

Enter the following names and numbers of hours worked.

Jason Martin, 10
Tim Jaynes, 40
Charles Jenkins, 20
Tina Smith, 15
Billy Joyner, 10
Ruby Harrison, 30

Step 4:   After entering the data for the last employee, the form should now look like Figure 8-11.

Step 5:   Click the Exit button to end the application.

Figure 8-11   The Pizza Payroll form completed

Step 6: Open the Code window and look at the class-level declarations section, which are shown as follows.

```
' Class-level declarations
Const payRate As Decimal = 6      ' Standard hourly pay rate
Dim names(5) As String            ' Employee names
Dim hours(5) As Integer           ' Hours worked
Dim grossPay(5) As Decimal        ' Gross pay
Dim totalGrossPay As Decimal      ' Total gross pay
Dim totalHours As Integer         ' Total hours worked
```

The payRate constant holds the hourly pay rate for each employee. The arrays, names, hours and grossPay, are used as parallel arrays in the following manner: Employee 1's name is stored in names(0), hours worked are stored in hours(0) and gross pay is stored in grossPay(0). This continues for the other employees. The totalGrossPay variable is used to hold the total gross pay for all employees, and the totalHours variable is used to hold the total labor hours for all employees.

Step 7: Look at the code for the btnCalcPay_Click event procedure. The code is as follows.

```
Private Sub btnCalculate_Click(ByVal sender As System.Object, _
          ByVal e As System.EventArgs) Handles btnCalculate.Click
    ' Call the Sub procedures to calculate
    ' and display each employee's gross pay, the
    ' total payroll, and the total labor hours worked.
    GetData()
    CalcPay()
    DisplayPayrollData()
End Sub
```

This event procedure calls three Sub procedures. Look at the code for the GetData Sub procedure, which follows.

```
Sub GetData()
    ' Get the names of the six employees
    ' and the hours worked by each
    Dim count As Integer     ' Loop counter

    For count = 0 To 5
        names(count) = InputBox("Enter the name of employee " & _
                              "number " & (count + 1).ToString, _
                              "Employee Name")
        hours(count) = Val(InputBox("Enter the hours worked by " & _
                              names(count), "Hours Worked"))
    Next count
End Sub
```

This procedure uses a loop to ask the user for the names of six employees and the hours worked by each. The names are stored in the names array and the hours worked are stored in the hours array. Now look at the CalcPay Sub procedure, which is as follows.

```
Sub CalcPay()
    ' This procedure calculates and displays each
    ' employee's gross pay.
    Dim count As Integer ' Loop counter

    ' Calculate the gross pay.
    For count = 0 To 5
        grossPay(count) = hours(count) * payRate
    Next count

    ' Calculate the total of all the gross pay.
    For count = 0 To 5
        totalGrossPay += grossPay(count)
    Next count

    ' Calculate the total of all the hours.
    For count = 0 To 5
        totalHours += hours(count)
    Next count
End Sub
```

The first loop calculates each employee's gross pay and stores the results in the grossPay array. When this loop has finished, the gross pay for employee 1 will be stored in grossPay(0), the gross pay for employee 2 will be stored in gross Pay(1), and so forth.

The second loop calculates the total of all the employee gross pay. It does this by summing all the values in the grossPay array. The sum is stored in the total GrossPay class-level variable.

The third loop calculates the total of all the hours worked by all the employees. It does this by summing all the values in the hours array. The sum is stored in the totalHours class-level variable.

Step 8: Look at the code for the DisplayPayrollData procedure, which is as follows.

```
Sub DisplayPayrollData()
    ' Displays the payroll data for each employee
    ' and the total gross pay and total hours worked.
    Dim count As Integer ' Loop counter

    ' Display each employee's data
    For count = 0 To 5
        lstPayData.Items.Add("Name: " & names(count) & _
            " Hours: " & hours(count) & " Gross Pay: " & _
            FormatCurrency(grossPay(count)))
    Next count

    ' Display the total gross pay for all employees
    lblTotalPayroll.Text = FormatCurrency(totalGrossPay)

    ' Display the total hours for all employees
    lblLaborHours.Text = totalHours.ToString
End Sub
```

This procedure uses a loop to display each employee's name, hours, and gross pay in the `lstPayData` list box. The total gross pay and the total hours worked are displayed in the `lblTotalPayroll` and `lblTotalHours` labels.

Creating Parallel Relationships between Arrays, List Boxes, and Combo Boxes

Recall that the items stored in a list box or a combo box have a built-in index. The index of the first item is 0, the index of the second item is 1, and so forth. Because this indexing scheme corresponds with the way that array subscripts are used, it is possible to create parallel relationships between list boxes, combo boxes, and arrays.

For example, assume that an application has a list box named `lstPeople`. The following statements are used to store three names in the list box.

```
lstPeople.Items.Add("Jean James")
lstPeople.Items.Add("Kevin Smith")
lstPeople.Items.Add("Joe Harrison")
```

After these statements execute, "Jean James" will be stored at index 0, "Kevin Smith" will be stored at index 1, and "Joe Harrison" will be stored at index 2. Also assume that the application has an array of strings named `phoneNumbers`. This array will hold the phone numbers of the three people whose names are stored in the list box. The following statements are used to store phone numbers in the array.

```
phoneNumbers(0) = "555-2987"
phoneNumbers(1) = "555-5656"
phoneNumbers(2) = "555-8897"
```

The phone number that is stored at element 0 ("555-2987") belongs to the person whose name is stored at index 0 in the list box ("Jean James"). Likewise, the phone number that is stored at element 1 belongs to the person whose name is stored at index 1 in the list box, and so forth. When the user selects a name from the list box, the following statement can be used to display that person's phone number:

```
MessageBox.Show(phoneNumbers(lstPeople.SelectedIndex))
```

Recall that the SelectedIndex property holds the index of the item in the list box that has been selected. This statement uses that value as a subscript in the `phoneNumbers` array.

It is possible for the SelectedIndex property to hold a value that is outside the bounds of the parallel array, however. When no item is selected, the SelectedIndex property holds -1. The following code provides error checking.

```
With lstPeople
    If .SelectedIndex > -1 And _
        .SelectedIndex < phoneNumbers.Length Then
            MessageBox.Show(phoneNumbers(.SelectedIndex))
    Else
            MessageBox.Show("That is not a valid selection.")
    End If
End With
```

Searching Arrays

It is common for applications to not only store and process information stored in arrays, but to search arrays for specific items. A straightforward method of searching an array is the sequential search. The *sequential search* is a very simple algorithm. It uses a loop to sequentially examine the elements in an array, one after the other, starting with the first one. It compares each element with the value being searched for, and stops when the value is found, or the end of the array is encountered. If the value being searched for is not in the array, the algorithm will unsuccessfully search to the end of the array.

The pseudocode for a sequential search is as follows. In the pseudocode, found is a Boolean variable, position and subscript are integers, and array is an array of any type. searchValue is the value being searched for. When the algorithm is completed, if the found variable is false, then the search value was not found in the array. If found is true, position will contain the subscript of the array element containing the search value.

```
found = False
subscript = 0
Do While found is False and subscript < array's length
    If array(subscript) = searchValue Then
        found = True
        position = subscript
    End If
    subscript += 1
End While
```

For example, assume that an application stores test scores in an array of single precision variables named scores. The following code searches the array for an element containing 100.

```
' Search for a 100 in the array.
found = False
count = 0
Do While Not found And count < scores.Length
    If scores(count) = 100 Then
        found = True
        position = count
    End If
    count += 1
Loop
' Was 100 found in the array?
If found Then
    MessageBox.Show("Congratulations! You made a 100 on test " & _
                (position + 1).ToString, "Test Results")
Else
    MessageBox.Show("You didn't score a 100, but keep trying!", _
                "Test Results")
End If
```

Sorting an Array

Often, the data in an array must be sorted in *ascending order*, which means its values are arranged from lowest to highest. The lowest value will be stored in the first element and the highest value will be stored in the last element. To sort an array in ascending order, use the `Array.Sort` method. The general format of the method is:

```
Array.Sort(ArrayName)
```

ArrayName is the name of the array you wish to sort. For example, assume that the following declaration exists in an application:

```
Dim numbers() As Integer = { 7, 12, 1, 6, 3 }
```

The following statement will sort the array in ascending order.

```
Array.Sort(numbers)
```

After the statement executes, the values in the array will appear in this order: 1, 3, 6, 7, 12. When you pass an array of strings to the `Array.Sort` method, the array is sorted in alphabetical order. For example, assume that the following declaration exists:

```
Dim names() As String = { "Sue", "Kim", "Alan", "Bill" }
```

The following statement will sort the array in alphabetical order:

```
Array.Sort(names)
```

After the statement executes, the values in the array will appear in this order: "Alan", "Bill", "Kim", "Sue".

Dynamically Sizing Arrays

Visual Basic .NET allows you to change the number of elements in an array at run-time with the *ReDim statement*. The general format of the ReDim statement is

```
ReDim [Preserve] Arrayname(UpperSubscript)
```

The word `Preserve` is optional. If it is used, any values that already exist in the array will be preserved. If `Preserve` is not used, the existing values in the array are destroyed. *Arrayname* is the name of the array being resized. *UpperSubscript* is the new upper subscript, and should only be a positive whole number.

For example, the following statement resizes the dynamic array names to so that 25 is the upper subscript. After this statement has executed, `names` will have a total of 26 elements. Because the `Preserve` key word is used, any values that were originally stored in `names` will still be there.

```
ReDim Preserve names(25)
```

When you do not know at design time the number of elements you will need in an array, you can declare an array with no subscripts, and then use the `ReDim` statement later to give it a size. For example, suppose you want to write a test-averaging application that can average any number of tests. You would initially declare an array with no subscripts, as follows.

```
Dim scores() As Single
```

This statement creates an object variable that references `Nothing`, but is capable of referencing an array of Single values. Later, when the application has determined the number of test scores, a

ReDim statement can be used to give the array a size. The following code shows an example of such an operation.

```
numScores = Val(InputBox("Enter the number of test scores."))
If numScores > 0 Then
    ReDim scores(numScores - 1)
Else
    MessageBox.Show("You must enter 1 or greater.")
End If
```

This code asks the user to enter the number of test scores. If the user enters a value that is greater than 0, the ReDim statement sizes the array with numScores – 1 being the upper subscript. (Because the subscripts begin at 0, the upper subscript will be numScores – 1.)

✓ **Checkpoint**

8.8 values is an array of 100 integers. Write a For…Next loop that totals all the values stored in the array.

8.9 points is an array of integers. You do not know the size of the array. Write code that calculates the average of the values in the array.

8.10 serialNumbers is an array of strings. Write the code that sorts the array in ascending order.

8.11 What is displayed by the message boxes in the following code segment? (You may need to use a calculator.)

```
Dim times(4) As Integer
Dim speeds(4) As Integer
Dim dists(4) As Integer
speeds(0) = 18
speeds(1) = 4
speeds(2) = 27
speeds(3) = 52
speeds(4) = 100

Dim count As Integer
For count = 0 To 4
    times(count) = count
Next count

For count = 0 To 4
    dists(count) = times(count) * speeds(count)
Next count

For count = 0 To 4
    MessageBox.Show(times(count) & " " & speeds(count) & _
        " " & dists(count))
Next count
```

8.12 Assume that sales is an array of 20 elements. Write a statement that resizes the array to 50 elements. If the array has existing values, they should be preserved.

8.13 Assume that validNumbers is an array of integers. Write code that searches the array for the value 247. If the value is found, display a message indicating its position in the array. If the value is not found, display a message indicating so.

▶ 8.4 Sub Procedures and Functions that Work with Arrays

CONCEPT

YOU MAY PASS ARRAYS AS ARGUMENTS TO SUB PROCEDURES AND FUNCTIONS. YOU MAY ALSO RETURN AN ARRAY FROM A FUNCTION. THESE CAPABILITIES ALLOW YOU TO WRITE SUB PROCEDURES AND FUNCTIONS THAT PERFORM GENERAL OPERATIONS WITH ARRAYS.

Passing Arrays as Arguments

Quite often you will want to write Sub procedures or functions that process the data in arrays. For example, procedures can be written to store data in an array, display an array's contents, sum or average the values in an array, etc. Usually such procedures accept an array as an argument.

For example, the following Sub procedure accepts an integer array as an argument and displays the sum of the array's elements.

```
Sub DisplaySum(ByVal a() As Integer)
    ' Displays the sum of the elements in the
    ' argument array.
    Dim total As Integer = 0     ' Accumulator
    Dim count As Integer         ' Loop counter

    For count = 0 To (a.Length - 1)
        total += a(count)
    Next
    MessageBox.Show("The total is " & total.ToString)
End Sub
```

Notice that the parameter variable is declared as an array with no upper subscript specified inside the parentheses. The parameter is an object variable that will reference the array that is passed as an argument. To call the procedure, simply pass the name of an array, as shown in the following code.

```
Dim numbers() As Integer = { 2, 4, 7, 9, 8, 12, 10 }
DisplaySum(numbers)
```

When this code executes, the `DisplaySum` procedure is called and the `numbers` array is passed as an argument. The procedure will calculate and display the sum of the elements in `numbers`.

Passing Arrays By Value and By Reference

Array parameters may be declared either as `ByVal` or `ByRef`. Be aware, however, that the `ByVal` key word does not restrict a procedure from accessing and modifying the argument array's elements. For example, look at the following `SetToZero` procedure.

```
Sub SetToZero(ByVal a() As Integer)
    ' Set all the elements of the array argument
    ' to zero.
    Dim count As Integer     ' Loop counter

    For count = 0 To a.Length - 1
        a(count) = 0
```

```
      Next
   End Sub
```

This procedure accepts an integer array as its argument and sets each element of the array to 0. Suppose we call the procedure, as shown in the following code.

```
Dim numbers() As Integer = { 1, 2, 3, 4, 5 }
SetToZero(numbers)
```

After the procedure executes, the numbers array will contain the values 0, 0, 0, 0, and 0.

Although the ByVal key word does not restrict a procedure from accessing the elements of an array argument, it does prevent an array argument from be assigned to another array. For example, the following procedure accepts an array as its argument, and then assigns the parameter to another array.

```
Sub ResetValues(ByVal a() As Integer)
   ' Assign the array argument to a
   ' new array. Does this work?
   Dim newArray() As Integer = {0, 0, 0, 0, 0}
   a = newArray
End Sub
```

Suppose we call the procedure, as shown in the following code.

```
Dim numbers() As Integer = { 1, 2, 3, 4, 5 }
ResetValues(numbers)
```

After the procedure executes, the numbers array will still contain the values 1, 2, 3, 4, and 5. If the parameter array had been declared with the ByRef key word, however, the assignment would have affected the argument, and the numbers array would contain the values 0, 0, 0, 0, and 0 after the procedure executed.

Returning an Array from a Function

It is also possible to return an array from a function. For example, the following function prompts the user to enter four names. The four names are then returned in an array.

```
Function GetNames() As String()
   ' Get four names from the user
   ' and return them as an array
   ' of strings.
   Dim names(3) As String
   Dim input As String
   Dim count As Integer

   For count = 0 To 3
       input = InputBox("Enter name " & (count + 1).ToString)
       names(count) = input
   Next
   Return names
End Function
```

Notice that the function has a return type of String(), which indicates that it returns an array of strings. The return value can be assigned to any array of strings. The following code shows the function's return value being assigned to customers.

```
Dim customers() As String
customers = GetNames()
```

After the code executes, the `customers` array will contain the names entered by the user.

The array that is returned from a function must be assigned to an array of the same data type. For example, if a function returns an array of integers, its return value can only be assigned to an array of integers.

In Tutorial 8-3 you examine an application that has several functions that work with arrays.

TUTORIAL 8-3:

Examining an application with functions that work with arrays

In this tutorial you examine the Sales Data application, which asks the user for sales figures for a series of days . The application then calculates and displays the total sales, average sales, highest amount of sales for a given day, and lowest amount of sales for a given day.

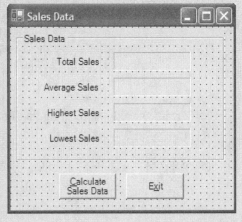

Figure 8-12   Sales Data form

Step 1: Start Visual Basic .NET and open the Sales Data project, which is stored in the \Chap8\Sales Data folder. The application's form is shown in Figure 8-12. The Calculate Sales Data button is named `btnCalculate`.

Step 2: Open the Code window and scroll down to the `GetSalesData` function. The code follows.

```
Function GetSalesData(ByRef s() As Decimal) As Boolean
    ' Prompts the user for the sales figures and store them
    ' in the argument array. Returns true if the procedure
    ' was successful, or false if not.
    Dim salesData() As Decimal   ' To hold sales data
    Dim numDays As Integer       ' Number of days
    Dim count As Integer         ' Loop counter
    Dim status As Boolean        ' Indicates success or failure

    numDays = Val(InputBox("For how many days do you have sales?"))
    If numDays > 0 Then
        ReDim salesData(numDays - 1)
        For count = 0 To (numDays - 1)
            salesData(count) = Val(InputBox("Enter the sales for " & _
                            "day " & (count + 1).ToString))
```

```
        Next count
        s = salesData
        status = True
    Else
        MessageBox.Show("Enter at least 1.")
        status = False
    End If
    Return status
End Function
```

Note that the array parameter, s, is declared ByRef, and that this function returns a Boolean value. First, the function asks the user to enter the number of days for which there are sales figures. If the user enters a number greater than zero, the salesData array is resized to hold the sales figures. In the For...Next loop, the user is asked to enter the sales for each day, and the numbers are stored in the salesData array. After the loop finishes, the salesData array, which now holds all the sales figures, is assigned to the parameter array, s. The Boolean status variable is set to true, which indicates that the data was collected.

If the user enters zero or less for the number of days, a message is displayed asking the user to enter at least one. The Boolean status variable is then set to false, indicating that no data was collected. The function's last action is to return the value in the status variable.

Step 3:   Continue scrolling in the Code window to examine the GetTotal, GetAverage, GetHighest, and GetLowest functions. Their code follows.

```
Function GetTotal(ByVal n() As Decimal) As Decimal
    ' Calculate and return the total of the
    ' values in the array argument.
    Dim total As Decimal = 0     ' Accumulator
    Dim count As Integer         ' Loop counter

    For count = 0 To (n.Length - 1)
        total += n(count)
    Next
    Return total
End Function

Function GetAverage(ByVal n() As Decimal) As Decimal
    ' Calculate and return the average of the
    ' values in the array argument.
    Dim average As Decimal

    average = GetTotal(n) / n.Length
    Return average
End Function

Function GetHighest(ByVal n() As Decimal) As Decimal
    ' Returns the highest value in the array argument
    Dim count As Integer         ' Loop counter
    Dim highest As Decimal       ' Temporary holder
```

```
        highest = n(0)
        For count = 1 To (n.Length - 1)
            If n(count) > highest Then
                highest = n(count)
            End If
        Next count
        Return highest
    End Function

    Function GetLowest(ByVal n() As Decimal) As Decimal
        ' Returns the lowest value in the array argument
        Dim count As Integer      ' Loop counter
        Dim lowest As Decimal     ' Temporary holder
        lowest = n(0)
        For count = 1 To (n.Length - 1)
            If n(count) < lowest Then
                lowest = n(count)
            End If
        Next count
        Return lowest
    End Function
```

Step 4: Scroll back to the top of the Code window and look at the `btnCalculate_Click` event procedure. The code follows.

```
    Private Sub btnCalculate_Click(ByVal sender As System.Object, _
        ByVal e As System.EventArgs) Handles btnCalculate.Click
        Dim sales() As Decimal   ' To hold sales data
        Dim total As Decimal     ' To hold the total sales
        Dim average As Decimal   ' To hold the average sales
        Dim highest As Decimal   ' To hold the highest sales
        Dim lowest As Decimal    ' To hold the lowest sales

        If GetSalesData(sales) Then
            ' Calculate total, average, highest,
            ' and lowest sales
            total = GetTotal(sales)
            average = GetAverage(sales)
            highest = GetHighest(sales)
            lowest = GetLowest(sales)
            ' Display the results
            lblTotal.Text = FormatCurrency(total)
            lblAverage.Text = FormatCurrency(average)
            lblHighest.Text = FormatCurrency(highest)
            lblLowest.Text = FormatCurrency(lowest)
        End If
    End Sub
```

This procedure calls the functions and displays the resulting sales data on the Label controls.

Step 5: Run the application, click the Calculate Sales Data button, and enter the following input.

Number of days: **5**
Sales for day 1: **1357.89**
Sales for day 2: **1564.25**
Sales for day 3: **927.12**
Sales for day 4: **1032.69**
Sales for day 5: **1468.27**

Step 6: The form should display the sales data shown in Figure 8-13.

Step 7: End the application.

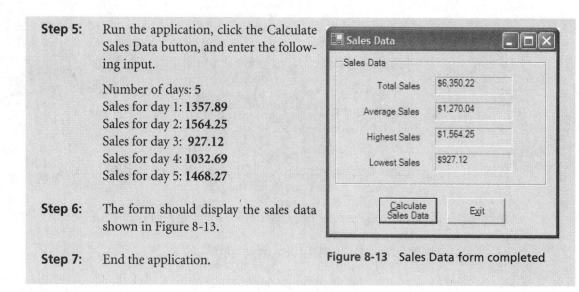

Figure 8-13   Sales Data form completed

▶ 8.5   Multidimensional Arrays

CONCEPT

YOU MAY CREATE ARRAYS WITH MORE THAN TWO SUBSCRIPTS TO HOLD COMPLEX SETS OF DATA.

Two-Dimensional Arrays

The arrays presented so far have had only one subscript. An array with one subscript is a *single-dimension array*, and is useful for storing and working with a single set of data. Sometimes, though, it is necessary to work with multiple sets of data. For example, in a grade-averaging program a teacher might record all of one student's test scores in an array. If the teacher has 30 students, that means he or she will need 30 arrays to record the scores for the entire class. Instead of declaring 30 individual arrays, it would be better to declare a two-dimensional array.

A *two-dimensional array* is like an array of arrays and can be used to hold multiple sets of values. It is best to think of a two-dimensional array as having rows and columns of elements, as shown in Figure 8-14. This figure shows an array having three rows (numbered 0, 1, and 2) and four columns (numbered 0, 1, 2, and 3). There are a total of 12 elements in the array.

	column 0	column 1	column 2	column 3
row 0				
row 1				
row 2				

Figure 8-14   Rows and columns

To declare a two-dimensional array, two sets of upper subscripts are required, the first one for the rows and the second one for the columns. The general format of a two-dimensional array declaration is:

```
Dim ArrayName(UpperRow, UpperColumn) As DataType
```

Let's take a closer look at the syntax.

◆   *ArrayName* is the name of the array.

◆   *UpperRow* is the value of the array's highest row subscript. This must be a positive whole number.

◆   *UpperColumn* is the value of the array's highest column subscript. This must be a positive whole number.

◆   *DataType* is a Visual Basic .NET data type.

An example declaration of a two-dimensional array with three rows and four columns follows, and is shown in Figure 8-15. The highest row subscript is 2 and the highest column subscript is 3.

```
Dim scores(2, 3) As Single
```

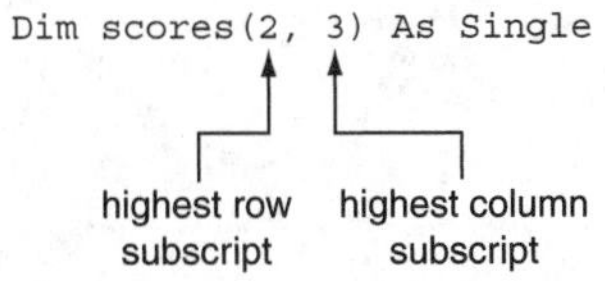

Figure 8-15   Declaration of a two-dimensional array

When data in a two-dimensional array is processed, each element has two subscripts, the first for its row and the second for its column. Using the `scores` array as an example, the elements in row 0 are referenced as

```
scores(0, 0)
scores(0, 1)
scores(0, 2)
scores(0, 3)
```

The elements in row 1 are

```
scores(1, 0)
scores(1, 1)
scores(1, 2)
scores(1, 3)
```

And the elements in row 2 are

```
scores(2, 0)
scores(2, 1)
scores(2, 2)
scores(2, 3)
```

Figure 8-16 illustrates the array with the subscripts shown for each element.

	column 0	column 1	column 2	column 3
row 0	scores(0, 0)	scores(0, 1)	scores(0, 2)	scores(0, 3)
row 1	scores(1, 0)	scores(1, 1)	scores(1, 2)	scores(1, 3)
row 2	scores(2, 0)	scores(2, 1)	scores(2, 2)	scores(2, 3)

Figure 8-16   Subscripts for each element of the `scores` array

To access one of the elements in a two-dimensional array, you must use both subscripts. For example the following statement stores the number 95 in `scores(2, 1)`.

```
scores(2, 1) = 95
```

Programs that process two-dimensional arrays can do so with nested loops. For example, the following code prompts the user to enter a score, once for each element in the array.

```
For row = 0 To 2
    For col = 0 To 3
        num = Val(InputBox("Enter a score."))
        scores(row, col) = num
    Next col
Next row
```

And the following code displays all the elements in the `scores` array.

```
For row = 0 To 2
    For col = 0 To 3
        lstOutput.Items.Add(scores(row, col).ToString)
    Next col
Next row
```

In Tutorial 8-4 you examine an application that stores sales figures in a two-dimensional array. The application sums the values in each row of the two-dimensional array and sums the values in the entire array.

TUTORIAL 8-4:

Examining an application that sums the rows of a two-dimensional array

In a company with three divisions, each division keeps its total sales for each quarter. This application uses an array with three rows (one for each division) and four columns (one for each quarter) to store the company's sales data.

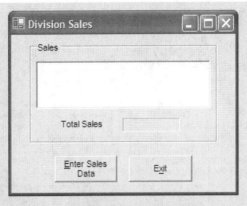

Figure 8-17   The Division Sales form

Step 1:   Start Visual Basic .NET and open the Division Sales project, which is stored in the \Chap8\Division Sales folder on the student disk.

Step 2:   Run the application. The form shown in Figure 8-17 appears.

Step 3:   Click the Enter Sales Data button. The application will use a series of input boxes to prompt you for each division's sales for each quarter. Because there are three divisions and four quarters for each division, you will see a total of 12 input boxes. As the input boxes prompt you, enter the following sales data.

Division 1, quarter 1: **31000.00**
Division 1, quarter 2: **29000.00**
Division 1, quarter 3: **32000.00**
Division 1, quarter 4: **39000.00**

Division 2, quarter 1: **56000.00**
Division 2, quarter 2: **54000.00**
Division 2, quarter 3: **41000.00**
Division 2, quarter 4: **54000.00**

Division 3, quarter 1: **29000.00**
Division 3, quarter 2: **28000.00**
Division 3, quarter 3: **25000.00**
Division 3, quarter 4: **32000.00**

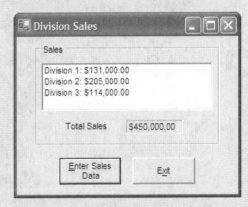

Figure 8-18   Completed Division Sales form

After you enter the data for the division 3, quarter 4, the form should appear as shown in Figure 8-18.

Step 4:   Click the Exit button to end the application.

Step 5:   Open the Code window and look at the class-level declaration of a two-dimensional array named `sales`, as follows.

```
Dim sales(2, 3) As Decimal ' Corporate sales figures.
```

As mentioned earlier, the array has three rows (one for each division) and four columns (one for each quarter) to store the company's sales data. The row subscripts are 0, 1, and 2, and the column subscripts are 0, 1, 2, and 3. Figure 8-19 illustrates how the quarterly sales figures are stored in the array.

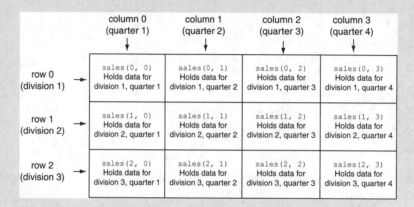

Figure 8-19 Division and quarter data stored in `Sales` elements

Step 6: Look at the `btnEnterSalesData_Click` event procedure. Nested loops, shown here, display the 12 input boxes to gather the sales data from the user.

```
' Get input from the user.
For divElement = 0 To 2
    For qtrElement = 0 To 3
    sales(divElement, qtrElement) = _
        Val(InputBox("Enter sales for division " & _
            (divElement + 1).ToString & ", quarter " & _
            (qtrElement + 1).ToString, "Input Sales Data"))
    Next qtrElement
Next divElement
```

The code that follows uses another set of nested loops to calculate the total sales for each division and the total sales for the company.

```
' Calculate and display the totals.
For divElement = 0 To 2
    ' Initialize the division accumulator.
    divTotal = 0
    ' Total the division sales.
    For qtrElement = 0 To 3
        ' Add the element to the accumulators.
        divTotal += sales(divElement, qtrElement)
        total += sales(divElement, qtrElement)
    Next qtrElement
    ' Display the division total.
    lstOutput.Items.Add("Division " & (divElement + 1).ToString & _
        ": " & FormatCurrency(divTotal))
Next divElement
' Display the total sales of all divisions.
lblTotalSales.Text = FormatCurrency(total)
```

Two accumulators are used in the loops: `divTotal`, to sum each division's total sales, and `total`, to sum all the sales data. Let's take a closer look at the nested loops.

The outer loop iterates three times, once for each division in the company. Here is the first line of the loop.

```
For divElement = 0 To 2
```

The first operation performed by the outer loop is to initialize the `divTotal` accumulator, as follows.

```
' Initialize the division accumulator.
divTotal = 0
```

The `divTotal` accumulator must be initialized because the inner loop uses it to calculate the total sales for each division. The inner loop iterates four times, once for each sales quarter.

```
' Total the division sales.
For qtrElement = 0 To 3
' Add the element to the accumulators.
divTotal += sales(divElement, qtrElement)
total += sales(divElement, qtrElement)
Next qtrElement
```

The inner loop also uses the `total` accumulator to calculate the total of all the values in the array. Because `total` holds a running total of all the elements in the array, it is not initialized during the loop iterations.

After the inner loop has completed a cycle, which is four iterations, the outer loop displays the division total in the `lstOutput` list box.

```
' Display the division total.
lstOutput.Items.Add("Division " & (divElement + 1).ToString & _
        ": " & FormatCurrency(divTotal))
Next divElement
```

When the outer loop has completed its three iterations, the following code copies the contents of total to the `lblTotalSales` control.

```
' Display the total sales of all divisions.
lblTotalSales.Text = FormatCurrency(total)
```

Implicit Sizing and Initialization of Two-Dimensional Arrays

As with a single-dimensional array, you may provide an initialization list for a two-dimensional array. Recall that when you provide an initialization list for an array, you cannot provide the upper subscript numbers. When initializing a two-dimensional array, you must provide the comma to indicate the number of dimensions. Here is an example of a two-dimensional array declaration with an initialization list.

```
Dim numbers(,) As Integer = {{1, 2, 3}, {4, 5, 6}, {7, 8, 9}}
```

Notice that the initialization values for each row are enclosed in their own set of braces. In this example, the initialization values for row 0 are {1, 2, 3}, the initialization values for row 1 are {4, 5, 6}, and the initialization values for row 2 are {7, 8, 9}. So, this statement declares an array with three rows and three columns. The same statement could also be written as:

```
Dim numbers(,) As Integer = {{1, 2, 3}, _
                             {1, 2, 3}, _
                             {1, 2, 3}}
```

In either case, the values are assigned to the numbers array in the following manner:

numbers(0, 0) is set to 1
numbers(0, 1) is set to 2
numbers(0, 2) is set to 3

numbers(1, 0) is set to 4
numbers(1, 1) is set to 5
numbers(1, 2) is set to 6

numbers(2, 0) is set to 7
numbers(2, 1) is set to 8
numbers(2, 2) is set to 9

Using the For Each Loop to Sum a Two-Dimensional Array

Tutorial 8-4 demonstrates the use of nested loops to calculate the sum of each row and the sum of all values in a two-dimensional array. If you only want to sum the contents of the array, it is simpler to use the For Each loop. In the following code, total is an accumulator (initialized to 0), element is an integer variable, and numbers is a two-dimensional array of integers.

```
For Each element In numbers
    total += element
Next element
```

After the loop has completed, total will contain the sum of all the elements in the numbers array.

Summing the Columns of a Two-Dimensional Array

You may also use nested loops to sum the columns in a two-dimensional array. The following code sums each column of an array named values, which has five rows and three columns. The outer loop controls the column subscript and the inner loop controls the row subscript. The variable total accumulates the sum of each column.

```
' Sum the columns.
For col = 0 To 2
    ' Initialize the accumulator.
    total = 0
    ' Sum a column.
    For row = 0 To 4
        total += values(row, col)
```

```
        Next row
        ' Display the sum of the column.
        MessageBox.Show("Sum of column " & col.ToString & _
                        " is " & total.ToString)
    Next col
```

Three-Dimensional Arrays and Beyond

Visual Basic .NET allows you to create arrays with up to 32 dimensions. Here is an example of a three-dimensional array declaration:

```
Dim seats(9, 11, 14) As Decimal
```

This array can be thought of as 10 sets of 12 rows, with each row containing 15 columns. This array might be used to store the prices of seats in an auditorium, where there are 15 seats in a row, 12 rows in a section, and a total of 10 sections.

Figure 8-20 illustrates the concept of a three-dimensional array as pages of two-dimensional arrays.

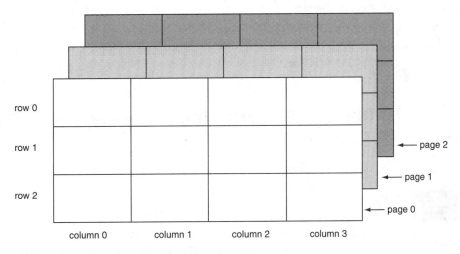

Figure 8-20   A three-dimensional array

Arrays with more than three dimensions are difficult to visualize but can be useful in some programming problems. For example, in a factory warehouse where cases of widgets are stacked on pallets, an array with four dimensions could be used to store a part number for each widget. The four subscripts of each element could represent the pallet number, case number, row number, and column number of each widget. Similarly, an array with five dimensions could be used if there were multiple warehouses.

✓ Checkpoint

8.14   Declare a two-dimensional array of integers named `grades`. It should have 30 rows and 10 columns.

8.15   How many elements are in the following array?

```
Dim sales(5, 3) As Decimal
```

8.16   Write a statement that assigns 56893.12 to the first column of the first row of the `sales` array declared in Checkpoint 8.15.

8.17 Write a statement that displays in a message box the contents of the last column of the last row of the array `sales` declared in Checkpoint 8.15.

8.18 Declare a two-dimensional array named `settings` large enough to hold the following table of information.

12	24	32	21	42
14	67	87	65	90
19	1	24	12	8

8.19 How many rows and columns does the array declared in the following statement have?

```
Dim matrix(,) As Integer = {{2, 4, 7, 0, 3}, _
        {6, 5, 12, 8, 6}, {9, 0, 14, 6, 0}, _
        {16, 7, 9, 13, 10}}
```

8.20 A video rental store keeps videos on 50 racks with 10 shelves each. Each shelf holds 25 videos. Declare a three-dimensional array of strings large enough to represent the store's storage system. Each element of the array will hold a video's name.

▶ 8.6 Focus on GUI Design: The Enabled Property, the Timer Control, and Splash Screens

CONCEPT

YOU DISABLE CONTROLS BY SETTING THEIR ENABLED PROPERTY TO FALSE. THE TIMER CONTROL ALLOWS YOUR APPLICATION TO EXECUTE A PROCEDURE AT REGULAR TIME INTERVALS. SPLASH SCREENS ARE FORMS THAT APPEAR AS AN APPLICATION BEGINS EXECUTING.

The Enabled Property

Most controls have a Boolean property named Enabled. When a control's *Enabled property* is set to false, it is considered disabled, which means it cannot receive the focus and cannot respond to events generated by the user. In addition, many controls appear dimmed, or grayed out, when their Enabled property is set to false. For example, Figure 8-21 shows a form with labels, a text box, a group box, radio buttons, a list box, and buttons. All of these controls have their Enabled property set to false.

By default, a control's Enabled property is set to true. If you change a control's Enabled property to false at design time, the control will be initially disabled when the application runs.

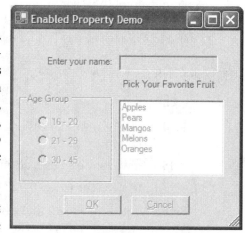

Figure 8-21 Controls with Enabled property set to false

You can also change the Enabled property's value with code at run time. For example, assume an application has a radio button named `radBlue`. The following statement disables the control.

```
radBlue.Enabled = False
```

Sometimes you do not want the user to access controls. For example, consider an application that calculates the price of two different models of a new car. One model comes only in red, yellow, and black, while the other model comes only in white, green, and orange. As soon as the user selects a model, the application can disable the colors not available for that model.

The Timer Control

The *Timer control* allows an application to automatically execute code at regular time intervals. This is useful when you want an application to perform an operation at certain times or after an amount of time has passed. For example, a Timer control can perform simple animation by moving a graphic image across the screen, or it can cause a form to be hidden after a certain amount of time.

You double-click the Timer tool in the toolbox to place a Timer control on a form. Because the Timer control is invisible at run-time, it appears in the component tray at design time. The standard prefix for a Timer control's name is `tmr`.

Timer Events

When you place a Timer control on a form, it responds to `Tick` events as the application is running. A `Tick` event is generated at regular time intervals. If the control has a `Tick` event procedure, it is executed each time a `Tick` event occurs. Therefore, the code that you write in the `Tick` event procedure executes at regular intervals.

To create a `Tick` event procedure code template, double-click a Timer control that has been placed in the component tray.

Timer Control Properties

The Timer control has two important properties: Enabled and Interval. When the Enabled property is set to true, the Timer control responds to `Tick` events. When the Enabled property is set to false, the Timer control does not respond to `Tick` events and any code in the control's `Tick` event procedure does not execute.

The *Interval property* can be set to a value of 1 or greater. The value stored in the Interval property is the number of milliseconds that elapse between timer events. A millisecond is a thousandth of a second, so setting the Interval property to 1000 will cause a timer event to occur every second.

WARNING:

 If you set the Interval property to 0 a run-time error will occur.

In Tutorial 8-5 you examine an application that demonstrates a Timer control.

TUTORIAL 8-5:

The Timer control demo

Step 1: Start Visual Basic .NET and open the Timer Demo project, which is stored in the \Chap8\Timer Demo folder. The application's form is shown in Figure 8-22. Notice that the Timer control appears as a stopwatch in the component tray.

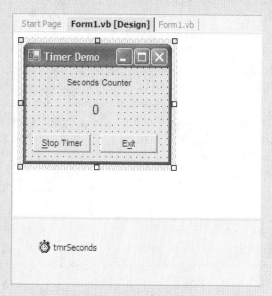

Figure 8-22 The Timer Demo form

Step 2: Run the application. The form shown in Figure 8-23 appears.

Step 3: The number appearing under the Seconds Counter label is initially set to 0, but it increments every second. After a few seconds, click the Stop Timer button to halt the timer.

Figure 8-23 The Timer Demo application running

Step 4: Notice that when you clicked the Stop Timer button, the button's text changed to Start Timer. Click the button again to start the timer.

Step 5: After a few seconds, click the Exit button to end the application.

Step 6: With the Design window open, select the Timer control.

Step 7: With the Timer control selected, look at the Properties window. The name of the control is `tmrSeconds`. Its Enabled property is initially set to true, and its Interval property is set to 1000.

Step 8: Open the Code window and notice that a class-level variable named `seconds` is declared.

Step 9: Look at the `tmrSeconds_Tick` event procedure. The code is as follows.

```
Private Sub tmrSeconds_Tick(ByVal eventSender As System.Object, _
        ByVal eventArgs As System.EventArgs) Handles tmrSeconds.Tick
    ' Update the seconds display by one second.
    seconds += 1
    lblCounter.Text = seconds.ToString
End Sub
```

Each time the `tmrSeconds_Tick` event procedure executes, it adds 1 to `seconds` and then copies its value to the `lblCounter` label. Because the Timer control's Interval property is set to 1000, this event procedure executes every second (unless the Timer control's Enabled property is set to false).

Step 10: The button that stops and starts the timer is named `btnToggleTimer`. Look at the `btnToggleTimer_Click` event procedure. The code is as follows.

```
Private Sub btnToggleTimer_Click(ByVal sender As System.Object, _
        ByVal e As System.EventArgs) Handles btnToggleTimer.Click
    ' Toggle the timer.
    If tmrSeconds.Enabled = True Then
        tmrSeconds.Enabled = False
        btnToggleTimer.Text = "&Start Timer"
    Else
        tmrSeconds.Enabled = True
        btnToggleTimer.Text = "&Stop Timer"
    End If
End Sub
```

The code tests the value of the `tmrSeconds.Enabled` property. If the property is set to true, the code sets it to false and changes the button's text to "&Start Timer". Otherwise, it sets the property to true and changes the button's text to "&Stop Timer".

Splash Screens

A *splash screen* is a form that is displayed while an application is loading. Splash screens usually show logos, and assure the user that a slowly loading application is in the process of starting up. Most major applications, such as Microsoft Word, Excel, and others display a splash screen while starting up.

Forms have a property named *TopMost* which may be set to true or false. When set to true, it causes the form to always be displayed on top of other forms. By default this property is set to false. Splash screens should always appear on top of the other forms in an application, so you set this property to true for any form that is to become a splash screen. Splash screens should also be displayed in modeless style (with the `Show` method) so the application will continue to process code while the splash screen is displayed.

A splash screen should automatically disappear after a short time period. You can place a Timer control on a splash screen form, set its Interval property to the desired time interval, and then code a

Tick event procedure to close the form. Tutorial 8-7 leads you through the process of creating a splash screen.

TUTORIAL 8-6:

Creating a splash screen

Step 1: Start Visual Basic .NET and begin a new Windows application project. Name the project Splash Demo.

Step 2: Name the application's form frmMain and place the following controls on it.

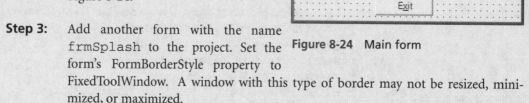

- ◆ A label on the form with the text "This is the main form."

- ◆ An Exit button that ends the application.

Your form should appear similar to Figure 8-24.

Figure 8-24 Main form

Step 3: Add another form with the name frmSplash to the project. Set the form's FormBorderStyle property to FixedToolWindow. A window with this type of border may not be resized, minimized, or maximized.

Step 4: Add the labels and Picture Box control shown in Figure 8-25 to the frmSplash form. Set the Picture Box control's SizeMode property to StretchImage. The graphic image that is shown in the figure is stored in the file C:\Program Files\Microsoft Visual Studio .NET\Common7\Graphics\icons \Office\Graph04.Ico. If this file is not installed on your system, substitute another image or omit the PictureBox control from the form. Set the form's

Figure 8-25 Splash screen form

Text property to "Loading" and change the form's BackColor property to a light color.

Step 5: Set the form's TopMost property to true. This will ensure that the form is always displayed on top of the other forms on the screen.

Step 6: Place a Timer control on the form. Name the Timer tmrTimer, set its Interval property to 5000, and set its Enabled property to true.

Step 7: Double-click the `tmrTimer` control to insert a code template for its `Tick` event procedure. Complete the event procedure so it appears as the following code.

```
Private Sub tmrTimer_Tick(ByVal sender As System.Object, _
          ByVal e As System.EventArgs) Handles tmrTimer.Tick
   ' Close the form
   Me.Close()
End Sub
```

Step 8: Open the Project Properties Pages dialog box and select `frmMain` as the startup object. (Right-click the project's entry in the Solution Explorer window, then select Properties from the pop-up menu to display the dialog box.)

Step 9: You must write code in the `frmMain` form's `Load` event procedure that displays the splash screen. Double-click the `frmMain` form in the Design window to create a code template for the `Load` event procedure. Complete the event procedure by writing the following code shown in bold.

```
Private Sub frmMain_Load(ByVal sender As System.Object, _
          ByVal e As System.EventArgs) Handles MyBase.Load
   Dim splashForm As New frmSplashScreen()

   ' Display the splash screen
   splashForm.Show()
End Sub
```

Step 10: Save the project and run it. The splash screen should appear as shown in Figure 8-26.

Step 11: The Timer control should unload the splash screen form after five seconds have elapsed.

Step 12: On the main form, click the Exit button to end the application.

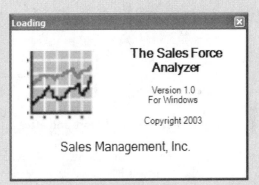

Figure 8-26 Splash screen

▶ 8.7   Focus on GUI Design: Anchoring and Docking Controls

CONCEPT

CONTROLS HAVE TWO PROPERTIES, ANCHOR AND DOCK, THAT ALLOW YOU TO CONTROL THE CONTROL'S POSITION ON THE FORM WHEN THE FORM IS RESIZED AT RUN TIME.

The Anchor Property

You may have noticed that when a control is placed on a form, and the user resizes the form at run time, the position of the control does not change with respect to the top and left edges of the form. For example, look at the form shown in Figure 8-27. The image on the left shows the form before the user has resized it and the image on the right shows the form after the user has resized it.

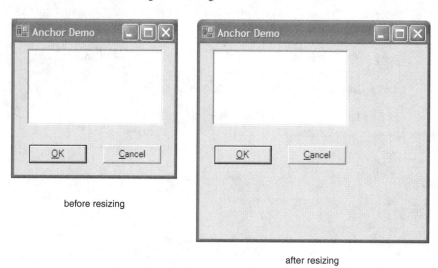

before resizing

after resizing

Figure 8-27   A form before and after the user resized it

Notice that after the user has resized the form, the positions of the list box and buttons did not change. Controls have an *Anchor property* which allows you to "anchor" the control to one or more edges of a form. When a control is anchored to a form's edge, the distance between the control's edge and the form's edge will remain constant, even when the user resizes the form.

When you click the Anchor property in the Properties window, the pop-up window shown in Figure 8-28 appears.

Notice that the top and left bars are selected. This indicates that the control is anchored to the top and left edges of the form, and is the Anchor property's default setting. To change the Anchor property's setting, simply select the bars that correspond to all the edges of the form that you wish to anchor the control to. For example, Figure 8-29 shows how the Anchor property will appear when the control is anchored to the bottom and right edges.

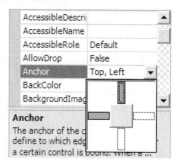

Figure 8-28   The Anchor property selected

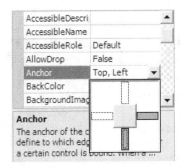

Figure 8-29 Anchor property set to the bottom and right edges

Figure 8-30 shows a form before and after it has been resized. This time, the button controls are anchored to the bottom and right edges and the list box is anchored to the top and left edges.

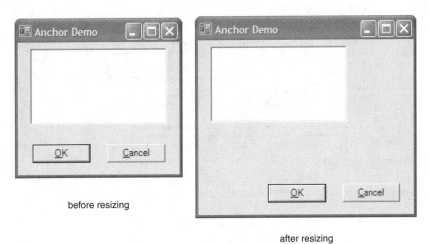

Figure 8-30 Buttons anchored to the bottom and right edges

It is possible to anchor a control to opposing sides, such the top and the bottom, or the left and the right. This will cause the control to be resized when the form is resized. For example, look at Figure 8-31. The PictureBox control is anchored to all four edges of the form, and its SizeMode property is set to StretchImage. When the form is resized, the PictureBox control is also resized.

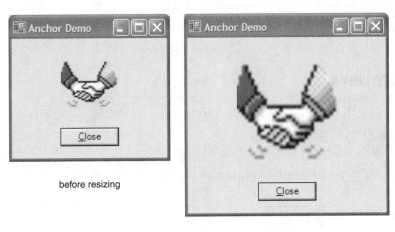

Figure 8-31 PictureBox control anchored to all four edges of the form

The Dock Property

When a control is docked, it is positioned directly against one of the edges of a form. Additionally, the length or width of a docked control is changed to match the length or width of the form's edge. For example, the form in Figure 8-32 has four docked buttons. A button is docked to each of the form's edges.

Notice that the buttons are automatically sized to fill up the edge that they are docked to. You use the *Dock property* to dock a control against a form's edge. When you select the Dock property in the Properties window, the pop-up window shown in Figure 8-33 appears. The figure illustrates how each button in the pop-up window affects the control.

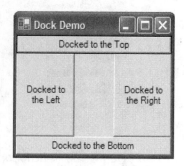

Figure 8-32 Form with docked buttons

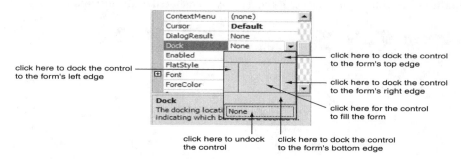

Figure 8-33 Dock property selected

Note that the square button in the center causes the control to fill the entire form.

✓ Checkpoint

8.21 A form has check box controls named `chkFreePizza` and `chkFreeCola`, and a radio button control named `radLifeTimeMember`. Write code that enables the check boxes if the radio button is selected.

8.22 If you want a Timer control to execute its `Tick` event procedure every half second, what value do you store in its Interval property?

8.23 How do you make sure that a form is always displayed on top of other forms?

8.24 What is the purpose of the Anchor property?

8.25 What is the purpose of the Dock property?

▶ 8.8 Random Numbers

CONCEPT

VISUAL BASIC .NET PROVIDES THE TOOLS TO GENERATE RANDOM NUMBERS AND INITIALIZE THE SEQUENCE OF RANDOM NUMBERS WITH A SEED VALUE.

Some applications, such as games and simulations, require the use of randomly generated numbers. Visual Basic .NET provides the intrinsic function Rnd, which returns a random number, and the Randomize statement, which initializes the sequence of numbers returned by the Rnd function.

Visual Basic .NET uses an algorithm to generate a sequence of random numbers. When the Rnd function is called, it returns a number from the sequence. The numbers that Visual Basic .NET generates in the sequence depend on a *seed* value. If Visual Basic .NET uses the same seed value each time it generates the sequence, it will always generate the same numbers. Therefore, you should make sure that Visual Basic .NET uses a new seed value each time your application uses a sequence of random numbers. The *Randomize statement* is used to accomplish this. Here is the Randomize statement's general format:

```
Randomize [Number]
```

The brackets indicate that the argument *Number* is optional. The argument is any number or numeric expression you wish to use as the seed value. If you omit the argument, Visual Basic .NET uses the system time returned from your computer's clock as the seed. Unless you want to generate the same sequence of random numbers each time you run your application, you should not provide an argument.

Once you have used the Randomize statement to initialize the sequence of random numbers, you can use the Rnd function to retrieve random numbers. The *Rnd function* returns a single precision random number between 0.0 and 1.0. The function's general format is:

```
Rnd [(Number)]
```

The argument, *Number* is shown in brackets, indicating that it is optional. In most cases, you will not provide an argument, but here is a description of how the argument affects the number returned by Rnd:

- If *Number* is less than 0, it is used as a seed to generate a new sequence of numbers.
- If *Number* is 0, Rnd returns the last random number generated.
- If *Number* is greater than 0, Rnd returns the next random number in the sequence.
- If *Number* is omitted, Rnd returns the next random number in the sequence.

For example, suppose the following statements are executed:

```
Randomize
x = Rnd
y = Rnd
z = Rnd
```

The Randomize statement initializes the sequence of random numbers using the system time. Then the Rnd function is called three times and its return values are stored in the variables x, y, and z. The numbers stored in x, y, and z will be single precision values between 0.0 and 1.0.

Generating Random Integers Within a Range

If you wish to generate a random integer between 1 and another number, use a statement in the following general format:

```
RandomNumber = 1 + Int(Rnd * UpperNumber)
```

This statement uses the intrinsic function Int. The Int function accepts a numeric argument and returns the integer portion of the argument. For instance, the function call Int(3.7) returns 3. *UpperNumber* is the upper limit of the range of random numbers. If you wish to generate a random number in the range 1 through 10, *UpperNumber* should be set to 10.

If you wish to generate a random integer within a range where the lower limit is something other than 1, use a statement in the following general format:

```
RandomNumber = Int(LowerNumber + Rnd * (UpperNumber - LowerNumber))
```

In the statement, *LowerNumber* is the lower limit of the range and *UpperNumber* is the upper limit of the range. For example, if you want to generate a random number in the range -10 through 10, *LowerNumber* should be set to -10 and *UpperNumber* should be set to 10.

Look at the following code as an example of random number use. When executed, it plays a number guessing game with the user, where the application generates a random number in the range of 1 through 10 and prompts the user to guess the number.

```
' Play a number guessing game.
Dim randomNum As Integer ' To hold the random number
Dim guess As Integer      ' To hold the user's guess

' Initialize the sequence of random numbers.
Randomize
' Generate a random number in the
' range 1 through 10.
randomNum = 1 + Int(Rnd * 10)
' Get the user's guesses.
MessageBox.Show("I am thinking of a number between 1 and 10. " & _
                "Can you guess what it is?")
Do
    guess = Val(InputBox("Enter your guess."))
    If guess = randomNum Then
        MessageBox.Show("You guessed it!")
    ElseIf guess > randomNum Then
        MessageBox.Show("That is too high. Guess again.")
    ElseIf guess < randomNum Then
        MessageBox.Show("That is too low. Guess again.")
    End If
Loop Until guess = randomNum
```

✓ Checkpoint

8.26 Describe the purpose of the `Randomize` statement.

8.27 What happens if the same seed value is used each time a sequence of random numbers is generated?

8.28 If you do not specify a seed value with the `Randomize` statement, what value does Visual Basic .NET use as the seed value?

8.29 Describe the random number returned by the `Rnd` function.

8.30 What is the purpose of the `Int` function?

8.31 Write a statement that assigns a random integer in the range of 1 through 100 to the variable `randomNumber`.

8.32 Write a statement that assigns a random integer in the range of 100 through 400 to the variable `randomNumber`.

▶ 8.9 Focus on Problem Solving: Building the Demetris Leadership Center Application

CONCEPT

IN THIS SECTION YOU BUILD AN APPLICATION THAT PROCESSES DATA STORED IN PARALLEL ARRAYS.

The Demetris Leadership Center (DLC) publishes the books, videos, and audiocassettes listed in Table 8-1.

Table 8-1

Demetris Leadership Center products

Product Title	Product Description	Product Number	Unit Price
Six Steps to Leadership	Book	914	$12.95
Six Steps to Leadership	Audiocassette	915	$14.95
The Road to Excellence	Video	916	$18.95
Seven Lessons of Quality	Book	917	$16.95
Seven Lessons of Quality	Audiocassette	918	$21.95
Seven Lessons of Quality	Video	919	$31.95
Teams are Made, not Born	Book	920	$14.95
Leadership for the Future	Book	921	$14.95
Leadership for the Future	Audiocassette	922	$16.95

The vice president of sales has asked you to write a sales-reporting program that

◆ Prompts the user for the units sold of each product.

◆ Displays a sales report showing detailed sales data for each product and the total revenue from all products sold.

The application will need a main form named `frmMain`, a splash screen form named `frm Splash`.

The `frmMain` Form

Figure 8-34 shows a sketch of `frm Main` with the form's controls labeled.

Table 8-2 lists each of the form's controls (excluding the menu controls) along with any relevant property setting.

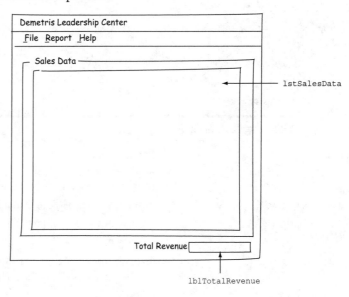

Figure 8-34 Sketch of `frmMain` form

Table 8-2

`frmMain` controls and property settings

Control Type	Control Name	Properties
Form	`frmMain`	Text: "Demetris Leadership Center"
GroupBox	(Default)	Text: "Sales Data"
Label	(Default)	Text: "Total Revenue"
Label	`lblTotalRevenue`	Text: " " BorderStyle: Fixed3D
MainMenu	(Default)	See Table 8-3 for details

Figure 8-35 shows a sketch of the menu system on `frmMain`. Table 8-3 lists the MenuItem object names, text, and shortcut keys.

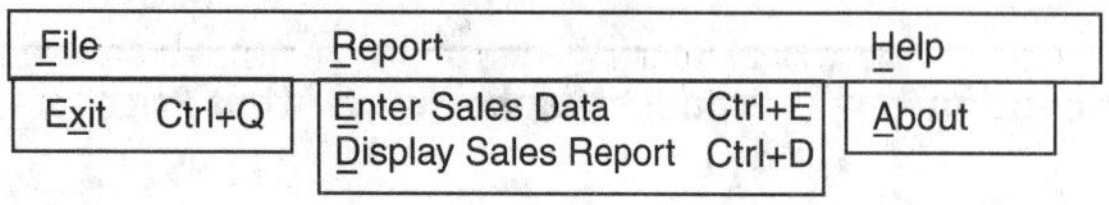

Figure 8-35   Menu system on `frmMain`

Table 8-3

`frmMain` MenuItem names, text, and shortcut keys

MenuItem Name	Text	Shortcut Key
`mnuFile`	&File	
`mnuFileExit`	E&xit	Ctrl+Q
`mnuReport`	&Report	
`mnuReportData`	&Enter Sales Data	Ctrl+E
`mnuReportDisplay`	&Display Sales Report	Ctrl+D
`mnuHelp`	&Help	
`mnuHelpAbout`	&About	

Table 8-4 describes the form's class -level declarations.

Table 8-4

Class-level declarations in `frmMain`

Name	Description
`maxSubscript`	A constant, which is set to 8. This constant is the upper subscript of the class-level arrays, and the upper limit of counters used in loops that process information in the arrays.
`prodNames`	An array of strings. This array holds the names of the DLC products.
`desc`	An array of strings. This array holds the descriptions of the DLC products.
`prodNums`	An array of integers. This array holds the product numbers of the DLC products.
`prices`	An array of Decimal variables. This array holds the prices of the DLC products.
`unitsSold`	An array of integers. This array holds the number of units sold for each of the DLC products.

The arrays `prodNames`, `desc`, `prodNums`, `prices`, and `unitsSold` are used as parallel arrays.

Table 8-5 lists and describes the methods in `frmMain`.

Table 8-5

frmMain methods

Method	Description
InitArrays	This Sub procedure copies the names, descriptions, product numbers, and unit prices of the DLC products to the class-level arrays.
mnuFileExit_Click	Ends the application.
mnuReportData_Click	Prompts the user for sales data.
mnuReportDisplay_Click	Calculates and displays the revenue for each product and the total revenue.
mnuHelpAbout_Click	Displays an About box.
Load	Displays the splash screen and calls the InitArrays Sub procedure.

The **frmSplash** Form

This application will display a splash screen from the main form's Load event procedure. Figure 8-36 shows a sketch of the splash screen form, `frmSplash`.

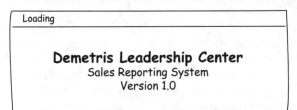

Loading

Demetris Leadership Center
Sales Reporting System
Version 1.0

Figure 8-36   frmSplash **form**

The splash screen will have a Timer control that will automatically close the form after five seconds. It will be displayed in modeless style. While it is on the screen, the `InitArrays` sub procedure will execute.

TUTORIAL 8-7:

Building the Demetris Leadership Center sales-reporting application

Step 1:   Start Visual Basic .NET and begin a new Windows application project named Demetris Sales.

Step 2:   Name the initial form `frmMain`. Set the form up as shown in Figure 8-37. Refer to Table 8-2 for the control names and their property settings, and to Figure 8-34 for the locations of the controls in the control arrays. Refer to Figure 8-35 for the menu layout, and to Table 8-3 for the MenuItem properties. Be sure to select `frmMain` as the startup object.

Figure 8-37 `frmMain`

Step 3: Write the following class-level declarations in the `frmMain` form's code.

```
' Class-level declarations
Const maxSubscript As Integer = 8       ' Array upper subscript
Dim prodNames(maxSubscript) As String   ' Product names
Dim desc(maxSubscript) As String        ' Descriptions
Dim prodNums(maxSubscript) As Integer   ' Product numbers
Dim prices(maxSubscript) As Decimal     ' Unit prices
Dim unitsSold(maxSubscript) As Integer  ' Units sold
```

Step 4: Write the following procedures in the `frmMain` form's code.

```
Private Sub frmMain_Load(ByVal sender As System.Object, _
        ByVal e As System.EventArgs) Handles MyBase.Load
    ' Create an instance of the splash screen.
    Dim splashForm As New frmSplash()
    ' Display the splash screen in modeless style.
    splashForm.Show()
    ' Initialize the arrays with product data.
    InitArrays()
End Sub

Sub InitArrays()
    ' Initialize the arrays.
    ' First product
    prodNames(0) = "Six Steps to Leadership"
    desc(0) = "Book"
    prodNums(0) = 914
    prices(0) = 12.95
```

```
                    ' Second product
                    prodNames(1) = "Six Steps to Leadership"
                    desc(1) = "Audiocassette"
                    prodNums(1) = 915
                    prices(1) = 14.95

                    ' Third product
                    prodNames(2) = "The Road to Excellence"
                    desc(2) = "Video"
                    prodNums(2) = 916
                    prices(2) = 18.95

                    ' Fourth product
                    prodNames(3) = "Seven Lessons of Quality"
                    desc(3) = "Book"
                    prodNums(3) = 917
                    prices(3) = 16.95

                    ' Fifth product
                    prodNames(4) = "Seven Lessons of Quality"
                    desc(4) = "Audiocassette"
                    prodNums(4) = 918
                    prices(4) = 21.95

                    ' Sixth product
                    prodNames(5) = "Seven Lessons of Quality"
                    desc(5) = "Video"
                    prodNums(5) = 919
                    prices(5) = 31.95

                    ' Seventh product
                    prodNames(6) = "Teams Are Made, Not Born"
                    desc(6) = "Book"
                    prodNums(6) = 920
                    prices(6) = 14.95

                    ' Eighth product
                    prodNames(7) = "Leadership for the Future"
                    desc(7) = "Book"
                    prodNums(7) = 921
                    prices(7) = 14.95

                    ' Ninth product
                    prodNames(8) = "Leadership for the Future"
                    desc(8) = "Audiocassette"
                    prodNums(8) = 922
                    prices(8) = 16.95
    End Sub

    Private Sub mnuFileExit_Click(ByVal sender As System.Object, _
            ByVal e As System.EventArgs) Handles mnuFileExit.Click
        ' End the application.
        End
    End Sub
```

```
Private Sub mnuReportData_Click(ByVal sender As System.Object, _
        ByVal e As System.EventArgs) Handles mnuReportData.Click
    ' Prompt the user for sales data.
    Dim count As Integer ' Loop counter

    ' Get unit sales for each product.
    For count = 0 To maxSubscript
        unitsSold(count) = Val(InputBox("Enter unit sold of " & _
                            "product number " & prodNums(count), _
                            "Enter Sales Data"))
    Next count
End Sub

Private Sub mnuReportDisplay_Click(ByVal sender As
System.Object, _
        ByVal e As System.EventArgs) Handles mnuReportDisplay.Click
    ' Calculates and displays the revenue for each
    ' product and the total revenue.
    Dim count As Integer ' Loop counter
    Dim revenue As Decimal
    Dim totalRevenue As Decimal

    ' Display the sales report header.
    lstSalesData.Items.Add("SALES REPORT")
    lstSalesData.Items.Add("--------------------")

    ' Display sales data for each product.
    For count = 0 To maxSubscript
        ' Calculate product revenue.
        revenue = unitsSold(count) * prices(count)
        ' Display the product data.
        lstSalesData.Items.Add("Product Number: " & _
            prodNums(count))
        lstSalesData.Items.Add("Name: " & prodNames(count))
        lstSalesData.Items.Add("Description: " & desc(count))
        lstSalesData.Items.Add("Unit Price: " & _
            FormatCurrency(prices(count)))
        lstSalesData.Items.Add("Units Sold: " & _
            unitsSold(count))
        lstSalesData.Items.Add("Product Revenue: " & _
            FormatCurrency(revenue))
        lstSalesData.Items.Add("")
        ' Accumulate revenue.
        totalRevenue = totalRevenue + revenue
    Next count
    ' Display total revenue.
    lblTotalRevenue.Text = FormatCurrency(totalRevenue, 2)
End Sub

Private Sub mnuHelpAbout_Click(ByVal sender As System.Object, _
        ByVal e As System.EventArgs) Handles mnuHelpAbout.Click
    ' Display an About box.
    MessageBox.Show("Displays a sales report for DLC.", "About")
End Sub
```

Step 5: Add the splash screen form to the project, and name the form `frm Splash`. Set the form's FormBorder-Style property to FixedToolWindow, and set its TopMost property to true. Set the form's Text property to "Loading". Select a light color for the form's BackColor property. The form should appear similar to Figure 8-38.

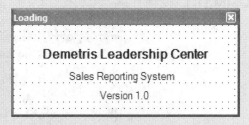

Figure 8-38   `frmSplash` form

Step 6: Add a Timer control named `tmrTimer` to the `frmSplash` form. Set the control's Interval property to 5000, and set its Enabled property to true.

Step 7: Write the following `Tick` event procedure for the `tmrTimer` control.

```
Private Sub tmrTimer_Tick(ByVal sender As System.Object, _
        ByVal e As System.EventArgs) Handles tmrTimer.Tick
    ' Close the splash screen
    Me.Close()
End Sub
```

Step 8: Save the project.

Step 9: Run the application. The splash screen should appear, then automatically close after five seconds.

Step 10: When the main form appears, click the Report menu, then click Enter Sales Data. You will be prompted with input boxes to enter the units sold for each of the DLC products. Enter the following values:

Product number 914:	**140**
Product number 915:	**85**
Product number 916:	**129**
Product number 917:	**67**
Product number 918:	**94**
Product number 919:	**142**
Product number 920:	**109**
Product number 921:	**65**
Product number 922:	**43**

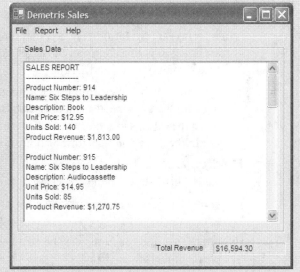

Figure 8-39   Main form completed

Step 11: Click the Report menu, then click Display Sales Report. Your form should now appear as Figure 8-39. Scroll through the sales data displayed in the list box.

Step 12: End the application.

SUMMARY

An array is a like group of variables with a single name. All of the variables within an array are called elements and are of the same data type.

You access the individual variables in an array through a subscript, which is a number that pinpoints a specific element within an array. Subscript numbering begins at zero. When you declare an array, you specify the upper subscript.

Visual Basic .NET allows you to implicitly size an array by omitting the upper subscript in the declaration statement and providing an initialization list. An array initialization list is a set of numbers enclosed in a set of braces, with the numbers separated by commas.

You process array elements the way you process regular variables, but when working with array elements, you must provide a subscript.

Visual Basic .NET allows you to store a subscript number in a variable, then use the variable as a subscript. This makes it possible to use a loop to cycle through an entire array, performing the same operation on each element.

Visual Basic .NET performs array bounds checking at run time. This means it does not allow a statement to use a subscript that is outside the range of subscripts for an array.

The `For Each...Next` loop is a special loop designed specifically to access values from arrays and array-like structures.

Arrays in Visual Basic .NET have a Length property that holds the number of elements in the array.

To sum the numbers stored in an array, you must use a loop with an accumulator variable to add all the elements. To average the numbers stored in an array, first sum all the values and then divide the sum by the total number of elements. This chapter also discusses algorithms to find the highest and lowest values in an array.

To copy the values in one array to another, use a loop to copy the individual elements.

Parallel arrays are two or more arrays that hold related data, and the related elements in each array are accessed with a common subscript. You can also create a parallel relationship between list boxes, combo boxes, and arrays.

The sequential search algorithm uses a loop to examine the elements in an array sequentially, starting with the first one. It compares each element with the value being searched for and stops when the value is found or the end of the array is encountered. If the value being searched for is not in the array, the algorithm will unsuccessfully search to the end of the array.

The `Array.Sort` method sorts the elements of an array in ascending order, which means the lowest value will be stored in the first element and the highest value will be stored in the last element.

Visual Basic .NET allows you to change the number of elements in an array at run time with the `ReDim` statement.

Sub procedures and functions may be written to accept arrays as arguments. Functions may also be written to return an array.

A single dimension array has one subscript, and is useful for storing and working with a single set of data. Two-dimensional arrays can hold multiple sets of values. It is best to think of a two-dimensional array as having rows and columns of elements.

To declare a two-dimensional array, two sets of upper subscripts are required, the first one for the rows and the second one for the columns. You may also implicitly size a two-dimensional array by omitting the upper subscripts from the declaration and providing an initialization list.

When data in a two-dimensional array is processed, each element has two subscripts, one for its row and one for its column.

You may use nested loops to sum the rows or columns of a two-dimensional numeric array.

You may use the `For Each...Next` loop to sum all the values in a numeric two-dimensional array.

Visual Basic .NET allows you to create arrays with with up to 32 dimensions.

When a control's Enabled property is set to false, it is considered disabled, which means it cannot receive the focus, cannot respond to events generated by the user, and appears dimmed or grayed out on the form.

The Timer control allows an application to automatically execute code at regularly timed intervals. The Timer control is invisible at run-time. At design time it appears in the component tray. The standard prefix for a Timer control's name is `tmr`.

The Timer control responds to `Tick` events. When a `Tick` event occurs, the `Tick` event procedure is executed.

When the Timer control's Enabled property is set to true, the Timer control responds to `Tick` events. When the Enabled property is set to false, the Timer control does not respond to `Tick` events and the code in the `Tick` event procedure does not execute.

The Timer control's Interval property can be set to a positive nonzero value that is the number of milliseconds to elapse between `Tick` events.

A splash screen is a form that is displayed while an application is loading. Splash screens usually show logos, and assure the user that a slowly loading application is in the process of starting up.

The Anchor property allows you to "anchor" a control to one or more edges of a form. When a control is anchored to a form's edge, the distance between the control's edge and the form's edge will remain constant, even when the user resizes the form.

You use the Dock property to dock a control against a form's edge. When a control is docked, it is positioned directly against one of the edges of a form. Additionally, the length or width of a docked control is changed to match the length or width of the form's edge.

The `Rnd` function returns a single precision random number between 0.0 and 1.0.

The `Randomize` statement initializes the sequence of random numbers returned by the `Rnd` function with a seed value.

Key Terms

Anchor property	ReDim statement
Array bounds checking	Rnd function
Ascending order	Seed value
Dock property	Sequential search
Element	Single dimension array
Enabled property	Splash screen
For Each...Next loop	Subscript
Index	Timer control
Interval property	TopMost property
Parallel arrays	Two-dimensional array
Randomize statement	Variable array

Review Questions

Fill-in-the-blank

1. You access the individual variables in an array through a(n)_____, which is a number that pinpoints a specific element within an array.

2. The _____ loop is a special loop designed specifically to access values from arrays and array-like structures.

3. _____ arrays are two or more arrays that hold related data, and the related elements in each array are accessed with a common subscript.

4. The _____ algorithm uses a loop to examine the elements in an array sequentially, starting with the first one

5. The _____ statement can be used to resize an array at run time.

6. The _____ property holds the number of elements in an array.

7. Declaring a two-dimensional array requires two sets of _____ .

8. When a control's _____ property is set to false, it is considered disabled.

9. The _____ property causes the distance between a control's edge and the form's edge to remain constant, even when the form is resized.

10. The _____ property causes a control to be positioned directly against one of the form's edges.

11. The _____ control allows an application to automatically execute code at regularly timed intervals.

12. The Timer control's _____ property specifies the number of milliseconds between timer events.

13. A(n) _____ is a window that is displayed while an application is loading.

14. The _____ value is used to initialize a sequence of random numbers.

15. The _____ function generates a random number.

Multiple Choice

1. All of the variables within an array are called

    a. Boxes

    b. Elements

    c. Subvariables

    d. Intersections

2. The number that identifies a specific element within an array is the
    a. Element specifier

    b. Determinator

    c. Locator

    d. Subscript

3. This is the lower subscript of an array.

    a. 1

    b. { }

    c. 0

    d. -1

4. Array bounds checking occurs at
   a. Run time
   b. Design time
   c. Break time
   d. All of the above

5. You can use this property to determine the number of elements in an array.
   a. Size
   b. Elements
   c. Length
   d. NumberElements

6. To access related data in a set of parallel arrays, access the elements in the arrays with
   a. The same array name
   b. The same subscript
   c. The index -1
   d. The `GetParallelData` function

7. Which statement resizes the numbers array to have 20 elements?
   a. `ReDim numbers(19)`
   b. `ReDim numbers(20)`
   c. `Resize numbers() To 19`
   d. `Resize numbers() To 20`

8. Which statement resizes the array `numbers` and does not erase the values already stored in the array?
   a. `ReDim numbers(99)`
   b. `ReDim Preserve numbers(99)`
   c. `Preserve numbers(99)`
   d. `ReSize Preserve numbers(99)`

9. An apt analogy for two-dimensional array elements is as
   a. Feet and inches
   b. Books and pages
   c. Lines and statements
   d. Rows and columns

10. Which statement disables the control `lblResult`?
    a. `lblResult.Disabled = True`
    b. `Disable lblResult`
    c. `blResult.Enabled = False`
    d. `lblResult.Dimmed = True`

11. The Timer control Interval property may be set to what type of value
    a. 0 or greater
    b. A fractional number
    c. A negative number
    d. 1 or greater

12. You can use this property to cause a control to fill an entire form.
    a. Fill
    b. Dock
    c. Anchor
    d. Stretch

13. What statement initializes the sequence of random numbers with a seed value?
    a. `InitRandom`
    b. `Rnd`
    c. `Seed`
    d. `Randomize`

14. This property causes a form to be displayed on top of all the other currently displayed forms.
    a. TopMost
    b. Top
    c. OnTop
    d. Front

True or False

Indicate whether each of the following statements is true or false.
1. T F: The upper subscript must be a positive whole number.
2. T F: Numeric array elements are automatically initialized to -1.
3. T F: You may not use a named constant as a subscript in an array declaration.
4. T F: Visual Basic .NET allows you to use a variable as a subscript when processing an array with a loop.
5. T F: You get an error message at design time when you write code that attempts to access an element outside the bounds of an array.
6. T F: The value stored in an array's Length property is the same as the array's upper subscript.
7. T F: You should use a loop to copy the values of one array to another array.
8. T F: Parallel arrays are useful when the related data is of unlike types.
9. T F: The `ReDim` statement may be used with any array.
10. T F: The value stored in the Timer control's Interval property specifies an interval in seconds.
11. T F: It is possible to anchor a control to a form's opposing edges.
12. T F: When a control is docked to a form's edge, the width or height of the control will be adjusted to match the size of the form's edge.

Short Answer

1. Write code that declares a string array with three elements, then stores your first, middle, and last names in the array's elements.

2. What values are displayed by the following code?

```
Dim values(4) As Integer
Dim count As Integer

For count = 0 To 4
```

```
     values(count) = count + 1
Next count

For count = 0 To 4
    MessageBox.Show(values(count).ToString)
Next count
```

3. The following code segment declares a 20-element array of integers called `fish`. When completed, the code should ask how many fish were caught by fishermen 1 through 20 and store this information in the array. Complete the program.

```
Private Sub btnFishCatchArray_Click()
    Dim fish(19) As Integer
    '
    ' You must finish this program. It should ask how
    ' many fish were caught by fisherman 1 - 20 and
    ' store this information in the array Fish.

End Sub
```

4. What is the output of the following code segment? (You may need to use a calculator.)

```
Const Rate As Single = 0.1
Dim balance(4) As Decimal
Dim due As Decimal
Dim count As Integer
balance(0) = 100
balance(1) = 250
balance(2) = 325
balance(3) = 500
balance(4) = 1100
For count = 0 To 4
    due = balance(count) * Rate
    MessageBox.Show(due.ToString)
Next count
```

5. Write a statement that assigns 145 to the first column of the first row of the array declared in the following statement.

```
Dim numberArray(9, 11) As Integer
```

6. Write a statement that assigns 18 to the last column of the last row of the array declared in the previous question.

7. An application uses a Timer control named `tmrClock`. Write a statement that stops the timer from responding to timer events.

8. Where does the `Randomize` statement get its seed value if you do not provide one?

What Do You Think?

1. The following code totals the values in two arrays: `numberArray1` and `numberArray2`. Both arrays have 25 elements. Will the code print the correct sum of values for both arrays? Why or why not?

```
Dim total As Integer = 0 ' Accumulator
For count = 0 To 24
    total += numberArray1(count)
Next count
MessageBox.Show("Total for numberArray1 is " & _
                total.ToString)
For count = 0 To 24
    total += numberArray2(count)
Next count
MessageBox.Show("Total for numberArray2 is " & _
                total.ToString)
```

2.   How many elements are in the following array?

```
Dim sales(5, 3) As Single
```

3.   How many elements are in the following array?

```
Dim values(3, 3) As Single
```

4.   If you are writing an application that must perform a lot of startup operations, would you choose to display the splash screen as a modal or modeless form? Why?

5.   An application uses a Timer control named `tmrControl`. Write a programming statement that sets the time between timer events at three seconds.

6.   Why is a computer's system time a good source of seed values?

Find the Errors

1.   `Dim readings(-1) As Integer`
2.   ```
Dim table(10) As Integer ' Stores 11 values
Dim i As Integer
Dim maxNum As Integer = 11
For i = 0 To maxNum
    table(i) = Val(InputBox("Enter the next value:"))
Next i
```
3.   `Dim values(3) = { 2, 4, 6 }`
4.   ```
' tmrTimer is a Timer control
tmrTimer.Interval = 0
```

Algorithm Workbench

1.   `names` is a string array with 20 elements. Write code with a `For Each...Next` loop that prints each element of the array.

2.   In an application you need to store the populations of 12 countries. Declare two arrays that may be used in parallel to store the names of the countries and their populations.

3.   Write a loop that uses the arrays you declared in question 3 to print each country's name and its population.

4.   The arrays `numberArray1` and `numberArray2` have 100 elements. Write code that copies the values in `numberArray1` to `numberArray2`.

5.   Write the code for a sequential search that determines whether the value -1 is stored in the array `values`. The code should print a message indicating whether the value was found.

6. An application has stores the following data about employees:

    Name, stored in a list box named `lstNames`.

    Employee number, stored in an array of strings named `empNums`.

    There is a parallel relationship between the list box and the array. Assume that the user has selected an employee's name from the list box. Write code that displays in a message box the employee number for the selected employee.

7. Declare a two-dimensional array of integers named `grades`. It should have 30 rows and 10 columns.

8. `values` is a two-dimensional array of single precision numbers with 10 rows and 20 columns. Write a `For Each`...`Next` loop that sums all the elements in the array and stores the sum in the variable `total`.

9. Write nested code using `For`...`Next` loops that performs the same operation asked for in question 8.

10. An application uses a two-dimensional array declared as follows. Write code that sums each row in the array and displays the result.

    ```
    Dim days(29, 5) As Integer
    ```

11. Write code that sums each column in the array in question 10.

12. Write code that uses a `For Each`...`Next` loop to sum all of the elements in the array in question 10.

13. Write a code that assigns a random integer in the range of 1 through 50 to the varibable `num`.

14. Write a code that assigns a random integer in the range of -100 through 500 to the varibable `num`.

PROGRAMMING CHALLENGES

1. Largest/Smallest Array Values

Create an application that lets the user enter 10 values into an array. The application should display the largest and smallest values stored in the array. Figure 8-40 shows an example of the application's form after all 10 values have been entered, with the largest and smallest values displayed.

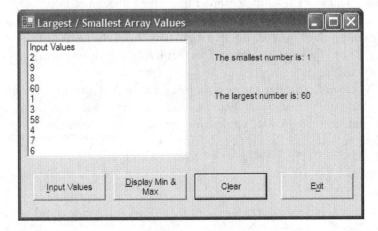

Figure 8-40 Largest/Smallest Array Values form

2. Rainfall Statistics

Create an application that lets the user enter the rainfall for each of the 12 months into an array. The application should calculate and display the following statistics: total rainfall for the year, the average monthly rainfall, and the months with the highest and lowest amounts of rainfall. Figure 8-41 shows an example of the application's form after each month's rainfall amount has been entered and the statistics have been displayed.

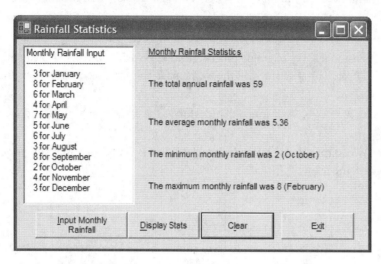

Figure 8-41   Rainfall Statistics form

3. Random Sentences

Create an application that will produce random sentences as output. Do so by using five arrays of strings, one each for nouns, adjectives, verbs, prepositions, and articles. Each array should hold several words of that part of speech. For example, the articles array could hold the words "the", "a", "some", "another", and "one"; the nouns array could hold "Martian", "baby", "skunk", "computer", and "mosquito"; the prepositions array could hold "around", "through", "under", "over" and "by"; and so forth.

The application should generate sentences by randomly choosing eight words (randomly generating eight array indices) from these arrays, always constructing sentences by using its parts of speech in the following order: article, adjective, noun, verb, preposition, article, adjective, noun.

For example, a sentence might be "The shiny computer flew over a huge mosquito." In this example, "The" and "a" were randomly chosen from the articles array, "shiny" and "huge" from the adjectives array, "computer" and "mosquito" from the nouns array, "flew" from the verbs array, and "over" from the prepositions array. Be careful to produce sentences that have the proper spacing, upper- and lowercase, and a period at the end.

Design your form with buttons to display the next sentence, to clear all sentences currently displayed, and to close the application. Display your sentences one per line in a list box. Allow enough room to display at least 10 sentences. Figure 8-42 shows an example of the form using a list box. The figure shows the form with three sentences already generated.

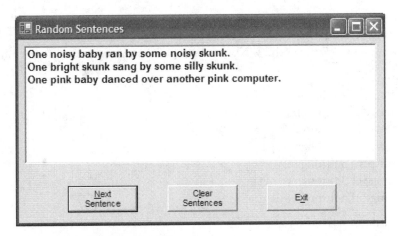

Figure 8-42   Random Sentences form

4. Driver's License Exam

The local Registry of Motor Vehicles office has asked you to create an application that grades the written portion of the driver's license exam. The exam has 20 multiple-choice questions. Here are the correct answers to the questions.

1. B	6. A	11. B	16. C
2. D	7. B	12. C	17. C
3. A	8. A	13. D	18. B
4. A	9. C	14. A	19. D
5. C	10. D	15. D	20. A

Your application should store the correct answers in an array. A form, such as the one shown in Figure 8-43, should allow the user to enter answers for each question.

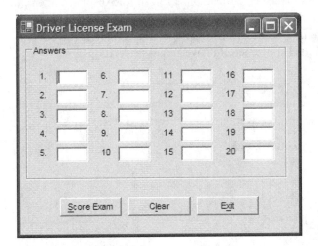

Figure 8-43   Driver's License Exam form

When the user clicks the Score Exam button, the application should display another form showing whether each question was answered correctly or incorrectly, and whether the student passed or failed the exam. A student must correctly answer 15 of the 20 questions to pass the exam.

Input validation: Only accept the letters A, B, C, or D as answers.

5. PIN Verifier

The National Commerce Bank has hired you to create an application that verifies a customer personal identification number (PIN). A valid PIN is a seven-digit number that meets the following specifications:

Digit 1: Must be in the range of 7 through 9
Digit 2: Must be in the range of 5 through 7
Digit 3: Must be in the range of 0 through 4
Digit 4: Must be in the range of 0 through 9
Digit 5: Must be in the range of 6 through 9
Digit 6: Must be in the range of 3 through 6
Digit 7: Must be in the range of 4 through 8

Notice that each digit must fall into a range of numbers. Your application should have two arrays: `minimum` and `maximum`. The `minimum` array should hold the minimum values for each digit, and the `maximum` array should hold the maximum values for each digit.

The application should allow the user to enter seven digits on a form similar to the one shown in Figure 8-44. When the verify button is clicked, the application should use the `minimum` and `maximum` arrays to verify that the numbers fall into acceptable ranges.

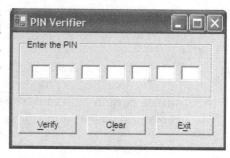

Figure 8-44 PIN Verifier form

Design Your Own Forms

6. Employee Directory

Create an employee directory application that shows employee names in a list box on the main form. When the user selects a name from the list box, the application should display that employee's ID number, department name, and telephone number on a separate form.

The application should store the employee ID numbers, department names, and telephone numbers in separate arrays. The arrays and the list box should have a parallel relationship.

7. Grade book

A teacher has five students who have taken four tests. The teacher uses the following grading scale to assign a letter grade to a student, based on the average of his or her four test scores.

Test Score	Letter Grade
90–100	A
80–89	B
70–79	C
60–69	D
0–59	F

Create an application that uses an array of strings to hold the five student names, an array of five strings to hold the five students' letter grades, and five arrays of four single precision numbers to hold each student's set of test scores.

Equip the application with a menu or a set of buttons that allows the application to perform the following:

♦ Display a form that allows the user to enter or change the student names and their test scores.

◆ Calculate and display each student's average test score and a letter grade based on the average.

The application should display a splash screen when it executes.

Input validation: Do not accept test scores less than zero or greater than 100.

8. Grade Book Modification

Modify the grade book application in Programming Challenge 7 so it drops each student's lowest score when determining the test score averages and letter grades.

9. Charge Account Validation

Create an application that allows the user to enter a charge account number. The application should determine whether the number is valid by comparing it to the numbers in the following list.

5658845	4520125	7895122	8777541	8451277	1302850
8080152	4562555	5552012	5050552	7825877	1250255
1005231	6545231	3852085	7576651	7881200	4581002

The list of numbers should be stored in an array. A sequential search should be used to locate the number entered by the user. If the user enters a number that is in the array, the program should display a message saying the number is valid. If the user enters a number that is not in the array, the program should display a message indicating the number is invalid.

10. Lottery Application

Create an application that simulates a lottery. The application should have an array of five integers and should generate a random number in the range of 0 through 9 for each element in the array. The user should then enter five digits that the application will compare to the numbers in the array. A form should be displayed showing how many of the digits matched. If all of the digits match, display a form proclaiming the user as a grand prize winner.

11. Soccer Team Score Application

A soccer team needs an application to record the number of points its players score during a game. Create an application that asks how many players the team has, and then asks for the names of each player. The program should size an array of strings so it is large enough to hold the player names, and size an array of integers to it is large enough to hold the number of points scored by each player. The application should have a menu system or buttons that perform the following:

◆ Display a form allowing the user to enter the players' names.

◆ Display a form that can be used during a game to record the points scored by each player.

◆ Display the total points scored by each player and by the team.

The application should display a splash screen when it executes.

Input validation: Do not accept negative numbers as points.

CHAPTER 9

Files, Printing, and Structures

▶ 9.1 Introduction

This chapter begins by discussing how to save data to sequential text files and then read the data back into an application. The chapter then shows you how to use the Open-FileDialog, SaveFileDialog, ColorDialog, and FontDialog controls to equip your application with standard Windows dialog boxes for opening and saving files and for selecting colors and fonts. Next we discuss the PrintDocument control and how to print reports from your application. Last, the chapter shows you how package units of data together into structures.

▶ 9.2 Using Files

CONCEPT

A FILE IS A COLLECTION OF DATA STORED ON A COMPUTER'S DISK. INFORMATION CAN BE SAVED TO FILES AND LATER REUSED.

The applications you have created so far require you to re-enter data each time the program runs. This is because the data kept in controls and variables is stored in RAM, and disappears once the program stops running. To retain data between the times it runs, an application must have a way of saving it.

Data is saved in a *file*, which is stored on a computer's disk. Once the data is saved in a file, it will remain there even after the program stops running, and can be retrieved and used at a later time. In this chapter you write applications that create their own files and save data there. These applications do not rely on the user re-entering data each time the application runs.

The Process of Using a File

There are always three steps that must be taken when a file is used by an application:

1. The file must be opened. If the file does not yet exist, opening it means creating it.

2. Data is either written to the file or read from the file.

3. When the application is finished using the file, the file is closed.

When a Visual Basic .NET application is actively working with data, the data is located in random-access memory, usually in variables and/or control properties. When data is written into a file, it is copied from the variables or control properties. Figure 9-1 illustrates this.

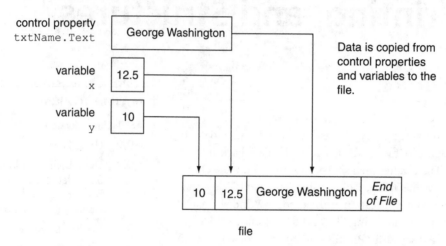

Figure 9-1   Writing data to a file

When data is read from a file, it is copied from the file into variables and/or control properties. Figure 9-2 illustrates this.

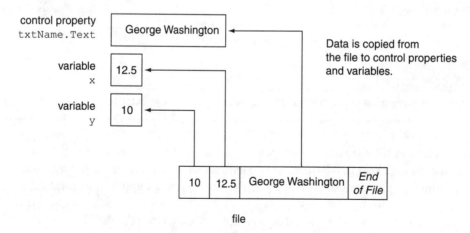

Figure 9-2   Reading data from a file

The terms input file and output file are often used. An *input file* is a file that a program reads data from. It is called an input file because the data stored in it serves as input to the program. An *output file* is a file that a program writes data to. It is called an output file because the program stores output in the file.

File Types and Access Methods

There are two types of files: text and binary. A *text file* contains plain text, and may be opened in a text editor such as Notepad. Data in *binary files* is stored as pure binary data, and you cannot view their contents with a text editor.

There are also two methods of accessing files: sequential-access and random-access. A *sequential-access file* is like a stream of data that must be read from its beginning to its end. To read an item that is stored in the middle or at the end of a sequential-access file, an application must read all the items in the file before it.

Data in a *random-access file* may be accessed in any order. An application may immediately jump to any item in a random-access file without first reading the preceding items. The difference between sequential-access and random-access files is like the difference between a cassette tape and a CD. When listening to a CD, you don't need to listen to or fast-forward over unwanted songs. You simply jump to the track that you want to listen to.

Because most Visual Basic .NET programmers prefer to use databases instead of random-access or binary files, we only discuss sequential-access text files in this chapter. Binary and random-access files are discussed in Appendix C.

Writing to Files with `StreamWriter` Objects

In order to write data to a sequential text file, you use a *StreamWriter object*. A `StreamWriter` object is an instance of the *StreamWriter class*. This class provides the methods necessary for writing data to a sequential file.

Creating a `StreamWriter` Object and Opening a File

The steps necessary to create and use a `StreamWriter` object are:

1. Declare an object variable.
2. Open a file and create a `StreamWriter` object to access the file. Store the `StreamWriter` object's memory address in the object variable you created in step 1.

To declare an object variable that you can use to reference a `StreamWriter` object, use a `Dim` statement in the following general format:

```
Dim ObjectVar As System.IO.StreamWriter
```

`ObjectVar` is the name of the object variable. As with other variables, you may use the `Private` or `Public` access specifier if you are declaring the object variable at the class-level or module-level.

Next you must create an instance of the `StreamWriter` object and store its address in the object variable. Visual Basic .NET provides two different methods for doing this: `System.IO.File.CreateText` and `System.IO.File.AppendText`. Here is the general format of the `System.IO.File.CreateText` method.

```
System.IO.File.CreateText(Filename)
```

`Filename` is a string or a string variable specifying the name of the file on the disk, such as "Customers.dat". The name can include the path to the file as well. For example, in the filename "A:\Customers.dat", the A: specifies that the file is located in drive A:. This method creates the file specified by

Filename and returns the address of a `StreamWriter` object that may be used to write data to the file. If the file already exists when this method executes, its contents are erased.

Here is the general format of the `System.IO.File.AppendText` method.

```
System.IO.File.AppendText(Filename)
```

Once again, *Filename* is a string or a string variable specifying the name of the file on the disk, including optional path information. This method creates the file specified by *Filename* and returns the address of a `StreamWriter` object that may be used to write data to the file. If the file already exists when this method executes, data written to the file will be appended to the end of the existing data. If the file does not already exist, it will be created.

Let's study some examples of how these methods are used. Look at the following code.

```
Dim phoneFile As System.IO.StreamWriter
phoneFile = System.IO.File.CreateText("phonelist.txt")
```

The first statement creates an object variable named `phoneFile`. The second statement creates a file named phonelist.txt. If the file already exists, its contents will be erased. The address of a `Stream Writer` object is assigned to the `phoneFile` variable, which is then ready to be used to write data to the file.

Another example follows. This code stores the file name in a variable and uses the `System.IO.File.AppendText` method.

```
Dim customerFile As System.IO.StreamWriter
Dim filename As String = "customers.txt"
customerFile = System.IO.File.AppendText(filename)
```

This code declares an object variable named `customerFile` and opens a file named customers.txt. If the file does not exist, it is created. If the file already exists, it is opened and data that is written to the file will be appended to the existing data. The address of a `StreamWriter` object is assigned to the `customerFile` variable, which is then ready to be used to write data to the file.

File Locations

When you open a file you may specify its path along with its filename. For example, "A:\names.txt" specifies that names.txt is in the root folder of a floppy disk in drive A:, and "C:\MyData\Data.txt" specifies that Data.txt is in the \MyData folder on drive C:. In the following code segment, the file pricelist.txt is created in the root folder of drive A:.

```
Dim priceFile As System.IO.StreamWriter
priceFile = System.IO.File.CreateText("A:\pricelist.txt")
```

In the following code, the file memo.txt is created in the C:\WordProc folder.

```
Dim memoFile As System.IO.StreamWriter
memoFile = System.IO.File.CreateText("C:\WordProc\memo.txt")
```

These examples specify not only the file's name, but the file's location as well. If you specify only a file name, however, such "phonelist.txt" or "customers.txt", Visual Basic .NET will assume the file's location to be the same folder from which the application is running. Normally this is a folder named bin, which is located under the folder that contains the application's project files.

For example, Sherry uses a computer running Windows XP, and she logs into her computer with the user name Sherry. She has created a Visual Basic .NET application in the following folder on her hard drive:

C:\Documents and Settings\Sherry\My Documents\Assignment12

Her application uses the following code to create a file:

```
Dim textFile As System.IO.StreamWriter
textFile = System.IO.File.CreateText("mytext.txt")
```

Because she did not specify a path for the file, the file will be created in the project's bin folder, which is at the following location:

C:\Documents and Settings\Sherry\My Documents\Assignment12\bin

WARNING:

 It is possible to move an application's executable file to a location other than the project's bin directory. This will also change the default location in which files are created.

Writing Data to a File

The *WriteLine method* is a member of the `StreamWriter` class, and is used to write a "line" of data to a file. Here is the general format of the method.

```
ObjectVar.WriteLine(Data)
```

ObjectVar is the name of a `StreamWriter` object variable. *Data* is the data that is to be written to the file. *Data* can be a constant or the name of a variable. The method writes the data to the file and then writes a newline character immediately after the data. A *newline character* is an invisible character[*] that separates text by breaking it into another line when displayed on the screen.

To further understand how the method works, let's look at an example. Assume an application opens a file and writes three students' first names and their scores to the file with the following code.

```
Dim studentFile As System.IO.StreamWriter
studentFile = System.IO.File.CreateText("StudentData.txt")
studentFile.WriteLine("Jim")
studentFile.WriteLine(95)
studentFile.WriteLine("Karen")
studentFile.WriteLine(98)
studentFile.WriteLine("Bob")
studentFile.WriteLine(82)
```

You can visualize the data being written to the file in the following manner:

Jim<*Newline*>95<*Newline*>Karen<*Newline*>98<*Newline*>Bob<*Newline*>82<*Newline*>

The newline characters are represented here as <*Newline*>. You do not actually see the newline characters, but when the file is opened in a text editor such as Notepad, its contents will appear as

---

[*] The newline character is actually stored as two characters: a carriage return (character code 13) and a linefeed character (character code 10).

shown in Figure 9-3. As you can see from the figure, each newline character causes the data that follows it to be displayed on a new line.

TIP: Each time the `WriteLine` method executes, it creates a line in the file. This is why it is named `"WriteLine"`.

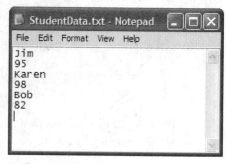

Figure 9-3   File contents displayed in Notepad

In addition to separating the contents of a file into lines, the newline character also serves as a delimiter. A *delimiter* is an item that separates other items. When you write data to a file using the `WriteLine` method, newline characters will separate the individual items of data. Later you will see that the data must be separated in order for it to be read from the file.

Writing a Blank Line to a File

The `WriteLine` method can be used to write a blank line to a file. Simply call the method without an argument, as shown in the following example:

```
textFile.WriteLine()
```

Closing a File

The opposite of opening a file is closing it. The `StreamWriter` class has a method named `Close` that closes a file. Here is the method's general format.

```
ObjectVar.Close()
```

`ObjectVar` is the name of a `StreamWriter` object variable. After the method executes, the file was opened with `ObjectVar` is closed. For example, `salesFile` is an object variable that references a `StreamWriter` object. The following statement closes the file associated with `salesFile`.

```
salesFile.Close()
```

Your application should always close files when finished with them. This is because Visual Basic .NET creates one or more buffers when a file is opened. A *buffer* is a small "holding section" of memory. When an application writes data to a file, that data is first written to the buffer. When the buffer is filled, all the information stored there is written to the file. This technique increases the system's performance because writing data to memory is faster than writing it to a disk. The `Close` method writes any unsaved information remaining in the file buffer and releases the memory that was allocated by the `StreamWriter` object.

NOTE: *Once a file is closed, you must reopen it to perform operations on it.*

In Tutorial 9-1 you examine an application that writes data about three of your friends to a file.

TUTORIAL 9-1:

Examining an application that writes data to a file

Step 1: Start Visual Basic .NET and open the File WriteLine demo project which is stored in the \Chap9\File WriteLine Demo folder. The application form is shown in Figure 9-4.

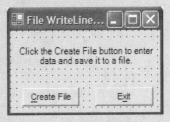

Step 2: Open the Code window and look at the btnCreateFile_Click event procedure. The code is as follows.

Figure 9-4   File Write Line Demo form

```
Private Sub btnCreateFile_Click(ByVal sender As System.Object, _
        ByVal e As System.EventArgs) Handles btnCreateFile.Click
    ' This procedure prompts the user for data and
    ' saves it to a file.
    Dim filename As String     ' File name
    Dim friendName As String   ' To hold a name
    Dim age As Integer         ' To hold an age
    Dim address As String      ' To hold an address
    Dim count As Integer       ' Loop counter
    Dim friendFile As System.IO.StreamWriter   ' Object variable

    ' Get the file name from the user.
    filename = InputBox("Enter the filename.", "Filename Needed")
    ' Open the file.
    friendFile = System.IO.File.CreateText(filename)
    ' Get the data for three friends and write it
    ' to the file.
    For count = 1 To 3
        ' Get the data.
        MessageBox.Show("Get ready to enter data for friend " & _
                count.ToString)
        friendName = InputBox("Enter your friend's name.")
        age = Val(InputBox("Enter your friend's age."))
        address = InputBox("Enter your friend's address.")
        ' Write the data to the file.
        friendFile.WriteLine(friendName)
        friendFile.WriteLine(age)
        friendFile.WriteLine(address)
    Next
    ' Close the file.
    friendFile.Close()
End Sub
```

This procedure asks the user to enter a name for the file that will be created. The name is stored in the filename variable, and used in the following statement, which opens the file.

```
friendFile = System.IO.File.CreateText(filename)
```

The `For...Next` loop performs three iterations, each time prompting the user to enter the name, age, and address of a friend. The user's input is stored in the variables `friendName`, `age`, and `address`. Once the data is entered, it is written to the file with the following statements.

```
friendFile.WriteLine(friendName)
friendFile.WriteLine(age)
friendFile.WriteLine(address)
```

The file is then closed.

Step 3: Run the application and click the Create File button. You are prompted to enter the filename. When you enter the filename, you must provide the path of a disk location that can be written to. For example, **A:\MyFriends.txt** will create the file MyFriends.txt on a floppy disk in drive A. **C:\Temp\MyFriends.txt** will create the file MyFriends.txt in the C:\Temp folder. Enter a path and filename and make a note of it because you will use the same file later in this tutorial and again in Tutorial 9-2.

NOTE: *If you are working in a school computer lab, you may be restricted to saving files only to certain disk locations. Ask your instructor or lab manager for these locations.*

Step 4: Enter the following names, ages, and addresses as you are prompted for this data. After you have entered the data for the third friend, the application returns to the main form. Click the Exit button.

	Name	**Age**	**Address**
Friend 1	Jim Weaver	30	P. O. Box 124
Friend 2	Mary Duncan	24	47 Elm Street
Friend 3	Karen Warren	28	24 Love Lane

Step 5: In Windows, open the Notepad text editor.

TIP: If you cannot find Notepad on your system, click the Windows Start button, then click Run. In the Run dialog box, type **Notepad.exe** and click the OK button.

In Notepad, open the file you created in step 3. (Click File, then click Open. In the Open dialog box type the path and filename you used in step 3 in the file name text box. Click the Open button.) The contents of the file should appear as shown in Figure 9-5.

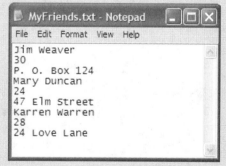

Figure 9-5 Contents of the file displayed in Notepad

As you can see, each record is written to a separate line in the file. This is because a newline character separates each record.

Step 6: Close Notepad.

Appending to a File

Appending to a file means to write new data to the end of the data that already exists in the file. When an existing file is opened with the `System.IO.File.AppendText` method, any data that is written to the file will be appended to the file's existing data. If the file does not exist, it is created. For example, assume the file A:\MyFriends.txt exists and contains the following data, from the previous tutorial.

Jim Weaver
30
P. O. Box 124
Mary Duncan
24
47 Elm Street
Karen Warren
28
24 Love Lane

The following code opens the file in append mode and writes additional data to the file.

```
' Declare an object variable
Dim friendFile As System.IO.StreamWriter
' Open the file.
friendFile = System.IO.File.AppendText("A:\MyFriends.txt")
' Write the data.
friendFile.WriteLine("Bill Johnson")
friendFile.WriteLine(30)
friendFile.WriteLine("36 Oak Street")
' Close the file.
friendFile.Close()
```

After this code executes, the MyFriends.txt file will contain the following data.

Jim Weaver
30
P. O. Box 124
Mary Duncan
24
47 Elm Street
Karen Warren
28
24 Love Lane
Bill Johnson
30
36 Oak Street

The `Write` Method

The *Write method* is also a member of the `StreamWriter` class, and is used to write an item of data to a file without writing the newline character. Here is the general format of the method.

```
ObjectVar.Write(Data)
```

ObjectVar is the name of a StreamWriter object variable. *Data* is the data that is to be written to the file. *Data* can be a constant or the name of a variable. This method can be used to write data to a file without terminating the line with a newline character. For example, assume an application has a StreamWriter object variable named outputFile, as well as the following variables.

```
Dim name As String = "Jeffrey Smith"
Dim idNum As Integer = 47895
Dim phone As String = "555-7864"
```

The contents of all three variables may be written to a single line in the file with the following code.

```
outputFile.Write(name)
outputFile.Write(" ")
outputFile.Write(idNum)
outputFile.Write(" ")
outputFile.WriteLine(phone)
```

The first statement writes the name variable to the file. The second statement writes a space character (" "). The third statement writes the idNum variable, and the fourth statement writes another space. The last statement uses the WriteLine method to write the phone variable, followed by a newline character. This code will write the following line to the file:

```
Jeffrey Smith 47895 555-7864
```

Reading Files with StreamReader Objects

To read data from a sequential text file, you use a *StreamReader object*. A StreamReader object is an instance of the *StreamReader class*, which provides methods for reading data from a file. The process of creating a StreamReader object is similar to that of creating a StreamWriter object, which we discussed in the previous section. First, you declare an object variable with a declaration statement in the following general format.

```
Dim ObjectVar As System.IO.StreamReader
```

ObjectVar is the name of the object variable. As with other variables, you may use the Private or Public access specifier if you are declaring the object variable at the class level or module level.

Now you must create an instance of the StreamReader object and store its address in the object variable with the *System.IO.File.OpenText method*. The method's general format is:

```
System.IO.File.OpenText(Filename)
```

Filename is a string or a string variable specifying the path and/or name of the file to open. This method opens the file specified by *Filename* and returns the address of a StreamReader object that may be used to write data to the file. If the file does not exist, a run-time error occurs.

The following code shows an example of how to use these statements.

```
Dim customerFile As System.IO.StreamReader
customerFile = System.IO.File.OpenText("customers.txt")
```

The first statement creates an object variable named `customerFile`. The second statement opens the file customers.txt and returns the address of a `StreamReader` object that may be used to read data from the file. The address of the `StreamReader` object is assigned to the `customerFile` variable.

Reading Data From a File

The *`ReadLine` method* is a member of the `StreamReader` class, and is used to read a "line" of data to a file. Here is the general format of the method.

```
ObjectVar.ReadLine()
```

`ObjectVar` is the name of a `StreamReader` object variable. The method reads a line from the file associated with *`ObjectVar`* and returns the data that was read as a string. For example, assume that `customerFile` is a `StreamReader` object variable and `customerName` is a string variable. The following statement reads a line from the file and stores it in the `customerName` variable.

```
customerName = customerFile.ReadLine()
```

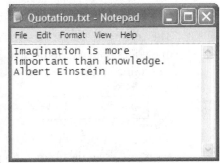

Data is read from a sequential file's beginning to its end. When the file is opened, its *read position*, which is the position of the next item to be read, is set to the first item in the file. As data is read, the read position advances through the file. For example, consider the file, Quotation.txt, shown in Figure 9-6. As you can see from the figure, the file has three lines.

Quotation.txt - Notepad
File Edit Format View Help
Imagination is more
important than knowledge.
Albert Einstein

Figure 9-6 Text file with three lines

Suppose an application opens the file with the following code.

```
Dim textFile As System.IO.StreamReader
textFile = System.IO.File.OpenText("Quotation.txt")
```

When this code opens the file, its read position is at the beginning of the first line, as illustrated in Figure 9-7.

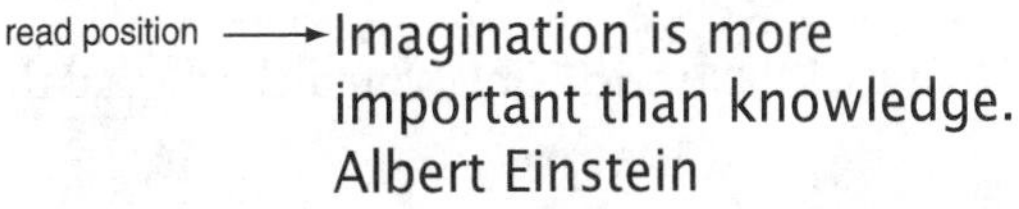

read position
Imagination is more
important than knowledge.
Albert Einstein

Figure 9-7 Initial read position

Now, suppose the application uses the following statement to read a line from the file. In the statement, assume that `input` is a string variable.

```
input = textFile.ReadLine()
```

This statement will read a line from the file, beginning at the current read position. After the statement executes, the input variable will contain the string "Imagination is more". The file's read position will be advanced to the next line, as illustrated in Figure 9-8.

read position ⟶ Imagination is more
important than knowledge.
Albert Einstein

Figure 9-8   Read position after first line is read

If the ReadLine method is called again, the second line will be read from the file and the file's read position will be advanced to the third line. After all the lines have been read, the read position will be at the end of the file.

Closing the File

You close files that are opened with a StreamReader object with the Close method. The general format is:

```
ObjectVar.Close()
```

Determining Whether a File Exists

The System.IO.File.OpenText method will cause a run-time error if the file it is trying to open does not exist. To prevent an error, you should use the *System.IO.File.Exists method* to determine whether a file exists before you attempt to open it. The general format of the method is:

```
System.IO.File.Exists(Filename)
```

Filename is the name of a file, which may include the path. The method returns true if the file exists, or false if the file does not exist. The following code shows an example of how to use the method to determine if a file exists prior to trying to open the file.

```
If System.IO.File.Exists(filename) Then
        ' Open the file.
    inputFile = System.IO.File.OpenText(filename)
Else
    MessageBox.Show(filename & " does not exist.")
End If
```

In Tutorial 9-2 you examine an application that uses the ReadLine statement to read the file you created in Tutorial 9-1.

TUTORIAL 9-2:

Examining an application that reads a file

Step 1:   Start Visual Basic .NET and open the File ReadLine Demo project, which is stored in the \Chap9\File ReadLine Demo folder. Run the application. The form is shown in Figure 9-9.

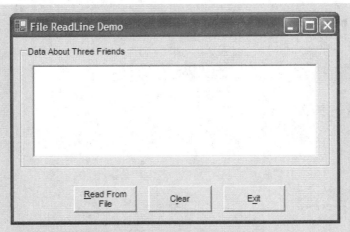

Figure 9-9   File ReadLine Demo form

Step 2:   Click the Read From File button. An input box will appear asking for the filename. Enter the path and filename that you used to create the file in step 3 of Tutorial 9-1. When you click the OK button on the input box, the data is read from the file and displayed in the list box, as shown in Figure 9-10. If you did not type the path and filename exactly as you did in Tutorial 9-1, you will see a message box indicating the file was not found. In that case, click the Read From File button again, this time entering the correct path and filename.

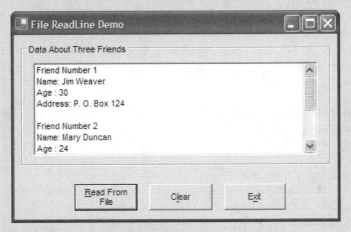

Figure 9-10   File ReadLine Demo form completed

Step 3:   Click the Exit button to end the application.

Step 4:   Open the Code window and look at the `btnRead_Click` event procedure. Notice that the following `If` statement is used to determine whether the file exists before an attempt is made to open it.

```
If System.IO.File.Exists(filename) Then
```

Inside the `If` statement, a `For...Next` loop performs three iterations, each time reading a line from the file. The lines are read into the `friendName`, `age`, and `address` variables, then added to the list box.

```
        For count = 1 To 3
           ' Read a record from the file.
           friendName = friendFile.ReadLine()
           age = Val(friendFile.ReadLine())
           address = friendFile.ReadLine()
           ' Display the data in the list box.
           lstFriends.Items.Add("Friend Number " & count.ToString)
           lstFriends.Items.Add("Name: " & friendName)
           lstFriends.Items.Add("Age : " & age.ToString)
           lstFriends.Items.Add("Address: " & address)
           lstFriends.Items.Add("") ' Add a blank line
        Next count
```

Detecting the End of a File

The File ReadLine Demo application in Tutorial 9-2 is written to read three records from the file because it is known that exactly three records are stored in the file. In many cases, however, the amount of data in a file is unknown. When this is the case, you use the *Peek method* to determine when the end of the file has been reached. The general format of the Peek method is:

```
ObjectVar.Peek
```

ObjectVar is an object variable referencing a StreamReader object. This method looks ahead in the file, without moving the current read position, and returns the very next character that will be read. If the current read position is at the end of the file (where there are no more characters to read), the method returns -1. Here is an example of a Do While loop that uses the Peek method to determine when the end of the Scores.txt file has been reached. The loop reads all the lines from the file and adds them to the lstResults list box.

```
Dim scoresFile As System.IO.StreamReader    ' Object variable
Dim input As String
scoresFile = System.IO.File.OpenText("Scores.txt")

Do Until scoresFile.Peek = -1
   input = scoresFile.ReadLine()
   lstResults.Items.Add(input)
Loop
scoresFile.Close()
```

TUTORIAL 9-3:

Examining an application that detects the end of a file

Step 1: Start Visual Basic .NET and open the File Demo project, which is stored in the \Chap9\File Demo folder on the student disk. Run the application. The form is shown in Figure 9-11.

Figure 9-11   File Demo form

Step 2:   Click the Create File button. An input box appears asking you "How many numbers do you want to enter?" Enter **5** and press Enter.

Step 3:   Because you indicated you want to enter five numbers, the application will prompt you five times with an input box to enter a number. Enter the following numbers: **2, 4, 6, 8,** and **10**. The application writes these numbers to a file.

Step 4:   After you have entered the last number, click the Read File button. The application reads the numbers from the file and prints them on the form as shown in Figure 9-12.

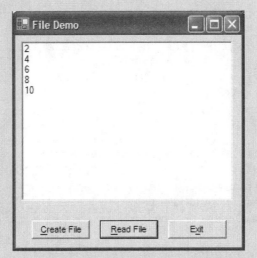

Figure 9-12   File Demo form with numbers displayed

Step 5:   Click the Exit button to end the application.

Step 6:   Open the Code window and look at the `btnCreate_Click` event procedure. The code is as follows.

```
Private Sub btnCreate_Click(ByVal sender As System.Object, _
        ByVal e As System.EventArgs) Handles btnCreate.Click
    ' This procedure creates the file and stores
    ' the numbers entered by the user.
    Dim outputFile As System.IO.StreamWriter ' Object variable
    Dim maxNumbers As Integer    ' The number of values
    Dim count As Integer         ' Loop counter
    Dim filename As String       ' The filename
    Dim number As Integer        ' User input
    ' Get the number of numbers from the user.
    maxNumbers = Val(InputBox("How many numbers do you " & _
            "want to enter?"))
    ' Create the file.
    outputFile = System.IO.File.CreateText("Numbers.txt")
    ' Get the numbers and write them to the file.
    For count = 1 To maxNumbers
        number = Val(InputBox("Enter a number."))
        outputFile.WriteLine(number)
    Next count
    ' Close the file.
    outputFile.Close()
End Sub
```

First the user is asked how many numbers he or she wants to enter. This value is stored in maxNumbers. Next, the file is created and a loop prompts the user to enter a series of numbers, writing each one to the file. After the loop completes its iterations, the file is closed.

Step 7: Now look at the btnRead_Click event procedure. The code is as follows.

```
Private Sub btnRead_Click(ByVal sender As System.Object, _
        ByVal e As System.EventArgs) Handles btnRead.Click
    ' This procedure opens the file, reads all the values
    ' from the file, and adds them to the list box.
    Dim inputFile As System.IO.StreamReader ' Object variable
    Dim count As Integer         ' Loop counter
    Dim filename As String       ' The filename
    Dim number As Integer        ' User input

    If System.IO.File.Exists("Numbers.txt") Then
        inputFile = System.IO.File.OpenText("Numbers.txt")
        lstOutput.Items.Clear()
        Do Until inputFile.Peek = -1
            lstOutput.Items.Add(inputFile.ReadLine)
        Loop
        inputFile.Close()
    Else
        MessageBox.Show("File not found.", "Error")
    End If
End Sub
```

This procedure uses the `System.IO.File.Exists` method to determine that the Numbers.txt file exists. If so, the file is opened, the list box is cleared, and the following loop is executed:

```
Do Until inputFile.Peek = -1
        lstOutput.Items.Add(inputFile.ReadLine)
Loop
```

This loop repeats until the `Peek` method returns -1, indicating that the end of the file has been reached. In each iteration, a line is read from the file and added to the list box. Because the loop repeats until the end of the file is reached, it can read any number of items from the file.

Other *StreamReader* Methods

The `StreamReader` class also provides the `Read` and `ReadToEnd` methods, which we will briefly discuss. The general format of the `Read` method is:

```
ObjectVar.Read
```

ObjectVar is the name of a `StreamReader` object variable. The *Read method* reads only the next character from a file and returns the character code for that character. To convert the character code to a character, use the *Chr function*, as shown in the following code.

```
Dim textFile As System.IO.StreamReader
Dim input As String = ""

textFile = System.IO.File.OpenText("names.txt")
Do While textFile.Peek <> -1
   input &= Chr(textFile.Read)
Loop
textFile.Close()
```

This code opens the file names.txt. The `Do While` loop, which repeats until it reaches the end of the file, executes the following statement:

```
input &= Chr(textFile.Read)
```

This statement gets the character code for the next character in the file, converts it to a character with the `Chr` function, and concatenates that character to the string variable `input`. When the loop has finished, the string variable `input` will contain the entire contents of the file names.txt.

The general format of the `ReadToEnd` method is:

```
ObjectVar.ReadToEnd
```

ObjectVar is the name of a `StreamReader` object variable. The *ReadToEnd method* reads and returns the entire contents of a file, beginning at the current read position. Here is an example.

```
Dim textFile As System.IO.StreamReader
Dim input As String
```

```
textFile = System.IO.File.OpenText("names.txt")
input = textFile.ReadToEnd
textFile.Close()
```

The statement `input = textFile.ReadToEnd` reads all of the file's contents and stores it in the variable `input`.

Working with Arrays and Files

Saving the contents of an array to a file is a straightforward procedure: Use a loop to step through each element of the array, writing its contents to the file. For example, assume an application has the following array declaration:

```
Dim values(9) As Integer
```

The following code opens a file named Values.txt and writes the contents of each element of the values array to the file.

```
Dim outputFile as System.IO.StreamWriter
outputFile = System.IO.File.CreateText("values.txt")
For count = 0 To (values.Length - 1)
    outputFile.WriteLine(values(count))
Next count
outputFile.Close()
```

Reading the contents of a file into an array is equally straightforward. The following code opens the Values.txt file and reads its contents into the elements of the values array.

```
Dim inputFile as System.IO.StreamReader
inputFile = System.IO.File.OpenText("values.txt")
For count = 0 To (values.Length - 1)
    values(count) = Val(inputFile.ReadLine)
Next count
inputFile.Close()
```

NOTE: *This code segment does not check for the end of the file, therefore it assumes that there are enough values in the file to fill the array.*

If You Want to Know More: Using the **Imports** *Statement*

.NET classes such as `StreamWriter` and `StreamReader`, are organized in program structures known as namespaces. A *namespace* serves as a container for declarations.

For example, one of the .NET namespaces is `System.IO`. The `System.IO` namespace contains classes for reading and writing data to and from files. The `StreamWriter` and `StreamReader` classes are both declared in the `System.IO` namespace. That is why you prefix the names of these classes with `System.IO` when you declare objects of their types. Without the `System.IO` prefix, Visual Basic .NET doesn't know where to find these classes. A class name that is prefixed by its namespace name is called a *fully qualified class name*.

Visual Basic .NET allows you to use an `Imports` statement to eliminate the need of prefixing class names with their namespace names. The general format of the `Imports` statement is:

```
Imports Namespace
```

Namespace is the name of a valid namespace. For example, the following statement specifies the `System.IO` namespace.

```
Imports System.IO
```

The `Imports` statement must appear before all other declarations in a file, and cannot appear inside a class declaration or inside a module declaration. For example, a form file that uses an `Imports` statement might appear as:

```
Imports System.IO

Public Class frmMain
    Inherits System.Windows.Forms.Form
        '(more code appears here...)
End Class
```

Placing the statement `Imports System.IO` at the top of a code file eliminates the need to prefix the `StreamWriter` and `StreamReader` class names with `System.IO`. For example, the following code may be used to declare `outputFile` as a `StreamReader` object variable.

```
Dim outputFile as StreamWriter
```

You may place as many `Imports` statements as necessary in a file.

✓ Checkpoint

9.1   What are the three steps in the process of using a file?

9.2   What type of object variable must you create to open a file for writing? For reading?

9.3   Write a statement that creates the file Test.txt so that you may write data to it. If the file already exists, its contents should be erased.

9.4   Write a statement that writes the contents of the variable x to a line in the file you opened in checkpoint 9.3.

9.5   Write a statement that opens the file Test.txt for reading.

9.6   Write a statement that reads a line from the file you opened in checkpoint 9.5, into the variable x.

9.7   How do you determine that a file already exists?

9.8   When reading a file, how do you determine that you have reached end of the file?

▶ 9.3 The OpenFileDialog, SaveFileDialog, FontDialog, and ColorDialog Controls

CONCEPT

VISUAL BASIC .NET PROVIDES DIALOG CONTROLS THAT EQUIP YOUR APPLICATIONS WITH STANDARD WINDOWS DIALOG BOXES FOR OPERATIONS SUCH AS OPENING FILES, SAVING FILES, AND SELECTING FONTS AND COLORS.

The OpenFileDialog and SaveFileDialog Controls

So far, the applications in this chapter that open a file either specify the filename as part of the code or require the user to enter the path and filename. Most Windows users, however, are accustomed to using a dialog box to browse their disk for a file to open or for a location to save a file. You can use the OpenFileDialog and SaveFileDialog controls to equip your applications with the standard dialog boxes that most Windows applications use for opening or saving a file.

The OpenFileDialog Control

The *OpenFileDialog control* can display a standard Windows Open dialog box. Figure 9-13 shows such a dialog box as it appears in Windows XP.

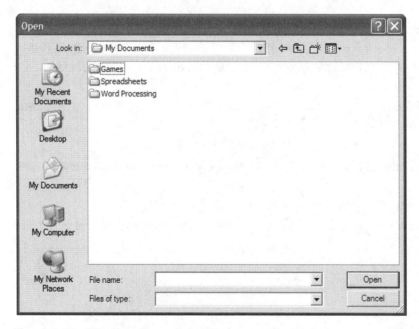

Figure 9-13   Windows Open dialog box

The Open dialog box is very useful in applications that work with files. It gives users the ability to browse their disks for a file to open, instead of typing a long path and filename.

Adding the OpenFileDialog Control to Your Project

You double-click the OpenFileDialog tool in the toolbox to place an OpenFileDialog control on a form. (You may have to scroll through several tools to locate it.) Because the control is invisible at run time, it appears in the component tray at design time. We will use the prefix `ofd` when naming the control.

Displaying an Open Dialog Box

You display an Open dialog box by calling the OpenFileDialog control's `ShowDialog` method. Here is the method's general format.

```
ControlName.ShowDialog()
```

ControlName is the name of the OpenFileDialog control. For example, assuming `ofdOpen File` is the name of an OpenFileDialog control, the following statement calls its `ShowDialog` method.

```
ofdOpenFile.ShowDialog()
```

This method returns one of the values `DialogResult.OK` or `DialogResult.Cancel` indicating which button, OK or Cancel, the user clicked to dismiss the dialog box. When the user selects a file with the Open dialog box, the file's path and name are stored in the control's Filename property. For example, the following code displays an Open dialog box and determines whether the user has selected a file. If so, the filename is displayed.

```
If ofdOpenFile.ShowDialog() = DialogResult.OK Then
    MessageBox.Show(ofdOpenFile.FileName)
Else
    MessageBox.Show("You selected no file.")
End If
```

The Filter Property

The Open dialog box has a "Files of type" list box. This list box displays a filter that specifies the type of files that are visible in the dialog box. Filters typically use the wildcard character (`*`) followed by a file extension. For example, the `*.txt` filter specifies that only files that end in .txt (which are text files) are displayed, and the `*.doc` filter specifies that only files that end in `.doc` (which are Microsoft Word files) are displayed. The `*.*` filter allows all files to be displayed.

For example, the dialog box in Figure 9-14 shows the list box dropped down, containing the `*.txt` and `*.*` filters.

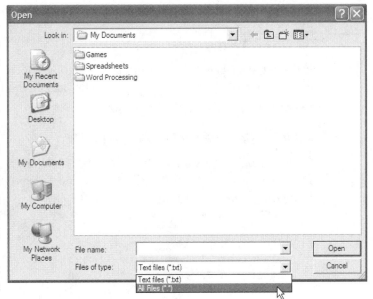

Figure 9-14 Open dialog box with `*.txt` and `*.*` filters

You set the filters that are displayed in the Files of type list box by using the control's *Filter property*. This property may be set in the Properties window at design time, or with code at run time. When storing a value in the Filter property, you store a string containing both a description of the filter and the filter itself. The description and the filter are separated with the pipe (|) symbol. For example, assuming an application has an OpenFileDialog control named ofdOpenFile, the following statement sets the Filter property for text files only.

```
ofdOpenFile.Filter = "Text files (*.txt)|*.txt"
```

The part of the string that appears before the pipe symbol is the description of the filter and is displayed in the Files of type list box. The part of the string that appears after the pipe symbol is the actual filter. In our example, the description of the filter is Text files (*.txt) and the filter is *.txt.

The pipe symbol is also used to separate multiple filters. For example, the following statement stores two filters in ofdOpenFile.Filter: *.txt and *.*.

```
ofdOpenFile.Filter = "Text files (*.txt)|*.txt|All Files (*.*)|*.*"
```

The description of the first filter is Text files (*.txt) and the filter is *.txt. The description of the second filter is All files (*.*) and the filter is *.*.

The InitialDirectory Property

By default the Open dialog box displays the current directory (or folder). You may specify another directory to be initially displayed by storing its path in the *InitialDirectory property*. For example, the following code stores the path C:\Data in ofdOpenFile.InitialDirectory before displaying an Open dialog box.

```
ofdOpenFile.InitialDirectory = "C:\Data"
ofdOpenFile.ShowDialog()
```

When the Open dialog box is displayed, it will show the contents of the directory C:\Data.

The Title Property

By default, the Open dialog box displays the string "Open" in its title bar. You may change this by storing a string in the control's *Title property*. The value in the Title property is displayed in the dialog box's title bar.

Using the Open Dialog Box to Open a File

The following code assumes that ofdOpenFile is the name of an OpeFileDialog control. It demonstrates how to set the Filter, InitialDirectory, and Title properties, display the Open dialog box, retrieve the filename entered by the user, and open the file.

```
' Configure the Open dialog box and display it.
With ofdOpenFile
    .Filter = "Text files (*.txt)|*.txt|All files (*.*)|*.*"
    .InitialDirectory = "C:\Data"
    .Title = "Select a File to Open"
    If .ShowDialog() = DialogResult.OK Then
        inputFile = System.IO.File.OpenText(.Filename)
    End If
End With
```

The SaveFileDialog Control

The *SaveFileDialog control* can display a standard Windows Save As dialog box. Figure 9-15 shows such a dialog box as it appears in Windows XP.

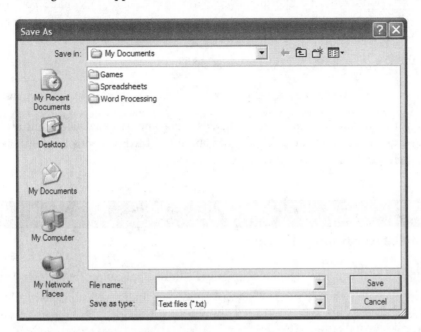

Figure 9-15   Windows Save As dialog box

The *Save As dialog box* is also useful in applications that work with files. It gives users the ability to browse their disks for a location to save a file to, as well as specifying the file's name.

The SaveFileDialog control has much in common with the OpenFileDialog control. You double-click the SaveFileDialog tool in the toolbox to place the control on a form. Because the control is invisible at run time, it appears in the component tray at design time. We will use the prefix `sfd` when naming the control.

You display a Save As dialog box by calling the SaveFileDialog control's `ShowDialog` method. Here is the method's general format.

```
ControlName.ShowDialog()
```

ControlName is the name of the SaveFileDialog control. For example, assuming `sfdSave File` is the name of a SaveFileDialog control, the following statement calls its `ShowDialog` method.

```
sfdSaveFile.ShowDialog()
```

This method returns one of the values `DialogResult.OK` or `DialogResult.Cancel` indicating which button, OK or Cancel, the user clicked to dismiss the dialog box.

The Filename property will hold the name of the file selected or entered by the user. The Filter, InitialDirectory, and Title properties work with the Save As dialog box the same way they do with the Open dialog box. The following code assumes that `sfdSaveFile` is the name of a common dialog control. It demonstrates how to set the Filter, InitialDirectory, and Title properties, display the Save As dialog box, retrieve the filename entered by the user, and open the file.

```
' Configure the Save As dialog box and display it.
With sfdSaveFile
    .Filter = "Text files (*.txt)|*.txt|All files (*.*)|*.*"
    .InitialDirectory = "C:\Data"
    .Title = "Save File As"
    ' If the user selected a file, open it for output.
    If .ShowDialog() = DialogResult.OK Then
        inputFile = System.IO.File.OpenText(.Filename)
    End If
End With
```

In Tutorial 9-4 you gain experience using the OpenFileDialog and SaveFileDialog controls by creating a simple text editor application. You will also learn about the TextBox control's MultiLine property, WordWrap property, and TextChanged event.

TUTORIAL 9-4:

Creating a simple text editor application

In this tutorial you will create a simple text editing application that allows you to create documents, save them, and open existing documents. The application will use a multi-line TextBox control to hold the document text. It will also the a menu system shown in Figure 9-16.

```
 File              Help
┌──────────────┐┌──────────┐
│ New...  Ctrl+N││ About    │
│ Open... Ctrl+O│└──────────┘
│ Save    Ctrl+S│
│ Save As...    │
├──────────────┤
│ Exit    Ctrl+Q│
└──────────────┘
```

Figure 9-16 Simple Text Editor menu system

Table 9-1 lists the MenuItem objects in the menu system shown in Figure 9-16, with the contents of their Text and Shortcut properties.

Table 9-1

MenuItem objects and their Text and Shortcut properties

MenuItem Object Name	Text Property	Shortcut Property
mnuFile	&File	(None)
mnuFileNew	&New...	CtrlN
mnuFileOpen	&Open...	CtrlO
mnuFileSave	&Save	(None)
mnuFileSaveAs	Save& As...	CtrlS
mnuFileExit	E&xit	CtrlQ
mnuHelp	&Help	(None)
mnuHelpAbout	&About	(None)

Notice that some of the menu item Text property values end with ellipses (...). It is a standard Windows convention for a menu item's text to end with ellipses if the menu item displays a dialog box.

Step 1: Start Visual Basic .NET and begin a new Windows application project. Name the project Simple Text Editor.

Step 2: Set the form's Name property to **frmMain** and change its file name in the Solutions Explorer window to frmMain.vb.

Step 3: Set the form's Text property to **Simple Text Editor**. Create a MainMenu control on the form and add the MenuItem objects listed in Table 9-1. Set their Text and Short-cut properties to the values shown in the table. The form should appear similar to Figure 9-17.

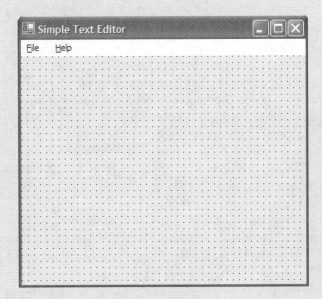

Figure 9-17   Simple Text Editor form

Step 4: Add a TextBox control to the form. Set its name to txtDocument and clear the contents of its Text property. TextBox controls have a Boolean property named *MultiLine*, which is set to false by default. When this property is set to true, the height of the Text Box control may be enlarged and its text may span multiple lines. Set the MultiLine property of the txtDocument control to True. TextBox controls also have a *Word-Wrap property* that, when set to true, cause lines to word-wrap. By default WordWrap is set to true. Use the Properties window to confirm that the txtDocument control's WordWarp property is set to true.

Step 5: Enlarge the size of the txtDocument control so it fills most of the form, as shown in Figure 9-18.

Figure 9-18 Simple Text Editor form with text box enlarged

Step 6: Select the txtDocument control's Anchor property in the Properties window. Set the Anchor property to Top, Bottom, Left, Right. This will cause the TextBox control to automatically resize if the user resizes the form.

Step 7: Add an OpenFileDialog control and a SaveFileDialog control to the form. Name the OpenFileDialog control ofdOpenFile. Name the SaveFileDialog control sfdSaveFile.

Step 8: Set the Title property of the ofdOpenFile control to **Open File**. Set the Title property of the sfdSaveFile control to **Save File As**. Set the Filter property of both controls to **Text Files (*.txt) | *.txt**.

Step 9: Open the Code window and write the following comments and class-level declarations.

```
' Class-level variables

' documentName holds the document file name
Dim documentName As String = ""

' isChanged holds true when the document has
' been changed since it was last saved. It holds
' false when the document has not been changed
' since it was last saved.
Dim isChanged As Boolean = False
```

The documentName variable will hold the file name under which the text box's contents are saved. The Boolean isChanged variable will be used to indicate whether the contents of the text box have changed since last saved. When isChanged is set to true, it indicates that the current contents of the text box have been changed since last saved. When this is the case, the user should be warned.

Step 10: Any time a TextBox control's Text property changes, a TextChanged event is triggered. In this step you will write a TextChanged event procedure for the txtDocument control, which will set the isChanged variable to true. With the Code window still open, select txtDocument in the class name drop-down list box, and then select TextChanged in the method name drop-down list box. A code template for the txtDocument_TextChanged event procedure should appear. Complete the procedure by entering the code shown in bold.

```
Private Sub txtDocument_TextChanged(ByVal sender As Object, _
       ByVal e As System.EventArgs) _
       Handles txtDocument.TextChanged
    ' Update the isChanged variable to indicate that
    ' the text has changed.
    isChanged = True
End Sub
```

Step 11: Now you will write the following Sub procedures: ClearDocument, OpenDocument, SaveDocument, and SaveAs. The ClearDocument procedure clears the txtDocument control's Text property, sets documentName to an empty string, and sets isChanged to false. The OpenDocument procedure displays an Open dialog box, opens the file selected by the user, and reads its contents into the text box. The SaveDocument procedure saves the contents of the text box to the file specified by the documentName variable. The SaveAs procedure saves the contents of the text box to the file selected by the user in Save As dialog box. The code for these procedures follows.

```
Sub ClearDocument()
    ' Clear the contents of the text box.
    txtDocument.Clear()
    ' Clear the document name.
    documentName = ""
    ' Set isChanged to False.
    isChanged = False
End Sub

Sub OpenDocument()
    ' Use the OpenFileDialog control to get
    ' a file name.
    Dim inputFile As System.IO.StreamReader

    If ofdOpenFile.ShowDialog = DialogResult.OK Then
        documentName = ofdOpenFile.FileName
        inputFile = System.IO.File.OpenText(documentName)
        txtDocument.Text = inputFile.ReadToEnd
        inputFile.Close()
    End If
End Sub

Sub SaveDocument()
    ' Save the current document under the name
    ' stored in documentName.
    Dim outputFile As System.IO.StreamWriter
```

```
            outputFile = System.IO.File.CreateText(documentName)
            outputFile.Write(txtDocument.Text)
            outputFile.Close()
            ' Update the isChanged variable.
            isChanged = False
        End Sub

        Sub SaveAs()
            If sfdSaveFile.ShowDialog = DialogResult.OK Then
                documentName = sfdSaveFile.FileName
                SaveDocument()
            End If
        End Sub
```

Step 12: Write the Click event procedures for the menu items that appear on the File menu. The code follows.

```
Private Sub mnuFileNew_Click(ByVal sender As System.Object, _
        ByVal e As System.EventArgs) Handles mnuFileNew.Click
    ' Begin a new document.
    If isChanged = True Then
        ' Document has been changed and is not saved
        If MessageBox.Show("The current document is not saved. " & _
            "Are you sure?", "Confirm", MessageBoxButtons.YesNo) _
                = DialogResult.Yes Then
            ClearDocument()
        End If
    Else
        ' Document has not changed
        ClearDocument()
    End If
End Sub

Private Sub mnuFileOpen_Click(ByVal sender As System.Object, _
        ByVal e As System.EventArgs) Handles mnuFileOpen.Click
    ' Open an existing text file.
    If isChanged = True Then
        ' Document has been changed and is not saved
        If MessageBox.Show("The current document is not saved. " & _
            "Are you sure?", "Confirm", MessageBoxButtons.YesNo) _
                = DialogResult.Yes Then
            ClearDocument()
            OpenDocument()
        End If
    Else
        ' Document has not changed
        ClearDocument()
        OpenDocument()
    End If
End Sub
```

```
Private Sub mnuFileSave_Click(ByVal sender As System.Object, _
        ByVal e As System.EventArgs) Handles mnuFileSave.Click
    ' Save the current document under its existing name.
    If documentName = "" Then
        ' The document has not been saved, so
        ' use Save As dialog box.
        If sfdSaveFile.ShowDialog = DialogResult.OK Then
            documentName = sfdSaveFile.FileName
            SaveDocument()
        End If
    Else
        SaveDocument()
    End If
End Sub

Private Sub mnuFileSaveAs_Click(ByVal sender As System.Object, _
        ByVal e As System.EventArgs) Handles mnuFileSaveAs.Click
    ' Save the current document under a new name.
    If sfdSaveFile.ShowDialog = DialogResult.OK Then
        documentName = sfdSaveFile.FileName
        SaveDocument()
    End If
End Sub

Private Sub mnuExit_Click(ByVal sender As System.Object, _
        ByVal e As System.EventArgs) Handles mnuExit.Click
    ' End the application with the Close method so the
    ' Closing event will trigger.
    Me.Close()
End Sub
```

Step 13: Write the `Click` event procedure for the About menu item on the Help menu. The code follows.

```
Private Sub mnuHelpAbout_Click(ByVal sender As System.Object, _
        ByVal e As System.EventArgs) Handles mnuHelpAbout.Click
    ' Display an about box.
    MessageBox.Show("Simple Text Editor version 1.0")
End Sub
```

Step 14: We want to warn the user if he or she attempts to exit the application without saving the contents of the text box, so a `frmMain_Closing` event procedure must be written. In the class name drop-down list box, select (Base Class Events). In the method name drop-down list box select Closing. A code template for the `frmMain_Closing` event procedure should appear. Complete the event procedure by entering the following code, shown in bold.

```
Private Sub frmMain_Closing(ByVal sender As Object, _
        ByVal e As System.ComponentModel.CancelEventArgs) _
        Handles MyBase.Closing
```

```
              ' If the document has not been changed, confirm
              ' before exiting.
              If isChanged = True Then
                  If MessageBox.Show("The current document is not saved. " & _
                          "Are you sure you want to exit?", "Confirm", _
                          MessageBoxButtons.YesNo) = DialogResult.Yes Then
                      e.Cancel = False
                  Else
                      e.Cancel = True
                  End If
              End If
      End Sub
```

Step 15: Save the project, and run the application. If you entered all the code correctly, you should see the form shown in Figure 9-19.

Figure 9-19   Simple Text Editor form

Step 16: Enter some text into the text box. Experiment with each of the menu commands to see if the application operates correctly. When you are finished, exit.

The ColorDialog and FontDialog Controls

The ColorDialog Control

The *ColorDialog control* displays a standard Windows Color dialog box. Figure 9-20 shows a default Color dialog box, on the left. When the user clicks the Define Custom Colors button, the dialog box expands to become the fully open Color dialog box shown on the right.

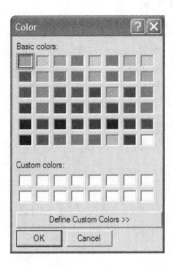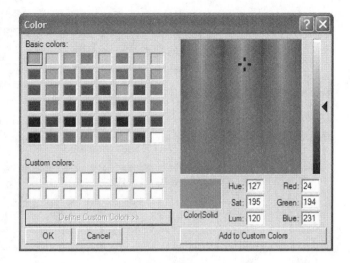

Color dialog box   fully open Color dialog box

Figure 9-20   Windows Color dialog box

You double-click the ColorDialog tool in the toolbox to place the control on a form. Because the control is invisible at run-time, it appears in the component tray at design time. We will use the prefix cd when naming the control.

You display a Color dialog box by calling the ColorDialog control's ShowDialog method. For example, assuming cdColor is the name of a ColorDialog control, the following statement calls its ShowDialog method.

```
cdColor.ShowDialog()
```

This method returns one of the values DialogResult.OK or DialogResult.Cancel indicating which button, OK or Cancel, the user clicked to dismiss the dialog box. The Color property will hold a value representing the color selected by the user. This value can be used with control properties that designate color, such as ForeColor and BackColor. For example, the following code displays the Color dialog box and then sets the color of the text displayed by the lblMessage label to that selected by the user.

```
If cdColor.ShowDialog() = DialogResult.OK Then
    lblMessage.ForeColor = cdColor.Color
End If
```

By default, black is initially selected when the color dialog box is displayed. If you wish to set the initially selected color, you must set the Color property to the desired color value. For example, the following code sets the initially selected color to blue.

```
cdColor.Color = Color.Blue
If cdColor.ShowDialog() = DialogResult.OK Then
    lblMessage.ForeColor = cdColor.Color
End If
```

The following code sets the initially selected color to the color of the lblMessage label before displaying the dialog box.

```
cdColor.Color = lblMessage.ForeColor
If cdColor.ShowDialog() = DialogResult.OK Then
    lblMessage.ForeColor = cdColor.Color
End If
```

The FontDialog Control

The *FontDialog control* displays a standard Windows Font dialog box. Figure 9-21 shows the default Font dialog box on the left, and a Font dialog box with a Color drop-down list on the right.

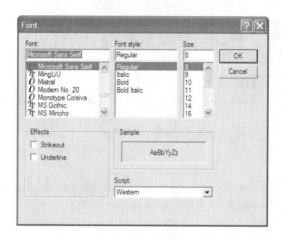

default Font dialog box

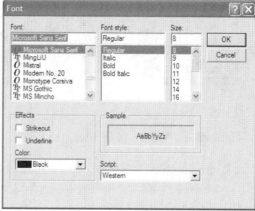

Font dialog box with color choices displayed

Figure 9-21   Windows Font dialog box

You double-click the FontDialog tool in the toolbox to place the control on a form. Because the control is invisible at run-time, it appears in the component tray at design time. We will use the prefix `fd` when naming the control.

You display a Font dialog box by calling the FontDialog control's `ShowDialog` method. For example, assuming `fdFont` is the name of a FontDialog control, the following statement calls its `ShowDialog` method.

```
fdFont.ShowDialog()
```

By default, the Font dialog box does not allow the user to select a color. This is controlled by the FontDialog control's ShowColor property, which may be set to true or false. When set to true, the Font dialog box will appear with a Color drop-down list, as shown on the right in Figure 9-21.

The `ShowDialog` method returns one of the values `DialogResult.OK` or `Dialog Result.Cancel` indicating which button, OK or Cancel, the user clicked to dismiss the dialog box. The Font property will hold a value representing the font settings selected by the user. The Color property will hold a value representing the color selected by the user. For example, the following code displays the Font dialog box and then sets the `lblMessage` control's font to that selected by the user.

```
If fdFont.ShowDialog() = DialogResult.OK Then
    lblTest.Font = fdFont.Font
End If
```

The following code displays a Font dialog box with a drop-down list of colors. It then sets the `lblMessage` control's font and color to the values selected by the user.

```
fdFont.ShowColor = True
If fdFont.ShowDialog() = DialogResult.OK Then
    lblTest.Font = fdFont.Font
    lblTest.ForeColor = fdFont.Color
End If
```

✓ Checkpoint

9.9 Why is it a good idea to use the Open and Save As dialog boxes in applications that work with files?

9.10 What is the purpose of the following OpenFileDialog and SaveFileDialog properties?

Filter

InitialDirectory

Title

Filename

9.11 You want an Open dialog box to have the following filters: text files (*.txt), Word files (*.doc), and all files (*.*). What string would you store in the Filter property?

9.12 When the user selects a color with the Color dialog box, where is the color value stored?

9.13 When the user selects font settings with the Font dialog box, where are the font setting values stored?

9.14 How do you display a Font dialog box with a drop-down list of colors?

9.15 When the user selects a color with the Font dialog box, where is the color value stored?

▶ 9.4 The PrintDocument Control

CONCEPT

THE PRINTDOCUMENT CONTROL ALLOWS YOU TO PRINT DATA TO THE PRINTER.

The *PrintDocument control* gives your application the ability to print output on the printer. You double-click the PrintDocument tool in the toolbox to place a PrintDocument control on a form. Because the control is invisible at run time, it appears in the component tray at design time. We will use the prefix pd when naming the control.

The `Print` Method and the `PrintPage` Event

The PrintDocument control has a *Print method* that starts the printing process. The method's general format is:

```
PrintDocumentControl.Print()
```

When the `Print` method is executed, it triggers a `PrintPage` event. It is in the `PrintPage` event procedure that you must write code to handle the actual printing. To create a `PrintPage` event procedure code template, simply double-click the PrintDocument control in the component tray. An example code template for a PrintDocument control named `pdPrint` follows.

```
Private Sub pdPrint_PrintPage(ByVal sender As System.Object, _
        ByVal e As System.Drawing.Printing.PrintPageEventArgs) _
        Handles pdPrint.PrintPage

End Sub
```

Inside the `PrintPage` event procedure, you write code that sends text to the printer using a specified font and color, at a specified location. You accomplish this with the `e.Graphics.DrawString` method. We will use the following general format of the method:

```
e.Graphics.DrawString(String, New Font(FontName, Size, _
                      Style), Brushes.Black, HPos, VPos)
```

String is the string that is to be printed. *FontName* is a string holding the name of the font to use. `Size` is the size of the font, measured in points. *Style* is the font style. Typically, the valid values are `FontStyle.Bold`, `FontStyle.Italic`, `FontStyle.Regular`, `FontStyle.Strikeout`, and `FontStyle.Underline`. *HPos* is the horizontal position of the output. This is the distance of the output, in points, from the left margin of the paper. *VPos* is the vertical position of the output. This is the distance of the output, in points, from the top margin of the paper. The `Brushes.Black` argument specifies that output should printed in black.

For example, the following code is a `PrintPage` event procedure that prints the contents of a TextBox control, `txtInput`, in a regular 12-point Times New Roman font. The horizontal and vertical coordinates of the output are 10 and 10.

```
Private Sub pdPrint_PrintPage(ByVal sender As System.Object, _
        ByVal e As System.Drawing.Printing.PrintPageEventArgs) _
        Handles pdPrint.PrintPage
    e.Graphics.DrawString(txtInput.Text, New Font("Times New Roman", _
                    12, FontStyle.Regular), Brushes.Black, 10, 10)
End Sub
```

The following code is a `PrintPage` event procedure that prints the string "Sales Report" in a bold 18-point Courier font. The horizontal and vertical coordinates of the output are 150 and 80.

```
Private Sub pdPrint_PrintPage(ByVal sender As System.Object, _
        ByVal e As System.Drawing.Printing.PrintPageEventArgs) _
        Handles pdPrint.PrintPage
    e.Graphics.DrawString("Sales Report", New Font("Courier", 18, _
                    FontStyle.Bold), Brushes.Black, 150, 80)
End Sub
```

The following code is a `PrintPage` event procedure that prints the contents of a file. In the code, assume that `filename` is a string variable containing the name of the file whose contents are to be printed.

```
Private Sub pdPrint_PrintPage(ByVal sender As System.Object, _
        ByVal e As System.Drawing.Printing.PrintPageEventArgs) _
        Handles pdPrint.PrintPage
```

```
        Dim inputFile As System.IO.StreamReader
        Dim x As Integer = 10
        Dim y As Integer = 10

        inputFile = System.IO.File.OpenText(filename)
        Do While inputFile.Peek <> -1
            e.Graphics.DrawString(inputFile.ReadLine, _
                    New Font("Courier", 10, FontStyle.Regular), _
                    Brushes.Black, x, y)
            y += 12
        Loop
        inputFile.Close()
    End Sub
```

The variables x and y are used to specify the horizontal and vertical positions of each line of printed output. Notice the statement y += 12 that appears inside the loop. This increases the vertical distance of each line by 12 points from the top of the page. The output is printed in a 10 point font, so there will be 2 points of space between each line.

In Tutorial 9-5 you will modify the Simple Text Editor application you created in Tutorial 9-4 by adding a Print command to the File menu.

TUTORIAL 9-5:

Adding printing capabilities to the Simple Text Editor application

Step 1:   Start Visual Basic .NET and load the Simple Text Editor project you created in Tutorial 9-4.

Step 2:   Add a Print menu item to the File menu, as shown in Figure 9-22. Name the Menu Item object mnuFilePrint. Set its Text to **&Print** and its Shortcut property to CtrlP. Place separator bars above and below the item.

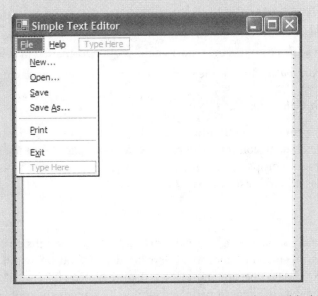

Figure 9-22   Print menu item and separator bars added

Step 3:   Add a PrintDocument control to the form. Name the control `pdPrint`.

Step 4:   Double-click the `pdPrint` control to create a code template for the `pdPrint_PrintPage` event procedure. Complete the event procedure by entering the following code shown in bold.

```
Private Sub pdPrint_PrintPage(ByVal sender As System.Object, _
        ByVal e As System.Drawing.Printing.PrintPageEventArgs) _
        Handles pdPrint.PrintPage
    ' Print the contents of the text box.
    e.Graphics.DrawString(txtDocument.Text, _
                    New Font("MS Sans Serif", 12, _
                    FontStyle.Regular), Brushes.Black, 10, 10)
End Sub
```

Step 5:   Add the following `mnuFilePrint_Click` event procedure.

```
Private Sub mnuFilePrint_Click(ByVal sender As System.Object, _
        ByVal e As System.EventArgs) Handles mnuFilePrint.Click
    ' Print the current document.
    pdPrint.Print()
End Sub
```

Step 6:   Run the application. Enter some text into the text box or load an existing file. Test the new Print command. The contents of the text box should be printed on the printer.

Step 7:   Exit the application.

Printing Reports

Reports typically have the following common parts:

◆   A *report header* is printed first and contains the name of the report, the date and time the report was printed, and other general information about the data in the report.

◆   The *report body*, which contains the report's data, is often formatted in columns.

◆   An optional *report footer* contains the sum of one or more columns of data.

Printing Reports with Columnar Data

Report data is typically printed in column format, with each column having an appropriate heading. To properly align printed data in columns, you must use a monospaced font to ensure that all characters occupy the same amount of space, and use the `String.Format` method to format the data into columns. Let's take a closer look at each of these topics.

Monospaced Fonts

Most printers are normally set to a proportionally spaced font like MS sans serif. In a proportionally spaced font, the amount of space occupied by a character depends on the width of the character. For example, the letters "m" and "w" occupy more space than the letters "i" and "j". Because of this, you may have trouble getting data to align properly in columns. To remedy the problem, you should select a monospaced font, such as Courier New. All the characters in a monospaced font use the same amount of space on the printed page.

Using `String.Format` to Align Data along Column Boundaries

The `String.Format` method is a very versatile tool for formatting strings. In this section we will discuss how to use the method to align data along column boundaries. The method is used in the following general format:

```
String.Format(FormatString, Arg0, Arg1 [,...])
```

`FormatString` is a string that contains text and/or formatting specifications. `Arg0` and `Arg1` are arguments that are to be formatted. The `[,...]` notation indicates that more arguments may follow. The method returns a string that contains the data provided by the arguments `Arg0`, `Arg1`, etc, formatted with the specifications found in `FormatString`.

Let's look at an example of how this method may be used to format data into columns. The following code produces a string with the numbers 10, 20, and 30 aligned into columns that are ten characters wide each. The resulting string is stored in the variable `str`.

```
Dim str As String
Dim x, y, z As Integer
x = 10
y = 20
z = 30
str = String.Format("{0, 10}{1, 10}{2, 10}", x, y, z)
```

The string `"{0, 10}{1, 10}{2, 10}"` is the format string. The variable x is argument 0, the variable y is argument 1, and the variable z is argument 2. This illustrated in Figure 9-23.

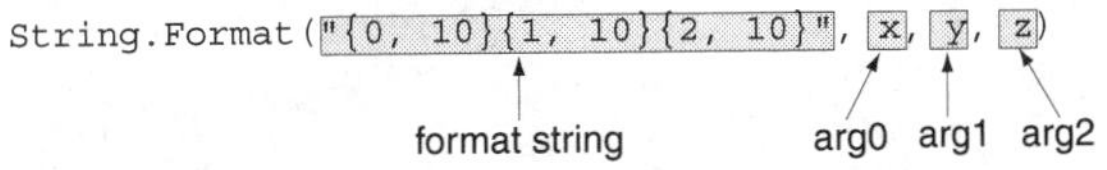

Figure 9-23 Arguments of the `String.Format` method

The contents of the format string specify how the data is to be formatted. Notice that the string has three sets of numbers inside curly braces. The first set is `{0, 10}`. This specifies that argument zero (which is the variable x) is to be placed in a column that is ten spaces wide. The second set is `{1, 10}`. This specifies that argument one (which is the variable y) is to be placed in a column that is ten spaces wide. The third set is `{2, 10}`. This specifies that argument two (which is the variable z) is to be placed in a column that is ten spaces wide. Figure 9-24 labels all these parts. There are no spaces between the sets.

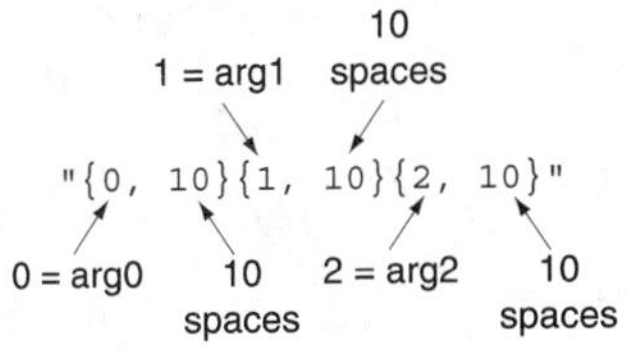

Figure 9-24 Format specifications

After the last statement in the previous code executes, the variable `str` will contain the string " 10 20 30". The numbers will be placed in columns of ten spaces each, as illustrated in Figure 9-25.

Notice that the numbers are right-justified inside the columns. If you use a negative for a column width in the format string, the value that appears in that column will be left justified. For example, using the variables x, y, and z from the previous code example, the method call

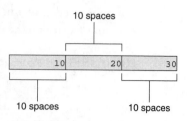

Figure 9-25 Column widths

```
String.Format("{0, -10}{1, -10}{2, -10}", x, y, z)
```

will produce the string "10   20   30   ".

Let's examine a code sample that prints a sales report with a header, two columns of data, and a footer. The data is printed from the following parallel arrays:

```
Dim names As String() = {"John Smith", "Jill McKenzie", _
                         "Karen Suttles", "Jason Mabry", _
                         "Susan Parsons"}
Dim sales As Decimal() = {2500.0, 3400.0, 4200.0, _
                          2200.0, 3100.0}
```

The `names` array contains five salespeople's names and the `sales` array contains each salesperson's sales. The `For...Next` loop in the following event procedure prints each line of data and uses an accumulator, `total`, to sum the sales amounts. The contents of `total` are printed in the footer to show the total sales.

```
Private Sub pdPrint_PrintPage(ByVal sender As System.Object, _
        ByVal e As System.Drawing.Printing.PrintPageEventArgs) _
        Handles pdPrint.PrintPage

    Dim count As Integer      ' Loop counter
    Dim total As Decimal = 0  ' Accumulator
    Dim vertPosition As Integer ' Vertical printing position

    ' Print the report header
    e.Graphics.DrawString("Sales Report", New Font("Courier New", 12, _
            FontStyle.Bold), Brushes.Black, 150, 10)
    e.Graphics.DrawString("Date and Time: " & Now.ToString, _
            New Font("Courier New", 12, FontStyle.Bold), _
            Brushes.Black, 10, 38)
    ' Print the column headings
    e.Graphics.DrawString(String.Format("{0, 20}{1, 20}", _
            "NAME", "SALES"), New Font("Courier New", 12, _
            FontStyle.Bold), Brushes.Black, 10, 66)
    ' Print the body of the report
    vertPosition = 82
    For count = 0 To 4
        e.Graphics.DrawString(String.Format("{0, 20}{1, 20}", _
            names(count), FormatCurrency(sales(count))), _
            New Font("Courier New", 12, _
            FontStyle.Regular), Brushes.Black, 10, _
```

```
            vertPosition)
        total += sales(count)
        vertPosition += 14
    Next count
    ' Print the report footer
    e.Graphics.DrawString("Total Sales: " & FormatCurrency(total), _
            New Font("Courier New", 12, FontStyle.Bold), _
            Brushes.Black, 150, 165)
End Sub
```

The report printed by this code will appear similar to the following.

```
                Sales Report

    Date and Time: 6/24/2003 11:12:34 AM

            Name              Sales
        John Smith          $2,500.00
      Jill McKenzie         $3,400.00
      Karen Suttles         $4,200.00
        Jason Mabry         $2,200.00
      Susan Parsons         $3,100.00

        Total Sales: $15,400.00
```

✓ Checkpoint

9.16 How do you trigger a PrinterDocument control's `PrintPage` event?

9.17 Assume that an application has a PrintDocument control named `pdPrint`. Write a statement that may be placed in the control's `PrintPage` event procedure and will print your first and last name in an 18 point bold MS sans Serif font. Print your name at 100 points from the page's left margin and 20 points from the page's top margin.

9.18 Name the three parts that most reports have.

9.19 What is the difference between a proportionally spaced font and a monospaced font?

9.20 Assume that an application has a PrintDocument control named `pdPrint`. Write a statement that may be placed in the control's `PrintPage` event procedure and will print the contents of the variables a and b in a 12 point regular Courier New font. The contents of a should be printed in a column that is 12 characters wide, and the contents of b should be printed in a column that is eight characters wide. Print the data at 10 points from the page's left margin and 50 points from the page's top margin.

9.21 Rewrite the answer you wrote to Checkpoint 9.20 so the contents of the variable a are left-justified.

▶ 9.5 Structures

CONCEPT

VISUAL BASIC .NET ALLOWS YOU TO CREATE YOUR OWN DATA TYPES, IN WHICH YOU MAY GROUP MULTIPLE DATA FIELDS.

So far you have created applications that keep data in individual variables. If you need to group items together, Visual Basic .NET allows you to create arrays. The limitation of arrays, however, is that all the fields must be of the same data type. Sometimes a relationship exists between items of different types. For example, a payroll system might use the variables shown in the following declaration statements.

```
Dim empNumber As Integer     ' Employee number
Dim firstName As String      ' Employee's first name
Dim lastName As String       ' Employee's last name
Dim hours As Single          ' Number of hours worked
Dim payRate As Decimal       ' Hourly pay rate
Dim grossPay As Decimal      ' Gross pay
```

All of these variables are related because they can hold data about the same employee. The `Dim` statements, however, create separate variables and do not establish a relationship between the variables.

Instead of creating separate variables that hold related data, you can create a structure that holds all the related data. A *structure* is a data type that you create, which contains one or more variables known as fields. The fields can be of different data types. Once a structure has been created, variables of the structure may be declared.

You create a structure at the class- or module-level with the *Structure statement*. We will use the following general format of the `Structure` statement.

```
[AccessSpecifier] Structure StructureName
    FieldDeclarations
End Structure
```

AccessSpecifier is shown in brackets, indicating that it is optional. If you use the `Public` access specifier, the structure is accessible to statements outside the class or module. If you use the `Private` access specifier, the structure is accessible only to statements in the class or module. *StructureName* is the name of the structure. *FieldDeclarations* is one or more declarations of fields. Field declarations appear as regular `Dim` statements. Here is an example of a `Structure` statement.

```
Structure EmpPayData
    Dim empNumber As Integer
    Dim firstName As String
    Dim lastName As String
    Dim hours As Single
    Dim payRate As Decimal
    Dim grossPay As Decimal
End Structure
```

This statement creates a structure named `EmpPayData`. The `EmpPayData` type has six fields: `empNumber`, `firstName`, `lastName`, `hours`, `payRate`, and `grossPay`.

TIP: Notice that the name of the structure is written in Pascal-casing. Recall that in Pascal-casing, the first character of the name is uppercase. This serves as a visual reminder that the structure name is not a variable name.

TIP: If you want a structure to be available to multiple forms in a project, place the `Structure` statement, with the `Public` access specifier, in a standard module.

The `Structure` statement does not create a variable. It simply creates a new data type by telling Visual Basic .NET what the data type is made of. You declare variables of a structure with `Dim` statements, just as you would with any other data type. For example, the following statement declares a variable called `deptHead`:

```
Dim deptHead As EmpPayData
```

This statement declares `deptHead` as an `EmpPayData` variable. The `deptHead` variable can store six values. This is because the `EmpPayData` data type is made of six fields, as illustrated in Figure 9-26.

You access the fields with the dot operator. For example, the following statements assign values to all six fields of the `deptHead` variable.

```
deptHead.empNumber = 1101
deptHead.firstName = "Joanne"
deptHead.lastName = "Smith"
deptHead.hours = 40
deptHead.payRate = 25
deptHead.grossPay = deptHead.hours * deptHead.payRate
```

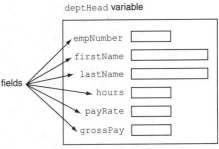

Figure 9-26   The `deptHead` variable

In addition, the following statement adds the `empNumber` field to the `lstEmployeeList` list box.

```
lstEmployeeList.Items.Add(deptHead.empNumber)
```

You may use the `With` statement with structure variables to simplify your code, as shown in the following example.

```
With deptHead
    .empNumber = 1101
    .firstName = "Joanne"
    .lastName = "Smith"
    .hours = 40
    .payRate = 25
    .grossPay = .hours * .payRate
End With
```

Passing Structure Variables to Procedures and Functions

Like regular variables, you may pass structure variables to procedures and functions. For example, the following procedure accepts an `EmpPayData` variable as its argument. Notice that the argument is passed by reference.

```
Sub CalcPay(ByRef employee As EmpPayData)
    ' This procedure accepts an EmpPayData variable
```

```
    ' as its argument. The employee's gross pay
    ' is calculated and stored in the grossPay
    ' field.
    With employee
        .grossPay = .hours * .payRate
    End With
End Sub
```

Arrays as Structure Members

Structures may contain arrays as fields, but an array field cannot be declared with an initial size. For example, look at the following `Structure` statement.

```
Structure StudentRecord
    Dim name As String
    Dim testScores() As Single
End Structure
```

After declaring a structure variable, you can use the `ReDim` statement to establish a size for the array. You then access the array elements with a subscript, as shown in the following example.

```
Dim student As StudentRecord
ReDim student.TestScores(4)
student.name = "Mary McBride"
student.testScores(0) = 89
student.testScores(1) = 92
student.testScores(2) = 84
student.testScores(3) = 96
student.testScores(4) = 91
```

Arrays of User-Defined Data Structure Variables

You may also declare an array of structure variables. For example, the following statement declares `employees` as an array of 10 `EmpPayData` variables.

```
Dim employees(9) As EmpPayData
```

To access the individual variables in the array, use a subscript as shown in the following statement.

```
employees(0).empNumber = 1101
```

This statement assigns 1101 to the `empNumber` field of `employees(0)`.

When you are working with an array of structure variables and the structure contains an array as one of its fields, you must use the `ReDim` statement to establish a size for the array field of each element. For example, recall that the `StudentRecord` type discussed in the previous section has a field named `testScores`, which is an array of five numbers. Suppose an application declares an array of the `StudentRecord` variables as follows.

```
Dim students(9) As StudentRecord
```

A loop, such as the following, can be used to set a size for each `testScores` array.

```
For i = 0 To 9
   ReDim students(i).testScores(4)
Next i
```

You can work with the array fields once they have been given a size. For example, the following statement stores 95 in `testScores(0)` which belongs to `students(5)`.

```
students(5).testScores(0) = 95
```

TUTORIAL 9-6:

Examining an application with a structure

In this tutorial you examine a modified version of the File WriteLine Demo project that you examined in Tutorial 9-1. This version of the project uses a structure to store the friend data.

Step 1: Start Visual Basic .NET and open the structure file write demo project, which is stored in the \Chap9\Structure File WriteLine Demo folder.

Step 2: Open the Code window. The following `Structure` statement is used to create the `FriendInfo` structure.

```
' Declare a structure to hold friend information.
Structure FriendInfo
    Dim name As String        ' To hold a name
    Dim age As Integer        ' To hold an age
    Dim address As String     ' To hold an address
End Structure
```

Step 3: Look at the `btnSave_Click` event procedure, which is as follows. The procedure declares the structure variable `MyFriend` to hold the names, ages, and addresses entered by the user. The `WriteLine` statement writes the contents of the structure variable's fields to the file.

```
Private Sub btnCreateFile_Click(ByVal sender As System.Object, _
        ByVal e As System.EventArgs) Handles btnCreateFile.Click
    ' This procedure prompts the user for data and
    ' saves it to a file.
    Dim filename As String    ' File name
    Dim count As Integer      ' Loop counter
    Dim myFriend As FriendInfo ' Structure variable
    Dim friendFile As System.IO.StreamWriter    ' Object variable
```

```
        ' Get the file name from the user.
        filename = InputBox("Enter the filename.", "Filename Needed")
        ' Open the file.
        friendFile = System.IO.File.CreateText(filename)
        ' Get the data for three friends and write it
        ' to the file.
        For count = 1 To 3
            ' Get the data.
            MessageBox.Show("Get ready to enter data for friend " & _
                            count.ToString)
            myFriend.name = InputBox("Enter your friend's name.")
            myFriend.age = Val(InputBox("Enter your friend's age."))
            myFriend.address = InputBox("Enter your friend's address.")
            ' Write the data to the file.
            friendFile.WriteLine(myFriend.name)
            friendFile.WriteLine(myFriend.age)
            friendFile.WriteLine(myFriend.address)
        Next count
        ' Close the file.
        friendFile.Close()
    End Sub
```

Step 4: Run the application and, as you did in Tutorial 9-1, click the Save Data to File button. Enter a filename and data for three of your friends. The procedure saves the data to the file.

Step 5: End the application.

✓ **Checkpoint**

9.22 Write a `Structure` statement that creates a structure named `Movie`. The structure should have fields to hold the following data about a movie.

Name of the movie

The movie's director

The movie's producer

The year the movie was released

9.23 Write a statement that declares a variable of the `Movie` structure that you wrote in Checkpoint 9.22.

9.24 Write statements that store the following data in the variable you declared in Checkpoint 9.23. (Do not use the `With` statement.)

Name of the movie: Wheels of Fury

The movie's director: Arlen McGoo

The movie's producer: Vincent Van Dough

The year the movie was released: 2003

9.25 Rewrite the statements you wrote in checkpoint 9.24 using the `With` statement.

▶ 9.6 Focus on Problem Solving: Modifying the Demetris Leadership Center Application

In Chapter 8 you created a sales reporting application for the Demetris Leadership Center. The application prompts the user to enter the number of units sold of each product and displays a sales report showing the revenue from each product and the total revenue from all products sold. In this section you modify the application in the following ways:

◆ You replace the parallel arrays with a single array of structure variables.

◆ You equip the application with the option of saving the units sold to a file and later retrieving the data.

◆ You add the capability of printing the sales report.

The Structure

In the original version of this application, you declared a group of arrays to hold the product names, descriptions, product numbers, prices, and units sold. The arrays were processed as parallel arrays. In this exercise you will replace the arrays with the following structure and structure variable array declaration:

```
Structure ProductData
    Dim name As String          ' Product name
    Dim desc As String          ' Description
    Dim prodNum As Integer      ' Product number
    Dim price As Decimal        ' Unit price
    Dim unitsSold As Integer    ' Units sold
End Structure

' Array upper subscript
Const maxSubscript As Integer = 8

' Array of ProductData
Dim products(maxSubscript) As ProductData
```

The New Menu Items

Recall that the application's File menu only has one item: Exit. You will add the following four new items to the File menu: Open File, Save As, Clear Sales Figures, and Print Sales Report. The menu with the new items inserted is shown in Figure 9-27. Notice that three separator bars are also added.

Table 9-2 lists the new menu controls with their texts and shortcut keys.

Figure 9-27 File menu with new items

Table 9-2

New menu controls

Name	Text	Shortcut key
mnuFileOpen	&Open File	Ctrl+O
mnuFileSaveAs	&Save As	Ctrl+S
mnuFileClear	C&lear Sales Figures	Ctrl+C
mnuFilePrint	&Print Sales Report	Ctrl+P

You will also add the procedures described in Table 9-3 to the frmMain module.

Table 9-3

New procedures for frmMain

Method	Description
mnuFileOpen_Click	Uses an OpenFileDialog control to display an Open dialog box. The file name selected by the user passed to the ReadFile procedure.
mnuFileSaveSaveAs_Click	Uses a SaveFileDialog control to display a Save As dialog box. The user selects or enters a filename, which is passed to the SaveFile procedure.
mnuFileClear_Click	Sets the unitsSold field of each element of the products array to 0, clears the contents of the lstSalesData list box, and clears the contents of the lblTotalRevenue control.
mnuFilePrint_Click	Uses the PrintDocument control to print a sales report that shows the revenue of each product and the total revenue.
ReadFile	Accepts a file name as its argument. The file is opened and its contents are read into the unitsSold fields of the structure variables in the products array.
SaveFile	Accepts a file name as its argument. The file is opened and the contents of the unitsSold fields of the elements in the products array are written to it.

TUTORIAL 9-7:

Modifying the Demetris Leadership Center sales-reporting application

Step 1: Start Visual Basic .NET and load the Demetris Leadership Center sales-reporting application that you created in Chapter 8, Tutorial 8-8.

Step 2: Add the following controls to the frmMain form:

- An OpenFileDialog control. Name the control ofdOpenFile.
- A SaveFileDialog control. Name the control sfdSaveFile.
- A PrintDocument control. Name the control pdPrint.

Step 3: The current version of this application has the following class-level array declarations:

```
Dim prodNames(maxSubscript) As String   ' Product names
Dim desc(maxSubscript) As String        ' Descriptions
Dim prodNums(maxSubscript) As Integer   ' Product numbers
Dim prices(maxSubscript) As Decimal     ' Unit prices
Dim unitsSold(maxSubscript) As Integer  ' Units sold
```

Replace these array declarations with the following declarations.

```
Structure ProductData
    Dim name As String              ' Product name
    Dim desc As String              ' Description
    Dim prodNum As Integer          ' Product number
```

```
                    Dim price As Decimal            ' Unit price
                    Dim unitsSold As Integer        ' Units sold
                End Structure

                ' Array upper subscript
                Const maxSubscript As Integer = 8

                ' Array of ProductData
                Dim products(maxSubscript) As ProductData
```

Step 4:   The InitArrays procedure initializes the parallel arrays. Modify it to initialize the product array instead. The new code follows.

```
Private Sub InitArrays()
    ' Initialize the arrays.
    ' First product
    products(0).name = "Six Steps to Leadership"
    products(0).desc = "Book"
    products(0).prodNum = 914
    products(0).price = 12.95

    ' Second product
    products(1).name = "Six Steps to Leadership"
    products(1).desc = "Audiocassette"
    products(1).prodNum = 915
    products(1).price = 14.95

    ' Third product
    products(2).name = "The Road to Excellence"
    products(2).desc = "Video"
    products(2).prodNum = 916
    products(2).price = 18.95

    ' Fourth product
    products(3).name = "Seven Lessons of Quality"
    products(3).desc = "Book"
    products(3).prodNum = 917
    products(3).price = 16.95

    ' Fifth product
    products(4).name = "Seven Lessons of Quality"
    products(4).desc = "Audiocassette"
    products(4).prodNum = 918
    products(4).price = 21.95

    ' Sixth product
    products(5).name = "Seven Lessons of Quality"
    products(5).desc = "Video"
    products(5).prodNum = 919
    products(5).price = 31.95

    ' Seventh product
    products(6).name = "Teams Are Made, Not Born"
    products(6).desc = "Book"
    products(6).prodNum = 920
    products(6).price = 14.95
```

```
                              ' Eighth product
                              products(7).name = "Leadership for the Future"
                              products(7).desc = "Book"
                              products(7).prodNum = 921
                              products(7).price = 14.95

                              ' Ninth product
                              products(8).name = "Leadership for the Future"
                              products(8).desc = "Audiocassette"
                              products(8).prodNum = 922
                              products(8).price = 16.95
                          End Sub
```

Step 5: Modify the mnuReportData_Click event procedure so it stores the user's input in the products array. The procedure follows, with the modified code shown in bold.

```
Private Sub mnuReportData_Click(ByVal sender As System.Object, _
        ByVal e As System.EventArgs) Handles mnuReportData.Click
    ' Prompt the user for sales data.
    Dim count As Integer ' Loop counter

    ' Get unit sales for each product.
    For count = 0 To maxSubscript
        products(count).unitsSold = _
            Val(InputBox("Enter units sold of " & _
            "product number " & products(count).prodNum, _
            "Enter Sales Data"))
    Next count
End Sub
```

Step 6: Modify the mnuReportDisplay_Click event procedure so it displays data in the products array. The procedure follows, with the modified code shown in bold.

```
Private Sub mnuReportDisplay_Click(ByVal sender As System.Object, _
        ByVal e As System.EventArgs) Handles mnuReportDisplay.Click
    ' Calculates and displays the revenue for each
    ' product and the total revenue.
    Dim count As Integer ' Loop counter
    Dim revenue As Decimal
    Dim totalRevenue As Decimal

    ' Display the sales report header.
    lstSalesData.Items.Add("SALES REPORT")
    lstSalesData.Items.Add("--------------------")
    ' Display sales data for each product.
    For count = 0 To maxSubscript
        ' Calculate product revenue.
        revenue = products(count).unitsSold * _
            products(count).price
        ' Display the product data.
```

```
            lstSalesData.Items.Add("Product Number: " & _
                products(count).prodNum.ToString)
            lstSalesData.Items.Add("Name: " & products(count).name)
            lstSalesData.Items.Add("Description: " & _
                products(count).desc)
            lstSalesData.Items.Add("Unit Price: " & _
                FormatCurrency(products(count).price))
            lstSalesData.Items.Add("Units Sold: " & _
                products(count).unitsSold.ToString)
            lstSalesData.Items.Add("Product Revenue: " & _
                FormatCurrency(revenue))
            lstSalesData.Items.Add("")
            ' Accumulate revenue.
            totalRevenue = totalRevenue + revenue
        Next count
        ' Display total revenue.
        lblTotalRevenue.Text = FormatCurrency(totalRevenue)
    End Sub
```

Step 7:   In the Design window, select the MainMenu control and add the menu items listed in Table 9-2 to the File menu. Refer to Figure 9-27 for each control's position.

Step 8:   Add the mnuFileOpen_Click and mnuFileSaveAs_Click event procedures. The code follows.

```
Private Sub mnuFileOpen_Click(ByVal sender As System.Object, _
        ByVal e As System.EventArgs) Handles mnuFileOpen.Click
    ' Let the user select a file to open, and pass the
    ' selected file name to the ReadFile procedure.
    With ofdOpenFile
        .Filter = "Text Files (*.txt)|*.txt|All Files (*.*)|*.*"
        .Title = "Select a File to Open"
        If .ShowDialog = DialogResult.OK Then
            If .FileName <> "" Then
                ReadFile(.FileName)
            Else
                MessageBox.Show("No file selected.", "Error")
            End If
        End If
    End With
End Sub

Private Sub mnuFileSaveAs_Click(ByVal sender As System.Object, _
        ByVal e As System.EventArgs) Handles mnuFileSaveAs.Click
    ' Let the user select or enter a file name to save the
    ' data to. Pass the file name to the SaveFile procedure.
    With sfdSaveFile
        .Filter = "Text Files (*.txt)|*.txt|All Files (*.*)|*.*"
        .Title = "Save File As"
        If .ShowDialog = DialogResult.OK Then
            If .FileName <> "" Then
```

```
                                SaveFile(.FileName)
                            Else
                                MessageBox.Show("File not saved.", "Error")
                            End If
                        End If
                    End With
                End Sub
```

Step 9: Add the mnuFileClear_Click event procedure. The code follows.

```
Private Sub mnuFileClear_Click(ByVal sender As System.Object, _
        ByVal e As System.EventArgs) Handles mnuFileClear.Click
    ' This procedure clears the sales data from the
    ' list box and the total revenue label, and sets
    ' the unitSold array's elements to zero.
    Dim count As Integer      ' loop counter

    ' Clear the list box.
    lstSalesData.Items.Clear()
    ' Clear the total revenue label.
    lblTotalRevenue.Text = ""
    ' Clear the unitsSold array.
    For count = 0 To maxSubscript
        products(count).unitsSold = 0
    Next
End Sub
```

Step 10: Add the mnuFilePrint_Click event procedure. The code follows.

```
Private Sub mnuFilePrint_Click(ByVal sender As System.Object, _
        ByVal e As System.EventArgs) Handles mnuFilePrint.Click
    ' Call the Print method to start printing.
    pdPrint.Print()
End Sub
```

Step 11: In the Design window, double-click the pdPrint control to create a code template for the pdPrint_PrintPage event procedure. Complete the procedure as follows.

```
Private Sub pdPrint_PrintPage(ByVal sender As System.Object, _
        ByVal e As System.Drawing.Printing.PrintPageEventArgs) _
        Handles pdPrint.PrintPage

    ' This procedure prints the sales report.
    Dim count As Integer          ' Loop counter
    Dim revenue As Decimal
    Dim totalRevenue As Decimal
    Dim vertPos As Integer
    Dim formatStr As String =
        "{0,27}{1,15}{2,10}{3,8}{4,12}{5,10}"
```

```
                              ' Print the report header.
                              e.Graphics.DrawString("Demetris Leadership Center " & _
                                          Sales Report", New Font("Courier New", _
                                          10, FontStyle.Bold), Brushes.Black, 150, 10)
                              e.Graphics.DrawString("Date and Time: " & Now.ToString, _
                                          New Font("Courier New", 10, FontStyle.Bold), _
                                          Brushes.Black, 10, 38)
                              ' Print the column headings.
                              e.Graphics.DrawString(String.Format(formatStr, "Product", _
                                       "Desc", "Prod Num", "Price", "Units Sold", _
                                       "Revenue"), New Font("Courier New", 10, _
                                       FontStyle.Bold), Brushes.Black, 10, 66)
                              ' Set the vertical position for the first item.
                              vertPos = 80
                              ' Print sales data for each product.
                              For count = 0 To maxSubscript
                                  ' Calculate the unit revenue.
                                  revenue = products(count).unitsSold * _
                                      products(count).price
                                  ' Accumulate the total revenue.
                                  totalRevenue += revenue
                                  ' Print the unit data.
                                  e.Graphics.DrawString(String.Format(formatStr, _
                                          products(count).name, products(count).desc, _
                                          products(count).prodNum, _
                                          FormatCurrency(products(count).price), _
                                          products(count).unitsSold, _
                                          FormatCurrency(revenue)), _
                                          NewFont("Courier New", 10, FontStyle.Regular), _
                                          Brushes.Black, 10, vertPos)
                                  vertPos += 14
                              Next
                              ' Print the report footer.
                              e.Graphics.DrawString("Total Revenue: " & _
                                       FormatCurrency(totalRevenue), _
                                       New Font("Courier New", 12, _
                                       FontStyle.Bold), Brushes.Black, 150, vertPos)
                          End Sub
```

Step 12: Write the code for the `ReadFile` and `SaveFile` Sub procedures, as follows.

```
Sub ReadFile(ByVal filename As String)
    ' Read the contents of the specified file
    ' into the unitsSold array.
    Dim inputFile As System.IO.StreamReader
    Dim count As Integer = 0  ' Loop counter

    ' Open the file.
    inputFile = System.IO.File.OpenText(filename)
    ' Read the data.
```

```
            Do While (inputFile.Peek <> -1) And _
                (count <= maxSubscript)
                products(count).unitsSold = inputFile.ReadLine
                count += 1
        Loop
        ' Close the file.
        inputFile.Close()
    End Sub

    Sub SaveFile(ByVal filename As String)
        ' Save the contents of the unitsSold array.
        Dim outputFile As System.IO.StreamWriter
        Dim count As Integer     ' Loop counter

        ' Open the file.
        outputFile = System.IO.File.CreateText(filename)
        ' Save the data.
        For count = 0 To maxSubscript
            outputFile.WriteLine(products(count).unitsSold)
        Next
        ' Close the file.
        outputFile.Close()
    End Sub
```

Step 13: Save the project.

Step 14: Run the application. The splash screen should appear. It should automatically close after five seconds.

Step 15: When the main form appears, click the Report menu, then click Enter Sales Data. You will be prompted with input boxes to enter the units sold for each of the DLC products. Enter the following values:

Product number 914: **140**
Product number 915: **85**
Product number 916: **129**
Product number 917: **67**
Product number 918: **94**
Product number 919: **142**
Product number 920: **109**
Product number 921: **65**
Product number 922: **43**

Step 16: Click the Report menu, then click Display Sales Report. The form should now show the revenue for each product and the total revenue, as shown in Figure 9-28.

Figure 9-28 Form with sales data shown

Step 17:   Click the File menu, then click Save As. The Save As dialog box should appear. In the File name text box enter SalesData.txt, then click the Save button. This saves the units sold numbers to the file SalesData.txt.

Step 18:   On the main form, click File on the menu bar, then click Clear Sales Figures on the File menu. The units sold and revenue for each product, as well as the total revenue, should clear.

Step 19:   Click the File menu then click Open File. The Open dialog box should appear Select the SalesData.txt file and click the Open button.

Step 20:   Click the Report menu, then click Display Sales Report. The form should now show the revenue for each product and the total revenue.

Step 21:   Click the File menu, then click Print Sales Report. The application should print a report on your printer like the following:

```
                    Demetris Leadership Center Sales Report

Date printed: 6/25/2003
Time printed: 11:30:13 AM

        ProductDescProd NumPriceUnits SoldRevenue

        Six Steps to LeadershipBook914$12.95140$1,813.00
        Six Steps to LeadershipAudiocassette915$14.9585$1,270.75
        The Road to ExcellenceVideo916$18.95129$2,444.55
        Seven Lessons of QualityBook917$16.9567$1,135.65
        Seven Lessons of QualityAudiocassette918$21.9594$2,063.30
        Seven Lessons of QualityVideo919$31.95142$4,536.90
        Teams Are Made, Not BornBook920$14.95109$1,629.55
        Leadership for the FutureBook921$14.9565$971.75
        Leadership for the FutureAudiocassette922$16.9543$728.85

        Total Revenue:  $16,594.30
```

Step 22:   Exit the application.

SUMMARY

Data is saved in a file, which is stored on a computer's disk.

Three steps must be taken when an application uses a file: The file must be opened (which creates the file if it does not exist), data is either written to the file or read from the file, and the file is closed.

There are two types of files: text and binary. There are also two methods of accessing the data in files: sequential-access and random-access. This chapter only covers sequential-access text files, which are like streams of data that must be read from beginning to end.

To write data to a file you create a `StreamWriter` object. To read data from a file you create a `StreamReader` object.

The `System.IO.File.CreateText` method creates a file and returns the address of a `StreamWriter` object. If the file already exists, its contents are erased. The `System.IO.File.AppendText` method opens a file and returns the address of a

StreamWriter object. If the file already exists, new output is appended to the existing output. If the file does not exist, it is created. The System.IO.File.OpenText method opens a file and returns the address of a StreamReader object.

WriteLine is a StreamWriter method that writes a line of data to a file, terminating the line with a newline character. Write is a StreamWriter method that writes an item of data to a file without terminating the output with a newline character.

ReadLine is a StreamReader method that reads, and then returns, a line of data from a file.

When a sequential file is opened, its read position is set to the first item in the file. As data is read, the read position advances through the file.

Close is both a StreamWriter and a StreamReader method that closes a file.

The System.IO.File.Exists method determines if a specified file exists.

Peek is a StreamReader method that can be used to determine if the end of a file has been reached.

You save the contents of an array to a file using a loop that steps through each element of the array, writing its contents to the file.

By specifying a namespace with the Imports statement, you can refer to names in that namespace without fully qualifying them.

The OpenFileDialog control can display a standard Windows Open dialog box. The SaveFileDialog control can display a standard Windows Save As dialog box. The ColorDialog control can display a standard Windows Color dialog box. The FontDialog control can display a standard Windows Font dialog box.

The PrintDocument control gives your application the ability to print output on the printer. You write the code that handles the actual printing in the PrintPage event procedure. You trigger a PrintPage event by calling the Print method.

In the PrintPage event procedure, you use the e.Graphics.DrawString method to send output to the printer.

Reports typically have a header, a body, and a footer.

To properly align printed data in columns, you must use a monospaced font to ensure that all characters occupy the same amount of space, and use the String.Format method to format the data into columns.

A structure is a data type that you create, which contains one or more variables known as fields. The fields can be of different data types. You create a structure with the Structure statement. Once you have created a structure, you may declare variables of it.

KEY TERMS

AppendText method	CreateText method
Binary file	Delimiter
Buffer	File
Chr function	Filename property
Close method	Filter property
Color dialog box	Font dialog box
ColorDialog control	FontDialog control

InitialDirectory property
Input file
Multiline
Newline character
Open dialog box
OpenFileDialog control
`OpenText` method
Output file
Peek method
`Print` method
PrintDocument control
`PrintPage` event procedure
Random Access File
Read method
Read position
`ReadLine` method
`ReadToEnd` method
Report body

Report footer
Report header
Save As dialog box
SaveFileDialog property
Sequential access file
`StreamWriter` class
`StreamWriter` object
Structure
`Structure` statement
`System.IO.File.AppendText` method
`System.IO.File.CreateText` method
`System.IO.File.Exists` method
`System.IO.File.OpenText` method
Title property
WordWrap property
`Write` method
`WriteLine` method

Review Questions

Fill-in-the-blank

1. Before a file can be used, it must be _____.
2. When a file is opened, a _____ is created, which is a small "holding section" of memory that data is first written to.
3. When it is finished using a file, an application should always _____ it.
4. To write data to a sequential file, you use a _____ object.
5. To read data from a sequential file, you use a _____ object.
6. The _____ method writes a line to a file.
7. The _____ method reads a line from a file.
8. The _____ character is a delimiter that marks the end of a line in a file.
9. The _____control allows you to print data directly to the printer.
10. You write code that handles printing in the _____ event procedure.
11. All of the characters printed with a _____ font occupy the same amount of space.
12. The _____ control displays an Open dialog box for selecting or entering a file name.
13. The _____ control displays a Save As dialog box for selecting or entering a file.
14. The _____ control displays a Color dialog box for selecting a color.
15. The _____ control displays a Font dialog box for selecting a font.
16. A(n) _____is a data type that you create, containing one or more variables, which are known as fields.

Multiple Choice

1. What are the two types of files?

    a. Real and integer

    b. Microsoft Access and Microsoft Word

    c. Text and binary

    d. Encrypted and decrypted

2. You use this type of object to write data to a file.
    a. `FileWriter`
    b. `OuputFile`
    c. `File`
    d. `StreamWriter`

3. You use this type of object to read data from a file.
    a. `FileReader`
    b. `StreamReader`
    c. `File`
    d. `Inputfile`

4. This method creates a file if it does not exist, and erases the contents of the file if it already exists.
    a. `System.IO.File.OpenText`
    b. `System.IO.File.AppendText`
    c. `System.IO.File.CreateText`
    d. `System.IO.File.OpenNew`

5. This method creates a file if it does not exist. If it already exists, data that is written to it will be added to the end of its existing contents.
    a. `System.IO.File.OpenText`
    b. `System.IO.File.AppendText`
    c. `System.IO.File.CreateText`
    d. `System.IO.File.OpenNew`

6. This statement writes a line of data to a file, terminating it with a newline character.
    a. `WriteLine`
    b. `SaveLine`
    c. `StoreLine`
    d. `Write`

7. This statement writes an item of data to a file, and does not terminate it with a newline character.
    a. `WriteItem`
    b. `SaveItem`
    c. `StoreItem`
    d. `Write`

8. This statement reads a line from a file.
    a. `Read`
    b. `ReadLine`
    c. `GetLine`
    d. `Input`

9. You use this method to detect when the end of a file has been reached.
   a. `End`
   b. `Peek`
   c. `LastItem`
   d. `FileEnd`

10. You use this method to determine if a file exists.
    a. `System.File.Exists`
    b. `File.IO.Exists`
    c. `System.IO.File.Exists`
    d. `Exists.File`

11. Assuming that `ofdOpen` is an OpenFileDialog control, the following statement displays the dialog box.
    a. `ofdOpen.Display()`
    b. `Show(ofdOpen)`
    c. `ofdOpen.OpenDialog()`
    d. `ofdOpen.ShowDialog()`

12. This property determines the types of files displayed in an Open or a Save As dialog box.
    a. FileTypes
    b. Filter
    c. Types
    d. FileDisplay

13. This property determines the directory, or folder, that is first displayed in an Open or a Save As dialog box.
    a. InitialDirectory
    b. InitialFolder
    c. Location
    d. Path

14. When the user selects a file with an Open or Save As dialog box, the file's path and name are stored in what property?
    a. Filename
    b. PathName
    c. File
    d. Item

15. When a PrintDocument control's `Print` method is executed, it triggers this event.
    a. `StartPrint`
    b. `PrintPage`
    c. `PagePrint`
    d. `SendPage`

16. Inside the appropriate PrintDocument event procedure, you use this method to actually send output to the printer.
    a. `e.Graphics.DrawString`
    b. `e.PrintText`

     c.   `e.Graphics.SendOutput`

     d.   `Print`

17.   You can use this method to align data into columns.

     a.   `Align`

     b.   `Format.Align`

     c.   `Format.Column`

     d.   `String.Format`

18.   This statement allows you to create a data type that contains one or more variables, known as fields.

     a.   `UserDefined`

     b.   `DataType`

     c.   `Structure`

     d.   `Fields`

True or False

Indicate whether each of the following statements is true or false.

1.   T F: A file must be opened before it can be used.

2.   T F: An input file is a file that a program writes data to.

3.   T F: To read a record that is stored in the middle or at the end of a sequential-access file, an application must read all the records in the file before it.

4.   T F: The `System.IO.File.CreateText` method creates a `StreamReader` object and returns its memory address.

5.   T F: If you specify only a file name when opening a file, Visual Basic .NET will assume the file's location to be the same folder from which the application is running.

6.   T F: In addition to separating the contents of a file into lines, the newline character also serves as a delimiter.

7.   T F: If you call the `WriteLine` method with no argument, it will write a blank line to the file.

8.   T F: A file's read position is set to the end of the file when a file is first opened.

9.   T F: The `Peek` method causes the read position to advance by one character.

10.   T F: The Title property holds the name of the file the user selected with an Open or Save As dialog box.

11.   T F: You can specify the font to use when sending output to the printer.

12.   T F: You must use a proportionally-spaced font when aligning data in columns.

13.   T F: A structure may hold variables of different data types.

14.   T F: `Structure` statements can appear inside a procedure or function.

15.   T F: Structures may not contain arrays.

16.   T F: You many declare an array of structure variables.

Short Answer

1.   What are the three steps that must be taken when a file is used by an application?

2.   What happens when you close a file with the `Close` method?

3.   What is a file's read position? Where is the read position when a file is first opened for reading?

4. What is the difference between the `WriteLine` method and the `Write` method?

5. What happens when you use the `System.IO.File.OpenText` method to open a file that does not exist?

6. What has happened when the `Peek` method returns -1?

7. What does the `ReadLine` method return when it reads a blank line?

8. What does the `Read` method return?

9. What is the difference between the `Print` method and the `PagePrint` event procedure?

10. Where must `Structure` statements appear?

What Do You Think?

1. How do you think a file buffer increases system performance?

2. Why should you use the `Peek` method before the `ReadLine` method rather than after it?

3. You are using the `ReadLine` method to read data from a file. After each line is read, it is added to a list box. What error can potentially occur, and how do you prevent it?

4. An application has the forms `frmMain` and `frmGetData`, and the module `MainModule`. You want a structure to be available only to procedures in the `MainModule` module. Where do you place the `Structure` statement, and which access specifier do you use, `Public` or `Private`?

5. Despite the fact that an application properly aligns the contents of a report into columns using the `String.Format` method, on paper the columns do not align as they should. What is the problem?

Find the Errors

What is wrong with the following code?

1.
```
Dim myFile As System.IO.StreamReader
myFile = System.IO.File.CreateText("names.txt")
```

2.
```
If Not System.Exists(filename) Then
    MessageBox.Show(filename & " does not exist.")
End If
```

3.
```
Do Until myFile.Peek = ""
    input = myFile.ReadLine()
    lstResults.Items.Add(input)
Loop
```

4. (Assume that `ofdOpen` is an OpenFileDialog control.)
```
ofdOpen.Filter = "Text files (*.txt)&*.txt"
```

5. (Assume that `pdPrint` is a PrintDocument control.)
```
Private Sub pdPrint_PrintPage(ByVal sender As System.Object, _
        ByVal e As System.Drawing.Printing.PrintPageEventArgs) _
        Handles pdPrint.PrintPage
    pdPrint.Print("Hello World!", New Font("Times New Roman", _
                12, FontStyle.Regular), Brushes.Black, 10, 10)
End Sub
```

6. The following Structure statement appears in a form.

```
Structure PersonInfo
    Dim name As String
    Dim age As Integer
    Dim phone As String
End Structure
```

The following statement appears in the same form:

```
PersonInfo.name = "Jill Smith"
```

Algorithm Workbench

1. A file named DiskInfo.txt already exists. You wish to add data to the data already in the file. Write the statements necessary to open the file.

2. You wish to create a new file named NewFile.txt and write data to it. Write the statements necessary to open the file.

3. An application uses a list box named `lstInventory`. Write code that writes the contents of the list box to the file Inventory.txt.

4. An application has an array of integers named `numbers`. Write code that writes the contents of the array to the file numbers.txt.

5. Write a `Structure` statement that creates a structure to hold the following data about a savings account. The structure should be declared in a standard module and be available to all modules in the project.
    Account number (string)
    Account balance (demical)
    Interest rate (single)
    Average monthly balance (demical)

6. Assume that `CustomerData` is a structure. The following statement declares `customers` as an array of 10 `CustomerData` variables.

    ```
    Dim customers(9) As CustomerData
    ```

    Write a statement that stores "Jones" in the `lastName` field of the `customers(7)`.

7. You have the following variables: `prodName`, `prodNum`, and `prodPrice`. Write a `String.Format` statement that returns a string with `prodName`'s value in a column of 10 spaces, `prodNum`'s value in a column of 8 spaces, and `prodPrice`'s value in a column of 6 spaces.

8. An application uses an OpenFileDialog control named `ofdOpen`. Write statements that will display an Open dialog box with the initial directory C:\Becky\Images and use the following filters: JPEG images (*.jpg) and GIF images (*.gif).

PROGRAMMING CHALLENGES

1. Employee Data, Part 1

Create an application that allows the user to enter the following employee data: first name, middle name, last name, employee number, department, telephone number, telephone extension, and e-mail address. The valid selections for department are accounting, administration, marketing, MIS, and sales. Once the data is entered, the user should be able to save it to a file. Figure 9-29 shows an example of the application's form.

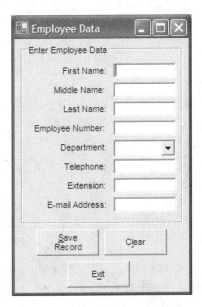

Figure 9-29   Employee Data form for saving employee records

The form shown in Figure 9-29 has a combo box for selecting the department; a Save Record button, which writes the record to a file; a Clear button that clears the text boxes; and an Exit button. Write code in the `Form_Load` procedure that allows the user to enter the name of the file.

2.   Employee Data, Part 2

Create an application that reads the records stored in the file created by the application in Programming Challenge 1.

Write code in the form's `Load` procedure that allows the user to enter the name of the file and opens it. The form shown in Figure 9-30 has a Next Record button, which reads a record from the file and displays its fields; a Clear button which clears the labels; and an Exit button. When the user clicks the Next Record button, the application should read the next record from the file and display it. When the end of the file is encountered, a message should be displayed.

3.   Student Test Scores

A teacher has six students and wants you to create an application that stores their grade data in a file and prints a grade report. The application should have a structure that stores the following student data: name (a string), test scores (an array of five singles), and average test score (a single). Because the teacher has six students, the application should use an array of six structure variables.

The application should allow the user to enter data for each student, and calculate the average test score. Figure 9-31 shows an example form.

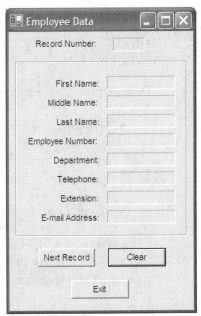

Figure 9-30   Employee Data form for reading employee records

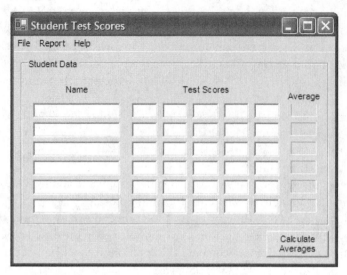

Figure 9-31 Student Test Scores form

The user should be able to save the data to a file, read the data from the file, and print a report showing each student's test scores and average score. The form shown in Figure 9-31 uses a menu system. You may use Buttons instead if you prefer.

Input validation: Do not accept test scores less than zero or greater than 100.

4. Video Collection

Create an application that stores data about your video collection in a file. The application should have a structure to hold the following fields: video name, year produced, running time, and rating. The application should allow the user to save the data to a file, search the file for a video by name, and print a report listing all the video records in the file. Figure 9-32 shows an example form.

Figure 9-32 Video Collection form

Design Your Own Forms

5. Random Number File Generator

Create an application that generates a series of 100 random numbers in the range of 1 through 1000. Save the series of numbers to a file.

6. Number Analysis

Create an application that reads the numbers from the file your application created for Programming Challenge 5. (If you have not completed that assignment, use the file named NumberSet.txt in the \Chap9 folder on the student disk. It contains a series of 100 real numbers.) Your application should perform the following:

- ◆ Display the total of the numbers
- ◆ Display the average of the numbers
- ◆ Display the highest number in the file
- ◆ Display the lowest number in the file

7. Font and Color Tester

Create an application that tests the way different fonts and color combinations appear. The application should display some text in a label, and have a menu with the items Select Font and Select Color.

The Select Font menu item should display a Font dialog box with a color drop-down list. The application should change the text displayed in the label to the font and color selected in the dialog box.

The Select Color menu item should display a Color dialog box. The application should change the background color of the label to the color selected in the dialog box.

8. Simple Text Editor Modification

Modify the Simple Text Editor application that you created in this chapter by adding a View menu to the menu system. The View menu should have two items: Font and Color.

The Font menu item should display a Font dialog box with a color drop-down list. The application should change the text displayed in the text box to the font and color selected in the dialog box.

The Color menu item should display a Color dialog box. The application should change the background color of the text box to the color selected in the dialog box.

9. Image Viewer

You can load an image into a PictureBox control at run time by using the `Image.FromFile` method. For example, assume that `picImage` is a PictureBox control and `filename` is a variable containing the name of a graphic file. The following statement loads the graphic file into the Picture-Box control:

```
picImage.Image = Image.FromFile(filename)
```

Create an application that has a PictureBox control on a form. The PictureBox control should be configured so it fills the entire area of the form and resizes when the user resizes the form.

The application should have a File menu with an Open command. The Open command should display an Open dialog box, displaying files of the following graphic types:

- Bitmaps (*.bmp)
- Jpegs (*.jpg)
- Gifs (*.gif)

When the user selects a file with the Open dialog box, the application should display the image in the PictureBox control.

10. Employee Data, Part 3

Create an application that performs the following operations with the employee file created by the application in Programming Challenge 1:

- Uses an Open dialog box to allow the user to select the file
- Allows the user to enter a new employee record and then saves the record to the file
- Allows the user to enter an employee number and searches for a record containing that employee number. If the record is found, the record is displayed.
- Display all records, one after the other
- Prints an employee record

Equip your application with either a menu system or a set of Buttons to perform these operations.

11. Customer Accounts

Create an application that uses a structure to store the following data about a customer account: last name, first name, customer number, address, city, state, ZIP code, telephone number, account balance, and date of last payment. The application should allow the user to save customer account records to the file, search the file for a customer by last name or customer number, and print a report listing all the customer records in the file.

Input validation: When entering a new record, make sure the user enters data for all fields. Do not accept negative numbers for account balance.

12. Rainfall Statistics File

In Programming Challenge 2 of Chapter 8 you created an application that allows the user to enter the amount of rainfall for each month and then displays rainfall statistics. Modify the application so it can save the monthly rainfall amounts entered by the user to a file and read the monthly rainfall amounts from a file.

13. Charge Account Number File

In Programming Challenge 9 of Chapter 8 you created an application that allows the user to enter a charge account number and determines whether the number is valid by comparing it to the numbers in an array. Modify the application so it compares the number to the numbers in a file. Create the file using Notepad or another text editor.

CHAPTER 10

10

Working with Databases

▶ 10.1 Introduction

$\mathbf{M}$ost businesses store their company data in databases, and Visual Basic allows you to work with many different types of databases. This chapter discusses basic database terminology and introduces fundamental database concepts. ADO .NET is presented as a tool for accessing databases. Many fundamental techniques for working with databases in code are presented.

▶ 10.2 What Is a Database?

CONCEPT

THE DATA IN A DATABASE IS ORGANIZED IN TABLES, ROWS, AND COLUMNS.

In addition to working with sequential files, as discussed in Chapter 9, Visual Basic allows you to write applications that work with databases, such as those created with Microsoft Access. A *database* may be thought of as a collection of tables which hold related data. The data stored in a *table* is organized in rows and columns. Figure 10-1 shows an example of a table that holds inventory data.

A *field* is an individual piece of information pertaining to an item. In a database table, each column is a field. The table in Figure 10-1 has four columns or fields. The first column contains part numbers, the second column contains descriptions, the third column contains prices, and the fourth column contains quantities on hand.

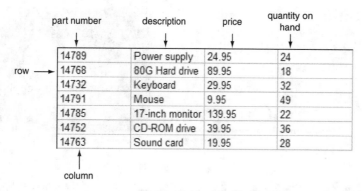

Figure 10-1   Database table

A *record* is a complete set of data about a single item, consisting of one or more fields. In a database table, each row is a record. For example, the third row in the table contains the following record:

Part number: 14732

Description: Keyboard

Price: 29.95

Quantity on hand: 32

Database tables usually have a primary key. A *primary key* is a field, or the combination of multiple fields, that uniquely identify each row in the table. For example, in the inventory table, the part number column would be a good choice for the primary key because no two parts will have the same part number.

✓ **Checkpoint**

10.1   How are database tables organized?

10.2   What is a field?

10.3   What is a record?

10.4   How do records and fields relate to rows and columns?

10.5   What is a primary key?

▶ **10.3   ADO .NET**

CONCEPT

ADO .NET IS A DATABASE TECHNOLOGY THAT ALLOWS YOU TO CONNECT YOUR VISUAL BASIC .NET APPLICATIONS TO A VARIETY OF DATA SOURCES.

The previous version of Visual Basic supported a database component known as ADO, which stands for ActiveX Data Objects. Visual Basic .NET supports Microsoft's newest generation of database technology, known as ADO .NET. *ADO .NET* is an extremely powerful data access component. In this chapter you will learn fundamental techniques for accessing and manipulating databases using ADO .NET.

Setting Up an Application to Work with a Database

Setting your application up to work with a database involves three steps:

1. Create a connection to a data source.

2. Create a data adapter to facilitate the transfer of data from the data source to your application, and vice versa.

3. Create a dataset to hold the data in memory while your application works with it.

The Data Connection

The first step is to create a connection to a data source. As the name implies, a *data source* is source of data. Although we will focus exclusively on databases, there are many different types of data sources, such as spreadsheets, e-mail repositories, text files, etc. Furthermore, the data source may be located on the same computer as the application that is accessing it, or it may be located on a server that the computer is connected to over a network. You use a connection object to establish a connection with a data source. The *connection object*'s task is to provide the low-level functionality to interact with a data source.

The Data Adapter

The second step is to create a data adapter. A *data adapter* is an object that provides the required methods for retrieving from the data source and updating the data in the data source after your application has made a change to it.

The Dataset

The third step is to create a dataset. A *dataset* is an in-memory cache of records that is separate from the data source but still allows you to work with the data. Think of it as a holding area for information retrieved from a data source. Your application does not directly search and manipulate the data in the data source, but performs its operations on the data held in the dataset.

Once the data has been loaded into the dataset, the connection to the data source is not utilized until data within the dataset has been modified and a request to update the source has been initiated. All changes to the data take place within the dataset and must be applied to the source. This type of data manipulation was adopted to minimize network traffic and take advantage of the processing capabilities of the client.

Figure 10-2 illustrates that application code works with the dataset. Data is transferred from the data source to the dataset, or vice-versa, through the data adapter.

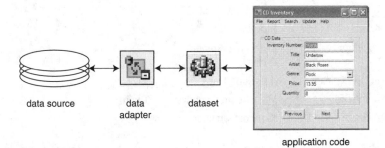

Figure 10-2 Flow of data

✓ **Checkpoint**

10.6 What are the three steps involved in setting an application up to work with a database?

10.7 What is a data source?

10.8 What is a data adapter?

10.9 What is a dataset?

10.10 When your application manipulates data, does it perform the manipulation on the dataset or the data source?

▶ 10.4 Focus on Problem Solving: The Sounds Incredible Music Store CD Inventory Application

CONCEPT

IN THIS CHAPTER YOU DEVELOP AN APPLICATION THAT PERFORMS BASIC OPERATIONS ON A DATABASE, SUCH AS ADDING CHANGING, AND DELETING RECORDS, AND SEARCHING FOR DATA.

This chapter's Focus on Problem Solving exercise is divided among the remaining sections. You have been asked by the manager of the Sounds Incredible music store to create an application that manages a database of the store's inventory of compact discs. The application should allow the user to browse through all the records in the database, search for a specific record, add new records, delete records, and update existing records. In addition it should calculate the total retail value of the CD inventory.

The manager has already created a database with Microsoft Access. The database is stored in a file named CDInventory.mdb, located in the \Chap10 folder on the student disk. It contains one table named `tblCompactDiscs`, which holds the inventory data. It is recommended that table names be prefixed with `tbl`. Table 10-1 lists the data currently stored in the table.

Table 10-1

Records for the `tblCompactDiscs` database table

Inventory number	Title	Artist	Genre	Price	Quantity
17865	Tonal Experience	Loud Ones	Rock	14.95	5
17853	Missing Card	Joe Looney Band	Rock	12.95	7
17452	All That Jazz	Nick Robertson	Jazz	15.95	2
17369	Best of Beethoven	Clyde Philharmonic Orchestra	Classical	11.95	1
18965	Alone in New Orleans	Nick Robertson	Jazz	15.95	3
16877	Down in the Dirt	Mainstream Cowboys	Country	13.95	6
16522	Mozart, Please	Hazelton Symphony Orchestra	Classical	14.95	2
15936	Undertow	Black Roses	Rock	13.95	8
17852	Crimson Moon	Audrey Kline	Country	14.95	4

Each field in the database has a name. The recommended prefix for field names is `fld`. The field names in the `tblCompactDiscs` table will be `fldInvNumber`, `fldTitle`, `fldGenre`, `fld Price`, and `fldQuantity`.

Database fields are also assigned a data type. The data types available for fields are determined by the type of database and are not the same as the Visual Basic data types. For example, Table 10-2 describes most of the data types available in Microsoft Access. Table 10-3 compares these Access data types to the Visual Basic data types.

Table 10-2

Microsoft Access data types

Field Data Type	Description
Text	Text and numbers, such as names and addresses, phone numbers, and postal codes. A Text field can contain from 0 to 255 characters.
Memo	Lengthy text and numbers, such as comments or explanations. A Memo field can contain up to 1.2 billion characters.
Number	Numerical data on which you intend to perform mathematical calculations, except calculations involving money. The Number data types are byte, integer, long integer, single, and double.
Date/Time	Dates and times. The same field can store both a date and a time. All dates are stored in U.S. format (MM/DD/YYYY). Internally, a floating-point number stores the date in the whole number portion, and the fractional portion stores the number of minutes since midnight.
Currency	Used where a field contains monetary values. Do not use the Number data type for currency values, because numbers to the right of the decimal are rounded off during calculations. The Currency data type maintains a fixed number of digits to the right of the decimal.
AutoNumber	Sequential numbers automatically inserted by the database engine. Numbering begins at 1.
Yes/No	Holds values of Yes/No, True/False, On/Off. Corresponds to Visual Basic's Boolean type.
OLE Object	Objects created in other programs using the OLE protocol. Managed by OLE Image, or picture box controls.

Table 10-3

Comparison of Microsoft Access and Visual Basic data types

Access Data Type	Visual Basic Data Type
Text	String
Memo	String
Number (byte)	Byte
Number (integer)	Integer
Number (long integer)	Long integer
Number (single)	Single
Number (double)	Double
Date/Time	Date
Currency	Decimal
AutoNumber	Long
Yes/No	Boolean
OLE Object	String

Data-Aware Controls

The ADO .NET dataset gives your application access to data in a database table. In order to work with the data, you must bind one or more data-aware controls to the dataset. A *data-aware control* is one that can automatically display data from a particular row and column of a table in a dataset. Most of the controls in Visual Basic .NET are data aware.

Data-aware controls have a DataBindings property which is composed of several subproperties. For example, the TextBox control has a DataBindings property, and within it is a Text subproperty. The Text subproperty holds the name of a column, and is used to bind that column to the control's Text property. At run time, the text box control displays the data in the selected column of a specific row.

TIP: Before binding a data-aware control to a dataset, you must have already configured the connection, data adapter and dataset objects.

The `BindingContext` and `CurrencyManager` Objects

All Windows forms in Visual Basic .NET have a built-in object named *BindingContext*. This object manages all of the data bindings for the controls on the form. A `CurrencyManager` object is added to a form when you connect the form to a data source. The *CurrencyManager object* gives you a simple way to navigate among the rows in a database table. One row in the database table is always the current row. The `CurrencyManager` object provides a way to select different rows as the current row. The data-aware controls always display data from the current row, so each time a new row is selected, the data displayed on the form is updated.

Tutorial 10-1 guides you through the steps of adding an ADO .NET dataset to an application, connecting it to the CDInventory.mdb database, binding data-aware controls to the dataset, and using the `CurrencyManager` object to navigate among the rows in the database table.

TUTORIAL 10-1:

Creating an application that works with a database

The folder \Chap10\CD Inventory on the student CD contains a partially completed project named CD Inventory. It also contains a Microsoft Access database file named CDInventory.mdb. In this tutorial you will complete the application so it displays data from the database, adds new records, modifies and deletes existing records, searches for records, and reports data from calculations made on the records.

NOTE: *Before starting this tutorial, copy the CD Inventory folder and the CDInventory.mdb file from the student disk to a location on your hard drive.*

Figure 10-3   The CD Inventory main form

Step 1:   Start Visual Basic and open the CD Inventory project. The `frmMain` form is shown in Figure 10-3.

The controls on the form are named `txtInvNumber`, `txtTitle`, `txtArtist`, `cboGenre`, `txtPrice`, `txtQuantity`, `btnPrevious`, and `btnNext`.

Establishing the database connection.

Step 2:   The Server Explorer tab appears at the left of the Visual Basic .NET main window, near the ToolBox. Figure 10-4 shows how the tab might appear, depending on how your windows are configured. Click the Server Explorer tab to open the Server Explorer window.

TIP: If you do not see the Server Explorer tab, click View on the menu bar, then click Server Explorer. You can also press Ctrl+Alt+S on the keyboard.

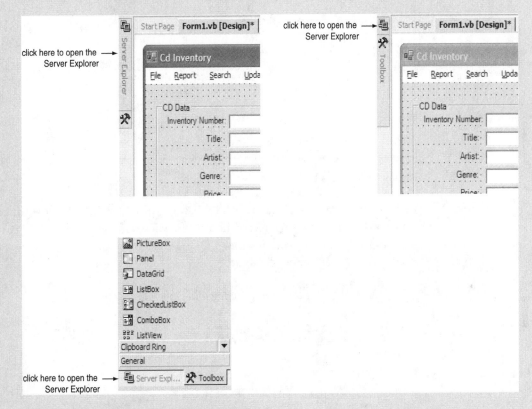

Figure 10-4   Server Explorer tab locations

Step 3:   Click the Connect to database icon in the Server Explorer window, as shown in Figure 10-5. This should cause the Data Link Properties dialog box to appear, as shown in Figure 10-6.

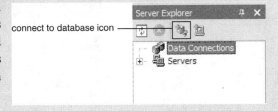

Figure 10-5   Connect to database icon

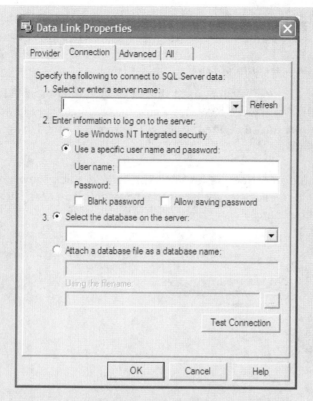

Figure 10-6   Data Link Properties dialog box

Step 4:   Click the Provider tab. This tab gives you a list of providers, which allow you to access different types of data sources. Choose the Microsoft Jet 4 OLE DB Provider, as shown in Figure 10-7. Microsoft Jet 4 OLE DB is a provider that allows you to connect to a Microsoft Access database.

NOTE: *OLE DB stands for object linking and embedding database.*

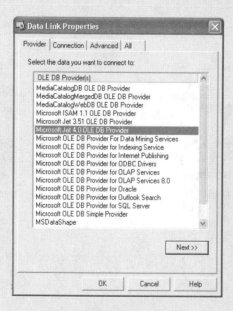

Figure 10-7   Provider tab

Step 5:   Click the Connection tab. The dialog box should appear as shown in Figure 10-8. Under the heading "1. Select or enter a database name", click the button with the ellipsis (...) and browse to the location of the CDInventory.mdb database file. This will be the same folder holding the project files.

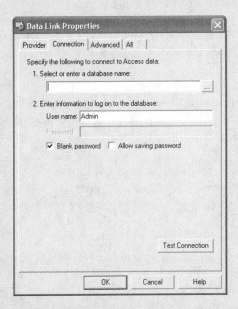

Figure 10-8   Data Link dialog window

Step 6:   Click the Test Connection button. You should see a message box displaying "Test connection succeeded." Click the OK button to dismiss the dialog box.

> **NOTE:**   *If you get an error message indicating that the connection failed after you click the Test Connection button, repeat steps 3 through 6 and make sure you select the CDInventory.mdb file as the database.*

Step 7:   In the Server Explorer window, expand the Data Connections tree until you see the entry for `tblCompact Discs`, as shown in Figure 10-9.

Step 8:   Click and drag the `tblCompactDiscs` table name onto the `frmMain` form.

Notice that there are now two new items in the component tray. The first is named `OleDbConnection1`. This is the connection object which has the capability to make a connection to the CDInventory.mdb database. The second is named `OleDbDataAdapter1`. This is the data adapter object which is capable of transferring data between the database and a dataset.

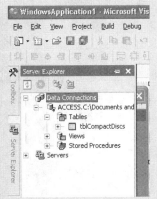

Figure 10-9   The Server Explorer expanded tree

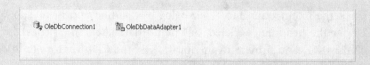

Figure 10-10   New connection and data adapter

Now that the connection and data adapter objects have been added we need to select each one and apply some changes to their properties.

Step 9:   Click the `OleDbConnection1` object in the component tray. In the properties window scroll down until you see the Name property. Change the name from `OleDbConnection1` to `conCompactDiscs`. Note that we use the `con` prefix for connection object names.

Step 10:   Click the `OleDbDataAdapter1` icon in the component tray. In the properties window scroll until you see the Name property. Change the name from `OleDdataAdapter1` to `daCompactDiscs`. Note that we use the `da` prefix for data adapter object names.

Step 11:   Notice that while the `daCompactDiscs` object is selected, the following links appear in the lower portion of the Properties window: Configure Data Adapter, Generate Dataset, and Preview Data. This is shown in Figure 10-11. Click the Configure Data Adapter link.

The Data Adapter Configuration Wizard dialog box, shown in Figure 10-12, will be displayed.

Figure 10-11   Data adapter properties

Figure 10-12   Data Adapter Configuration Wizard

For this application, click the Next command button accepting all of the defaults until you reach the final window and then click Finish. The data adapter has now been configured correctly for general access to all the data in the database table.

Step 12: Click the Generate Dataset link at the bottom of the properties dialog box. The Generate Dataset dialog box will appear. Click the New button under "Choose a Dataset" and type `dsCompactDiscs` in the text box. The dialog box should appear as shown in Figure 10-13. Click OK.

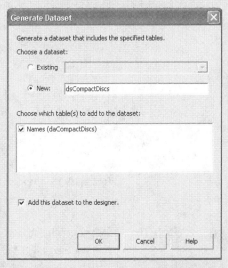

The name you entered for the dataset name, `dsCompactDiscs`, will not be the name of a dataset object, but will serve as a data type name for the dataset. Visual Basic .NET creates a dataset object and assigns it the name `DsCompactDiscs1`. This object is added to the component tray, which should now appear as shown in Figure 10-14.

Figure 10-13 Generate Dataset dialog

Figure 10-14 Completed component tray

We have successfully configured the connection to our Microsoft Access database.

Now you will need to bind the controls on the form to the ADO.NET `DsCompactDiscs1` dataset. The text box at the top of the form is `txtInvNumber`.

Step 13: In the Design window, select the `txtInvNumber` text box.

Step 14: Click the plus sign next to the DataBindings property in the Properties window to expand its contents. The DataBindings property has three subproperties: (Advanced), Tag, and Text.

> **NOTE:** *Because Text is a subproperty of DataBindings, it can be referred to as the DataBindings.Text property.*

Step 15: Select the Text subproperty and click the down arrow. You see a drop-down box that displays an entry for the `DsCompactDiscs1` dataset, as shown in Figure 10-15.

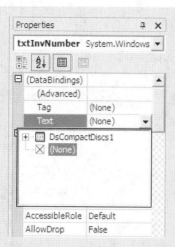

Figure 10-15 Text subproperty

Step 16: Click the plus sign next to DsCompactDiscs1 and continue to expand the tree until you see the fldInvNumber field. Click fldInvNumber to set the binding. Now the txtInvNumber text box is bound to the fldInvNumber field in the dataset.

Step 17: Bind the remaining controls to the appropriate field in the DsCompactDiscs1 dataset in the following manner:

- Select txtTitle and set its DataBindings.Text property to fldTitle.
- Select txtArtist and set its DataBindings.Text property to fldArtist.
- Select cboGenre and set its DataBindings.Text property to fldGenre.
- Select txtPrice and set its DataBindings.Text property to fldPrice.
- Select txtQuantity and set its DataBindings.Text property to fld Quantity.

Step 18: Open the Code window and add the following class-level declaration.

```
' Class-level declaration
Dim currManager As CurrencyManager
```

This code declares a variable that we will use to reference the form's built-in CurrencyManager object. In the next step you will write code that connects this variable to the CurrencyManager object.

Step 19: Now we need to write code that will fill the DsCompactDiscs1 dataset. This is done with the data adapter's *Fill* method. The general format of the Fill method is:

```
DataAdapter.Fill(DataSet)
```

DataAdapter is the name of a data adapter object, and *DataSet* is the name of the dataset object to fill. After this method executes, the dataset object will contain a table of data.

Add a Load event procedure to the form and complete it as follows.

```
Private Sub frmMain_Load(ByVal sender As System.Object, _
          ByVal e As System.EventArgs) Handles MyBase.Load
    ' Fill the data set.
    daCompactDiscs.Fill(DsCompactDiscs1)
    ' Get a reference to the CurrencyManager object.
    currManager = Me.BindingContext(DsCompactDiscs1, _
                          "tblCompactDiscs")

End Sub
```

The first statement uses the daCompactDiscs data adapter's Fill method to retrieve data from the database and fill the DsCompactDiscs1 dataset. After this statement executes, the DsCompactDiscs1 dataset will contain the tblCompactDiscs table, which was read from the database. The next statement is:

```
currManager = Me.BindingContext(DsCompactDiscs1, _
                          "tblCompactDiscs")
```

This statement causes our currManager variable to reference the CurrencyManager object for the tblCompactDiscs table in the DsCompactDiscs1 dataset. We will use the currManager variable to navigate among the rows in the tblCompactDiscs table.

Step 20: Save the project and run the application. The application's form should appear, as shown in Figure 10-16. Because you bound the controls to fields in the dataset, the form displays the data stored in the dataset's first row. This proves that we have successfully connected to the database and retrieved the data from the tblCompactDiscs table. Now we need to add the ability to navigate from record to record. End the application.

Step 21: As you saw in the previous step, the first row of the dataset table is automatically displayed when the application runs. When the user clicks the Next button, the next row in the table should be displayed. Likewise, when the Previous button is clicked, the previous row should be displayed.

Figure 10-16 CD Inventory form

The CurrencyManager object has a *Position property* that holds the number of the current row. Row numbers are zero-based, so the first row in the table is row 0. By adding one to this property, we select the next row as the current row. The CurrencyManager object also has a Count property that holds the number of rows in the table. We will use this property to determine when we have reached the last row in the table.

Add the following `btnNext_Click` event procedure.

```
Private Sub btnNext_Click(ByVal sender As System.Object, _
        ByVal e As System.EventArgs) Handles btnNext.Click
    ' Advance to the next row in the table.
    If currManager.Position < (currManager.Count - 1) Then
        currManager.Position += 1
    Else
        MessageBox.Show("No more records.")
    End If
End Sub
```

NOTE: *Because row numbering starts at zero, we know that we have reached the last row when* `currManager.Position` *is equal to* `currManager.Count -1`.

Step 22: Add the following `btnPrevious_Click` event procedure.

```
Private Sub btnPrevious_Click(ByVal sender As System.Object, _
        ByVal e As System.EventArgs) Handles btnPrevious.Click
    ' Move back to the previous row in the table.
    If currManager.Position > 0 Then
        currManager.Position -= 1
    Else
        MessageBox.Show("First record reached.")
    End If
End Sub
```

Step 23: Save the project and run the application. When the form first appears it should display the contents of the first row in the table. Click the Next button to see the data in the next row. Do this repeatedly until you reach the end of the table.

Step 24: Click the Previous button repeatedly until you reach the first row in the table.

Step 25: End the application.

We have a good start with the application, but we need to add more functionality like adding, deleting and changing records.

Adding New Records and Saving Existing Records

Adding a new record to a database involves the following steps.

- ◆ Create a new empty row with the same column layout as the table that you wish to add the row to.
- ◆ Populate the columns of the new row with data.
- ◆ Add the new row to the table.
- ◆ Save the updated table to the data source.

Let's take a closer look at each step.

Creating a New Empty Row

To create a new empty row you first declare an object variable that can reference the row. Here is the general format of such a declaration.

```
Dim ObjectVar As System.Data.DataRow
```

ObjectVar is the name of the object variable. For example, the following statement declares *newRow* as an object variable that can be used to reference a row.

```
Dim newDataRow As System.Data.DataRow
```

Next you create the row and let the object variable reference it with a statement in the following general format:

```
ObjectVar = DataSet.Table.NewRow
```

ObjectVar is the object variable, `DataSet` is the name of the dataset, `Table` is the name of the table. After the statement executes, `ObjectVar` will reference a new empty row that has the same column layout as the rows in `Table`. For example, the following statement will be used in our CD Inventory application. The object variable is `newDataRow`, `DsCompactDiscs1` is the name of the dataset, and `tblCompactDiscs` is the name of the table.

```
newDataRow = DsCompactDiscs1.tblCompactDiscs.NewRow
```

NOTE: *The new row is not part of the dataset yet.*

Populating the Columns of the New Row

Once you have an object variable that references a new row, you can use the row's `Item` method to assign a value to a column. The general format of such a statement is:

```
ObjectVar.Item(ColumnName) = NewValue
```

ObjectVar is the object variable that references the new row. `ColumnName` is the name of the column that you are assigning a new value to. `NewValue` is the new value. You must write such an assignment statement for each column of the row.

For example, in our CD Inventory application, the column names are `fldInvNumber`, `fldTitle`, `fldArtist`, `fldGenre`, `fldPrice`, and `fldQuantity`. Assuming that `newDataRow` is an object variable that references a new row, the following statements could be used to copy new values to the row's columns. Assume that `newInvNumber`, `newTitle`, `newArtist`, `newGenre`, `newPrice`, and `newQuantity` are variables containing the new data.

```
newDataRow.Item("fldInvNumber") = newInvNumber
newDataRow.Item("fldTitle") = newTitle
newDataRow.Item("fldArtist") = newArtist
newDataRow.Item("fldGenre") = newGenre
newDataRow.Item("fldPrice") = newPrice
newDataRow.Item("fldQuantity") = newQuantity
```

Adding the New Row to a Table

After you have stored the new data into the columns of the new row, you must add the new row to the table. You do so with a statement in the following general format:

```
DataSet.Table.Rows.Add(ObjectVar)
```

DataSet is the name of the dataset and *ObjectVar* is the name of the object variable that references the new row. After the statement executes, the row referenced by *ObjectVar* will be added to the table. For example, the following statement could be used in the CD Inventory application to add the new row referenced by newDataRow to the tblCompactDiscs table.

```
DsCompactDiscs1.tblCompactDiscs.Rows.Add(newDataRow)
```

Saving the Updated Table to the Data Source

Adding a row to a table does not add a row to the underlying data source. If you want a new row to become part of the database file that the table was created from, you must use the data adapter's *Update method*. Here is the method's general format:

```
DataAdapter.Update(DataSet)
```

DataAdapter is the name of a data adapter and *DataSet* is the name of a data set. After this statement executes, the changes that have been made to the data set will be saved to the data adapter's data source. For example, the following statement updates the data source connected to the daCompactDiscs data adapter with the DsCompactDiscs1 dataset.

```
daCompactDiscs.Update(DsCompactDiscs1)
```

In Tutorial 10-2 you will add the capability of saving new records to the database.

TUTORIAL 10-2:

Modifying the CD Inventory application to add records

Step 1: Start Visual Basic .NET and open the CD Inventory project. Add a new standard module to the project named CDInventoryModule. Complete the module's code as follows.

```
Module CDInventoryModule
    ' Module-level declarations
    Public newInvNumber As String
    Public newTitle As String
    Public newArtist As String
    Public newGenre As String
    Public newPrice As Decimal
    Public newQuantity As Integer
End Module
```

This module declares six global variables that will be used by the `frmAdd` form to save the new record data.

Step 2:   Open the `frmAdd` form, which is shown in Figure 10-17.

Create a code template for the OK button's `Click` event procedure, and complete it as shown in the following bold code.

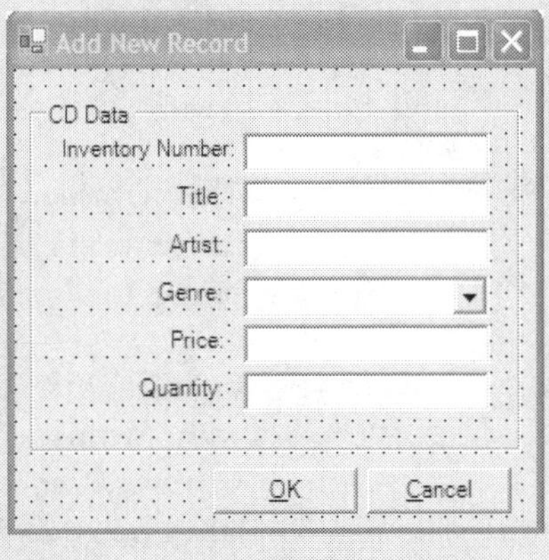

Figure 10-17 The `frmAdd` form

```
Private Sub btnOk_Click(ByVal sender As System.Object, _
        ByVal e As System.EventArgs) Handles btnOk.Click
    ' Copy the new data to the global variables.
    newInvNumber = txtInvNumber.Text
    newTitle = txtTitle.Text
    newArtist = txtArtist.Text
    newGenre = cboGenre.Text
    newPrice = Val(txtPrice.Text)
    newQuantity = Val(txtQuantity.Text)
    ' Signal that OK was clicked.
    Me.DialogResult = DialogResult.OK
    ' Close the form.
    Me.Close()
End Sub
```

This code copies the data from the text boxes and the combo box on the form into the global variables. The following statements appear next:

```
' Signal that OK was clicked.
Me.DialogResult = DialogResult.OK
```

Forms have a property named DialogResult, which may be set at run time. The Dialog Result property holds a value that represents a button, and can be tested after the form closes. This code stores the value DialogResult.OK in the property, indicating that the OK button was pressed. After the form closes, we will test this property to determine which button the user clicked. The last statement in the procedure closes the form.

Step 3:   Create a code template for the Cancel button's `Click` event procedure, and complete it as shown in the following bold code.

```
Private Sub btnCancel_Click(ByVal sender As System.Object, _
        ByVal e As System.EventArgs) Handles btnCancel.Click
    ' Signal that Cancel was clicked.
    Me.DialogResult = DialogResult.Cancel
```

```
        ' Close the form.
        Me.Close()
    End Sub
```

The only action taken by this procedure is to store the value `DialogResult.Cancel` in the form's DialogResult property. This indicates that the user clicked the Cancel button to dismiss the form. The form is then closed.

Step 4: Open the `frmMain` form. The form has a MainMenu control that is already filled with menu items. The Update menu has the following items: Add, Save All Changes, Cancel All Changes, and Delete. The names of these menu items are `mnuUpdateAdd`, `mnuUpdateSave`, `mnuUpdateCancel`, and `mnuUpdateDelete`.

Create a code template for the `mnuUpdateAdd_Click` event procedure, and then complete the procedure with the following code shown in bold.

```
Private Sub mnuUpdateAdd_Click(ByVal sender As System.Object, _
        ByVal e As System.EventArgs) Handles mnuUpdateAdd.Click
    ' Add a new record to the database.
    Dim addNewRecordForm As New frmAdd()
    If addNewRecordForm.ShowDialog = DialogResult.OK Then
        AddNewRecord()
    End If
End Sub
```

This procedure creates an instance of the `frmAdd` form and then opens it with the `ShowDialog` method. The `If` statement tests the return value of the `Show Dialog` method. The `ShowDialog` method returns the value in the form's DialogResult property. Recall that the OK button on the `frmAdd` form returns `Dialog Result.OK` and the Cancel button returns `DialogResult.Cancel`. In this code, if the ShowDialog method returns DialogResult.OK, we call the Add NewRecord Sub procedure, which you will write in the next step.

Step 5: Write the `AddNewRecord` Sub procedure, as follows.

```
Private Sub AddNewRecord()
    ' This procedure adds a new record to the
    ' database.
    Dim newDataRow As System.Data.DataRow

    ' Create a new row with the same layout
    ' as the tblCompactDiscs table.
    newDataRow = DsCompactDiscs1.tblCompactDiscs.NewRow
    ' Copy the new data to the new row.
    newDataRow.Item("fldInvNumber") = newInvNumber
    newDataRow.Item("fldTitle") = newTitle
    newDataRow.Item("fldArtist") = newArtist
    newDataRow.Item("fldGenre") = newGenre
    newDataRow.Item("fldPrice") = newPrice
    newDataRow.Item("fldQuantity") = newQuantity
    ' Add the new row to the dataset.
```

```
        DsCompactDiscs1.tblCompactDiscs.Rows.Add(newDataRow)
        ' Update the database file.
        daCompactDiscs.Update(DsCompactDiscs1)
    End Sub
```

This procedure creates a new row, and then copies the data from the global variables into the row's columns. It then adds the new row to the dataset's table, and saves the table changes to the database file.

Step 6:   Save the project and run the application. At the main form, click Update on the menu bar, then click Add. The `frmAdd` menu should appear.

Step 7:   Enter the following data on the `frmAdd` form:

Inventory number: **18567**
Title: **December Moon**
Artist: **Hans Rose**
Genre: **Jazz**
Price: **18.95**
Quantity: **6**

Step 8:   Use the Next button to navigate to the end of the table. You should see the record you just entered displayed last.

Step 9:   Exit the application.

Saving Existing Records

Next you will code the Update menu's Save All Changes and Cancel All Changes commands. While the user is navigating the records in the database, he or she can make changes to the data. These changes only affect the dataset, and are not stored in the database file until the data adapter's `Update` method is called. The Save All Changes command will call the `Update` method to save all the changes that have been made to the dataset. The Cancel All Changes command will cancel all changes that have been made to the dataset by reloading the data from the data source.

TUTORIAL 10-3:

Coding the Save All Changes and Cancel All Changes commands

Step 1:   Start Visual Basic .NET and open the CD Inventory project. Open the `frmMain` form and create a code template for the `mnuUpdateSave_Click` event procedure. Complete the procedure as shown in the following bold code.

```
Private Sub mnuUpdateSave_Click(ByVal sender As System.Object, _
    ByVal e As System.EventArgs) Handles mnuUpdateSave.Click
    ' Save changes made to the dataset.
    Dim savedPosition As Integer
```

```
      ' Save the current position.
      savedPosition = currManager.Position
      ' Move the current position to force the data
      ' in the currently displayed bound controls to
      ' update the dataset.
      currManager.Position += 1
      ' Update the data source.
      daCompactDiscs.Update(DsCompactDiscs1)
      ' Go back to the saved position.
      currManager.Position = savedPosition
   End Sub
```

Before this procedure saves the contents of the dataset to the data source, it must overcome a limitation of data-bound controls. When the user makes a change to a record that is displayed in the data-bound controls, the changes are not transferred to the dataset until the user moves to another record. For example, suppose the user changes the `fldPrice` field of a record that is displayed on the form, and then saves it. The price change is not saved because it has not been transferred from the text box to the dataset.

To overcome this limitation, this procedure first copies the value in `currManager.Position` to the variable `savedPosition`. This saves the current row position. The procedure then adds one to `currManager.Position`. This forces any changes that have been made to the currently displayed record to be transferred to the dataset. (The `CurrencyManager` object will not cause a run-time error if you attempt to move beyond the last record, so this will work even when the last record is displayed.)

Next, the procedure calls the data adapter's `Update` method, and then copies `savedPosition` back to `currManager.Position`.

Step 2: Create a code template for the `mnuUpdateCancel_Click` event procedure. Complete the procedure as shown in the following bold code.

```
   Private Sub mnuUpdateCancel_Click(ByVal sender As System.Object, _
         ByVal e As System.EventArgs) _
      Handles mnuUpdateCancel.Click
      ' Refill the dataset from the datasource.
      daCompactDiscs.Fill(DsCompactDiscs1)
      currManager.Refresh()
   End Sub
```

This procedure simply reloads the data from the data source into the dataset, replacing any changes that have been made with the data that was last saved. The `Currency Manager` object's `Refresh` method forces the contents of data-bound controls to be refreshed.

Step 3: Save the project and run the application. Locate the following record:

Inventory number: 16877
Title: Down in the Dirt
Artist: Mainstream Cowboys
Genre: Country
Price: 13.95
Quantity: 6

Step 4: Change the price to 16.95. Click Update on the menu bar, and then click Save All Changes. The record is now saved to the database file with the new price.

Step 5: Exit the application, and then start it again. Confirm that the price for the record you changed in step 3 is 16.95.

Step 6: End the application.

Removing Records

The `CurrencyManager` object has a *RemoveAt method* that removes a specified row from the table. The general format of the method is:

```
ObjectVar.RemoveAt(Index)
```

ObjectVar is an object variable that references the `CurrencyManager` object, and *Index* is the position of the row that is to be removed. For example, the following statement can be used in the CD Inventory application to remove the record stored at the current row:

```
currManager.RemoveAt(currManager.Position)
```

The row is only removed from the dataset. For the deletion to become permanent, the dataset must be saved to the data source with the data adapter's `Update` method.

TUTORIAL 10-4:

Coding the Delete command

Step 1: Start Visual Basic .NET and open the CD Inventory project. Open the `frmMain` form and create a code template for the `mnuUpdateDelete_Click` event procedure. Complete the procedure as shown in the following bold code.

```
Private Sub mnuUpdateDelete_Click(ByVal sender As System.Object, _
        ByVal e As System.EventArgs) _
        Handles mnuUpdateDelete.Click
    If MessageBox.Show("Are you sure you want to delete " & _
                        "this record?", "Confirm", _
                        MessageBoxButtons.YesNo) _
                        = DialogResult.Yes Then
        ' Remove the current record from the dataset.
        currManager.RemoveAt(currManager.Position)
```

```
                            ' Save the dataset to the database file.
                            daCompactDiscs.Update(DsCompactDiscs1)
                            ' Refresh the data-bound controls.
                            currManager.Refresh()
                    End If
                End Sub
```

Step 2: Save the project and run the application. Locate the following record:

Inventory number: 16877
Title: Down in the Dirt
Artist: Mainstream Cowboys
Genre: Country
Price: 16.95
Quantity: 6

Step 3: Click Update on the menu bar, and then click Delete. The record is now deleted from the database.

Step 4: End the application.

Inventory Value Report

The Sounds Incredible manager needs to be able to see the total retail value of the store's inventory. To calculate the inventory retail value, we must compute the sum of the retail prices of all the items in inventory. For each record we must multiply `fldQuantity` times `fldPrice`. This gives us the total retail value for that item. We sum the total retail values of each record, and we have the total retail value of the entire inventory.

To perform these calculations, we will write a loop that steps through each row of the table, multiplying the `fldQuantity` field by the `fldPrice` field. You access a specific field in a row with an expression in the following format:

```
DataSet.Table(Index).Field
```

DataSet is the name of the dataset, *Table* is the name of the table, *Index* is a row number, and *Field* is the name of a field. This expression returns the value stored in the specified field. For example, in our CD Inventory application, the following expression returns the value stored in the `fldPrice` field of row 3:

```
DsCompactDiscs1.tblCompactDiscs(3).fldPrice
```

Remember that the first row numbers is zero, so this expression returns the value of the `fldPrice` field in the fourth row.

The table has a Count property that holds the number of rows. You may determine the number of rows in a table with an expression in the following general format:

```
DataSet.Table.Count
```

In our CD Inventory application, we will use the table's Count property to set the upper limit of a loop that calculates the total retail value of the inventory.

TUTORIAL 10-5:

Coding the Inventory Value command

Step 1: Start Visual Basic .NET, open the CD Inventory project, and open the `frmMain` form. The MainMenu control has a Report menu with one item: Inventory Value. The name of this MenuItem object is `mnuReportValue`. Create a code template for the `mnuReportValue_Click` event procedure. Complete the procedure as shown in the following bold code.

```
Private Sub mnuReportValue_Click(ByVal sender As System.Object, _
        ByVal e As System.EventArgs) _
        Handles mnuReportValue.Click
    ' Calculates and displays the total retail value
    ' of the inventory.
    Dim i As Integer              ' Loop counter
    Dim total As Decimal = 0      ' Accumulator

    ' Sum the retail value of each item.
    With DsCompactDiscs1
        For i = 0 To (.tblCompactDiscs.Count - 1)
            total += (.tblCompactDiscs(i).fldPrice * _
                        .tblCompactDiscs(i).fldQuantity)
        Next i
    End With
    MessageBox.Show("Total Retail Value of Inventory: " & _
                    FormatCurrency(total), "Retail Value")
End Sub
```

Step 2: Save the project and run the application. Click Report on the menu bar, then click Inventory Value. A message box should appear displaying the total retail value of the inventory.

Step 3: End the application.

Searching for CDs by inventory number, artist and title

The last feature we will add to our application is the ability to search the database for records by inventory number, artist, or title. For this application we will write simple linear search procedures to locate items. In chapter 11 we will introduce more sophisticated database searching techniques using SQL.

TUTORIAL 10-6:

Coding the search commands

Step 1: Start Visual Basic .NET, open the CD Inventory project, and open the `frmMain` form. The MainMenu control has a Search menu with the following items: Search by Inventory Number, Search by Artist, and Search by Title. The names of these Menu

Item objects are `mnuSearchInvNumber`, `mnuSearchArtist`, and `mnuSearchTitle`. Create a code template for the `mnuSearchInvNumber_Click` event procedure. Complete the procedure as shown in the following bold code.

```
Private Sub mnuSearchInvNumber_Click(ByVal sender As _
      System.Object, ByVal e As System.EventArgs) _
      Handles mnuSearchInvNumber.Click
   ' Find a record by its inventory number.
   Dim searchNumber As Integer ' Inv number to search for
   Dim recNum As Integer        ' Record number of found record

   ' Get the inventory number to search for.
   searchNumber = Val(InputBox("Enter the inventory number " & _
                              "to search for.", "Search"))
   recNum = FindByInvNumber(searchNumber)
   If recNum <> -1 Then
      currManager.Position = recNum
   Else
      MessageBox.Show("Record not found.", "Search")
   End If
End Sub
```

This procedure asks the user to enter an inventory number to search for. That value is then passed as an argument to the `FindByInvNumber` function, which you will write in the next step. The `FindByInvNumber` function will search for a record containing the inventory number passed as an argument. If the record is found, its row number is returned and the `CurrencyManager` object's Position property is changed to that row number. If the record is not found, the function returns -1.

Step 2: Write the code for the `FindByInvNumber` function, as follows.

```
Private Function FindByInvNumber(ByVal invNum As Integer)
   ' Search for a record with a specific inventory
   ' number and return it's row number. If the record
   ' can't be found, return -1.
   Dim i As Integer = 0        ' Loop counter
   Dim recNum As Integer        ' Record number of found record
   Dim isFound As Boolean = False  ' Flag variable

   With DsCompactDiscs1
      Do Until (i >= .tblCompactDiscs.Count) Or isFound
         If .tblCompactDiscs(i).fldInvNumber _
            = invNum Then
            ' Update the flag
            isFound = True
         Else
            ' Increment the counter.
            i += 1
         End If
      Loop
      ' Was the record found?
```

```
                    If isFound Then
                        recNum = i
                    Else
                        recNum = -1
                    End If
                End With
                ' Return the results.
                Return recNum
            End Function
```

This procedure steps through each row in the table, searching for a row where the fldInvNumber field matches the value passed as an argument. If a row is found, its row number is returned. If the row is not found, -1 is returned.

Step 3: Create a code template for the mnuSearchArtist_Click event procedure. Complete the procedure as shown in the following bold code.

```
Private Sub mnuSearchArtist_Click(ByVal sender As _
        System.Object, ByVal e As System.EventArgs) Handles _
        mnuSearchArtist.Click
    ' Find a record by a specific artist.
    Dim byArtist As String  ' Artist to search for
    Dim recNum As Integer   ' Record number of found record

    ' Get the inventory number to search for.
    byArtist = InputBox("Enter the artist to search for.", _
                        "Search")
    ' Search, beginning at row 0.
    recNum = FindByArtist(byArtist, 0)
    If recNum <> -1 Then
        currManager.Position = recNum
        Do Until recNum = -1
            If MessageBox.Show("Search for more records?", _
                        "Search", MessageBoxButtons.YesNo) _
                        = DialogResult.Yes Then
                ' Get the next record number.
                recNum = FindByArtist(byArtist, recNum + 1)
                If recNum <> -1 Then
                    ' Display the found record.
                    currManager.Position = recNum
                Else
                    MessageBox.Show("No more records.", "Search")
                End If
            Else
                recNum = -1
            End If
        Loop
    Else
        MessageBox.Show("Record not found.", "Search")
    End If
End Sub
```

When we searched for a record by its inventory number, we were only concerned with finding the first record with a matching `fldInvNumber` field. That is because no two records exist with the same field number. It must be taken into consideration that multiple records might exist with the same artist name stored in `fldArtist`. This procedure allows the user to search for multiple records.

First, the procedure asks the user to enter an artist to search for. That value is then passed as the first argument to the `FindByArtist` function, and the number zero is passed as the second argument. The second argument specifies the row number to begin the search. The `FindByArtist` function will search for a record beginning at the specified row containing the artist name that you passed as the first argument. If the record is found, the `CurrencyManager` object's Position property is changed to the record's row number, and a loop begins which allows the user to search for another record.

Step 4: Write the code for the `FindByArtist` function, as follows.

```
Private Function FindByArtist(ByVal byArtist As String, _
        ByVal row As Integer)
    ' Search for a record by a specific artist, beginning at
    ' a specific row. If found, return the record's row number.
    ' If a record can't be found, return -1.
    Dim i As Integer            ' Loop counter
    Dim recNum As Integer          ' Record number of found record
    Dim isFound As Boolean = False' Flag variable

    ' Initialize the counter.
    i = row
    ' Search for the first record.
    With DsCompactDiscs1
        Do Until (i >= .tblCompactDiscs.Count) Or isFound
            If .tblCompactDiscs(i).fldArtist.ToUpper _
                = byArtist.ToUpper Then
                    ' Update the flag
                    isFound = True
            Else
                ' Increment the counter.
                i += 1
            End If
        Loop
        ' Was the record found?
        If isFound Then
            recNum = i
        Else
            recNum = -1
        End If
    End With
    ' Return the results.
    Return recNum
End Function
```

This procedure begins at the row specified by the row parameter, searching for a row where the `fldArtist` field matches the value passed as an argument. Note that a case-insensitive comparison is performed. If a row is found, its row number is returned. If the row is not found, -1 is returned.

Step 5:   Create a code template for the `mnuSearchTitle_Click` event procedure. Complete the procedure as shown in the following bold code.

```
Private Sub mnuSearchTitle_Click(ByVal sender As _
          System.Object, ByVal e As System.EventArgs) _
          Handles mnuSearchTitle.Click
    ' Find a record with a specific title.
    Dim title As String  ' title to search for
    Dim recNum As Integer   ' Record number of found record
    ' Get the inventory number to search for.
    title = InputBox("Enter the title to search for.", "Search")
    ' Search, beginning at row 0.
    recNum = FindByTitle(title, 0)
    If recNum <> -1 Then
        currManager.Position = recNum
        Do Until recNum = -1
            If MessageBox.Show("Search for more records?", _
                      "Search", MessageBoxButtons.YesNo) _
                      = DialogResult.Yes Then
                ' Get the next record number.
                recNum = FindByTitle(title, recNum + 1)
                If recNum <> -1 Then
                    ' Display the found record.
                    currManager.Position = recNum
                Else
                    MessageBox.Show("No more records.", "Search")
                End If
            Else
                recNum = -1
            End If
        Loop
    Else
        MessageBox.Show("Record not found.", "Search")
    End If
End Sub
```

Like the `mnuSearchArtist_Click` procedure, this procedure allows the user to search for multiple records with the same search criterion. It uses the `FindByTitle` function to perform the search.

Step 6:   Write the code for the `FindByTitle` function, as follows.

```
Private Function FindBytitle(ByVal title As String, _
                          ByVal row As Integer)
```

```
' Search for a record with a specific title, beginning at
' a specific row. If found, return the record's row number.
' If a record can't be found, return -1.
Dim i As Integer                ' Loop counter
Dim recNum As Integer           ' Record number of found record
Dim isFound As Boolean = False' Flag variable

' Initialize the counter.
i = row
' Search for the first record.
With DsCompactDiscs1
    Do Until (i >= .tblCompactDiscs.Count) Or isFound
        If .tblCompactDiscs(i).fldTitle.ToUpper _
                = title.ToUpper Then
                ' Update the flag
                isFound = True
        Else
                ' Increment the counter.
                i += 1
        End If
    Loop
    ' Was the record found?
    If isFound Then
        recNum = i
    Else
        recNum = -1
    End If
End With
' Return the results.
Return recNum
End Function
```

Step 7: Save the project and run the application. Click Search on the menu bar, then click By Inventory Number. An input box should appear asking you to enter an inventory number. Enter **17369** and click OK. The application should locate the record shown in Figure 10-18.

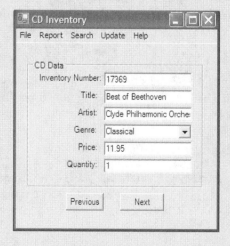

Figure 10-18 CD Inventory form with search results

Step 8:   Now you will test the Search by Artist capability. Click Search on the menu bar, then click By Artist. An input box should appear asking you to enter the artist to search for. Enter **Nick Robertson** and click OK. The application should locate the first record with Nick Robertson stored in the `fldArtist` field, as shown in Figure 10-19. You should also see a message box asking "Search for more records?"

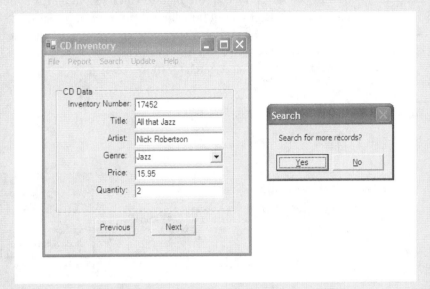

Figure 10-19   CD Inventory form with search results

Step 9:   Click the Yes button on the message box. The application locates the next record with Nick Robertson stored in the `fldArtist` field, as shown in Figure 10-20. The message box asking "Search for more records?" is displayed again.

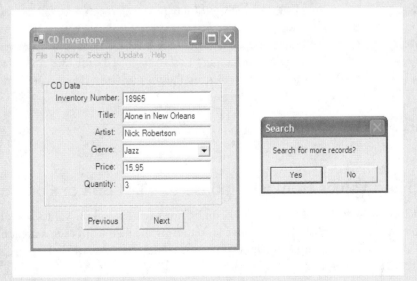

Figure 10-20   CD Inventory form with search results

Step 10: Click the Yes button on the message box. There are no more records meeting the search criterion, so a message box is displayed with the message "No more records". Click the OK button to dismiss the message box. The last record that was found is now displayed on the form.

Step 11: Now you will search for a record by title. Click Search on the application's menu bar, then click By Title. An input box should appear prompting you to enter the CD title. Enter **Mozart, Please** and click OK. The application should locate the first record with Mozart, Please stored in `fldTitle`, as shown in Figure 10-21. You should also see a message box asking "Search for more records?"

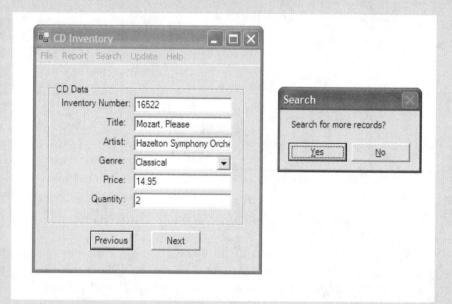

Figure 10-21 CD Inventory form with search results

Step 12: Click the Yes button on the message box. There are no more records meeting the search criterion, so a message box is displayed with the message "End of records". Click the OK button to dismiss the message box. The last record that was found is now displayed on the form.

Step 13: End the application.

Copying Values from a Database to a List Box or Combo Box

Sometimes you want to use a list box or combo box to display all the values stored in a database field. A simple way to accomplish this is to use a loop to copy the field from each database record to the list box or combo box. For example, the following code copies the value of each record's `fldTitle` field to the `lstTitles` list box.

```
Dim i As Integer
    With DsCompactDiscs1
    For i = 0 To (.tblCompactDiscs.Count - 1)
```

```
        lstRecords.Items.Add(.tblCompactDiscs(i).fldTitle)
    Next
End With
```

You can also bind a list box or combo box to a database table. There are three properties that you must set to bind the list box or combo box to the table: DataSource, DisplayMember, and ValueMember.

First, you set the DataSource property to the table that you wish to bind the control to. Next you pick two fields from the table that you want to access with the list box or combo box. One of the fields will be displayed in the list, and the other field will be retrieved when the user selects an item from the list. You set the DisplayMember property to the name of the field whose contents you wish to display in the list box or combo box, then set the ValueMember property to the field you want to retrieve when the user makes a selection. This can be the same field that you selected for the DisplayMember property, but in most cases it will be different.

At run time, the list box or combo box will display the field that you selected for the DisplayMember property, for all the rows in the table. When the user selects an item in the list, the control accesses the row containing that value, and it retrieves the contents of the field you selected for the ValueMember property. To retrieve the contents of that field, you use the SelectedValue property.

For example, suppose we have a list box named `lstRecords` in the CD Inventory application. We set the DataSource property to `DsCompactDiscs1.tblCompactDiscs`. That binds the control to the `tblCompactDiscs` table. Next we select `fldTitle` for the DisplayMember property, and we select `fldInvNumber` for the ValueMember property. At run time, the list box will display the `fldTitle` field for each row in the table, as shown in Figure 10-22.

Figure 10-22 List box bound to the `tblCompactDiscs` table

The following statement could be used to display the inventory number for the title that is selected in the list box.

```
MessageBox.Show(lstRecords.SelectedValue)
```

Working with Radio Buttons and Databases

Radio buttons normally appear in a group, and represent a set of choices that the user may choose from. When there is a set of valid choices for a database field, you might want to present those choices with radio buttons.

For example, suppose a database table has a field named `fldPet`, which holds the type of pet that a person owns. Assume that the valid values for the field are the strings "Dog", "Cat", "Bird", "Other", and "None". An application that is connected to the table might have a set of radio buttons similar to Figure 10-23.

Code similar to the following can be used to update the `fldPet` field of a record. In the code, `rowNum` is a variable holding the row number of the record being changed.

Figure 10-23 Radio buttons

```
If radDog.Checked = True Then
    DsDataSet1.tblData(rowNum).fldPet = "Dog"
ElseIf radCat.Checked = True Then
    DsDataSet1.tblData(rowNum).fldPet = "Cat"
ElseIf radBird.Checked = True Then
    DsDataSet1.tblData(rowNum).fldPet = "Bird"
ElseIf radOther.Checked = True Then
    DsDataSet1.tblData(rowNum).fldPet = "Other"
ElseIf radNone.Checked = True Then
```

```
        DsDataSet1.tblData(rowNum).fldPet = "None"
    End If
    daAdapter.Update(DsDataSet1)
```

✓ Checkpoint

10.11   What is a data-aware control?

10.12   What is a `BindingContext` object?

10.13   What is a `CurrencyManager` object?

10.14   What do providers allow you to do?

10.15   When you use the Server Explorer to connect to a database, two objects are automatically created in the component tray. What types of objects are these?

10.16   What does the data adapter's `Fill` method do?

10.17   In code, how do you determine the number of the current row of a table?

10.18   How do you create a new row in a table?

10.19   How do you save a modified table to its data source?

10.20   How do you remove a record from a table?

SUMMARY

A field is an individual piece of information pertaining to an item. A record is a complete set of data about a single item, consisting of one or more fields.

A database may be thought of as a collection of tables which hold related data. The data stored in a table is organized in rows and columns. Each column is a field and an entire row is a record.

A primary key is a field, or the combination of multiple fields, that uniquely identify each row in the table.

ADO .NET is an extremely powerful data access component that allows your Visual Basic .NET applications to access the data stored in databases.

The first step is to create a connection to a data source. As the name implies, a data source is source of data. The second step is to create a data adapter. A data adapter is an object that provides the required methods for retrieving from the data source and updating the data in the data source after your application has made a change to it. The third step is to create a dataset. A dataset is an in-memory cache of records that is separate from the data source but still allows you to work with the data.

A data-aware control is one that can automatically display data from a particular row and column of the ADO .NET dataset. Most of the controls in Visual Basic .NET are data aware.

All Windows forms in Visual Basic .NET have a built-in object named `BindingContext`. This object manages all of the data bindings for the controls on the form. A `CurrencyManager` object is added to a form when you connect the form to a data source. The `CurrencyManager` object gives you a simple way to navigate among the rows in a database table.

You use the Server Explorer window to connect to a database at design time. This automatically creates a connection object and a data adapter object.

The data adapter's `Fill` method is used to fill a dataset with data from a data source.

The `CurrencyManager` object has a Position property that holds the number of the current row. Row numbers are zero-based, so the first row in the table is row 0.

Adding a new record to a database involves these steps: Create a new empty row with the same column layout as the table that you wish to add the row to, populate the columns of the new row with data, add the new row to the table, and then save the updated table to the data source.

The data adapter's `Update` method saves a modified table to its data source.

The `CurrencyManager` object's `RemoveAt` method removes a specified row from a table.

You access a specific field in a row with an expression in the following format:
> `DataSet.Table(Index).Field`

You may use a loop to copy data from a database into a list or combo box. You may also bind a list or combo box to a column in a table.

You can present a list of valid choices for a database field with radio buttons, and then write code that updates that field with the data selected by the user.

KEY TERMS

ADO .NET	Field
`BindingContext` object	`Fill` method
Connection object	Position property
`CurrencyManager` object	Primary key
Data adapter	Record
Data source	`RemoveAt` method
Data-aware control	Table
Database	`Update` method
Dataset	

Review Questions

Fill-in-the-blank

1. The data stored in a database table is organized in _____ and _____.

2. A(n) _____ is a field, or the combination of multiple fields, that uniquely identify each row in the table.

3. A _____ is an individual piece of information pertaining to an item.

4. A _____ is a complete set of data about a single item, consisting of one or more fields.

5. A _____ is an object that provides the required methods for retrieving from the data source and updating the data in the data source after your application has made a change to it

6. A _____ is an in-memory cache of records that is separate from the data source but still allows you to work with the data.

7. All Windows forms in Visual Basic .NET have a built-in object named _____, which manages all of the data bindings for the controls on the form.

8. The _____ object gives you a simple way to navigate among the rows in a database table.

9. A _____ control is one that can automatically display data from a particular row and column of a dataset table.

10. You use the _____ window to connect to a database at design time.

Multiple Choice

1. In a database table, each column is a(n)
   a. Element
   b. Field
   c. Record
   d. Database

2. In a database table, each row is a(n)
   a. Element
   b. Field
   c. Record
   d. Database

3. The recommended prefix for database table names is
   a. `tbl`
   b. `tab`
   c. `dtb`
   d. `dat`

4. The recommended prefix for field names is
   a. `dbf`
   b. `tbf`
   c. `fie`
   d. `fld`

5. This ADO .NET object facilitates the transfer of data between a data source and a dataset.
   a. Table
   b. DBTable
   c. TableConnect
   d. DataAdapter

6. This type of control can display data from a database field.
   a. Read-write
   b. Data-aware
   c. Field-aware
   d. Database

7. The DataBindings.Text property of a TextBox control holds
   a. The name of a database
   b. The name of an ADO data control
   c. The name of a database table
   d. The name of a field, or column

8. This data adapter method saves a modified table to a data source.
   a. `Save`
   b. `Update`

    c.   `SaveRecord`

    d.   `AddNew`

9. This method creates a new blank row that may be edited and added to the table.

    a.   `NewRow`

    b.   `AddRow`

    c.   `CreateEmpty`

    d.   `AddNew`

10. This method deletes a row from the table.

    a.   `DeleteRow`

    b.   `RemoveAt`

    c.   `DeleteCurrent`

    d.   `EraseRow`

True or False

Indicate whether each of the following statements is true or false.

1. T F: You think of a column in a database table as a record.

2. T F: Combo box controls are data-aware.

3. T F: Before binding a data-aware control to an ADO .NET dataset, you must already have already configured its data adapter.

4. T F: Microsoft Jet is the provider you select when working with Microsoft Access databases.

5. T F: The first row in a table is row number 1.

6. T F: `Update` is a dataset method.

7. T F: In addition to saving a new record, the `Update` method can also be used to save changes to an existing record.

8. T F: The `NewRow` method creates a new record and automatically saves it to the table.

9. T F: `Fill` is a dataset method.

10. T F: Setting the `CurrencyManager` object will not cause a run-time error if you attempt to move beyond the last row.

Short Answer

1. In general, what are the steps necessary to set up a Visual Basic .NET application to work with a database?

2. What is the difference between a data source and a dataset?

3. What is the purpose of a data adapter?

4. You wish to bind a TextBox control to a column named `fldGrossPay`. How do you do this?

5. What type of object must you work with to perform simple navigation among the rows in a table?

6. What method do you call to load a dataset with a database table?

7. How do you make a specific row the "current" row?

8. You've made a change to a row in a table. How do you save the changes to the data source?

What Do You Think?

1. ADO .NET can be used to access many different types of databases. For example, you can work with databases created with Microsoft Access, Oracle, Foxpro, and others. What is the advantage of using a technology such as ADO .NET over writing code to directly access each specific type of database?

2. How could you "bookmark" the current row in a table?

3. Why must you configure an ADO .NET dataset before you can configure any data-aware controls that use it?

4. Why is it a good idea to call the data adapter's `Update` method before exiting an application?

Find the Errors

For each of the following code segments, assume that `daAdapter` is a data adapter, `DsDataSet1` is a dataset, `tblInfo` is a table, `fldIDnumber` is a column in the table, and `newDataRow` is an object variable that will reference a row.

```
1.   DsDataSet1.Fill(daAdapter)

2.   Dim newDataRow As System.DataSet.DataRow

3.   newDataRow = DsDataSet1.NewRow

4.   newDataRow("fldIDnumber") = "574K8892"

5.   DsDataSet1.tblInfo.Add(newDataRow)

6.   DsDataSet1.Update(daAdapter)
```

Algorithm Workbench

For each Algorithm Workbench question, assume the application has a data adapter named `daAdapter`, a dataset named `DsEmployees1`, and a table named `tblEmpInfo`.

1. Write code that steps through each record, from first to last, and accumulates the total of all the records' `fldHours` field (which is an integer).

2. Rewrite the code you wrote in question 1 so it steps through each record from last to first.

3. Write code that searches from the first record for a record with "Suffolk" stored in the `fldLastName` field. If the record is not found, display a message indicating this.

4. Write code that searches from the first record for a record where the `fldPayRate` field is greater than 25.50. If the record is not found, display a message indicating this.

5. Write code that accumulates the total of the `fldHours` field (an integer) for each record where `fldLastName` is "Jones".

6. Write code that copies each record's `fldIDnumber` field to the `lstIDnumber` list box.

PROGRAMMING CHALLENGES

1. Stock Trader, Part 1

First, create a database named `Stocks` using Microsoft Access. The database should have a table named `tblStocks`. Table 10-4 lists the fields you should create in the table.

Table 10-4

Fields required for `tblStocks` table

Field name	Data type	Description
fldStockName	Text	Holds the name of the stock.
fldTicker	Text	Holds the stock ticker symbol.
fldShares	Number (integer)	Holds the number of shares purchased.
fldPurchasePrice	Currency	Holds the price per share of the stock when it was purchased.
fldPcommission	Currency	Holds the amount of commission paid to the stock broker when the stock was purchased.
fldSoldPrice	Currency	Holds the price per share of the stock when it was sold.
fldScommission	Currency	Holds the amount of commission paid to the stock broker when the stock was sold.
fldGainLoss	Currency	Holds the capital gain or loss realized from the sale of the stock. A capital gain is the amount of profit made (minus all commissions), and a capital loss is the amount of loss (plus all commissions).
fldExchange	Text	Holds the name of the stock exchange where the stock is traded. Valid values are "New York Stock Exchange", "American Stock Exchange", or "NASDAQ".

Next, create an application with a form similar to the one shown in Figure 10-24.

Connect the application to the `Stocks` database, add and configure the appropriate ADO .NET objects. Next create the First, Next, Previous, and Last buttons. These buttons should display the first row, next row, previous row, and last row in the table.

Bind the text boxes and the label control to the appropriate fields. (Bind a label control to the `fld GainLoss` field, because this field is not entered by the user but calculated by your application.) You will have to write code that updates the Stock Exchange radio buttons, based on the value in the `Exchange` field.

Also add buttons to add a new record, save changes to the current record, and delete the current record. When a record is added, your application must calculate a value for the `fldGainLoss` field. A capital gain is the amount of profit made (minus all commissions), and a capital loss is the amount of loss (plus all commissions).

NOTE: *If you prefer, you may substitute a menu system for the command buttons shown in the figure.*

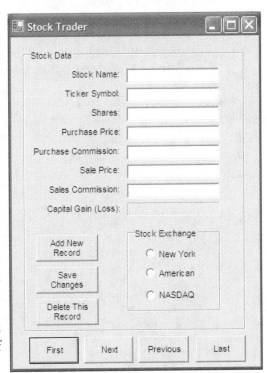

Figure 10-24 Stock Trader form

Design Your Own Forms

2. Custom Navigation Buttons

Modify the CD Inventory application so the form contains a First Record and Last Record button. The First Record button should display the first row in the table and the Last Record button should display the last row in the table.

3. Stock Trader, Part 2

Add a total capital gain/loss report capability to the Stock Trader application you created in Programming Challenge 2. The application should display the total capital gain or loss from all the stocks in the database.

4. CDs by Artist Report

Add a CDs by Artist item to the CD Inventory application's Report menu. It should display the number of CDs by a particular artist in inventory. Allow the user to enter the artist's name.

5. Sales Form

Add a Sales form to the CD Inventory application that calculates the total of a sale. The form should allow the user to search for a particular CD and enter the quantity being purchased. The total of the sale, including a 6% sales tax, should be displayed. In addition, the record's `fldQuantity` field should be updated by subtracting from it the quantity purchased.

Input Validation: Display an error message if the user attempts to purchase a quantity greater than what is stored in the `fldQuantity` field.

6. Reorder Report

Add a Reorder Report item to the CD Inventory application's Report menu. The reorder report should display a list of all CDs that should be reordered. A CD should be reordered if its quantity is less than 2.

CHAPTER

11

Advanced Database Programming and SQL

▶ 11.1 Introduction

This chapter introduces the Structured Query Language (SQL) and gives a tutorial on different SQL statements. Techniques for using SQL to search for data using the ADO .NET are discussed. The DataGrid control, which displays data in rows and columns, similar to a spreadsheet, is introduced. The chapter concludes with a primer on good database design.

▶ 11.2 Introduction to SQL

CONCEPT

SQL IS A STANDARD LANGUAGE FOR MANIPULATING DATABASES. YOU CREATE SQL STATEMENTS TO SEARCH FOR, INSERT, CHANGE, AND DELETE RECORDS.

A Brief History

SQL was developed in the mid-1970s by IBM as a means to access data in a prototype relational database management system known as System R. System R grew into SQL/DS and later was transformed into DB2. DB2 is now IBM's flagship database management system.

Other producers of relational database management systems (RDBMS) became aware of SQL and were able to adopt it when the publication of a technical article that contained the syntax and functions of the language put SQL into the public domain. Honeywell introduced the first commercially available SQL product in 1976, and Oracle followed in 1980 with a database management system built entirely around SQL.

In the mid-1980s ANSI and later ISO took on the task of defining standards for the language. As these standards were developed and adopted by software companies, the option of creating an application that was not tied to a particular database engine became a reality. Now it is possible to write a large application that can be ported to another database engine with a simple change to one line of code!

Today, SQL is the standard for data storage, retrieval, and manipulation. All of the major players in the RDBMS arena utilize SQL because not offering the language would result in greatly decreased or nonexistent market share.

Overview of SQL

You retrieve and/or manipulate data in SQL by executing statements, which are also called *queries*. SQL has its own syntax and set of key words. Although in our Visual Basic .NET exercises we focus primarily on the `Select` statement, this section provides a quick tutorial on several SQL statements.

Finding Records with the `Select` Statement

The *Select statement* is used to find records within a table. The statement can specify any or all columns in the table and can also provide criteria to narrow the selection results. The syntax is

```
Select ColumnNameList From TableName Where ColumnName = Criteria;
```

In the syntax, `ColumnNameList` is one or more columns or fields, `TableName` is the name of a table, and `Criteria` is a value to search for within the column. Notice that the statement ends with a semicolon.

Substituting an asterisk (*) for the first instance of `ColumnName` will produce a result set with all of the columns. For example, the following `Select` statement searches the table `tblEmployees` for all records with "Smith" stored in `fldLastName`.

```
Select * From tblEmployees Where fldLastName = "Smith";
```

The `Select` statement returns a *dynaset*, which is a set of records matching the search criteria. For example, the previous statement returns a dynaset consisting of all the records with "Smith" stored in `fldLastName`. Depending on how the SQL statement is written, a dynaset may or may not have all the fields that appear in the table, and may consist of fields from multiple tables.

SQL statements are often written across multiple lines and include indentation. For example, the previous example can also be written as

```
Select
    *
From
    tblEmployees
Where
    fldLastName = "Smith";
```

Complex SQL statements are easier to read when written this way.

Specifying Selection Criteria

Without the ability to define which records to search for by supplying column related criteria, the `Select` statement would be practically worthless. Seldom is every record in the table the desired result of a query. For example, consider a Microsoft Access database with a table named `tblNames`. The table has the columns described in Table 11-1.

Table 11-1

Columns in the `tblNames` table

Column	Type	Size	Required?	Indexed?
fldKey	AutoNumber	Long Integer	Yes	Yes, no duplicates
fldFirst	Text	20	Yes	No
fldLast	Text	20	Yes	No
fldMiddle	Text	15	No	No
fldStreet	Text	40	Yes	No
fldCity	Text	25	Yes	No
fldState	Text	2	Yes	No
fldPostalCode	Text	10	Yes	Yes, duplicates OK
fldTelephone	Text	13	No	No
fldEmail	Text	48	No	No

Because there is no `Where` clause, the following statement will return every column in every record in the `tblNames` table.

```
Select
    *
From
    tblNames;
```

You can also use logical operators such as `And` and `Or` to provide multiple criteria. The following statement will return all of the columns of the records with `fldCity` equal to "Ontario" and with `fldLast` equal to "Jones".

```
Select
    *
From
    tblNames
Where
    fldCity = "Ontario"
    And fldLast = "Jones";
```

Altering the Table Structure with the `Alter` Statement

Sometimes you only want certain columns returned from a `Select` statement. For example, suppose your company is planning to do some e-mail marketing and needs the first names, last names, and e-mail address for all customers who live in a city named Bristol. The following statement returns such a list. The list that is returned will only include the columns `fldFirst`, `fldLast`, and `fldEmail`.

```
Select
    fldFirst,
    fldLast,
    fldEmail
From
    tblNames
Where
    fldCity = "Bristol";
```

However, this command returns a list of names and e-mail addresses for customers in Bristol, Virginia, Bristol, Tennessee and Bristol England! How can the result set be generated for the U.S. cities only?

One option would be to include a range of values for `fldPostalCode` that correspond only to U.S. postal codes, but that could be cumbersome if there will be many mailings targeted to specific countries. The most practical solution would be to alter the table structure to add a country column. In SQL you use an *Alter statement* to alter the structure of a table. The following statement adds a column named `fldCountry` to the `tblNames` table.

```
Alter Table
   tblNames
Add Column
   fldCountry char(25) not null;
```

In the statement, `char(25)` indicates that the field is character, or text, and its size is 25 characters. The `not null` directive specifies that the field is required, and that all records entered into the table must have a value in this field. The resulting table structure is shown in Table 11-2.

Table 11-2

Modified structure of the `tblNames` table

Column	Type	Size	Required?	Indexed?
fldKey	AutoNumber	Long Integer	Yes	Yes, no duplicates
fldFirst	Text	20	Yes	No
fldLast	Text	20	Yes	No
fldMiddle	Text	15	No	No
fldStreet	Text	40	Yes	No
fldCity	Text	25	Yes	No
fldState	Text	2	Yes	No
fldPostalCode	Text	9	Yes	Yes, duplicates OK
fldTelephone	Text	13	No	No
fldEmail	Text	48	No	No
fldCountry	Text	25	Yes	No

Now the following statement may be used to select the records for customers in the United States only.

```
Select
   fldFirst,
   fldLast,
   fldEmail
From
   tblNames
Where
   fldCity = "Bristol" And fldCountry = "USA";
```

Adding Records with the *Insert* Statement

The *Insert statement* is the primary method for adding records to a table. The syntax is

```
Insert Into TableName (
     ColumnName1,
     ColumnName2,
     etc.)
Values(
     Value1,
     Value2,
     etc.);
```

The column names are separated by commas and listed inside parentheses. The values that are to be inserted into the columns must follow the same order as the column names. For example, *Value1* will be inserted into *ColumnName1*, *Value2* will be inserted into *ColumnName2*, and so forth.

If the table structure requires a value in a column and no data is present in the insert statement, the record will not be entered and an error will result. You must also present the values properly formatted. Character values must be enclosed in either single or double quotes, and columns that have been defined as numeric must not have values enclosed in quotation marks. If an improper format is presented in the Insert statement, the record will not be inserted and an error will result. If a column has been defined as an AutoNumber you do not need to supply any data because the database engine will provide the necessary value.

For example, the following Insert statement adds a new record to the tblNames table.

```
Insert Into tblNames (
    fldFirst,
    fldMiddle,
    fldLast,
    fldStreet,
    fldCity,
    fldState,
    fldPostalCode,
    fldTelephone,
    fldEmail
    fldCountry)
Values (
    "John",
    "Q",
    "Doe",
    "22 Oak Forest Lane",
    "Anytown",
    "NC",
    "29090-9090",
    "(555) 555-5555",
    "jqdoe@bestisp.com"
    "USA");
```

You can see that the values are listed in the same order as their corresponding fields. "John" will be stored in fldFirst, "Q" will be stored in fldMiddle, "Doe" will be stored in fldLast, and so forth.

Notice that the `fldKey` column is not specified in the statement. Because it has been defined as an AutoNumber column, an integer value is assigned automatically. This value will usually be the value of the `fldKey` column in the last record inserted, plus one.

Now consider the following statement:

```
Insert Into tblNames (
    fldFirst,
    fldMiddle,
    fldLast,
    fldStreet,
    fldCity,
    fldState,
    fldPostalCode,
    fldTelephone,
    fldEmail
    fldCountry)
Values (
    "Jane",
    "R",
    "Jones",
    "41 Cliff Side",
    "Anytown",
    NC,
    "29090-9090",
    "(555) 555-5555",
    "jrjones@bestisp.com"
    "USA");
```

This statement will generate an error and not be inserted. Can you see why? The value for the `fldState` column was not enclosed in quotes. The following statement will also generate an error. Can you see why?

```
Insert Into tblNames (
    fldFirst,
    fldMiddle,
    fldLast,
    fldStreet,
    fldCity,
    fldState,
    fldTelephone,
    fldEmail
    fldCountry)
Values (
    "Jane",
    "R",
    "Jones",
    "41 Cliff Side",
    "Anytown",
    "NC",
    "(555) 555-5555",
    "jrjones@bestisp.com"
    "USA");
```

The column `fldPostalCode` was defined as a required field but no value was provided in the statement.

Deleting Records with the `Delete` Statement

The *`Delete` statement* is used to remove a record or records from a database. To delete every record in a table, the syntax is

```
Delete From TableName;
```

WARNING:

Be very careful when using this form of the `Delete` statement because it will remove every record in the table.

For example, look at the following statement.

```
Delete From tblNames;
```

This statement will remove every record in the database! Hopefully last night's backup was a good one if this is not what you intended to do.

A *selective deletion* removes records that meet specified criteria. To perform a selective deletion, use a `Where` clause with the `Delete` statement. The syntax is

```
Delete From
      TableName
Where
      ColumnName = Criteria;
```

For example, the following statement will delete the record with "29090-9090" stored in the `fldPostalCode` field.

```
Delete from
    tblNames
Where
    fldPostalCode = "29090-9090";
```

If you want to delete all the records for customers in the 29090 area you would use the following command.

```
Delete From
    tblNames
Where
    Left(fldPostalCode, 5) = "29090";
```

The `Left` function returns a specified number of leftmost characters from a string. This statement will delete all records where the five leftmost characters of the `fldPostalCode` field are "29090". The following statement deletes all records that have an e-mail address at mycollege.edu. The `Right` function returns a specified number of rightmost characters from a string.

```
Delete From
    tblNames
Where
    Right(fldEmail, 13) = "mycollege.edu";
```

The following statement will result in an error. Can you see why?

```
Delete From
    tblNames
Where
    fldState = NC;
```

This statement will fail because NC is not enclosed in quotation marks.

Updating Records with the Update Statement

The *Update statement* is used to change the contents in one or more columns in a table. As with Delete, the Update statement can affect every record in a table or selected records. To change the contents of every record in a table, use the following syntax.

```
Update TableName
Set ColumnName = Value ;
```

WARNING

 Be very careful when using this form of the Update statement because it will change every record in the table!

For example, look at the following statement.

```
Update tblNames
Set fldTelephone = "(555)555-1212";
```

After executing this statement, you will need to call your friendly database administrator and ask to have the tblNames table restored because everyone in the table now has the same telephone number!

To perform a *selective update*, which means to change the contents of selected records, use the following syntax.

```
Update
        TableName
Set
        ColumnName = Value
Where
        ColumnName = Criteria.
```

For example, the following statement locates records with "(555) 555-5555" stored in fldTele phone and changes that field to "(555) 555-1212" for those records only.

```
Update
    tblNames
Set
    fldTelephone = "(555) 555-1212"
Where
    fldTelephone = "(555) 555-5555";
```

After submitting this command, however, you might want to take a coffee break. As you recall, the fldTelephone column is not indexed, so the database engine will have to search the table sequentially to find the matching record. If the table contains many records, the search for the record meeting the given criteria could take a long time.

A better strategy is to specify the `fldKey` column for the search. Because the `fldKey` column was defined as being uniquely indexed, the record will be found and the update applied almost immediately. An example follows.

```
Update
   tblNames
Set
   fldTelephone = "(555) 555-1212"
Where
   fldKey = 12345;
```

Using SQL in the Server Explorer

Recall from Chapter 10 that Visual Basic .NET's Server Explorer feature allows you to connect to a database so an application can work with it. It is also possible to execute SQL statements in the Server Explorer. In Tutorial 11-1 you open a sample database and practice executing several SQL statements.

TUTORIAL 11-1:

Executing SQL statements in the Server Explorer

Step 1: A Microsoft Access database file named Customers.mdb is in the \Chap11\Customers folder on the student disk. Copy this file to a location on your hard drive. The database has a table named `tblNames`. The five records that are already stored in the table are shown in Table 11-3.

Table 11-3

Contents of the `tblNames` table

fldKey	fldFirst	fldLast	fldMiddle	fldStreet	fldCity	fldState	fldPostalCode	fldTelephone	fldEmail
1	Jason	Bedford	Alexander	27 Elm Street	Canton	NC	27777-0027	555-1234	jbedford@fakeisp.com
2	William	Jones	Wallace	147 Pine Street	Sonoma	CA	44444-0147	555-3434	wjones@fakeisp.com
3	Emily	Smith	Lynn	P.O. Box 77	Carterville	NC	28888-0077	555-9898	esmith@fakeisp.com
4	Susan	Bolden	Gillian	77 Long Drive	Smithville	SC	99999-5632	555-6655	sbolden@fakeisp.com
5	Charles	Barnette	William	P.O. Box 656	Carterville	NC	28888-0656	555-7889	cbarnette@fakeisp.com

Step 2: The Server Explorer tab appears at the left of the Visual Basic .NET main window, near the ToolBox. Figure 11-1 shows how the tab might appear, depending on how your windows are configured. Click the Server Explorer tab to open the Server Explorer window.

> TIP: If you do not see the Server Explorer tab, click View on the menu bar, then click Server Explorer. You can also press Ctrl+Alt+S on the keyboard.

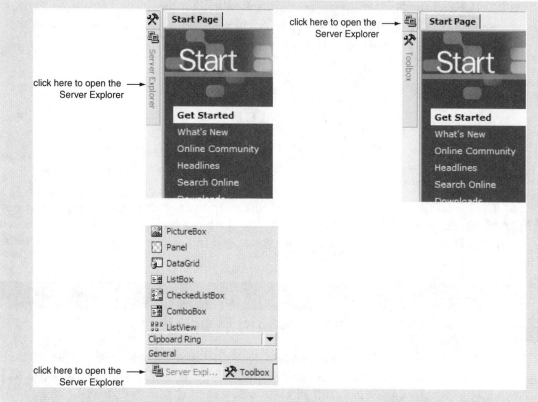

Figure 11-1   Server Explorer tab locations

Step 3:   Click the Connect to database icon in the Server Explorer window, as shown in Figure 11-2. This should cause the Data Link Properties dialog box to appear, as shown in Figure 11-3.

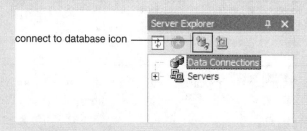

Figure 11-2   Connect to database icon

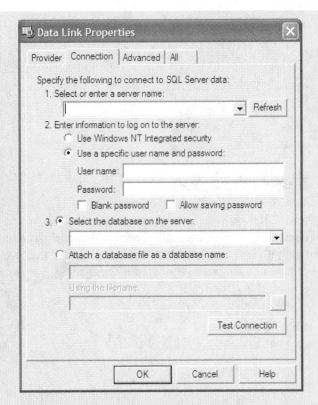

Figure 11-3   Data Link Properties dialog box

Step 4:   In the Data Link Properties dialog box, click the Provider tab and choose Microsoft Jet 4.0 OLE DB Provider. Recall from Chapter 10 that Microsoft Jet is the provider that allows you to connect to an Access database.

Step 5:   Click the Connection tab and browse to the Customer.mdb database that you copied in step 1. Click the Test Connection button to test the connection to the database. You should see a message box indicating "test connection succeeded." Click the OK button.

Step 6:   In the Server Explorer window, expand the tree underneath Data Connections until the table `tblNames` is displayed, as shown in Figure 11-4.

Figure 11-4   Server Explorer tree expanded

Step 7:   Right click `tblNames` and click Retrieve Data from Table. A window, shown in Figure 11-5, will open with the records from `tblNames` displayed. The query toolbar should also appear above the data window with buttons representing different methods of database interaction.

> TIP: If you do not see the query toolbar, click View, then ToolBars. On the Toolbars menu, click Query.

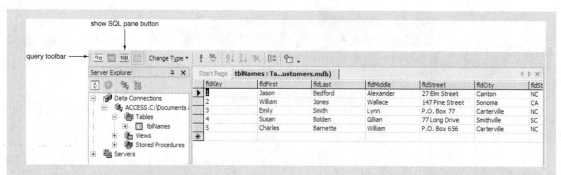

Figure 11-5   Records displayed with query toolbar

Step 8:   Click the show SQL pane button, shown in Figure 11-5. A new window will open, as shown in Figure 11-6, with a basic SQL statement that returns all records in the table. This statement was generated by default when you selected Retrieve Data from Table. Below the SQL statement pane is a window that allows you to view the records returned from the SQL statement.

fldKey	fldFirst	fldLast	fldMiddle	fldStreet	fldCity	fldSt
1	Jason	Bedford	Alexander	27 Elm Street	Canton	NC
2	William	Jones	Wallace	147 Pine Street	Sonoma	CA
3	Emily	Smith	Lynn	P.O. Box 77	Carterville	NC
4	Susan	Bolden	Gillian	77 Long Drive	Smithville	SC
5	Charles	Barnette	William	P.O. Box 656	Carterville	NC

```
SELECT    *
FROM      tblNames
```

Figure 11-6   SQL pane opened

Step 9:   In the SQL Statement window highlight the SQL statement and delete it.

Step 10:   Now type the following SQL statement, which will return every record with "NC" stored in the `fldState` field.

```
Select * From tblNames Where fldState = "NC";
```

Click the exclamation point button (!) on the SQL toolbar to execute the statement. The records that are returned by the statement are now displayed. After you have examined the records, highlight the SQL statement and delete it.

Step 11:   Enter the following statement in the SQL pane:.

```
Update tblNames Set fldTelephone = "555-1212" Where fldKey = 2;
```

This statement locates the record with 2 stored in `fldKey` and changes the `fldTelephone` field to "555-1212". Click the Execute button to update the data in `fldTelephone` in record 2. A message box appears indicating "1 row affected by last query."

Step 12: The `Update` statement does not return any records, so the results pane remains blank. To verify that the record has been updated, highlight and delete the SQL statement, enter `Select * From tblNames;` and execute the statement. Find the record with 2 in `fldKey` and look at the `fldTelephone` field. It has been changed to 555-1212.

✓ Checkpoint

11.1   What does SQL stand for?

11.2   What company first developed SQL?

11.3   What is the purpose of the `Select` statement?

11.4   What is a dynaset?

11.5   What happens when you substitute an asterisk (*) for the column names in a `Select` statement?

11.6   How do you provide multiple search criteria?

11.7   What is the purpose of the `Alter` statement?

11.8   What is the purpose of the `Insert` statement?

11.9   How do you delete records from a database?

11.10   What is the purpose of the `Update` statement?

▶ 11.3   Using SQL with ADO .NET

CONCEPT

THE ADO .NET DATA ADAPTER CAN MANIPULATE THE DATA IN ITS DATASET WITH SQL STATEMENTS.

You can use the ADO .NET data adapter, which was introduced in Chapter 10, to execute SQL statements on a database. In this section we discuss techniques for processing SQL statements with a data adapter.

Configuring the SelectCommand.CommandText Property at Design Time

The first technique we will discuss for processing SQL is configuring the data adapter's *SelectCommand. CommandText* property at design time. (CommandText is a subproperty of the SelectCommand property.) Once you have created a data adapter object and configured it, select it. In the Properties window expand the SelectCommand property, as shown in Figure 11-7.

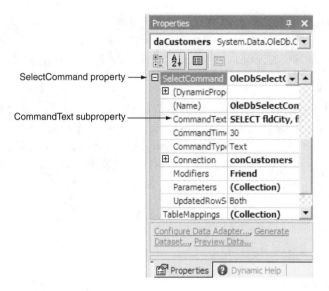

Figure 11-7 The SelectCommand property

To configure the property so it processes an SQL statement, select the CommandText subproperty, then click the ellipses button (...) to open the Query Builder dialog box, as shown in Figure 11-8.

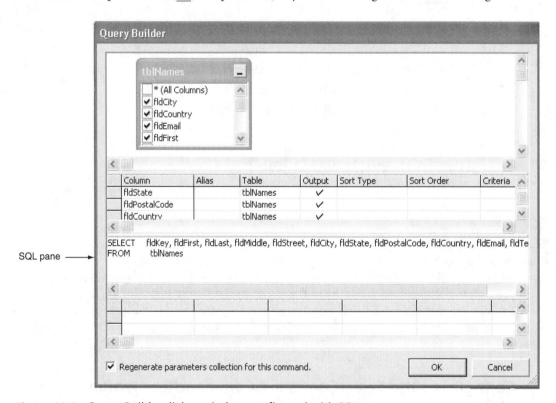

Figure 11-8 Query Builder dialog window configured with SQL statement

The Query Builder provides an area known as the SQL pane. You enter an SQL statement into the SQL pane, click the OK button, and the SQL statement becomes the contents of the SelectCommand. CommandText property. Subsequently, the results of the SQL statement become the contents of the dataset.

TUTORIAL 11-2:

Configuring the Data Adapter's SelectCommand property at design time

Step 1:   Under the \Chap11 folder on the student disk, there is a folder named Customer Data. This folder contains the Customers Data project that you will modify in this tutorial. Copy this folder to the same location on your hard drive that you copied the Customers.mdb file in Tutorial 11-1.

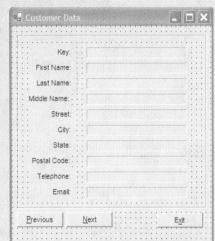

Figure 11-9   The Customer Data form

Step 2:   Start Visual Basic .NET and open the Customers Data project. The application's form is shown in Figure 11-9. The form contains a group of labels for displaying database fields. You will connect the form to the Customers.mdb database and bind these labels to its fields.

Step 3:   Open the Server Explorer and then click the connect to database icon. The Data Link Properties dialog box should appear.

> **TIP:**   To get the Data Link Properties dialog box you can also right-click the Data Connections entry in the Server Explorer. On the pop-up menu select the Add Connection item.

Step 4:   Click the Provider tab and choose Microsoft Jet 4.0 OLE DB Provider.

Step 5:   Click the Connection tab and browse to your Customers.mdb database at the "Select or enter a database name" prompt. Click the Test Connection button to test the database connection. If the test succeeded, click Ok to dismiss the window. If the test failed, repeat steps 2 – 4 to select the correct file.

Step 6:   In the Server Explorer window, expand the Data Connection tree until you see `tblNames` under Tables. Click and drag `tblNames` onto your form. A connection object named `OleDbConnection1` and a data adapter object named `OleDbDataAdapter1` will be created in the component tray. Change the name of the `OleDbConnection1` object to `conCustomers`, and change the name of the `OleDbDataAdapter1` object to `daCustomers`.

Step 7:   Select the `daCustomers` control and select its SelectCommand.CommandText property. Click the ellipses button to open the Query Builder. Replace the SQL command that you see in the SQL pane with the following command:

```
Select * From tblNames Where fldState = "NC"
```

This is shown in Figure 11-10. (Do not place a semicolon at the end of the statement.) This command will return only the records with "NC" stored in `fldState`.

NOTE: *The Query Builder will show an error message if you terminate your SQL statements with a semicolon.*

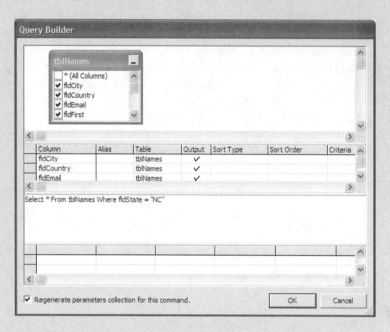

Figure 11-10 Command entered into the Query Builder

Step 8: With the data adapter still selected, click the Generate Dataset link beneath the properties window. Select New, change the name in the text box to dsCustomers and click Ok. A dataset object named DsCustomers1 is added to the component tray. We will keep this default name for the dataset.

Step 9: The form has a group of labels with the following names: lblKey, lblFirst, lblLast, lblMiddle, lblStreet, lblCity, lblState, lblPostalCode, lblTelephone, and lblEmail. Set each label's DataBindings.Text property to the appropriate field in the DsCustomers1 data set. For example, follow these steps to bind the lblKey control to the fldKey field:

  ◆ Select the lblKey control.

  ◆ In the Properties window select DataBindings, then select Text.

  ◆ In the drop-down list, expand the DsCustomers1 entry, and then expand the tblNames entry.

  ◆ Select fldKey.

Step 10: Open the Code window and write the following class-level declaration for a variable to reference the CurrencyManager object.

```
' Class-level declaration
Dim currManager As CurrencyManager
```

Step 11: Create a code template for the form's Load event procedure. Complete the event procedure with the following code, shown in bold.

```
        Private Sub frmMain_Load(ByVal sender As System.Object, _
            ByVal e As System.EventArgs) Handles MyBase.Load
          ' Populate the dataset.
          daCustomers.Fill(DsCustomers1)
          ' Get the CurrencyManager object's address.
          currManager = Me.BindingContext(DsCustomers1, "tblNames")
        End Sub
```

Step 12: The form has a Previous button named `btnPrevious`, a Next button named `btnNext`, and an Exit button named `btnExit`. Create `Click` event procedure templates for these buttons, and then complete the event procedures with the following code, shown in bold.

```
        Private Sub btnPrevious_Click(ByVal sender As System.Object, _
            ByVal e As System.EventArgs) Handles btnPrevious.Click
          ' Move to the previous record.
          If currManager.Position > 0 Then
              currManager.Position -= 1
          Else
              MessageBox.Show("First record reached.")
          End If
        End Sub


        Private Sub btnNext_Click(ByVal sender As System.Object, _
            ByVal e As System.EventArgs) Handles btnNext.Click
          ' Advance to the next row in the table.
          If currManager.Position < (currManager.Count - 1) Then
              currManager.Position += 1
          Else
              MessageBox.Show("No more records.")
          End If
        End Sub


        Private Sub btnExit_Click(ByVal sender As System.Object, _
            ByVal e As System.EventArgs) Handles btnExit.Click
           ' End the application.
           End
        End Sub
```

Step 13: Save the project and run the application. Use the Next and Previous buttons to view the records. You should only see the records that were returned from the SQL statement, which are the customers in North Carolina.

Step 14: Click the Exit button to end the application.

Using the SelectCommand.CommandText Property in Code

You may also set the data adapter's SelectCommand.CommandText property to an SQL statement in code. The general format is

```
DataAdapter.SelectCommand.CommandText = "SQL statement"
DataAdapter.Fill(DataSet)
```

The first step is to store a string containing a valid SQL statement in the SelectCommand property. Then you call the data adapter's `Fill` method to refresh the records stored in the dataset. After the `Fill` method is called, the dataset will contain the records returned by the SQL statement.

For example, look at the following code.

```
Dim sql as String
sql = "Select * From tblNames Where fldState = 'NC';"
daCustomers.SelectCommand.CommandText = sql
daCustomers.Fill(DsCustomers1)
```

First a string variable, `sql`, is declared to hold the SQL statement. The `Select` statement, which returns all records with "NC" stored in `fldState`, is stored in the variable. The variable is then assigned to the data adapter's SelectCommand.CommandText property. The `Fill` method is called to update the dataset with the records returned from the SQL statement. Statements, like those discussed in Chapter 10 which use the `CurrencyManager`, may then be executed to process the records in the dataset.

Testing for an Empty Dataset

The dataset has a property of the same name as the database table. This property has its own Count property which contains the number of rows in the table. You can access the Count property with an expression in the following general format:

```
DataSet.Table.Count
```

If the `Select` statement assigned to the data adapter's SelectCommand.CommandText property finds no records matching the search criteria, an empty dataset will be returned and the dataset will contain no records. You can test the table's Count property to determine the number of records it contains. For example, the following code displays a message if the `DsCustomers1` dataset's `tblNames` table is empty.

```
If DsCustomers1.tblNames.Count = 0 Then
   MessageBox.Show("No records found.")
End If
```

TUTORIAL 11-3:

Setting the SelectCommand property at run time

Step 1: Start Visual Basic .NET and open the CustomerData project from Tutorial 11-2.

Step 2: Select the daCustomers control. Select the control's SelectCommand property and store the statement **Select * From tblNames;** in the CommandText property. This configures the control to display all the records in the tblNames table.

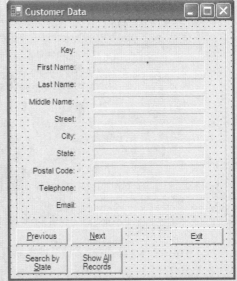

Step 3: In the Form window add a button named btnSearch with the caption "Search by State" and a button named btnShowAll with the text "Show All Records". Arrange the controls on the form to resemble Figure 11-11.

Step 4: The btnSearch button will allow the user to search for customers in a specific state. It will display an input box asking for a state abbreviation and then pass that as an argument to the

Figure 11-11 Form with btnSearch and btnShowAll buttons added

FindByState procedure, which you will write in the next step. Create a code template for the btnSearch_Click procedure, and then complete it with the following code shown in bold.

```
Private Sub btnSearch_Click(ByVal sender As System.Object, _
        ByVal e As System.EventArgs) Handles btnSearch.Click
    ' Prompt the user for a state abbreviation
    ' and search for customers in that state.
    Dim state As String  ' To hold user input
    state = InputBox("Enter a state abbreviation")
    FindByState(state)
    If DsCustomers1.tblNames.Count = 0 Then
        MessageBox.Show("No records found.", "Search Results")
        GetAllRecords()
    End If
End Sub
```

This procedure calls the FindByState Sub procedure, which will fill the dataset with records matching the search criteria. If no records are found, a message is displayed and the GetAllRecords Sub procedure is called. This procedure refills the dataset with all the records in the databse. You will write the GetAllRecords Sub procedure momentarily.

Step 5: Now you will write the FindByState Sub procedure. This procedure accepts an argument containing a state abbreviation. It then builds an SQL statement to search for records with that value in fldState. Enter the following code for the procedure.

```
Private Sub FindByState(ByVal state As String)
    ' Find records by state.
    Dim sql As String
```

```
        sql = "Select * From tblNames Where fldState = '" _
                & state & "';"
        DsCustomers1.Clear()
        daCustomers.SelectCommand.CommandText = sql
        daCustomers.Fill(DsCustomers1)
        currManager.Refresh()
    End Sub
```

First, this procedure builds the SQL statement and stores it in the `sql` string variable. Then, the dataset's `Clear` method is called. The `Clear` method removes all the rows currently stored in the dataset's tables. Next, the SQL statement is stored in the data adapter's SelectCommand.CommandText property, and the `Fill` method is called. Last, the `CurrencyManager` object's `Refresh` method is called. This forces the bound controls to be reset to display the currently loaded data.

Step 6: The `btnShowAll` button will display all the records in the `tblNames` table. Create a code template for the button's `Click` event procedure, and then complete the procedure with the following code shown in bold.

```
Private Sub btnShowAll_Click(ByVal sender As System.Object, _
        ByVal e As System.EventArgs) Handles btnShowAll.Click
    ' Populate the dataset with all records.
    GetAllRecords()
End Sub
```

Step 7: Now write the `GetAllRecords` Sub procedure. The code follows.

```
Private Sub GetAllRecords()
    ' Get all records.
    daCustomers.SelectCommand.CommandText = " Select * " & _
        "From tblNames;"
    DsCustomers1.Clear()
    daCustomers.Fill(DsCustomers1)
    currManager.Refresh()
End Sub
```

Step 8: Save the project and run the application. Click the Search by State button and enter **NC** into the input box. Click the OK button. The dataset should now filled with records with "NC" stored in the `fldState` field.

Step 9: Click the Search by State button and enter **CA** into the input box. Click the OK button. The dataset should now be filled with records with "CA" stored in the `fldState` field.

Step 10: Click the Show All Records button. The dataset should now be filled will all records in the table.

Step 11: End the application.

✓ **Checkpoint**

11.11 How do you configure a data adapter at design time to execute an SQL command?

11.12 How do you process a new SQL statement in code?

11.13 After completing the step you described in checkpoint 11.12, what must you do to cause the dataset to be updated with the results of the SQL statement?

11.14 How do you determine in code whether a `Select` statement finds no records matching the search criteria?

▶ 11.4 Using the DataGrid Control with ADO .NET

CONCEPT

THE DATAGRID CONTROL DISPLAYS DATABASE RECORDS IN ROWS AND COLUMNS, SIMILAR TO A SPREADSHEET.

The *DataGrid control* is used to create a data grid, which displays the information in a dataset in row and column order. Each row in the data grid corresponds to a record in the dataset, and each column in the data grid references the corresponding field. The data grid does not contain a copy of the data in a dataset, but references the dataset directly. If a change is made to a row or field in the data grid, that change is realized within the dataset, but not in the data source until the data adapter's `Update` method is called.

Data Grid Properties and Methods

The DataGrid control provides several properties, methods, and event procedures. Table 11-4 describes several data grid properties, Table 11-5 describes several data grid methods, and Table 11-6 describes several data grid event procedures.

Table 11-4

Several DataGrid control properties

Property	Description
AllowSorting	Enables or disables the option of sorting by clicking on a column heading.
ReadOnly	When set to true, the data in the data grid cannot be edited, deleted, or added to. When set to false, new records may be added, existing records may be changed, and records may be deleted.
CaptionText	Returns or sets the text for the caption.
CaptionVisible	Returns or sets the grid's visible status.
Enabled	Returns or sets the grid's user interactivity status. When true, the user may interact with the grid. When false, no interaction is allowed.
CurrentRowIndex	Returns or sets the row that has the focus.
DataSource	Returns or sets the data source that is associated with this data grid.

Table 11-5

Several data grid methods

Method	Description
Refresh	Repaints the data grid.
ResetBindings	Refreshes the data derived from the data source.
Focus	Sets the focus and activates this data grid.
Show	Sets this data grid's Visible property to true so it will be displayed.

Table 11-6

Several data grid event procedures

Event procedure	Description
Click	Executes when this data grid is clicked.
DoubleClick	Executes when this data grid is double-clicked.
Scroll	Executes when the user scrolls this data grid.

Creating a Data Grid Control

You add a data grid to a form just as you add any other control: either double-click its tool in the toolbox, then resize the control, or click its tool in the toolbox and draw the control on the form. After you have added a DataGrid control to your form, you normally perform the following:

- ◆ Associate a table in an existing dataset with the DataGrid control.
- ◆ Format the appearance of the data grid's columns.

The DataGrid control has a DataSource property, which you set to the name of the table you wish to display.

TUTORIAL 11-4:

Creating a Data Grid control

Step 1: Start Visual Basic .NET and begin a new Windows application project. Name the project **Customer DataGrid**.

Step 2: Widen the form so it fills up a good portion of the screen, such as 800 pixels. (Check the Size.Width property to determine the width of the form.) Type **Customer Database** as the form's Text property.

Step 3: Create a button named `btnExit` with the text "E&xit". Write a `Click` event procedure for the button that ends the application. Also, create a button named `btnSave` with the text "&Save." Figure 11-12 shows how the form should look at this point.

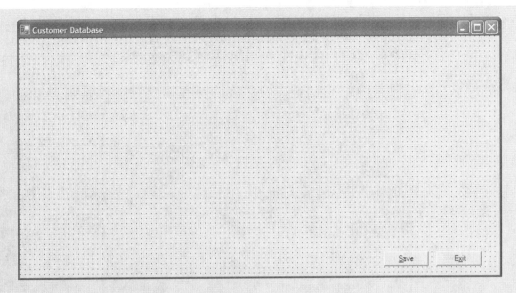

Figure 11-12   Customer Database form

Step 4: Use the Server Explorer to create a connection to the Customers.mdb database that you used in the previous tutorial. Use the Microsoft Jet 4.0 OLE DB provider.

Step 5: After you have created a connection to the database, expand the tree in the Server Explorer window until the `tblNames` table is displayed. Click and drag the `tblNames` table onto the form. A connection object and data adapter object will be created in the component tray. Rename the connection object `conCustomers` and rename the data adapter `daCustomers`.

Step 6: Select the data adapter, then select the SelectCommand.CommandText property to open the Query Builder. In the Query Builder, enter the following SQL statement in the SQL pane:

```
Select  fldLast, fldFirst, fldMiddle, fldStreet, fldCity, fldState,
        fldPostalCode, fldCountry, fldEmail, fldTelephone,
        fldKey
 From   tblNames
```

This command selects all of the fields in the `tblNames` table. We could have used the statement `Select * From tblNames`, but in most cases the columns in the dataset would be generated in alphabetical order. When we specify each field name in a `Select` statement, the columns are generated in the order that their field names appear in the statement.

Step 7: Click the OK button to close the Query Builder, then click the Generate Dataset link in the Properties window. In the Generate Dataset dialog box, select New and change the dataset's name from `DataSet1` to `dsCustomers` and click OK. The `DsCustomers1` control will appear in the component tray.

Step 8: Open the toolbox and create a DataGrid control on the form. Size the data grid so it occupies most of the form, as shown in Figure 11-13. Name it `dgdDatabase`. Note that `dgd` is the standard prefix for DataGrid controls.

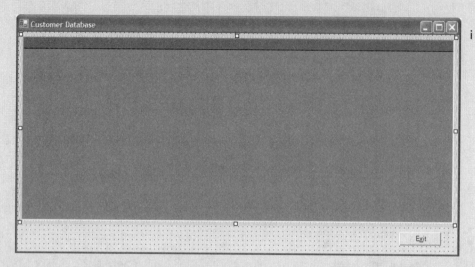

Figure 11-13 DataGrid control placed

Step 9: Select the data grid and then find its DataSource property Properties window. Select the property, then click the down-arrow that appears. In the drop-down box select the `DsCustomers1.tblNames`. The connection from the dataset to the data grid is now established. Note the table's field names are displayed as each column's heading.

Step 10: Change the data grid's CaptionText property to **Customers**. This establishes a title that is displayed in the grid's title bar. The form should resemble Figure 11-14.

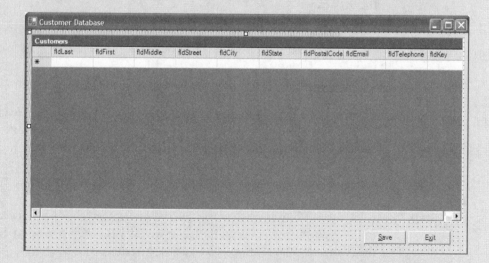

Figure 11-14 DataGrid control with columns displayed and CaptionText set

Step 11: Although the field names are helpful to you, the programmer, they are not usually appropriate as column headings in a data grid. You should change the column headings to something more straightforward for the application user. Find the data grid control's TableStyles property in the Properties window. Click the ellipses (**...**) button to activate the DataGridTable Style Collection Editor dialog box, as shown in Figure 11-15.

Figure 11-15 DataGridTableStyle Collection Editor dialog box

Step 12: Click the Add button. This adds a DataGridTableStyle object to the dialog box. The dialog box should now appear as shown in Figure 11-16.

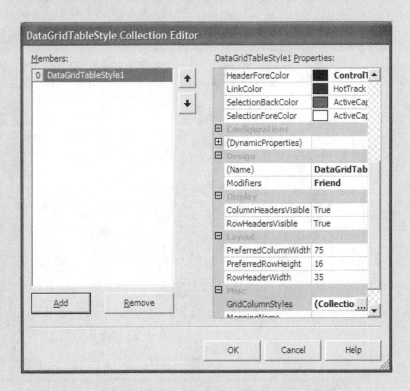

Figure 11-16 DataGridTableStyle Collection Editor dialog box

Step 13: In the column on the right (the DataGridTableStyle1 Properties column) select the MappingName property. Set the MappingName property to the name of the database table, **tblNames**. (If tblNames does not appear in the drop-down list, type it into the property.) Next, click the ellipses button that appears next to the GridColumnStyles property. The DataGridColumn Style Collection Editor dialog box, shown in Figure 11-17, should appear.

Figure 11-17 DataGridColumnStyle Collection Editor dialog box

Step 14: Click the Add button. This adds a DataGridTextBoxColumn object to the dialog box. The dialog box should now appear as shown in Figure 11-18.

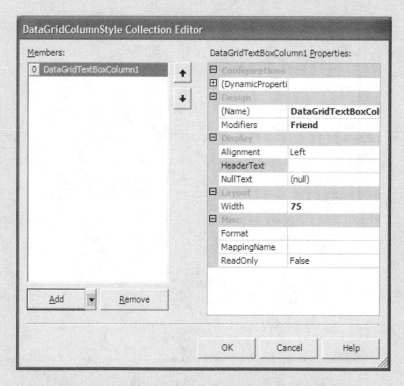

Figure 11-18 DataGridColumnStyle Collection Editor dialog box

Step 15:   Now you are ready to assign a column heading to a database field. In the column on the right (the DataGridTextBoxColumn1 Properties column), there are two properties: HeaderText and MappingName. You select a database field in the MappingName property, and you enter text in the HeaderText property. The text that you enter for the HeaderText property will appear as the column heading for the database field you selected in the MappingName property.

Select the the MappingName property, then click the down-arrow that appears next to it. In the drop-down box select `fldLast`. In the HeaderText property type **Last**.

Step 16:   Click the Add button again. This adds another DataGridTextBoxColumn object to the dialog box. Select the the MappingName property, then click the down-arrow that appears next to it. In the drop-down box select `fldFirst`. In the HeaderText propert type **First**.

Step 17:   Continue clicking the Add button to add a DataGridTextBoxColumn object for each field in the database. Table 11-7 shows the MappingName and HeaderText settings for each object. Note that you have already added objects for the first two fields, `fldLast` and `fldFirst`.

Table 11-7

MappingName and HeaderText settings

MappingName	HeaderText
fldLast	Last
fldFirst	First
fldMiddle	Middle
fldStreet	Street
fldCity	City
fldState	State
fldPostalCode	PostalCode
fldCountry	Country
fldEmail	Email
fldTelephone	Telephone
fldKey	Key

After adding the last object, the dialog box should appear similar to Figure 11-20.

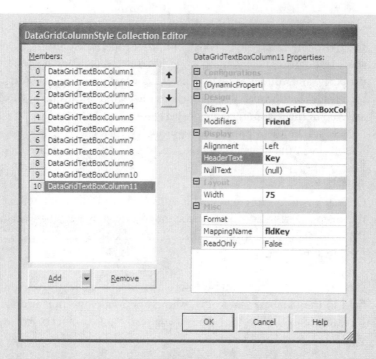

Figure 11-19   DataGridColumnStyle Collection Editor with all objects added

TIP: Each object that is displayed in the Members pane of the Data GridColumnStyle collection editor corresponds to a column in the data grid. Notice that a number appears to the left of each object's name. The order that the objects appear in the Members pane is the order that the columns appear in the data grid. You can move a column in the order by selecting it, then clicking the up-arrow or down-arrow button.

Step 18:   Click the OK button. This returns you to the DataGridTableStyle Collection Editor dialog box. Click the OK button on this dialog box as well. The form should now appear similar to Figure 11-20, with the column headers displayed.

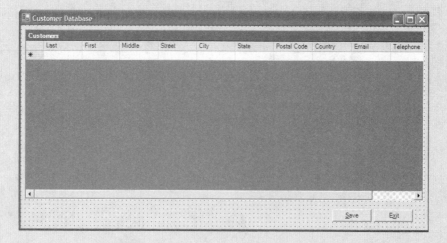

Figure 11-20   Column headers displayed

Step 19: Create a code template for the `btnSave` button's `Click` event procedure. Complete the procedure by entering the following code, shown in bold.

```
Private Sub btnSave_Click(ByVal sender As System.Object, _
        ByVal e As System.EventArgs) Handles btnSave.Click
    ' Save the dataset.
    daCustomers.Update(DsCustomers1)
End Sub
```

Step 20: Save the project and run the application. The form should appear as shown in Figure 11-21.

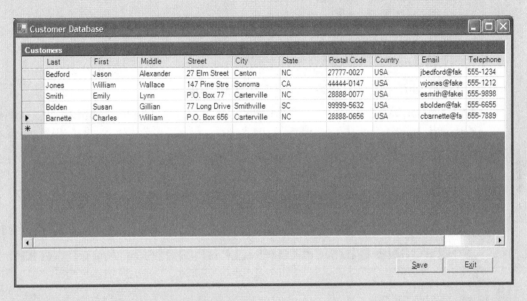

Figure 11-21   Records displayed in data grid

Step 21: The default value of a DataGrid control's ReadOnly property is false, which means that data in the DataGrid control may be edited, deleted, or added to. Notice that a blank record appears at the bottom of the grid. When you enter data into the blank record, a new record is added to the dataset. Add the following new record to the dataset:

Last name: **Clark**
First name: **Sara**
Middle name: **Lisa**
Street: **427 Hemlock Lane**
City: **Gainesville**
State: **GA**
Postal Code:**57574-4456**
Country: **USA**
Email: **slclark@mycollege.edu**
Telephone: **555-9989**

Step 22: Notice that a small button appears to the left of each record. You select a record by clicking the button that appears next to it. Once you have selected a record, you can delete it by pressing the Delete key on the keyboard. Select the record for Charles Barnette and delete it.

Step 23: You can directly edit records in the data grid. Select Jason Bedford's telephone number and change it to **555-7878**.

Step 24: The changes you have made only affect the dataset. To make the changes permanent, they must be saved to the data source. Click the Save button to execute the data adapter's `Update` method.

Step 25: End the application.

✓ Checkpoint

11.15 What DataGrid control property do you set to associate the control with a dataset?

11.16 By default, what does ADO .NET provide as column headings for the DataGrid control?

11.17 What do you do to prevent the user from changing, deleting, or adding to the data in a DataGrid control?

▶ 11.5 Focus on Problem-Solving: Enhancing the Sounds Incredible Music Store CD Inventory Application

In Chapter 10 you developed an inventory database application for the Sounds Incredible music store. The application allows the user to add, change, delete, and search for records. Now you will enhance the application by adding a form with a data grid for displaying the results when the user searches by artist name.

TUTORIAL 11-5:

Modifying the CD Inventory application

Step 1: Start Visual Basic .NET and open the CD Inventory project that you created in Chapter 10. Make sure you have an open connection to the CDInvnetory database in the Server Explorer window.

Step 2: Find the `mnuSearchArtist_Click` event procedure. Replace the current code as follows:

```
Private Sub mnuSearchArtist_Click(ByVal sender As System.Object, _
        ByVal e As System.EventArgs) _
        Handles mnusearchArtist.Click
```

```
' Find a record by a specific artist.
Dim showGridForm As New frmShowGrid()

showGridForm.ShowDialog()
End Sub
```

This procedure displays an instance of the `frmShowGrid` form, which you will create in the next step.

Step 3:   Add a new form named `frmShowGrid` with the caption **Search Results**.

Step 4:   Drag the `tblNames` table from the Server Explorer window to the form. This adds a connection object and a data adapter. Rename the connection object `conCompactDiscs`, and rename the data adapter `daCompactDiscs`.

Step 5:   Use the Query Builder to add the following SQL statement to the data adapter's SelectCommand.CommandText property:

```
SELECT   fldInvNumber, fldTitle, fldArtist, fldGenre, fldPrice,
         fldQuantity
FROM     tblCompactDiscs
```

Step 6:   With the data adapter selected, click the Configure Dataset link in the Properties window. Name the new dataset `dsCDGrid`, and click the OK button. A dataset object named `DsCDGrid1` should appear in the component tray.

Step 7:   Add a DataGrid control to the form. Set its name to `dgdRecords` and its Data-Source property to `DsCDGrid1`. Size the form and data grid to appear similar to Figure 11-22.

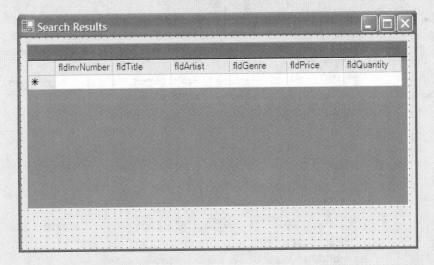

Figure 11-22   Form and data grid

Step 8:   The column headings currently read `fldInvNumber`, `fldTitle`, `fldArtist`, `fldGenre`, `fldPrice`, and `fldQuantity`. Change them to **Inv Number**, **Title**, **Artist**, **Genre**, **Price**, and **Quantity**, respectively.

Step 9: Add a Close button (named `btnClose`) to the lower right corner of the form. The form should now resemble Figure 11-23.

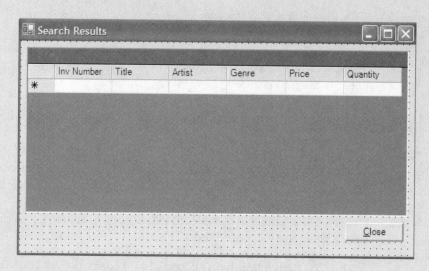

Figure 11-23 Search Results form

Step 10: Write the following code for the form's `Load` procedure.

```
Private Sub frmShowGrid_Load(ByVal sender As System.Object, _
        ByVal e As System.EventArgs) Handles MyBase.Load
    ' Load the grid with selected records.
    Dim sql As String    ' To hold the SQL statement.
    Dim artist As String ' To hold the artist name.
    ' Get the artist name.
    artist = InputBox("Enter the artist name.")
    ' Build the SQL statement.
    sql = "Select * From tblCompactDiscs " _
        & "Where fldArtist = '" & artist & "';"
    ' Run the SQL statement and refresh the controls.
    DsCDGrid1.Clear()
    daCompactDiscs.SelectCommand.CommandText = sql
    daCompactDiscs.Fill(DsCDGrid1)
    dgdRecords.Refresh()
    ' If no records were found, display a message.
    If DsCDGrid1.tblCompactDiscs.Count = 0 Then
        MessageBox.Show("No records found.", "Search Results")
    End If
End Sub
```

This procedure uses an input box to ask the user for an artist name. It then builds an SQL statement to search the dataset for all records with that artist name. If no records are found a message box is displayed indicating so.

Step 11: Write the following code for the `btnClose` button's `Click` event procedure.

```
Private Sub btnClose_Click(ByVal sender As System.Object, _
    ByVal e As System.EventArgs) Handles btnClose.Click
    ' Close this form.
    Me.Close()
End Sub
```

Step 12: Save the project and run the application. Click Search on the menu bar, and then click By Artist on the Search menu.

Step 13: An input box appears asking you to enter the artist's name. Enter **Nick Robertson** and click OK. The `frmShowGrid` form appears with all records containing the artist name Nick Robertson, as shown in Figure 11-24.

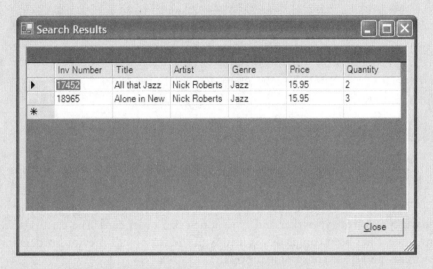

Figure 11-24 Search Results form with Nick Robertson records displayed

Step 14: Click the Close button to close the form. Search for records with other artist names, including some that do not appear in the database. When you are finished, exit the application.

▶ 11.6 If You Want to Know More About SQL: Good Database Design

Relational database management systems, commonly referred to as RDBMS, have become the standard model for data storage and retrieval. There are three reasons why the relational model is so attractive and has become so widespread:

- ◆ Flexibility—The relational structure allows a variety of data views.
- ◆ Efficiency—Redundancy is eliminated and space is saved.
- ◆ Data integrity is maintained—Data modification anomalies are greatly reduced.

Defining Relational Data

In simple terms, a *relational database* is comprised of a series of tables, each containing a unique set of data, including a unique primary key. The tables are connected or related to each other by the primary key. Think of it as a parent-child relationship: For every set of child data there is a set of parent data. Let's take a look at a paper database that is simple in structure, but with very labor-intensive data entry and many opportunities for mistakes.

The success of Acme Advanced Widgets has made it necessary to move from its time-honored and semi-reliable paper order entry and tracking system to a computerized system. Acme has determined that no commercial software can adequately handle its business, so it has contracted with Ace Consulting to take its paper and convert it to data. Ace Consulting's database guru, Amy, has followed Acme's paper trail and has devised the plan for the transformation. One of Acme's order cards looks like this:

```
Customer:          Ralph Fitzroy
Address:           102 South Fleming
                   Farmingdale SC 38888
Telephone:         (555) 555-1212
Item:              Baby Blue Portable Widget
Quantity:          1
Price:             49.95
Order Date:        01/01/1997
Ship Date:         01/02/1997
Shipping Charge:   4.95
```

For every order placed, Laura, Acme's top-notch sales and customer service associate, sits down at her trusty Selectric typewriter and types a new 3x5 order card. The card is placed in the orders tray and, after it has been completed, is filed with the customer's previous orders in date order. This is a very time- and space-consuming process.

Amy's quick perusal of the order-taking process indicated that Acme needed at least four tables in their database: `tblCustomer`, `tblProduct`, `tblOrder`, and `tblPayment`.

Next, Amy created the table structures shown in Tables 11-8 through 11-11 in Access. The tables show each field's properties as reported in Access.

Table 11-8

The `tblCustomer` table

Column	Field properties	Indexed?
fldKey	AutoNumber	Yes (no duplicates), primary key
fldFirstName	Text, size: 25	No
fldLastName	Text, size: 25	Yes (duplicates)
fldStreet	Text, size: 40	No
fldCity	Text, size: 25	Yes (duplicates)
fldState	Text, size: 2	Yes (duplicates)
fldZip	Text, size: 10	Yes (duplicates)
fldTelephone	Text, size: 14	No
fldEmail	Text, size: 32	No
fldEntryDate	Date/Time	No

The `tblCustomer` table contains the customer's name and contact information as well as two additional fields, `fldKey` and `fldEntryDate`. The `fldKey` field is the primary key that uniquely identifies this record. It is the field that will identify it to its child, the `tblOrder` table. The value for the `fldKey` field is generated automatically every time a new customer is added to the table. The value for the `fldEntryDate` field is also generated automatically for every new entry. Amy added the `fldEntryDate` column because she knew that Acme would want to do some customer longevity and aging reports.

Table 11-9

The `tblProduct` table

Column	Field properties	Indexed?
fldKey	Numeric (long integer)	Yes (no duplicates), primary key
fldProductName	Text, field size: 30	No
fldDescription	Text, field size: 64	No
fldCost	Numeric (decimal), precision: 18 digits, decimal places: 2	No
fldWeight	Numeric (single), decimal places: 2	No
fldEntryDate	Date/time	No

Table 11-10

The `tblOrder` table

Column	Field properties	Indexed?
fldKey	Numeric (long integer)	Yes (no duplicates), primary key
fldCustomerKey	Numeric (long integer)	Yes (duplicates OK)
fldProductKey	Numeric (long integer)	Yes (duplicates OK)
fldCost	Currency, decimal places: 2	No
fldQuantity	Numeric (integer)	No
fldEntryDate	Date/time	No

Amy created the `tblOrder` table to take advantage of relationships between customers and orders, and between products and orders. The table has a field for both the customer key and the product key. When Laura enters an order in the computerized system she will only have to provide the customer's key to link the order to a particular customer and the product key to reference a particular product.

The `fldCost` column is added to enable history report generation. Amy could have left `fldCost` out, after all, the cost for the product can be referenced by the key in the product table. Acme will require some sales history reporting but as the cost of raw materials changes over time, so will the product cost. If the product cost is derived by a reference to the product table, only the current product cost can be used, resulting in inaccurate history figures. This table design allows the product cost to be saved at the time of the order for future analysis and reporting.

Table 11-11

The `tblPayment` table

Column	Field properties	Indexed?
fldKey	Numeric (long integer)	Yes (no duplicates), primary key
fldOrderKey	Numeric (long integer)	Yes (duplicates OK)
fldPayment	Currency, decimal places: 2	No
fldEntryDate	Date/time	No

The `tblPayment` table requires only two entries by Acme's accounting department: `fldOrderKey` and `fldPayment`. The `fldOrderKey` field references the `tblOrder` record, which in turn references both the `tblCustomer` table and the `tblProduct` table. Figure 11-25 shows the relationships between the tables as displayed in the Access Relationships window.

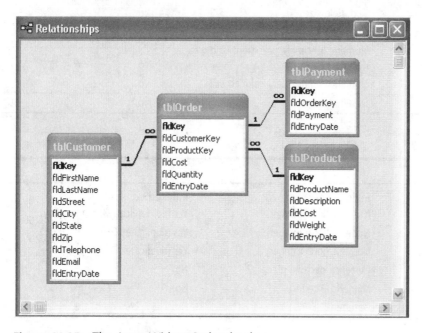

Figure 11-25   The Acme Widget Order database

Amy enlisted Laura's help in entering test data based on a selection of her order cards. Laura was ecstatic to learn that even though Frank Harrison ordered one of every widget, she only had to enter his name once. Tables 11-12 through 11-15 list the test data that Laura entered.

Table 11-12

Entries for the `tblCustomer` table

fldKey	fldFirstName	fldLastName	fldStreet	fldCity	fldState	fldZip	fldTelephone	fldEmail	fldEntryDate
1	Frank	Harrison	121 S. Main	Chesterfield	OH	45621-3265	(555) 555-1212	fharrison@bestisp.com	2/24/2003
2	Janice	Potts	195 N. Ashe	Bear Creek	MN	65214	(555) 555-2323	jpotts@mycollege.edu	2/24/2003
3	Harry	Jones	23 West Haven	Clyde	NC	28719	(555) 555-3434	hjones@bestisp.com	2/24/2003
4	Lisa	Hicks	PO Box 34245	Jonesboro	TN	37629	(555) 555-5656	lhicks@easttn.com	2/24/2003

Table 11-13

Entries for the `tblProduct` table

fldKey	fldProductName	fldDescription	fldCost	fldWeight	fldEntryDate
1	Baby Blue Advanced Widget	A beautiful piece designed to complement any seaside home.	49.95	5.10	2/24/2003
2	Translucent Basic Widget	A widget that bares its soul.	39.95	5.10	2/24/2003
3	Rainbow Basic Widget	A nostalgic early '70s widget.	39.95	5.10	2/24/2003
4	Forest Green Advanced Widget	A widget for the country estate.	59.95	5.50	2/24/2003
5	Heavy Metal Basic Widget	A widget built for harsh environments.	69.95	0.00	2/24/2003
6	Baby's First Widget	A small-scale, nonfunctioning widget.	9.95	0.00	2/24/2003

Table 11-14

Entries for the `tblOrder` table

fldKey	fldCustomerKey	fldProductKey	fldCost	fldQuantity	fldEntryDate
1	4	1	49.95	1	2/24/2003
2	4	2	39.95	1	2/24/2003
3	4	3	39.95	1	2/24/2003
4	4	4	59.95	1	2/24/2003
5	4	5	69.95	1	2/24/2003
6	4	6	9.95	1	2/24/2003
7	1	2	39.95	1	2/24/2003
8	2	3	39.95	1	2/24/2003
9	3	5	69.95	1	2/24/2003
10	3	6	9.95	3	2/24/2003
11	1	6	9.95	1	2/24/2003

Table 11-15

Entries for the `tblPayment` table

fldKey	fldOrderKey	fldPayment	fldEntryDate
1	1	49.95	2/24/2003
2	2	39.95	2/24/2003
3	3	39.95	2/24/2003
4	4	59.95	2/24/2003
5	5	69.95	2/24/2003
6	6	9.95	2/24/2003
7	7	39.95	2/24/2003
8	8	39.95	2/24/2003
9	9	69.95	2/24/2003
10	10	29.85	2/24/2003
11	11	9.95	2/24/2003

Once the data had been entered, Amy wrote a series of SQL queries to produce sample reports to present to Acme's Computerization Task Force for its approval.

The following query produces a simple product list for Acme's upcoming Web site and its printed catalog, *The Weekly Widget.*

```
Select
    fldProductName As Name,
    fldDescription As Description,
    fldCost As Cost,
    fldKey As Key
From
    tblProduct
Order By
    fldProductName;
```

The result of the query is shown in Table 11-16.

Table 11-16

Results of product list query

Name	Description	Cost	Key
Baby Blue Advanced Widget	A beautiful piece designed to complement any seaside home.	49.95	1
Baby's First Widget	A small scale, nonfunctioning widget.	9.95	6
Forest Green Advanced Widget	A widget for the country estate.	59.95	4
Heavy Metal Basic Widget	A widget built for harsh environments.	69.95	5
Rainbow Basic Widget	A nostalgic early '70s widget.	39.95	3
Translucent Basic Widget	A widget that bares its soul.	39.95	2

Amy could have substituted an asterisk for individual field names in the Select clause, but that would have given her all of the data in the table. fldEntryDate is not germane to the purpose of this query so Amy had to specify the fields she wanted.

Notice that Amy use the As key word with each field name.

```
fldProductName As Name,
fldDescription As Description,
fldCost As Cost,
fldKey As Key
```

The As key word provides a new name for the resulting column. When the query executes, it will return a set of records with the columns Name, Description, Cost, and Key. These names are more appropriate than the database field names for report columns.

The From clause simply identifies the table that holds the information. Amy added Order By ProductName to put the products in alphabetical order. The seasonal catalog will also have a list by price for the cost-conscious widget buyer, so all Amy will have to do is change the Order By clause to Order By Cost, ProductName. This change will order the list by item cost first, then item description. If more than one item has the same cost, the items will be placed in alphabetical order in that cost.

The following query produces a sales summery report grouped by the product.

```
Select
    tblProduct.fldProductName As Product
    Sum(tblOrder.fldQuantity) As Quantity,
    Sum(tblOrder.fldCost * tblOrder.fldQuantity) As Total
From
    tblProduct,
    tblOrder
Where (tblProduct.fldKey = tblOrder.fldProductKey)
Group By tblProduct.fldProductName
```

Running the query gives the results shown in Table 11-17.

Table 11-17

Results of sales summary report query

Product	Quantity	Total
Baby Blue Advanced Widget	2	99.9
Baby's First Widget	5	49.75
Forest Green Advanced Widget	3	179.85
Heavy Metal Basic Widget	2	139.9
Rainbow Basic Widget	2	79.9
Translucent Basic Widget	3	119.85

Let's look at the sales report query and see how it works. The first task was to define the fields Amy wanted to use. The first directive tells the database engine she wants to see the `fldProductName` field from the `tblProduct` table and the sum of both `fldQuantity` and `fldCost` times `fldQuantity` in the `tblOrder` table.

Next she had to link the two tables. As you may recall, `tblOrder` has been related to `tblProduct` by the field `fldProductKey` as illustrated in Figure 11-26.

The first task is to tell the database engine that the `fldKey` field in `tblProduct` and the `fldProductKey` field in `tblOrder` relate these two tables. This is done in the following `Where` clause.

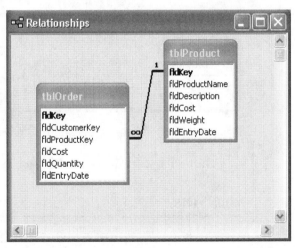

Figure 11-26   Relationship between `tblOrder` and `tblProduct`

```
Where (tblProduct.fldKey = tblOrder.fldProductKey)
```

Note that the criterion for joining these two tables is surrounded by parentheses. As with many languages, SQL recognizes a set of parentheses to establish execution precedence. In this example Amy wanted to ensure that the table relationship was established before she narrowed her search.

Finally she needed to specify the field that would be used to provide the grouping point for the query. In this case it is `fldProductName`, so she added the following directive.

```
Group By tblProduct.fldProductName
```

She could have also used the product record's `fldKey` field because it, like the product name, uniquely identifies this record.

The following query provides a basic sales summary by the customer's state.

```
Select
    tblCustomer.fldState AS State,
    Sum(tblOrder.fldQuantity) AS Quantity,
    Sum(tblOrder.fldCost) AS Sales
From
    tblCustomer, tblOrder
Where
    (tblCustomer.fldKey = tblOrder.fldCustomerKey)
Group By
    tblCustomer.fldState;
```

Figure 11-27 illustrates the relationship between the `tblCustomer` table and the `tblOrder` table.

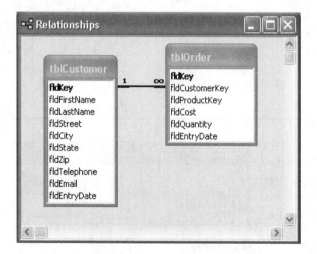

Figure 11-27   Relationship between `tblCustomer` and `tblOrder`

The results of the query are shown in Table 11-18.

Table 11-18

Results of sales summary by customer state report query

State	Quantity	Sales
MN	1	39.95
NC	8	239.7
OH	2	49.9
TN	6	269.7

This simple query provided some interesting information. North Carolina had the most sales, Tennessee had the highest sales, and the southeastern region of the United States had the most and highest sales by far. The Acme marketing department next asked Amy to write a query that would reveal which product sold the most in the region. Her fourth example was the sales by region by product query, as follows.

```
Select
    tblCustomer.fldState AS State,
    tblProduct.fldProductName AS Product,
    Sum(tblOrder.fldQuantity) AS Quantity,
    Sum(tblOrder.fldCost * tblOrder.fldQuantity) AS Sales
From
    tblCustomer,
    tblOrder,
    tblProduct
Where
    ((tblCustomer.fldKey = tblOrder.fldCustomerKey) And
    (tblProduct.fldKey = tblOrder.fldProductKey))
Group By
    tblCustomer.fldState,
    tblProduct.fldProductName;
```

Figure 11-28 illustrates the relationships between tblCustomer, tblOrder, and tblProduct.

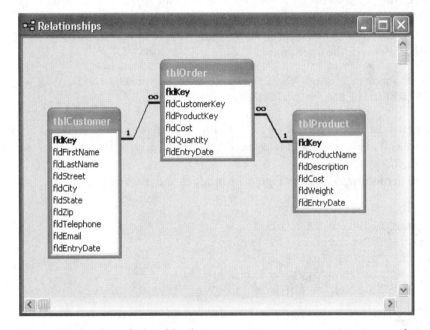

Figure 11-28 The relationships between tblCustomer, tblOrder, and tblProduct.

The sales region by product query produced the results shown in Table 11-19.

Table 11-19

Results of the sales region by product query

State	Product	Quantity	Sales
MN	Rainbow Basic Widget	1	39.95
NC	Baby Blue Advanced Widget	1	49.95
NC	Baby's First Widget	3	29.85
NC	Forest Green Advanced Widget	2	119.9
NC	Heavy Metal Basic Widget	1	69.95

Table 11-19 *continued*

Results of the sales region by product query

State	Product	Quantity	Sales
NC	Translucent Basic Widget	1	39.95
OH	Baby's First Widget	1	9.95
OH	Translucent Basic Widget	1	39.95
TN	Baby Blue Advanced Widget	1	49.95
TN	Baby's First Widget	1	9.95
TN	Forest Green Advanced Widget	1	59.95
TN	Heavy Metal Basic Widget	1	69.95
TN	Rainbow Basic Widget	1	39.95
TN	Translucent Basic Widget	1	39.95

This query was a bit more complicated, utilizing more tables and a more complex grouping requirement. Because Amy was looking for information on both the region and the product, she had to tap the three tables that held that data. Recall that since the `tblOrder` table holds the key reference to both the `tblCustomer` and `tblProduct` tables, Amy had to specify in the following `Where` clause the relationships between the three tables.

```
Where ((tblCustomer.fldKey = tblOrder.fldCustomerKey) and
       (tblProduct.fldKey = tblOrder.fldProductKey))
```

Note that Amy established the order of execution with three sets of parenthesis, a set around each relationship reference and one around both references. The results revealed that the largest selling item was Baby's First Widget.

Amy's last query demonstrated sales by region, by product, and by price range.

```
Select
    tblCustomer.fldState AS State,
    tblProduct.fldProductName AS Product,
    tblOrder.fldCost as Cost,
    Sum(tblOrder.fldQuantity) AS Quantity,
    Sum(tblOrder.fldCost * tblOrder.fldQuantity) AS Sales
From
    tblCustomer,
    tblOrder,
    tblProduct
Where
    (tblOrder.fldCost > 20 and tblOrder.fldCost < 60) and
    ((tblCustomer.fldKey = tblOrder.fldCustomerKey) and
    (tblProduct.fldKey = tblOrder.fldProductKey))
Group By
    tblCustomer.fldState,
    tblProduct.fldProductName,
    tblOrder.fldCost;
```

Table 11-20 shows the results of the query.

Table 11-20

Results of sales by region, by product, and by price range query

State	Product	Cost	Quantity	Sales
MN	Rainbow Basic Widget	39.95	1	39.95
NC	Baby Blue Advanced Widget	49.95	1	49.95
NC	Forest Green Advanced Widget	59.95	2	119.9
NC	Translucent Basic Widget	39.95	1	39.95
OH	Translucent Basic Widget	39.95	1	39.95
TN	Baby Blue Advanced Widget	49.95	1	49.95
TN	Forest Green Advanced Widget	59.95	1	59.95
TN	Rainbow Basic Widget	39.95	1	39.95
TN	Translucent Basic Widget	39.95	1	39.95

The intent was to produce a report that excluded the lowest- and highest-priced widgets. Acme believed its mid-range products were the foundation of the company's sales so Amy gave them an SQL query to test its theory.

Amy added `tblOrder.fldCost` to the `Select` clause as a reference point for the marketing analysts and added a cost range to the `Where` clause. In previous queries all of the records were read and processed, but this query was only looking for a range, so Amy inserted the range criteria before the relationship joins. Her reasoning was that it would be a waste of computer resources to pull all of the records in the relationship chain of an order and then discover that the cost was outside of the range. Adding the cost-range check at the beginning was the most efficient method; if a product's cost were outside of the range, the order record would be rejected without performing the record joining. Note that some more advanced SQL engines perform this type of optimization on their own before processing the query.

Finally, Amy added the `tblOrder.fldCost` field to the `Group By` clause because some SQL engines, such as Microsoft Access, require a field specified in the `Select` clause to also be included in the `Group By` clause. Amy had to be careful where she added `tblOrder.fldCost` in the clause because inserting it in the wrong place could skew the results and invalidate the query. SQL `Group By` execution precedence is from left to right, so she appended the line to the clause because `tblCustomer.fldState` and `tblProduct.fldProductName` were the fields of most concern in the grouping.

All of these queries use the `fldCost` field in the `tblOrder` table instead of in the `tblProduct` table because Amy was concerned about accurate historical data. If the `tblProduct.fld Cost` field had been used, query results with any reference to `fldCost` could have been skewed if widget prices had changed. `tblProduct.fldCost` contains only the current cost: `tblOrder.fldCost` contains the price that was actually paid.

Amy's presentation was a success. Laura loves the system and the marketing team is off mulling over the data and pondering new ways to mine the future database. It is critical to note that all of this potential was realized using only the information that Laura already kept on her 3x5 order cards!

SUMMARY

Structured Query Language (SQL) is the standard database language for data storage, retrieval and manipulation.

The `Select` statement is used to find records within a table that match search criteria. The `Select` statement returns a dynaset, which is a set of records matching the search criteria.

The `Alter` statement is used to alter a database table's structure.

The `Insert` statement is used to add records to a database table.

The `Delete` statement is used to delete records from a database table.

A selective deletion removes records that meet specified criteria.

The `Update` statement is used to change the contents in one or more columns in a table.

A selective update changes the contents only of selected records.

You may configure a data adapter object's SelectCommand.CommandText property at design time with an SQL statement. The records that are returned from the SQL statement will then become the source of records for the dataset.

In code you may assign a string containing a valid SQL statement a data adapter object's Select Command.CommandText property. After you call the `Fill` method, the records that are returned from the SQL statement will then become the source of records for the dataset.

If an SQL statement returns no records to the *DataSet.Table*.Count property will be set to zero.

The DataGrid control is designed to display the information in a dataset in row and column order. Each row in the data grid corresponds to a record in the dataset and each column in the data grid references the corresponding field in the dataset.

You associate a data grid with a dataset using the data grid's DataSource property.

A relational database is comprised of a series of tables, each containing a unique set of data, including a unique primary key. The tables are connected, or related, to each other by the primary key.

KEY TERMS

`Alter` statement	`Select` statement
Data grid control	SelectCommand.CommandText property
`Delete` statement	Selective deletion
Dynaset	Selective update
`Insert` statement	Structured Query Language (SQL)
Queries	`Update` statement
Relational database	

Review Questions

Fill-in-the-blank

1. _____ is the standard database language for data storage, retrieval, and manipulation.

2. The _____ statement is used to find records within a table that match search criteria.

3. The `Select` statement returns a(n) _____, which is a set of records matching the search criteria.

4. The _____ statement is used to modify a database table's structure.

5. The _____ statement is used to add records to a database table.

6. To remove records from a database table, use the _____ statement.

7. To modify the contents of records in a database table, use the _____ statement.

8. In code you may assign a string containing a valid SQL statement to the ADO data adapters's _____ property.

9. After you call the _____ method, the records that are returned from an SQL statement will then become the source of records for the ADO data control.

10. The _____control is designed to display `Dataset` data in row and column format.

Multiple Choice

1. Which company developed the first implementation of SQL?

    a. Honeywell

    b. IBM

    c. DEC

    d. None of the above

2. The SQL statement used to search for records in a database is
    a. `Search`
    b. `Find`
    c. `Select`
    d. `Extract`

3. The SQL statement used to change the structure of a database table is
    a. `Alter`
    b. `Change`
    c. `Modify`
    d. `Structure`

4. The SQL statement used to add records to a database is
    a. `Add`
    b. `Insert`
    c. `Save`
    d. `New`

5. The SQL statement used to change the contents of records in a database is
    a. `Revise`
    b. `Change`
    c. `Modify`
    d. `Update`

6. The SQL statement used to remove records from a database is
    a. `Remove`
    b. `Delete`
    c. `Erase`
    d. `Extract`

7. The records returned from an SQL statement in ADO .NET are called a

    a. Dataset

    b. Resultset

    c. Queryset

    d. Returnset

8. To make sure an SQL statement returns all the columns from a table, use this character as the column name.
   a. ?
   b. #
   c. *
   d. &

9. To specify an SQL statement as the source of data for an ADO .NET data control, you must configure what ADO data adapter property?
   a. ConnectionString
   b. DataSource
   c. CommandText
   d. SqlSource

10. To associate a DataGrid control to an ADO .NET data adapter, you must configure what data grid property?
    a. ConnectionString
    b. DataSource
    c. RecordSource
    d. SqlSource

True or False

Indicate whether each of the following statements is true or false.

1. T F: SQL is an obscure language used only within Visual Basic .NET.

2. T F: The statement `Select * From tblTable;` will return all the columns of all the records in the table `tblTable`.

3. T F: SQL statements may span multiple lines and may include indentation.

4. T F: SQL does not support the `And` and `Or` logical operators.

5. T F: It is not possible to modify the structure of a table with an SQL statement.

6. T F: If a table structure requires a value in a column and no data is present in the insert statement, the record will not be entered and an error will result.

7. T F: In an `Insert` statement, you may store values enclosed in quotes in numeric fields.

8. T F: The statement `Delete From tblTable;` will not delete any records because a `Where` clause has not been provided.

9. T F: The statement `Update tblTable Set fldNum = 0;` will change every record in the table `tblTable`.

10. T F: A data grid does not contain a copy of the data in a dataset, but references the dataset directly.

Short Answer

1. What is the difference between the `Insert` statement and the `Update` statement?

2. How do you specify that only certain columns be returned from a `Select` statement?

3. What two steps do you take in code when issuing a new SQL command for the data adapter to execute?

4. What is the standard prefix for a DataGrid control name?

5. How do you configure a DataGrid control so the user cannot change its contents?

What Do You Think?

1. Without the ability to define which records to search for by supplying column- related criteria, the `Select` statement would be practically worthless. Why?

2. Sometimes you only want certain columns returned from a `Select` statement. Why?

3. How is the dataset that is returned from a `Select` statement different from the database table that the `Select` statement searches?

4. Why is it always a good idea to provide search criteria when using the `Delete` statement?

5. Since it is possible to configure the data adapter with an SQL command at design time, why would you want to do the same in code?

6. Why would you normally want to change the column headings displayed by a DataGrid control?

Find the Errors

The following SQL statements contain errors. Find each one.

```
1.  Select
        *
    From
        tblNames
    Where
        fldCity = "Redmond"
        fldState = "WA";

2.  Select
        fldFirst
        fldLast
    From
        tblNames;

3.  Insert Into tblNames (
        fldFirst ,
        fldMiddle,
        fldLast,
        fldStreet,
        fldCity,
        fldState,
        fldTelephone,
        fldEmail)
    Values (
        "Josh",
        "J",
        "Smith",
        "123 Grayson Ave.",
        "Mayberry",
        "NC",
        "(555) 555-5555",
        jjsmith@bestisp.com);
```

Algorithm Workbench

For the following questions, assume a database contains a table named `tblCustomers`.

1. Write an SQL statement that returns all columns of all the records in the `tblCustomers` table.

2. Write an SQL statement that returns the following columns of all the records in `tblCustomers`: `fldFirst`, `fldLast`, and `fldCity`.

3. Write an SQL statement that returns all the columns of the records in `tblCustomers` that have "San Diego" stored in `fldCity`.

4. Write an SQL statement that returns all the columns of the records in `tblCustomers` that have "Washington" stored in `fldCity` and for which `fldAge` is less than 30.

5. Write an SQL statement that adds a new column named `fldEmail` to `tblCustomers`. The column should store text up to 30 characters in length.

6. Write an SQL statement that adds a new record to `tblCustomers`. Store 45789 in `fldId`, "Jimmy" in `fldFirst`, "McGregor" in `fldLast`, "Sacremento" in `fldCity`, and 28 in `fldAge`.

7. Write an SQL statement that deletes all records from `tblCustomers` with "Smith" stored in `fldLast`.

8. You need to locate every record in `tblCustomers` that has 28667 stored in `fldPostalCode` and change that value to 28999. Write an SQL statement that makes the change.

PROGRAMMING CHALLENGES

1. Customer List Box

Create an application with a list box similar to that in Figure 11-29. When the Get Names button is clicked, the list box should display the first and last names of all the customers in the Customers database.

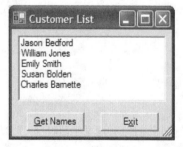

Figure 11-29   Customer List box form

The application should use an data adapter control configured with an SQL command to retrieve the records.

2. Search by State

Modify the Customers Database application you created in Tutorial 11-2 to include a Search button, a Show All button, and a No Update button as shown in Figure 11-30.

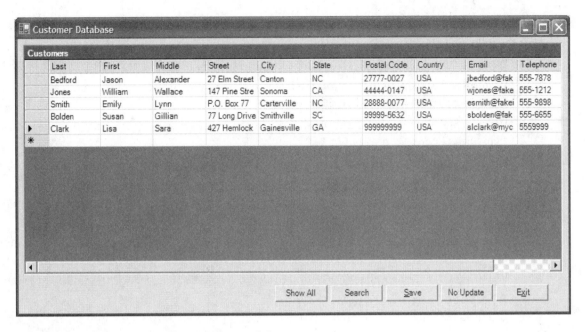

Figure 11-30   Customer Database with search by state

When the Search button is clicked, the application should prompt the user for a state abbreviation (such as CA, NC, SC, etc.). It should then only display the records for customers in that state in the DataGrid control. When the Show All button is clicked the application should display all records. When the No Update button is clicked, the application should throw away the current contents of the data grid and reload the data from the data source.

Design Your Own Forms

3.   Stock Trader Modification

In Chapter 10, Programming Challenges 1 and 3, you created the Stock Trader application. Add the capability to enter a dollar value and search for stocks where the purchase price is less than the dollar value entered. Use an SQL statement to find the records and display them in a DataGrid control.

4.   CD Inventory Search By Title Modification

Modify the CD Inventory application from Chapter 10 so the Search By Title menu item uses an SQL statement to search for all the CDs with a specified title. The resulting records should be displayed in a read-only DataGrid control.

5.   CD Inventory Search by Quantity Modification.

Add a new "Search by Quantity" menu item to the CD Inventory application from Chapter 10. When the user selects this menu item, the application should ask for a maximum quantity. It should then use an SQL statement to find all the CDs with a quantity-on-hand of no more than the specified amount. The resulting records should be displayed in a read-only DataGrid control.

6.   CD Inventory Search by Price and Genre Modification

Add a new "Search by Price and Genre" menu item to the CD Inventory application from Chapter 10. When the user selects this menu item, the application should ask for a genre (such as rock, jazz, country, etc.), and a maximum price. The application should use an SQL statement to search for all the CDs within the specified genre and with a price that does not exceed the specified maximum price. The resulting records should be displayed in a read-only DataGrid control.

CHAPTER 12

Classes, Exceptions, Collections, and Scrollable Controls

▶ 12.1 Introduction

This chapter introduces abstract data types and shows you how to create them with classes. The process of analyzing a problem and determining its classes is discussed, and techniques for creating objects, properties, and methods are introduced. Next, the chapter introduces exceptions and discusses error-handling techniques. Collections, which are structures for holding groups of objects, are also covered. The Object Browser, which allows you to see information about the classes, properties, methods, and events available to your project, is discussed. The chapter concludes by showing you how to create scrollable controls.

▶ 12.2 Classes and Objects

CONCEPT

CLASSES ARE PROGRAM STRUCTURES THAT DEFINE ABSTRACT DATA TYPES AND THAT ARE USED TO CREATE OBJECTS.

One of the most exciting developments in computer software over the last 20 years has been object-oriented programming, nicknamed OOP. *Object-oriented programming* is a way of designing and coding applications such that interchangeable software components can be used to build larger programs. Object-oriented programming languages, such as ALGOL, SmallTalk, and C++, first appeared in the early 1980s. The legacy from these languages has been the gradual development of object-like visual tools for building programs. In Visual Basic .NET, for example, forms, buttons, check boxes, list boxes, and other controls are ideal examples of objects. Object-oriented designs help us produce programs that are well suited to ongoing development and expansion.

Abstract Data Types

An *abstract data type (ADT)*, is a data type created by a programmer. ADTs are very important in computer science and especially significant in object-oriented programming. An *abstraction* is a general model of something—a definition that includes only the general characteristics of an object. For example, the term "dog" is an abstraction. It defines a general type of animal. The term captures the essence of what all dogs are without specifying the detailed characteristics of any particular breed of dog or any individual animal. According to Webster's New Collegiate Dictionary, a dog is "a highly variable carnivorous domesticated mammal (*Canis familiaris*) probably descended from the common wolf."

In real life, however, there is no such thing as a mere dog. There are specific dogs, each sharing common characteristics such as paws, fur, whiskers, and a carnivorous diet. For example, Travis owns a rottweiler named Bailey, and Shirley owns a poodle named Snuggles. In this analogy the abstraction, dog, is like a data type and the specific dogs (Bailey and Snuggles) are instances of the type.

Classes

A *class* is a program structure that defines an abstract data type. You create a class then create instances of the class. All class instances share common characteristics. For example, Visual Basic .NET controls and forms are classes. In the toolbox each icon represents a class. When you select the button tool from the toolbox and place it on a form, as in Figure 12-1, you are creating an instance of the button class. An instance is also called an *object*.

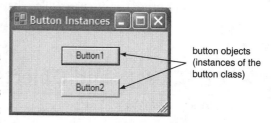

Class Properties, Methods, and Event Procedures

The way a program communicates with each object is determined by the properties and methods defined in the object's class. The button class, for example, has properties such as Location, Text, and Name. Each button object contains its own unique set of property values. In the example shown in Figure 12-1, the two buttons have different values in their Location and Text properties.

Figure 12-1   Instances of the button class

Methods are shared by all instances of a class. For example, the button class has a method named `Focus`, which is the same for all button objects.

Event procedures are also methods, but they are specific to individual objects. For example, a form with several buttons will almost always have different code written in each button's `Click` event procedure.

Object-Oriented Design

Object-oriented programming is not just a matter of randomly dropping classes into a program. The challenge is to design classes in such a way that the resulting objects will effectively cooperate and communicate. The primary goal of object-oriented design is to address the needs of the application or problem being solved. A secondary goal is to design classes that can outlive the current application and possibly be useful in future programs.

The first step, after creating the program specifications, is to analyze the application requirements. *Object-oriented analysis*, as it is called, often starts with a detailed specification of the problem to be solved. A term often applied to this process is *finding the classes*. A famous sculptor once said that inside every block of marble is a work of art waiting to be discovered. So, too, in every problem and every application there are classes waiting to be found. It is the designer's job to discover just what those classes are.

Finding the Classes

Classes are the fundamental building blocks of object-oriented applications. When designing object-oriented programs, we first select classes that reflect physical entities in the application domain. For example, the user of a record-keeping program for a college might describe some of the application's requirements as follows:

> We need to keep a **list of students** that lets us track the courses they have completed. Each student has a **transcript** that contains all information about his or her completed courses. At the end of each semester, we will calculate the grade point average of each **student**. At times, users will search for a particular **course** taken by a student.

Notice the highlighted nouns and noun phrases in this description: list of students, transcript, student, and course. These would ordinarily become classes in the program's design.

Looking for Control Structures

Classes can also be discovered in the description of processing done by an application or in the description of control structures. For example, if the application involved scheduling college classes for students another description from the program specifications might be:

> We also want to schedule classes for students, using the college's master schedule to determine the times and room numbers for each student's class. When the optimal arrangement of classes for each student has been determined, each student's class schedule will be printed and distributed.

In this description, we anticipate a need for a controlling agent that could be implemented as a class. We might call it `Scheduler`, a class that matches up each student's schedule with the college master schedule.

Describing the Classes

The next step, after finding the classes in an application, is to describe the classes in terms of attributes and operations. *Attributes* are characteristics of each object that will be implemented as properties. Attributes describe the properties that all objects of the same class have in common. Classes also have *operations*, which are actions the class objects may perform or messages to which they can respond. Operations are implemented as class methods. Table 12-1 describes some of the important attributes and operations of the record-keeping application that we described earlier.

Table 12-1

Sample attributes and operations

Class	Attributes (properties)	Operations (methods)
Student	LastName, FirstName, IdNumber	Display, Input
StudentList	AllStudents, Count	Add, Remove, FindStudent
Course	Semester, Name, Grade, Credits	Display, Input
Transcript	CourseList, Count	Display, Search, CalcGradeAvg

The complete set of attributes and operations is often incomplete during the early stages of design, because it is difficult to anticipate all the application requirements. As a design develops, the need often arises for additional properties and methods that improve communication between objects. Rather than a weakness, however, this ability to accommodate ongoing modifications is one of the strengths of the object-oriented design process.

Interface and Implementation

The *class interface* is the portion of the class that is visible to the application programmer. The program written to use a class is sometimes called the *client program*, in reference to the client-server relationship between a class and the programs that use it. The class interface provides a way for clients to communicate (send messages) to class objects. In Visual Basic .NET, a class interface is created by declaring public properties, methods, and events.

The *class implementation* is the portion of a class that is hidden from client programs; it is created from private member variables, private properties, and private methods. The hiding of data and procedures inside a class is achieved through a process called *encapsulation*. In this, it might be helpful to visualize the class as a "capsule" around its data and procedures.

✓ Checkpoint

12.1   Give some examples of objects in Visual Basic .NET.

12.2   A text box tool appears in the toolbox and a text box control has been placed on a form. Which represents the TextBox class and which is an instance of the TextBox class?

12.3   When analyzing a problem, how do we select the classes?

12.4   What is an attribute of a class? How are attributes implemented?

12.5   What is an operation of a class? How are they implemented?

12.6   What is a class interface?

12.7   What is the class implemetation?

▶ 12.3   Creating a Class

CONCEPT

TO CREATE A CLASS IN VISUAL BASIC .NET, YOU CREATE A CLASS DECLARATION. THE CLASS DECLARATION SPECIFIES THE MEMBER VARIABLES, PROPERTIES, METHODS, AND EVENTS THAT BELONG TO THE CLASS.

You create a class in Visual Basic .NET by creating a class declaration. We will use the following general format when writing class declarations:

```
Public Class ClassName
        MemberDeclarations
End Class
```

ClassName is the name of the class. *MemberDeclarations* is one or more declarations of members of the class. Follow these steps to add a class declaration to a project.

1. Click the Add New Item button (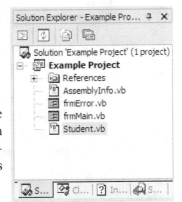) on the toolbar, or click Project on the menu bar, then click Add Class. The Add New Item dialog box, shown in Figure 12-2, should appear. Make sure that Class is selected in the Templates pane. Notice that in the figure, the name Class1.vb appears in the Name text box. In this example, Class1.vb is the default name for the file that the class declaration will be stored in, and Class1 is the default name for the class.

NOTE: *The default name may be different, depending on the number of classes already in the project.*

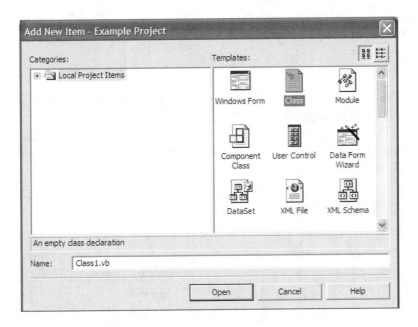

Figure 12-2   Add New Item dialog box

2. Change the default name that is displayed in the Name text box to the name you wish to give the new class file. For example, if you wish to name the new class Student, enter Student.vb in the Name text box.

3. Click the Open button.

A new, empty class declaration will be added to your project. The empty class declaration will be displayed in the Code window and an entry for the new class file will appear in the Solution Explorer window. The Solution Explorer window in Figure 12-3 shows two forms and one class: frmError, frmMain, and Student.

Figure 12-3   The Solution Explorer window showing two forms and one class

Member Variables

A *member variable* is a variable that is declared inside a class declaration. The variable is a member of the class. A member variable declaration has the following general format:

```
AccessSpecifer VariableName As DataType
```

AccessSpecifier determines the accessibility of the variable. Variables declared with the Public access specifier may be accessed by statements outside the class declaration. Variables declared with the Private access specifier may be accessed only by statements inside the class declaration. *VariableName* is the name of the variable, and *DataType* is the variable's data type. For example, the following code declares a class named Student. The class has three member variables: lname, fname, and id.

```
Public Class Student
    Public lname As String    ' Holds last name
    Public fname As String    ' Holds first name
    Public id As String       ' Holds ID number
End Class
```

Notice that each of the member variables is declared as Public, which means that statements outside the class declaration may access them.

As with structures, a class declaration does not create an instance of the class. It only establishes a blueprint for the class's organization. To actually work with the class, you must create *class objects*, which are instances of the class.

Creating an Instance of a Class

Creating an instance of a class is a two-step process: You declare an object variable, and then you create an instance of the class in memory and assign its address to the object variable. Although there are only two steps in the process, there are two different techniques for performing these steps. The first method performs both steps in one line of code, as shown in the following example.

```
Dim freshman As New Student()
```

This statement creates an object variable named freshman. The New key word causes the class instance to be created in memory. The object's address is assigned to freshman.

The second method requires two lines of code, as shown in the following example.

```
Dim freshman As Student
freshman = New Student()
```

The Dim statement in the first line creates an object variable named freshman. By default, the object variable is initialized to the value Nothing. The second line uses the New keyword to create an instance of the Student class and assigns its memory address to the freshman variable.

When you create instances of a class, each instance has its own copy of the class's member variables.

Accessing Members

Once you have created a class object, you can work with its Public members in code. You access the Public members of a class object with the dot (.) operator. Assuming that freshman is an object variable that references a `Student` class object, the following statements store values in the object's `Public` member variables.

```
freshman.fname = "Joy"
freshman.lname = "Robinson"
freshman.id = "23G794"
```

It might have occurred to you that the member variables `fname`, `lname`, and `id` can work as properties of the `Student` class. Implementing properties as public member variables is not the best approach, however. Suppose you wish to validate the data being stored in a property, or perform a calculation when a property is updated. In those cases, properties cannot be implemented as public member variables. Instead, Visual Basic .NET allows you to implement properties as property procedures.

Property Procedures

A *property procedure* is a function that behaves like a property. The general format of a property procedure is:

```
Public Property PropertyName() As DataType
     Get
             Statements
     End Get
     Set(ParameterDeclaration)
             Statements
     End Set
End Property
```

PropertyName is the name of the property procedure, and hence the name of the property that the procedure implements. *DataType* is the data type of the property. Notice that the procedure has two sections: a `Get` section and a `Set` section. The *Get section* holds the code that is executed when the property value is retrieved, and the *Set section* holds the code that is executed when a value is stored in the property.

TIP: Properties are almost always declared with the `Public` access specifier so they can be accessed from outside their enclosing class module.

TIP: After you type the first line of a property procedure, Visual Basic .NET will build a code template for the rest of the procedure.

For example, let's add a TestAverage property to the `Student` class, which will hold the student's test score average. Because the average test score is a number in the range of 0.0 through 100.0, we want to validate any value stored in the TestAverage property. Therefore, we will implement the TestAverage property as a property procedure that validates any data stored in the property. The modified code for the class follows.

```
Public Class Student
    ' Member variables
    Public lname As String    ' Holds last name
    Public fname As String    ' Holds first name
    Public idNum As String    ' Holds ID number
    Private testAvg As Single' Holds test average
```

```
' TestAverage Property procedure
Public Property TestAverage() As Single
    Get
        Return testAvg
    End Get
    Set(ByVal value As Single)
        If value >= 0.0 And value <= 100.0 Then
            testAvg = value
        Else
            MessageBox.Show("Invalid test average.", "Error")
        End If
    End Set
End Property
End Class
```

Notice that a private member variable named `testAvg` has been added to the class. This member variable will hold the actual value that is stored in the TestAverage property. We have declared the variable as private to prevent code outside the class from storing values directly in it. To store a test average in an object, the property procedure must be used. This allows us to perform validation on the value before it is stored in an object.

Let's look at the `Get` and `Set` sections of the property procedure. The code for the `Get` section follows.

```
Get
    Return testAvg
End Get
```

The `Get` section does only one thing: it returns the value stored in the `testAvg` member variable. Here is the code for the `Set` section:

```
Set(ByVal value As Single)
    If value >= 0.0 And value <= 100.0 Then
        testAvg = value
    Else
        MessageBox.Show("Invalid test average.", "Error")
    End If
End Set
```

The `Set` section has a declaration for a parameter named `value`. When a number is stored in the TestAverage property, the `Set` section is executed and the number being stored in the property is passed into the `value` parameter. The procedure determines if `value` is within the range of 0.0 through 100.0. If it is, then it is stored in the `testAvg` member variable. If it is not, an error message is displayed.

The following code shows an example of the TestAverage property in use.

```
Dim freshman As Student
freshman = New Student()
freshman.TestAverage = 82.3
```

The last statement stores the value 82.3 in the TestAverage property. Because a value is being stored in the property, this statement causes the `Set` section of the TestAverage property procedure to execute. The number 82.3 is passed into the `value` parameter. Because 82.3 is within the range of 0.0

through 100.0, it is stored in the object's `testAvg` member variable. The following statement will cause an error message to be displayed:

```
freshman.TestAverage = 107.0
```

In this case, 107.0 is passed into the `value` parameter, which causes the message box with the error message to be displayed.

Any statement that retrieves the value in the TestAverage property will cause the property procedure's `Get` section to execute. For example, the following code assigns the value in the TestAverage property to the variable `average`.

```
average = freshman.TestAverage
```

This statement causes the property's `Get` section to execute, which returns the value stored in the `testAvg` member variable. The following code displays the value in the TestAverage property in a message box.

```
MessageBox.Show(freshman.TestAverage.ToString)
```

Now, let's modify the `Student` class so the following properties are implemented as property procedures: FirstName, LastName, IdNumber, and TestAverage. The code follows.

```
Public Class Student
    ' Member variables
    Private lname As String     ' Holds last name
    Private fname As String     ' Holds first name
    Private id As String        ' Holds ID number
    Private testAvg As Single    ' Holds test average

    ' LastName property procedure
    Public Property LastName() As String
        Get
            Return lname
        End Get
        Set(ByVal value As String)
            lname = value
        End Set
    End Property

    ' FirstName property procedure
    Public Property FirstName() As String
        Get
            Return fname
        End Get
        Set(ByVal value As String)
            fname = value
        End Set
    End Property

    ' IdNumber property procedure
    Public Property IdNumber() As String
        Get
            Return id
        End Get
        Set(ByVal value As String)
```

```
              id = value
        End Set
    End Property

    ' TestAverage property procedure
    Public Property TestAverage() As Single
        Get
            Return testAvg
        End Get
        Set(ByVal value As Single)
            If value >= 0.0 And value <= 100.0 Then
                testAvg = value
            Else
                MessageBox.Show("Invalid test average.", "Error")
            End If
        End Set
    End Property
End Class
```

Read-Only Properties

Sometimes it is useful to make a property read-only. Client programs can query a *read-only property* to get its value, but cannot modify it. The general format of a read-only property procedure is:

```
ReadOnly Property PropertyName() As DataType
    Get
            Statements
    End Get
End Property
```

The first line of a read-only property procedure begins with the `Readonly` key word. Notice that the procedure has no `Set` section. It is only capable of returning a value. For example, the following code demonstrates a read-only TestGrade property that we might add to our `Student` class.

```
    ' TestGrade property procedure
    ReadOnly Property TestGrade() As Char
        Get
            Dim grade As Char
            Select Case testAvg
                Case 90 To 100
                    grade = "A"
                Case 80 To 90
                    grade = "B"
                Case 70 To 80
                    grade = "C"
                Case 60 To 70
                    grade = "D"
                Case Else
                    grade = "F"
            End Select
            Return grade
        End Get
    End Property
```

This property returns one of the following character values, depending on the contents of the `testAvg` member variable: "A", "B", "C", "D", or "F".

A compiler error will occur if a client program attempts to store a value in a read-only property. For example, the following statement will result in an error:

```
freshman.TestAverage = "A"        ' Error
```

Removing Objects and Garbage Collection

It is a good habit to remove objects that are no longer needed, allowing the application to free memory for other purposes. To remove an object, set all the object variables that reference it to `Nothing`. For example, the following statement sets the object variable `freshman` to `Nothing`.

```
freshman = Nothing
```

After this statement executes, the `freshman` variable will no longer reference an object. If the object that it previously referenced is no longer referenced by any other variables, it will be removed from memory by the Visual Basic .NET garbage collector. The *garbage collector* is a process that destroys objects when they are no longer needed.

NOTE: *The garbage collector might not remove an object from memory immediately after the last reference to it has been removed. The system uses an algorithm to determine when it should periodically remove unused objects. As the amount of available memory decreases, the garbage collector removes unreferenced objects more often.*

Going Out of Scope

Like all variables, an object variable that is declared inside a procedure is local to that procedure. If an object is referenced only by a procedure's local object variable, the object is automatically removed from memory by the garbage collector after the procedure ends. This is called *going out of scope*. For example, look at the following procedure.

```
Sub CreateStudent()
    Dim sophomore As Student
    sophomore = New Student()
    sophomore.FirstName = "Travis"
    sophomore.LastName = "Barnes"
    sophomore.IdNumber = "17H495"
    sophomore.TestAverage = 94.7
End Sub
```

This procedure declares an object variable named `sophomore`. An instance of the `Student` class is created and referenced by the `sophomore` variable. When this procedure ends, the instance of the class that is referenced by `sophomore` is automatically removed by the garbage collector.

An object is not removed from memory if there are still references to it. For example, assume an application has a global module-level variable named `g_studentVar`. Look at the following code.

```
Sub CreateStudent()
    Dim sophomore As Student
    sophomore = New Student()
    sophomore.FirstName = "Travis"
    sophomore.LastName = "Barnes"
```

```
        sophomore.IdNumber = "17H495"
        sophomore.TestAverage = 94.7
        g_studentVar = sophomore
    End Sub
```

The last statement in the procedure assigns g_studentVar to the object referenced by sophomore. This means that both g_studentVar and sophomore reference the same object. When this procedure ends, the object referenced by sophomore will not be removed from memory because it is still referenced by the module-level variable g_studentVar.

Comparing Object Variables with the **Is** Operator

Multiple object variables can reference the same object in memory. For example, the following code declares two object variables: collegeStudent and transferStudent. Both object variables are made to reference the same instance of the Student class.

```
    Dim collegeStudent As Student
    Dim transferStudent As Student
    collegeStudent = New Student()
    transferStudent = collegeStudent
```

After this code executes, both collegeStudent and transferStudent will reference the same object. You cannot use the = operator in an If statement to determine whether two object variables reference the same object. Instead, you use the *Is operator*. For example, the following statement will properly determine if collegeStudent and transferStudent reference the same object.

```
    If collegeStudent Is transferStudent Then
        ' Perform some action
    End If
```

You can use the Not operator with the Is operator to determine whether two variables do not reference the same object. Here is an example:

```
    If Not (collegeStudent Is transferStudent) Then
        ' Perform some action
    End If
```

If you wish to compare an object variable to the special value Nothing, you will have to use the Is operator, as shown in the following code.

```
    If collegeStudent Is Nothing Then
        ' Perform some action
    End If
```

Creating an Array of Objects

You can create an array of object variables, and then create an object for each element of the array to reference. The following code declares mathStudents as an array of 10 object variables. It then uses a loop to assign each element of the array to an object:

```
Dim mathStudents(9) As Student
Dim i As Integer
For i = 0 To 9
    Set mathStudents(i) = New Student()
Next i
```

You can use another loop to release the memory used by the array, as shown in the following statements:

```
Dim i As Integer
For i = 0 To 9
    Set mathStudents(i) = Nothing
Next i
```

Writing Sub Procedures and Functions that Work with Objects

You can easily write Sub procedures and functions that accept object variables as arguments. For example, the following procedure accepts an object variable that references an instance of the Student class as its argument and displays the student's grade.

```
Sub DisplayStudentGrade(ByVal s As Student)
    ' Displays a student's grade.
    MessageBox.Show("The grade for " & s.FirstName & _
        " " & s.LastName & " is " & s.TestGrade.ToString)
End Sub
```

The parameter, s, is an object variable that can reference an instance of the Student class. To call the procedure, simply pass an object variable that references a Student object, as shown in the following code.

```
DisplayStudentGrade(freshman)
```

When this statement executes, the DisplayStudentGrade procedure is called and the freshman object variable is passed as an argument. Inside the procedure, the variable s will reference the same object that freshman references.

Passing Objects By Value and By Reference

Object variable parameters may be declared either as ByVal or ByRef. Be aware, however, that the ByVal key word does not restrict a procedure from accessing and modifying the object that the argument references. For example, look at the following ClearStudent procedure.

```
Sub ClearStudent(ByVal s As Student)
    s.FirstName = ""
    s.LastName = ""
    s.IdNumber = ""
    s.TestAverage = 0.0
End Sub
```

An object variable referencing a Student object is passed into this procedure as an argument. The procedure clears the FirstName, LastName, IdNumber, and TestAverage properties of the object referenced by the argument. For example, look at the following code:

```
freshman.FirstName = "Joy"
freshman.LastName = "Robinson"
freshman.IdNumber = "23G794"
freshman.TestAverage = 82.3
' Display Joy Robinson's grade.
DisplayStudentGrade(freshman)
' Clear the properties of the object.
ClearStudent(freshman)
```

After the `ClearStudent` procedure executes, the properties of the object referenced by the `freshman` variable will be cleared.

Although the `ByVal` key word does not restrict a procedure from accessing the object referenced by an argument, it does prevent an argument from being assigned to another object. For example, the following procedure accepts an object variable as its argument, and then assigns the parameter to another object.

```
Sub ResetStudent(ByVal s As Student)
    ' Assign the argument to a
    ' new object. Does this work?
    Dim newStudent As Student
    newStudent = New Student()
    newStudent.FirstName = "Bill"
    newStudent.LastName = "Owens"
    newStudent.IdNumber = "56K789"
    newStudent.TestAverage = 84.6
    s = newStudent
End Sub
```

Suppose we call the procedure, as shown in the following code.

```
freshman.FirstName = "Joy"
freshman.LastName = "Robinson"
freshman.IdNumber = "23G794"
freshman.TestAverage = 82.3
ResetStudent(freshman)
```

After the `ResetStudent` procedure executes, the object referenced by the `freshman` variable will still contain the data for Joy Robinson. If the parameter variable had been declared with the `ByRef` key word, however, the assignment would have affected the `freshman` variable. In that case, the `freshman` variable would no longer reference the object containing Joy Robinson's data, but would reference the object containing the data for Bill Owens.

Returning an Object from a Function

It is also possible to return an object from a function. For example, the following function prompts the user to enter the data for a `Student` class object. The object is then returned.

```
Function GetStudent() As Student
    ' Get student data and return it as an object.
    Dim s As Student
    s = New Student()
    s.FirstName = InputBox("Enter the student's first name.")
```

```
        s.LastName = InputBox("Enter the student's last name.")
        s.IdNumber = InputBox("Enter the student's ID number.")
        s.TestAverage = InputBox("Enter the student's test average.")
        Return s
    End Function
```

The following code shows the function's return value being assigned to the freshman object variable.

```
Dim freshman As Student
freshman = GetStudent()
```

Class Methods

A *class method* is a Sub procedure or function that is a member of the class. The method performs some operation on the data stored in the class. You write methods inside the class declaration. For example, suppose we wish to add a Clear method to the Student class, as shown in the following code. To simplify the code listing, the property procedures have been omitted.

```
Public Class Student
    ' Member variables
    Private lname As String     ' Holds last name
    Private fname As String     ' Holds first name
    Private id As String        ' Holds ID number
    Private testAvg As Single   ' Holds test average

    (Property procedures appear here.)

    ' Clear method
    Public Sub Clear()
        fname = ""
        lname = ""
        id = ""
        testAvg = 0.0
    End Sub
End Class
```

The Clear method clears the private member variables that hold the student's first name, last name, ID number, and test average. The following statement calls the method using the object referenced by freshman.

```
freshman.Clear()
```

Constructors

A *constructor* is a class method that is automatically called when an instance of the class is created. It is helpful to think of constructors as initialization routines. They are useful for initializing member variables or performing other startup operations. To create a constructor, simply create a Sub procedure named New in the class. (Alternatively, you can select New from the method name drop-down list and a code template will be created for you.) Each time an instance of the class is created, the New procedure will be executed.

For example, suppose we wish to add to the Student class a constructor that initializes the private member variables. The code follows.

```
Public Class Student
    ' Member variables
    Private lname As String      ' Holds last name
    Private fname As String      ' Holds first name
    Private id As String         ' Holds ID number
    Private testAvg As Single    ' Holds test average
    ' Constructor
    Public Sub New()
        fname = fname = ""
        lname = fname = ""
        id = id = ""
        testAvg = 0.0
    End Sub
```

(The rest of this class is omitted.)

```
End Class
```

Assuming that `freshman` is an object variable, we create an instance of the class with the following statement:

```
freshman = New Student()
```

When this statement executes, an instance of the `Student` class is created and its constructor is executed. The result is that `freshman.LastName`, `freshman.FirstName`, and `freshman.IdNumber` will hold the string "(unknown)" and `freshman.TestAverage` will hold 0.0.

Finalizers

A *finalizer* is a class method named `Finalize`, which is automatically called just before an instance of the class is destroyed. If you wish to execute code immediately before an object is destroyed, create a `Finalize` method in the class. Because of the syntax of the `Finalize` method, it is recommended that you let Visual Basic .NET create a code template. Select `Finalize` in the method name drop-down list, and the following code template will be created.

```
Protected Overrides Sub Finalize()
    MyBase.Finalize()

End Sub
```

Any code that you wish to execute should be placed after the `MyBase.Finalize()` statement. The `Finalize` method isn't nearly as useful as the `New` method. As previously mentioned, the garbage collector uses an algorithm to determine when it should periodically release all unreferenced objects from memory. Therefore, you cannot predict exactly when the `Finalize` method will be executed.

Displaying Messages in the Output Window

Before beginning our class-building tutorial, we should discuss a valuable debugging tool: the Output window. The Output window, shown in Figure 12-4, normally appears at the bottom of the Visual Basic .NET environment while an application is running. This window displays various messages while an application is being compiled.

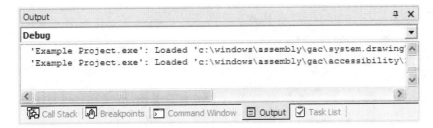

Figure 12-4 Output window

You can display your own messages in the Output window with the `Debug.WriteLine` method. The method has the following general format:

```
Debug.WriteLine(Output)
```

Output is a constant or a variable whose value is to be displayed in the Output window. We will use this method in the Tutorial 12-1 to display status messages from a class constructor and finalizer. The constructor will be modified as follows.

```
' Constructor
Public Sub New()
    Debug.WriteLine("Student object being created.")
    fname = ""
    lname = ""
    id = ""
    testAvg = 0.0
End Sub
```

The `Debug.WriteLine` method will display a message in the Output window each time a `Student` object is created in memory. We will also add a similar statement to the `Finalize` method, as follows.

```
Protected Overrides Sub Finalize()
    MyBase.Finalize()
    Debug.WriteLine("Student object being destroyed.")
End Sub
```

This will let us know when the garbage collector destroys an object. Each time a `Student` object is removed from memory, the `Debug.Writeline` method will display a message in the output window.

In Tutorial 12-1 you will create the `Student` class we have been using as an example, and use it in an application that saves student data to a file.

TUTORIAL 12-1:

Creating the Student Data application

Step 1: Start Visual Basic .NET and begin a new Windows application project. Name the project Student Data.

Step 2: Set up the application's form as shown in Figure 12-5.

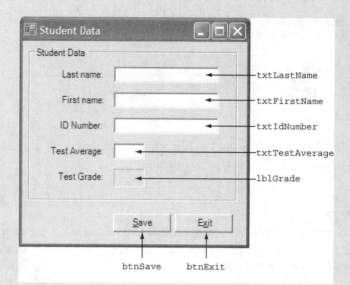

Figure 12-5 Student Data form

Step 3: Perform the following steps to add a new class to the project:

- Click Project on the menu bar, then click Add Class.

- In the Add New Item dialog box, make sure Class is selected in the Templates pane. In the Name text box, type Student.vb.

- Click the Open button.

A new class file is created and opened in the Code window. The contents of the class appear as follows.

```
Public Class Student

End Class
```

Step 4: Complete the class by entering the following code shown in bold.

```
Public Class Student
    ' Member variables
    Private lname As String     ' Holds last name
    Private fname As String     ' Holds first name
    Private id As String        ' Holds ID number
    Private testAvg As Single   ' Holds test average

    ' Constructor
    Public Sub New()
        Debug.WriteLine("Student object being created.")
        fname = ""
        lname = ""
        id = ""
        testAvg = 0.0
    End Sub
```

```
    ' LastName property procedure
Public Property LastName() As String
    Get
        Return lname
    End Get
    Set(ByVal value As String)
        lname = value
    End Set
End Property


    ' FirstName property procedure
Public Property FirstName() As String
    Get
        Return fname
    End Get
    Set(ByVal value As String)
        fname = value
    End Set
End Property


    ' IdNumber property procedure
Public Property IdNumber() As String
    Get
        Return id
    End Get
    Set(ByVal value As String)
        id = value
    End Set
End Property


    ' TestAverage property procedure
Public Property TestAverage() As Single
    Get
        Return testAvg
    End Get
    Set(ByVal value As Single)
        If value >= 0.0 And value <= 100.0 Then
            testAvg = value
        Else
            MessageBox.Show("Invalid test average.", "Error")
        End If
    End Set
End Property


    ' TestGrade property procedure
ReadOnly Property TestGrade() As Char
    Get
        Dim grade As Char
        Select Case testAvg
            Case 90 To 100
```

```
                                    grade = "A"
                        Case 80 To 90
                                    grade = "B"
                        Case 70 To 80
                                    grade = "C"
                        Case 60 To 70
                                    grade = "D"
                        Case Else
                                    grade = "F"
                End Select
                Return grade
            End Get
        End Property


        ' Clear method
        Public Sub Clear()
            fname = ""
            lname = ""
            id = ""
            testAvg = 0.0
        End Sub
    End Class
```

Step 5: Now you will add a finalizer that displays a message in the output window. In the method name drop-down list, select `Finalize`. A code template should appear. Complete the template by entering the statement shown in bold in the following code.

```
Protected Overrides Sub Finalize()
    MyBase.Finalize()
    Debug.WriteLine("Student object being destroyed.")
End Sub
```

Step 6: Open the application's form in the Design window. Double-click the `btnSave` button to create a code template for its `Click` event procedure. Complete the event procedure by entering the following code, shown in bold.

```
Private Sub btnSave_Click(ByVal sender As System.Object, _
        ByVal e As System.EventArgs) Handles btnSave.Click
    Dim studentRecord As Student

    ' Create the Student class instance.
    studentRecord = New Student()
    ' Get the data from the form.
    GetData(studentRecord)
    ' Display the test grade.
    lblGrade.Text = studentRecord.TestGrade
    ' Save the record.
    SaveRecord(studentRecord)
    ' Confirm that the record was saved.
    MessageBox.Show("Record saved.", "Confirmation")
```

```
    ' Clear the form.
    ClearForm()
End Sub
```

Step 7:   Write the following Sub procedures in the same form.

```
Private Sub GetData(ByVal s As Student)
    ' Get the data from the text boxes and store
    ' in the object referenced by s.
    s.LastName = txtLastName.Text
    s.FirstName = txtFirstName.Text
    s.IdNumber = txtIdNumber.Text
    s.TestAverage = txtTestAverage.Text
End Sub

Private Sub SaveRecord(ByVal s As Student)
    ' Save the properties of the object referenced
    ' by s to the file.
    Dim outputFile As System.IO.StreamWriter

    ' Open the file.
    outputFile = System.IO.File.AppendText("Students.txt")
    ' Save the properties.
    outputFile.WriteLine(s.FirstName)
    outputFile.WriteLine(s.LastName)
    outputFile.WriteLine(s.TestAverage)
    outputFile.WriteLine(s.TestGrade)
    ' Close the file.
    outputFile.Close()
End Sub

Private Sub ClearForm()
    ' Clear the form.
    txtFirstName.Clear()
    txtLastName.Clear()
    txtIdNumber.Clear()
    txtTestAverage.Clear()
    lblGrade.Text = ""
    ' Reset the focus.
    txtLastName.Focus()
End Sub
```

Step 8:   Write the following Click event procedure for the btnExit button.

```
Private Sub btnExit_Click(ByVal sender As System.Object, _
        ByVal e As System.EventArgs) Handles btnExit.Click
    ' End the application.
    End
End Sub
```

Step 9: Save the project and run the application. On the application's form, enter the following data:

Last name: **Green**
First name: **Sara**
ID number: **27R8974**
Test average: **92.3**

Click the Save button to save the student data to a file. A message box appears indicating that the record was saved. Notice that the message "Student object being created" is displayed in the output window. This message was displayed by the `Student` class constructor. Click the OK button on the

Step 10: Click the Exit button. If the message "Student object being destroyed" has not yet been displayed by the class's Finalize `method`, it will be when you click the Exit button.

If You Want to Know More: Using a Class in More Than One Project

It is possible to use a class in more than one project. For example, suppose you are creating several applications that work with student data. Instead of rewriting the `Student` class for each project, you can create the class once, and then add it to the other projects.

Follow these steps to add an existing class to a project.

1. Click Project on the menu bar, and then click Add Existing Item.
2. The Add Existing Item dialog box appears. Use the dialog box to locate the class file that you want to add to the project. When you locate the file, select it and click the Open button. The class is now added to the project.

✓ Checkpoint

12.8 How do you add a class module to a project?

12.9 What two steps must you perform when creating an instance of a class?

12.10 How do you remove an object from memory?

12.11 If an object is created inside a procedure, it is automatically removed from memory when the procedure ends, if no variables declared at the class or module level reference it. What is this called?

12.12 What are member variables?

12.13 What is a property procedure?

12.14 What does the `Get` section of a property procedure do?

12.15 What does the `Set` section of a property procedure do?

12.16 What is a constructor? What is the `Finalize` method?

▶ 12.4   Exceptions and Error Handling

CONCEPT

EXCEPTIONS SIGNAL ERRORS OR UNEXPECTED EVENTS THAT OCCUR WHILE AN APPLICATION IS RUNNING.

You have seen that run-time errors cause a Visual Basic .NET application to display an error message and halt execution. You can prevent many run-time errors by carefully coding your application. For example, dividing a number by zero will cause a run-time error. The following code can be used to prevent a run-time error by preventing a division by zero:

```
' Divide num1 by num2 if num2 is not zero.
If num2 <> 0 Then
    result = num1 / num2
Else
    MessageBox.Show("ERROR: Cannot divide by zero.")
End If
```

Some errors, however, are caused by conditions outside the application and cannot be avoided. For example, suppose an application creates a file on the disk and the user deletes it. Later the application attempts to open the file to read from it, and because it does not exist, a run-time error occurs. As a result, the application halts with an error message.

In Visual Basic .NET, run-time errors are caused by exceptions. An *exception* is an event or condition that happens unexpectedly, and causes the application to halt. To detect that an exception has occurred, and prevent it from halting your application, Visual Basic .NET allows you to create error handlers. An *error handler* is a section of code that gracefully responds to exceptions. The process of intercepting and responding to exceptions is called *error trapping*.

Handling an Exception

To handle an exception, an application can use a `Try...Catch` statement. We will look at several variations of the `Try..Catch` statement, beginning with the following general format.

```
Try
        TryBlock
Catch
        CatchBlock
End Try
```

TryBlock is a section of code known as a `Try` block. A *Try block* is one or more statements that are always executed, and can potentially cause an exception. It is said that the code in the *TryBlock* is protected because the application will not halt if the *TryBlock* causes an exception. *CatchBlock* is a section of code known as a `Catch` block. A *Catch block* is one or more statements that are executed if the `Try` block causes an exception.

For example, the following code handles a division by zero error.

```
Try
    result = num1 / num2
Catch
    MessageBox.Show("An error has occurred.")
End Try
```

This code executes the statement `result = num1 / num2`. If an exception occurs while this statement is executing (such as division by zero), the application does not halt, but executes `Catch` block. In this case an error message is displayed in a message box. The following shows another example. This code attempts to open a file named names.txt. If an exception occurs, an error message is displayed in a message box.

```
Dim inputFile As System.IO.StreamReader
Try
    inputFile = System.IO.File.OpenText("names.txt")
Catch
    MessageBox.Show("An error has occurred.")
End Try
```

A problem with this example is that it responds with the same nondescript error message regardless of the cause of the exception. There are several conditions that can cause an exception when the `System.IO.File.OpenText` method executes. Here are a few.

- The file is not found

- The path does not exist

- The application does not have permission to open the file

- An empty string, or the value `Nothing`, was passed as an argument to the method

You can use an expanded version of the `Try...Catch` statement to determine the cause of the exception. Here is the general format.

```
Try
      TryBlock
Catch ExceptionVar As ExceptionType
      CatchBlock
(More Catch statements may appear.)
End Try
```

The code *ExceptionVar* `As` *ExceptionType* (which appears immediately after the `Catch` key word) is a variable declaration. *ExceptionVar* is the variable name and *Exception Type* is a specific Visual Basic .NET exception type. When a `Catch` statement handles an exception, the *ExceptionVar* variable will reference an object that contains data about the exception.

Each exception that occurs has a specific type. There is a multitude of exception types in Visual Basic .NET. For example, Table 12-2 lists all the types of exceptions that may occur when executing the `System.IO.File.OpenText` method.

Table 12-2

Possible types of exceptions that may result from the `System.IO.File.OpenText` method

Exception Type	Cause
SecurityException	The application does not have the required permission to open the file.
ArgumentException	The argument is a zero-length string, contains only white space, or contains one or more invalid characters.
ArgumentNullException	The value Nothing was passed as the argument.
PathTooLongException	The length of file and path name passed as the argument exceeds the system-defined maximum length.
DirectoryNotFoundException	The directory specified in the file's path does not exist.
FileNotFoundException	The file does not exist.
NotSupportedException	A colon (:) appears in the middle of the string passed as the argument.

TIP: The function and method reference in Appendix B provides information on exceptions. Also, you can see a list of exceptions for any method by looking at the method's help page in the Visual Basic .NET help system. The list of exceptions shown in Table 12-2 can be found on the help page for the `System.IO.File.Open Text` method.

The `System.IO.File.OpeText` method causes an exception of the type `FileNotFoundException` when it attempts to open a file that does not exist. It causes an exception of the type `DirectoryNotFoundException` when the directory specified in the file's path does not exist. Here is an example of a `Try...Catch` statement that handles both of these types of exceptions.

```
Try
    inputFile = System.IO.File.OpenText("globby.txt")
Catch ex As FileNotFoundException
    MessageBox.Show("File not found.")
Catch ex As DirectoryNotFoundException
    MessageBox.Show("Directory not found.")
End Try
```

In this code, the statement in the `Try` block is executed. If an exception occurs, Visual Basic .NET examines the `Catch` statements in the order they appear. If the exception type specified in a `Catch` statement matches the type of exception that has occurred, that `Catch` statement's `Catch` block is executed. This code handles only two types of exceptions: `FileNotFoundException` and `DirectoryNotFoundException`. It displays the message "File not found." when an exception of the type `FileNotFoundException` occurs, or "Directory not found." when an exception of the type `DirectoryNotFoundException` occurs.

What Happens When an Exception is Not Handled?

If an exception occurs that is not handled by a `Catch` statement, Visual Basic .NET will halt the application and display the appropriate error message. For example, the previously shown code handles only two types of exceptions. If an exception other than those handled occurs, such as a `SecurityException`, the application will halt as if there were no error handling.

Extracting an Error Message from the Exception Variable

When an exception occurs, Visual Basic .NET creates an object in memory that holds data regarding the exception. When a `Catch` statement handles an exception, its exception variable will reference that object. Exception objects have a property named Message that holds the system-defined error message for that particular type of exception. Sometimes you might want to use the system-defined error message instead of writing one of your own. The following code shows an example.

```
Try
    inputFile = System.IO.File.OpenText("globby.txt")
Catch ex As FileNotFoundException
    MessageBox.Show(ex.Message)
Catch ex As DirectoryNotFoundException
    MessageBox.Show(ex.Message)
End Try
```

The `Exception` Type

There is one exception type named *Exception* that may be used to handle any type of exception. You can use a `Catch` statement with a variable of this type when you want to intercept all of the exceptions that might occur, and have access to the exception object that holds the system-defined error message.

For example, the following function can be used to open a file for reading. It accepts the file's name (including the path, if desired) as an argument. If an exception of any type occurs, the system-defined error message is displayed and the function returns the value `Nothing`. If the file is successfully opened, the function returns a reference to a `StreamReader` object.

```
Function OpenFileForReading(ByVal filename As String) _
        As System.IO.StreamReader
    Dim fileObject As System.IO.StreamReader
    Try
        fileObject = System.IO.File.OpenText(filename)
    Catch ex As Exception
        MessageBox.Show(ex.Message, "Error")
        fileObject = Nothing
    End Try
    Return fileObject
End Function
```

The following code demonstrates how the function is called.

```
inputFile = OpenFileForReading("customers.txt")
If Not (inputFile Is Nothing) Then
    ' Read data from the file.
End If
```

The `Try...Finally` Statement

There is one more version of the Try statement we should discuss: the `Try...Finally` statement. The general format is:

```
Try
      TryBlock
Catch [ExceptionVar As ExceptionType]
      CatchBlock
(More Catch statements may appear.)
Finally
      FinallyBlock
End Try
```

The `Try` and `Catch` parts of the statement are identical to the versions we have studied so far. In addition, this statement adds a `Finally` statement with an accompanying *FinallyBlock*. *FinallyBlock* is a section of code known as a *Finally block*, which is one or more statements that are always executed after the `Try` block has executed, and after any `Catch` blocks have executed. The statements in the *FinallyBlock* execute whether an exception occurs or not.

For example, the following Sub procedure accepts two string arguments: `filename` and `file Contents`. The procedure uses the `OpenFileForReading` function discussed earlier to open the file specified by `filename`. It then reads the entire file's contents into the `fileContents` variable.

```
Sub ReadEntireFile(ByVal filename As String, _
                   ByRef fileContents As String)
   ' Reads the entire contents of a file
   ' into a string.
   Dim fileObject As System.IO.StreamReader

   fileObject = OpenFileForReading(filename)
   If Not (fileObject Is Nothing) Then
      Try
            fileContents = fileObject.ReadToEnd
      Catch ex As Exception
            MessageBox.Show(ex.Message)
            fileContents = Nothing
      Finally
            fileObject.Close()
      End Try
   End If
End Sub
```

This procedure uses a `Try...Finally` statement to trap any errors that might occur as a result of the `ReadToEnd` method. The `Finally` statement closes the file, regardless of whether an error occurred or not.

✓ Checkpoint

12.17 What is the difference between a `Try` block, a `Catch` block, and a `Finally` block?

12.18 What happens is an exception occurs, but is not handled?

12.19 Once an exception is caught, how do you access the system-defined error message for that exception?

▶ 12.5 Collections

A *collection* is similar to an array. It is a single unit that contains several items. You can access the individual items in a collection with an index, which is similar to an array's subscript. The difference between an array's subscripts and a collection's indices is that a collection's indices begin at one. You might recall that an array's subscripts begin at zero.

Another difference between arrays and collections is that collections automatically expand as items are added to them and shrink as items are removed from them. Also, the items stored in a collection do not have to be of the same type.

Visual Basic .NET provides a class named `Collection`. When you create a collection in an application, you are creating an instance of the `Collection` class. So, creating a collection is identical to creating any other class object. The following statements declare an object variable named `customers`, then assign a new `Collection` instance to it.

```
Dim customers As Collection
customers = New Collection()
```

You can also create a `Collection` instance and assign it to an object variable in one statement:

```
Dim customers As New Collection()
```

Adding Items to a Collection

You add items to a collection with the *Add method*. The general format is:

```
Object.Add(Item [, Key] [, Before] [,After]))
```

Object is the name of an object variable that references a collection. The *Item* argument is the object, variable, or value that is to be added to the collection. *Key* is an optional string expression that is associated with the item and can be used to search for it. (*Key* must be unique for each member of a collection.) Before discussing the optional *Before* and *After* arguments, let's look at an example statement that adds a class object to a collection. Assume that `customers` references a collection and `custData` references an object containing customer data for a customer named Smith. The following statement adds `custData` to the collection, with the key value "Smith".

```
customers.Add(custData, "Smith")
```

Before is an optional argument that can be used when you want to insert an item before an existing member. It can be either a string that identifies the existing member's key or a number specifying the existing member's index. The optional *After* argument works just like the *Before* argument, except that the new item is inserted after the existing member. The following statement is an example of using the *Before* argument.

```
customers.Add(custData, "Smith", "Thomas")
```

This statement adds `custData` to the `customers` collection, with the key value "Smith". The `custData` object is positioned before an object with the key value "Thomas". Now let's look at an example that specifies an *After* argument.

```
customers.Add(custData, "Smith", , "Reece")
```

This statement adds `custData` to the `customers` collection, with the key value "Smith". The `custData` object is positioned after an object with the key value "Reece".

If you do not specify a `Before` or `After` value, the new member will be added to the end of the collection. You cannot use both *Before* and *After*.

Add Method Exceptions

An exception of the `ArgumentException` type will occur when you attempt to add a member with the same `Key` as an existing member, when you specify both a `Before` and an `After` argument, or when the `Before` or `After` argument refers to a nonexistent member. Here is a code example that shows how to handle the exception.

```
Try
    customers.Add(custData, "Smith")
Catch ex as ArgumentException
    MessageBox.Show(ex.Message)
End Try
```

Accessing Items by Their Indices

You may access an item in a collection by its index, using either of the following general formats.

```
Object(Index)
Object.Item(Index)
```

Consider an application with a collection named `names`. The following code gets five names from the user, adding them to the `names` collection.

```
For i = 1 To 5
    name = InputBox("Enter name.")
    names.Add(name)
Next i
```

Both of the following statements display the name at index 3 in a message box.

```
MessageBox.Show(names(3))
MessageBox.Show(names.Item(3))
```

The IndexOutOfRange Exception

An exception of the `IndexOutOfRange` type will occur if you use an index that does not match the index of any item in the collection. Here is a code example that shows how to handle the exception.

```
Try
    custData = customers.Item(5)
```

```
Catch ex as IndexOutOfRangeException
   MessageBox.Show(ex.Message)
End Try
```

The Count property

Each collection has a *Count property* that holds the number of items stored in the collection. Suppose the application also has a list box named `lstNames` and a collection named `names`. The following code uses the Count property as the upper limits of the `ForNext` loop.

```
Dim i As Integer
   For i = 1 To names.Count
      lstNames.Items.Add(names(i))
   Next i
End Sub
```

Storing Class Objects in a Collection

Collections are very useful for storing class objects. For example, consider an application that uses the `Student` class discussed earlier in this chapter. Suppose the application creates a collection named `studentCollection`. with the following statement:

```
Dim studentCollection As New Collection()
```

The following statement can be used to store `studentData`, an instance of the `Student` class, in the `studentCollection` collection:

```
studentCollection.Add(studentData)
```

Adding a Member with a Key Value

When you provide a value for the `Add` method's *Key* argument, the key value is associated with the item. You can then use that key value to search for the item. For example, the following statement adds `studentData`, an instance of the `Student` class, to the `studentCollection` collection and uses the IdNumber property as a key value.

```
studentCollection.Add(studentData, studentData.IdNumber)
```

Because the value stored in the IdNumber property is associated with the class object as a key value, you can use the `Item` method (discussed next) to search for the class object.

WARNING:

 If you attempt to add an item with a key value that an existing member is already using, an exception of the type `ArgumentException` occurs.

Searching for an Item by Key Value with the `Item` Method

You have already seen how the `Item` method can be used to retrieve an item with a specific index. It can also be used to retrieve an item with a specific key value. When used this way, the general format of the method is:

```
Object.Item(Expression)
```

Object is the name of a collection. *Expression* can be either a numeric or a string expression. If *Expression* is a string, the `Item` method returns the member with the key value that matches the string. If no member exists with an index or key value matching *Expression*, an exception of the type `IndexOutOfRangeException` occurs. (If *Expression* is a numeric expression, it is used as an index value and the `Item` method returns the member at the specified index location.)

For example, the following code searches the `studentCollection` collection for an item with the key value "49812".

```
Dim s as Student
s = studentCollection.Item("49812")
```

After this code executes, the `s` variable will reference the object returned from the `Item` method.

The following code uses the `Item` method to retrieve members by index. It retrieves each member from the collection and displays the value of the LastName property in a message box.

```
Dim i As Integer
Dim results As Student

For i = 1 To studentCollection.Count
    results = studentCollection.Item(i)
    MessageBox.Show(results.LastName)
Next i
```

Using References Versus Copies

When an item in a collection is of a fundamental Visual Basic .NET data type, such as Integer or Single, you retrieve only a copy of the member. For example, suppose the following code is used to add strings to a collection named `numbers`:

```
Dim input As Integer
input = InputBox("Enter an integer value.")
numbers.Add(input)
```

Suppose the following code is used to retrieve the integer stored at index 1 and to change its value.

```
Dim n As Integer
n = names(1)
n = 0
```

Because n is only a copy of a value in the collection, the item stored at index 1 is left unchanged.

When an item in a collection is a class object, however, you retrieve a reference to it, not a copy. For example, the following code retrieves the member of the `studentCollection` collection with the key value 49812, and changes the value of its LastName property to "Griffin".

```
Dim s as Student
s = studentCollection.Item("49812")
s.LastName = "Griffin"
```

Because a reference to the member is returned, the LastName property of the object in the collection is modified.

Using the `For Each...Next` Loop with a Collection

You may also use the `For Each...Next` loop to access the individual members of a collection, eliminating the need to compare a counter variable against the collection's Count property. For example, the following code prints the LastName property of each member of the `studentCollection` collection.

```
Dim s As Student
For Each s In studentCollection
    MessageBox.Show(s.LastName)
Next s
```

Removing Members

Use the *Remove method* to remove a member from a collection. The general format is:

```
Object.Remove(Expression)
```

Object is the name of a collection. *Expression* can be either a numeric or string expression. If it is a numeric expression, it is used as an index value and the member at the specified index location is removed. If *Expression* is a string, the member with the key value that matches the string is removed. If an index is provided, and it does not match an index of any item in the collection, an exception of the `IndexOutOfRangeException` type occurs. If a key value is provided, and it does not match the key value of any item in the collection, an exception of the `ArgumentException` type occurs.

For example, the following statement removes the member with the key value "49812" from the `studentCollection` collection:

```
studentCollection.Remove("49812")
```

The following statement removes the member at index location 7 from the `studentCollection` collection:

```
studentCollection.Remove(7)
```

Here are two code examples that show how to handle the exceptions that the `Remove` method might cause.

```
Try
    studentCollection.Remove(5)
Catch ex as IndexOutOfRangeException
    MessageBox.Show(ex.Message)
End Try

Try
    studentCollection.Remove("46812")
Catch ex as ArgumentException
    MessageBox.Show(ex.Message)
End Try
```

Writing Sub Procedures and Functions that Work with Collections

You can easily write Sub procedures and functions that accept collections as arguments, and functions that return collections. Remember that a collection is an instance of a class, so follow the same guidelines for passing any class object as an argument, or returning a class object from a function.

Relating the Items in Multiple Collections

Sometimes it is useful to store related data in two or more collections. For example, assume a company assigns a unique employee number to each employee. An application that calculates gross pay has the following collections.

```
Dim hoursWorked As New Collection()   ' To hold hours worked
Dim payRates As New Collection()      ' To hold hourly pay rates
```

The hoursWorked collection is used to store the number of hours each employee has worked, and the payRates collection is used to store each employee's hourly pay rate.

When an item is stored in the hoursWorked or payRates collections, it is stored with the employee's number as the key. For instance, let's say James Bourne's ID number is 55678. He has worked 40 hours and his pay rate is $12.50. The following statements add his data to the appropriate collections.

```
hoursWorked.Add(40, "55678")
payRates.Add(12.5, "55678")
```

To calculate his gross pay, we need to retrieve his data from each collection, using his ID number as the key:

```
grossPay = hoursWorked.Item("55678") * payRate.Item("55678")
```

The following code expands on this idea. In addition to the hoursWorked and payRates collection, this code uses a collection to hold the employee names, and a collection to hold the employee ID numbers.

```
Dim empNumbers As New Collection()    ' To hold employee numbers
Dim employees As New Collection()     ' To hold employee names
Dim hoursWorked As New Collection()   ' To hold hours worked
Dim payRates As New Collection()      ' To hold hourly pay rates
Dim empNum As String                  ' To retrieve an emp number
Dim empName As String                 ' To retrieve an emp name
Dim grossPay, hours, rate As Decimal  ' Used in pay calculations
Dim i As Integer                      ' Loop counter

' Add each employee's number to the
' empNumbers collection.
empNumbers.Add("55678")
empNumbers.Add("78944")
empNumbers.Add("84417")

' Add the employee names to the employees
' collection, with the employee ID number
' as the key.
employees.Add("James Bourne", "55678")
```

```
employees.Add("Jill Davis", "78944")
employees.Add("Kevin Franklin", "84417")

' Add each employee's hours worked to the
' hoursWorked collection, with the employee
' ID number as the key.
hoursWorked.Add(40, "55678")
hoursWorked.Add(35, "78944")
hoursWorked.Add(20, "84417")

' Add each employee's hours pay rate to the
' payRates collection, with the employee
' ID number as the key.
payRates.Add(12.5, "55678")
payRates.Add(18.75, "78944")
payRates.Add(9.6, "84417")

' Compute and display each employee's
' gross pay.
For i = 1 To employees.Count
    ' Get an employee number to use as a key.
    empNum = empNumbers(i)
    ' Get this employee's name
    empName = employees.Item(empNum)
    ' Get the hours worked for this employee.
    hours = hoursWorked.Item(empNum)
    ' Get the pay rate for this employee.
    rate = payRates.Item(empNum)
    ' Calculate this employee's gross pay.
    grossPay = hours * rate
    MessageBox.Show("Gross pay for " & empName & _
            " is " & FormatCurrency(grossPay))
Next
```

✓ Checkpoint

12.20   How do collections differ from arrays?

12.21   How do you add members to a collection?

12.22   How is a key value useful when you are adding an item to a collection?

12.23   How do you search for a specific member of a collection?

12.24   How do you remove a member from a collection?

▶ 12.6   Focus on Problem Solving: Creating the Student Collection Application

Campus Systems, Inc. is developing software for a university and has hired you as a programmer. Your first assignment is to develop an application that allows the user to select a student's ID number from a list box to view the data about the student. The user should also be able to add new student records and delete student records. The application will use the `Student` class and a collection of `Student` class objects. A test application with two forms has already been created for you.

TUTORIAL 12-2:

Examining the existing forms

Step 1:   Start Visual Basic .NET and open the Student Collection project, which is located on the student disk in the \Chap12\Student Collection folder.

The project already has the two forms, shown in Figures 12-6 and 12-7. The `frmMain` form has a list box, `lstIdNumbers`, that will display a list of student ID numbers. When a student's ID number is selected from the list box, the data for that student will be displayed in the following Label controls: `lblLastName`, `lblFirstName`, `lblIdNumber`, `lblTestAverage`, and `lblGrade`. The Add Student button causes the `frmAdd` form to be displayed. The Remove button removes the student whose ID number is currently selected.

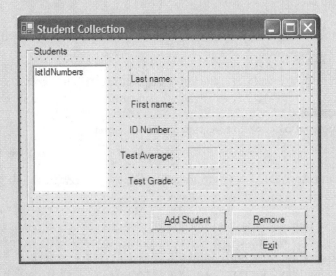

Figure 12-6 `frmMain` form

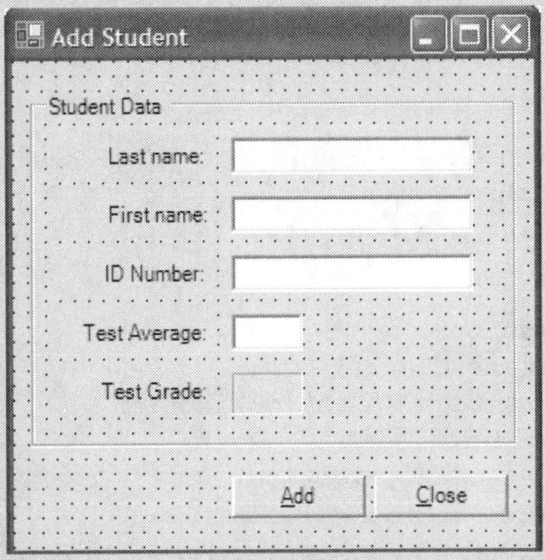

Figure 12-7 `frmAdd` form

Step 2:   Add the `Student` class that you created in Tutorial 12-1 to the project. (Click Project on the menu bar, then click Add Existing Item. Browse to the folder containing the Student.vb file. Select the Student.vb file and click Open.)

Step 3:   Add a standard module to the project. Name the module `StudentCollectionModule`. Complete the module by entering the following code shown in bold.

```
Module StudentCollectionModule
    Public studentCollection As Collection
End Module
```

This statement declares `studentCollection` as an object variable that will reference a collection. Because it is declared as `Public`, it will be available to all the forms in the project.

Step 4:   Now you will write the code for the `frmMain` form. Add the following `Load` event procedure to the form.

```
Private Sub frmMain_Load(ByVal sender As System.Object, _
            ByVal e As System.EventArgs) Handles MyBase.Load
    ' Create the collection.
    studentCollection = New Collection()
End Sub
```

Step 5:   Add the `btnAdd_Click` event procedure, `UpdateListBox` Sub procedure, and `ClearForm` Sub procedure as follows.

```
Private Sub btnAdd_Click(ByVal sender As System.Object, _
            ByVal e As System.EventArgs) Handles btnAdd.Click
    ' Display the Add Student form.
    Dim addStudentForm As New frmAdd()

    ' Display the form.
    addStudentForm.ShowDialog()
    ' Update the contents of the list box.
    UpdateListBox()
End Sub

Private Sub UpdateListBox()
    ' Update the list box contents.
    Dim s As Student

    ' Clear the list box.
    lstIdNumbers.Items.Clear()
    ' Load the ID numbers in the collection
    ' into the list box.
    For Each s In studentCollection
        lstIdNumbers.Items.Add(s.IdNumber)
    Next
    ' Select the first item in the list.
    If lstIdNumbers.Items.Count > 0 Then
```

```
            lstIdNumbers.SelectedIndex = 0
        Else
            ClearForm()
        End If
    End Sub

    Private Sub ClearForm()
        ' Clear the form.
        lblFirstName.Text = ""
        lblLastName.Text = ""
        lblIdNumber.Text = ""
        lblTestAverage.Text = ""
        lblGrade.Text = ""
    End Sub
```

The btnAdd_Click event procedure displays the frmAdd form, which allows the user to add a new student object to the collection. After the frmAdd form is closed, the UpdateListBox procedure is called. This procedure calls the ClearForm procedure to clear any data currently displayed. It then adds all of the student ID numbers in the studentCollection collection to the lstIdNumbers list box.

Step 6: Add the btnRemove_Click event procedure, as follows.

```
    Private Sub btnRemove_Click(ByVal sender As System.Object, _
            ByVal e As System.EventArgs) Handles btnRemove.Click
        ' Remove the selected student from the collection.
        Dim index As Integer

        If lstIdNumbers.SelectedItem <> "" Then
            If MessageBox.Show("Are you sure?", "Confirm Deletion", _
                MessageBoxButtons.YesNo) = DialogResult.Yes Then

                ' Retrieve the student's data from the collection.
                index = lstIdNumbers.SelectedIndex
                Try
                    studentCollection.Remove(lstIdNumbers.
                    SelectedItem)
                    lstIdNumbers.Items.Remove(index)
                    UpdateListBox()
                Catch ex As Exception
                    MessageBox.Show(ex.Message)
                End Try
            End If
        End If
    End Sub
```

Step 7: Now you will write the lstNumbers_SelectedIndexChanged event procedure. This event procedure will execute any time the selected item in the list box changes. To create a code template for the procedure, open the form in the Design window and then double-click the lstIdNumbers list box. The code follows.

```
Private Sub lstIdNumbers_SelectedIndexChanged(ByVal sender As _
        System.Object, ByVal e As System.EventArgs) _
        Handles lstIdNumbers.SelectedIndexChanged
    ' Update the selected student data.
    Dim studentData As Student

    If lstIdNumbers.SelectedItem <> "" Then
        ' Retrieve the student's data from the collection.
        Try
            studentData = _
                studentCollection.Item(lstIdNumbers.SelectedItem)
        Catch ex As Exception
            MessageBox.Show(ex.Message)
            studentData = Nothing
        End Try
        ' Display the student data.
        If Not (studentData Is Nothing) Then
            DisplayData(studentData)
        End If
    End If
End Sub
```

This event procedure displays, in the Label controls, the data for the student whose ID number is selected in the list box.

Step 8:   Write the DisplayData Sub procedure, as follows.

```
Private Sub DisplayData(ByVal s As Student)
    ' Get the data from the text boxes and store
    ' in the object referenced by s.
    lblLastName.Text = s.LastName
    lblFirstName.Text = s.FirstName
    lblIdNumber.Text = s.IdNumber
    lblTestAverage.Text = s.TestAverage
    lblGrade.Text = s.TestGrade
End Sub
```

This procedure copies the data from a Student class object to the Label controls.

Step 9:   Write the btnExit_Click event procedure, as follows

```
Private Sub btnExit_Click(ByVal sender As System.Object, _
        ByVal e As System.EventArgs) Handles btnExit.Click
    ' End the application.
    End
End Sub
```

Step 10:   Now you will write the code for the frmAdd form. Add the btnAdd_Click event procedure, the GetData Sub procedure, the AddRecord Sub procedure, and the ClearForm Sub procedure, as follows.

```
Private Sub btnAdd_Click(ByVal sender As System.Object, _
        ByVal e As System.EventArgs) Handles btnAdd.Click
    Dim studentRecord As Student

    ' Create the Student class instance.
    studentRecord = New Student()
    ' Get the data from the form.
    GetData(studentRecord)
    ' Display the test grade.
    lblGrade.Text = studentRecord.TestGrade
    ' Save the record.
    AddRecord(studentRecord)
    ' Confirm that the record was saved.
    MessageBox.Show("Record added.", "Confirmation")
    ' Clear the form.
    ClearForm()
End Sub

Private Sub GetData(ByVal s As Student)
    ' Get the data from the text boxes and store
    ' in the object referenced by s.
    s.LastName = txtLastName.Text
    s.FirstName = txtFirstName.Text
    s.IdNumber = txtIdNumber.Text
    s.TestAverage = txtTestAverage.Text
End Sub

Private Sub AddRecord(ByVal s As Student)
    ' Add the object referenced by s to the collection.
    ' Use the student ID number as the key.
    Try
        studentCollection.Add(s, s.IdNumber)
    Catch ex As Exception
        MessageBox.Show(ex.Message)
    End Try
End Sub

Private Sub ClearForm()
    ' Clear the form.
    txtFirstName.Clear()
    txtLastName.Clear()
    txtIdNumber.Clear()
    txtTestAverage.Clear()
    lblGrade.Text = ""
    ' Reset the focus.
    txtLastName.Focus()
End Sub
```

Step 11: Add the `btnClose_Click` event procedure, as follows.

```
Private Sub btnClose_Click(ByVal sender As System.Object, _
        ByVal e As System.EventArgs) Handles btnClose.Click
```

```
        ' Close the form.
        Me.Close()
    End Sub
```

Step 12: Save the project and run the application. Click the Add Student button, and add the following students:

Student 1
Last name: **Green**
First name: **Sara**
ID number: **27R8974**
Test average: **92.3**

Student 2
Last name: **Robinson**
First name: **Joy**
ID number: **89G4561**
Test average: **97.3**

Student 3
Last name: **Williams**
First name: **Jon**
ID number: **71A4478**
Test average: **78.6**

Step 13: Close the frmAdd form. The main form should now appear as shown in Figure 12-8.

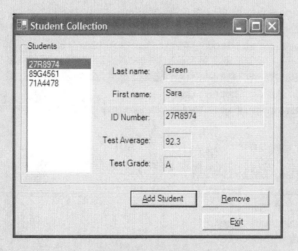

Figure 12-8 Main form with students added

Step 14: Select a student's ID number in the list box. That student's data is displayed in the Label controls.

Step 15: Remove each student one-at-a-time by selecting an ID number and then clicking the Remove button. Click Yes when asked "Are you sure?"

Step 16: Exit the application. Leave the Student Collection project loaded for the next tutorial.

▶ 12.7   The Object Browser

THE OBJECT BROWSER IS A DIALOG BOX THAT ALLOWS YOU TO BROWSE THE MANY CLASSES AND COMPONENTS THAT ARE
AVAILABLE TO YOUR PROJECT.

The *Object Browser* is a dialog box that displays information about objects. You can use the Object
Browser to examine classes that you have created, as well as the namespaces, classes, and other components that Visual Basic .NET makes available to your project. Tutorial 12-3 guides you through the process of using the Object Browser to examine the classes you created in the student collection project.

TUTORIAL 12-3:

Using the Object Browser

Step 1:   Start Visual Basic .NET and open the student collection project you created in Tutorial 12-2.

Step 2:   Open the Object Browser by performing one of the following actions.

   ◆   Click View on the menu bar, then click Other Windows, then click Object
       Browser.

   ◆   Press the F2 key on the keyboard.

   The Object Browser window, shown in Figure 12-9 appears. The left pane is the
   objects pane, and the right pane is the members pane. You select an object in the
   objects pane and information about that object appears in the members pane.

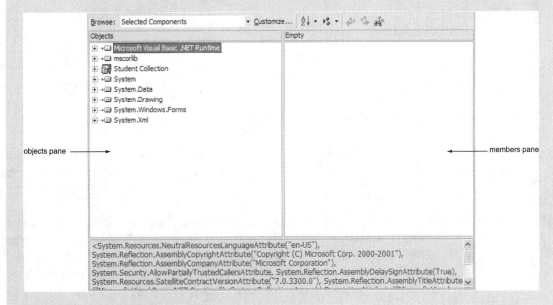

Figure 12-9   The Object Browser window

Step 3:   Notice that a Student Collection entry appears in the objects pane. Click the small plus sign that appears to the left of this entry to expand it. The entry {} Student_Collection appears. The braces ({}) indicate that Student_Collection is a namespace. Visual Basic .NET has created a namespace for this project and named it Student_Collection. The contents of the project are stored in this namespace. Click the small plus sign that appears to the left of this entry to expand it. Now entries appear for `frmAdd`, `frmMain`, `Student`, and `StudentCollectionModule`.

Step 4:   Click the entry for `Student`. All of the members of the `Student` class should now be listed in the members pane, as shown in Figure 12-10. If you click an entry in the members pane, a brief summary of the member is displayed below the pane. If you double-click an entry, the Code window appears with the cursor positioned at the selected item's declaration statement.

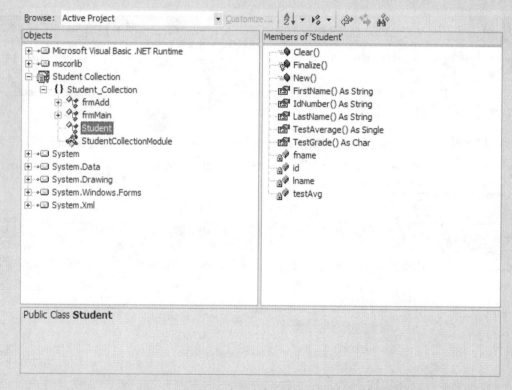

Figure 12-10   Members of the `Student` class displayed in the members pane

Step 5:   Click some of the other entries under {} Student_Collection in the object window, such as `frmMain` and `StudentCollectionModule`, to view their members in the members window.

Step 6:   Because the standard Visual Basic .NET controls are classes, the Object Browser can be used to examine them as well. Sometimes this is useful in determining what methods and properties a control has. For example, let's look at the TextBox class. Click the find ( ) button. The Find Symbol dialog box, shown in Figure 12-11 should appear. Type **TextBox** in the Find what box and click the Find button. The results of the search will appear at the bottom of the screen in a Find Symbol Results window. Close the Find Symbol dialog box and double-click the entry for TextBox (System.Windows.Forms) that appears in the Find Symbol Results window. The TextBox class should appear selected in the objects pane and the members of the TextBox class should appear in the members pane.

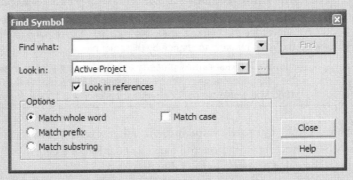

Figure 12-11   The Find Symbol dialog box

Step 7:   Close the Object Browser.

▶ 12.8   Focus on GUI Design: Scroll Bars and Track Bars

CONCEPT

THE HSCROLLBAR, VSCROLLBAR, AND TRACKBAR CONTROLS PROVIDE A GRAPHICAL WAY TO ADJUST A NUMBER WITHIN A RANGE OF VALUES.

The HScrollBar, VScrollBar, and TrackBar controls allow the user to adjust a value within a range of values. The *HScrollBar control* is used to create a horizontal scroll bar, the *VScrollBar control* is used to create a vertical scroll bar, and the *TrackBar control* is used to create a track bar. Examples of these controls are shown in Figure 12-12. We will refer to these controls as scrollable controls.

Table 12-3 lists the important properties of the scrollable controls.

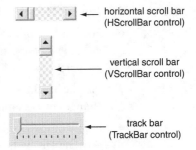

Figure 12-12   Horizontal and vertical scroll bars and a track bar

Table 12-3

Scrollable control properties

Property	Description
Minimum	The scroll bar or track bar's minimum value.
Maximum	The scroll bar or track bar's maximum value.
Value	The scroll bar or track bar's current value.

Table 12-3 *continued*

Scrollable control properties

Property	Description
LargeChange	The amount by which the Value property changes when the user clicks the scroll bar or track bar area around the slider. Track bars also respond to the Page Up and Page Down keys, which cause the Value property to change by this amount.
SmallChange	The amount by which the Value property changes when the user clicks one of the scroll arrows at either end of a scroll bar. Track bars also respond to the arrow keys, which cause the Value property to change by this amount.
TickFrequency	This is a TrackBar control property only. This property holds the number of units between the tick marks on the control. For example, if Minimum is set to 0 and Maximum is set to 1000, you would set the TickFrequency property to 100 to draw ten tick marks.

Scrollable controls hold a numeric value in their Value property. The user increases or decreases the Value property by interacting with the scroll bar. The position of a control's slider corresponds with the number stored in its Value property in the following ways.

- When a horizontal scroll bar or a track bar's slider is moved toward the left, the number in the Value property decreases, toward the value stored in the Minimum property.

- When a horizontal scroll bar or a track bar's slider is moved toward the right, the number in the Value property increases, toward the value stored in the Maximum property.

- When a vertical scroll bar's slider is moved up, the number in the Value property decreases, toward the value stored in the Minimum property.

- When a vertical scroll bar's slider is moved down, the number in the Value property increases, toward the value stored in the Maximum property.

The number stored in the Minimum property is the Value property's minimum value, and the number stored in the Maximum property is its maximum value.

The user changes the contents of the Value property by moving the scrollable control's slider. The user may do this by clicking the scroll arrows that appear at either end of a scroll bar, by clicking the area around the slider, or by dragging the slider. TrackBar controls also respond to the Page Up, Page Down, and arrow keys on the keyboard. The following list summarizes the affect of these actions.

- For the HScrollBar and VScrollBar controls, when the user clicks one of the scroll arrows at either end of a scroll bar, the Value property changes by the amount stored in the SmallChange property.

- For the TrackBar control, when the user presses any of the arrow keys, the Value property changes by the amount stored in the SmallChange property.

- For all of the scrollable controls, when the user clicks the area around the slider, the Value property changes by the amount stored in the LargeChange property.

- For the TrackBar control, when the user presses the Page Up or Page Down key, the Value property changes by the amount stored in the LargeChange property.

NOTE: *The Value property cannot reach the number stored in the Maximum property by way of the slider being moved. The largest value that can be reached by moving the slider is Maximum - LargeChange + 1. However, you can store the Maximum value in the Value property with an assignment statement.*

The scrollable controls trigger a `Scroll` event when the user moves the slider with any of these actions. To perform an operation each time a scrollable control's slider changes position, you write a `Scroll` event procedure.

We will use `hsb` as the prefix for a HScrollBar control name, `vsb` as the prefix for a VScrollBar control name, and `tb` as the prefix for a TrackBar control name. In Tutorial 12-4 you examine an application that uses each of these scrollable controls.

TUTORIAL 12-4:

Working with scrollable controls

Step 1:   Start Visual Basic .NET and load the Scrollable Control Demo project, which is located in the\Chap12\Scrollable Control Demo folder on the student disk. The application's form is shown in Figure 12-15. This application converts centigrade temperatures to Fahrenheit and meters to feet, and moves a graphic image across the form. The user changes the centigrade temperature with a VScrollBar control named `vsbCent`, changes the distance in meters with an HScrollBar control named `hsb Meters`, and moves the graphic of the sailboat with a TrackBar control named `tbBoat`.

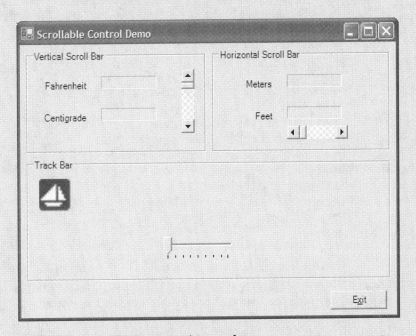

Figure 12-13   Scrollable Control Demo form

Table 12-4 shows initial property settings for the scroll bar controls.

Table 12-4

Property settings for `vsbCent` and `hsbMeters`

Property	`vsbCent` setting	`hsbMeters` setting
Min	-100	0
Max	100	100
LargeChange	20	20
SmallChange	1	1

Step 2: Run the application and experiment with the scroll bars. The application changes the centigrade temperature and converts it to Fahrenheit when you interact with the vertical scroll bar. It changes the meters value and converts it to feet when you interact with the horizontal scroll bar. It also moves the graphic images of the sailboat when you interact with the track bar.

Step 3: End the application. Open the Code window and locate the `vsbCent_Scroll` event procedure. The code is as follows.

```
Private Sub vsbCent_Scroll(ByVal sender As System.Object, _
        ByVal e As System.Windows.Forms.ScrollEventArgs) _
        Handles vsbCent.Scroll
    ' Update the temperatures.
    Dim fahr As Single ' To calculate Fahrenheit temp.
    Dim cent As Single ' To hold centigrade temp.

    ' Get the negative of vsbCent.Value because
    ' the maximum value is at the bottom of the
    ' scroll bar and the minumum is at the top.
    cent = -(vsbCent.Value)
    ' Calculate fahrenheit temperature.
    fahr = (9.0 / 5.0) * cent + 32
    ' Display the values.
    lblCent.Text = cent.ToString
    lblFahr.Text = fahr.ToString
End Sub
```

This procedure treats the number stored in the scroll bar's Value property as a centigrade temperature. It gets the number stored there, converts it to Fahrenheit, and displays both the centigrade and Fahrenheit temperatures in the Label controls. Note that the negative of the number stored in the Value property is assigned to the `cent` variable. This is because the VScrollBar control is at its minimum value when the slider is at the top, and is at its maximum value when the slider is at the bottom. This logic seems counterintuitive to this application, so we reverse it by getting the negative of the Value property.

Step 4: Now look at the `hsbMeters_Scroll` event procedure. The code follows.

```
Private Sub hsbMeters_Scroll(ByVal sender As System.Object, _
        ByVal e As System.Windows.Forms.ScrollEventArgs) _
        Handles hsbMeters.Scroll
```

```
        ' Update the distances.
        ' 1 meter = 3.281 feet.
        lblMeters.Text = hsbMeters.Value.ToString
        lblFeet.Text = (hsbMeters.Value * 3.281).ToString
    End Sub
```

This procedure treats the number stored in the scroll bar's Value property as a distance measured in meters. The value is copied to the lblMeters control, then converted to feet. The distance in feet is copied to the lblFeet control.

Step 5:   Now look at the tbBoat_Scroll event procedure. The code follows.

```
    Private Sub tbBoat_Scroll(ByVal sender As System.Object, _
             ByVal e As System.EventArgs) Handles tbBoat.Scroll
        ' Move the boat by storing tbBoat's Value
        ' property in picBoat's Left property.
        picBoat.Left = tbBoat.Value
    End Sub
```

This procedure stores the number in the track bar's Value property in the picture box's Left property. As the track bar's Value property changes, so does the position of the sail boat image.

✓ Checkpoint

12.25   How do you establish the range of values that may be stored in a scrollable control's Value property?

12.26   What is the difference between the SmallChange and LargeChange properties?

12.27   When does a scrollable control's Scroll event occur?

Summary

Object-oriented programming is a way of designing and coding applications that allows interchangeable software components to be used to build larger programs.

An abstract data type (ADT) is a data type created by a programmer.

A class is a program structure that defines an abstract data type.

An object is an instance of a class.

The primary goal of object-oriented design is to address the needs of the application or problem being solved. A secondary goal is to design classes that can outlive the current application and possibly be useful in future programs.

The class interface is the portion that is visible to the application programmer who uses the class. The program written by such a person is also called the client program, in reference to the client-server relationship between a class and the programs that use it.

The class implementation is the portion of a class that is hidden from client programs; it is created from private member variables, private properties, and private methods.

There are two steps that must occur when an instance of a class is created. You declare an object variable, and then you create an instance of the class in memory and assign its address to the object variable. Each instance of a class has its own unique copy of the class's member variables.

You access the members, properties, and methods of a class object with the dot (.) operator.

Properties are generally implemented as property procedures. A property procedure is a function that behaves like a property. Property procedures have two sections: Get and Set. The Get section is executed anytime the value of the property is retrieved. The Set section is executed any time a value is stored in the property.

A read-only property cannot be set by a client program. It is implemented as a property procedure declared with the ReadOnly key word, and does not have a Set section.

To remove an object, set all the object variables that reference it to Nothing and it will be removed from memory by the Visual Basic .NET garbage collector. The garbage collector is a process that destroys objects when they are no longer needed.

An object variable that is declared inside a procedure is local to that procedure. If an object is referenced only by a procedure's local object variable, the object is automatically removed from memory by the garbage collector after the procedure ends.

Use the Is operator to compare two object variables, to determine if they reference the same object.

You can create arrays of objects, and you can write Sub procedures and functions that work with objects.

A class method is a Sub procedure or function that is a member of the class. The method performs some operation on the data stored in the class. You write methods inside the class declaration.

A constructor is a class method that is automatically called when an instance of the class is created. It is helpful to think of constructors as initialization routines. They are useful for initializing member variables or performing other startup operations. To create a constructor, simply create a Sub procedure named New in the class.

A finalizer is a class method named Finalize, which is automatically called just before an instance of the class is destroyed.

The Output window normally appears at the bottom of the Visual Basic .NET environment while an application is running. This window displays various messages while an application is being compiled. You can display your own messages in the Output window with the Debug.WriteLine method.

You can use the Add Existing Item dialog box top add an existing class to project.

An exception is an event or condition that happens unexpectedly, and causes the application to halt. An error handler is a section of code that gracefully responds to exceptions. The process of intercepting and responding to exceptions is called error trapping. To handle an exception, an application can use a Try...Catch or a Try...Finally statement.

A Try block is one or more statements in a Try that are always executed, and can potentially cause an exception. A Catch block is one or more statements that are executed if the Try block causes an exception. A Finally block is one or more statements that are always executed after the Try block has executed, and after any Catch blocks have executed.

A collection is a structure that holds a group of items. It automatically expands and shrinks to accommodate the items added to it, and allows items to be stored with an associated key value, which may be searched for.

The Count property holds the number of items that are stored in a collection. The Add method is used to store an item in a collection. The Item method is used to search for an item in a collection. The Remove method is used to remove an item from a collection.

The Object Browser is used to display information about the classes, properties, methods, and events available to a project.

The HScrollBar, VScrollBar, and TrackBar controls provide a graphical way to adjust a number within a range of values.

KEY TERMS

Abstract data type (ADT)	HScrollBar (horizontal scroll bar) control
Abstraction	Is operator
Add method	Item method
Attributes	LargeChange property
Catch block	Maximum property
Class	Member variable
Class declaration	Minimum property
Class implementation	Object
Class interface	Object Browser
Class method	Object-oriented analysis
Class object	Object-oriented programming (OOP)
Client program	Operations
Collection	Output window
Constructor	Property procedure
Count property	Read-only property
Encapsulation	Remove method
Error trapping	Set section
Error-handler	SmallChange property
Exception	TickFrequency property
Exception type	TrackBar control
Finalizer	Try block
Finally block	Try...Catch and
Finding the classes	Try...Finally statements
Garbage collector	Value property
Get section	VScrollBar (vertical scroll bar) control
Going out of scope	

Review Questions

Fill-in-the-blank

1. A(n) _____ is a data type created by a programmer.

2. A(n) _____ is a program structure that defines an abstract data type.

3. An object is a(n) _____ of a class.

4. The _____ is the portion of a class that is visible to the application programmer who uses the class.

5. The _____ is the portion of a class that is hidden from client programs.

6. A(n) _____ procedure is a function that behaves like a class property.

7. The _____ section is executed when a client program retrieves the value of a property.

8. The _____ section executes when a client program stores a value in a property.

9. A(n) _____ property cannot be set by a client program.

10. A(n) _____ is a Sub procedure or function that is a member of the class.

11. A(n) _____ is a class method that is automatically called when an instance of the class is created.

12. A(n) _____ is a class method that is automatically called just before an instance of the class is destroyed.

13. You can display messages for debugging purposes in the _____ window.

14. A(n) _____ is an event or condition that happens unexpectedly, and causes the application to halt.

15. A(n) _____ is a structure that holds a group of items.

16. The _____ is a dialog box that displays information about the classes, properties, methods, and events available to a project.

Multiple Choice

1. This is a program structure that defines an abstract data type.

    a. Variable

    b. Exception

    c. Class

    d. Class object

2. The variable `status` is declared inside a class. `status` is a
    a. Global variable

    b. Constructor

    c. Finalizer

    d. Member variable

3. An object is automatically released when all references to it are set to
    a. `Nothing`

    b. `Empty`

    c. `Clear`

    d. `Done`

4. This section of a property procedure returns the value of the property.
    a. `Value`

    b. `Property`

    c. `Get`

    d. `Set`

5. This section of a property procedure stores a value of the property.
   a. `Value`
   b. `Property`
   c. `Get`
   d. `Let`

6. A class constructor is a Sub procedure by this name.
   a. `New`
   b. `Constructor`
   c. `Finalizer`
   d. `Main`

7. A class finalizer is a Sub procedure by this name.
   a. `New`
   b. `Finalizer`
   c. `Finalize`
   d. `Main`

8. This section is missing from a read-only property procedure.
   a. `Get`
   b. `Set`
   c. `Store`
   d. `Save`

9. This process runs periodically to free the memory used by all unreferenced objects.
   a. Garbage collector
   b. Memory collector
   c. Housekeeper
   d. RAM dumper

10. You must use this operator to determine whether two object variables reference the same object.
    a. `=`
    b. `<>`
    c. `Is`
    d. `Equal`

11. In a `Try...Catch` or `Try...Finally` statement, this is one or more statements that are always executed, and can potentially cause an exception.
    a. `Try` block
    b. `Catch` block
    c. Exception block
    d. `Finally` block

12. In a `Try...Catch` or `Try...Finally` statement, this is one or more statements that are executed in response to an exception.
    a. `Try` block
    b. `Catch` block
    c. Exception block
    d. `Finally` block

13. In a `Try...Catch` or `Try...Finally` statement, this is one or more statements that are always executed, and are executed last, after any potential exceptions have been handled.
    a. `Try` block
    b. `Catch` block
    c. Exception block
    d. `Finally` block

14. Which method is used to store an item in a collection?
    a. `Store`
    b. `Insert`
    c. `Add`
    d. `Collect`

15. Which method to search for an item in a collection?
    a. `Find`
    b. `Item`
    c. `Search`
    d. `Member`

16. Which method removes an item from a collection?
    a. `Remove`
    b. `Item`
    c. `Delete`
    d. `Erase`

17. This property holds the number of items stored in a collection.
    a. `Items`
    b. `Number`
    c. `Count`
    d. `Members`

18. Which of the following displays information about the classes, properties, methods, and events available to a project?
    a. Object Browser
    b. Object Navigator
    c. Class Browser
    d. Class Resoruce List

19. Which property sets the amount by which the Value property changes when the user clicks the scroll bar area around a slider?
    a. LargeChange
    b. SmallChange
    c. UnitChange
    d. ValueChange

20. Which property sets the amount by which the Value property changes when the user clicks one of the scroll arrows at either end of the scroll bar?
    a. LargeChange
    b. SmallChange
    c. UnitChange
    d. ValueChange

21. Which event occurs when a scrollable control's slider changes to a new position?
    a. `Scroll`
    b. `Update`
    c. `Increment`
    d. `Change`

True or False

Indicate whether each of the following statements is true or false.

1. T F: Public properties are part of the class interface.

2. T F: Private member variables are part of the class interface.

3. T F: A class's `New` procedure must be called from a client program.

4. T F: A class method may be either a procedure or a function.

5. T F: A run-time error will occur when you attempt to add a member with the same key as an existing member.

6. T F: You can use both the *Before* and *After* arguments of the `Add` method at the same time.

7. T F: When retrieving an item from a collection, and the item is of the integer data type, you retrieve only a copy of the member.

8. T F: By default a vertical scroll bar is at its minimum value when the slider is at the bottom and is at its maximum value when the slider is at the top.

9. T F: The Object Browser does not display information about the standard Visual Basic .NET controls.

10. T F: If you attempt to retrieve an item from a collection and specify a non-existent index, a run-time error is generated.

Short Answer

1. How is a class interface created in Visual Basic .NET?

2. What is encapsulation?

3. In the statement `Dim newStudent As Student`, which is the class and which is the object variable?

4. How do you create a read-only property?

5. How is an object different from a class?

6. Do the icons in the Visual Basic .NET tool box represent classes, or objects?

7. How are properties different from methods?

8. What is the difference between retrieving a collection item that is of a fundamental Visual Basic .NET data type and retrieving one that is a class object?

9. What is encapsulation?

10. What happens to an object that is created inside a procedure when the procedure finishes?

What Do You Think?

1. While developing an application you create a class named `BankAccount` and you declare an object variable of the `BankAccount` type named `checking`. Which is the abstract data type, `BankAccount` or `checking`?

2. Look at the following problem description and identify the potential classes.

   We need to keep a list of customers and record our business transactions with them. Each time a customer purchases a product, an order is filled out. Each order shows a list of items that are kept in our central warehouse.

3. Does each button on the same form manipulate its own copy of the Visible property?

4. In a student record-keeping program, what attributes might be assigned to a college transcript class?

5. Why are member variables usually declared private in classes?

6. At the end of the following example, how many Student objects exist?

```
Dim st1 As New Student()
Dim st2 As Student
st2 = st1
```

7. At the end of the following example, how many Student objects exist?

```
Dim st1 As New Student
Dim st2 As Student
st2 = st1
st1 = Nothing
```

Find the Errors

For each of the following questions assume Customer is a class. Find the errors.

1. `Dim Customer as New customerData()`

2. `Dim customerData as Customer`
   `customerData.LastName = "Smith"`

3. `customerData = Nothing`
   `customerData.LastName = "Smith"`

4.
```
Public Property LastName() As String
   Set
        Return lname
   End Get
   Get(ByVal value As String)
        lname = value
   End Set
End Property
```

5. `Dim customerCollection as Collection`
   `customerCollection.Add customerData`

Algorithm Workbench

1. An application declares an array of objects with the statement
   `Dim employees(9) As Employee`
   Write a loop that creates 10 instances of the class and assigns them to the elements of the array.

2. Code a Dim statement that declares an object variable of the class type Transcript. The statement should not create an instance of the class.

3. Code a statement that creates a Transcript class object and assigns it to the variable from the previous question.

4. Code a statement that releases the memory used by the object variable used in the previous two questions.

5. Code a single statement that both declares an object variable and creates a new instance of the `Transcript` class.

6. Write the property procedures for a property named CustomerNumber that assigns a string value to a member variable named `custNum`.

7. `nameCollection` references a collection. Write a Try...Catch statement that stores your last name in the collection, with the number 475 as the key. The statement should respond to any exception that might occur.

PROGRAMMING CHALLENGES

1. E-Mail Address Book

Write a program that lets the user display and modify an address book containing names, e-mail addresses, and phone numbers. The program should contain a class named `Address`. The `Address` class should contain the following information about one person: name, e-mail address, phone, and comments. The application should also have a collection named `addressList`, which stores a collection of `Address` objects.

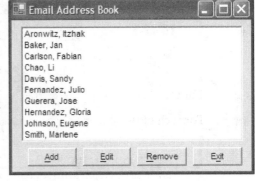

Figure 12-14   E-mail Address Book form

The main window, shown in Figure 12-16, displays the names from the address book in a list box. The user should be able to input new names and addresses, using a form similar to the one shown in Figure 12-14.

Figure 12-15   Add New Name form

2. Carpet Price Calculator

The Westfield Carpet Company has asked you to write an application that calculates the price of carpeting. To calculate the price of a carpet you multiply the area of the floor (width times length) by the price per square foot of carpet. For example, the area of a floor that is 12 feet long and 10 feet wide is 120 feet. To cover that floor with carpet that costs $8 per square foot would cost $960.

You should create a class named `Rectangle` with the following properties:

Width: A single
Length: A single
Area: A single

The Area property should be read-only. Provide a method named `CalcArea` that calculates width times length and stores the result in the Area property.

Next, create a class named `Carpet` with the following properties:

Color: A string
Style: A string
Price: A decimal

The application should have a form similar to the one in Figure 12-16. (The carpet price is the price per square foot.) When the Calculate button is clicked, the application should copy the data in the text boxes into the appropriate object properties, then display the area and price.

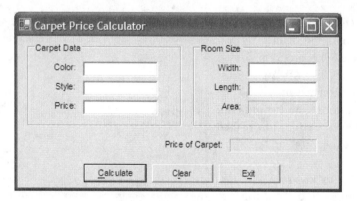

Figure 12-16   Carpet Price Calculator form

3. Scrollable Tax Calculator

Create an application that allows you to enter the amount of a purchase, and then displays the amount of sales tax on that purchase. Use a scrollable control such as a scroll bar or a track bar to adjust the tax rate between 0% and 10%. The form should appear similar to Figure 12-17.

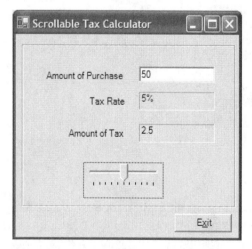

Figure 12-17   Scrollable Tax Calculator form

Design Your Own Forms

4. Saving the Student Collection

Modify the student collection application from this chapter so it saves the collection in a file or a database before the program exits. When the program starts up, load the collection from the file or database.

5. `Motor` Class

Create an application that tracks electric motors in a manufacturing plant. The application should have a `Motor` class with the following properties:

MotorId: Five-digit string, such as "02340"
Description: String
RPM: Single, values in the range 10 to 10000
Voltage: Single, values in the range 1 to 500
Status: String, three characters.

The Status values are:

ON: Motor is online and running.
OFF: Motor is online but not running.
MNT: Motor is undergoing maintenance and cleaning.
NA: Motor is not available.

The application should be able to store at least ten `Motor` class objects in an array. Create an input form in the application that allows users to input new motor records to be added to the array. Create another form that displays all the motors in the array in a list box.

6. `Motor Collection`

Modify the application you created in the Programming Challenge 5 so it uses a collection instead of an array to hold the `Motor` class objects. When the application ends, it should save the contents of the collection to a file or a database. When the application starts up, it should load the data from the file or database into the collection. Be sure to write the appropriate error handlers.

7. Account Class

You are a programmer for the Home Software Company. You have been assigned to develop a class that models the basic workings of a bank account. The class should have the following properties:

Balance: Holds the current account balance.
IntRate: Holds the interest rate for the period.
Interest: Holds the interest earned for the current period.
Transactions: Holds the number of transactions for the current period.

The class should also have the following methods:

MakeDeposit	Takes an argument, which is the amount of the deposit. This argument is added to the Balance property.
Withdraw	Takes an argument that is the amount of the withdrawal. This value is subtracted from the Balance property, unless the withdrawal amount is greater than the balance. If this happens, an error message is displayed.

`CalcInterest`   This method calculates the amount of interest for the current period, stores this value in the Interest property, and adds it to the Balance property.

Demonstrate the class in an application that performs the following tasks:

◆ Allows deposits to be made to the account.

◆ Allows withdrawals to be taken from the account.

◆ Calculates interest for the period.

◆ Reports the current account balance at any time.

◆ Reports the current number of transactions at any time.

8. Inventory Item Class

Create an application that stores inventory records for a retail store. The application should have an `Inventory` class with the following properties:

InvNumber: A string used to hold an inventory number. Each item in the inventory should have a unique inventory number.

Description: A string that holds a brief description of the item.

Cost: A decimal value that holds the amount that the retail store paid for the item.

Retail: A decimal value that holds the retail price for the item.

OnHand: An integer value that holds the number of items on hand. This value cannot be less than 0.

The application should store Inventory class objects in a collection. Create an input form in the application that allows users to input new inventory items to be added to the collection. The user should also be able to look up items by their inventory number.

9. Inventory Class Modification

Modify the application you created in Programming Challenge 8 so it saves the contents of the collection to a file or a database. When the application starts up, it should load the data from the file or database into the collection. Be sure to write the appropriate error handlers.

10. Cash Register

Create an application that serves as a simple cash register for a retail store. Use the `Inventory` class you created in Programming Challenge 8 to store data about the items in the store's inventory. When the application starts up, it should load the entire store's inventory from a file or a database into a collection of `Inventory` class objects.

When a purchase is made, the cashier should select an item from a list box. (If an item's OnHand property is set to zero, the item should not be available in the list box.) The item's description, retail price, and number of units on hand should be displayed on the form when selected. The cashier should enter the quantity being purchased, and the application should display the sales tax and the total of the sale. (The quantity being purchased cannot exceed the number of units on hand.) The quantity being purchased should be subtracted from the item's OnHand property.

When the application ends, the contents of the collection should be saved to the file or database.

CHAPTER

13

Inheritance, Custom Controls, and Using the Clipboard

13.1 Introduction

F irst, this chapter introduces you to inheritance. Inheritance is an object-oriented programming feature that allows you to base a class on an existing class. Next, we discuss how to create custom controls. The ability to equip your applications with clipboard copy, cut, and paste operations is then covered.

MAJOR TOPICS

▶13.1 Introduction

▶13.2 Introduction to Inheritance

▶13.3 Creating Custom Controls

▶13.4 Sharing Text with the Clipboard

▶ 13.2 Introduction to Inheritance

CONCEPT

INHERITANCE ALLOWS A NEW CLASS TO BE BASED ON AN EXISTING CLASS. THE NEW CLASS INHERITS THE ACCESSIBLE MEMBER VARIABLES, METHODS, AND PROPERTIES OF THE CLASS IT IS BASED ON.

An important aspect of object-oriented programming is inheritance. *Inheritance* allows you to create new classes that inherit, or derive, characteristics of existing classes. For example, you might start with the Student class that we discussed in Chapter 12, which has only general information for all types of students. But special types of students might require the creation of classes such as Graduate Student, ExchangeStudent, StudentEmployee, and so on. These new classes would share all the characteristics of the Student class, and they would each add the new characteristics that make them specialized.

In an inheritance relationship, there is a base class and a derived class. The *base class* is the generalized class that other classes may be based on. The *derived class* is based on the base class, and inherits characteristics from it. You can think of the base class as the parent and the derived class as the child.

751

Let's look at an example. The following `Vehicle` class has two properties, implemented as property procedures: Passengers and MilesPerGallon. The Passengers property uses the `numPassengers` member variable and the MilesPerGallon property uses the `mpg` member variable.

```
Public Class Vehicle
    ' Private member variables
    Private numPassengers As Integer      ' Number of passengers
    Private mpg As Single                 ' Miles per gallon

    ' Passengers property
    Public Property Passengers() As Integer
        Get
            Return numPassengers
        End Get
        Set(ByVal value As Integer)
            numPassengers = value
        End Set
    End Property

    ' MilesPerGallon property
    Public Property MilesPerGallon() As Single
        Get
            Return mpg
        End Get
        Set(ByVal value As Single)
            mpg = value
        End Set
    End Property
End Class
```

The `Vehicle` class holds only general data about a vehicle. By using it as a base class, however, we can create other classes that hold more specialized data about specific types of vehicles. For example, look at the following code for a `Truck` class.

```
Public Class Truck
    Inherits Vehicle
    ' Private member variables
    Private cargoWeight As Single    ' Maximum cargo weight
    Private fourWheelDr As Boolean   ' Four wheel drive

    ' MaxCargoWeight property
    Public Property MaxCargoWeight() As Single
        Get
            Return cargoWeight
        End Get
        Set(ByVal value As Single)
            cargoWeight = value
        End Set
    End Property

    ' FourWheelDrive property
    Public Property FourWheelDrive() As Boolean
        Get
            Return fourWheelDr
        End Get
```

```
        Set(ByVal value As Boolean)
            fourWheelDr = value
        End Set
    End Property
End Class
```

Notice the second line of this class declaration:

```
Inherits Vehicle
```

This statement indicates that this class is derived from the `Vehicle` class. Because it is derived from the `Vehicle` class, the `Truck` class inherits all the `Vehicle` class member variables, methods, and properties that are not declared as private. In addition to the inherited base class members, the `Truck` class adds two properties of its own: MaxCargoWeight, which hold the maximum cargo weight, and FourWheelDrive, which indicates whether the truck is four wheel drive.

The following statements create an instance of the `Truck` class.

```
Dim pickUp as Truck
pickUp = New Truck()
```

And the following statements store values in all of the object's properties.

```
pickUp.Passengers = 2
pickUp.MilesPerGallon = 18
pickUp.MaxCargoWeight = 2000
pickUp.FourWheelDrive = True
```

Notice that values are stored not only in the MaxCargoWeight and FourWheelDrive properties, but also the Passengers and MilesPerGallon properties. The `Truck` class inherits the Passengers and MilesPerGallon properties from the vehicle class.

Overriding Properties and Methods

Sometimes a property procedure or method in a base class does not work adequately for a derived class. When this happens, you can *override* the base class property procedure or method by writing one with the same name in the derived class. When an object of the derived class accesses the property or calls the method, Visual Basic .NET will execute the overridden version in the derived class instead of the version in the base class.

For example, the `Vehicle` class has the following property procedure.

```
Public Property Passengers() As Integer
    Get
        Return numPassengers
    End Get
    Set(ByVal value As Integer)
        numPassengers = value
    End Set
End Property
```

The `Set` section of this property procedure simply stores any value that is passed to it in the `numPassengers` variable. Suppose that in the `Truck` class we want to restrict the number of passengers to either 1 or 2. We can override the Passengers property procedure by writing another version of it in the `Truck` class.

First, we must add the `Overridable` key word to the property procedure in the `Vehicle` class, as follows.

```
Public Overridable Property Passengers() As Integer
    Get
        Return numPassengers
    End Get
    Set(ByVal value As Integer)
        numPassengers = value
    End Set
End Property
```

The *Overridable key word* indicates that the procedure may be overridden in a derived class. If we do not add this key word to the declaration, a compiler error will occur when we attempt to override the procedure. The general format of a property procedure with the `Overridable` key word is:

```
Public Overridable Property PropertyName() As DataType
    Get
            Statements
    End Get
    Set(ParameterDeclaration)
            Statements
    End Set
End Property
```

NOTE: *A private property cannot be overridable.*

Next, we write the overridden property procedure in the `Truck` class, as follows.

```
' Passengers property
Public Overrides Property Passengers() As Integer
    Get
        Return MyBase.Passengers
    End Get
    Set(ByVal value As Integer)
        If value >= 1 And value <= 2 Then
            MyBase.Passengers = value
        Else
            MessageBox.Show("Passengers must be 1 or 2.", "Error")
        End If
    End Set
End Property
```

Notice that this procedure uses the *Overrides key word*. This indicates that it overrides a procedure in the base class. The general format of a property procedure that overrides a base class property procedure is:

```
Public Overrides Property PropertyName() As DataType
      Get
              Statements
      End Get
      Set(ParameterDeclaration)
              Statements
      End Set
End Property
```

Let's look at how the procedure works. The Get section has the following statement:

```
Return MyBase.Passengers
```

The *MyBase key word* refers to the base class. The expression MyBase.Passengers refers to the base class's Passengers property. So, this statement simply returns the value that is returned from the base class's Passengers property.

The Set section uses an If statement to validate that value is 1 or 2. If value is 1 or 2, the following statement is executed.

```
MyBase.Passengers = value
```

This statement stores value in the base class's Passenger property. If value is not 1 or 2, an error message is displayed. So, the following code will cause the error message to appear.

```
Dim pickUp As Truck
pickUp = New Truck()

pickUp.Passengers = 5
```

The complete code for the modified Vehicle and Truck class follows.

```
Public Class Vehicle
    ' Private member variables
    Private numPassengers As Integer     ' Number of passengers
    Private mpg As Single                ' Miles per gallon

    ' Passengers property
    Public Overridable Property Passengers() As Integer
        Get
            Return numPassengers
        End Get
        Set(ByVal value As Integer)
            numPassengers = value
        End Set
    End Property

    ' MilesPerGallon property
    Public Property MilesPerGallon() As Single
        Get
            Return mpg
        End Get
        Set(ByVal value As Single)
            mpg = value
```

```
            End Set
        End Property
End Class

Public Class Truck
    Inherits Vehicle

    ' Private member variables
    Private cargoWeight As Single     ' Maximum cargo weight
    Private fourWheelDr As Boolean    ' Four wheel drive

    ' MaxCargoWeight property
    Public Property MaxCargoWeight() As Single
        Get
            Return cargoWeight
        End Get
        Set(ByVal value As Single)
            cargoWeight = value
        End Set
    End Property

    ' FourWheelDrive property
    Public Property FourWheelDrive() As Boolean
        Get
            Return fourWheelDr
        End Get
        Set(ByVal value As Boolean)
            fourWheelDr = value
        End Set
    End Property

    ' Passengers property
    Public Overrides Property Passengers() As Integer
        Get
            Return MyBase.Passengers
        End Get
        Set(ByVal value As Integer)
            If value >= 1 And value <= 2 Then
                MyBase.Passengers = value
            Else
                MessageBox.Show("Passengers must be 1 or 2.", "Error")
            End If
        End Set
    End Property
End Class
```

Overriding Methods

Class methods may be overridden in the same manner as property procedures. The general format of an overridable base class Sub procedure is:

```
Public Overridable Sub ProcedureName()
    Statements
End Sub
```

The general format of an overridable base class function is:

```
Public Overridable Function ProcedureName() As DataType
      Statements
End Sub
```

NOTE: *A private procedure or function cannot be overridable.*

The general format of a Sub procedure that overrides a base class Sub procedure is:

```
AccessSpecifier Overridable Sub ProcedureName()
      Statements
End Sub
```

The general format of a function that overrides a base class function is:

```
AccessSpecifier Overrides Function ProcedureName() As DataType
      Statements
End Sub
```

Because the derived class cannot access the private members of the base class, the overridable methods in the base class cannot be declared as private. The methods in the derived class that override the base class methods can be declared as private, however.

Overriding the `ToString` Method

By now you are familiar with the ToString method that all of the Visual Basic .NET data types provide. This method returns a string representation of the data stored in a variable or object.

Every class that you create in Visual Basic .NET is automatically derived from a built-in class named *Object*. The Object class has a method named ToString which returns a fully-qualified class name. You can override this method so it returns a string representation of the data stored in a class. For example, we can add the following ToString method to the Vehicle class:

```
' Overriden ToString method
Public Overrides Function ToString() As String
   ' Return a string representation
   ' of a vehicle.
   Dim str As String

   str = "Passengers: " & numPassengers.ToString & _
         " MPG: " & mpg.ToString
   Return str
End Function
```

This method returns a string showing a vehicle's number of passengers and the miles-per-gallon. When a method is declared with the Overrides key word, it is also implicitly declared as Overridable. So, we can override this ToString method in the Truck class, as follows.

```
' Overriden ToString method
Public Overrides Function ToString() As String
   ' Return a string representation
```

```
' of a vehicle.
Dim str As String

str = MyBase.ToString & " Max. Cargo: " & _
      cargoWeight.ToString & " 4WD: " & _
      fourWheelDr.ToString
Return str
End Function
```

This method calls `MyBase.ToString`, which is the `Vehicle` class's `ToString` method. To that method's return value, it concatenates string versions of the `cargoWeight` variable and the `fourWheelDr` variable. The resulting string is then returned. Look at the following code to see how all this works.

```
Dim bigTruck As New Truck()
bigTruck.Passengers = 2
bigTruck.MilesPerGallon = 14
bigTruck.MaxCargoWeight = 8000
bigTruck.FourWheelDrive = True
MessageBox.Show(bigTruck.ToString)
```

This code will display the following string in a message box:

```
Passengers: 2 MPG: 14 Max. Cargo: 8000 4WD: True
```

Base Class and Derived Class Constructors

Recall from Chapter 12 that a constructor is a Sub procedure named `New` that is a member of a class. The constructor is automatically called when an instance of the class is created. It is possible for both a base class and a derived class to have constructors. For example, look at the following classes, `Parent` and `Child`.

```
Public Class Parent
    Public Sub New()
        MessageBox.Show("This is the base class constructor.")
    End Sub
End Class

Public Class Child
    Inherits Parent

    Public Sub New()
        MessageBox.Show("This is the derived class constructor.")
    End Sub
End Class
```

When an instance of the derived class is created, the base class constructor is called first, and then the derived class constructor is called. So, creating an instance of the `Child` class will cause the message "This is the base class constructor." to be displayed, followed by the message "This is the derived class constructor."

NOTE: *Notice that the* `Overridable` *and* `Overrrides` *key words are not used with constructors.*

Protected Members

In addition to `Private` and `Public`, we will also study the `Protected` access specifier. The `Protected` access specifier may be used to in the declaration of a base class member, such as:

```
Protected cost As Decimal
```

This statement declares a protected variable named `cost`. *Protected* base class members are like private members, except they may be accessed by methods and property procedures in derived classes. To all other code, however, protected class members are just like private class members.

TUTORIAL 13-1:

Completing an application that uses inheritance

In this tutorial you will complete an application that keeps records about the number of course hours completed by computer science students. You will create a class named `GeneralStudent`, which will have properties to hold the following data: first name, last name, ID number, math hours completed, communications hours completed, humanities hours completed, elective hours completed, and total hours completed. This class will have a method named `UpdateHours` that will calculate the total hours completed when any of the other hours are changed. In addition, the class will override the `ToString` method.

You will also create a class named `CsStudent`, which will be derived from the `GeneralStudent` class. The `CsStudent` class will have a property to hold the number of computer science hours completed. This class will override the `General Student` class's `UpdateHours` method to add the number of computer science hours.

Step 1: Start Visual Basic .NET and open the Computer Science Student project located in the \Chap13\Computer Science Student folder on the student disk. The forms have already been built for you. Figure 13-1 shows the `frmMain` form and Figure 13-2 shows the `frmDisplayStudents` form.

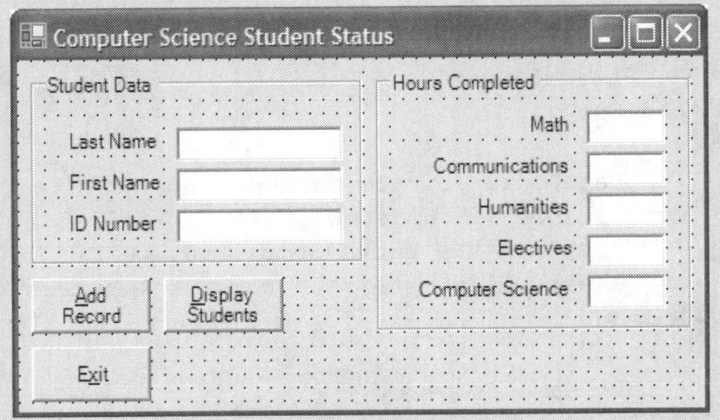

Figure 13-1 The `frmMain` form

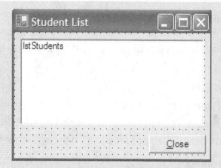

Figure 13-2   The `frmDisplayStudents` form

Step 2:   Add a new class named `GeneralStudent` to the project. The code for the class follows.

```
Public Class GeneralStudent
    'Private member variables
    Private lname As String     ' Last name
    Private fname As String     ' First name
    Private idNum As String     ' ID number
    Private mathHrs As Single   ' Math hours completed
    Private commHrs As Single   ' Communications hours
                                  completed
    Private humHrs As Single    ' Humanities hours completed
    Private electHrs As Single  ' Elective hours completed
    Protected hoursComp As Single' Total Hours completed


  ' Constructor
    Public Sub New()
        ' Initialize the private member variables.
        lname = "(Unknown)"
        fname = "(Unknown)"
        idNum = "(Unknown)"
        mathHrs = 0
        commHrs = 0
        humHrs = 0
        electHrs = 0
        hoursComp = 0
    End Sub


    ' UpdateHours Private method
    Overridable Sub UpdateHours()
        ' Update the hours completed.
        hoursComp = mathHrs + commHrs + humHrs + electHrs
    End Sub


    ' Last Name property
    Public Property LastName() As String
        Get
            Return lname
```

```vb
            End Get
            Set(ByVal value As String)
                lname = value
            End Set
    End Property


    ' First name property
    Public Property FirstName() As String
        Get
                Return fname
        End Get
        Set(ByVal value As String)
                fname = value
        End Set
    End Property


    ' IdNumber property
    Public Property IdNumber() As String
        Get
                Return idNum
        End Get
        Set(ByVal value As String)
                idNum = value
        End Set
    End Property


    ' MathHours property
    Public Property MathHours() As Single
        Get
                Return mathHrs
        End Get
        Set(ByVal value As Single)
                mathHrs = value
                UpdateHours()
        End Set
    End Property


    ' CommunicationsHours property
    Public Property CommunicationsHours() As Single
        Get
                Return commHrs
        End Get
        Set(ByVal value As Single)
                commHrs = value
                UpdateHours()
        End Set
    End Property


    ' HumanitiesHours property
    Public Property HumanitiesHours() As Single
```

```
            Get
                Return humHrs
            End Get
            Set(ByVal value As Single)
                humHrs = value
                UpdateHours()
            End Set
        End Property


        ' ElectiveHours property
        Public Property ElectiveHours() As Single
            Get
                Return electHrs
            End Get
            Set(ByVal value As Single)
                electHrs = value
                UpdateHours()
            End Set
        End Property


        ' HoursCompleted property (read-only)
        ReadOnly Property HoursCompleted() As Single
            Get
                Return hoursComp
            End Get
        End Property


        ' Overridden ToString method
        Public Overrides Function ToString() As String
            ' Return the student data as a string.
            Dim str As String

            str = "Name: " & lname & ", " & fname & _
                " Completed Hours: " & _
                hoursComp.ToString
            Return str
        End Function

    End Class
```

Step 3:   Add another class named `CsStudent` to the project. This class will be derived from the `GeneralStudent` class. The code for the class follows.

```
    Public Class CsStudent
        Inherits GeneralStudent

        ' Private member variables
        Private csHrs As Single           ' CS hours completed
        ' Constructor
        Public Sub New()
            ' Initialize the private member variable.
            csHrs = 0
        End Sub
```

```
    ' Overridden UpdateHours method
    Public Overrides Sub UpdateHours()
        MyBase.UpdateHours()
        hoursComp += csHrs
    End Sub

    ' CSHours property
    Public Property CSHours() As Single
        Get
            Return csHrs
        End Get
        Set(ByVal value As Single)
            csHrs = value
        End Set
    End Property

End Class
```

Step 4: Add a standard module named ComputerScienceStudentModule to the project. This module will declare a global object variable named g_csStudentCollection, which will be used to create a collection to hold CsStudent objects. The code for the module follows.

```
Module ComputerScienceStudentModule
    ' Module-level declaration
    Public g_csStudentCollection As Collection
End Module
```

Step 5: Now you will write the event procedures and Sub procedures for the frmMain form. First, write the form's Load event procedure, which creates the collection. The code follows.

```
Private Sub frmMain_Load(ByVal sender As System.Object, _
        ByVal e As System.EventArgs) Handles MyBase.Load
    ' Create the collection.
    g_csStudentCollection = New Collection()
End Sub
```

Step 6: Next, write the btnAdd_Click procedure, the GetData Sub procedure, the AddStudent Sub procedure, and the ClearForm Sub procedure. The code follows.

```
Private Sub btnAdd_Click(ByVal sender As System.Object, _
        ByVal e As System.EventArgs) Handles btnAdd.Click
    ' Add the data entered on the form to the collection.
    Dim csData As CsStudent

    csData = New CsStudent()
    GetData(csData)
    AddStudent(csData)
    ClearForm()
```

```
        csData = Nothing
    End Sub

    Private Sub GetData(ByVal csData As CsStudent)
        ' Get the data from the form.
        csData.LastName = txtLastName.Text
        csData.FirstName = txtFirstName.Text
        csData.IdNumber = txtIdNumber.Text
        csData.MathHours = Val(txtMath.Text)
        csData.CommunicationsHours = Val(txtComm.Text)
        csData.HumanitiesHours = Val(txtHum.Text)
        csData.ElectiveHours = Val(txtElect.Text)
        csData.CSHours = Val(txtCompSci.Text)
    End Sub

    Private Sub AddStudent(ByVal csData As CsStudent)
        ' Add a CsStudent object to the collection and use
        ' the IdNumber property as the key.
        Try
            g_csStudentCollection.Add(csData, csData.IdNumber)
        Catch ex As Exception
            MessageBox.Show(ex.Message)
        End Try
    End Sub

    Private Sub ClearForm()
        ' Clear the form.
        txtLastName.Clear()
        txtFirstName.Clear()
        txtIdNumber.Clear()
        txtMath.Clear()
        txtComm.Clear()
        txtHum.Clear()
        txtElect.Clear()
        txtCompSci.Clear()
        ' Set the focus.
        txtLastName.Focus()
    End Sub
```

Step 7: Write the `btnDisplay_Click` and `btnExit_Click` event procedures. The code follows.

```
Private Sub btnDisplay_Click(ByVal sender As System.Object, _
        ByVal e As System.EventArgs) Handles btnDisplay.Click
    ' Display a form showing all the students
    ' in the collection.
    Dim displayForm As New frmDisplayStudents()

    displayForm.ShowDialog()
End Sub
```

```
                Private Sub btnExit_Click(ByVal sender As System.Object, _
                    ByVal e As System.EventArgs) Handles btnExit.Click
                    ' End the application.
                    End
                End Sub
```

Step 8: Now you will write the code for the frmDisplayStudents form. This form has only two event procedures: frmDisplayStudents_Load, and btnClose_Click. The code follows.

```
                Private Sub frmDisplayStudents_Load(ByVal sender As _
                    System.Object, ByVal e As System.EventArgs) _
                    Handles MyBase.Load
                    Dim cs As CsStudent

                    For Each cs In g_csStudentCollection
                        lstStudents.Items.Add(cs.ToString)
                    Next
                End Sub

                Private Sub btnClose_Click(ByVal sender As System.Object, _
                    ByVal e As System.EventArgs) Handles btnClose.Click
                    ' Close this form.
                    Me.Close()
                End Sub
```

Step 9: Save the project and run the application. On the main form, add data for a fictitious student, then click the Add Record button. Repeat this for at least two more students. Click the Display Students button to see a list of the students you have added. Figure 13-3 shows an example.

Step 10: Click the Close button and then end the application.

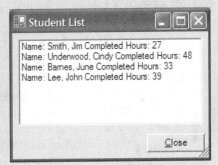

Figure 13-3   Student list displayed

✓ Checkpoint

13.1 The beginning of a class declaration follows. What is the name of the base class, and what is the name of the derived class?

```
Public Class Fly
    Inherits Insect
```

13.2 What does a derived class inherit from its base class?

13.3 What is overriding?

13.4 What key word must you include in the declaration of a property procedure or method in order for it to be overridden in a derived class?

13.5 What key word must you include in the declaration of a property procedure or method in order for it to override one that exists in the base class?

13.6 When both a base class and a derived class have a constructor, which executes first?

13.7 What is a protected base class member?

▶ 13.3 Creating Custom Controls

CONCEPT

VISUAL BASIC .NET ALLOWS YOU TO CREATE YOUR OWN CUSTOM CONTROLS THAT MAY BE USED ON APPLICATION FORMS.

In addition to the standard controls, such as labels, buttons, and text boxes, Visual Basic .NET allows you to create your own custom controls. A *custom control* is a control that is designed by a programmer for a specific purpose. When you create a custom control, you create a class that is derived from the `System.Windows.Forms.UserControl` class. You then add to this class the ingredients necessary for your custom control, such as properties, methods, and other controls.

The process of creating a custom control is straightforward. Tutorial 13-2 guides you through the steps of creating a TimeZone control. Before we begin the tutorial, however, we need to look at the `DateAdd` function, which we will use in the control.

The *DateAdd function* adds an interval of time to a Date variable. The interval can be expressed in seconds, minutes, hours, days, months, etc. Here is the function's general format:

```
DateAdd(Interval, Number, DateValue)
```

Interval is a value that represents the interval we are adding to the date. For example, the value `DateInterval.Second` specifies that we are adding seconds to the date, and the value `DateInterval.Hour` specifies that we are adding hours to the date. *Number* is the number of intervals we are adding. *DateValue* is the Date value that we are adding to. The function returns the resulting Date value. For example, look at the following code.

```
' Declare two Date variables
Dim systemTime As Date
Dim anotherTime As Date

' Get the system time.
systemTime = Now
' Make anotherTime equal to
' systemTime plus six hours.
anotherTime = DateAdd(DateInterval.Hour, 6, systemTime)
' Display the time
MessageBox.Show(anotherTime.ToLongTimeString)
```

This code retrieves the system time and stores it in the `systemTime` variable. The `DateAdd` function is then used to add six hours to the value in `systemTime`, the result being stored in the variable `anotherTime`. Notice that the last statement displays the value `anotherTime.ToLongTimeString` in a message box. The Date variable's *ToLongTimeString method* returns the variable's time value in long format.

TIP: To subtract an interval from a Date variable, pass a negative number as the
        `Number` argument to the `DateAdd` function.

TUTORIAL 13-2:

Creating the TimeZone custom control

In this tutorial you will create the TimeZone custom control, which displays the current time in the Pacific, Mountain, Central, and Eastern time zones.

Step 1:   Start Visual Basic .NET and begin a new project. As shown in Figure 13-4, select Windows Control Library in the Templates pane of the New Project Dialog box. In the Name text box, type **TimeZone Control**. Click the OK button.

The form for this project appears without a title bar or a border, as shown in Figure 13-5. This makes sense because you are creating a control that will be placed on a form.

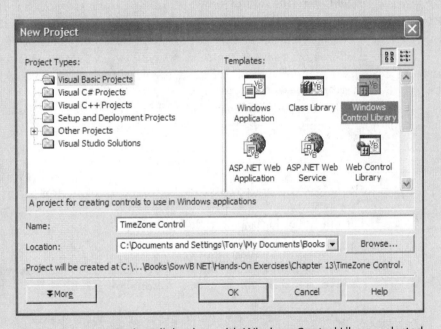

Figure 13-4   New Project dialog box with Windows Control Library selected

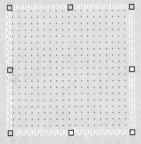

Figure 13-5   The custom control form

Step 2: Think of the borderless form as canvas on which you will construct the visual part of your custom control. The default name for the control is `UserControl1`. In the Properties window change the control's name to **TimeZone**. In the Solution Explorer window, change the name of the UserControl1.vb entry to TimeZone.vb.

Step 3: Set the control form up as shown in Figure 13-6. The labels with borders will be used to display the time in different time zones. Name the labels `lblPacific`, `lblMountain`, `lblCentral`, and `lblEastern`.

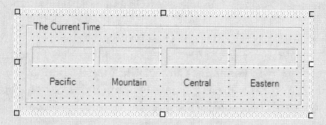

Figure 13-6 The control form

Step 4: Open the code window and notice that the class is already set up for you, as shown in Figure 13-7.

```
Public Class TimeZone
    Inherits System.Windows.Forms.UserControl

    Windows Form Designer generated code

End Class
```

Figure 13-7 Generated class code for the TimeZone control

Enter the following class-level declarations.

```
' TimeZone Custom control
Private sysTime As Date  ' To hold the current time
Private tzone As String  ' Zone property
```

The `sysTime` variable will hold the current time (retrieved from the computer's internal clock), and the `tzone` variable will hold the value of the control's Zone property.

Step 5: Create the following property procedure for the Zone property.

```
' Zone property
Public Property Zone() As String
    Get
        Return tzone
    End Get
    Set(ByVal value As String)
        tzone = value.Trim.ToLower
        ' Test for valid values.
```

```
                    If tzone <> "pacific" And tzone <> "mountain" And _
                       tzone <> "central" And tzone <> "eastern" Then
                       ' Display an error message.
                       MessageBox.Show("Invalid value for Zone property", _
                                       "Error")
                       tzone = ""
                    Else
                       tzone = value
                    End If
            End Set
         End Property
```

The Set section tests the value argument to determine whether it contains a valid property value. If the argument contains an invalid value, the procedure displays an error message.

Step 6:   Create the following Load event procedure, which assigns the default value "Eastern" to the TimeZone property.

```
Private Sub TimeZone_Load(ByVal sender As Object, _
            ByVal e As System.EventArgs) Handles MyBase.Load
      ' Initialize TimeZone property to
      ' EST by default.
      tzone = "Eastern"
End Sub
```

Step 7:   Create the following Sub procedures, which are the control's methods.

```
Public Sub ShowTime()
    ' Display the current time.
    sysTime = Now   ' Get the time from the system.
    If tzone.ToLower.Trim = "eastern" Then
        ShowEastern()
    ElseIf tzone.ToLower.Trim = "central" Then
        ShowCentral()
    ElseIf tzone.ToLower.Trim = "mountain" Then
        ShowMountain()
    ElseIf tzone.ToLower.Trim = "pacific" Then
        ShowPacific()
    End If
End Sub


Private Sub ShowEastern()
    ' This procedure displays the times with Eastern
    ' as the default time zone.

    ' Display the times.
    lblEastern.Text = sysTime.ToLongTimeString
    lblCentral.Text = DateAdd(DateInterval.Hour, -1, _
                              sysTime).ToLongTimeString
```

```
            lblMountain.Text = DateAdd(DateInterval.Hour, -2, _
                                    sysTime).ToLongTimeString
            lblPacific.Text = DateAdd(DateInterval.Hour, -3, _
                                    sysTime).ToLongTimeString
    End Sub

    Private Sub ShowCentral()
        ' This procedure displays the times with Central
        ' as the default time zone.

        ' Display the times.
        lblEastern.Text = DateAdd(DateInterval.Hour, 1, _
                                    sysTime).ToLongTimeString
        lblCentral.Text = sysTime.ToLongTimeString
        lblMountain.Text = DateAdd(DateInterval.Hour, -1, _
                                    sysTime).ToLongTimeString
        lblPacific.Text = DateAdd(DateInterval.Hour, -2, _
                                    sysTime).ToLongTimeString
    End Sub

    Private Sub ShowMountain()
        ' This procedure displays the times with Mountain
        ' as the default time zone.

        ' Display the times.
        lblEastern.Text = DateAdd(DateInterval.Hour, 2, _
                                    sysTime).ToLongTimeString
        lblCentral.Text = DateAdd(DateInterval.Hour, 1, _
                                    sysTime).ToLongTimeString
        lblMountain.Text = sysTime.ToLongTimeString
        lblPacific.Text = DateAdd(DateInterval.Hour, -1, _
                                    sysTime).ToLongTimeString
    End Sub

    Private Sub ShowPacific()
        ' This procedure displays the times with Pacific
        ' as the default time zone.

    ' Display the times.
        lblEastern.Text = DateAdd(DateInterval.Hour, 3, _
                                    sysTime).ToLongTimeString
        lblCentral.Text = DateAdd(DateInterval.Hour, 2, _
                                    sysTime).ToLongTimeString
        lblMountain.Text = DateAdd(DateInterval.Hour, 1, _
                                    sysTime).ToLongTimeString
        lblPacific.Text = sysTime.ToLongTimeString
    End Sub
```

The ShowTime procedure retrieves the current time from the computer's internal clock with the Now function and stores it in the sysTime variable. It then calls one of the methods ShowEastern, ShowCentral, ShowMountain, or ShowPacific, depending on the value in the tzone member variable.

The `ShowEastern` procedure assumes we are in the Eastern time zone. It displays the current system time in the `lblEastern` label, and then uses the `DateAdd` function to calculate the time for the other time zones. The `ShowCentral`, `ShowMountain`, and `ShowPacific` procedures perform the same operation, assuming that we are in the Central, Mountain, and Pacific time zones respectively.

Step 8: Save the project.

Step 9: Compile the control by clicking Build on the menu bar, then clicking Build Time-Zone Control. If you typed everything correctly, the project should compile. It will not execute, however. To execute the control, we must include it in another project. In the next tutorial we will create a Windows application and use the TimeZone control.

Step 10: Close the solution.

Using a Custom Control in a Project

When you compile a custom control, Visual Basic .NET creates a file with the extension .DLL in the project's bin folder. Once you have created a custom control you must add a reference to its .DLL file to any projects that should be able to use the control. When you add a reference to the custom control to a project, an icon representing the custom control will appear in the Visual Basic .NET toolbox when you open that project. Tutorial 13-3 guides you through the process of adding a reference to the Time-Zone control to a project.

TUTORIAL 13-3:

Adding the TimeZone control to a project

Step 1: Start Visual Basic .NET and begin a new Windows application project. Name the project Custom Control Demo.

Step 2: Now you will add the TimeZone Custom control to the toolbox. Right-click anywhere in the Windows Form section of the toolbox. The pop-up menu shown in Figure 13-8 should appear. Click Customize Toolbox. The Customize Toolbox dialog box, shown in Figure 13-9 should appear.

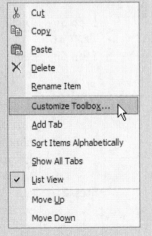

Figure 13-8   Toolbox pop-up menu

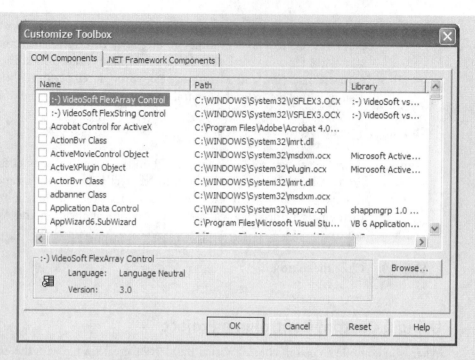

Figure 13-9 Customize Toolbox dialog box

NOTE: *The entries shown in the Customize Toolbox dialog box on your system may not be the same ones shown in Figure 13-9.*

Step 3: Click the .NET Framework Components tab.

Step 4: Click the Browse button. A Browse dialog box will appear. Browse to bin folder under the TimeZone Control project folder. You should see the file TimeZoneControl.dll. Select this file and click the Open button.

Step 5: On the Customize Toolbox dialog box, click OK.

Step 6: Scroll down in the toolbox until you see the TimeZone tool, as shown in Figure 13-10.

Step 7: Double-click the TimeZone tool. A TimeZone control should appear on the form. Notice that the default name is TimeZone1. We will use the default name in this project.

Figure 13-10 TimeZone tool in the toolbox

Step 8: Resize the form and add the buttons shown in Figure 13-11. Name the buttons `btnPacific`, `btnMountain`, `btnCentral`, and `btnEastern`.

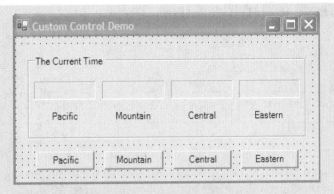

Figure 13-11   Custom Control Demo form

Step 9:   Create the following `Click` event procedures for the buttons.

```
Private Sub btnPacific_Click(ByVal sender As System.Object, _
        ByVal e As System.EventArgs) Handles btnPacific.Click
    TimeZone1.Zone = "Pacific"
    TimeZone1.ShowTime()
End Sub

Private Sub btnMountain_Click(ByVal sender As System.Object, _
        ByVal e As System.EventArgs) Handles btnMountain.Click
    TimeZone1.Zone = "Mountain"
    TimeZone1.ShowTime()
End Sub

Private Sub btnCentral_Click(ByVal sender As System.Object, _
        ByVal e As System.EventArgs) Handles btnCentral.Click
    TimeZone1.Zone = "Central"
    TimeZone1.ShowTime()
End Sub

Private Sub btnEastern_Click(ByVal sender As System.Object, _
        ByVal e As System.EventArgs) Handles btnEastern.Click
    TimeZone1.Zone = "Eastern"
    TimeZone1.ShowTime()
End Sub
```

Step 10:   Save the project and run the application. Click the Pacific button. The application should display the current time in the Pacific label, with the corresponding times in the Mountain, Central, and Eastern labels. Experiment with the other buttons.

Step 11:   End the application.

✓ **Checkpoint**

13.8   In a nutshell, what is a custom control?

13.9   What class is a custom control derived from?

13.10   Once you have created a custom control, how do you compile it?

13.11   How do you add a custom control to the toolbox?

▶ 13.4   Sharing Text with the Clipboard

CONCEPT

YOU CAN ACCESS THE WINDOWS CLIPBOARD WITH THE VISUAL BASIC .NET CLIPBOARD METHODS.

Visual Basic .NET's *Clipboard methods* allow you to share data with other Windows applications. One of the Clipboard methods is the *SetDataObject method* for storing text in the clipboard. When copying text to the clipboard, use one of the following general formats.

```
Clipboard.SetDataObject(Text)
Clipboard.SetDataObject(Text, Remain)
```

The argument, *Text*, is the text you wish to store in the clipboard. When you use the first format of the SetDataObject method, the text will be deleted from the clipboard when the application exits. In the second format, the argument *Remain* is a Boolean value. If *Remain* is True, the text will remain in the clipboard after the application exits. If *Remain* is False, the text will not remain in the clipboard after the application exits.

For example, the following statement stores the contents of a text box named txtInput in the clipboard. The text will remain after the application terminates.

```
Clipboard.SetDataObject(txtInput.Text, True)
```

The *GetDataObject method* returns the contents of the clipboard. It can be used to retrieve text, graphics, or an object. Because it can be used to retrieve different types of data, the syntax is somewhat complex. The general format for retrieving text is:

```
ClipBoard.GetDataObject().GetData(dataFormats.Text)
```

This form of the method returns the text that is currently stored in the clipboard. If there is no text in the clipboard, it returns Nothing. For example, the following statement copies the text in the clipboard to the lblMessage label.

```
Dim str As String
str = Clipboard.GetDataObject().GetData(DataFormats.Text)
If str Is Nothing Then
    MessageBox.Show("str is nothing")
Else
    lblMessage.Text = str
End If
```

In Tutorial 13-4 you build an application that uses the clipboard to copy, cut, and paste text with other Windows applications.

TUTORIAL 13-4:

Completing the Clipboard Demo application

Step 1: Start Visual Basic .NET and open the Clipboard Demo project, which is located in the \Chap13\Clip board Demo folder on the student disk. The application's form is shown in Figure 13-12. The text box is named txtInput. The menu system has the following menu items:

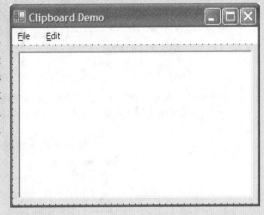

File
  Exit
Edit
  Copy
  Cut
  Paste
  Select All

Figure 13-12   Clipboard Demo form

The mnuFileExit_Click event procedure is already written for you.

Step 2: Create the mnuEditCopy_Click and mnuEditCut_Click event procedures. The code is as follows.

```
Private Sub mnuEditCopy_Click(ByVal sender As System.Object, _
      ByVal e As System.EventArgs) Handles mnuEditCopy.Click
   ' This procedure copies the selected
   ' text to the clipboard.
   Clipboard.SetDataObject(txtInput.SelectedText)
End Sub

Private Sub mnuEditCut_Click(ByVal sender As System.Object, _
      ByVal e As System.EventArgs) Handles mnuEditCut.Click
   ' This procedure cuts the selected
   ' text and copies it to the clipboard.
   Clipboard.SetDataObject(txtInput.SelectedText)
   ' Erase the selected text.
   txtInput.SelectedText = ""
End Sub
```

Both event procedures are similar. First, the selected text in the txtInput text box is passed as an argument to the Clipboard.SetDataObject method. This copies the selected text to the clipboard. The mnuEditCut_Click procedure then erases the selected text from txtInput.

Step 3: Create the mnuEditPaste_Click event procedure, which pastes the text in the clipboard into txtInput. The code is as follows.

```
Private Sub mnuEditPaste_Click(ByVal sender As System.Object, _
      ByVal e As System.EventArgs) Handles mnuEditPaste.Click
```

```
        ' This procedure pastes the text in the
        ' clipboard to the text box.
        Dim str As String

        str = Clipboard.GetDataObject().GetData(DataFormats.Text)
        If Not (str Is Nothing) Then
            txtInput.SelectedText = str
        End If
    End Sub
```

Step 4: Create the `mnuEditSelectAll_Click` event procedure, which selects all the text in `txtInput`. The code is as follows.

```
    Private Sub mnuEditSelectAll_Click(ByVal sender As System.Object, _
            ByVal e As System.EventArgs) _
            Handles mnuEditSelectAll.Click
        ' This procedure selects all the text
        ' in the text box.
        txtInput.SelectionStart = 0
        txtInput.SelectionLength = txtInput.Text.Length
    End Sub
```

Step 5: Most Windows applications disable the Paste command when the clipboard contains no text, and disable the Copy and Cut commands when no text is selected. Create the following `mnuEdit_Popup` event procedure, which performs this action when the Edit menu is clicked. (To create the code template for the procedure, select mnuEdit in the object box, then select Popup in the method name box.)

```
    Private Sub mnuEdit_Popup(ByVal sender As Object, _
            ByVal e As System.EventArgs) Handles mnuEdit.Popup
        ' This procedure enables or disables the
        ' Copy, Cut, and Paste commands.
        ' If there is no text in the clipboard
        ' disable the Paste command.
        If Clipboard.GetDataObject().GetData(DataFormats.Text) _
            Is Nothing Then
            mnuEditPaste.Enabled = False
        Else
            mnuEditPaste.Enabled = True
        End If
        ' If no text is selected disable the
        ' Copy and Cut commands.
        If txtInput.SelectionLength = 0 Then
            mnuEditCopy.Enabled = False
            mnuEditCut.Enabled = False
        Else
            mnuEditCopy.Enabled = True
            mnuEditCut.Enabled = True
        End If
    End Sub
```

Step 6: Save the project and run the application. Click the Edit menu. Notice that the Copy and Cut commands are disabled. If there is no previously copied text in the clipboard, the Paste command will also be disabled.

Step 7: While the application is running, execute Notepad. (If you cannot find Notepad on your Programs menu, click Start, then click Run. In the Run dialog box, type Notepad.exe in the text box and click OK.)

Step 8: Enter some text into the Clipboard Demo application's `txtInput` text box.

Step 9: Click the Select All menu item on the Edit menu. Notice that all the text in the `txtInput` text box is selected.

Step 10: Click the Copy command on the Edit menu. In Notepad, select Paste from the Edit menu. The text that you copied from the `txtInput` text box is pasted into Notepad.

Step 11: Delete the text in Notepad and type some different text. Copy the text from Notepad and paste it into the Clipboard Demo application.

Step 12: In the Clipboard Demo application, highlight the text in the `txtInput` text box and click the Cut command on the Edit menu. The text should be erased from the `txtInput` text box.

Step 13: In Notepad click Paste on the Edit menu. The text you cut from the Clipboard Demo application should be pasted into Notepad.

Step 14: End the application and close Notepad.

✓ Checkpoint

13.12 What does the `Clipboard.SetDataObject` method do?

13.13 What does the `Clipboard.GetDataObject` method do?

13.14 What statement would you write to store the string "Hello World" in the clipboard?

13.15 What statement would you write to paste the contents of the clipboard into the `txtEditor` text box?

SUMMARY

Inheritance allows you to create new classes that inherit, or derive, characteristics of existing classes. In an inheritance relationship, there is a base class and a derived class. The base class is the generalized class that other classes may be based on. The derived class is based on the base class, and inherits characteristics from it. You can think of the base class as the parent and the derived class as the child.

Sometimes a property procedure or method in a base class does not work adequately for a derived class. When this happens, you can override the base class property procedure or method by writing one with the same name in the derived class.

You must use the `Overridable` key word in the declaration of a method or property procedure in a base class that is to be overridden. You must use the `Overrides` key word in the declaration of a method or property procedure in a derived class that overrides another one in the base class.

Every class that you create in Visual Basic .NET is automatically derived from a built-in class named `Object`. The `Object` class has a method named `ToString` which returns a fully-qualified class name. You can override this method so it returns a string representation of the data stored in a class.

It is possible for both a base class and a derived class to have constructors. When an instance of the derived class is created, the base class constructor is called first, and then the derived class constructor is called.

Protected base class members are like private members, except they may be accessed by methods and property procedures in derived classes. To all other code, however, protected class members are just like private class members.

Visual Basic .NET allows you to create your own custom controls. A custom control is a control that is designed by a programmer for a specific purpose.

The `DateAdd` function adds an interval of time to a Date variable.

The Date variable's `ToLongTimeString` method returns the variable's time value in long format.

When you compile a custom control, Visual Basic .NET creates a file with the extension .DLL in the project's bin folder. Once you have created a custom control you must add a reference to its .DLL file to any projects that should be able to use the control. When you add a reference to a custom control's .DLL file to a project, an icon for the custom control appears in the Visual Basic .NET toolbox when you open that project.

Visual Basic .NET's `Clipboard` methods allow you to share data with other Windows applications. The `Clipboard.SetDataObject` method is used for storing text in the clipboard, and the `ClipBoard.GetDataObject` method is used for retrieving data from the clipboard.

KEY TERMS

Base class	`Object` class
`Clipboard` methods	`Overridable` key word
Custom control	Override
`DateAdd` function	`Overrides` key word
Derived class	`Protected` access specifier
`GetDataObject` method	`SetDataObject` method
`GetDataObject` method	`SetDataObject` method
Inheritance	`ToLongTimeString` method
`MyBase` key word	

Review Questions

Fill-in-the-blank

1. _____ is an object-oriented programming feature that allows you to create new classes that inherit, or derive, characteristics of existing classes.

2. A(n) _____ class is a generalized class that other classes may be based on.

3. A(n) _____ class is based on another class, and inherits characteristics from it.

4. You can _____ a base class property procedure or method by writing one with the same name in a derived class.

5. _____ base class members are like private members, except they may be accessed by methods and property procedures in derived classes.

6. A _____ control is a control that is designed by a programmer for a specific purpose.

7. Visual Basic .NET's _____ methods allow you to share data with other Windows applications.

Multiple Choice

1. In an inheritance relationship, this class is usually a generalized class that other, more specialized, classes are derived from.
   a. Derived
   b. Base
   c. Protected
   d. Public

2. These base class members are not inherited by a derived class.
   a. Private
   b. Public
   c. Protected
   d. ReadOnly

3. This key word indicates that the procedure may be overridden in a derived class.
   a. Private
   b. Overrides
   c. Public
   d. Overridable

4. This key word indicates that a procedure in a derived class overrides a procedure in the base class.
   a. Private
   b. Overrides
   c. Public
   d. Overridable

5. When used in a derived class, this key word refers to the base class.
   a. BaseClass
   b. Base
   c. MyBase
   d. Parent

6. Every class that you create in Visual Basic .NET is automatically derived from a built-in class with this name,
   a. Object
   b. SuperClass
   c. Parent
   d. System

7. Class members declared with this access specifier are like private members, except they may be accessed by methods and property procedures in derived classes.
    a. `Special`
    b. `Secret`
    c. `Public`
    d. `Protected`

8. A custom control is a class that is derived from
    a. `System.UserControl`
    b. `System.Windows.Forms.UserControl`
    c. `System.Windows.CustomControl`
    d. `System.Forms.Control`

9. This function adds an interval of time to a Date variable.
    a. `AddDate`
    b. `AddInterval`
    c. `DateAdd`
    d. `AddTime`

10. Date variables have this method which returns the variable's time value in long format.
    a. `ToLongTimeString`
    b. `LongTime`
    c. `ToLongFormat`
    d. `FormatLong`

11. When starting a custom control, you select this type of project.
    a. Custom Control
    b. Empty Control
    c. Windows Control Library
    d. Virtual Control

12. When you compile a custom control, Visual Basic .NET creates a file with this extension.
    a. .CTL
    b. .VCC
    c. .VB
    d. .DLL

13. Which `Clipboard` method stores text in the clipboard?
    a. `StoreClip`
    b. `SetDataObject`
    c. `StoreText`
    d. `SetText`

14. Which method retrieves text from the clipboard?
    a. `GetClip`
    b. `GetText`
    c. `ReadText`
    d. `GetDataObject`

True or False

Indicate whether each of the following statements is true or false.

1. T F: A private property or method cannot be overridden.
2. T F: The `ToString` method cannot be overridden.
3. T F: Protected base class members cannot be accessed by derived classes.
4. T F: Once you compile a custom control, its icon is automatically added to the toolbox for all projects you create.
5. T F: A custom control form has no border or title bar.
6. T F: You can store data in the clipboard, but it always is erased when the application ends.

Short Answer

1. Class A has the following members:

   Private member variable `x`
   Public member variable `y`
   Public property `Data`
   Protected method `UpdateData`

   Class B is derived from class A. Which of class A's members are inherited by class B?

2. When a property procedure or method in a base class does not work adequately for a derived class, what can you do?

3. Class B is derived from class A. Class A's `UpdateData` method has been overridden in class B. How can the `UpdateData` method in class B call the `UpdateData` method in class A?

4. How do you add a custom control to a project?

What Do You Think?

1. An application at an animal hospital uses two classes: `Mammal` and `Dog`. Which do you think is the base class and which is the derived class? Why?

2. Why does it make sense that you cannot use the `Overridable` key word in a private base class member declaration?

3. The form on which you draw a custom control appears different from a regular project's form. What is the difference? Why does a custom control's form appear this way?

4. Why should you give careful consideration to the project name you give a custom control project?

5. In an application that supports Copy, Cut, and Paste operations, when do you want to disable the Copy and Cut commands? When do you want to disable the Paste command?

Find the Errors

1. The following code appears in a base class:

```
Private Overridable Function GetData() As Integer
    Statements
End Sub
```

2. The following code appears in a base class:

```
Public Overridable Function GetData() As Integer
    Statements
End Sub
```

And the following code appears in a derived class:

```
' This function overrides the base class function.
Public Function GetData() As Integer
    Statements
End Sub
```

3. ```
   ' Retrieve text from the clipboard and store
      ' it in the txtInput control.
   Clipboard.SetDataObject(txtInput.Text)
   ```

Algorithm Workbench

1. Look at the ffollowing code for the Book class.

```
Public Class Book
    ' Private member variables
    Private bookTitle As String
    Private bookAuthor As String
    Private bookPublisher As String
    Private isbnNumber As String

    ' Constructor
    Public Sub New()
      bookTitle = ""
      bookAuthor = ""
      bookPublisher = ""
      isbnNumber = ""
    End Sub

    ' Title Property
    Public Property Title() As String
      Get
            Return bookTitle
      End Get
      Set(ByVal value As String)
          bookTitle = value
      End Set
    End Property

    ' Author property
    Public Property Author() As String
      Get
            Return bookAuthor
      End Get
      Set(ByVal value As String)
          bookAuthor = value
      End Set
    End Property

    ' Publisher property
      Public Property Publisher() As String
          Get
                Return bookPublisher
```
```

```
            End Get
            Set(ByVal value As String)
                bookPublisher = value
            End Set
        End Property

        ' Isbn property
        Public Property Isbn() As String
            Get
                Return isbnNumber
            End Get
            Set(ByVal value As String)
                isbnNumber = value
            End Set
        End Property
    End Class
```

Design a class named `TextBook` that is derived from the `Book` class. The `TextBook` class should have the following properties:

- Course (string). This property holds the name of the course that the textbook is used for.
- OrderQuantity (integer). This property holds the number of books to order for the course.

The OrderQuantity property cannot be negative, so provide error checking in the property procedure.

2. An application has a text box named `txtIngredients`. It also has a menu item object named `mnuEditCopy` that should copy the selected text from `txtIngredients` to the clipboard. Write the code that should appear in the `mnuEditCopy_Click` event procedure.

3. The application described in question 1 also has a menu item object named `mnuEditCut` that should cut the selected text from `txtIngredients` to the clipboard. Write the code that should appear in the `mnuEditCut_Click` event procedure.

4. The application described in question 1 also has a menu control named `mnuEditPaste` that should paste the text in the clipboard into the `txtIngredients` control. Write the `mnuEditPaste_Click` event procedure.

PROGRAMMING CHALLENGES

1. Fahrenheit to Centigrade Custom control

Create a custom control named FtoC. It should accept a temperature in Fahrenheit and convert it to centigrade. The formula to make the conversion is

$$Centigrade = (Fahrenheit - 32) * 0.5556$$

The control should appear similar to that shown in Figure 13-13. Demonstrate the control in an application.

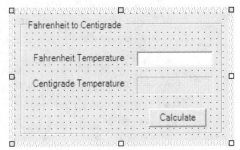

Figure 13-13   FtoC control

Design Your Own Forms

Programming Challenges 2, 3, and 4 are continuations of the same project.

2. Design a Base Class

Begin a new project named Customer Information, and design a class named `Person` with the following properties:

- LastName (string)
- FirstName (string)
- Address (string)
- City (string)
- State (string)
- Zip (string)
- Phone (string)

Implement the properties as public property procedures.

Create a form that allows you to store data in each property of a `Person` object.

3. Design a Derived `Customer` Class

Open the Customer Information project you created in Programming Challenge 2. Design a new class named `Customer`, which is derived from the `Person` class. The `Customer` class should have the following properties:

- CustomerNumber (integer)
- MailingList (Boolean)
- Comments (string)

The CustomerNumber property will be used to hold a unique number for each customer. The Mailing List property will be set to true if the customer wishes to be on a mailing list, or false if the customer does not wish to be on a mailing list. The comments property holds miscellaneous comments about the customer.

Modify the form so it allows you to store data in each property of a `Customer` object. To enter the customer comments, use a TextBox control with its Multiline and WordWrap properties set to true.

4. Design a Derived `PreferredCustomer` Class

A retail store has a preferred customer plan where customers may earn discounts on all their purchases. The amount of a customer's discount is determined by the amount of the customer's cumulative purchases in the store.

- When a preferred customer spends $500, he or she gets a 5% discount on all future purchases.
- When a preferred customer spends $1000, he or she gets a 6% discount on all future purchases.
- When a preferred customer spends $1500, he or she gets a 7% discount on all future purchases.
- When a preferred customer spends $2000 or more, he or she gets a 10% discount on all future purchases.

Open the Customer Information project that you modified in Programming Challenge 3. Design a new class named `PreferredCustomer`, which is derived from the `Customer` class. The `PreferredCustomer` class should have the following properties:

- PurchasesAmount (decimal)
- DiscountLevel (single)

Modify the application's form so it allows you to store data in each property of a `PreferredCustomer` object. Add the object to a collection, using the customer number as a key. Allow the user to lookup a preferred customer by the customer number, edit the customer data, and remove a customer from the collection.

5. Fahrenheit to Centigrade Control Modification

Modify the FtoC Custom control you created in Programming Challenge 1 so it has a Copy button. When the button is pressed, it should copy the centigrade temperature to the clipboard. Demonstrate this feature by incorporating the control in an application, converting a Fahrenheit temperature, and copying it to the clipboard, then pasting it to Notepad.

APPENDIX

User Interface Design Guidelines

When developing an application you should carefully plan the design of its user interface. A correctly designed user interface should be simple, self-explanatory, and without distracting features. This appendix covers several important areas of user interface design.

Adhere to Windows Standards

The users of your application are probably experienced with other Windows applications. They will expect your application to provide the features and exhibit the behavior that is common to all Windows applications. The guidelines provided in this appendix cover many of the Windows standards. In addition, you should carefully study applications such as Microsoft Word and Microsoft Excel to observe their forms, menus, controls, and behavior.

Provide a Menu System

Avoid using too many buttons on a form. If an application provides many commands or operations for the user to choose from, place them in a menu system. Of course, an application that uses a menu system will have some menus and menu commands that are unique to that application. There are many menu commands, however, that are common to most, if not all, applications. Windows applications that use a menu bar normally have the following standard menus.

- **File menu commands** New, Open, Close, Save, Save As, Print, and Exit
- **Edit menu commands** Copy, Cut, Paste, and Select All. If an application provides searching capabilities, such as Find or Replace commands, they are typically found on the Edit menu.
- **Help menu commands** About

Color

You may be tempted to make your forms colorful and exciting. This is generally not a good idea, however. The color combinations that you consider to be attractive may not be appealing to others. The following are some general guidelines on the use of color.

- **Use dark text on a light background.** The combination of certain colors for text and background can make the text difficult to read. Use a dark color, such as black, for text and a light color, such as gray, for the background. The contrast between dark and light colors makes the text easier to read.

- **Use predefined Windows colors.** Windows uses a predefined set of colors for forms, controls, text, etc. These colors may be customized by the user. To ensure that your application conforms to the color scheme selected by the user, you should use the predefined system colors. To find the system colors in the properties window, select a color-related property such as BackColor. Then, click the property's down-arrow button to display a pop-up list of colors. Select the System tab to display the system colors.

- **Avoid bright colors.** Bright colors are discouraged because they can distract the user and make the application appear cluttered and unprofessional. In addition, many users have color-defective vision and cannot distinguish the difference between some colors.

Text

The use of nonstandard or multiple fonts can be distracting and cause your forms to be difficult to read. Here are some suggestions on the use of fonts.

- **Use the default MS sans serif font only.** Sans serif is the standard font used by most applications. Italic and underlined fonts are less readable than plain fonts, so avoid using them.

- **Use the standard font size.** When possible, limit the font size to the default 8 point. If you must use a larger size do not use a font larger than 12 point.

- **Limit your exceptions to these rules.** If you insist on changing the font and/or font size, do so sparingly. In addition, do not use more than two fonts and two font sizes on a form.

Define a Logical Tab Order

Recall from Chapter 3 that a control's TabIndex property specifies the control's position in the tab order. The user expects the focus to shift in a logical order when he or she presses the Tab key. Typically, the control in the upper-left corner of the form will be the first in the tab order. The control that appears below it or next to it will be the next. The tab order will continue in this fashion. If the focus shifts randomly around the form, the user will become confused and frustrated.

Assign Tooltips

Recall from Chapter 5 that a tooltip is a small box that is displayed when you hold the mouse cursor over control for a few seconds. The box gives a short description of what the button does. You can define tooltips for a form by creating a ToolTip control.

Provide Keyboard Access

Many users are proficient with the keyboard and can perform operations with it faster than with the mouse. For their convenience, you should develop your applications so they support both mouse and keyboard input. Here are some suggestions.

- **Use keyboard access keys.** Assign keyboard access keys to buttons, option buttons, check boxes, and menu items.

- **Assign a default button.** If a form uses buttons, you should always make the one that is most frequently clicked the default button. You do this by selecting the button as the form's AcceptButton. Recall from Chapter 3 that when a button is selected in a form's AcceptButton property, the button's `Click` event procedure is triggered anytime the user presses the Enter key while the form is active.

◆ **Assign a cancel button.** If a form has a cancel button, you should select it in the form's CancelButton property. Recall from Chapter 3 that when a button is selected in a form's CancelButton property, the button's `Click` event procedure is triggered anytime the user presses the Escape key while the form is active.

Group Controls

If a form has several controls, try to simplify the form's layout by grouping related controls inside group boxes. This will visually break the form's surface area up into separate sections and make it more understandable for the user.

Form Location

Use the form's Location property (which has two subproperties: X and Y) to position the form in the center of the screen.

Provide a Splash Screen

If your application takes a noticeable amount of time to load, provide a splash screen. Splash screens occupy the user's attention while they are waiting and provide reassurance that your application is properly loading.

Function and Method Reference

This appendix provides a quick reference for the functions and methods that are discussed in this book. Each entry provides the general format of the function or method and lists the types of any exceptions that may be caused. (This is not a complete list of all the Visual Basic .NET functions an methods. For information on a function or method that is not listed here, consult the Visual Basic .NET help system.)

Add method—collections

Object.Add(*Item [, Key] [, Before] [,After]))*

Object is the name of an object variable that references a collection. The *Item* argument is the object, variable, or value that is to be added to the collection. *Key* is an optional string expression that is associated with the item and can be used to search for it. (*Key* must be unique for each member of a collection.) *Before* is an optional argument that can be used when you want to insert an item before an existing member. It can be either a string that identifies the existing member's key or a number specifying the existing member's index. The optional *After* argument works just like the *Before* argument, except that the new item is inserted after the existing member. If you do not specify a *Before* or *After* value, the new member will be added to the end of the collection. You cannot use both *Before* and *After*.

Exception	Condition
ArgumentException	Occurs when the key value already exists in the collection, or when both the *Before* and *After* arguments are provided.

Add method—dataset

DataSet.*Table*.Rows.Add(*ObjectVar*)

DataSet is the name of the dataset and *ObjectVar* is the name of the object variable that references the new row. After the statement executes, the row referenced by *ObjectVar* will be added to the table.

Exception	Condition
ArgumentNullException	The row object referenced by ObjectVar is Nothing.
ArgumentException	The row is already inserted into the table, or belongs to another table.
ConstraintException	This action violates a constraint.
NoNullAllowedException	A column in the row is null and the column does not allow null values.

Add method—ListBox Control

ListBox.Items.Add(Item)

ListBox is the name of the list box control. Item is the item that is to be added to the Items property.

Exception	Condition
SystemException	The system does not have enough available memory to accommodate the addition of this item.

AppendText—System.IO.File

System.IO.File.AppendText(Filename)

Filename is a string or a string variable specifying the name of the file on the disk, including optional path information. This method creates the file specified by Filename and returns the address of a StreamWriter object that may be used to write data to the file. If the file already exists when this method executes, data written to the file will be appended to the end of the existing data. If the file does not already exist, it will be created.

Exception	Condition
SecurityException	The calling application does not have the required permission.
ArgumentException	The filename or path is invalid.
ArgumentNullException	Filename is set to Nothing.
PathTooLongException	The path in Filename exceeds the maximum limit for the system.
DirectoryNotFoundException	The directory specified does not exist.
FileNotFoundException	The file specified does not exist.
NotSupportedException	Filename contains a colon (:) in the middle of the string.

Chr function

Chr(CharacterCode)

CharacterCode is an integer character code. The function returns the character that corresponds to the character code.

Exception	Condition
`ArgumentException`	The character code is less than -32768 or > 65535.

`Clear` method—**ListBox Control**

`ListBox.Items.Clear()`

Erases all the items in a list box's Items property.

`Clear` method—**TextBox Control**

`TextBox.Clear()`

Clears the Text property of a TextBox control.

`Close` method—**BinaryReader** class

`ObjectVar.Close()`

`ObjectVar` is the name of a `BinaryReader` object variable. After the method executes, the file opened with `ObjectVar` is closed.

`Close` method—**BinaryWriter** class

`ObjectVar.Close()`

`ObjectVar` is the name of a `BinaryWriter` object variable. After the method executes, the file opened with `ObjectVar` is closed.

`Close` method—**Form** class

`Me.Close()`

Closes a form. The Me key word references the current instance of the form. A form executing the `Me.Close()` statement is calling its own `Close` method.

Exception	Condition
`InvalidOperationException`	The form was closed while a handle was being created.

`Close` method—**StreamReader** class

`ObjectVar.Close()`

`ObjectVar` is the name of a `StreamReader` object variable. After the method executes, the file opened with `ObjectVar` is closed.

`Close` method—**StreamWriter** class

`ObjectVar.Close()`

`ObjectVar` is the name of a `StreamWriter` object variable. After the method executes, the file opened with `ObjectVar` is closed.

`CreateText` method—**System.IO.File**

`System.IO.File.CreateText(Filename)`

Filename is a string or a string variable specifying the name of the file. This method creates the file specified by *Filename* and returns the address of a `StreamWriter` object that may be used to write data to the file. If the file already exists when this method executes, its contents are erased.

Exception	Condition
`SecurityException`	The calling application does not have the required permission.
`ArgumentException`	The filename or path is invalid.
`ArgumentNullException`	*Filename* is set to `Nothing`.
`PathTooLongException`	The path in *Filename* exceeds the maximum limit for the system.
`DirectoryNotFoundException`	The directory specified does not exist.
`FileNotFoundException`	The file specified does not exist.
`NotSupportedException`	*Filename* contains a colon (:) in the middle of the string.

DateAdd function

`DateAdd(`*Interval, Number, DateValue*`)`

Adds a time interval to a date. *Interval* is a value that represents the interval we are adding to the date. For example, the value `DateInterval.Second` specifies that we are adding seconds to the date, and the value `DateInterval.Hour` specifies that we are adding hours to the date. *Number* is the number of intervals we are adding. *DateValue* is the Date value that we are adding to. The function returns the resulting Date value.

Exception	Condition
`ArgumentException`	The *Interval* argument is invalid.
`ArgumentOutOfRangeException`	The resulting date is before 00:00:00 on January 1 of the year 1, or later than 23:59:59 on December 31, 9999.
`InvalidCastException`	The *DateValue* argument cannot be converted to a Date data type.

EOF Function

`EOF(`*FileNumber*`)`

Tests a random-access file to determine if the end of the file has been reached. *FileNumber* is the number of the file to test. The function returns true if the end of the file has already been reached, or false otherwise.

Exception	Condition
`IOException`	*FileNumber* does not exist, or the file's mode is invalid.

FileClose method

```
FileClose(FileNumber)
```

Closes a random-access file. *FileNumber* is the file number associated with the file.

FileOpen method

```
FileOpen(FileNumber, FileName, OpenMode.Random, _
    AccessMode, OpenShare.Default, RecordLength)
```

Opens a random-access file. *FileNumber* is an integer that you use to identify the file. *FileName* is the name of the file, which can include the file's path. *AccessMode* specifies how the file will be accessed, and can be one of these values: `OpenAccess.Default`, `OpenAccess.Read`, `OpenAccess.ReadWrite`, or `OpenAccess.Write`. Note that a random-access file can be opened for both reading and writing with `OpenAccess.ReadWrite`. *RecordLength* is the size of the records that will be stored in the file.

Exception	Condition
ArgumentException	An invalid value for *AccessMode* was specified, or a write-only file was opened for input, or a read-only file was opened for output, or *RecordLength* is negative (and not -1).
IOException	*FileNumber* is < -1 or > 255 or already in use. This exception is also caused when *FileName* is invalid or the file is already opened.

FileGet method

```
FileGet(FileNumber, Item, RecordNumber)
```

Reads a record from a random-access file. *FileNumber* is the number of the file. This is the same number you specified as the *FileNumber* argument with the *FileOpen* method. *Item* is a variable that will hold the record. *RecordNumber* is the number of the record to read.

Exception	Condition
ArgumentException	*RecordNumber* is < 1 (and not -1)
IOException	*FileNumber* does not exist or file mode is invalid for this operation.

FilePut method

```
FilePut(FileNumber, Item, RecordNumber)
```

Writes a record to a random-access file. *FileNumber* is the number of the file. This is the same number you specified as the *FileNumber* argument with the *FileOpen* method. *Item* is the record to be written. *RecordNumber* is the number of the record to write.

Exception	Condition
ArgumentException	*RecordNumber* is < 1 (and not -1)

|IOException|*FileNumber* does not exist or file mode is invalid for this operation.|

Fill method—DataAdapter

DataAdapter.Fill(*DataSet*)

DataAdapter is the name of a data adapter object, and *DataSet* is the name of the dataset object to fill. After this method executes, the dataset object will contain a table of data.

DrawString method

e.Graphics.DrawString(*String*, New Font(*FontName*, _

　　　　Size, *Style*), Brushes.Black, *HPos*, *VPos*)

String is the string that is to be printed. *FontName* is a string holding the name of the font to use. Size is the size of the font, measured in points. *Style* is the font style. Typically, the valid values are FontStyle.Bold, FontStyle.Italic, FontStyle.Regular, Font Style.Strikeout, and FontStyle.Underline. *HPos* is the horizontal position of the output. This is the distance of the output, in points, from the left margin of the paper. *VPos* is the vertical position of the output. This is the distance of the output, in points, from the top margin of the paper. The Brushes.Black argument specifies that output should printed in black.

Exists method—System.IO.File

System.IO.File.Exists(*Filename*)

Filename is the name of a file, which may include the path. The method returns true if the file exists, or false if the file does not exist.

Exception	Condition
ArgumentException	The filename or path is invalid.
ArgumentNullException	*Filename* is set to Nothing.
PathTooLongException	The path in *Filename* exceeds the maximum limit for the system.
NotSupportedException	*Filename* contains a colon (:) in the middle of the string.

Format method—String class

String.Format(*FormatString*, *Arg0*, *Arg1* [, ...])

FormatString is a string that contains text and/or formatting specifications. *Arg0* and *Arg1* are arguments that are to be formatted. The [, ...] notation indicates that more arguments may follow. The method returns a string that contains the data provided by the arguments *Arg0*, *Arg1*, etc., formatted with the specifications found in *FormatString*.

Exception	Condition
ArgumentNullException	*FormatString* is set to Nothing.
FormatException	The format is invalid.

FormatCurrency function

FormatCurrency(*NumericExpression* [,*DecimalPoints* [,*IncludeLeading Digit* [,*UseParensForNegatives* [,*GroupDigits*]]]])

Formats a number as currency, such as dollars and cents. The number will also include a dollar sign or other currency symbol. The value of *NumericExpression* is the number to be formatted. *DecimalPoints* is the number of decimal points the formatted number is rounded to. (By default the number is rounded to two places.) See the FormatNumber function for descriptions of the *IncludeLeadingDigit*, *UseParensForNegatives*, and *GroupDigits* arguments.

Exception	Condition
ArgumentException	The number of digits specified by DecimalPoints is greater than 99.
InvalidCastException	*NumericExpression* is not numeric.

FormatDateTime function

FormatDateTime(*DateExpression* [, *Format*])

Formats a date expression. *DateExpression* is the date expression, such as the name of a Date variable, which is to be formatted. The second argument, *Format*, which is optional, is a value that tells Visual Basic how to format the date. It may be one of the following: DateFormat.GeneralDate, DateFormat. LongDate, DateFormat.ShortDate, DateFormat.LongTime, or DateFormat.ShortTime.

Exception	Condition
ArgumentException	The format is invalid.

FormatNumber function

FormatNumber(*NumericExpression* [,*DecimalPoints* [,*IncludeLeadingDigit* [,*UseParensForNegatives* [,*GroupDigits*]]]])

Returns a string containing a formatted number. The value of *NumericExpression* is the number to be formatted. *DecimalPoints* is the number of decimal points the formatted number is rounded to. (By default the number is rounded to two places.)

IncludeLeadingDigit can be one of the following values: TriState.True or TriState.False, or TriState.UseDefault. If TriState.True is passed, the number is formatted to include a leading zero if it is fractional. For example, the number .27 would be formatted as 0.27. If TriState.False is passed, no leading zero is used. If TriState.UseDefault is passed, or no argument is passed, the computer's regional settings are used.

UseParensForNegatives can also be one of the values TriState.True or TriState.False, or TriState.UseDefault. If TriState.True is passed as the argument, the formatted number is placed inside parentheses if it is negative. If TriState.False is passed as this argument, negative numbers are not placed inside parentheses. If

`TriState.UseDefault` is passed, or no argument is passed, the function uses the regional settings.

GroupDigits can also be one of the values `TriState.True` or `TriState.False`, or `TriState.UseDefault`. If `TriState.True` is passed, or no argument is passed, the function inserts commas into the formatted number, according to the regional settings specifications. If `TriState.False` is passed as the argument, no commas are inserted.

Exception	Condition
`InvalidCastException`	*NumericExpression* is not numeric.

`FormatPercent` function

`FormatPercent(`*NumericExpression* `[,`*DecimalPoints* `[,`*IncludeLeadingDigit* `[,`*UseParensForNegatives* `[,`*GroupDigits*`]]]])`

Formats the numeric argument *NumericExpression* as a percent. It does this by multiplying the argument by 100, then rounding it two decimal places and adding a percent sign. *Decimal Points* is the number of decimal points the formatted number is rounded to. (By default the number is rounded to two places.) See the `FormatNumber` function for descriptions of the *IncludeLeadingDigit*, *UseParensForNegatives* and *GroupDigits* arguments.

Exception	Condition
`InvalidCastException`	*NumericExpression* is not numeric.

`GetDataObject`—`Clipboard`

`ClipBoard.GetDataObject().GetData(dataFormats.Text)`

This form of the method returns the text that is currently stored in the clipboard. If there is no text in the clipboard, it returns `Nothing`.

Exception	Condition
`ExternalException`	The data could not be retrieved from the clipboard.
`ThreadStateException`	The ApartmentState property of the application is not set to ApartmentState.STA.

`GetItemChecked` method—CheckedListBox Control

CheckedListBox`.GetItemChecked(`*Index*`)`

CheckedListBox is the name of the CheckedListBox control. *Index* is the index of an item in the list. If the item is checked, the method returns true. Otherwise, it returns false.

Exception	Condition
`ArgumentException`	Index is < 0 or >= the number of items in the list box.

`IndexOf` method

StringExpression`.IndexOf(`*SearchString*`)`

StringExpression`.IndexOf(`*SearchString, Start*`)`

`StringExpression.IndexOf(SearchString, Start, Count)`

In the first format, `SearchString` is the string or character to search for within `String Expression`. The method returns the character position, or index, of the first occurrence of `SearchString` if it is found within `StringExpression`. If `SearchString` is not found, the method returns -1.

Exception	Condition
`ArgumentNullException`	`SearchString` is `Nothing`.
`ArgumentOutOfRangeException`	`Start` is negative, `Count` is negative, `Start` is less than 0 or beyond the end of `StringExpression`, or `Count` plus `Start` is less than 0 or beyond the end of `StringExpression`.

InputBox function

`InputBox(Prompt [, Title] [, Default] [, Xpos] _`

`        [, Ypos])`

Displays an input box and returns the input typed by the user. The brackets are drawn around the `Title`, `Default`, `Xpos`, and `Ypos` arguments to indicate that they are optional. The first argument, `Prompt`, is a string that is displayed to the user in the input box. Normally, this string is a prompt requesting the user to enter a value. `Title` is a string that appears in the input box's title bar. If you do not provide a value for `Title`, the name of the project appears. `Default` is a string value that is initially displayed in the input box's text box. This value serves as the default input. If you do not provide a value for `Default`, the input box's text box will initially appear empty. `Xpos` and `Ypos` specify the input box's location on the screen. `Xpos` is an integer that specifies the distance of the input box's leftmost edge from the left edge of the screen. `Ypos` is an integer that specifies the distance of the topmost edge of the input box from the top of the screen. `Xpos` and `Ypos` are both measured in twips. (A *twip* is 1/1440th of an inch.) If `Xpos` is omitted, Visual Basic centers the input box horizontally on the screen. If `Ypos` is omitted, Visual Basic places the input box near the top of the screen, approximately one third the distance down.

Insert method

`ListBox.Items.Insert(Index, Item)`

`ListBox` is the name of the list box control. `Index` is an integer argument that specifies the position where `Item` is to be placed in the Items property. `Item` is the item to add to the list.

Exception	Condition
`ArgumentOutOfRangeException`	Index is less than 0 or greater than or equal to the number of items in the list box.

Int function

`Int(Number)`

Returns the integer portion of the argument `Number`.

Exception	Condition
`ArgumentNullException`	`Number` was not specified.
`ArgumentException`	`Number` is not numeric.

IPmt function

IPmt(*InterestRate, Period, NumPeriods, -Amount*)

Returns the required interest payment for a specific period on a loan. It assumes the loan has a fixed interest rate, with fixed periodic payments. *InterestRate* is the periodic interest rate. *Period* specifies which period you wish to calculate the interest payment for. (*Period* must be at least 1, and no more than the total number of periods of the loan.) *NumPeriods* is the number of periods of the loan. *Amount* is the loan amount (expressed as a negative number).

Exception	Condition
ArgumentException	*Period* is invalid.

IsNumeric function

IsNumeric(*StringExpression*)

Returns true if *StringExpression* contains a number, or false if the string's contents cannot be recognized as a number.

Item method—System.Data.DataRow

ObjectVar.Item(*ColumnName*)

ObjectVar is an object variable that references the new row. *ColumnName* is the name of the column. This expression returns the value stored in the column, or can be used in an assignment statement to store a value in the column.

Exception	Condition
IndexOutOfRangeException	The column cannot be found.
InvalidCastException	Occurs when setting a value whose data type does not match that of the column.
DeletedRowInaccessibleException	The row has been deleted.

LCase function

LCase(*StringExpression*)

Returns the lowercase equivalent of *StringExpression*.

Left function

Left(*StringExpression, Length*)

Extracts a specified number of characters from the left side of a string. The function returns a string that is the rightmost *Length* number of characters of *StringExpression*.

Exception	Condition
ArgumentException	*Length* is less than zero.

Len function

Len(*StringExpression*)

Returns the number of characters in *StringExpression*.

Length method

StringExpression.Length

Returns the number of characters in a string.

LTrim function

LTrim(*StringExpression*)

Returns a copy of *StringExpression* with the leading spaces stripped away. The leading spaces are any spaces that pad the left side of the string.

Mid function

Mid(*StringExpression*, *Start*[, *Length*])

Extracts characters from the middle of *StringExpression* and returns them as a string. The second argument, *Start*, indicates the starting position of the string that is to be extracted. The third argument, *Length*, indicates the number of characters to extract (including the starting character). If *Length* is omitted, Mid will return all the characters from the starting position to the end of the string.

Exception	Condition
ArgumentException	*Start* is less than or equal to zero or *Length* is less than zero.

NewRow method—System.Data.DataRow

DataSet.*Table*.NewRow

ObjectVar is the object variable, *DataSet* is the name of the dataset, *Table* is the name of the table. Returns the address of a new empty row that has the same column layout as the rows in *Table*.

Now property

Now

Returns a Date value containing the current date and time.

Open method—System.IO.File

System.IO.File.Open(*Filename*, *FileMode*)

Filename is a string or a string variable specifying the path and/or name of the file to open. *FileMode* is a value specifying the mode in which the file will be opened. Valid modes are FileMode.Append, FileMode.Create, FileMode.CreateNew, FileMode.Open, FileMode.OpenOrCreate, and FileMode.Truncate. This method opens the file specified by *Filename* and returns the address of a FileStream object.

Exception	Condition
SecurityException	The calling application does not have the required permission.
ArgumentException	The filename or path is invalid.
ArgumentNullException	*Filename* is set to Nothing.
ArgumentOutOfRangeException	FileMode is invalid.
PathTooLongException	The path in *Filename* exceeds the maximum limit for the system.
DirectoryNotFoundException	The directory specified does not exist.
IOException	The file already exists.
FileNotFoundException	The file specified does not exist.
NotSupportedException	*Filename* contains a colon (:) in the middle of the string.
UnauthorizedAccessException	*Filename* specifies a directory or a read-only file, or the operation is not supported.

OpenText method—System.IO.File

```
System.IO.File.OpenText(Filename)
```

Filename is a string or a string variable specifying the path and/or name of the file to open. This method opens the file specified by *Filename* and returns the address of a StreamReader object that may be used to write data to the file. If the file does not exist, a run-time error occurs.

Exception	Condition
SecurityException	The calling application does not have the required permission.
ArgumentException	The filename or path is invalid.
ArgumentNullException	*Filename* is set to Nothing.
PathTooLongException	The path in *Filename* exceeds the maximum limit for the system.
DirectoryNotFoundException	The directory specified does not exist.
FileNotFoundException	The file specified does not exist.
NotSupportedException	*Filename* contains a colon (:) in the middle of the string.

Peek method—StreamReader class

```
ObjectVar.Peek
```

ObjectVar is an object variable referencing a StreamReader object. This method looks ahead in the file, without moving the current read position, and returns the very next character that will be read. If the current read position is at the end of the file (where there are no more characters to read), the method returns -1.

Pmt function

`Pmt(`*`InterestRate, NumPeriods, -Amount`*`)`

Returns the periodic payment amount for a loan. *`InterestRate`* is the periodic interest rate. *`NumPeriods`* is the number of periods of the loan. `Amount` is the loan amount (expressed as a negative number).

Exception	Condition
`ArgumentException`	*`Period`* is zero.

PPmt function

`PPmt(`*`InterestRate, Period, NumPeriods, -Amount`*`)`

Returns the principal payment for a specific period on a loan. It assumes the loan has a fixed interest rate, with fixed periodic payments. *`InterestRate`* is the periodic interest rate. *`Period`* specifies which period you wish to calculate the interest payment for. (*`Period`* must be at least 1, and no more than the total number of periods of the loan.) *`NumPeriods`* is the number of periods of the loan. `Amount` is the loan amount (expressed as a negative number).

Exception	Condition
`ArgumentException`	*`Period`* is invalid. It must specify a value greater than 1 and less than *`NumPeriods`*.

Print method—PrintDocument control

`PrintDocumentControl``.Print()`

When the `Print` method is executed, it triggers a `PrintPage` event. It is in the `PrintPage` event procedure that you must write code to handle the actual printing.

Exception	Condition
`InvalidPrinterException`	The printer that is named in the PrinterSettings. PrinterName property does not exist.

Randomize statement

`Randomize [`*`number`*`]`

Initializes the Visual Basic .NET random number generator. The argument *`number`* is any number or numeric expression you wish to use as a seed value.

Read method—StreamReader class

`ObjectVar``.Read`

`ObjectVar` is the name of a `StreamReader` object variable. The `Read` method reads only the next character from a file and returns the character code for that character. To convert the character code to a character, use the `Chr` function.

ReadLine method—StreamReader class

`ObjectVar``.ReadLine()`

ObjectVar is the name of a `StreamReader` object variable. The method reads a line from the file associated with *ObjectVar* and returns the data that was read as a string.

Exception	Condition
OutOfMemoryException	There is not enough memory to hold the string that will be read.
IOException	An I/O error has occurred.

ReadToEnd method—**StreamReader** class

ObjectVar.ReadToEnd

ObjectVar is the name of a `StreamReader` object variable. The `ReadToEnd` method reads and returns the entire contents of a file, beginning at the current read position.

Exception	Condition
OutOfMemoryException	There is not enough memory to hold the string that will be read.
IOException	An I/O error has occurred.

Remove method—collections

Object.Remove(*Expression)*

Object is the name of a collection. *Expression* can be either a numeric or string expression. If it is a numeric expression, it is used as an index value and the member at the specified index location is removed. If *Expression* is a string, the member with the key value that matches the string is removed.

Exception	Condition
ArgumentException	*Expression* is not specified, or specifies an index that is invalid.
IndexOutOfRangeException	*Expression* specifies an item that is not in the collection.

Remove method—**ListBox** control

ListBox.Items.Remove(*Item*)

ListBox is the name of the list box control. *Item* is the item you wish to remove.

RemoveAt method—**CurrencyManager**

ObjectVar.RemoveAt(*Index*)

Removes a row in the dataset. *ObjectVar* is an object variable that references the `CurrencyManager` object, and *Index* is the position of the row that is to be removed.

Exception	Condition
IndexOutOfRangeException	*Index* specifies a row that does not exist.

RemoveAt method—ListBox control

`ListBox.Items.RemoveAt(Index)`

`ListBox` is the name of the list box control. `Index` is the index of the item to be removed.

Exception	Condition
`ArgumentOutOfRangeException`	`Index` is less than zero or greater than or equal to the number of items in the list box.

Right function

`Right(StringExpression, Length)`

Extracts a specified number of characters from the right side of a string. The function returns a string that is the rightmost `Length` number of characters of `StringExpression`.

Exception	Condition
`ArgumentException`	`Length` is less than zero.

Rnd statement

`Rnd [(number)]`

Returns a single precision random number between 0.0 and 1.0. The argument, `Number` is shown in brackets, indicating that it is optional. If `Number` is less than 0, it is used as a seed to generate a new sequence of numbers. If `Number` is 0, `Rnd` returns the last random number generated. If `Number` is greater than 0, `Rnd` returns the next random number in the sequence. If `Number` is omitted, `Rnd` returns the next random number in the sequence.

RTrim function

`RTrim(StringExpression)`

Returns a copy of `StringExpression` with the trailing spaces stripped away. The trailing spaces are any spaces that pad the right side of the string.

SetDataObject—Clipboard

`Clipboard.SetDataObject(Text)`

`Clipboard.SetDataObject(Text, Remain)`

The argument, `Text`, is the text you wish to store in the clipboard. In the second format, the argument `Remain` is a Boolean value. If `Remain` is `True`, the test will remain in the clipboard after the application exits. If `Remain` is `False`, the text will not remain in the clipboard after the application exits.

Exception	Condition
`ExternalException`	The data could not be retrieved from the clipboard.
`ThreadStateException`	The ApartmentState property of the application is not set to ApartmentState.STA .
`ArgumentNullException`	The value of `Text` is `Nothing`.

Show method—**Form** class

ObjectVariable.Show()

ObjectVariable is the name of an object variable that references an instance of a form. This method displays the form in modeless style.

Show method—**MessageBox** Class

MessageBox.Show(*Message*)

MessageBox.Show(*Message, Caption*)

MessageBox.Show(*Message, Caption, Buttons*)

MessageBox.Show(*Message, Caption, Buttons, Icon*)

MessageBox.Show(*Message, Caption, Buttons, Icon, _*

DefaultButton)

When MessageBox.Show is executed, a message box (which is a Windows dialog box) appears on the screen. In the first format shown, *Message* is a string that is displayed in the message box. In the second format, *Caption* is a string to be displayed in the message box's title bar. In the third format, *Buttons* is a value that specifies which buttons to display in the message box. In the fourth format, *Icon* is a value that specifies an icon to display in the message box. In the fifth format, the *DefaultButton* argument is a value that specifies which button to select as the default button. The default button is the button that is clicked when the user presses the Enter key.

Exception	Condition
InvalidEnumArgumentException	The *Buttons*, *Icon*, or *DefaultButton* value is invalid.
InvalidOperationException	The call was made from a process that was not running in user interactive mode.

ShowDialog method—**Form** class

ObjectVariable.ShowDialog()

ObjectVariable is the name of an object variable that references an instance of a form. This method displays the form in modal style.

Sort method—**Array** class

Array.Sort(*ArrayName*)

Sorts the contents of an array in ascending order. *ArrayName* is the name of the array you wish to sort.

Exception	Condition
ArgumentNullException	The array is set to Nothing.
RankException	The array is multidimensional.
InvalidOperationException	An exception was thrown by the comparer.

Today property

Today

Returns a `Date` value containing the current date.

ToLower method

StringExpression`.ToLower`

Returns the lowercase equivalent of a string expression.

ToString method

VariableName`.ToString`

Returns a string representation of the calling variable or the object referenced by the variable.

ToUpper method

StringExpression`.ToUpper`

Returns the uppercase equivalent of a string expression.

Trim function

`Trim(`*StringExpression*`)`

Returns a copy of *StringExpression* with the leading and trailing spaces stripped away. The leading spaces are any spaces that pad the left side of the string, and the trailing spaces are any spaces that pad the right side of the string.

Trim method

StringExpression`.Trim`

Returns a copy of the string expression with all leading and trailing spaces removed.

TrimEnd method

StringExpression`.TrimEnd`

Returns a copy of the string expression with all trailing spaces removed.

TrimStart method

StringExpression`.TrimStart`

Returns a copy of the string expression with all leading spaces removed.

UCase function

`UCase(`*StringExpression*`)`

Returns the uppercase equivalent of *StringExpression*.

Update method—data adapter

DataAdapter`.Update(`*DataSet*`)`

DataAdapter is the name of a data adapter and *DataSet* is the name of a data set. After this statement executes, the changes that have been made to the data set will be saved to the data adapter's data source.

Exception	Condition
SystemException	The source table could not be found.
DBConcurrencyException	The Update method attempted an INSERT, UPDATE, or DELETE statement which affected no records.

Val function

Val(*StringExpression*)

Returns the numeric value of the *StringExpression*.

Exception	Condition
OverflowException	The value is too large.
InvalidCastException	The number is badly formed.
ArgumentException	The value passed as the argument cannot be converted to a string.

Write method—BinaryWriter class

ObjectVar.Write(*Data*)

ObjectVar is the name of a BinaryWriter object variable. *Data* is the data that is to be written to the file. *Data* can be a constant or the name of a variable.

Exception	Condition
IOException	An I/O error occurred.

Write method—StreamWriter class

ObjectVar.Write(*Data*)

ObjectVar is the name of a StreamWriter object variable. *Data* is the data that is to be written to the file. *Data* can be a constant or the name of a variable. This method can be used to write data to a file without terminating the line with a newline character.

Exception	Condition
IOException	An I/O error has occurred.
ObjectDisposedException	The StreamWriter object's buffer is full, or AutoFlush is true, and the StreamWriter object is closed.
NotSupportedException	The StreamWriter object's buffer is full, or AutoFlush is true, and the contents of the buffer cannot be written because the stream is fixed-size and the object is at the end of the stream.

WriteLine method—Debug

```
Debug.WriteLine(Output)
```

Output is a constant or a variable whose value is to be displayed in the Output window.

WriteLine method—StreamWriter class

```
ObjectVar.WriteLine(Data)
```

ObjectVar is the name of a `StreamWriter` object variable. *Data* is the data that is to be written to the file. *Data* can be a constant or the name of a variable. The method writes the data to the file and then writes a newline character immediately after the data.

Exception	Condition
`IOException`	An I/O error has occurred.

APPENDIX

Binary and Random-Access Files

Chapter 9 introduced you to sequential file operations. All of the files you worked with in that chapter were text files. That means that data is stored in the files as text. Even the numbers that you store in a text file are converted to text. When you read an item from a text file, it is read as a string. Sometimes text files are convenient to work with because you can open them in programs such as Notepad.

Visual Basic .NET also lets you create binary files. Data stored in a binary file is stored in its raw binary format. Binary files are sometimes smaller than text files, and the data that is read from them does not have to be converted before math or other operations are performed on them. Although you might be able to open a binary file in Notepad, you cannot read its contents because the file is not formatted as text.

To open a binary file, you first create a `FileStream` object, then create either a `BinaryWriter` or `BinaryReader` object. For example the following code creates a new binary file named myfile.dat. A `BinaryWriter` object can then be used to write binary data to the file.

```
Dim outputFile As System.IO.BinaryWriter
Dim fs As System.IO.FileStream
fs = System.IO.File.Open("myfile.dat", FileMode.Create)
outputFile = New System.IO.BinaryWriter(fs)
```

The `System.IO.File.Open` method in this code takes two arguments. The first argument is the path name of the file. The second argument specifies the mode in which the file will be opened. Valid modes are `FileMode.Append`, `FileMode.Create`, `FileMode.CreateNew`, `FileMode.Open`, `FileMode.OpenOrCreate`, and `FileMode.Truncate`. You can view detailed descriptions of each of these modes by searching for "FileMode Enumeration" in the Visual Basic .NET help system.

The `BinaryWriter` class has a `Write` method that writes data in binary form to a file. The following code shows how an integer is written to a file. Assume that age is an integer variable.

```
age = Val(InputBox("Enter your age."))
outputFile.Write(age)
```

To close a binary file, use the `Close` method, as shown in the following statement.

```
outputFile.Close()
```

Reading data from a binary file is also straightforward. The following code shows how a binary file may be opened, an integer value read from it, and then closed.

```
Dim inputFile As System.IO.BinaryReader
Dim fs As System.IO.FileStream
Dim age As Integer
fs = System.IO.File.Open("myfile.dat", FileMode.Open)
inputFile = New System.IO.BinaryReader(fs)
age = inputFile.ReadInt32()
inputFile.Close()
```

Table C-1 lists some of the `BinaryReader` methods for reading data from a file.

Table C-1

Some of the `BinaryReader` methods for reading data

Method	Description
PeekChar	Reads the next available item as a character from the file and does not advance the read position. Returns -1 if there are no more items in the file.
Read	Reads the next character from the file and advances the read position to the next item in the file.
ReadBoolean	Reads a Boolean value from the file and advances the read position to the next item in the file.
ReadByte	Reads a Byte value from the file and advances the read position to the next item in the file.
ReadBytes	Reads an array of Byte values from the file and advances the read position to the next item in the file.
ReadChar	Reads a Char value from the file and advances the read position to the next item in the file.
ReadChars	Reads an array of Char values from the file and advances the read position to the next item in the file.
ReadDecimal	Reads a Decimal value from the file and advances the read position to the next item in the file.
ReadDouble	Reads a Double value from the file and advances the read position to the next item in the file.
ReadInt16	Reads a Short value from the file and advances the read position to the next item in the file.
ReadInt32	Reads an Integer value from the file and advances the read position to the next item in the file.
ReadInt64	Reads a Long value from the file and advances the read position to the next item in the file.
ReadSingle	Reads a Single value from the file and advances the read position to the next item in the file.

Random-Access Files

Random-access files provide an efficient way of storing and retrieving data in such a way that records may be modified selectively. Sequential files may only be processed in sequential order, hence the name *sequential*. Processing begins at the first item and continues in sequence to the last item, unless the process is halted and the file closed. A random-access file, on the other hand, does not have to be processed in sequence. You can select any item in the file, read it, and modify it in place.

Fields, Records, and Structures

In Chapter 10 you learned that a field is an individual piece of data pertaining to a single item, and a record is a collection of related fields. For example, a set of fields might be a person's name, age, address, and phone number. Together, all those fields that pertain to one person make up a record.

Random-access files are designed to hold data organized in records. Each record in a random-access file is identified by a unique integer. The first record is record 1, the second record is record 2, and so forth. The records in a random-access file must all be the same length, for a very good reason: The physical position of any record can be found by multiplying the record number by the record length.

Structures provide a convenient way to organize information into records. For example, the following structure declaration could be used to create a record.

```
Structure PersonData
    Public Name As String
    Public Age As Integer
    Public Address As String
    Public City As String
    Public State As String
    Public PostalCode As String
    Public Telephone as String
End Structure
```

A problem arises when you store strings in a random-access file, because strings are variable-length. To declare a string with a fixed length, prefix its declaration with the following attribute:

```
<VBFixedString(Length)>
```

Length is the fixed length of the string. The following structure declaration uses this attribute, and is suitable for holding data that will be written to a random-access file:

```
Structure PersonData
    <VBFixedString(25)> Public Name As String
    Public Age As Integer
    <VBFixedString(25)> Public Address As String
    <VBFixedString(15)> Public City As String
    <VBFixedString(2)>  Public State As String
    <VBFixedString(10)> Public PostalCode As String
    <VBFixedString(15)> Public Telephone as String
End Structure
```

Opening a Random-Access File

The `FileOpen` method is used to open a random-access file. The method's general format is:

```
FileOpen(FileNumber, FileName, OpenMode.Random, _
        AccessMode, OpenShare.Default, RecordLength)
```

FileNumber is an integer that you use to identify the file. *FileName* is the name of the file, which can include the file's path. *AccessMode* specifies how the file will be accessed, and can be one of these values: `OpenAccess.Default`, `OpenAccess.Read`, `OpenAccess.ReadWrite`, or

`OpenAccess.Write`. Note that a random-access file can be opened for both reading and writing with `OpenAccess.ReadWrite`. *RecordLength* is the size of the records that will be stored in the file.

You can determine the size of a record with the `Len` function. The general format is:

```
Len(Object)
```

Object is any variable or object. The function returns the size of *Object*.

For example, look at the following code. It declares `person` as a `PersonData` structure variable. It then passes person to a Sub procedure, `GetData`, which stores data in `person`. It then opens a random access-file named CustomerData.dat. The `Len` function is used to determine the length of the `person` variable.

```
Dim person As PersonData
GetData(person)
FileOpen(1, "CustomerData.dat", OpenMode.Random, _
    OpenAccess.ReadWrite, OpenShare.Default, Len(person))
```

Writing Records to a Random-Access File

You use the `FilePut` method to write a record to a random-access file. The general format is:

```
FilePut(FileNumber, Item, RecordNumber)
```

FileNumber is the number of the file. This is the same number you specified as the *FileNumber* argument with the *FileOpen* method. *Item* is the record to be written. *RecordNumber* is the number of the record to write. For example, the following statement writes the *person* variable to file number 1 as record number 1.

```
FilePut(1, person, 1)
```

Reading Records from a Random-Access File

You use the `FileGet` method to read a record from a random-access file. The general format is:

```
FileGet(FileNumber, Item, RecordNumber)
```

FileNumber is the number of the file. This is the same number you specified as the *FileNumber* argument with the *FileOpen* method. *Item* is a variable to hold the record being read. *Record-Number* is the number of the record to read. For example, the following statement reads record number 5 and stores it in the *person* variable.

```
FileGet(1, person, 5)
```

Testing for the End of a Random-Access File

The `EOF` function determines if the end of a random-access file has been reached. The general format is:

```
EOF(FileNumber)
```

FileNumber is the number of the file to test. The function returns true if the end of the file has already been reached, or false otherwise. For example, the following loop reads each record from a file into the `person` variable, and passes person to a function named `DisplayData`.

```
recNum = 1
Do Until EOF(1)
    FileGet(1, person, recNum)
    DisplayData(person)
    recNum += 1
Loop
```

Closing a Random-Access File

Use the `FileClose` method to close a random-access file. The general format is:

```
FileClose(FileNumber)
```

FileNumber is the file number associated with the file.

APPENDIX

Converting Mathematical Expressions to Programming Statements

In mathematical expressions it is not always necessary to use an operator for multiplication. For example, the expression *2xy* is understood to mean "2 times *x* times *y*." Visual Basic .NET, however, requires an operator for any mathematical operation. Table D-1 shows some mathematical expressions that perform multiplication and the equivalent Visual Basic .NET expression.

Table D-1

Math expressions in Visual Basic .NET

Mathematical expression	Operation	Visual Basic .NET equivalent
6B	6 times B	`6 * b`
(3)(12)	3 times 12	`3 * 12`
4xy	4 times *x* times *y*	`4 * x * y`

When converting mathematical expressions to Visual Basic programming statements, you may have to insert parentheses that do not appear in the mathematical expression. For example, look at the following expression:

$$X = \frac{A + B}{C}$$

To convert this to a Visual Basic statement, `a + b` will have to be enclosed in parentheses:

```
x = (a + b) / c
```

Table D-2 shows more mathematical expressions and their Visual Basic .NET equivalents.

Table D-2

More math expressions in Visual Basic .NET

Mathematical expression	Visual Basic expression
$Y = 3\dfrac{X}{2}$	$y = x / 2 * 3$
$Z = 3BC + 4$	$z = 3 * b * c + 4$
$A = \dfrac{3X + 2}{4A - 1}$	$a = (3 * x + 2) / (4 * a - 1)$

Answers to Checkpoints

Chapter 1

1.1 The Central Processing Unit (CPU), main memory, secondary storage, input devices, and output devices.

1.2 A unique number assigned to each section of memory. Its purpose is to identify a memory location.

1.3 Program instructions and data are stored in main memory while the program is operating. Main memory is volatile, and loses its contents when power is removed from the computer. Secondary storage holds data for long periods of time—even when there is no power to the computer.

1.4 Operating Systems and Application Software.

1.5 A set of well-defined steps for performing a task or solving a problem.

1.6 To ease the task of programming. Programs may be written in a programming language and then converted to machine language.

1.7 Procedural and object-oriented.

1.8 It means that an application responds to events that occur, or actions that take place, such as the clicking of a mouse.

1.9 A property is data stored in an object. A method is an action that an object performs.

1.10 Because the default name is not descriptive. It does not indicate the purpose of the control.

1.11 A Text Box.

1.12 Text1

1.13 No. The + symbol is an illegal character for control names.

1.14 The program's purpose, information to be input, the processing to take place, and the desired output.

1.15 Planning helps the programmer create a good design, and avoid errors that may not otherwise be anticipated.

1.16 It means to imagine what the computer screen looks like when the program is running. This is the first step in creating an application's forms, or windows.

1.17 A diagram that graphically depicts a program's flow.

1.18 A cross between human language and a programming language.

1.19   Run time errors are the type of mistakes that do not prevent an application from executing, but cause it to produce incorrect results. For example, a mistake in a mathematical formula is a common type of run time error.

1.20   To find and correct run-time errors.

1.21   Testing is a part of each design step. Flowcharts should be tested, code should be desk-checked, and the application should be run with test data to verify it produces the correct output.

1.22   The Solution Explorer window shows a file-oriented view of a project. It allows you to quickly navigate among the files in your project.

1.23   The Properties window shows, and allows you to change, most of the currently selected object's properties, and those properties' values.

1.24   The Dynamic Help window displays a list of help topics that changes as you perform operations. The topics that are displayed are relevant to the operation you are currently performing.

1.25   The standard toolbar contains buttons that execute frequently used commands. The layout toolbar contains buttons for formatting the layout of controls on a form.

1.26   Design time is the mode in which you build an application. Run time is the mode in which you are running an application. Break time is the mode in which an application is suspended for debugging purposes.

1.27   The standard toolbar contains buttons that execute frequently used menu commands. The toolbox, however, provides buttons for placing controls.

1.28   A Tooltip is a small box that is displayed when you hold the mouse cursor over a button on the Toolbar or in the Toolbox for a few seconds. The box gives a short description of what the button does.

Chapter 2

2.1   Text

2.2   With the form selected, double-click the Label control tool in the toolbox.

2.3   To resize the control's bounding box.

2.4   TopLeft, TopCenter, TopRight, MiddleLeft, MiddleCenter, MiddleRight, BottomLeft, BottomCenter, and BottomRight.

2.5   Select it and press the Delete key.

2.6   When you resize the PictureBox, the image size adjusts to fit within it.

2.7   The title bar shows [run], which indicates that Visual Basic .NET is in run time.

2.8   1) On the Visual Studio .NET Start Page click the name of the project.

2) On the Visual Studio .NET Start Page click the Open Project button, then use the Open Project dialog box to locate the project's solution or project file. Select the file and click Open.

3) Click File on the menu bar, then click New, then click Project. Use the Open Project dialog box to locate the project's solution or project file. Select the file and click Open.

2.9   Alphabetic and categorized. You select alphabetic mode by clicking the alphabetic button. You select categorized mode by clicking the categorized button. When the alphabetic button is clicked, the properties are displayed in alphabetical order. When the categorized button is clicked, related properties are listed in groups.

2.10   Text is listed under the Appearance category. Name is listed under the Design category.

2.11   By selecting it from the list of objects displayed in the object box's drop-down list.

2.12   If a control will be accessed in code, or will have code associated with it (such as an event procedure), you will assign it a name. Otherwise, keep the control's default name.

2.13   A property that may only have one of two values: True or False.

2.14   `btnShowName_Click()`

2.15   Nothing. The line is a remark, and is ignored.

2.16   A remark is a note of explanation that documents something in a program.

2.17   `lblSecretAnswer.Visible = False`

2.18   It causes an application to terminate.

2.19   A code region is a section of code that may be collapsed, or hidden from view.

2.20   You expand a code region by clicking the plus sign that appears in the margin next to the name of the region. You collapse an expanded code region by clicking the minus sign that appears next to the name of the region.

2.21   The background color of the Label's text changes.

2.22   The color of the Label's text changes.

2.23   FormBorderStyle

2.24   You cannot move them until they are unlocked.

2.25   Right-click over an empty spot on the Form, then select Lock Controls from the pop-up menu.

2.26   Just like you locked them: Right-click over an empty spot on the Form, then select Lock Controls from the pop-up menu.

2.27   `lblTemperature.Caption = "48 degrees."`

2.28   When AutoSize is set to false, the bounding box of its Label control remains, at run time, the size that it was given at design time. If the text that is copied into the Label's Text property is too large to fit in the control's bounding box, then the text is only partially displayed. When a label's AutoSize property is set to true, the label's bounding box will automatically resize to accommodate the text stored in the label's Text property.

2.29   The BorderStyle property may have one of the following values: None, FixedSingle, and Fixed 3D. When set to None, the label will have no border. (This is the default value.) When set to FixedSingle, the label will have outlined with a border that is a single pixel wide. When set to Fixed3D the label will have recessed 3D appearance.

2.30   `lblName.TextAlign = ContentAlignment.TopRight`
       `lblName.TextAlign = ContentAlignment.BottomLeft`
       `lblName.TextAlign = ContentAlignment.TopCenter`

2.31   Click Help on the menu bar, then click Dynamic Help.

2.32   Click the index button on the Dynamic Help window, or click Help on the menu bar, then click Index.

2.33   By selecting Visual Basic and Related in the Filter by drop-down list.

2.34   A help screen that is displayed for the currently selected item when the F1 key is pressed.

2.35   Compile Errors and Run Time Errors.

Chapter 3

3.1   Text

3.2   `lblMessage.Caption = txtInput.Text`

3.3   Hello Jonathon, how are you?

3.4   The line continuation character is actually two characters: a space followed by an underscore character. It allows you to break a long programming statement into two or more lines.

3.5   The control is accepting keyboard and/or mouse input from the user.

3.6   `txtLastName.SetFocus`

3.7   The order in which controls receive the focus when the user presses the Tab key.

3.8   The TabIndex property, which contains a numeric value, determines the position of a control in the tab order. The control that has the lowest TabIndex value (usually 0) on a form is the first in the tab order. The control with the next highest TabIndex (usually 1) will be the next in the tab order. This sequence continues.

3.9   In the order that controls are created.

3.10   That control is skipped in the tab order.

3.11   The & character has two effects. First, it assigns an access key to the button. In this case, the access key is Alt+M, because the & is in front of the letter M. Second, it causes the letter M to appear underlined on the button.

3.12   An accept button is a form's button that is clicked when the user presses the Enter key. A cancel button is a form's button that is clicked when the user presses the Escape key. You select accept and cancel buttons with the form's AcceptButton and CancelButton properties.

3.13   A variable is a storage location in the computer's memory, used for holding information while the program is running.

3.14   A variable declaration is a statement that causes Visual Basic to create a variable in memory.

3.15   Only c, `interestRate` is written in camel casing.

3.16
`count`	Legal.
`rate*Pay`	Illegal. Cannot use the * character.
`deposit.amount`	Illegal. Cannot use a period.
`down_payment`	Legal. However, the name does not follow the standard convention of using a prefix to indicate its data type.

3.17   A variable declared inside a procedure.

3.18   The scope of a variable is the part of the program where the variable is visible, and may be accessed by programming statements. The lifetime of a variable is the time during which the variable exists in memory.

3.19   Integer: 0

Single: 0.0

Boolean: False

Byte: 0

Date: 12:00:00 AM January 1, 1

3.20   27

13

13

3.21   When a statement attempts to store a non-numeric value in a numeric variable or property.

3.22   It converts a string representation of a number to a numeric value, and does not generate a run-time error if the string cannot be converted to a number.

3.23   48.5

0

99

0

3.24   #02/20/2003 5:35:00 PM#

3.25   myDate = Now

3.26   3

3.27   21

2

17

18

3.28   29

3.29   It will execute.

3.30   A named constant is like a variable whose content is "read-only," and cannot be changed while the program is running.

3.31   Two decimal places.

3.32   Both the `FormatNumber` and `FormatCurrecny` functions allow you to format a number, rounded to a specified number of decimal places. Both format a number with comma separators. The `FormatCurrency` function, however, displays a currency symbol, such as a dollar sign.

3.33   "7.00%"

3.34   `DateFormat.LongDate`

3.35   You can make a form appear more organized by grouping related controls inside group boxes.

3.36   Controls on the form can only be positioned and sized along the form's grid dots.

3.37   Select the controls, click Format on the menu bar, click Align, then click Rights.

3.38   Select the controls, click Format on the menu bar, click Make Same Size, then click Both.

3.39   When the form is loaded into memory.

3.40   A compile error, or syntax error, will prevent an application from running. Examples are misspelled key words, incorrect use of operators or punctuation, etc. Compiler errors are often reported as soon as you type them A logic error is a programming mistake that does not prevent an application from running but causes the application to produce incorrect results. Examples are incorrect math statements, copying the wrong value to a variable, etc.

3.41   A breakpoint is a line of code that causes a running application to pause execution, and enter break mode. While the application is paused, you may perform debugging operations, such as examining variable contents and the values stored in control properties.

3.42   Single-stepping is a useful debugging technique for locating logic errors. In single-stepping, you execute an application's code one line at-a-time. After each line executes, you can examine variable and property contents. This process allows you to identify the line or lines of code causing the error.

Chapter 4

4.1   T, T, F, T, T, F, T

4.2   If the Boolean variable `isInvalid` is set to `True`.

4.3   Yes, they both perform the same operation.

4.4   The following statement is preferred, because the conditionally executed statement is indented.

```
If sales > 10000 Then
    commissionRate = 0.15
End If
```

The indention makes the statement easier to read.

4.5   A) 99

      B) 0

      C) 99

4.6   three times

4.7   One time by the `If...Then...ElseIf` statement and four times by the set of `If...Then` statements.

4.8

Logical Expression	Result
`True And False`	`False`
`True And True`	`True`
`False And True`	`False`
`False And False`	`False`
`True Or False`	`True`
`True Or True`	`True`
`False Or True`	`True`
`False Or False`	`False`
`True Xor False`	`True`
`True Xor True`	`False`
`Not True`	`False`
`Not False`	`True`

4.9   A) False

      B) False

      C) True

4.10   f, g, a, b, I, h, e, c, d

4.11   c, a, d, b

4.12   `DialogResult.Abort`

4.13   `MessageBox.Show("William" & ControlChars.CrLf &_`
                `"Joseph" & ControlChars.CrLf & _`
                `"Smith")`

4.14
```
Select Case quantity
    Case 0 To 9
        discount = 0.1
    Case 10 To 19
        discount = 0.2
    Case 20 To 29
        discount = 0.3
    Case Is >= 30
        discount = 0.4
    Else
        MsgBox "Invalid Data"
End Select
```

4.15   By examining its Checked property. If the property is set to true, the radio button is selected. If the property is set to false, the radio button is not selected.

4.16   Only one.

4.17   By examining its Checked property. If the property is set to true, the check box is selected. If the property is set to false, the check box is not selected.

4.18   Any or all of them.

4.19   By pressing the spacebar.

4.20   Local variables are visible only to statements in the same procedure as the variable's declaration. Class-level variables are visible to statements in all the procedures in the form that contains the variable's declaration.

4.21   The `Dim` statement for a class-level variable must be outside any procedure, and between the `Public Class` statement that appears at the top of the file and the `End Class` statement that appears at the bottom. Normally you place the `Dim` statement for a class-level variable near the top of a form's code, prior to the first procedure.

Chapter 5

5.1
```
input = InputBox("Enter a number", "Please Respond", 500)
```

5.2
```
input = InputBox("Enter a number", "Please Respond", 500, 100, 300)
```

5.3   0

5.4   Items.Count

5.5   11

5.6   SelectedItem

5.7   SelectedIndex

5.8
```
selectedName = lstNames.Items(1)
```

5.9   The loop is an infinite loop because it doesn't change the value of `count`.

5.10   10 times.

5.11   one time.

5.12   x is the counter and y is the accumulator.

5.13
```
Dim count As Integer = 5
Do While count >= 1
     lstOutput.Items.Add(count)
     count -= 1
Loop
```

5.14
```
Dim total As Integer = 0
Dim number As Integer

Do While total <= 300
     number = Val(InputBox("Enter a number"))
     total += number
Loop
```

5.15   Post-test

5.16   The loop iterates five times. The message box will display 10.

5.17
```
Dim count As Integer

For count = 0 To 100 Step 5
    lstOutput.Items.Add(count)
Next count
```

5.18
```
Dim count As Integer
Dim total As Integer
Dim num As Integer

total = 0
For count = 0 To 7
    num = Val(InputBox("Enter a number"))
    total += num
Next count
MessageBox.Show("The total is " & total.ToString)
```

5.19   The For loop

5.20   The Do While loop

5.21   The Do Until loop

5.22   1

1

2

2

1

2

3

1

2

5.23   600 times.

5.24   0

5.25   Items.Count

5.26   SelectedIndex

5.27   A drop-down combo box allows the user to type text into its text area. A drop-down list combo box does not allow the user to type text. It restricts the user to select an item from its list.

5.28   By retrieving the value in the Text property.

5.29   A drop-down list Combo Box.

5.30   If it is set to True, the Validating event of the control that focus is shifting *from* will fire.

5.31   A control's Validating event is triggered just before the focus shifts to another control whose Causes-Validation property is set to True.

5.32   True

5.33   The SelectionStart and SelectionLength properties can be used in code to automatically select the text in a Text Box. The SelectionStart property holds the position of the first selected character in the Text Box. The SelectionLength property holds the number of characters that are selected.

5.34
```
txtSerialNumber.SelectionStart = 0
txtSerialNumber.SelectionLength = _
    txtSerialNumber.Text.Length
```

5.35
```
With txtSerialNumber
    .SelectionStart = 0
    .SelLength = .Text.Length
End With
```

Chapter 6

6.1   If you enter 10, the following will be displayed:

I saw Elba

Able was I

If you enter 5, the following will be displayed:

Able was I

I saw Elba

6.2   Static local variables retain their value between procedure calls. Regular local variables do not.

6.3
```
Sub TimesTen(ByVal value As Integer)
    Dim result As Integer

    result = value * 10
    MessageBox.Show(result.ToString)
End Sub
```

6.4
```
TimesTen(25)
```

6.5
```
Sub PrintTotal(ByVal num1 As Single, ByVal num2 As Integer, _
            ByVal num3 As Long)
    Dim total As Single

    total = num1 + num2 + num3
    MessageBox.Show(total.ToString)
End Sub
```

6.6
```
PrintTotal(weight, count, units)
```

6.7   ByVal

6.8   A) `Distance`

B) Two

C) `rate` and `time`. They are both Singles.

D) Single

6.9
```
Function Days(ByVal years As Integer, ByVal months As Integer, _
            ByVal weeks As Integer) As Integer
```

6.10   `numDays = Days(y, m, w)`

6.11   `Function LightYears(ByVal miles As Long) As Single`

6.12   `distance = LightYears(m)`

6.13   `Function TimesTwo(number As Integer) As Integer`

           `Dim result as Integer`

           `result = number * 2`

           `Return result`

      `End Function`

6.14   Step Out. Ctrl+Shift+F8

6.15   Step Into. F8

6.16   Step Over. Shift+F8

Chapter 7

7.1   Make it the startup object.

7.2   `frm`

7.3   1. Click the add new item button on the tool bar, or click Project on the menu bar, then click Add Windows Form on the Project menu. The Add New Item dialog box, shown in Figure 7-2, should appear.

      2. Under Templates select Windows Form.

      3. Change the default name that is displayed in the Name text box to the name you wish to give the new form.

      4. A new blank form will be added to your project.

7.4   1. Right-click the form's entry in the Solution Explorer window.

      2. On the pop-up menu, click Exclude From Project.

7.5   A form file contains a form's code. It has the .vb extension.

7.6   When a modal form is displayed, no other form in the application can receive the focus until the modal form is closed. Also, when a statement displays a modal form, no other statements in that procedure will execute until the modal form is closed. A modeless form, however, allows the user to switch focus to another form while it is displayed. When a statement uses a method call to display a modeless form, the statements that follow the method call will continue to execute after the modeless form is displayed.

7.7   `resultsForm.ShowDialog()`

7.8   `resultsForm.Show()`

7.9   The form's `Activated` event procedure.

7.10   `infoForm.lblCustomer.Text = "Jim Jones"`

7.11   You can substitute the `Me` key word for the name of the currently active form. This can be useful when a form needs to call one of its own methods.

7.12   `Public average as Single`

7.13   Variable declarations, procedures, and/or functions that are not associated with a particular form.

7.14   .vb

7.15   1. Click the Add New Item button (🔳) on the toolbar, or click Project on the menu bar, then click Add Module. The Add New Item dialog box should appear.

2. Under Templates select Module.

3. Change the default name that is displayed in the Name text box to the name you wish to give the new module.

7.16   A name that clearly relates it to the Customers project, such as `CustomersModule`.

7.17   `Main`

7.18   a) Menu name: the name of a drop-down menu, which appears on the form's menu bar.

b) Menu command: A command that appears on a drop-down menu, and may be selected by the user.

c) Disabled menu command: A menu item that appears dimmed and cannot be selected by the user.

d) Checked menu command: A menu item that appears on a drop-down menu with a checkmark to its left.

e) Shortcut key: A key or combination of keys that cause a menu command to execute.

f) Submenu: Another menu that appears when a command on a drop-down menu is selected.

g) Separator bar: A horizontal bar used to separate groups of commands on a menu.

7.19   Shortcut keys are different from access keys in that a command's shortcut key may be used at any time the form is active, while a command's access key may only be used while the drop-down menu containing the command is visible.

7.20   `mnu`

7.21   `mnuFileSave`, `mnuFileSaveAs`, `mnuFilePrint`, and `mnuFileExit`.

7.22   By placing an ampersand (&) before a character in the Text property.

7.23   The item initially appears as a checked menu item, meaning it appears with a check mark displayed next to it.

7.24   By setting its Enabled property to false.

7.25   By setting the menu control's Checked property to true.

7.26   The MenuItem object's `Click` event procedure.

7.27   By right-clicking a control.

7.28   By setting the control's ContextMenu property to the name of the ContextMenu control.

Chapter 8

8.1   a. `Dim empNums(99) As Integer`

b. `Dim payRate(23) As Decimal`

c. `Dim miles() As Integer = { 10, 20, 30, 40, 50 }`

d. `Dim names(11) As String`

e. `Dim divisions() As String = { "North", "South", _`
   `"East", West" }`

8.2   The upper subscript (4) cannot appear inside the parentheses when an initialization list is provided.

8.3   a. 101

b. 3

c. 1

8.4 Visual Basic .NET does not allow a statement to use a subscript that is outside the range of subscripts for an array.

8.5
```
For count = 0 To 25
    MessageBox.Show(points(count).ToString)
Next count
```

8.6
```
Dim number As Integer
For Each number In points
    MessageBox.Show(number.ToString)
Next number
```

8.7
```
10.00
25.00
32.50
50.00
```

8.8
```
total = 0      ' Initialize accumulator.
For count = 0 To 99
    total += values(count)
Next count
```

8.9
```
total = 0' Initialize accumulator.
For count = 0 To (points.Length - 1)
    total += points(count)
Next count
average = total / points.Length
```

8.10 `Array.Sort(serialNumber)`

8.11
```
1 18 18
2 4 8
3 27 81
4 52 208
5 100 500
```

8.12 `ReDim Preserve sales(49)`

8.13
```
found = False
    count = 0
    Do While Not found And count < validNumbers.Length
    If validNumbers(count) = 247 Then
        found = True
        position = count
    End If
    count += 1
Loop
' Was 100 found in the array?
```

```
    If found Then
       MessageBox.Show("The value was found at position " & _
                       position.ToString)
    Else
       MessageBox.Show("The value was not found.")
    End If
```

8.14   `Dim grades(29, 9) As Integer`

8.15   24 elements (6 rows by 4 columns)

8.16   `sales(0, 0) = 56893.12`

8.17   `MessageBox.Show(sales(5, 3).ToString)`

8.18   `Dim settings(2, 4) As Integer`

8.19   Four rows and five columns.

8.20   `Dim videos(49, 9, 24) As String`

8.21
```
    If radLifeTimeMember.Checked = True Then
       chkFreePizza.Enabled = True
       chkFreeCola.Enabled = True
    End If
```

8.22   500

8.23   By setting the form's TopMost property to true.

8.24   It allows you to "anchor" the control to one or more edges of a form. When a control is anchored to a form's edge, the distance between the control's edge and the form's edge will remain constant, even when the user resizes the form.

8.25   It allows you to dock a control. When a control is docked, it is positioned directly against one of the edges of a form. Additionally, the length or width of a docked control is changed to match the length or width of the form's edge.

8.26   To initialize the sequence of random numbers with a seed value.

8.27   The same sequence is generated each time.

8.28   The system time returned from your computer's clock.

8.29   A single precision number in the range of 0.0 to 1.0.

8.30   To return the integer portion of a number.

8.31   `randomNumber = 1 + Int(Rnd * 100)`

8.32   `randomNumber = Int(100 + Rnd * (400 - 100)`

Chapter 9

9.1   Open the file, write data to the file or read data from the file, close the file.

9.2   `StreamWriter, StreamReader`

9.3   `outputFile = System.IO.File.CreateText("Test.txt")`

9.4   `outputFile.WriteLine(x)`

9.5   `inputFile = System.IO.File.OpenText("Test.txt")`

9.6   `x = inputFile.ReadLine`

9.7   With the `System.IO.File.Exists` method

9.8   With the `Peek` method. When `Peek` returns -1 the end of the file has been reached.

9.9   Most Windows users are accustomed to using a dialog box to browse their disk for a file to open, or for a location to save a file.

9.10   Filter—These list boxes display a filter that specifies the type of files that are visible in the dialog box. You store a string in the Filter property that specifies the filter(s) available in the list boxes.

InitialDirectory—You store the path of the directory whose contents are to be initially displayed in the dialog box.

Title—The string stored in this property is displayed in the dialog box's title bar.

Filename—The file name selected or entered by the user is stored in this property.

9.11   `Text files (*.txt)|*.txt|Word files (*.doc)|*.doc|All files(*.*)"`

9.12   The ColorDialog control's Color property.

9.13   The FontDialog control's Font property.

9.14   By setting the FontDialog control's ShowColor property to true before calling the `ShowDialog` method.

9.15   In the FontDialog control's Color property.

9.16   By calling the control's `Print` method.

9.17
```
e.Graphics.DrawString("Joe Smith", New Font("MS sans Serif", _
              18, FontStyle.Bold), Brushes.Black, 100, 20)
```

9.18   Header, body, and footer

9.19   The characters in a proportionally spaced font do not occupy the same amount of space. All the characters in a monospaced font use the same amount of space.

9.20
```
e.Graphics.DrawString(String.Format("{0,12}{1,8}", a, b), _
              New Font("Courier", 12, FontStyle.Regular), _
              Brushes.Black, 10, 50)
```

9.21
```
e.Graphics.DrawString(String.Format("{0,-12}{1,8}", a, b), _
              New Font("Courier", 12, FontStyle.Regular), _
              Brushes.Black, 10, 50)
```

9.22
```
Structure Movie
    name As String
    director As String
    producer As String
    year As Integer
End Structure
```

9.23   `Dim film As Movie`

9.24   Assuming the variable was named `film`,
```
film.name = "Wheels of Fury"
film.director = "Arlen McGoo"
film.strProducer = "Vincent Van Dough"
film.year = 2003
```

9.25   Assuming the variable was named `film`,

```
With film
    .name = "Wheels of Fury"
    .director = "Arlen McGoo"
    .strProducer = "Vincent Van Dough"
    .year = 2002
End With
```

Chapter 10

10.1   Database tables are organized in rows and columns.

10.2   An individual piece of information pertaining to an item.

10.3   A complete set of data about a single item, consisting of one or more fields.

10.4   A row in a table is an entire record. Each column is a field.

10.5   A field, or the combination of multiple fields, that uniquely identify each row in the table.

10.6   ◆   Create a connection to a data source.
    ◆   Create a data adapter to facilitate the transfer of data from the data source to your application.
    ◆   Create a dataset to hold the data in memory while your application works with it.

10.7   As the name implies, a data source is source of data. There are many different types of data sources, such as databases, spreadsheets, e-mail repositories, text files, etc.

10.8   An object that provides the required methods for retrieving from the data source and updating the data in the data source after your application has made a change to it.

10.9   An in-memory cache of records that is separate from the data source but still allows you to work with the data.

10.10   The dataset.

10.11   A control that can automatically display data from a particular row and column of the ADO .NET dataset.

10.12   An object that manages all of the data bindings for the controls on a form.

10.13   An object that is added to a form when you connect the form to a data source. The `CurrencyManager` object gives you a simple way to navigate among the rows in a database table.

10.14   Allows you to access different types of data sources.

10.15   A connection object and a data adapter object.

10.16   It fills a dataset with data.

10.17   By examining the `CurrencyManager` object's Position property.

10.18   First, declare an object variable of the System.DataRow type. Then, use the `NewRow` method to create a row. Now you can fill the new row with data using the Item property. Last, you add the row to the table with the `Add` method.

10.19   With the data adapter's `Update` method.

10.20   With the `CurrencyManager` object's `RemoveAt` method.

Chapter 11

11.1   Structured Query Language

11.2   IBM

11.3   To search for records within a database.

11.4   A set of records returned from a `Select` statement, matching its search criteria.

11.5   It will produce a result set with all of the columns.

11.6   With the `And` and `Or` operators.

11.7   To alter the structure of a database table. For example, it can be used to add a column.

11.8   To add a new record to a database.

11.9   With the `Delete` statement.

11.10   To change the contents of one or more columns in a table. It can affect selected records or every record.

11.11   Select its SelectCommand.CommandText property, click the ellipsis button, and enter the SQL command into Query Builder.

11.12   By assigning the SQL statement, as a string, in the data adapter's control's SelectCommand.CommandText property.

11.13   Call the data adapter's `Fill` method.

11.14   Test the *DataSet.Table*.Count property. If the SQL statement returned no records, it will be set to 0.

11.15   The DataSource property

11.16   Field names

11.17   By setting the DataGrid control's ReadOnly property to true.

Chapter 12

12.1   Forms, buttons, check boxes, list boxes, and other controls.

12.2   The TextBox tool represents the class and the TextBox control on the form is an instance of the class.

12.3   By finding the physical entities in the application domain.

12.4   Attributes describe the properties that all objects of the same class have in common. They are implemented as properties.

12.5   Actions the class objects may perform, or messages to which they can respond. They are implemented as methods.

12.6   The portion that is visible to the application programmer who uses the class.

12.7   The portion of a class that is hidden from client programs

12.8   1. Click the Add New Item button (▦) on the toolbar, or click Project on the menu bar, then click Add Class. The Add New Item dialog box should appear. Make sure that Class is selected in the Templates pane.

        2. Change the default name that is displayed in the Name text box to the name you wish to give the new class file.

        3. Click the Open button.

12.9   You declare an object variable, then you create an instance of the class in memory and assign its address to the variable.

12.10   An object is removed by setting the last variable that references it to `Nothing`.

12.11   Going out of scope.

12.12   Private variables in a class module.

12.13   A procedure that behaves like a class property.

12.14   It allows a client program to retrieve the value of a property

12.15   Allows a client program to set the value of a property

12.16   A constructor is a class method that is executed automatically when an instance of a class is created. The `Finalize` method is automatically called just before an instance of a class is destroyed.

12.17   A `Try` block is a block of code that is that appears in a `Try` statement. The `Try` block is always executed, and can potentially cause an exception. A `Catch` block is a block of code that is that appears in a `Catch` statement. The `Catch` block is executed when its `Catch` statement catches an exception. A `Finally` block is a block of code that is that appears in a `Finally` statement. The `Finally` block is one or more statements that are always executed after the `Try` block has executed, and after any `Catch` blocks have executed.

12.18   It is treated as though there is no exception handling. The application will halt and an error message will be displayed.

12.19   Use the exception variable to access its Message property.

12.20   One difference between arrays and collection objects is that collection objects automatically expand as items are added to them, and shrink as items are removed from them. Another difference is that the members of collections do not have to be of the same type.

12.21   With the `Add` method.

12.22   You can then use that key value to search for the item.

12.23   With the `Item` method.

12.24   With the `Remove` method.

12.25   By setting the Minimum and Maximum properties.

12.26   The SmallChange property sets the amount by which the Value property changes when the user clicks one of the scroll arrows at either end of a scroll bar, or uses the arrow keys to control a track bar. The LargeChange property sets the amount by which the Value property changes when the user clicks the scroll bar area around the slider.

12.27   It occurs when the slider changes positions.

Chapter 13

13.1   `Insect` is the base class and `Fly` is the derived class.

13.2   All of the base class's members (variables, properties, and methods) that are not declared as private.

13.3   Overriding is replacing a base class property procedure or method with one of the the same name in the derived class.

13.4   `Overridable`

13.5   `Overrides`

13.6   The base class constructor executes first, followed by the derived class constructor.

13.7   Protected base class members are like private members, except they may be accessed by methods and property procedures in derived classes. To all other code, however, protected class members are just like private class members.

13.8   A control that is that is created by you, the programmer.

13.9   `System.Windows.Forms.UserControl`

13.10   On the Build menu click Build *ProjectName*.

13.11   Right-click in the Windows Forms section of the toolbox. Click Customize Toolbox on the pop-up menu. Select the .NET Framework Components tab. Click the Browse button. Locate and select the custom control's .dll file and then click Open.

13.12   Copies text to the clipboard.

13.13   Returns the text that is currently stored in the clipboard, or Nothing if there is nothing in the clipboard.

13.14   `Clipboard.SetDataObject("Hello World")`

13.15   `txtEditor.Text = _`
        `Clipboard.GetDataObject().GetData(DataFormats.Text)`

Glossary

About box	A dialog box that usually displays brief information about the application.
Abstract data type (ADT)	A data type created by a programmer.
Abstraction	A model that includes only the general characteristics of an object.
Accept button	A button on a form that is clicked when the user presses the Enter key.
Access key	A key that is pressed in combination with the Alt key. Access keys allow the user to access buttons and menu items using the keyboard. Also known as a mnemonic.
Accumulator	The variable used to keep the running total.
`Activated` event procedure	A form event procedure that executes each time the user switches to a form from another form or another application.
`Add` method	A collection method for adding an item to the collection.
Address	A unique number assigned to each section of memory.
ADO .NET	An extremely powerful data access component that allows Visual Basic .NET applications to work with databases.
Algorithm	A set of well-defined steps for performing a task or solving a problem.
Alphabetic button	A button on the Properties window that causes properties to be displayed in alphabetic order.
`Alter` statement	The SQL statement used to alter a database table's structure.
Anchor property	A control property that allows you to "anchor" the control to one or more edges of a form.
`And` operator	A logical operator that combines two expressions into one. Both expressions must be true for the overall expression to be true.
`AppendText` method	See `System.IO.File.AppendText` method.
Application software	Programs that make the computer useful to the user. These programs solve specific problems, or perform general operations that satisfy the needs of the user.
Argument	A value passed to a Sub procedure or function.

Array bounds checking	A run time feature of Visual Basic that does not allow a statement to use a subscript that is outside the range of subscripts for an array.
Ascending order	When items are arranged in order, from lowest to highest.
Assignment operator	The equal sign (=). In an assignment statement, it copies the value on its right into the item on its left.
Assignment statement	A programming statement that uses the assignment operator to copy a value form one object to another.
Attributes	The data contained in an object. The characteristics of an object that will be implemented as properties.
Auto list box	A list box that appears while entering programming statements in the Code window. The Auto List box displays information that may be used to complete part of the statement.
Auto window	A debugging window that displays the value and data type of the variables that appear in the current statement, the three statements before, and the three statements after the current statement.
AutoSize property	A Label control property that, when set to true, causes the label's size to display all the text in the Text property.
BackColor property	A property that establishes the background color for text.
Base class	The class that a derived class is based on.
Binary file	A file whose contents are not stored as plain text, but as binary data.
Binary number	A number that is a sequence of 1s and 0s.
`BindingContext` object	Manages all of the data bindings for the controls on the form.
Boolean	A value that can be either true or false.
BorderStyle	A Label control property that determines the type of border, if any, that will appear around the control.
Bounding box	A transparent rectangular area that defines a control's size on a form.
Breakpoint	A line of code that causes a running application to pause execution, and enter break mode. While the application is paused, you may perform debugging operations, such as examining variable contents and the values stored in control properties.
Buffer	A small "holding section" of memory that data is first written to. When the buffer is filled, all the information stored there is written to the file.
Button	A rectangular button-shaped control that performs an action when clicked with the mouse.
`ByRef`	Key word used to declare a parameter variable, causing its argument to be passed by reference.
`ByVal`	Key word used to declare a parameter variable, causing its argument to be passed by value.
`Call`	A key word that may be optionally used to call a procedure.
Cancel button	A button on a form that is clicked when the user presses the Escape key.
Caption property	The property of many controls that determines text displayed somewhere on the control.
`Catch` block	A block of code that is that appears in a `Catch` statement. The `Catch` block is executed when its `Catch` statement catches an exception.
Categorized button	A button on the Properties window that causes related properties to be displayed in groups.

CausesValidation	A Boolean property. When the focus is shifting from Control A to Control B, and Control B's CausesValidation property is set to True, Control A's Validating event will fire.
Central processing unit (CPU)	The part of the computer that fetches instructions, carries out operations commanded by the instructions, and produces some outcome.
CheckBox control	A control which may appear alone or in groups, allow the user to make yes/no, or on/off, selections
CheckChanged event	An event that occurs when the state of a radio button or check box changes.
Checked property	A property of radio buttons and check boxes. It is set to true when the control is selected and false when the control is deselected. Also a MenuItem object property that may be set to true or false. When set to true, the object becomes a checked menu item.
Chr function	An intrinsic function that accepts a character code as an argument and returns the character that corresponds to the code.
Class	A program structure that defines an abstract data type.
Class declaration	A declaration that defines a class and member variables, properties, events, and methods.
Class implementation	The portion of a class that is hidden from client programs.
Class interface	The portion of a class that is visible to the application programmer who uses the class.
Class method	A method that is a member of a class.
Class object	An instance of a class.
Client program	A program written to use a class. This term is in reference to the client-server relationship between a class and the programs that use it.
Clipboard methods	Methods that allow you to share data with other applications via the Windows clipboard.
Close method	The StreamWriter or StreamReader method used to close a file.
Closed event procedure	A form event procedure that executes after a form has closed.
Closing event procedure	A form event procedure that executes as a form is in the process of closing, but before it has closed.
Code	The programming language statements used in an application.
Code region	A section of code that may be hidden from view, or collapsed, to improve the program's readability.
Code template	Code that is automatically inserted into an event procedure. It consists of the first and last lines of the procedure. You must add the code that appears between these two lines.
Code window	A text-editing window in which you write code.
Collection	An object that is similar to an array. It is a single unit that contains several items, and dynamically expands or shrinks in size as items are added to it or removed from it.
Color dialog box	A dialog box that allows the user to select a color.
ColorDialog control	Displays a Color dialog box.
Combined assignment operators	Operators that combine an arithmetic operator with an assignment operator.
ComboBox	A control that is the combination of a ListBox and a TextBox.

Compile errors	These are syntax errors, such as misspelled key words, incorrect use of operators or punctuation, etc. Statements containing compile errors are underlined with a jagged blue line.
Component tray	A resizable region at the bottom of the Design window that holds invisible controls.
Compound operators	See combined assignment operators.
Conditionally-executed statement	A statement that is only performed when a certain condition exists.
Connection object	An object that provides the low-level functionality to interact with to a data source.
Connector symbol	A flowcharting symbol that is used to connect two flowcharts. This symbol is used when a flowchart does not fit on a single sheet of paper or must be divided into sections.
Constructor	A class method that is automatically called when an instance of the class is created.
Contents button	A button on the Dynamic Help window that displays a table of contents in which related help topics are organized into groups.
Context menu	A pop-up menu that is displayed when the user right-clicks a form or control.
Context-sensitive help	A help screen that is displayed when the F1 key is pressed, for the item that is currently selected.
Control	An object, usually used as an on-screen element in a Visual Basic application.
`ControlChars.CrLf`	A value that can be concatenated with a string to produce multiple line displays.
Count property	A collection property that holds the number of items in the collection.
Counter	A variable that is regularly incremented or decremented each time a loop iterates.
`CreateText` method	*See* `System.IO.File.CreateText` method.
`CurrencyManager` object	An object that is added to a form when you connect the form to a data source. The `CurrencyManager` object gives you a simple way to navigate among the rows in a database table.
Custom control	A control that is designed by a programmer for a specific purpose.
Data adapter	Provides the required methods for retrieving or updating data in the data source.
Data grid control	A control designed to display the information in a dataset in row / column order.
Data source	A source of data such as a database, spreadsheet, etc.
Data type	The type of information that the variable can hold.
Data-aware control	A control that can display data from a column in a dataset.
Database	A collection of tables which hold related data.
Dataset	An in-memory cache of records that is separate from the data source but still allows you to work with the data.
`DateAdd` function	Adds an interval of time to a Date variable.
Decision structure	A program structure that allows a program to have more than one path of execution.
Default name	The name automatically assigned to a control when the control is first created.
`Delete` statement	The SQL statement used to delete records from a database table.

Delimiter	An item that separates other items.
Derived class	A class that is based on another class.
Design time	The mode in which you build an application.
Design window	Contains your application's forms. This is where you design your application's user interface by creating forms and placing controls on them.
Desk-checking	A process where the programmer starts reading code at the beginning and steps through each statement. A sheet of paper is often used in this process to jot down the current contents of variables and properties that change, and sketch what the screen looks like after each output operation. By stepping through each statement, many errors can be located and corrected.
Disk drive	A disk drive stores information by magnetically encoding it onto a circular disk.
Do Until loop	A looping structure that causes one or more statements to repeat until its test expression is true.
Do While loop	A looping structure that causes one or more statements to repeat as long as an expression is true.
Dock property	A control property that allows you to dock a control against a form's edge.
Dynamic Help window	Displays a list of help topics that changes as you perform operations. The topics that are displayed are relevant to the operation you are currently performing.
Dynaset	A set of records returned from an SQL statement.
Element	An individual variable in a variable array.
Empty string	Represented by two quotation marks, with no space between them.
Enabled property	A control property that, when set to false, disables the control. This means the control cannot receive the focus, cannot respond to events generated by the user, and appears dimmed or grayed out on the form.
Encapsulation	The hiding of data and procedures inside a class.
Error trapping	The process of intercepting and responding to exceptions.
Error-handler	A section of code that gracefully responds to exceptions.
Event procedure	A procedure that an object executes in response to an event.
Event-driven	A type of program that responds to events or actions that occur while the program is running.
Exception	An event or condition that happens unexpectedly, and causes the application to halt.
Exception type	An exception type that may be used to handle any type of exception.
Execution point	While single-stepping through an application's code, the execution point is the next line of code that will execute.
Exit Do	Stops the execution of a Do While or Do Until loop.
Exit For	Stops the execution of a For...Next loop.
Field	An individual piece of information pertaining to an item.
File	A collection of data stored on a computer's disk.
Filename property	A property of the OpenFileDialog and SaveFileDialog controls that holds the name of the file selected or entered by the user with the Open and Save As dialog boxes.

`Fill` method	A data adapter method that populates a data set with data.
Filter property	A property of the OpenFileDialog and SaveFileDialog controls used to set filters that control what file types are displayed in the Open and Save As dialog boxes.
Finalizer	A class method that is automatically called just before an object is destroyed.
`Finally` block	A block of code that is that appears in a `Finally` statement. The `Finally` block is one or more statements that are always executed after the `Try` block has executed, and after any `Catch` blocks have executed.
Finding the classes	The object-oriented analysis process of discovering the classes within a problem.
Flag	A Boolean variable that signals when some condition exists in the program.
Floating	When a window, such as the Project Explorer, Properties, or Form Layout window, is not docked.
Flowchart	A diagram that graphically depicts the "flow" of a method.
Focus	The control that has the focus is the one that receives the user's keyboard input or mouse clicks
`Focus` method	A method that gives the focus to a control.
Font dialog box	A dialog box that allows the user to select a font, a font style, and a size.
Font property	A property that indicates the size and style of a text font.
FontDialog control	Displays a Font dialog box.
`For Each...Next` loop	A loop designed specifically to access values from arrays and array-like structures.
`For...Next` loop	A loop specifically designed to initialize, test, and increment a counter variable.
ForeColor Property	A property that establishes the foreground color for text.
Form	A window onto which other controls are placed.
Formatting	The way a value is printed or displayed.
FormBorderStyle property	A property that configures a form's border. This property allows or prevents the resizing, minimizing, or maximizing of a window.
`frm`	Standard prefix for forms.
Function	A specialized routine that performs a specific operation, and then returns or produces information.
Function call	A statement that causes a function to execute.
Function procedure	Also known as a function. A type of procedure that performs an operation and returns a value.
Garbage collector	A process that destroys objects when they are no longer needed.
`Get` section	A section in a property procedure that allows a client program to retrieve the value of a property.
`GetDataObject` method	A `Clipboard` method that returns the text that is currently stored in the clipboard.
Global scope	The scope of a module-level or class-level variable that is declared with the `Public` access specifier.
Global variable	A module-level or class-level variable that is declared with the `Public` access specifier.

Going out of scope	What happens when an object is created inside a procedure, and is automatically removed from memory when the procedure ends.
Graphical user interface (GUI)	The graphical interface used by modern operating systems such as Windows 9x, NT, 2000, Me, and XP.
Group box	A rectangular border with an optional title that appears in the upper-left corner. (*See* GroupBox control.)
GroupBox control	A control that appears as a rectangular border with an optional title that appears in the upper-left corner. You group other controls by drawing them inside a GroupBox control.
Hardware	A computer's physical components.
Hide method	Removes a form from the screen, but does not remove it from memory.
Horizontal scroll bar	A horizontal slider bar that, when moved with the mouse, increases or decreases a value.
HScrollBar (horizontal scroll bar) control	Allows the user to adjust a value within a range of values.
If...Then	A statement that can cause other statements to execute under certain conditions.
If...Then...Else	A statement that will execute one group of statements if a condition is true, or another group of statements if the condition is false.
If...Then...ElseIf	A statement that is like a chain of If...Then...Else statements. They perform their tests, one after the other, until one of them is found to be true.
Implicit type conversion	When you assign a value of one data type to a variable of another data type, Visual Basic .NET attempts to convert the value being assigned to the data type of the variable.
Index	*See* subscript.
Index button	A button on the Dynamic Help window that displays a searchable alphabetized index of all the help topics.
Infinite loop	A loop that never stops repeating.
Inheritance	An object-oriented programming feature that allows you to create classes that are based on other classes.
InitialDirectory property	A property of the OpenFileDialog and SaveFileDialog controls used to set the path of the directory initially displayed in the Open and Save As dialog boxes.
Initialization	Specifying a starting value for a variable.
Input Box	A Windows dialog box that displays a message to the user, and has a Text Box that the user can enter information into
Input device	A device that collects information and sends it to the computer.
Input file	A file that a program reads data from.
Input validation	The process of inspecting input values and determining whether they are valid.
Insert statement	The SQL statement used to add records to a database table.
Integer division	A division operation in which the result is always an integer. If the result has a fractional part, it is discarded. Integer division is performed with the \ operator.
Integrated development environment (IDE)	An application that provides all the tools necessary for creating, testing, and debugging programs.

Intellisense	A feature of Visual Studio .NET that provides help and some automatic code completion while you are developing an application.
Interval property	A property of the timer control. The value stored in the Interval property is the number of milliseconds that elapse between timer events.
Intrinsic function	A function that is built into Visual Basic .NET.
IPmt	A function that returns the required interest payment for a specific period on a loan.
Is operator	Used to compare two object variables to determine whether they reference the same object.
IsNumeric function	An intrinsic function that accepts a string as its argument, and returns True if the string contains a number. The function returns False if the string's contents cannot be recognized as a number.
Item method	A collection method that searches for a specific member of the collection and returns a reference to it.
Items property	The items that are displayed in a list box or combo box are stored as strings in the Items property.
Items.Add method	A list box and combo box method that adds an item to the end of the control's Item property.
Items.Count property	Holds the number of items in a list box or combo box.
Items.Insert method	A list box and combo box method that adds an item at a specific index of the control's Item property.
Items.Remove method	A list box and combo box method that removes an item from the control's Item property.
Items.RemoveAt method	A list box and combo box method that removes an item at a specific index of the control's Item property.
Iteration	One execution of a loop's conditionally-executed statements.
Key words	Programming language words that have a special meaning. Key words may only be used for their intended purpose.
Label	A control that displays text that cannot be changed or entered by the user.
LargeChange property	A scroll bar or track bar property that holds the amount by which the Value property changes when the user clicks the scroll bar or track bar area around the slider. Track bars also respond to the Page Up and Page Down keys, which cause the Value property to change by this amount.
Leading space	A space that appears at the beginning of a string.
Length	A string method that returns the number of characters in the string.
Lifetime	The time during which the variable exists in memory
Line-continuation character	A space followed by an underscore character. This is used to break a long programming statement into two or more lines.
ListBox	A control that appears as a box containing a list of items.
ListBox control	A control that displays a list of items and also allows the user to select one or more items from the list.
Load event procedure	A procedure that is executed each time a form loads into memory.
Local variable	A variable declared inside a procedure.
Locals window	A debugging window that displays the current value and the data type of all the variables in the currently running procedure.

Logic error	A programming mistake that does not prevent an application from running but causes the application to produce incorrect results.
Logical operator	An operator, such as And or Or, that connects two or more relational expressions into one, or such as Not, which reverse the logic of an expression.
Loop	One or more programming statements that repeat.
Machine language	The language of 1s and 0s, which is the only language the CPU can process.
Main	A subprocedure that may be designated as the startup object.
Main memory	Also known as random-access memory, or RAM. This is where the computer stores information while programs are running.
MainMenu control	A control that consists of MenuItem objects, and is used to construct a menu system on a form.
Maximum property	A scroll bar or track bar property that holds the control's maximum value.
Me	A key word that may be substituted for the name of the currently active form or object.
Member variable	A variable that is declared inside a class declaration. The variable is a member of the class.
Menu designer	Allows you to create a custom menu system for any form in an application.
Menu system	A collection of commands organized in one or more drop-down menus.
MenuItem object	An object that is a menu name, menu command, or separator bar on a menu system.
Message box	A dialog box that displays a message to the user.
MessageBox.Show	A method that displays a Message Box.
Methods	The actions that an object performs.
Millisecond	1/1000 of a second.
Minimum property	A scroll bar or track bar property that holds the control's minimum value.
Mnemonic	A key that you press in combination with the Alt key to quickly access a control such as a button. Also known as an access key.
mnu	Standard prefix for menu controls.
Modal form	When a modal form displayed, no other form in the application can receive the focus until the modal form is closed. In addition, no other statements in the procedure that displayed the modal form will execute until the modal form is closed.
Modeless form	A modeless form allows the user to switch focus to another form while it is displayed. The statements that follow the modeless Show method call will continue to execute after the modeless form is displayed. Visual Basic will not wait until the modeless form is closed to execute these statements.
Modularize	To break an application's code into small, manageable procedures.
Module scope	The scope of a module-level variable declared with the Dim key word or the Private access specifier.
Multiline	A TextBox control property that, when set to true, allows the text box's text to span multiple lines.

`MyBase` key word	Refers to a derived class's base class.
Name property	A property that holds the control's name. Controls are accessed and manipulated in code by their names.
Named constant	Like a variable whose content is "read-only," and cannot be changed by a programming statement while the program is running.
Nested `If` statement	An `If` statement in the conditionally executed code of another `If` statement.
Nested loop	A loop inside of another loop.
New Project dialog box	Use this dialog box to indicate the type of application you are starting.
Newline character	An invisible character that separates text by breaking it into another line when displayed on the screen.
`Not`	A logical operator that reverses the "truth" of an expression. It makes a true expression false, and a false expression true.
Object	A programming element that contains data and actions. An instance of a class.
Object box	A drop-down list of the objects in the project which appears on the Properties window.
Object Browser	A dialog box that allows you to browse the many classes and components available to your project.
`Object` class	All classes are derived from the built-in `Object` class.
Object variable	A variable that holds the memory address of an object and allows you to work with the object.
Object-oriented analysis	During object-oriented design, The process of analyzing application requirements.
Object-oriented programming	A programming technique centered on creating objects. A way of designing and coding applications that has led to using interchangeable software components.
Open dialog box	A dialog box that gives users the capability of browsing their disks for a file to open, instead of typing a long path and filename.
OpenFileDialog control	Displays an Open dialog box.
`OpenText` method	*See* `System.IO.File.OpenText` method.
Operating system	A set of programs that manages the computer's hardware devices and controls their processes.
Operations	Actions performed by class objects.
Operator	Operators perform operations on one or more operands. An operand is usually a piece of data, like a number.
Options dialog box	Accessed from the Tools menu. This dialog box allows you to set various options in the Visual Basic environment.
`Or` operator	A logical operator that combines two expressions into one. One or both expressions must be true for the overall expression to be true. It is only necessary for one to be true, and it does not matter which.
Output device	A device that formats and presents output information.
Output file	A file that a program writes data to.
Output window	A window that displays various messages while an application is being compiled. You may write your own messages to the Output window with the `Debug.WriteLine` method.
`Overridable` key word	In a procedure declaration, indicates that the procedure may be overridden in a derived class.

Override	To override a property or method in a base class means to create one of the same name in a derived class. When an object of the derived class accesses the property or procedure, it accesses the one in the derived class instead of the one in the base class.
`Overrides` key word	In a procedure declaration, indicates that the procedure overrides a procedure in the base class.
Parallel arrays	Two or more arrays that hold related data, and the related elements in each array are accessed with a common subscript.
Parameter	A special variable that receives an argument being passed into a method, Sub procedure or function.
Pascal casing	A style of mixing upper- and lowercase characters in procedure, method, and class names. The first character in the name and the first character of each subsequent word in the name are capitalized. All other characters are lowercase.
`Peek` method	A `StreamReader` method that looks ahead in the file, without moving the current read position, and returns the very next character that will be read. Returns -1 when at the end of the file.
Picture box	A control that displays a graphic image.
PictureBox control	A control that can be used to display a graphic image.
`Pmt`	A function that returns the periodic payment amount for a loan.
Position property	A `CurrencyManager` property that holds the number of the current row.
Posttest loop	A loop that evaluates its test-expression after each iteration.
`PPmt`	A function that returns the principal payment for a specific period on a loan.
Precedence	A ranking system that determines which operator works firs in an expression where two operators share an operand.
Pretest loop	A loop that evaluates its test-expression before each iteration.
Primary key	A field, or the combination of multiple fields, that uniquely identify each row in a database table.
`Print` method	A method of the PrintDocument control that triggers a `Print-Page` event.
PrintDocument control	A control that provides the ability to print.
`PrintPage` event procedure	A PrintDocument control event procedure in which you write code that sends printed output to the printer.
Procedural programming	A programming technique centered on creating procedures.
Procedure	A set of programming language statements that are executed by the computer, one after the other.
Procedure call	A statement that calls, or executes, a procedure.
Procedure declaration	The code for a procedure.
Program	A sequence of instructions stored in the computer's memory. The instructions enable the computer to solve a problem or perform a task.
Programmer-defined names	Words or names defined by the programmer.
Programming languages	Languages that use words instead of numbers to program the computer.
Project	A group of files that make up a Visual Basic application.

Project file	A file ending with the .vbproj extension that contains data describing a Visual Basic .NET project.
Prompt	A string displayed, typically on a Form or in an Input Box, requesting the user to enter a value.
Properties	The data contained in an object.
Properties window	Shows and allows you to change most of the currently selected object's properties, and those properties' values.
Property procedure	A function that is a member of a class, and behaves like a property.
`Protected` access specifier	Protected base class members are like private members, except they may be accessed by methods and property procedures in derived classes. To all other code, however, protected class members are just like private class members.
Pseudocode	Statements that are a cross between human language and a programming language. Although the computer can't understand pseudocode, programmers often find it helpful to write an algorithm in a language that's "almost" a programming language, but still very human-readable.
`Public`	A key word used in the declaration of a module level variable or procedure, which makes it available to statements outside the module.
Queries	SQL statements that retrieve and/or manipulate data in a database.
RadioButton control	A control that usually appears in groups and allows the user to select one of several possible options.
RadioChecked property	A MenuItem object property that may be set to true or false. When set to true for a checked menu item, the item appears with a radio button instead of a check mark.
Random access file	A file whose records may be accessed in any order.
Random-access memory (RAM)	*See* main memory.
`Randomize` statement	Initializes the sequence of random numbers generated by the `Rnd` function with a seed value.
`Read` method	A `StreamReader` method that reads the next character from a file.
Read position	The position of the next item to be read from a file.
`ReadLine` method	A `StreamReader` method that reads a line of data from a file.
Read-only property	A property that whose value may be read, but may not be set by a client program.
`ReadToEnd` method	A `StreamReader` method that reads and returns the entire contents of a file, beginning at the current read position.
Record	A complete set of data about a single item, consisting of one or more fields.
`ReDim` statement	Resizes a dynamic array at run time.
Reference, pass by	An argument passing technique where the Sub procedure or function has access to the original argument. Any changes made to the parameter variable are actually performed on the original argument.
Relational database	A database that is comprised of a series of tables, each containing a unique set of data including a unique primary key.
Relational expression	An expression that uses a relational operator to compare values.

Relational operator	An operator that determines if a specific relationship, such as less than or greater than, exists between two values.
Remark	A note of explanation that documents something in a program.
Remove method	A collection method that removes a member.
RemoveAt method	A CurrencyManager method that removes a specified row from the table.
Repetition structure	*See* Loop.
Report body	The part of a report that contains the report's data, and is often formatted in columns.
Report footer	An optional part of a report that contains the sum of one or more columns of data.
Report header	The part of a report that is printed first and usually contains the name of the report, the date and time the report was printed, and other general information about the data in the report.
Rnd function	Generates a single precision random number in the range of 0.0 to 1.0.
Running total	A sum of numbers that accumulates with each iteration of a loop.
Run time	The mode in which you are running and testing an application.
Run time error	Errors that occur while a program is running. Run time errors are the type of mistakes that do not prevent an application from executing, but cause it to produce incorrect results. For example, a mistake in a mathematical formula is a common type of run time error.
Save As dialog box	A dialog box that gives users the capability of browsing their disks for a location to save a file to, as well as specifying the file's name.
SaveFileDialog property	Displays a Save As dialog box.
Scope	The part of the program where the variable is visible, and may be accessed by programming statements.
Search button	A button on the Dynamic Help window that allows you to search for help topics using key words.
Secondary storage	A device, such as a disk drive, that can hold information for long periods of time.
Seed value	A value used to determine the sequence of random numbers generated by the Rnd function.
Select Case	A statement in which one of several possible actions is taken, depending on the value of an expression.
Select statement	The SQL statement used to find records within a database table.
SelectCommand. CommandText property	A data adapter property that may be used to hold and execute an SQL statement.
SelectedIndex property	Holds the index of the selected item in a list box or combo box.
SelectedItem property	Holds the currently selected item of a list box or combo box.
SelectionLength	A Text Box property used to get or set the length of the selected text in the Text Box.
SelectionStart	A Text Box property used to get or set the starting position of the selected text in the Text Box.
Selective deletion	An operation that removes records that meet specified criteria from a database table.

Selective update	An operation that change the contents of selected records in a database table.
Sequence structure	A code structure where the statements are executed in sequence, without branching off in another direction.
Sequential access file	A file whose contents must be read from its beginning to its end.
Sequential search	An algorithm that uses a loop to search for a value in an array. The algorithm examines the elements in the array, one after the other, starting with the first one.
Set section	A section in a property procedure that executes when a client program sets the property to a value.
SetDataObject method	A Clipboard method for storing data in the clipboard.
Shortcut key	A key or combination of keys that cause a menu command to execute.
Shortcut property	A MenuItem object property that allows you to select a shortcut key.
Show method	Displays a modeless form and causes it to receive the focus.
ShowDialog method	Displays a modal form and causes it to receive the focus.
ShowShortcut property	A MenuItem object property that may be set to true or false. When set to true, the MenuItem object's shortcut key (selected with the Shortcut property) is displayed. When set to false, the shortcut key is not displayed.
Single dimension array	An array with one subscript, which is useful for storing and working with a single set of data.
Single-step	A debugging technique where you execute an application's programming statements one at a time. After each statement executes, you can examine variable and property contents. This process allows you to identify a line or lines of code causing a logic error.
SizeMode property	A PictureBox property that determines how the control will position and scale its graphic image.
Sizing handles	Small boxes that appear around a control when it is selected at design time. Sizing handles are use to enlarge or shrink the control.
SmallChange property	A scroll bar or track bar property that holds the amount by which the Value property changes when the user clicks one of the scroll arrows at either end of a scroll bar. Track bars also respond to the arrow keys, which cause the Value property to change by this amount.
Software	The programs that run on a computer.
Solution	A container for holding Visual Basic projects.
Solution file	A file that ends with the .sln extension and contains data describing a solution.
Splash screen	A form that is displayed while an application is loading.
Standard module	A module that contains code that are used by other modules in a project.
Startup object	The object that is initially displayed or executed when an application executes. The startup object may be a form or a Sub procedure named Main in a standard module.
Static	Key word used to declare static local variables.
Static local variable	Static local variables are not destroyed when a Sub procedure or function returns. They exist for the lifetime of the application, even though their scope is only the Sub procedure or function in which

they are declared. Because of this, they retain their values between procedure calls.

Step Into command	A debugging command that allows you to execute a single programming statement. (*See* single-step.) If the statement contains a call to a procedure or function, the next execution point that will be displayed is the first line of code in that procedure or function.
Step Out command	A debugging command executed while the application is in Break mode. Causes the remainder of the current procedure or function to complete execution without single stepping. After the procedure or function has completed, the line following the procedure or function call is highlighted, and single stepping may resume.
Step Over command	A debugging command executed while the application is in Break mode. Causes the currently highlighted line to execute. If the line contains a procedure or function call, however, the procedure or function is executed and you are not given an opportunity to single step through its statements. The entire procedure or function is executed, and the next line in the current procedure is highlighted.
Step value	The value added to the counter variable at the end of each iteration of a For...Next loop.
StreamWriter class	A class that provides methods for writing data to sequential files.
StreamWriter object	An instance of the StreamWriter class, used to write data to sequential files.
String concatenation	When one string is appended to another.
String literal	A group of characters inside a set of quotation marks.
Structure	A data type created by the programmer that contains one or more variables which are known as members.
Structure statement	The statement used to create a structure.
Structured Query Language (SQL)	The standard database language for data storage, retrieval and manipulation.
Sub procedure	A procedure that performs a specific task and does not return a value.
Subscript	A number that identifies a specific element within an array.
Syntax	Rules that must be followed when constructing a method. Syntax dictates how key words, operators and programmer-defined names may be used.
Syntax error	A syntax error is the incorrect use of a programming language element, such as a key word, operator, or programmer-defined word.
System.IO.File. AppendText method	A method that opens a text file for data to be written to it. If the file already exists, data will be appended to its current contents.
System.IO.File. CreateText method	A method that opens a text file for data to be written to it. If the file does not exist, it is created.
System.IO.File. Exists method	A method that returns true if the specified file exists, or false if it does not.
System.IO.File. OpenText method	A method that opens a text file for reading.
Tab order	The order in which controls receive the focus.
Tab order selection mode	In this mode you establish a tab order by clicking controls in the desired sequence. You activate the mode by clicking View on the menu bar, then clicking Tab Order.

TabIndex property	The TabIndex property contains a numeric value, which indicates the control's position in the tab order.
Table	A table is organized in rows and columns, and holds data in a database.
TabStop property	When set to True, causes a control to be skipped in the tab order.
Text box	A rectangular area on a form that accepts keyboard input. (Also see TextBox control.)
TextAlign Property	A property that aligns text within a control.
TextBox control	A control that allows you to capture input that the user has typed on the keyboard.
TickFrequency property	A TrackBar control property that holds the number of units between the tick marks on the control.
Timer control	Allows an application to automatically execute code at regular time intervals.
Title property	A property of the OpenFileDialog and SaveFileDialog controls used to set the string displayed in the Open and Save As dialog box title bars.
ToLongTimeString method	A Date method that returns the Date variable's time value in long format.
ToLower method	A string method that returns a lowercase version of a string.
Tool tip	A small box that is displayed when the user holds the mouse cursor over a control.
Toolbar, layout	Contains buttons for formatting the layout of controls on a form.
Toolbar, standard	Contains buttons that execute frequently used commands.
Toolbox	Contains buttons, or tools, for Visual Basic controls.
Tooltip	A small box that is displayed when you hold the mouse cursor over a button on the Toolbar or in the Toolbox for a few seconds. The box gives a short description of what the button does.
Tooltip control	A control that allows you to create tooltips for the other controls on a form.
TopMost property	A form property that, when set to true, causes the form to be displayed on top of all the other forms currently displayed.
ToString method	A method that returns the string representation of a variable.
ToUpper method	A string method that returns a uppercase version of a string.
TrackBar control	Allows the user to adjust a value within a range of values.
Trailing space	A space that appears at the end of a string.
Trim	A string method that returns a copy of the string without leading or trailing spaces.
TrimEnd	A string method that returns a copy of the string without trailing spaces.
TrimStart	A string method that returns a copy of the string without leading spaces.
Try block	A block of code that is that appears in a Try statement. The Try block is always executed, and can potentially cause an exception.
Try...Catch and Try...Catch... Finally statements	Statements that executes a block of code that might cause an exception to occur, and handles the exception.
Twip	One twip is 1/1440th of an inch. Twips are used as a measurement for positioning input boxes on the screen.
Two-dimensional array	Like an array of arrays, and can be used to hold multiple sets of values.

Type conversion error	A run time error that is generated anytime a non-numeric value that cannot be automatically converted to a numeric value is assigned to a numeric variable or property.
Type mismatch error	*See* type conversion error.
Unicode	A set of numeric codes that represent all the letters of the alphabet (both lower- and uppercase), the printable digits 0 through 9, punctuation symbols, and special characters. The Unicode system is extensive enough to encompass all the world's alphabets.
Update method	A data adapter method that saves a modified table to its data source.
Update statement	The SQL statement used to change the contents of one or more columns in a database table.
UseMnemonic property	A Label control property that may be set to true or false. When set to true, an ampersand character may be used in the Text property to establish an access key. When set to false, an ampersand character stored in the Text property is displayed as part of the text and no access key is defined.
Val function	An intrinsic function that converts a string representation of a number to a numeric value.
Validating event	Before the focus shifts from Control A to Control B, and Control B's CausesValidation property is set to True, Control A's Validating event will fire.
Value property	A scroll bar or track bar property that holds the control's current value.
Value, pass by	An argument passing technique where only a copy of the argument is passed to the parameter variable.
Variable	A variable is a storage location in the computer's memory, used for holding information while the program is running.
Variable array	A group of variables with a single name.
Variable declaration	A statement that causes Visual Basic to create a variable in memory.
Vertical scroll bar	A vertical slider bar that, when moved with the mouse, increases or decreases a value.
Visible property	A Boolean property that causes a control to be visible on the form, when set to True, or hidden when set to False.
VScrollBar (vertical scroll bar) control	Allows the user to adjust a value within a range of values.
Watch window	A debugging window that allows you to add the names of variables that you want to watch. This window displays only the variables that you have added.
With block	A set of statements enclosed in a With...End With statement.
With...End With	The With...End With statement allows you to create a With block. The statements inside a With block may perform several operations on the same object without specifying the name of the object each time.
WordWrap property	A TextBox control property that causes the contents of a multiline text box to word wrap.
Write method	A StreamWriter method that writes data to a file.
WriteLine method	A StreamWriter method used to write a line of data to a file.

Xor operator   A logical operator that combines two expressions into one. One expression (not both) must be true for the overall expression to be true. If both expressions are true, or both expressions are false, the overall expression is false.

Index